D0083519

Notable American Philanthropists

NOTABLE AMERICAN PHILANTHROPISTS

Biographies of Giving and Volunteering

Edited by
ROBERT T. GRIMM, JR.

An Oryx Book

GREENWOOD PRESS
Westport, Connecticut • London

Library of Congress Cataloging-in-Publication Data

Notable American philanthropists : biographies of giving and volunteering / edited by
Robert T. Grimm, Jr.
    p. cm.
   Includes index.
   ISBN 1–57356–340–4 (alk. paper)
   1. Philanthropists—United States—Biography. 2. Voluntarism—United States. I.
Grimm, Robert T.
HV27.N68 2002
361.7'4'092273—dc21   2002016953

British Library Cataloguing in Publication Data is available.

Library of Congress Catalog Card Number: 2002016953
ISBN: 1–57356–340–4

First published in 2002

Greenwood Press, 88 Post Road West, Westport, CT 06881
An imprint of Greenwood Publishing Group, Inc.
www.greenwood.com

Printed in the United States of America

The paper used in this book complies with the
Permanent Paper Standard issued by the National
Information Standards Organization (Z39.48–1984).

10 9 8 7 6 5 4 3 2 1

Copyright Acknowledgments

Every reasonable effort has been made to trace the owners of copyright materials in this book, but in some instances
this has proven impossible. The author and publisher will be glad to receive information leading to more complete
acknowledgments in subsequent printings of the book and in the meantime extend their apologies for any omissions.

For Laura

Contents

CONTENTS

Advisory Committee and Contributors

ADVISORY COMMITTEE MEMBERS

KATHRYN A. AGARD
Learning to Give Initiative
Council of Michigan Foundations

ELIZABETH T. BORIS
Center on Nonprofits and Philanthropy
The Urban Institute

A'LELIA BUNDLES
Madam C.J. Walker Biographer

DWIGHT F. BURLINGAME, CHAIR
The Center on Philanthropy at Indiana University
Indiana University–Purdue University Indianapolis

DONNA CHAVIS
Native Americans in Philanthropy

MICHAEL E. CORTÉS
Institute for Nonprofit Organization Management
University of San Francisco

RUTH CROCKER
Department of History
Auburn University

ROBERT T. GRIMM, JR.
The Center on Philanthropy
and Department of History
Indiana University

PETER DOBKIN HALL
Hauser Center for Nonprofit Organizations
John F. Kennedy School of Government
Harvard University

DAVID HAMMACK
Department of History
and Mandel Center for Nonprofit Organizations
Case Western University

LESLIE LENKOWSKY
Philanthropic Studies and Public Policy
The Center on Philanthropy at Indiana University

ROBERT L. PAYTON
Philanthropic Studies
Indiana University

CONTRIBUTORS

LESLEY AGARD
Kamehameha Schools

DIANNE C. ASHTON
Department of Philosophy and Religion
Rowan University

VIRGINIA BERNHARD
Department of History
University of St. Thomas, Houston

DREW M. BLANCHARD
The Center on Philanthropy at Indiana University

ADVISORY COMMITTEE AND CONTRIBUTORS

ELIZABETH BRAYER
Independent Historian
and George Eastman Biographer

ELEANOR L. BRILLIANT
School of Social Work
Rutgers University

A'LELIA BUNDLES
Madam C.J. Walker Biographer

DWIGHT F. BURLINGAME
The Center on Philanthropy
Indiana University–Purdue University Indianapolis

AMELIA CLARK
The Center on Philanthropy at Indiana University

STACY A. CORDERY
Department of History
Monmouth College

DONALD T. CRITCHLOW
Department of History
Saint Louis University

RUTH CROCKER
Department of History
Auburn University

DOUGLAS CZAJKOWSKI
Philanthropic Studies
Indiana University–Purdue University Indianapolis

HUGH DAVIS
Department of History
Southern Connecticut State University

JEROME DENUCCIO
English Department
Graceland University

JOELLEN EL BASHIR
Moorland-Spingarn Research Center
Howard University

KEVIN A. FORTWENDEL
Access Community Health Network (Chicago, Illinois)

DAMON W. FREEMAN
Department of History
Indiana University

MARYBETH GASMAN
Educational Policy Studies
Georgia State University

MICHAEL GERRITY
St. Joseph Hospital Foundation (Buffalo, New York)

ROBERTA K. GIBBONEY
School of Nursing
Indiana University

ROBIN GOLDSTEIN
Philanthropic Studies
Indiana University–Purdue University Indianapolis

JOHN J. GRABOWSKI
Department of History
Case Western Reserve University
and Western Reserve Historical Society

ROBERT T. GRIMM, JR.
The Center on Philanthropy
and Department of History
Indiana University

MICHAEL P. GRZESIAK
Kent State University

SUSAN HABER
The Center on Philanthropy at Indiana University and Independent Consultant

PETER DOBKIN HALL
Hauser Center for Nonprofit Organizations
John F. Kennedy School of Government
Harvard University

HEATHER E. HARMLESS
The Center on Philanthropy at Indiana University

JOSEPH C. HARMON
University Library
Indiana University–Purdue University Indianapolis

JAMES D. IVY
Independent Scholar

MARGARET J. KIMBALL
University Archives
Stanford University

JOHN M. KLOOS
Religious Studies
Benedictine University

THOMAS J. LAPPAS
Department of History
Indiana University

W. DAVID LASATER
University Development
Ball State University

LESLIE LENKOWSKY
Philanthropic Studies and Public Policy
The Center on Philanthropy at Indiana University

DAVID L. LIGHTNER
Department of History and Classics University of Alberta

PETER J. LING
Department of American and Canadian Studies
University of Nottingham, England

AL LYONS
The Center on Philanthropy at Indiana University

JAMES H. MADISON
Department of History
Indiana University, Bloomington

ALEXIS MANHEIM
Arthur A. Houghton, Jr. Library
Corning Community College

NANCY MCCALL
The Alan Mason Chesney Medical Archives
Johns Hopkins Medical Institutions

MARK MCGARVIE
School of Law
New York University

PATRICIA E. MCWILLIAMS
Indiana University–Purdue University Indianapolis

KYMBERLY A. MULHERN
Nokomis Foundation

GEORGE H. NASH
Independent Scholar and
Biographer of Herbert Hoover

LYNN O'CONNELL
Physician Assistant Foundation

KATHLEEN ODNE
Dean and Margaret Lesher Foundation

JOEL J. OROSZ
School of Public and Nonprofit Administration
Dorothy A. Johnson Center for Philanthropy

and Nonprofit Leadership
Grand Valley State University

FRANKLIN PARKER
College of Human Resources and Education
West Virginia University
Morgantown, West Virginia

ELIZABETH M. PETERSON
The Alan Mason Chesney Medical Archives
Johns Hopkins Medical Institutions

AMANDA PORTERFIELD
Religious Studies Program
University of Wyoming

NICHOLAS S. RACHEOTES
Department of History
Framingham State College

JAMES W. REED
Department of History
Rutgers University

KENNETH W. ROSE
Rockefeller Archive Center
Rockefeller University

REBECCA ROTH
Philanthropic Studies
Indiana University–Purdue University Indianapolis

DIANE L. SCHAEFER
Philanthropic Studies
Indiana University–Purdue University Indianapolis

JOEL SCHWARTZ
Hudson Institute

JUDITH SEALANDER
Department of History
Bowling Green State University

MICHAEL B. SMITH
Department of History
Indiana University

CLARICE STASZ
Department of History
Sonoma State University

LAMONT D. THOMAS
School of Arts and Sciences
University of Bridgeport

RICHARD W. TROLLINGER
Centre College

ADVISORY COMMITTEE AND CONTRIBUTORS

DIANE WINSTON
Religion Program
Pew Charitable Trusts

MARTIN MORSE WOOSTER
The Philanthropy Roundtable

CONRAD EDICK WRIGHT
Massachusetts Historical Society

BERTRAM WYATT-BROWN
Department of History
University of Florida

Foreword

Philanthropy in all its forms, from voluntary action to foundation grantmaking, is a hugely important force in North America. It has been important since the Native peoples of America created their communities and cultures. It continued so with the arrival of European explorers, new settlers, and Africans brought here by the slave trade, and it grew in force as increasingly complex modern societies emerged on the land. A source of local help to those in need, a force for reform of unjust systems and behaviors, and a builder of institutions we now take for granted, philanthropy is deeply embedded in our culture.

But in spite of this long presence and an admirable record of achievement, few people can name even a half dozen of the men and women who built and sustained philanthropy's place in American society—people later recognized as philanthropic leaders.

This collection of philanthropic profiles addresses that void. By including women and men from different times, social strata, and ethnic and national origins, this volume suggests the stunning diversity and depth of the philanthropic tradition in America. Each profile offers commentary on the possible origins of the person's philanthropic impulse, the actions that resulted, and the longer term significance of those actions. The profiles also sensibly mention the sometimes imperfect personalities behind the "good donor" or "do-gooder" image, reminding us of the prejudice, obsession, and neglectfulness that can be coupled with more admirable behavior. The profiles do not cover the organizations that evolved from the vision and original action of these pioneering people. Quite properly so. Those stories of change and adaptation belong in another volume.

It is fascinating how, taken together, these profiles bring alive issues that are part of contemporary interest in philanthropy and seem to run through much of its history in the United States. For example, some philanthropists concentrated their attention on immediate and full relief of suffering, while others focused on systemic reforms and root causes to relieve suffering in the future. Some drew their philanthropic fervor from religious traditions and feelings of righteous obligation, while others grounded their rationales for action in secular visions of fairness and decency. Many donors gave their time or money quietly and privately, while others used every opportunity to implore others to follow suit and be publicly accountable. Some trusted and therefore built enduring institutions that adapted as new philanthropic needs developed and changed, while others did their utmost to complete their work in their own lifetimes.

This wonderful collection of profiles is

likely to be used most often as a reference book (and its guides to further reading on each philanthropist are perfectly suited to this purpose); but this book can also be used in another way. Any random selection of a dozen entries in the collection will begin to generate understanding of the extraordinarily diverse landscape that American philanthropy presents. Approaching it this way can inspire readers to find their own philanthropic footing and style—and allow them to get busy in whatever fashion they choose. As these profiles suggest, at its best philanthropy can bring great personal fulfillment, create needed change in society, and tangibly demonstrate the fundamental values of freedom and pluralism that are integral to our history and future.

Susan V. Berresford
President, The Ford Foundation
New York, NY

Preface

Notable American Philanthropists: Biographies of Giving and Volunteering provides substantial profiles of individuals and families who made significant contributions to the American philanthropic tradition from the seventeenth century to today. This biographical encyclopedia defines philanthropy as a reciprocal relationship in which strategic voluntary association, voluntary giving, and voluntary action are directed toward an individual's or group's definition of the social or common good. Consequently, this volume encompasses men and women who, by their dedication to voluntary service or charitable donations, significantly shaped American life. Although philanthropists are often thought to be extremely wealthy, numerous individuals in the past made valuable contributions to American society with modest or little means or due to their volunteering and voluntary associations.

Entries covering individual American philanthropists run approximately 1,500 to 2,500 words in length, while family essays (e.g., the Rockefellers, Booths, and Guggenheims) generally range from 2,500 to 9,000 words. To reach a wide audience, the essays were written at the lower college and high school reading level. Each essay examines a philanthropist's early years, education, career, and then focuses upon his/her philanthropic philosophy and actions. All essay contributors paid particular attention to an individual's motivations and justifications for philanthropy, i.e., how each believed one should voluntarily associate or use personal wealth for philanthropic purposes. The contributors also included short samples of each philanthropist's writings and assessed the important societal contributions made by each individual's philanthropic activity. A bibliographic list of references, information on the location of personal papers and other manuscript sources, and a photograph (if available) accompany each profile. Additionally, cross-references to philanthropists profiled in the book are set in boldface type. Appendixes include a timeline of American philanthropy and bibliographies of videos and children's books.

To select the individuals included in this work, I worked with the Center on Philanthropy at Indiana University to form a national advisory committee composed of scholars, educators, and nonprofit practitioners. This committee assisted me in selecting individual philanthropists and made recommendations on essay content and foci as well as on individual entry authors. Dwight F. Burlingame, Associate Executive Director of the Center on Philanthropy at Indiana University, served as the Chair of the advisory committee.

After numerous e-mails, phone conversations, and in-person meetings with advisory members as well as extensive background research, I provided the advisory committee members with a lengthy list of possible candidates for the book, drafts of selection criteria and essay guidelines, and a sample essay. In October 1999, members of the advisory committee were flown to Indianapolis for a day-long discussion about these materials. During that meeting and through further conversations afterward, I settled on the following selection criteria for *Notable American Philanthropists*:

- Philanthropy is defined as a reciprocal relationship in which strategic voluntary association, voluntary giving, and voluntary action are directed toward an individual's or group's definition of the social or common good.
- Profiled individuals must be American, which is defined as those individuals who are citizens of, or lived a significant time in, the United States.
- Profiled individuals must be historical figures because the contributions and importance of philanthropists cannot be fully assessed until they have completed their life.
- The individuals will represent the major fields of philanthropy: arts, culture, and humanities; education; environment and animal related; health; human services; public benefit; and religion.
- The individuals will represent significant innovations, ideas, and approaches to American philanthropy.
- The individuals will represent the diversity (ethnicity, geography, sex, and social and political philosophy) of the American philanthropic tradition.

In three instances, I slightly altered the selection criteria. Believing that Englishman James Smithson's bequest represented an important event in the history of American philanthropy, the volume includes a piece on Smithson and the history of his bequest even though he never spent a day in the United States. In addition, I have provided two individual essays on living philanthropists (George Soros and William H. "Bill" Gates III) because they are well-known figures,

would be of interest to readers of this volume, and possess the potential to be notable American philanthropists. I also included a "tribe" biographical essay on American Indians because their giving tradition is more properly described collectively than individually.

With over 60 contributing authors participating in the project, this volume discusses the charitable actions of over 110 individuals in 80 essays. In most cases, the essay authors previously produced books or other material related to the profiled person(s) or their philanthropic fields. Indeed, the contributing author list includes numerous scholars notable for their work on certain individuals and/or the broad field of American philanthropy. In a few cases, some extremely bright, young scholars in philanthropic studies also contributed an essay. The reader will observe that numerous authors conducted some, or substantial, original research to complete their essays. I take pride in the fact that this book offers first-time information on Americans who are both well known and not so well known.

Although the contributions, approaches, and philosophies of the people in this volume are of great importance to all Americans, no current publication offers anything remotely comparable to *Notable American Philanthropists*. Consequently, the book fills an important gap in the current literature on American philanthropy and should interest a broad public. Indeed, the average reader will gain immense knowledge about American philanthropy by using this work. This book represents an essential source for all university and college libraries but draws special interest among the growing number of nonprofit management programs, American Humanics programs (training undergraduates for work in human service nonprofits), and service learning programs. *Notable American Philanthropists* also enhances all school libraries and public libraries, providing critical knowledge for teachers, administrators, and others involved or interested in the growing movement to include philanthropy and service learning in the K–12 curriculum. This work will also aid individuals and groups promoting voluntary service among children, youth, and adults and be an enjoyable read and reference for any professional working in or with the nonprofit sector as well as those in the media.

Acknowledgments

In January 1999, I went out for dinner with Dwight Burlingame, Larry Friedman, and David Hammack. Just prior to this meeting, Dwight had received a call from Donna Sanzone at Oryx Press. She asked if the Center on Philanthropy at Indiana University would be interested in producing a biographical work on American philanthropists. The four of us discussed the proposed project over dinner, and Larry encouraged me to undertake the project on the ride home that evening. A couple of days later, Dwight offered additional encouragement, and I began preliminary work on *Notable American Philanthropists* within the month.

During the two and a half years it took to prepare this book, the Lilly Endowment and the Indiana Humanities Council provided generous and substantial funding for the project (including research, office space, honorariums, and travel). Meanwhile, the Center on Philanthropy at Indiana University sponsored the project and made its vast resources available to me.

As with any book, I owe debts to many people. Dwight Burlingame devoted considerable amounts of time discussing the project with me and supporting the book's development in any way imaginable. This volume would not have become a reality without him. Leslie Lenkowsky generously offered his ideas and time and the publication is richly rewarded for it. Indeed, Dwight and Les are invaluable resources on philanthropy and I continue to learn much from them. David Hammack offered beneficial ideas and suggestions during the early phases of this project and Peter Dobkin Hall did likewise during the early and later stages of the work. While each wrote a biography of an important American philanthropist, A'Lelia Bundles and Ruth Crocker also charitably donated their time to this enterprise. During the formation of the project, I greatly appreciated that Kathryn A. Agard, Elizabeth T. Boris, Donna Chavis, Michael E. Cortés, Lawrence J. Friedman, Roberta K. Gibboney, Thomas J. Lappas, and Robert L. Payton took time out of their busy schedules to share their ideas and enhance the work.

While working on this book, I taught courses on philanthropy and the nonprofit sector to numerous undergraduate and executive education Masters students at Indiana University and shared my thoughts as well as parts of the book with them. I learned much from these discussions (in and outside of class) and am deeply grateful for their contributions to my understanding of American philanthropy and this endeavor. Moreover, this work is the product of over sixty contributing authors who diligently wrote and happily revised the essays presented within. I cannot express enough gratitude and appre-

ACKNOWLEDGMENTS

ciation for their efforts. I also appreciate the numerous Indiana University reference librarians who helped me locate important facts and information needed for the book. While working as a law librarian and historian, my wife, Laura L. Grimm, also spent more time assisting me with this book than anyone else. Using her library and historical skills, she tirelessly researched numerous topics, discussed and advised on issues arising from the book, and carefully reviewed every word. This book is gratefully dedicated to her.

Introduction

STUDYING AMERICAN PHILANTHROPY AND AMERICAN PHILANTHROPISTS

From 1951 to 1960, American graduate schools produced 10 dissertations related to philanthropy, charity, or nonprofits but produced 700 dissertations on the aforementioned topics from 1981 to 1990 (Hall, 1999). Furthermore, no academic centers or higher education programs on philanthropy existed in 1960. By 2001, approximately 60 academic centers and hundreds of academic programs at colleges and universities focused on this issue. In subsequent years, the number of centers and educational programs will surely increase. As a growing number of private and public elementary, middle, and high schools incorporate philanthropy and service learning, the study of philanthropy is also reaching into the K–12 curriculum. According to a 1999 survey conducted by the U.S. Department of Education, 64 percent of public schools and 83 percent of public high schools organize community service work and 32 percent of public schools and 50 percent of public high schools offer service-learning programs, which link the school's academic curriculum to service activities (Skinner and Chapman, 1999).

This introduction sketches some of the major forces behind the escalating attention to and study of charitable voluntary associations and charitable acts (such as volunteering time and donating money), using women's history as an example of the growing historical knowledge about philanthropy while emphasizing the advocacy of research on and academic programs related to charitable behaviors, rising interest in civil society, and greater recognition of the size, scope, and importance of giving and volunteering as societal agents in the increasing public regard for American philanthropy.

POST-BREMNER RESEARCH ON PHILANTHROPY: THE WOMEN'S HISTORY EXAMPLE

In 1956, historian Merle Curti led a two-day conference at Princeton University on the History of Philanthropy in an effort to address the lack of historical knowledge about philanthropy. A number of monographs resulted from this conference but none as popular, readable, and commercially enduring as Robert Bremner's *American Philanthropy* (1960), which was somewhat revised and republished in 1988. Bremner broadly defined philanthropy as the "improvement in the quality of human life" through efforts at the promotion of "the welfare, happiness, and culture of mankind"

(Bremner, 3). Thus, he broadly surveyed "voluntary activity in the fields of charity, education, humanitarian reform, social service, war relief, and foreign aid" (Bremner, 4). Although an important piece, the book exemplified post–World War II historians' tendency "to produce a new interpretive framework for American history" that focused "attention on what has united Americans rather than divided them" (Novick 1988, 333). In actuality, the vitality of American philanthropy is partly due to the number of philanthropists and voluntary associations that compete over definitions of the social good. Given the broad coverage of his relatively short work, Bremner only offered cursory attention to the majority of philanthropists mentioned and focused primarily on white men's experiences, offering—similar to most scholarship of the time—minor treatment of women's experiences as well as the experiences of groups such as blacks, American Indians, and Latinos.

Since Bremner's publication, a growing body of research documents how the aforementioned groups engaged in giving and volunteering. In the 1970s and early 1980s, for example, a recognizable historical field known as women's history began to emerge and address women's absence from most historical narratives. Rising out of the feminist movement, a few of these early histories of women found that philanthropy, since the early days of the American republic, represented a common way for women to enter public life. Linda Kerber's *Women of the Republic* described, for example, how the women of Philadelphia canvassed their city to raise funds for the welfare of Continental army soldiers. Kerber also cautioned against overlooking the importance of female philanthropic initiatives because such entities "provided an ideological justification for women's intrusion into politics" and "would become the standard model throughout the years of the early republic" (Kerber 1980, 104).

Nonetheless, a separate spheres ideology—the assumption that American history was divided exclusively by a female private sphere and a male public sphere—pervaded much of the scholarship of women's history until the mid-1980s. In the last two decades, historians of women have increasingly observed the ways in which the rhetoric of charitable associations, from Colonial America to the first half of the twentieth century, offered women a wedge into the public sphere. Christine Stansell's *City of Women* anticipated this sea-change when she argued that philanthropic groups, such as the Society for the Relief of Poor Widows, "gave women the . . . armor . . . to defend their reputations from the slurs women incurred when they ventured onto men's . . . terrain" (Stansell 1987, 69). In the last decade, historians also discovered that charitable associations not only offered women the opportunity to leave the home, but numerous charitable entities derived major funding from female donors and provided managerial and policy-making positions not available in the for-profit and government sectors of their time (see Ginzberg 1990; McCarthy 1990; Sander 1998; and Scott 1992).

AMERICAN PHILANTHROPY: INCREASING INTEREST AND GROWTH

While histories of women emerged, the U.S. Congress increasingly scrutinized private foundations and other aspects of philanthropy from the 1950s to the 1970s. Worried about the available information on philanthropy, John D. Rockefeller 3rd established the Commission on Private Philanthropy and Public Needs (1974) to expand the public's knowledge of philanthropy. Chaired by John H. Filer, the so-called Filer Commission published important research findings in *Giving in America: Toward a Stronger Voluntary Sector* (1975). This work spurred Rockefeller to fund what became the first of a growing number of academic centers that study philanthropy, the Program on Non-Profit Organizations at Yale University.

Concerned about some of the same issues as Rockefeller, John Gardner, a former U.S. Department of Health, Education, and Welfare secretary and president of the Carnegie

Corporation, drove the formation of Independent Sector (1980). As an umbrella organization for the nonprofit sector, this association wished to promote the values of charitable associations, giving, and volunteering. In proceeding years, Independent Sector, particularly its research committee led by Robert L. Payton, president of the Exxon Education Foundation, became instrumental in promoting the interdisciplinary study of philanthropy in educational programs and research centers throughout higher education. Similarly, Independent Sector began to produce statistics on charitable behaviors.

Breaking from the political atmosphere of the recent past, President Ronald Reagan and other political leaders began publicly espousing the virtues of the American voluntary spirit during the 1980s. Thereafter, the presidencies of George Bush, William Clinton, and George Walker Bush also exhibited considerable interest in encouraging the charitable activities of Americans.

The end of the Cold War (1989–1991) also heightened interest in philanthropy. Driven by the belief that voluntary action and associations represented the building blocks of prosperous democracies, scholars and politicians increasingly discuss how to translate America's civil society to emerging democracies in Eastern Europe and elsewhere. Civil society, a nebulous concept, is generally defined as "the space of uncoerced human association and also the set of relational networks—formed for the sake of family, faith, interest, and ideology," which "facilitate coordination and cooperation for mutual benefits" (Walzer, 1995, 7 and Putnam, 1995, 67). In his famous article "Bowling Alone" (1995), and subsequent book by the same name (2000), Robert Putnam questioned the health of American civil society and sparked public debates over the causes and varieties of civic engagement and disengagement.

Meanwhile, current statistics on the scope and size of philanthropy solidify its significance to American life. *Giving USA*, published by the American Association of Fundraising Counsel Trust for Philanthropy and prepared by the Center on Philanthropy at Indiana University, estimated that the charitable giving of Americans reached $203.5 billion in 2000. Through a national survey, Independent Sector's *The New Nonprofit Almanac IN BRIEF* reports that 70.1 percent of American households made charitable contributions and 55.5 percent of Americans volunteered in 1998. The same survey also states that Americans volunteered a total of 19.9 billion hours and estimates the total value of that time as $225.9 billion.

Expectedly, the media is providing more attention to Americans who are giving and volunteering or engaging in popular charitable endeavors. In July 2000, American philanthropy even graced the cover of *Time* magazine. *Notable American Philanthropists* intersects with and contextualizes the growing interest in philanthropy in the United States.

Robert T. Grimm, Jr.

WORKS CITED

Bremner, Robert. *American Philanthropy*. Chicago: University of Chicago, [1960], 1988.

Commission on Private Philanthropy and Public Needs. *Giving in America: Toward a Stronger Voluntary Sector*. Washington, DC: The Commission, 1975.

Ginzberg, Lori. *Women and the Work of Benevolence: Morality, Politics, and Class in the 19th-Century United States*. New Haven, CT: Yale University Press, 1990.

Giving USA: The Annual Report of Philanthropy for the Year 2000. New York: American Association of Fundraising Counsel Trust for Philanthropy, 2000.

Hall, Peter Dobkin. "The Work of Many Hands: A Response to Stanley N. Katz and the Origin of the 'Serious Study' of Philanthropy." *Nonprofit and Voluntary Sector Quarterly*, December 28, 1999, 522–534.

Kerber, Linda K. *Women of the Republic: Intellect and Ideology in Revolutionary America*. Chapel Hill: University of North Carolina Press, 1980.

McCarthy, Kathleen, ed. *Lady Bountiful Revisited: Women, Philanthropy, and Power*. New Brunswick, NJ: Rutgers University Press, 1990.

The New Nonprofit Almanac IN BRIEF: Facts and Figures on the Independent Sector 2001. Washington: Independent Sector, 2001.

Novick, Peter. *That Noble Dream: The 'Objectivity Question' and the American Historical Profession*. Cambridge: Cambridge University Press, 1988.

Putnam, Robert. "Bowling Alone: America's Declining Social Capital." *Journal of Democracy* 6, January 1995, 65–78.

———. *Bowling Alone: The Collapse and Revival of American Community*. New York: Simon & Schuster, 2000

Sander, Kathleen. *The Business of Charity: The Women's Exchange Movement, 1832–1900*. Urbana: University of Illinois Press, 1998.

Scott, Anne Firor. *Natural Allies: Women's Associations in American History*. Urbana: University of Illinois Press, 1992.

Skinner, Rebecca, and Chris Chapman. *Service-Learning and Community Service in K–12 Public Schools*. Washington, DC: National Center for Educational Statistics, U.S. Department of Education, 1999.

Stansell, Christine. *City of Women: Sex and Class in New York, 1789–1860*. Urbana: University of Illinois Press, 1987.

Walzer, Michael. "The Concept of Civil Society." In *Toward a Global Civil Society*. Providence: Berghahn Books, 1995, 7–27.

Notable American Philanthropists

A

JANE ADDAMS
(1860–1935)

Social Reformer, Pacifist, and Founder of Hull-House

INTRODUCTION

In the summer of 1892, the Ethical Culture Societies devoted its summer school to broadly discussing Philanthropy and Social Progress. Having founded Hull-House, one of the first American social settlements, three years earlier with her inheritance, Jane Addams served as one of the school's lecturers. In her address entitled "The Subjective Necessity for Social Settlements," she observed that "[t]he Settlement . . . is an experimental effort to aid in the solution of the social and industrial problems which are energized by the modern conditions of life in a great city" (Addams, 1990, 75). In subsequent years, social settlements would populate American urban areas and Addams would lead the settlement movement's transformation from experimental institutions to organizations that pushed for and created significant social reforms while working to reshape public conceptions of poverty. In her lifetime,

Addams's reform career would make her one of the most celebrated, as well as despised, women in America.

EARLY YEARS AND EDUCATION

On September 6, 1860, Jane Addams was born in Cedarville, Illinois to John Huy Addams and Sarah Weber Addams. Her ancestors had originally received land from William Penn, and John Addams emigrated from Pennsylvania to Illinois in 1844. In Illinois, John Addams became a prosperous businessman as well as a community leader, serving eight terms as an Illinois state senator. Jane Addams was the eighth of nine children (only four lived to maturity) born to John and Sarah Addams. She lost her mother when she was only two and grew up idolizing her father, who was the wealthiest and most prominent figure in town; however, she never grew close to her stepmother, Anna Haldeman Addams. As a child, Jane Addams suffered a number of illnesses, particularly tuberculosis of the spine, and consequently experienced a somewhat protected childhood.

In 1882, Addams graduated from the Rockford Female Seminary (Rockford, Illinois), an institution that strongly promoted a service ethic among its students. Graduating first in her class, she made plans to attend the Women's Medical College in Philadelphia and then provide medical care for the poor. Soon after beginning her studies in Philadelphia, she left the school due to health problems and never returned. Renowned physician S. Weir Mitchell prescribed his "rest cure" for Addams but such inactivity proved frustrating, and extended trips to Europe were found to be better for her health.

A member of the first generation of college-educated women (from the upper and upper-middle classes of society), Addams and her peers found few professional opportunities available to them. American society still dictated that women pursue a career as a wife and mother. Addams, however, had little, if any, interest in men and marriage and spent the 1880s searching for a purpose to her life. Like many other college-educated women, Addams ultimately constructed a career through full-time work in voluntary associations.

In 1888, Addams began to formulate the specifics of her philanthropic career by visiting Toynbee Hall in London. Started in 1884 by Anglican minister Samuel Barnett, Toynbee Hall was the first social settlement in London and aimed to improve the lives of poor people who were suffering the effects of rapid industrialization. Barnett's Toynbee Hall recruited male university students to settle in working-class neighborhoods; he believed that these university men would not only improve poverty conditions but also learn something about the "real world." Inspired, Addams decided to create a social settlement in America.

CAREER HIGHLIGHTS AND MAJOR PHILANTHROPIC CONTRIBUTIONS

In September 1889, twenty-nine-year-old Jane Addams and her college friend Ellen

Gates Starr founded the Hull-House social settlement by moving into a decaying mansion that was located in a densely populated and poor immigrant community on Chicago's south side. Subsequently developing a philosophy that was similar to Barnett's but also integrated her own experiences, Addams argued that privileged young people, particularly young women, needed a connection with the realities of the larger world. She worried that the rich and the poor, "the classes," were becoming too segregated from each other due to America's growing industrial society; the wealthy needed to interact with the poor so they would recognize that the poor were similar to them in most facets except opportunities. Consequently, Addams believed settlement activities mutually benefited the settlement workers and the people they served. Moreover, Addams argued, in a social justice tenor, "that the blessings which we associate with a life of refinement and cultivation can be made universal and must be made universal if they are to be permanent" (Addams, 1990, 69).

Addams started her social settlement at a time when the United States underwent a major transition. Driven by rising industrialization, urbanization, and immigration, America moved form a rural to a metropolitan society. An extremely high number of immigrants, 15 million, entered the United States from 1890 to the start of World War I. Unlike past immigration clusters from Western Europe, this group primarily came from Southern and Eastern Europe. Often, these immigrants also arrived poor, possessed few skills, and found unskilled work at the bottom of industrial society.

Although Addams's privileged background hardly prepared her for working among the poor, she rightly believed that moving to the center of a poor neighborhood represented the best way to learn about the problems of poverty, aid the poor, and find solutions to their problems. Quickly, Hull-House began to respond to its immigrant community's needs. Within its first decade, Hull-House settlement expanded from the original building and included an art gallery, gymnasium,

Jane Addams with children at the Mary Crane Nursery, c. 1930. Wallace Kirkland Papers (JAMC neg. 54), Jane Addams Memorial Collection, The University Library, University of Illinois at Chicago.

playground, cooperative boardinghouse, theater, and music school. The settlement also provided services ranging from nursery care to cooking, sewing, and carpentry classes.

For its first few years, Addams served as Hull-House's major financial supporter. When her father died in 1881, she had inherited $50,000 to $60,000, which constituted an impressive sum for the day, and used over $5,000 of that amount during the settlement's first year. As Hull-House expanded, the costs also rose. By 1893, she recognized that her assets would completely disappear if she did not broaden her institution's financial base. Fortunately, Addams found two women who became the financial sources behind Hull-House's expansion: Mary Rozet Smith and Louise deKoven Bowen. Giving over $100,000 during Addams's lifetime, Smith not only became a strong supporter of Hull-House but a confidant and lifetime companion of Addams. Bowen, also a friend of Addams, gave over $500,000 to Hull-House from 1895 to 1928

and took on numerous leadership positions in the settlement.

In a time when men controlled most societal wealth as well as other aspects of society, the fact that Hull-House was led by, and received major funding from, women illustrates how Addams cultivated a female network of reformers. Of course, men also served as Hull-House volunteers and donors but the Chicago settlement became famous for attracting women to the field of reform and helping cultivate the so-called progressive movement. Many women, who lived and worked at Hull-House, devoted large portions of their lives to settlement and other reform work, including **Florence Kelley**, who served as secretary of the National Consumers League from 1899 to 1932, and Julia Lathrop, who served as the first head of the federal government's Children's Bureau in 1912.

Although the poor were publicly characterized as lazy and immoral, Addams found her immigrant neighbors to be just the opposite. She and her fellow reformers soon observed that the poor were hindered by environmental conditions beyond their control and needed more than neighborhood services. Unlike contemporary philanthropist **Andrew Carnegie**, Addams did not believe that poor people could lift themselves out of poverty if they just applied enough effort. Further, she did not believe that free Carnegie libraries or even a free school such as **Peter Cooper**'s Cooper Union would work unless the environmental factors contributing to poverty were also addressed.

Undertaking an early social science approach, Hull-House gathered statistics on conditions in factories and tenements as well as neighborhood demographics. The 1895 publication of *Hull-House Maps and Papers*, an investigation of conditions in Chicago's Nineteenth Ward, represented the first systematic account of an urban immigrant community. *Hull-House Maps and Papers* included statistics on housing conditions, child labor, and weekly income as well as detailed maps. Armed with social science studies, Addams and other Hull-House reformers created the first factory inspection act in Illinois and advocated child labor laws, limitations on working hours for women, protection of immigrants, compulsory school attendance, and industrial safety legislation. The establishment of the nation's first juvenile court in Chicago (1899) was also the result of Hull-House activism.

Besides undertaking all types of reforms, Addams became a prolific writer and public speaker. Indeed, she became a national figure by authoring hundreds of magazine articles and twelve books, which covered her experiences and reform ideas. Her most famous work, the autobiographical *Twenty Years at Hull-House*, sold about 17,000 copies in the first year and 60,000 in her lifetime. Meanwhile, the settlement movement expanded from six settlements in 1891 to over 400 settlements by 1910. With Addams as the recognized leader of the settlement movement and Hull-House as the model settlement, Addams became even more famous. Prior to

World War I, she was probably the most famous woman in America. She used this celebrity status to promote progressive causes that reached beyond urban America, including women's suffrage. In 1912, she even seconded former President Theodore Roosevelt's presidential nomination at the Progressive Party convention and campaigned around the country for him.

After World War I erupted in Europe, Addams was recruited to lead the pacifist movement and conducted much of her wartime efforts through the Woman's Peace Party. Deeply disturbed by the war, she even promoted—unlike a number of fellow pacifists—the peace movement after the United States entered the war in 1917. Her pacifist activities stirred a highly negative reaction among the American public. Addams became largely characterized as a foolish, and later unpatriotic, American. Consequently, Addams spent much of the 1920s in Europe, working for the group she helped found, the Women's International League for Peace and Freedom, and then serving as its President. In 1931, Addams received the Nobel Peace Prize for her devotion to pacifist efforts.

CONCLUSION

By the 1930s, criticism of Addams had declined. When she died in 1935, she was hailed as an American hero. Although the social settlement movement never regained the popularity it had before the war, Addams and the social settlement movement had an important effect upon industrial America. They led reform movements that created juvenile courts, public parks, factory laws, the U.S. Children's Bureau, child labor regulations, tenement reforms, mother's pensions, and workmen's compensation. Settlement workers' consummate devotion to early social science methods developed university schools of social work and the professional social worker. Clearly, Addams and her fellow social settlement reformers left an enduring influence upon American society.

Robert T. Grimm, Jr.

FURTHER READING

Addams, Jane. *Twenty Years at Hull-House.* Urbana: University of Illinois Press, 1990.

Bryan, Mary Lynn McCree, and Allen F. Davis, eds. *100 Years at Hull-House.* Bloomington: Indiana University Press, 1990.

Davis, Allen F. *American Heroine: The Life and Legend of Jane Addams.* New York: Oxford University Press, 1973.

———. *Spearheads for Reform: The Social Settlements and the Progressive Movement, 1890–1914.* New York: Oxford University Press, 1967.

Elshtain, Jean Bethke. *Jane Addams and the Dream of American Democracy.* New York: Basic Books, 2002.

Hull-House Maps and Papers. New York: T.R. Crowell, 1895.

Sklar, Kathryn. "Who Funded Hull-House?" In Kathleen D. McCarthy, ed., *Lady Bountiful Revisited: Women, Philanthropy, and Power.* New Brunswick, NJ: Rutgers University Press, 1990, 94–115.

Stebner, Eleanor J. *The Women of Hull House: A Study in Spirituality, Vocation, and Friendship.* Albany: State University of New York Press, 1997.

PAPERS

Jane Addams's papers are at the Jane Addams Memorial Collection, University of Illinois–Chicago (Chicago, IL), and the Swarthmore College Peace Collection, Swarthmore College (Swarthmore, PA).

AMERICAN INDIAN PHILANTHROPY: FAMILY AND GIVING IN LAKOTA COMMUNITIES

INTRODUCTION

In his classic work, *Custer Died for Your Sins*, Vine Deloria, Jr. blamed the charitable efforts of missionaries and reformers for weakening Indian social structures and communities and for attacking many of its fundamental institutions. A Lakota from the Standing Rock reservation, Deloria also commented on the persistence of the Indian tradition of giving: "Indian religion taught that sharing one's goods with another human being was the highest form of behavior. The Indian people have tenaciously held to this tradition of sharing goods with other people in spite of all attempts by churches, government agencies, and schools to break them of the custom" (Deloria 1988, 121).

American Indians and philanthropists have had an ambiguous relationship at best. In extensively examining attempts to aid Indian people in their "plight," historians have criticized many nineteenth- and twentieth-century charitable organizations for their ethnocentric perspective on native cultures. Many groups, such as the New York State–based Lake Mohonk Council of the Friends of the Indian, attempted to make the Indians of the West look and act more like whites in the East. The cultural arrogance of many philanthropic groups, however well intentioned, contributed to a Federal Indian policy that used missionaries from the East and financial support from wealthy patrons to aid in the eradication of Indian religions, economies, and societies. What has often been left out of this picture is the way in which the attempts by benevolent non-Indians actually undermined a system of voluntary giving that predated the birth of the United States. The importance of philanthropy *within* Indian societies is at least as important to the history of U.S.-Indian relations, as the effect of non-Indian philanthropy on Native Americans. From contact through the present, divergent cultural perspectives on the meaning of gift giving, generosity, and the common good made misunderstandings endemic to Indian-white relations.

This piece offers a brief look at how generosity worked in the context of Lakota cul-

A group of Lakota chiefs photographed after meeting with General Miles on or near the Pine Ridge Reservation in 1891. Library of Congress: LC-USZ62-46735.

ture. It also examines how U.S. Indian policy lacked the flexibility to take into account this aspect of Lakota culture, and in fact attempted to root it out as anathema to the "advancement" of tribal people. By examining the experiences and ideas of two Lakota individuals—Black Elk and Mary Crow Dog—the diversity of American philanthropy will become apparent.

TRADITIONAL LAKOTA CULTURE

At the end of the nineteenth century, Native Americans in the West were under assault by white settlers, by soldiers, and by an Indian policy that sought to force nomadic plains tribes to become sedentary farmers with individual plots of land. Indians and non-Indians overtly criticized violence against individuals in massacres, such as Sand Creek in Colorado in 1864 and Wounded Knee in the Dakotas in 1890. Still, the more subtle attacks by missionaries and reformers were often viewed as beneficial. Yet, their attempt to provide for the welfare of individual Indians or nuclear families directly attacked a system of giving and a conception of the common good deeply ingrained within Lakota culture.

In traditional Lakota society, it has been well documented that obligations to an extended kin-network required individuals with even modest material possessions to share food, tools, and—during the reservation period—money with relatives. The Lakota did not conceive of family as a simple nuclear unit with limited obligations outside the sphere of mother, father, and children. Rather, the structure of a family consisted of an extended network of obligations, each individual ideally fulfilling his or her responsibility to other relatives. These obligations were further solidified by kin terms, which reinforced the belief that cousins, uncles, aunts, and grandparents were central members of a family. Indeed, kinship itself was less of a biological designation than a set of social relationships. Giving, in the sense of contributing to the common good, was not simply the province of the rich or an obligation to the church, but was a way of expressing one's basic humanity and membership in the community.

BLACK ELK (1863–1950)

At the dawn of the twentieth century, Catholic missions became one of the major sources of employment, food, and goods in the Lakota community. The large tract of land known as the Great Sioux Reservation, which covered about half of the present state of South Dakota, had been whittled away by a series of government actions at the end of the nineteenth century. With diminishing land and a dwindling buffalo population, the Lakota way of life was being eradicated. While the Lakota struggled with new economic realities, they retained many traditional beliefs and practices, especially regarding family responsibility and the redistribution of goods throughout the community. Many missionaries, however, sought to limit the sharing of money and goods by the Lakota. A clear example of this comes from the history of one of the most famous Lakota medicine men, Black Elk. Most people familiar with Black Elk know of him as a traditional medicine man who recorded his beliefs in an autobiography (*Black Elk Speaks*) cowritten with John Neihardt in the 1930s. Nonetheless, one can learn much about the ambiguous relationship between the ideal of Christian charity and the reality of missionary administration by looking at Black Elk's life after his conversion to Catholicism in the opening years of the twentieth century.

Black Elk became an important catechist for the church and traveled from his home reservation in Pine Ridge to other reservations in the West, spreading the word of the gospel and aiding other Catholic Indians. In many ways, the medicine-man-turned-Catholic was a model for the missionaries' goals. Still, many priests and other reformers sought to circumscribe what they viewed as unrestrained squandering of church resources by Black Elk. They objected to the way in which Black Elk redistributed his modest earnings with other Lakota. Father Eugene Buechel, S.J. wrote, "Black Elk is an efficient

Catechist, but like many full-bloods a very poor manager. He will always be a beggar, no matter how much money one would give him. . . . At the end of last [Catholic Indian] Congress I gave him $10.00 for extra work done. The next day he begged again for he had distributed the money among visitors from Standing Rock" [Lakota Reservation] (Demallie 1984, 22–23). As anthropologist Ray Demallie has indicated, this generosity to the point of poverty was a traditional pattern of Lakota leadership. Indeed, one of the precepts that attracted Black Elk to the Catholic faith was precisely this idea of Christian charity: also defined as giving to the point of poverty. In Black Elk's letters, the theme of Christian brotherhood is common, and it is likely that he saw elements of Christianity dovetailing with traditional beliefs. Still, the missionaries on the plains were not simply spreading the Christian religion, they were also inculcating Indian people with the values of the U.S. government, including respect for private property, a willingness to save and invest resources, and the superiority of the nuclear family.

Although it raised the ire of the Catholic leadership on the plains, Black Elk's generosity mimicked many traditional patterns of the Lakota past. Furthermore, Black Elk truly believed that the acceptance of Christianity was important for the Lakota people. In a letter to the *Catholic Herald*, Black Elk wrote, "There are many Indians in the U.S. but only a few belong to God's church; many are living unhappy lives. For this reason we should take in firmly what the priests tell us" (Demallie 1984, 20–21). He also warned, "Those who receive the blood of God's son unworthily will die and suffer. *My relatives*, this is very difficult, so think of these things" (Demallie 1984, 20–21) [emphasis added]. Such a quote reveals the seriousness of Black Elk's conviction and highlights his conception of the Christian Lakota community as a family. Clearly, the redistribution of wealth among Christian Lakota from the Standing Rock Reservation resulted from his belief that giving to the needy (especially other

Christians), without hesitation, was central to his Christianity.

Yet, the missionaries who so valued Black Elk as a catechist for the Catholic Church were also spreading the ideals of United States civilization. For many missionaries, individualism, economic development, and private ownership of land were more important traits to teach than generosity. The types of economic activity demonstrated by Black Elk indicated to missionaries that the Indian had not given up traditional practices and perhaps had not given up traditional religious or healing practices as well: activities that would undermine the missionaries' teachings. Nonetheless, the importance of generosity within Lakota society did not die out in the first third of the twentieth century. Indeed, later Lakota writers continued to comment on the persistence of this tradition. Despite their attempts and limited successes, the values from the pre-reservation period endured through the twentieth century.

MARY CROW DOG (1953–)

In the 1960s, Mary Crow Dog was a young Indian girl growing up in poverty on the Rosebud Reservation in South Dakota. Between Black Elk's conversion and the 1960s, Lakota communal land had been divided into small individual plots, many of which were sold to whites. As the reservations shrank, the assault on traditional cultures continued. Crow Dog spent her early years in an Indian boarding school, separated from her family and subject to the torments of teachers who failed to understand Lakota culture. During the same decade, many young Native Americans, living in cities after World War II, were banning together to form the American Indian Movement: a militant revitalization movement that was pan-tribal in nature and sought to enliven many traditional practices from many different native cultures. In an autobiography published in the early 1990s, *Lakota Woman*, Mary Crow Dog tells a story in which her life on the reservation changes drastically after her

involvement with the American Indian Movement and their activities at Rosebud and on the nearby Pine Ridge Reservation. From her story, one learns that the Lakota value of giving to the common good persisted into the 1970s, despite attempts by white reformers to curtail the relatively free flow of goods between Indian people.

For Crow Dog, the extended family network still existed among many of the older members of the Rosebud Reservation. Although her grandmother was Christian and encouraged her grandchildren to learn English and work in the white world, she remained very traditional in her conception of the extended family, or *tiospaye*. On the reservation, despite rather impoverished economic conditions, the expectation of generosity with material goods remained strong. Crow Dog describes this trend in the opening pages of her work: "Feeding every comer is still a sacred duty, and Sioux women seem always to be cooking from early morning until late at night. Fourth and fifth cousins still claim relationship and the privileges that go with it. Free enterprise has no future on the res" (Crow Dog 1991, 13). On the reservation and in the pan-tribal American Indian Movement, Crow Dog describes the free distribution of goods that permeated everyday life. In accordance with their traditional ways, children and visitors were taken in, fed, and given aid. Although some traditional social forms were sometimes less effective during difficult economic times, the ideal remained strong throughout the late twentieth century.

CONCLUSION

Lakota people have persistently conceived of "community" and "family" as integrated cultural and social institutions. The sharing of material goods with other members of the community, regardless of one's wealth, becomes easier to understand when viewed with an eye on its cultural origins in Lakota conceptions of the family. Although Native American cultures have frequently been romanticized in books, film, and other media, it is important to understand that while native communities have never been utopias, they support important cultural traditions that are part of American history. Ironically, what reformers and others attempted to limit was one of America's oldest philanthropic traditions.

Thomas J. Lappas

FURTHER READING

Crow Dog, Mary, and Richard Erodes. *Lakota Woman*. New York: Harper Perennial, 1991.

Deloria, Vine, Jr. *Custer Died for Your Sins, an Indian Manifesto*. Norman: University of Oklahoma Press, 1988. [Originally New York: Macmillan, 1969.]

———. *Spirit and Reason: The Vine Deloria, Jr. Reader*. Golden, CO: Fulcrum Publishing, 1990.

Demallie, Raymond J. *The Sixth Grandfather: Black Elk's Teachings Given to John G. Niehardt.* Lincoln: University of Nebraska Press, 1984.

Demallie, Raymond J., and Alfonso Ortiz, eds. *North American Indian Anthropology: Essays on Society and Culture*. Norman: University of Oklahoma Press, 1994.

Mauss, Marcel. *The Gift: Forms and Functions of Exchange in Archaic Societies*. Glencoe, IL: Free Press, 1954.

Neihardt, John G. *Black Elk Speaks: Being the Life Story of a Holy Man of the Oglala Sioux*. Lincoln: University of Nebraska Press, 1988. [Originally New York: William & Morrow, 1932.]

Wells, Roanld Austin. *The Honor of Giving: Philanthropy in Native America*. Indianapolis: Indian University Center on Philanthropy. 1998.

Wilson, James. *The Earth Shall Weep: A History of Native America*. New York: Atlantic Monthly Press, 1998.

B

LEONARD BACON
(1802–1881)

Editor, Minister, Promoter of Benevolent Associations,
and Pioneer in Charitable Trusteeship

INTRODUCTION

"The cause of active benevolence is the cause of God; and those who directly engage in it have so far the honor and happiness of being conformed to the highest standard of moral excellence" (Davis 1998, 28). With this statement, Leonard Bacon articulated the essence of his philosophy of life that led him to devote his energies to numerous voluntary associations. An influential editor, reformer, Congregational Church leader, and benevolent activist, he urged northern Protestants to enlist in a host of philanthropic activities.

EARLY YEARS AND EDUCATION

Born on February 2, 1802, Leonard Bacon was the first of seven children born to David and Alice Bacon, who served as Congregational missionaries to the Native Americans on the Michigan frontier until he was five. His parents then moved to the Western Re-

serve area of Ohio, where they established the town of Tallmadge as a Christian commonwealth that embodied New England institutions and ideas. David and Alice Bacon believed, true to their Congregationalist theology, that people were inherently sinful, but they also impressed upon their son the conviction, articulated by Timothy Dwight, **Lyman Beecher**, and other evangelical Protestants, that good works were essential for a Christian life and that individuals were moral agents accountable to God for their actions.

Due to serious financial difficulties, Bacon's parents were forced to abandon their godly experiment and return to Connecticut in 1812. With his family nearly destitute, an uncle's generosity enabled Bacon to attend Hartford Grammar School, which provided a rigorous classical education. He was subsequently admitted to Yale University as a scholarship student at the age of fifteen. Influenced by Beecher and other leading New

Leonard Bacon. Yale University Library.

England evangelicals who urged people to lead active Christian lives, Bacon participated in a number of student organizations at Yale University that emphasized moral uplift and religious benevolence.

Following his graduation from Yale University in 1820, Bacon, acting on his parents' fervent wish that he enter the ministry, studied at Andover Theological Seminary. The faculty at Andover—the premier seminary in the United States at the time—encouraged him to think systematically about philosophy and theology. Moreover, his professors, Beecher, and others urged him to actively engage in a number of philanthropic activities that embodied Samuel Hopkins's contention that one enhanced the glory of God by engaging in disinterested benevolence directed toward uplifting the downtrodden and advancing the Kingdom of God. For example, he labored for the Boston Society for the Moral and Religious Instruction of the Poor and played a leading role in the Andover Society of Inquiry Respecting Missions, which sought to send African Americans, both slave and free, to Liberia (on the coast of Africa). Even as a young theological student, he helped to shape the strategy of the American Colonization Society.

CAREER HIGHLIGHTS

In 1825, Bacon became pastor of the prestigious Center Church in New Haven, Connecticut. In July of that year, he married Lucy Johnson, whom he had met in Boston; the couple had nine children. Following her death in 1844, he married Catherine Terry, with whom he had five children. After nearly being dismissed by his congregation in the late 1820s, in part because he failed to generate a religious revival in his church, Bacon was able to regain their trust and affection. Indeed, at a time of declining permanency among New England pastors, his tenure at Center Church lasted for forty-one years. Most of his parishioners concurred with his adherence to the central tenets of the New Haven theology, which held that the millennium—the thousand years following the return of Christ to earth—must be accomplished by free moral agents who respond to rational appeals to turn to a benevolent God. Many members of his church also shared his interest in reform and philanthropic causes.

Bacon always considered his congregation his primary responsibility. Yet, from the beginning of his ministerial career, he was convinced that he must educate the American people on a broad range of social, political, and theological issues. Thus, as a writer, lecturer, and influential member of Congregational ecclesiastical bodies and numerous voluntary associations, he sought to connect his church and community to the larger world of organized benevolence, religious and reform journalism, social activism, and scholarship. Indeed, he wished to extend evangelical Protestantism and New England ideas and institutions to the rest of the nation and overseas.

Bacon used the press as a vehicle for the dissemination of his views to the general public, serving as a columnist or editor for several different papers for nearly sixty years. From 1826 until 1838, he was one of a committee that edited the *Christian Spectator*, a Connecticut evangelical magazine; his numerous articles focused largely on matters related to race, slavery, and the effort to convince African Americans to relocate in Liberia. As a leading advocate of colonization as a means of uplifting free blacks and eventually ending slavery, he also founded and edited the *Journal of Freedom* in the mid-1830s. In the early 1840s, he and other New Haven scholars and clergymen established the *New Englander*. For many years, Bacon served on the journal's editorial committee, and he contributed dozens of articles, including many on the organizations that constituted what historians have described as the "benevolent empire." From 1848 until 1861, he was senior editor of the *Independent*, an influential New York City religious newspaper that espoused benevolent activism, efforts to keep the territories free of slavery as well as the extension of Congregationalism to the West. In addition, he served as a columnist for the New York *Evangelist* in the 1840s, the *Congregationalist* in the 1860s, and the *Christian Union* in the 1870s. During the last fifteen years of his life, he taught theology and church history at Yale Divinity School.

MAJOR PHILANTHROPIC CONTRIBUTIONS

Indeed, Bacon devoted an enormous amount of time and energy to the temperance, colonization, antislavery, education, missionary, Bible, and other reform and benevolent causes. Beginning in the early 1820s, Bacon helped to establish and/or served as an officer or director of such voluntary associations as the Connecticut Colonization Society, the New Haven Anti-Slavery Association, the American Tract Society, the American Board of Commissioners for Foreign Missions, the Society for the Promotion of Collegiate and Theological Education at the West, the American Education Society, and the Connecticut Historical Society. As a respected and influential member of these organizations, he

helped to develop their strategy and philosophy, disseminate information to the public, recruit new members, and solicit contributions.

Saddled with debts from his college and seminary days, and with a large family to support on a minister's salary, Bacon was seldom able to contribute monetarily to the philanthropic associations that proliferated during his lifetime. Still, he effectively employed the press, the lecture hall, and the pulpit to proclaim the virtues of philanthropic action. He often reminded the members of his congregation that the accumulation of riches required hard work and patience and that it was incumbent upon them to contribute their wealth to good causes.

One of Bacon's most important contributions to American philanthropy was an 1847 article in the *New Englander*, which represented perhaps the first serious treatise on charitable trusteeship in the United States. In this article, he expressed concern that the executive committees of many voluntary organizations, such as the American Tract Society and the American Board of Commissioners for Foreign Missions (both of which he served as a member of the board of managers), were not sufficiently accountable to either their members or their churches. To guard against the perversion of their trust, he believed executive committees must be responsible to a streamlined and truly representative board of managers. Such boards, he argued, should in fact, and not just in theory, play a significant role in these associations by appointing members of executive committees and engaging in a substantive review of committees' actions during the previous year. Such an arrangement, he concluded, would best serve to inspire public confidence and safeguard the interests of these organizations and the larger religious community.

Clearly, Bacon was motivated by a number of considerations to write, speak, and organize on behalf of various voluntary associations. He believed, above all, that Christians were obligated to combat sin wherever it existed in the world and that the benevolent societies were the primary instruments for achieving this objective. These benevolent enterprises would, in turn, help to ensure the conversion of mankind to evangelical Protestantism in preparation for the return of Christ to earth for a thousand years. Evangelism, with its emphasis on the dangers to the soul and society posed by a rising tide of immorality and disorder, pointed to a conservative social philosophy. Bacon's involvement in the temperance, anti-Catholic, colonization, and missionary movements, as well as the Bible and tract societies represented, in part, an effort to restore order, morality, and racial and religious homogeneity in a society experiencing rapid industrialization, urbanization, immigration, and westward migration. Yet, his attachment to the concepts of immediate repentance for sin, free will, liberty, and social justice also moved him to champion public education, the abolition of slavery, temperance, fundamental rights for the freedmen following the Civil War, and other causes.

Indeed, a number of voluntary organizations that Bacon actively supported sought to achieve diverse, and sometimes contradictory, objectives. The Society for the Promotion of Collegiate and Theological Education at the West, which Bacon, Beecher, Horace Bushnell, and other Congregational activists founded in the early 1840s for the purpose of soliciting funds from eastern donors for fourteen colleges and seminaries in the West, illustrates this point. Simultaneously, this organization sought to extend education throughout the region; to provide an opportunity for poor, ambitious young men to receive a liberal, Christian education; to ensure the survival of a free, democratic society; to counter the disorder and irreligion that its founders believed to be prevalent in the West; to spread New England ideas and institutions (including the Congregational Church) to other parts of the United States; and to combat the Catholic influence that they feared was gaining ground in the new western settlements. In all, the Society's agenda reflected the complex mix of pessimism and optimism, fear and hope, and bigotry and compassion that motivated its founders.

CONCLUSION

Church leader, editor, and reform and benevolent activist, Leonard Bacon accomplished much during his lifetime. His efforts to launch, sustain, and publicize a host of voluntary associations that comprised the "benevolent empire," which sought to thoroughly Christianize America and to prepare the world for the thousand-year reign of Christ, profoundly influenced the ways that northern Protestants addressed the moral and social issues of the early and mid-nineteenth century.

Hugh Davis

FURTHER READING

Bacon, Theodore Dwight. *Leonard Bacon: A Statesman in the Church*. Edited by Benjamin W. Bacon. New Haven, CT: Yale University Press, 1931.

Banner, Lois. "Religious Benevolence as Social Control: A Critique of an Interpretation." *Journal of American History* 40, 1973, 23–41.

Bodo, John R. *The Protestant Clergy and Public Issues, 1812–1848*. Princeton, NJ: Princeton University Press, 1954.

Davis, Hugh. *Leonard Bacon: New England Reformer and Antislavery Moderate*. Baton Rouge: Louisiana State University Press, 1998.

Findlay, James. "Agency, Denominations and the Western Colleges, 1830–1860: Some Connections between Evangelicalism and Higher Education." *Church History* 50, 1981, 64–80.

Griffin, Clifford S. *Their Brothers' Keepers: Moral Stewardship in the United States, 1800–1865*. New Brunswick, NJ: Rutgers University Press, 1960.

PAPERS

Leonard Bacon's papers are located in the Yale University Archives (New Haven, CT).

ROGER NASH BALDWIN
(1884–1981)

Founder and Leader of the American Civil Liberties Union (ACLU)

INTRODUCTION

" 'The avoidance of any issue except the defense of the Bill of Rights has marked the Civil Liberties Union since its beginning' " (Lamson 1976, 155). These words, spoken by Roger Nash Baldwin, expressed the mission of the American Civil Liberties Union (ACLU) as well as the beliefs of an individual who would help transform the notion of civil liberties and strengthen the freedoms guaranteed in the Bill of Rights. For much of his life, Baldwin would defend individual rights by advocating policies enabling all Americans to express themselves as they wished.

EARLY YEARS AND EDUCATION

Little in Baldwin's early years suggested that he would become an advocate of civil liberties. Born on January 21, 1884, Baldwin was the first of six children of Lucy Cushing Nash and Frank Fenno Baldwin. Growing up in Wellesley, Massachusetts, Baldwin was a member of a prominent family of businessmen that traced its roots back to the Pilgrims. Baldwin led a privileged upper-middle-class childhood; he spent much of his childhood pursuing varied interests that ranged from bird watching to taking in many of the cultural opportunities available in nearby Boston, such as attending performances of the Boston Symphony.

After high school, Baldwin enrolled at Harvard University. While at Harvard, he began teaching night classes at the Cambridge Social Union, an adult education center established by Harvard professors and staffed by students. At the Cambridge Social Union, he taught 150 middle-aged men and women about the newly developing field of social science and gave weekly piano lessons. In 1905,

Baldwin received both a bachelor's and master's degree from Harvard University, and subsequently led his mother and five siblings on a one-year tour of Europe.

CAREER HIGHLIGHTS AND MAJOR PHILANTHROPIC CONTRIBUTIONS

Shortly after returning from Europe, Baldwin moved to St. Louis and accepted two positions: directing a neighborhood settlement house called Self-Culture Hall and teaching the first course in sociology at Washington University. Through his work at Self-Culture Hall, he became active in the social work movement. At the age of twenty-three, he left Self-Culture Hall to become chief probation officer of the recently established juvenile court.

By 1910, Baldwin had made a name for himself within the social reform movement and received several job offers from progressive organizations located on the East coast. Baldwin, however, decided to stay in St. Louis and accepted an offer to serve as secretary of the St. Louis Civic League. Moving from the field of social reform to civic reform, Baldwin worked with civic leaders to promote several reform initiatives that were also being implemented in other cities across the country, including campaigns against pollution and efforts to apply a civil service system to all areas of city government.

During his years in St. Louis, Baldwin's political thoughts were influenced by the writings of Emma Goldman, a leading anarchist. Goldman and her followers believed that the rights of the working class were being stifled by a capitalist system that relied on their work but shared little of the wealth created by the laborers. Subsequently, Baldwin became a strong supporter of labor organi-

Roger Nash Baldwin in 1934. Roger Nash Baldwin Papers, Public Policy Papers Division, Department of Rare Books and Special Collections, Princeton University Library.

zations, including radical ones like the International Workers of the World (IWW). Throughout the rest of his life, he would continue to believe that political and economic systems that were not capitalistic, particularly communism, offered a better model to protect an individual's rights.

With the outbreak of World War I, Baldwin became completely committed to pacifism and moved to New York City in 1917 to volunteer for the American Union Against Militarism (AUAM). The AUAM could trace its roots to an organization formed by three prominent social workers of the time: **Jane Addams**, Paul Kellogg, and **Lillian Wald**. Once the United States formally declared war on Germany, Baldwin believed that the AUAM's role should be to protect the rights of individuals who wished to express their opposition to the war. Baldwin established a Bureau of Conscientious Objectors (later named the Civil Liberties Bureau) within the AUAM to advocate for the fair treatment of Americans who did not want to serve in the

army. The goals of the Civil Liberties Bureau and the AUAM came into almost immediate conflict. While the AUAM was concerned with the plight of conscientious objectors, they primarily wished to work within the government to end American participation in World War I. At the same time, the Civil Liberties Bureau was bluntly attacking President Woodrow Wilson's administration for a policy of prosecuting conscientious objectors that refused military service. This difference in approach created tension within the Board of Directors of the AUAM, with Addams, Wald, and Kellogg protesting Baldwin's confrontational tactics and Norman Thomas and Crystal Eastman supporting his work. When it became apparent that the methods of the Civil Liberties Bureau and the AUAM were in conflict, the National Civil Liberties Bureau was formed as a separate organization with Baldwin as director.

As head of the National Civil Liberties Bureau, Baldwin worked diligently to protect the rights of conscientious objectors. Under his leadership, the Bureau lobbied military officials for fair treatment of conscientious objectors held in military prisons. It also advised potential conscientious objectors how to object to military service. In addition to conscientious objectors, the Bureau also took up the plight of the thousands of citizens who experienced repression of free speech because of the 1917 Espionage Act. Under this act, Americans who made speeches that interfered with recruiting and enlistment in the armed forces were prosecuted and received sentences of up to ten years in prison. The Bureau also provided support to members of the International Workers of the World who were brought up on charges of disrupting the war effort through work slowdowns. While the Bureau did not provide defense attorneys, it did organize public support for the workers and raised funds for their legal expenses.

In October 1918, Baldwin's pacifism was put to the ultimate test when he refused to report for his military physical examination and was arrested as a war resister. Baldwin pleaded guilty to the charge and was sentenced to one year in prison. While he served his sentence at the Essex County Jail, Baldwin's activism did not ebb. With the assistance of three fellow prisoners, he organized the Prisoners' Welfare League to try to improve prisoners' conditions. When the local sheriff found out about this organization, he transferred Baldwin to another prison to quiet the protests.

After nine months of incarceration, Baldwin was released from prison and married his first wife, Madeleine Doty, a writer, pacifist, and feminist whom he had originally met in St. Louis. Within the course of one year, he renewed his efforts to protect civil liberties and he helped found four new organizations dedicated to preserving Americans' freedom of speech. At the time of his release, hundreds of war protestors and conscientious objectors were still in jail. In fact, the U.S. Justice Department deported thousands of "radical" Americans because of their political views on World War I. These radicals were

writing to Baldwin, seeking advice and support. Consequently, Baldwin founded the Mutual Aid Society (1920), an organization that loaned funds to help underwrite the legal costs of left-wing radicals. He also launched the International Committee of Political Prisoners to raise money for these deported American citizens and to link them to helpful agencies in foreign countries. It was in this political and social context that Baldwin insisted that the National Civil Liberties Bureau expand its mission to the promotion of freedom of expression. To reflect its expanded mission, they renamed the organization the American Civil Liberties Union (ACLU), an organization Baldwin would guide for the next thirty years.

As director of the ACLU until 1950, Baldwin established the organization as a leading defender of the Bill of Rights and free expression. Over the years, he guided the ACLU to seek out test cases that would attempt to strengthen individual rights and gain the attention of American society. In Patterson, New Jersey, the ACLU defended the rights of striking factory workers to peaceably assemble and express their views, successfully overturning a 1796 law in the process. For years, the ACLU fought censorship by taking on city, state, and federal attempts to ban the importation and sale of objectionable books. The ACLU, for example, fought censors who wished to stop the distribution of such publications as *Ulysses, Strange Fruit, The Sex Side of Life, An American Tragedy, Lysistrata*, and *Nudist* magazine. Over the years, through repeated efforts of the ACLU, most obscenity standards were ruled unconstitutional.

During Baldwin's tenure, the ACLU also orchestrated one of the most famous cases of the twentieth century, the Scopes Monkey Trial (1925). When the state of Tennessee passed a law banning the teaching of evolution in the public schools, the ACLU sought out a teacher willing to test the statute's attack on free speech. John Scopes agreed to challenge the law and the ACLU coordinated his defense, which was headed up by the famous lawyer Clarence Darrow. Scopes was convicted under the law and ordered to pay a $100 fine. Upon appeal, his conviction was overturned, but—in a bittersweet victory for the ACLU—the Tennessee Supreme Court upheld the statute but acquitted Scopes because they believed his fine was excessive.

Baldwin also tried to advance international civil rights with his work in Japan and Germany following World War II. At the request of General Douglas MacArthur, Baldwin toured occupied Japan in 1947. During his time in Japan, he traveled and reported on censorship issues to MacArthur and met with other nongovernmental organizations (NGO) interested in civil liberties. In 1948, Baldwin spent the summer in Germany reviewing civil rights progress under American occupation. Upon retirement from the ACLU in 1950, Baldwin devoted much of his time to international civil liberties issues. He became active in the United Nations (UN) and chaired the International League for the Rights of Man, the only NGO in the UN to be devoted exclusively to human rights. In this position, Baldwin, Eleanor Roosevelt, and other leaders of the human rights movement worked to expand civil rights on a worldwide basis. Over the next 30 years, Baldwin would continue to contribute to this international movement.

CONCLUSION

As a social reformer and civil libertarian, Baldwin devoted over a half-century to the establishment and defense of individual rights and freedoms. As a result, Baldwin and his ACLU became major players in numerous public debates of the twentieth century. By engaging in and shaping a multitude of controversial issues, Baldwin and the ACLU also illustrated a major purpose of voluntary action and voluntary association, social change advocacy.

Kevin A. Fortwendel

FURTHER READING

Cottrell, Robert C. *Roger Nash Baldwin and the American Civil Liberties Union.* New York: Columbia University Press, 2000.
Lamson, Peggy. *Roger Baldwin: Founder of the American Civil Liberties Union.* Boston: Houghton Mifflin, 1976.

PAPERS

Roger Baldwin's papers are located in the Firestone Library at Princeton University (Princeton, NJ).

CLARA BARTON
(1821–1912)

Civil War Nurse and Founder of the American Red Cross

INTRODUCTION

"If I were to speak of war, it would not be to show you the glories of conquering armies but the mischief and misery they strew in their tracks; and how . . . some one must follow closely in their steps . . . toiling in the rain and darkness . . . with no thought of pride or glory . . . hearts breaking with pity, faces bathed in tears and hands in blood. This is the side which history never shows" (Oates 1994, n.p.). Although Clara Barton is best known for the nursing care she gave to wounded soldiers during the Civil War, earning her the name "Angel of the Battlefield," and her efforts to establish and shape the American Red Cross, her life also touched on other philanthropic causes, including the establishment of free public schools, women's suffrage, prison reform, and opportunities for African Americans. Barton, who devoted her life to humanitarian service, felt driven to help others. At times, her service seemed to even disregard her own physical and mental health.

EARLY YEARS AND EDUCATION

Clarissa Harlowe Barton, born on Christmas Day in 1821 in North Oxford, Massachusetts, was the youngest of five children. As a child, she was particularly close to her brother David, whom she nursed back to health during her early teens after he was badly injured in an accident. Indeed, she scarcely left his bedside for two years. Her mother, Sarah Barton, was a hard worker who believed in discipline and demanded that every task assigned be done. Her father, Stephen Barton, had served in the Indian wars under General Anthony Wayne before settling down as a farmer, and young Clara Barton never tired of hearing about his military experiences. Both parents influenced their daughter with their liberal politics, Universalist religious beliefs, and concern for social justice.

Barton was small in stature and extremely shy, but from an early age she demonstrated keen intellect, compassion, and independence. An excellent student, she started formal schooling when only four years old, became a teacher at age eighteen, and eleven years later furthered her education at the Clinton Liberal Institute, an advanced school for female teachers in New York state. Although she was a romantic and had several suitors, she told a cousin years later that she decided against matrimony early on, a decision that left her free to pursue the humanitarian causes to which she was devoted. In spite of this drive, she was forced to retreat for extended periods of time throughout her life because of bouts with depression and physical exhaustion.

CAREER HIGHLIGHTS

In 1839, Barton began her first teaching assignment in Worcester County, Massachusetts. From the beginning, she sought to establish a strong relationship with her students, built on mutual respect. Before long, she was in high demand, both for her enthusiastic teaching and for her ability to maintain discipline—even among the rowdiest boys. In the 1840s, she and her brother Stephen Barton worked to reorganize and improve the public schools in North Oxford, but eventually Barton longed to expand her horizons. Thus, after her studies at the Clinton Liberal Institute, she accepted a teaching position in Cedarville, New Jersey. Later, she moved to nearby Bordentown, where she agreed to teach without compensation, provided the town's leaders would equip a suitable place. Her goal was to prove the value of free public education, which she succeeded in doing, but she left when the school board authorized funding for a new school building and then insisted that it be headed by a man.

Disillusioned, Barton moved to Washington, DC, where she was befriended by Congressman Alexander DeWitt of Massachusetts and frequently attended sessions of Congress, which fueled her lifelong interest in politics. DeWitt also introduced her to Judge Charles Mason of the U.S. Patent Office, and Barton soon became one of the first women to be hired as a clerk-copyist there. However, many in the federal bureaucracy thought it improper for women and men to work side by side. Consequently, she lost her position when James Buchanan became president in 1856. She returned home for a brief time but her depression was aggravated by family problems including the poor health of her father and a favorite nephew, financial demands, and the tension of having to live with her brother and sister-in-law because she was unemployed. Four years later, she was recalled to the Patent Office and moved back to the nation's capital, residing in Washington when the conflict between North and South erupted into war.

MAJOR PHILANTHROPIC CONTRIBUTIONS

Like many, Barton was optimistic that the Civil War would be over quickly and deter-

A Civil War-era portrait of Clara Barton. Library of Congress; LC-USZ62-108564.

mined to do her part for the Union, declaring, "I'm well and strong and young—young enough to go to the front. If I can't be a soldier, I'll help soldiers" (Williams 1941, 63). Her first efforts, in 1861, consisted of gathering needed supplies—purchased with her own meager resources or donated by others—and distributing them to those in need behind the front lines. A year later, she obtained official clearance to aid soldiers on the battlefields, where she worked tirelessly to provide food, clothing, and medical supplies, seemingly oblivious to the danger. On many occasions, she labored with little or no sleep, moving among the sick and wounded to feed or soothe them, until she collapsed from exhaustion.

During the siege of Charleston (1863–1865), Barton continued to care for Union soldiers but also "came to understand the plight of the freed men and women" (Burton 1995, 27). Her mother, an abolitionist, had first opened her eyes to the evils of slavery. Although Barton's efforts to provide supplies

and teach some of the former slaves to read were small in comparison with the extent of their need, she did what she could and later described black soldiers as heroes. She wrote, "Whiter blood than theirs has often failed to exhibit traits as high and noble" (Burton 1995, 27). After the war, Barton also became acquainted with Frederick Douglass and continued to support Negro rights.

From 1865 to 1869, Barton organized a letter-writing campaign to search for missing soldiers, again using her own resources to meet the needs of those who were desperate for any information about their lost loved ones (though later the federal government reimbursed her for part of what she spent). She would compile lists of the missing soldiers and have them published in newspapers throughout the country, asking that anyone with information write to her so that she could then contact the family. She also worked closely with Dorrence Atwater, a prisoner of war at the dreaded Andersonville Prison in Georgia, who managed to compile a list of the prisoners who died while there. With a delegation from Washington, Atwater and Barton traveled to Georgia in 1865 to mark the graves.

For two years during the postwar period, Barton also embarked on lecture tours, which enabled her to become a well-known and respected figure throughout the North. She described her own experiences, acknowledged the important role that donors played in her success, and, at times, defended other leading women of the time, including Susan B. Anthony. Although Barton generally preferred to operate alone rather than actively participate in organizations led by others, she certainly identified with the women's suffrage movement and later criticized the prison system. Her assessment was based on a short-term appointment (in 1883) as superintendent of the Reformatory Prison for Women in Sherborn, Massachusetts, where she openly expressed her sympathy for the inmates and willingness to defend them.

In 1869, when Barton's health failed, her doctor ordered her to Europe to rest and recuperate. While in Geneva, Switzerland, Barton met founding members of the International Committee of the Red Cross, including Jean Henri Dunant and Gustave Moynier. This group had convened a conference in 1864 which resulted in the Geneva Convention, an agreement that regulated the fair treatment of prisoners and the sick or wounded during times of war. Although the United States was represented at this conference, it had not signed the treaty because of its policy against "entangling alliances."

With the outbreak of the Franco-Prussian War in 1870, Barton had the opportunity to observe the first efforts of the Red Cross. She volunteered to distribute aid in numerous cities, but was particularly known for her work in Strasbourg. There she launched an innovative program "based on the triple concept of self-help, petit capitalism, and home industry" (Burton 1995, 73) to provide for the impoverished citizens not by distributing donated clothing but by employing local women to make garments for two francs a day out of donated goods.

When Barton returned to the United States in 1873, she was still in a weakened condition, having served humanitarian causes in Europe much as she had in her own country, but she arrived home with a new purpose: to obtain American accession to the Geneva Convention and establish a Red Cross Society. After entering a sanitarium in Dansville, New York, to regain her health, she moved to Washington, DC, to lobby for her cause. She educated the public through brochures and speeches, made personal calls on cabinet heads and congressmen, and finally succeeded in establishing the American Association of the Red Cross in 1881. A year later, the United States signed the Geneva Treaty, and in 1884, the international organization approved the "American Amendment," so called because of its linkage to Barton's realization that the Red Cross could meet needs in times of peace as well as war.

Barton determined that the American Red Cross would "organize a system of national relief and apply the same in mitigating the sufferings caused by war, pestilence, famine and other calamities" such as floods, fires, earthquakes, and hurricanes (Barton 1898, 47). Indeed, the earliest relief efforts of the new society came in response to natural disasters. Barton or her trusted assistant, Dr. Julian Hubbell, personally supervised aid to the victims of forest fires in Michigan (1881); floods in the Mississippi and Ohio valleys (1882) and in Johnstown, Pennsylvania (1889); tornados in Illinois and yellow fever in Jacksonville, Florida (1888); famine in Texas (1885); earthquake (1886) and hurricanes (1893–1894) in South Carolina; and a tidal wave in Galveston, Texas (1900). Although in her seventies, Barton also headed up relief efforts for peasants starving in Russia (1892), Armenians fleeing massacres by the Turkish government (1896), and Cubans suffering in concentration camps (1897). She also personally oversaw wartime aid during the Spanish-American War (1898).

Throughout her presidency (1881–1904) of the organization, Barton represented the American Red Cross at international conferences in Europe, where she was always honored as a celebrity. At home, however, there was growing discontent with her leadership. The opposition cited her advanced age, lack of careful financial records, and the need for a management structure. Eventually, Barton was forced to resign. She spent her last eight years in her home at Glen Echo, near Washington, DC, or in Dansville, New York. Throughout this period, Barton was obsessed with communicating with the dead through mediums and séances. She died on April 12, 1912.

CONCLUSION

Barton exhibited selfless heroism, incredible generosity, and dogged determination to humanitarian service. At the same time, however, she often failed to take care of herself and repeatedly suffered breakdowns that kept her from the active life she craved. Bouts of depression and physical collapse, along with an inability to accept criticism and an unwillingness to share control with others, eventually led to her downfall. Nevertheless, she made important contributions to philanthropy in the United States, through direct service and establishing the American Red Cross, which continues as the leader in disaster relief today.

Roberta K. Gibboney

FURTHER READING

Barton, Clara. *The Red Cross in Peace and War.* Washington, DC: American Historical Press, 1898.

Burton, David H. *Clara Barton: In the Service of Humanity.* Westport, CT: Greenwood Press, 1995.

Oates, Stephen B. *A Woman of Valor: Clara Barton and the Civil War.* New York: Free Press, 1994.

Pryor, Elizabeth Brown. *Clara Barton: Professional Angel.* Philadelphia: University of Pennsylvania Press, 1987.

Williams, Blanche C. *Clara Barton: Daughter of Destiny.* Philadelphia: J. B. Lippincott, 1941.

PAPERS

Clara Barton's unpublished papers are collected in the Library of Congress (Washington, DC) (see Clara Barton, National Red Cross; and Theodore Roosevelt).

LYMAN BEECHER
(1775–1862)

Evangelist and Promoter of Voluntary Associations

INTRODUCTION

The Second Great Awakening—the wave of religious revivalism that swept the country between 1790 and 1840—has been referred to as an "organizing process" because it gave rise to a wide range of social reform initiatives. Connecticut evangelist Lyman Beecher played a key role in teaching Americans the possibilities of voluntary associations as instruments of social change. "The Fact is," Beecher would write reflecting on his career, "by voluntary efforts, societies, missions, and revivals, [the clergy] exert a deeper influence than" the past (Beecher 1961, I:253).

EARLY YEARS AND EDUCATION

A descendant of the early settlers of Connecticut, Lyman Beecher was born in New Haven, the son of David Beecher, a blacksmith and farmer, and Esther Lyman (the third of David Beecher's five wives). After receiving his primary education in country schools in New Haven and Guilford, Lyman Beecher entered Yale College in 1793. Timothy Dwight, the "Pope of New England Congregationalism," became president of the college at the beginning of Beecher's junior year. Poet, theologian, politician, educational innovator, and charismatic preacher, Dwight transformed the college—and saved Beecher from religious skepticism. Beecher became Dwight's protege and stayed on at Yale College after graduation (in 1797) to study theology. Dwight believed that democratic institutions depended on private morality and that the clergy had a particular responsibility for public morality as social and political activists. Beecher came to share these convictions.

CAREER HIGHLIGHTS AND MAJOR PHILANTHROPIC CONTRIBUTIONS

In 1799, Beecher was called to the pulpit of the Congregational Church in East Hampton, New York, where he honed his preaching and organizing skills. During the same year, he married Roxana Foote; the couple produced nine children. After his first wife's death in 1816, Beecher married Harriet Porter—having three sons and one daughter—and, after Porter's death, married Lydia Jackson. Prior to his first wife's death, he accepted a call from the church in Litchfield, Connecticut (1810)—arriving just as efforts to disestablish Congregationalism were moving into high gear. The clergy were in the thick of the battle and none was more political than his mentor, Dwight, who was the leader of the Federalist party in Connecticut.

Until 1817, the Congregational Church in Connecticut and Massachusetts was "established"—meaning that it was supported by taxation and enjoyed a variety of special legal privileges. Though Beecher worked closely with Dwight to defend the establishment, he privately began to doubt that coercion was the best way of maintaining vital and committed Christianity. His doubts were strengthened by his early experiments with voluntary associations. Early in his ministry at Litchfield, Beecher had attended the ordination of a colleague in a nearby town and had been appalled by the drunken spectacle that the assembled clergy made of themselves at the party following the religious service. "My alarm and shame, and indignation were intense," Beecher would recall, "and silently

I took an oath before God that I would never attend another ordination of that kind" (Beecher 1961, I:178).

Outraged, Beecher persuaded his fellow clergymen to take the lead in combating the "undue consumption of ardent spirits" because of their "deadly effect on health, intellect, the family, society, civil and religious institutions, and especially in nullifying the means of grace and destroying souls." Ministers were urged to offer "appropriate discourses" on intemperance, to abstain from using liquor at ecclesiastical meetings, and "to form voluntary associations" to promote temperance (Beecher 1961, I:179–180).

In his efforts on behalf of temperance, Beecher transcended the politically heated question of Congregational establishment to focus on an issue that—though it had important religious implications—could appeal to a broad public, regardless of its religious allegiance. Couching moral reform in pragmatic economic and nationalistic arguments, he also stressed the spiritual by calling on clergy and the faithful to lead the effort. Beecher's "experiment" showed the way in which the church, acting as a social force rather than a political one, could transform public life by enabling citizens to identify social problems as public issues and to weigh them morally.

Inspired by the success of this effort, Beecher sought to broaden the temperance initiative into a general movement for the "reformation of morals and the suppression of vice" because he saw such an effort as the ultimate solution to the problem of poverty (Beecher 1961, I:187). Once again, he moved beyond the church, seeking to build a coalition of like-minded clergy and influential laymen to lead the venture (to give it "weight and respectability"), but basing the effort organizationally on "local auxiliary societies" (Beecher 1961, I:185). The Yale College commencement was the ideal occasion for launching the movement because it was the most important annual public event in Connecticut, attracting not only the state's political, economic, and intellectual leaders,

This daguerreotype of Lyman Beecher was made in the late 1840s. Library of Congress; LC-USZ62-109964.

but also Yale alumni from throughout the Northeast. Decades later when Beecher reflected on these efforts, he claimed that he was moved to undertake them because he foresaw the downfall of the establishment and believed that the "voluntary system" of church support, combined with voluntary associations addressed to a variety of social evils, would make religion more, rather than less, influential.

The efforts of Beecher and other clergy to engage religion in public issues were controversial. The Calvinist doctrines on which Congregationalism was based argued that faith rather than good works was the key to salvation. Many religious conservatives felt that Beecher's social activism betrayed Calvinist principles by placing too much importance on good works and not enough on faith. Beecher, however, claimed to be faithful to Calvinism. He denied that good works were a means to salvation: For the faithful, Beecher argued, they were an essential ex-

pression of faith; for unbelievers, they were a means of leading them toward faith.

Arguments over these issues had been dividing New England Protestants since the Great Awakening of the 1740s, when the "New Lights," those favoring a return to the Calvinist emphasis on faith and conversion through appeals to the emotions, split from the "Old Lights" who favored more rational and humanitarian beliefs that stressed the value of good works. This division roughly paralleled emergent differences between the new upper class of urban merchants and manufacturers (who tended to favor the Old Lights) and farmers and artisans (who tended to favor the New Lights). In Massachusetts after 1800, these religious differences took the form of a bitter conflict between Trinitarian (Old Lights) and Unitarian (New Lights) Congregationalists for control of churches and appointments at Harvard College.

In 1826, the Hanover Street Church in

Boston, a Trinitarian congregation, called Lyman Beecher to lead the struggle against the Unitarians. Beecher, who by then had become an expert organizer and eloquent advocate, set immediately to work. Beecher organized the young men of his congregation into a voluntary association, which challenged Unitarian political candidates and took on social issues—corruption, intemperance, gambling, violations of the sabbath, theaters—that, they argued, had flourished under the Unitarian regime. They also organized an assortment of associations—lyceums (public lectures), libraries, and mechanics, temperance, and missionary societies—intended to rescue young people from the temptations of the city. These associations became models for organizations throughout the nation.

By the 1820s, Protestant evangelicalism, led by New England clergymen, had become a national movement as religious conservatives reorganized as national denominational bodies, sponsored religious publishing houses that were among the largest publishing enterprises in the country, founded schools and colleges, and supported "education societies" that underwrote the educations of pious and ambitious young men, who, after completing their degrees, went on to become either ministers or lay leaders in the evangelical movement. Because of the movement's social activism, it had a profound influence on politics and society in the decades before the Civil War. Beecher's strategic location in the national evangelical network assured the impact of his ideas.

In 1832, Beecher decided to go West, accepting the presidency of Lane Seminary and the pulpit at the Second Presbyterian Church of Cincinnati, Ohio. Beecher's tenure as Lane's president lasted only two years. When the seminary's trustees attempted to abolish student antislavery societies and to silence public discussion of slavery as an issue, Beecher resigned his presidency (though keeping his position as professor of theology). A group of dissenters, with generous support from eastern antislavery advocates, established Oberlin College, which became a major center of abolitionism.

During the eighteen years he spent in Ohio, Beecher consolidated his reputation as a national religious leader and eloquent proponent of voluntary associations. In his most famous oration, *A Plea for the West* (1835), Beecher offered a powerful vision of the public role of religion and the possibilities of associational action. "There must be permanent powerful literary and moral institutions, which, like the great orbs of attraction and light, shall send forth at once their power and their illumination, and without them all else will be ephemeral" (Beecher 1835, 19). Government alone could not be depended on to establish these institutions: "religious education and moral principle" were necessary to create the "habits of intellectual culture which spring up in alliance with evangelical institutions"—and they, in turn, produced the legislative will to create and sustain schools and other institutions of culture (Beecher 1835, 23).

Beecher also charged his discourse with a sense of millennial urgency, iterating themes about the interdependence of democracy and public morality drawn from the ideas of his old mentor, Timothy Dwight. Pointing to the need for schools in the West, Beecher argued that a "million and a half children without the means of education, and about an equal number of adults, either foreigners or native Americans, that are uneducated" were "most dangerous to liberty" because, "without intelligence, or conscience, or patriotism, or property, and driven on by demagogues," they had the power to "overrule all the property, and wisdom, and moral principles of the nation" (Beecher 1835, 47–49). Beecher devoted the bulk of *A Plea for the West* to a highly inflammatory peroration on the dangers posed to republican government by the growing immigrant population, especially Irish Catholics. This lapse into religious prejudice—which was said to have been responsible for stirring up the mob that destroyed the Ursuline convent in Charlestown, Massachusetts in August 1834—combined with eloquent appeals to the possibilities of democratic institutions, typified the tensions within American Protestantism in the nineteenth century.

After years of traveling the lecture circuit, fund-raising, writing, and preaching, Beecher's health broke down in 1850 and he decided to return to the East (first settling in Boston). By 1857, when his mental powers declined, he took up residence with his son, Henry Ward Beecher, a leading evangelical preacher who resided in Brooklyn, New York. Beecher died on January 10, 1863, and was buried in New Haven's Grove Street Cemetery.

Among Lyman Beecher's greatest legacies were his children. All seven of his sons became Congregational clergymen—the most notable being Henry Ward, who succeeded his father as the nation's leading evangelical preacher; Edward Ward, a leading religious journalist and antislavery advocate; and Charles Ward, a religious writer, hymnodist, and education reformer. Lyman Beecher's daughters, Harriet Beecher Stowe and Catherine Beecher, both became national figures, the former as the author of the hugely influential abolitionist novel *Uncle Tom's Cabin*, and the latter as an abolitionist, domestic reformer, and advocate for women's education.

CONCLUSION

Lyman Beecher made three key contributions to American philanthropy. First, he helped to make voluntary associations into sacred institutions, transforming them from the kinds of "self-created societies" that James Madison had denounced in *Federalist* #10 and George Washington had attacked in his "Farewell Address" as imperiling the American Republic, to legitimate and credible instruments through which private groups could act in the public interest. Second, he probably did more than any other American to legitimate associations as well as teach Americans how to use them. Beecher played an important role in popularizing the theological ideas of his friend and Yale theologian Nathaniel W. Taylor—ideas that tied evangelical fervor to social and political activism. This linkage was largely responsible for making the antebellum decades into America's first great age of reform and for the fact that voluntary associations were at the forefront of the great reform movements of the period—abolitionism, temperance, sabbatarianism, and efforts to relieve the sufferings of the dependent and disabled. Third, he helped to redefine the public role of religion, changing churches from being direct political actors into entities that endeavored to empower their members—acting as individuals—as moral agents in society, politics, and economic life.

Peter Dobkin Hall

FURTHER READING

Abzug, Robert H. *Cosmos Crumbling: American Reform and the Religious Imagination.* New York: Oxford University Press, 1994.

Beecher, Lyman. *The Autobiography of Lyman Beecher.* Barbara M. Cross, ed. 2 vols. Cambridge: Harvard University Press, 1961.

———. *A Plea for the West.* Cincinnati: Truman & Smith, 1835.

Bledstein, Burton J. *The Culture of Professionalism: The Middle Class and the Development of Higher Education in America.* New York: W.W. Norton & Company, 1976.

Foster, Charles O. *An Errand of Mercy: The Evangelical United Front, 1790–1837.* Chapel Hill: University of North Carolina Press, 1960.

Fraser, James W. *Pedagogue for God's Kingdom: Lyman Beecher and the Second Great Awakening.* Lanham, MD: University Press of America, 1985.

Henry, Stuart. *Unvanquished Puritan: A Portrait of Lyman Beecher.* Westport, CT: Greenwood Press, 1986.

Mathews, Donald G. "The Second Great Awakening as an Organizing Process, 1780–1830: An Hypothesis." *American Quarterly* 21, Spring 1969, 23–43.

Scott, Donald M. *From Office to Profession: The New England Ministry, 1750–1850.* Philadelphia: University of Pennsylvania Press, 1978.

Smith, Timothy L. *Revivalism and Social Reform: American Protestantism on the Eve of the Civil War.* New York: Harper & Row, 1957.

PAPERS

The papers of Lyman Beecher and several members of his family, covering the period 1704–1964, are located in the Yale University Library (New Haven, CT). Other papers can be found in the Beecher Family Papers, Archives and Special Collections, Mount Holyoke College (South Hadley, MA).

ANTHONY BENEZET
(1716–1784)

Educator, Abolitionist, and Social Reformer

INTRODUCTION

"Liberty is the right of every human creature, as soon as he breathes the vital air. And no human law can deprive him of the right which he derives from the law of nature' " (Jackson 1999, 106). This quote by Anthony Benezet epitomizes his guiding philosophy. Benezet spent his entire life giving to those in need and promoting equality for all people. His visions and actions were radical for his time but he made an impact on education and the abolitionist movement.

EARLY YEARS AND EDUCATION

Benezet was born in San Quentin, in Picardy, France, on January 31, 1713, to Judith and Jean Etienne Benezet. Benezet was the eldest of thirteen children, half of whom died in infancy. With the revocation of the Edict of Nantes, Protestant Huguenots, such as the Benezet family, faced persecution from the rule of King Louis XIV. This regime exhibited no tolerance for Protestants who refused to convert to Catholicism. Consequently, the Benezet family moved to Rotterdam, Holland, in 1715, desiring a more stable and safe place to live. Unhappy with their economic situation in Holland, the family moved again that same year to London, where they remained until 1731. Anthony Benezet received a formal liberal education in London and served as a mercantile apprentice. In London, the Benezet family was associated with the London Quakers; however, there is no evidence that they actually joined the sect. In France, Jean Etienne Benezet had been involved with the French Protestant group Inspires de la Vaunge, known for their nonviolent protest philosophies. They were also known as the Congeries Quakers. Anthony Benezet's exposure to the persecution of Huguenots in France and the witnessing of hostility toward immigrants in London, coupled with his introduction to nonviolent philosophies, greatly impacted his future ideology and lifestyle.

In 1731, the Benezet family moved to Philadelphia with hopes for a more peaceful and accepting environment. Shortly after their move, Anthony Benezet decided to join the Philadelphia Quakers Society of Friends. Benezet married Joyce Marriott on May 13, 1736. The couple had two children who died during infancy. Although Benezet received a formal education as a young man in London, most of his knowledge and views of the world came to fruition from his own studies. Benezet loved books, was a prolific reader, and, over the course of his life, built an enormous personal library. He studied philosophies from all over the world, taking what he could from others and applying it to his own thoughts and notions.

Benezet was also a great student of the sciences. He studied and taught both astronomy and biology. He mapped the stars and used microscopes in his teaching to identify and appreciate all of God's creations. Benezet also followed the scientific trends of medicine. He believed that proper maintenance of the body and mind was accomplished through exercise and proper rest. Benezet later incorporated this philosophy of physical exercise and rest into his curriculum, an unusual practice for Quaker schools.

CAREER HIGHLIGHTS AND MAJOR PHILANTHROPIC CONTRIBUTIONS

Benezet's love for learning inevitably brought him to the field of education. He began his teaching career by studying at the Germantown Academy and then taught at the Friends' English Public School from 1742 until 1754. In 1754, Benezet began a school for girls that went above and beyond the normal curriculum for women. In fact, it was the first school in Pennsylvania history to educate girls past the elementary level. Benezet began this school because he found the state of women's education deplorable. Consequently, he secured the money for the opening and maintenance of this school through fund-raising, something that became vital to his career and accomplishments.

Benezet also had a special affection for the poor and destitute no matter what race or gender. He felt that every human on Earth was equal and deserved a chance to live in harmony with God. Horrified by the ill treatment of the slaves and free African Americans, Benezet further derided the hypocrisy of American revolutionaries who were enslaving human beings. Benezet argued, "How many of those who distinguish themselves as the Advocates of Liberty, remain insensible and inattentive to the treatment of thousands and tens of thousands of our fellow man?" (Jackson 1999, 98). Long before the American Revolution, as early as 1750, Benezet began teaching free African-Americans in his home and continued this endeavor until his death in 1784. Benezet was inspired to this calling after securing a number of friendships with people in the African-American community, witnessing firsthand the appalling social conditions that free African Americans suffered under in Philadelphia. He believed that education was the means to self-empowerment, which could lift up the oppressed people in society.

From the 1750s to the 1760s, Benezet tirelessly lobbied the Society of Friends to build a school for African Americans. Twenty years later, his dreams were realized. In 1770, the Society of Friends raised enough funds to build a free school for African-American children. The school became known as the African School, and the first class included a mixture of twenty-two boys and girls. Over the next five years, over 250 African-American children received educational instruction from the school. Benezet remained heavily involved in the policymaking and curriculum coordination at the school until his death. During the 1770s, the economy experienced a downturn brought on by the American Revolution, and the Quakers found it increasingly difficult to raise funds for the African School. In 1780, with a lowered teaching stipend, the school could not hire an adequate instructor. As a result, Benezet took over as schoolmaster when he was sixty-seven years old and in ill health.

During the early 1770s, after the school's opening, the Quakers began a united antislavery campaign, due in large part to the petitioning and writing of Benezet. At the 1772 annual meeting of the Society of Friends, they decided to solidify their abolitionist appeal, requiring all of their members to emancipate their slaves or face expulsion. Benezet, from 1750 until his death, wrote prolifically, producing numerous self-financed antislavery pamphlets, tracts, and books. He completed one of his first major abolitionist tracts in 1767, *A Caution and Warning to Great-Britain and Her Colonies.* His most ambitious anti-slavery tract, *Some Historical Account of Guinea,* was published in 1788. Benezet used an anthropological and geographical approach in this tract to prove the equality of the African people. In 1775, Benezet also founded one of the first antislavery organizations, the Society for the Relief of Free Negroes Unlawfully Held in Bondage.

Benezet, unlike other abolitionists of the period, spent a substantial amount of time with the African-American community.

Through these experiences, Benezet differed from many abolitionists. Most white abolitionists of this time, even though they wanted to end slavery, did not consider the African-American people their equals. In opposition, Benezet proclaimed the races as equals and excoriated the claim of racial inequality as a "vulgar prejudice, founded on the pride and ignorance of the lordly masters, who have kept their Slaves at such a distance, as to be unable to form a right judgment of them" (Bruns 1971, 234). In many of his publications, Benezet demonstrated a combination of religious and Enlightenment sentiments to argue for the natural rights of all human beings. In fact, the use of popular Enlightenment theories strengthened his antislavery appeals because it helped secure a broader base of support. Benezet also wrote continually to others in France and England—people like Brissot, the Abbé Raynal, Marquis De Lafayette, and Jacob Bryant—who eventually had an influence on the abolition movements in Europe.

Benezet's philanthropy and fight for equality also extended to Native Americans. He strongly encouraged peaceable negotiation with Native Americans over land settlements. Benezet induced the formation of the Friendly Association for Regaining and Preserving Peace with the Indians by Pacific Measures in an effort to eradicate the violence and warfare between Native and European Americans, and to establish better treatment of the Native American. In 1784, Benezet also published *Observations on the Situation, Disposition, and Character of the Indian Natives of This Continent* in an effort to illustrate the Native American population as "rational beings as well as ourselves, with mental powers . . . equally with our own" (Kelley 1982, 75). In his writings, Benezet also condemned the use of hard liquor, especially as a bartering tool between various ethnic groups. He found it to be a wicked method of oppression and noted its addictive nature and the mental and physical decay that follows its use and abuse.

Benezet was also a pacifist, an element of the Quaker philosophy that he strictly abided by. His pacifism extended beyond the human world. He believed it was wrong to harm or disturb any creature in nature. Consequently, Benezet was also a conservationist. In a time when natural resources on the North American continent were abundant, he found it appalling to habitually waste any of the earth's natural capital. Later in life, Benezet even became a vegetarian, refusing to slay or eat animals. In his writings, he took a clear stance against the ill treatment of nature and believed that a natural harmony among people would follow a pure and decent relationship with nature. Benezet was not only a conservationist, he also strongly believed in keeping only a modest amount of materials and wealth. He believed the struggle for power and money was the root and force that kept the vicious spinning wheel of greed and slavery in motion.

CONCLUSION

Anthony Benezet's compassion and philanthropic efforts continued until his death. He spent the last months and weeks of his life preparing the African School for a successful future through effective fund-raising and acquiring suitable teachers to carry on the school's mission. He gave his entire estate to the school after the passing of his wife. Although not a huge sum, it enabled the school to hire another teacher and extend the building to include another floor and extra classrooms. As a true illustration of the impact and significance of his philanthropic efforts, over 400 African Americans attended Benezet's funeral.

Drew M. Blanchard

FURTHER READING

Benezet, Anthony. *Some Historical Account of Guinea: Its Situation, Produce, and the General Disposition of Its Inhabitants: with an Inquiry into the Rise and Progress of the Slave Trade, Its Nature, and Lamentable Effects.* London: J. Phillips, 1968 [1788].

———. *Some Observations on the Situation, Disposition, and Character of the Indian Natives of this Continent.* Philadelphia: Joseph Crukshank, 1784.

Benezet, Anthony, and William Warburton. *A Caution and Warning to Great-Britain and Her Colonies, in a Short Presentation of the Calamitous State of the Enslaved Negroes in the British Dominions.* Philadelphia: D. Hall and W. Sellers, 1767.

Bruns, Roger. "Anthony Benezet and the Natural Rights of the Negro." *Pennsylvania Magazine of History and Biography* 96 (1), 1972, 104–113.

———. "Anthony Benezet's Assertion of Negro History." *Journal of Negro History* 56 (3), 1971, 230–238.

Hornick, Nancy Slocum. "Anthony Benezet and the Africans' School: Toward a Theory of Full Equality." *Pennsylvania Magazine of History and Biography* 99 (4), 1975, 399–421.

Jackson, Maurice. "The Social and Intellectual Origins of Anthony Benezet's Antislavery Radicalism." *Pennsylvania History* 66 (supplement), 1999, 86–112.

Kashatus, William C. "A Reappraisal of Anthony Benezet's Activities in Educational Reform, 1754–1784." *Quaker History* 78 (1), 1989, 24–36.

Kelley, Donald Brooks. "A Tender Regard to the Whole Creation: Anthony Benezet and the Emergence of an Eighteenth-Century Quaker Ecology." *Pennsylvania Magazine of History and Biography* 106 (1), 1982, 69–88.

Vaux, Robert. *Memoirs of the Life of Anthony Benezet.* New York: Burt Franklin, 1969 [1817].

Wilson, Armistead. *Anthony Benezet from the Original Memoir.* New York: Books for Libraries Press, 1971 [1859].

PAPERS

Anthony Benezet's papers are located in the Special Collections Division of the Haverford College Library (Haverford, PA). The Benezet family papers, including papers of Anthony Benezet, are located in the William L. Clements Library in the Small Collections Division of the University of Michigan Libraries.

MARY MCLEOD BETHUNE
(1875–1955)

Civil Rights Activist and Founder of Bethune-Cookman College

INTRODUCTION

"Very early in my life, I saw the vision of what our women might contribute to the growth and development of the race—if they were given a certain type of intellectual training. . . . I longed to see their accomplishments recognized side by side with any women, anywhere. With that vision before me, my life has been spent." (McCluskey and Smith 1999, 84). In this 1926 statement, Mary McLeod Bethune explained her motivation for founding a school for black females in Daytona Beach, Florida. An educator and reformer, Bethune dedicated her life to improving the education and status of African Americans, particularly females, and fighting racial discrimination. Indeed, she was determined to educate as many African-American children and young adults as possible. Although she grew up with very little, Bethune was able to wield great power and affect change through her stature and intellect.

EARLY YEARS AND EDUCATION

Mary McLeod was born in Mayesville, South Carolina, in 1875. Her parents, Patsy and Samuel McLeod, were former slaves. Once set free, they built a strict, religious home for their seventeen children. With a small farm and a large family, all of the children had to help with the chores and Mary McLeod's job was helping to pick the cotton. Influenced by her grandmother, who instilled in her a respect for her African heritage, Mary McLeod became interested in learning at a young age. Upon the suggestion of her teacher, she enrolled in the Scotia Seminary in Concord, North Carolina, at age twelve. After graduating from the seminary, she won a scholarship to study at the Mission Training School of the Moody Bible Institute in Chicago, becoming the only African American among 1,000 students. While at the institute, she cultivated a deeper faith in God, which, in turn, provided the groundwork for all of her accomplishments. While in the Chicago area, she visited prisoners, served meals to the homeless, and provided counsel to those in poverty. She even hoped to become a missionary to Africa but the Moody Bible Institute told her that there were no openings for black missionaries in Africa.

After graduation, McLeod secured a teaching position at the Haines Institute in Augusta, Georgia. In this predominantly female institution, she acquired the skills needed to be a leader in education. From her mentor, Lucey Craft Laney, she learned much about educational philosophy as well as how to elicit community support. In 1897, she transferred to the Kendell Institute in Sumter, Georgia, and met Albertus Bethune. The two were married in 1898 and had a child in 1899.

CAREER HIGHLIGHTS AND MAJOR PHILANTHROPIC CONTRIBUTIONS

When Albertus Bethune took a sales job, the couple moved to Savannah, Georgia. Since Mary McLeod Bethune was well acquainted with many of the ministers in the area, this location turned out to be a boon to her missionary ambitions. These religious leaders respected Bethune and looked to her when the time came to establish educational institutions in the South. Reverend C.J. Uggans, a Presbyterian minister from Palatka, Florida, asked her to start a community school in his town. More interested in missionary work than housework, she took this position and moved to Florida without her husband; despite a lack of faith in her plans, Albertus Bethune later decided to join her.

Mary McLeod Bethune recognized that many African Americans were migrating to Florida in search of jobs and believed this population growth would necessitate more educational opportunities. After a time in Palatka, she moved on to Daytona Beach where she planned to establish a girls' school. It was at this point that Mary McLeod Bethune realized her charitable impulses would lead to a career in the United States, not missionary work in Africa.

In 1904, Bethune opened the doors of the Daytona Literary and Industrial School for Training Negro Girls. Families paid fifty cents a week to send their elementary school girls to the institution, but Bethune never refused to educate a child whose parents could not afford the tuition. Knowing that Daytona Beach was a vacation spot frequented by wealthy business people, she searched for a school benefactor and eventually found one in James Gamble of Proctor and Gamble. Moved and persuaded by Bethune's efforts, he supported the school during its early years. Bethune also convinced Gamble to become a trustee with the institution. Indeed, Bethune was skilled at convincing those in both the black and white communities that education was essential for black children. In 1923, the school merged with the Cookman Institute, in nearby Jacksonville, to become Bethune-Cookman College, a higher-education institution serving young women. As president of the college for over forty years, Bethune fought vehemently against the inequality that blacks faced and the quality of Bethune-Cookman College's graduates vindicated such efforts. Bethune-Cookman College is now the sixth largest member of the United Negro College Fund's thirty-nine-college contingency. Bethune's achievements in the area of education were recognized in 1935 when she received the National Association for the Advancement of Colored People's distinguished Spingarn Medal.

As Mary McLeod Bethune became more active in promoting the rights of African Americans and women, her relationship with

A 1949 portrait of Mary McLeod Bethune. Library of Congress; LC-USZ62-42476.

her husband became strained; her ambition left her unsatisfied with the accepted roles for women. With a heavy workload and grueling travel schedule, Bethune had little time for homemaking. Eventually, she divorced Albertus Bethune.

Given Bethune's success in the area of education, it is not surprising that she branched out into the political arena. She advocated antilynching laws, fair job and labor conditions, and job training for women as well as equality for all races. Bethune believed that women were the essential element in bringing about change in the United States. She argued that women, through their roles as mothers and teachers, could make significant changes by influencing children. Her trust and belief in women was affirmed when she was elected president of the National Association of Colored Women in 1924. Seeing the need for further work in the area of segregation and discrimination, Bethune founded the National Council of Negro

Women in 1930 to combat these problems. Considered a moderate by most, she worked side by side with other important mainstream African-American leaders, including college presidents Charles S. Johnson, Horace Mann Bond, Benjamin Mays, and **Frederick Douglass Patterson**.

Perhaps one of Bethune's greatest contributions came through her connections to those in power. In 1930, President **Herbert Hoover** invited her to the White House and asked her to serve on the White House Child Health and Protection Committee. Her connections within the White House continued through three administrations but were strongest during Franklin Roosevelt's presidency (1933–1945). As a result of her leadership role in the women's movement during the 1920s and 1930s, Bethune caught the attention of Eleanor Roosevelt, who invited Bethune to the White House for a luncheon she was giving for leaders of the National Council of Women of the United States.

During this luncheon, Bethune met Sara Delano Roosevelt, the mother of the president. Their friendship grew from this first encounter and became one of the most treasured friendships of her life.

Bethune's close relationships with the women of the Roosevelt family were instrumental in her appointment to many government positions. In addition to selecting Bethune to be Director of Negro Affairs for the National Youth Administration, Eleanor Roosevelt helped get Bethune involved in the National Counsel on Negro Affairs—popularly referred to as the "Black Cabinet." According to Roi Ottley, "By and large, they [the Black Cabinet] are cut from the same college-bred cloth. . . . They do their thinking and talking together. Studies are initiated by them, Negro sentiment tested frequently, abstractions harnessed, and eventually mature programs formulated" (Banks 1996, 116).

In her diligent pursuit of equality, Bethune helped integrate various areas of American life, ranging from the Red Cross to government cafeterias. She also showed great loyalty to the Roosevelts and was known for verbally attacking critics of the president and his wife—those on the right and the left. When Franklin died in 1945, Eleanor Roosevelt even sent Bethune one of his canes as a sign of gratitude.

In both 1937 and 1939, Bethune convened national conferences on racial problems in America. She noticed, as did W.E.B. DuBois, that although many had discussed this "problem," African Americans had rarely been asked for input. Bethune believed in interracial cooperation and insisted that it was essential to include African Americans in any plans that related to them. In her words, blacks and whites must share "together more fully in the benefits of freedom—not 'one as the hand and separate as the fingers,' but one as the clasped hands of friendly cooperation" (Bethune 1969, 255). Inspired by Bethune's energy and commitment, delegates attending these conferences wrote letters to Congress recommending policy changes.

CONCLUSION

Bethune contributed in many ways to the successes of African Americans and women in the United States. However, some of her work could have continued beyond her death, had she trained a protégé. Unfortunately, Bethune had a strong hold on her ideas. For instance, Bethune possessed many connections with philanthropists and politicians but clung tightly to the power, sometimes neglecting to pass on her skills or delegate responsibility to others. When Bethune died of a heart attack on May 18, 1955, many of the people who gave to and supported her efforts ceased their involvement. They were committed to Bethune, in many cases, rather than her causes. Nonetheless, she left a legacy of increased opportunities for African Americans and women.

Marybeth Gasman

FURTHER READING

Banks, William M. *Black Intellectuals: Race and Responsibility in American Life.* New York: W.W. Norton & Company, 1996.

Bethune, Mary McLeod. "Certain Unalienable Rights." in *What the Negro Wants*, ed. Rayford W. Logan. New York: Agathon Press, 1969.

Edgerton, John. *Speak Now against the Day: The Generation before the Civil Rights Movement in the South.* New York: Alfred E. Knopf, 1994.

Embree, Edwin. *13 against the Odds.* New York: Viking Press, 1942.

Howard-Pitney, David. *The Afro-American Jeremiad: Appeals for Justice in America.* Philadelphia: Temple University Press, 1990.

Keough, Leyla. "Mary McLeod Bethune." In *Africana: The Encyclopedia of the African and African American Experience*, ed. Kwane A. Appiah and Henry Louis Gates, Jr. New York: Basic Civitas Books, 1999, 229–230.

Love, Dorothy, ed. "Mary Jane McLeod Bethune." In *A Salute to Historic Black Women.* Chicago: Empack Publishing Company, 1984.

McCluskey, Audrey Thomas, and Elaine M. Smith, eds. *Mary McLeod Bethune: Building a Better World* [Essays and Selected Documents]. Bloomington and Indianapolis: Indiana University Press, 1999.

Smith, Elaine M. "Mary McLeod Bethune's 'Last Will and Testament': A Legacy for Race Vindication." *Journal of Negro History.* 81, Winter 1996, 105–122.

PAPERS

Mary McLeod Bethune's papers are located in the Special Collections of Bethune-Cookman College (Daytona Beach, FL) as well as in the Mary McLeod Bethune Collection, Amistad Research Center (New Orleans, LA).

BERNICE PAUAHI PAKI BISHOP
(1831–1883)

Hawaiian Aliʻi and Founder of Kamehameha Schools

INTRODUCTION

"I give, devise and bequeath all of the rest, residue and remainder of my estate real and personal, wherever situated unto the trustees below named, their heirs and assigns forever, to hold upon the following trusts, namely: to erect and maintain in the Hawaiian Islands two schools, each for boarding and day scholars, one for boys and one for girls, to be known as, and called the Kamehameha Schools" (*Wills and Deeds of Trust* 1957, 17–18).

With these words, Bernice Pauahi Paki Bishop created a legacy that has since grown into a $6 billion endowment that supports the largest independent prekindergarten through grade 12 school in the United States.

EARLY YEARS AND EDUCATION

Born December 19, 1831, in Honolulu, Hawaii to High Chiefs Abner Paki and Laura Konia, Pauahi Paki was the great-granddaughter of Kamehameha I, the warrior chief who united all the islands of Hawaii under his rule in 1810. For her first seven years, Pauahi Paki led a very pampered life, tended by doting relatives and servants who prepared her for the life and responsibilities of a member of traditional Hawaiian *aliʻi* (noble, chief). From them, she learned her native tongue and the culture and values of her Hawaiian ancestors. In 1839, King Kamehameha III decided that Paki and other high-ranking *aliʻi* children would be schooled in Western ways to fulfill their future leadership responsibilities. Indeed, he realized that they would need to interact on an equal basis with the many foreigners from around the world who were then pouring into Hawaii. Her teachers, Amos Starr Cooke and his wife Juliette Montague Cooke, were Protestant missionaries who had sailed to Hawaii from Boston, Massachusetts, in 1837.

Between June 1839 and June 1850, Pauahi Paki and her schoolmates lived with the Cookes at the Chiefs' Children's School and learned to speak, read, and write the English language fluently. They also received instruction in mathematics, algebra, geometry, astronomy, chemistry, literature, and history. Practical arts were required, so Paki learned to cook, clean, sew, and wash her own clothes, chores that *aliʻi* children would not typically be expected to do. By all accounts, Paki was a good student. Juliette Cooke observed that "Miss Bernice," as she became known at school, "is very fond of reading, likes history and is very well versed in it for a girl her age—she is fifteen—plays and sings well, paints prettily . . . makes her own dresses, is now studying chemistry and Euclid" (Williams 1992, 46).

In 1847, a young American named Charles Reed Bishop from Glens Falls, New York, became a regular visitor at the Cookes' school. A romantic attachment formed between Paki and Bishop and the couple was

An 1866 portrait of Bernice Pauahi Bishop, founder of Kamehameha Schools in Hawaii. Courtesy of Kamehameha Schools.

married on June 4, 1850, despite the bitter opposition of Paki's parents: they had hoped she would marry a chief, Lot Kapu'iwa, one of her schoolmates who later became King Kamehameha V. The Bishops proved to be compatible in all aspects and greatly interested in each other's endeavors throughout their thirty-four-year marriage. Their only marital disappointment was not having children of their own.

CAREER HIGHLIGHTS AND MAJOR PHILANTHROPIC CONTRIBUTIONS

Pauahi Bishop's training at the Chiefs' Children's School amply prepared her to execute her many family, household, social, and community responsibilities. She not only managed her home by participating in, as well as overseeing, the work of about thirty live-in servants, she also supervised management of the 16,000 acres of land that she inherited from her parents when she was still in her twenties. The lands included an eighty-nine-acre saltwater fishpond and fields of rice, sugarcane, bananas, sweet potatoes, and taro.

Civic and cultural activities filled much of her time. She was an active member or leader of organizations such as the Stranger's Friend Society (organized to aid the sick and destitute traveler), the Women's Sewing Society (providing clothing for the poor), and the Amateur Musical Society (conducting instrumental and vocal performances of all kinds). Brought up under the Cookes' Congregationalist teachings, she was a loyal and active church member to the end of her life. Pauahi Bishop also made herself available to Native Hawaiians who sought counseling. Charles Bishop's niece, Cordelia Allen, commented, "I was always interested to see her seated out under a large tamarind tree, surrounded by her people many of whom had come in from the country to advise with her (Black and Mellen 1965, 66–67).

An 1866 portrait of Charles Reed Bishop, husband of Bernice Pauahi Bishop. Courtesy of Kamehameha Schools.

A social and cultural leader noted for her graciousness, Pauahi Bishop hosted royalty, visiting dignitaries, friends, and relatives from Hawaii and abroad. A consummate hostess, her home was considered "the greatest centre of hospitality in Honolulu" (Kanahele 1986, 95) An avid traveler as well as art and music lover, she visited the continental United States several times and toured Europe with her husband in 1875–1876. In Rome they had an audience with Pope Pius IX and in England they were presented to Queen Victoria.

Charles Bishop was a widely respected and successful businessman. He established a bank in 1858, which today, as First Hawaiian Bank, is the state's oldest financial institution. Through banking, real estate, and other investments, Bishop became one of the wealthiest men in the kingdom. He also held various positions in government, such as member of the Privy Council (comprised of selected heads of governmental depart-

ments), House of Nobles under Kamehameha IV (which was extended as a commission for life under Kamehameha V), foreign minister under King Lunalilo, and president of the Board of Education under Kings Lunalilo and Kal'kaua and Queen Lili'uokalani.

Like his wife, he devoted a great deal of his time to civic activities and charitable works, ranging from serving on boards of directors (often as president or trustee for decades) to providing significant funding to educational, religious, health, and social organizations. His charitable work included the American Relief Fund, Queen's Hospital, Punahou School, Hilo Boys' Boarding School, Kapi'olani Maternity Home, Kawaiaha'o Seminary for Young Women, Central Union Church of Honolulu, and Kalaupapa Settlement for patients with Hansen's disease. Monetary bequests to some of these organizations ranged from $5,000 to more than $350,000. According to one source, Charles Bishop's generous charitable giving resulted from the words of multimillionaire mercantilist, financier, and philanthropist **George Peabody**, who wrote, "I found that there were men in life just as anxious to help the poor and destitute as I was to make money. I called in friends in whom I had confidence and asked them to be trustees for my first gift. They accepted. For the first time I felt a higher pleasure and greater happiness than making money—that of giving it away for good purposes" (Kent 1965, 297).

Pauahi Bishop wrote her will in October 1883, just five months after inheriting some 353,000 acres of land from her cousin Ruth Keʻelikʻlani. These lands, along with another 25,500 acres she inherited from her parents and an aunt, made her the largest private landowner in the Hawaiian kingdom with 9 percent of its total acreage. With a very wealthy husband and no children, Bishop was free to bequeath her estate as she wished. After modest gifts of money and life interests in property to attendants, friends, and relatives, she left the remainder of her estate to the founding of Kamehameha Schools.

Since a fire destroyed most of Pauahi Bishop's personal papers and letters in the 1906 San Francisco earthquake and fire, one can only speculate on her motives to endow a school. However, her husband sheds some light on the matter in his correspondence. He said that she wanted to honor the Kamehameha name and "decided that schools would be preferred, not for boys and girls of pure or part aboriginal blood exclusively, but that class should have preference; that is they should have the first right, provided, of course, that they took advantage of the opportunity and complied with the conditions and rules of the Will and of the Trustees and Estate" (Kent 1965, 145). Charles Bishop's reference to the conditions and rules represents his wife's directives to provide "a good education in the common English branches, and also instruction in morals and in such useful knowledge as may tend to make good and industrious men and women" (*Wills and*

Deeds of Trust 1957, 17–18). Following through on these mandates, the school initially offered basic academic courses and emphasized practical training in industrial arts; a highly regimented and military-style of organization for the boys; and Protestant Christian principles and practices.

In Charles Bishop's correspondence, he also makes references to Kamehameha IV and his queen, Emma, as another influence on Pauahi Bishop. These two *aliʻi* established Queen's Hospital and King Lunalilo endowed a home for the elderly prior to the writing of Pauahi Bishop's will. Later, after Pauahi Bishop's death, Queen Kapiʻolani would establish a maternity hospital and Queen Liliʻuokalani would endow a trust for orphans. All of these charitable institutions designated Native Hawaiians as their beneficiaries. Nearly all of these individuals were also Pauahi Bishop's schoolmates at the Chiefs' Children's School and members of her social circle throughout her adult life. They each used their prominence and resources to counteract the negative social, educational, and health conditions of nineteenth-century Hawaiians, and their legacies (collectively known today as the *aliʻi* trusts) still serve the people of Hawaii.

From early childhood, these *aliʻi* witnessed the steady physical and spiritual demise of Native Hawaiians. When Captain James Cook arrived in Hawaii in 1778 and opened the remote Hawaiian archipelago to the outside world, some of the results were disastrous. New ideas, customs, goods, and values weakened the traditional order of Hawaiian life and culture, which was centuries old. Furthermore, the introduction of foreign diseases such as syphilis, measles, mumps, and whooping cough, against which Hawaiians had no immunity, resulted in epidemics that killed tens of thousands of natives. When Pauahi Bishop was born in 1831, the native population was about 124,000. When she wrote her will in 1883, only 44,000 Hawaiians and part-Hawaiians remained.

In an 1887 address to students and staff of the newly opened Kamehameha School for Boys, Charles Bishop noted that his wife became deeply troubled by the declining population of Hawaiians and felt a lack of education helped precipitate that decrease. Bishop also said that Pauahi Bishop believed that "men from the East and men from the West would come to occupy them; skillful, industrious . . . looking mainly to their own interests" but she hoped "that there would come a turning point, when, through enlightenment, the adoption of regular habits and Christian ways of living, the natives would not only hold their own in numbers, but would increase again" (Kent 1965, 153).

After Pauahi Bishop's death on October 16, 1884, Charles Bishop, who had been named in her will as one of five trustees for her estate and coexecutor of her will, immediately set in motion the process that would result in the establishment of the Kamehameha Schools in 1887. He not only served as president of the Bernice Pauahi Bishop Estate's Board of Trustees, he was generous in using his own funds for the construction of several of the schools' initial buildings. He also deeded all the property back to the estate that his wife had granted him a life interest in, as well as some of his own properties. In addition, he founded and endowed the Bernice Pauahi Bishop Museum in 1889 as a memorial to his wife and repository for her and her family's priceless Hawaiian artifacts. Most of all, throughout the remainder of his life, Charles Bishop continued to guide the fiscal and educational policymaking of the trustees in directions that reinforced Pauahi Bishop's vision of a perpetual educational institution that would assist Native Hawaiians to become "good and industrious men and women" (*Wills and Deeds of Trust* 1957, 18).

CONCLUSION

Today, the Kamehameha Schools remain the sole beneficiary of Pauahi Bishop's perpetual trust known as the Bernice Pauahi Bishop Estate. In addition to owning 9 percent of the private property in Hawaii, the Bishop Estate has real estate and financial investments nationwide. Revenue generated by these assets has enabled Kamehameha Schools to subsidize between 85 and 95 percent of the cost of every student's education, and to provide supplemental financial aid to families of students who cannot afford the modest tuition and fees charged. Since its founding, Kamehameha Schools have graduated nearly 19,000 young Hawaiian men and women.

Currently, Kamehameha Schools encompass three college preparatory campuses (one K–12, the other two reaching K–12 status in 2005) enrolling 3,500 students. It also operates thirty-one preschools serving more than 1,000 three-and four-year-olds statewide, offers more than $17 million in college financial aid to Native Hawaiians annually, and provides other significant educational outreach services. Charles Bishop's words "Could the founder of these schools have looked into the future and realized the scenes before us this day, I am sure it would have excited new hopes in her breast, as it does in my own" are as meaningful today as they were at the school's first Founders Day in 1887 (Kent 1965, 153).

Lesley Agard

FURTHER READING

Black, Cobey, and Kathleen Mellen. *Princess Pauahi and Her Legacy*. Honolulu; Kamehameha Schools Press, 1965.

Heenan, David A., and Warren Bennis. *Co-Leaders; The Power of Great Leaders*. New York: John Wiley & Sons, 1999.

Kanahele, George S. *Pauahi, the Kamehameha Legacy*. Honolulu: Kamehameha Schools Press, 1986.

Kent, Harold W. *Charles Reed Bishop, Man of Hawaii*. Palo Alto, CA: Pacific Books, 1965.

Richards, Mary Atherton, ed. *Amos Starr Cooke and Juliette Montague Cooke: Their Autobiographies Gleaned from Their Journals and Letters*. Honolulu: The Daughters of Hawaii, 1987.

Williams, Julie S. *Princess Bernice Pauahi Bishop*. Honolulu: Kamehameha Schools Press, 1992.

Wills and Deeds of Trust: Bernice P. Bishop Estate, Bernice P. Bishop Museum, Charles R. Bishop Estate. 3rd ed. Honolulu: Printshop of Hawaii Company, 1957.

Bernice Pauahi Paki Bishop's papers are located at the Bernice Pauahi Bishop Museum and the Hawaii State Archives (both in Honolulu, HI). Charles Reed Bishop's papers are located at the Bernice Pauahi Bishop Museum, the Hawaii State Archives, the Bernice Pauahi Bishop Estate, Corporate Offices of the Kamehameha Schools, First Hawaiian Bank, Punahou Schools, and the Hawaiian Historical Society (all in Honolulu, HI).

BOOTH FAMILY

Ballington Booth (1857–1940)
and Maud Booth (1865–1948)

Commanders of the Salvation Army and Founders of the Volunteers of America

Evangeline Booth (1865–1950)

Commander of the Salvation Army

INTRODUCTION

William and Catherine Booth, founders of the Salvation Army (1878), spawned a global dynasty of religious philanthropists whose integration of spirituality and social service continues to reverberate. The Booths, British evangelicals, believed that individual and social salvation were linked, and they expected followers to care for the material as well as the religious needs of "down-out-outers," the poor among whom they worked. While William and Catherine focused their efforts in England, the Booth children commanded troops around the world. Three children and their spouses—Maud and Ballington Booth, Emma and Frederick Booth-Tucker, and Evangeline Booth—successively led the American Salvation Army from 1887 to 1934. Under their guidance, the Salvation Army grew from a small Christian evangelical mission to a large religious philanthropy with a nationwide network of shelters, hotels, soup kitchens, thrift shops, and rescue homes for prostitutes and unwed mothers.

While their outreach grew steadily, relations among the Booth family members were strained. When Maud and Ballington Booth received orders to prepare for reassignment outside the United States, they refused and started their own organization, the Volunteers of America. They subsequently had little to do with the Booth-Tuckers and less with Evangeline Booth, whom they blamed for inflaming public opinion and family sentiment against them. Notwithstanding familial enmity, both the Salvation Army and the Volunteers of America prospered, and while their paths increasingly diverged, both shared a religious commitment to help society's neediest.

BALLINGTON AND MAUD BOOTH

"Our work is not all bread and shelter. The underprivileged, the weak, and the unfortunate need more. They need sympathy, the warmth of fellowship, and the instilling of courage," (Wisbey 1994, 110). Although Ballington Booth spoke these words at the end of the Great Depression, they capture the mix of spiritual solicitude and social pragmatism that characterized his philanthropic mission over six decades. Working jointly with his wife, Maud Booth, the couple's leadership of the Salvation Army (1887–1896) and the Volunteers of America (1896–1940) wed religion and humanitarianism at a time when social service delivery was be-

Maud and Ballington Booth. Courtesy of The Salvation Army National Archives.

coming increasingly "scientific," and religion seemed less interested in this world than the next.

Early Years and Education

By dint of his birth, Ballington Booth was destined for a religious vocation. His parents had started the Salvation Army and expected their children to lead it. Ballington Booth, like his seven siblings, received most of his education at home in London. His parents, who were suspicious of worldly pursuits, wanted their brood to be Bible-centered soul winners. Even before he reached his teens, Ballington Booth displayed the requisite talents for crusades, including musical aptitude and oratorical command.

William Booth installed his progeny in key Salvation Army posts worldwide. When Ballington Booth was twenty-three, he headed the movement's Training Home for Men Officers in London. Three years later, he was sent to lead the forces in Australia (remaining

there for two years). Among the reasons he went abroad was his burgeoning relationship with Maud Charlesworth. The Booths had invited the teenaged girl into their home and assured her father that she and their son would not marry until she reached her majority.

Maud Charlesworth's childhood was very different than Ballington's insular upbringing. Her parents, Samuel and Maria Charlesworth, were financially comfortable, and her father descended from a long line of Anglican rectors. When she was still a toddler, her father left a comfortable country parish to work in a poor London church. While he hoped to bring the gospel to society's underprivileged, he still trained and educated his daughters to be Victorian gentlewomen. The girls had a good education and attended finishing school. Still, by assisting with her mother's outreach work to the needy, Maud Charlesworth was aware of the poverty around her.

Maud Charlesworth became acquainted with the Salvation Army when her mother brought her to one of their religious meetings. There, the sixteen-year-old found her life's work, smitten as much by Ballington Booth, who led the revival, as by the Army's boisterous crusade to the unchurched. When her mother died a few months later, Samuel Charlesworth gave her permission to assist Salvation Army work in France—as long as she kept a low profile (which meant staying out of uniform) and did not place herself in harm's way (in its early days, the Salvation Army was often attacked by crowds that disliked its militant evangelicalism). Yet, she obeyed neither restriction, entailing a fierce battle with her father over her involvement in what he deemed an irresponsible and sensational group. When her father refused permission for her to marry Ballington Booth, Maud Charlesworth, who was under age to wed without his consent, moved into the Booth household and worked in the Training Home for Women Officers. Soon after Ballington Booth returned from Australia, she came of age, and the two were wed. William

Booth subsequently appointed them commanders of the American Salvation Army.

Career Highlights and Major Philanthropic Contributions

When the Ballington Booths (as the couple was known) assumed leadership of the Salvation Army's work in America in 1887, the movement was held in low repute because its hallmarks—female preaching, rowdy services, and military parades—seemed contrary to traditional Christianity. Salvationists persevered in these practices believing they needed to attract attention to reach the unchurched. While the Ballington Booths continued the Salvation Army's lively antics, they also reached out to the rich and powerful whose good opinion could help the cause's reputation and finance its activities.

After two years in New York City, where the Army was headquartered, Maud Booth decided its mission to the poor should include the type of direct ministry that Salvationists pioneered in London. This outreach, dubbed the Cellar, Gutter, and Garrett Brigade, sent young women to live in the slums where they tended their neighbors: preparing food, cleaning homes, helping the sick, and caring for children. Rather than explicitly evangelize people who might be hostile to their faith, the women's actions testified to their beliefs. Although New Yorkers told Maud Booth that their slums were nothing like those in London, Salvationist "slum sisters" found much to do.

The following year, 1890, William Booth published *In Darkest England and the Way Out*, his blueprint for eradicating urban poverty. Booth linked social and spiritual salvation, making a case for meeting material needs as a prerequisite for saving souls. The Salvation Army subsequently expanded its social service delivery, and Ballington Booth oversaw the creation of several shelters for homeless men. Following the depression of 1893, the Salvation Army opened slum posts, homeless shelters, and rescue homes for so-called "fallen women" (often single mothers) nationwide.

The Ballington Booths became American citizens soon after their arrival. They wanted to demonstrate their attachment to their new homeland and to allay fears that foreigners ran the Salvation Army. In 1896, when word came from London that they must prepare for another posting, they were reluctant to comply. Buoyed by many supporters, the Booths resigned from the Salvation Army and started a new group, the Volunteers of America. While the new movement had many aspects in common with the Army (military titles, ranks, and uniforms), its differences were basic. The Volunteers of America was explicitly American and democratic (for example, leaders were elected). Moreover, it defined itself as a home missionary movement, an auxiliary to the churches, rather than a Protestant denomination such as the Salvation Army or Methodists.

The Ballington Booths made their greatest philanthropic contribution to American society through the Volunteers of America. While Ballington Booth devoted most of his time to strengthening the Volunteers' spiritual work and administering its organization, Maud Booth pioneered its work in prison reform. Early in their tenure, she received an invitation to speak at Sing Sing Prison in New York. Although she had visited prisons before, the plight of the prisoners she met on that trip touched her deeply and, for the next fifty years, her preeminent concerns were to improve the prison system and to assist prisoners and ex-convicts. "I would not have anyone think that I launched into this work with that foolish, unbalanced ardor of sentiment that looks upon all criminals as wronged unfortunates," she said. "But if Christ came to seek and save the lost . . . we ought to be able lovingly and tenderly to banish the past from our memory, pointing to the future with all it can hold if they will but make use today of Christ's good offer of forgiveness" (Wisbey 1994, 64–65).

In the early twentieth century, there were no advocacy groups lobbying for prisoners' rights or helping ex-convicts adjust to society. The prison system was more concerned with punishment than with reform and most people shunned those who had been incarcerated. Practical to her core, "Little Mother," as Maud Booth was called by prisoners, wanted to reform the worst aspects of prison life (such as the ball and chain, enforced idleness, and harsh discipline), assist the families of imprisoned men, and improve the ex-con's chances for rehabilitation. As a first step, she started Hope Hall, a home for discharged prisoners where residents could find comfort and fellowship as they acclimated to life outside prison. She also provided the families of those still in prison with financial assistance as well as meals and gifts at holiday time. Another of her programs was the Volunteer Prison League—a semiautonomous branch of the Volunteers of America—for prisoners and ex-cons interested in spiritual development. Race, religion, crime, or length of sentence had no bearing on membership; rather, the only conditions for joining were repentance for past wrongs and turning to God.

Maud Booth was not an innovator or a reformer of the first order but her great popularity gained an audience for a group that had little public sympathy or support. By addressing the need for prison reform and the importance of rehabilitation, she gave prisoners a human face and helped many Americans understand the need to change the penal system. In addition to prison work, the Booths also encouraged the Volunteers of America to be active in emergency relief, hospitals, shelters, and homes for unwed mothers. After World War I, the movement's focus increasingly shifted away from religion. Today, it is a nonsectarian philanthropic organization. Known for its responsiveness to local needs, the Volunteers of America is among the nation's largest providers of affordable housing for the elderly, low-income families, and people with mental or physical disabilities. The Ballington Booths' love for their adopted homeland, their desire to find practical expression for religious commitment, and their affirmation of each individual's dignity are among the legacies that continue to shape the Volunteers of America's mission.

Evangeline Booth. Courtesy of The Salvation Army National Archives.

EVANGELINE BOOTH

Evangeline Booth, head of the Salvation Army from 1904 to 1934, had a solid grasp of her adopted countrymen's religious preferences. An American, she said, "needs a religion that does something for him and in him, and provides something for him to do in the way of helping others" (Winston 1999, 188). Booth followed her own counsel, establishing the Army as a preeminent religious philanthropy. While she inherited an Army that most Americans viewed as a ragtag evangelical mission, she helped transform it into one of the nation's foremost charitable fund-raisers. Booth's savvy leadership enabled the Army to institutionalize its mission, making its provision of social services a religious good that transcended sectarian differences.

Early Years and Education

Born on Christmas Day in 1865, Evangeline Booth was viewed by her family as a special gift from God. Catherine Booth chose the name Eva after the heroine of *Uncle Tom's Cabin*, but William Booth registered the babe as Eveline. Called Eva by her family, she adopted the name Evangeline in later life because temperance crusader **Frances Willard** said it sounded more distinguished. The seventh of eight children, Evangeline Booth grew up in a home where religion was central. At five, she was preaching to her dolls; a few years later, William Booth found her exhorting the kitchen staff.

Evangeline Booth said she found her vocation at an early age when she saw a painting of a sinner calling out to Jesus. At that moment, she decided she, too, would live for others. "My life should be lived for the poor, the wicked, the helpless—they should have my life—have it all" (Wilson 1948, 46). Like her siblings, she was educated at home and began her ministry in her teens. At eighteen, stationed in a slum brigade, she won over skeptics by opening a toy hospital and working as a flower girl to better understand the lives of those around her. In later years, she wove these memories into "The Commander in Rags," a dramatic monologue that did double duty, illustrating her religious convictions while also raising funds.

Career Highlights and Major Philanthropic Contributions

After rising through the ranks of the Salvation Army in London, Evangeline Booth became Territorial Commissioner in Canada and Newfoundland. Under her leadership, the Salvation Army prospered and, after eight years, she was appointed head of the American Salvation Army in 1904. By then, the Army's street parades were a familiar sight and its social service network was expanding. Seeking to place the organization on firmer financial footing, Evangeline Booth made institution building her priority. The bottom line reflected her success. When she arrived in New York, Salvation Army property was valued at $1.5 million; thirty years later (in 1934), that figure was $48 million plus a capital account of $35 million.

During the 1910s, she expanded the Army's social programs and spotlighted its campaigns against the evils of the day, including cigarettes, alcohol, and "white slavery" (forcing or selling a woman into prostitution). However, the Salvation Army received its biggest boost when Booth received permission to provide social and welfare services to American troops stationed in France during World War I. Intuiting the troops' need for a woman's touch, Booth dispatched young women to "mother" American soldiers. While less than 250 Salvationists served in France, the praise they received suggested far greater numbers. Setting up "huts" near the front lines, Sallies, as Army women were called, sewed clothes, wrote letters, and prayed with the men. They also served coffee and doughnuts, frying thousands of crullers each day.

By the end of the war, the Salvation Army's reputation had changed from a street corner mission to a premier social service provider. Publicly downplaying their evangelical bent, Salvation Army leaders said their social service delivery was nonsectarian. Indeed, Americans of all (or no) religious faiths supported the Salvation Army's humanitarian work. During Evangeline Booth's tenure that work expanded rapidly. The Salvation Army transformed rescue homes from way stations for "fallen women" to homes for unwed mothers, and it also expanded its day care services, salvage work, men's shelters, and hotels for working women.

Evangeline Booth's biggest challenge came after the economy collapsed and the Great Depression started in 1929. As one of the few social service providers operating on a national scale, the Salvation Army was in a key position to offer assistance, especially in the years before the federal government was organized to do so. Following Evangeline Booth's well-known dislike for the dole, army leaders often asked recipients to work for their bed and bread. They also tried to keep families together, another of Evangeline and the Salvation Army's preferences.

In 1934, Evangeline achieved her life's goal: she was elected General of the Salvation

Army. As head of the international movement, she had to move to the London headquarters. When her tenure ended in 1939, however, she returned to New York City. Evangeline Booth had become an American citizen and she felt most at home in her adopted country. While she remained interested in the Salvation Army's welfare and enjoyed addressing Salvationist groups, she lived quietly in retirement and died in 1950.

In the years between 1904 and 1934, the Salvation Army's status changed from an outsider sect to a mainstream religious charity, and Evangeline Booth was at the center of that transformation. Her instinct for helping people in ways that directly addressed their needs—in breadlines or at the front lines—touched the public's imagination. Evangeline Booth had a grand scheme for the Salvation Army that was based on direct outreach to people in need. That she did not foist religion on those the Salvation Army helped insured the public's support, enabling it to become a national success story for religious philanthropy.

CONCLUSION

Many of the Booth family's contemporaries lauded them for putting together what other religious leaders had pulled asunder, Jesus's insistence on "caring for the least of my brothers" while also winning souls. By the end of the twentieth century, this "war on two fronts" gave rise to the largest charitable fund-raiser in the United States as the Salvation Army collected more money and helped more people than any other nonprofit organization. The Volunteers of America could not match its elder sibling's scope and size, but it continued to play an important role in social service delivery.

Roy Hattersley, in his biography of William and Catherine Booth, praised the couple's legacy in England in words that also describe the Booth children's accomplishments in America. "William Booth—believing in the Christian duty to help both the deserving and undeserving poor—stirred the conscience of a whole generation and contributed mightily to the great vision of social justice which, paradoxically, sprang from those hard times. No one did more to convince society that we are all members one of another" (Hattersley 2000, 438–439).

Diane Winston

FURTHER READING

Hattersley, Roy. *Blood and Fire: William and Catherine Booth and Their Salvation Army.* New York: Doubleday, 2000.

McKinley, Edward H. *Marching to Glory: The History of the Salvation Army in the United States, 1880–1992.* Grand Rapids, MI: William B. Eerdmans, 1995.

Walker, Pamela. *Pulling Down the Devil's Kingdom: The Salvation Army in Victorian England.* Berkeley: University of California Press, 2001.

Welty, Susan F. *Look Up and Hope! The Motto of the Volunteer Prison League: The Life of Maud Ballington Booth.* New York: Thomas Nelson, 1961.

Wilson, P.W. *General Evangeline Booth of the Salvation Army.* New York: Charles Scribner's Sons, 1948.

Winston, Diane. *Red Hot and Righteous: The Urban Religion of the Salvation Army.* Cambridge: Harvard University Press, 1999.

Wisbey, Herbert A., Jr. *Volunteers of America, 1896–1948: Era of the Founders.* Metairie, LA: Volunteers of America, 1994.

PAPERS

Some of Maud Ballington Booth's papers are located at the Special Collections Department, University of Iowa Libraries (Iowa City, IA). Maud and Ballington Booth's papers are also located at the Volunteers of America Headquarters (Alexandria, VA). Evangeline Booth's papers are at the Salvation Army Headquarters, Salvation Army Archives (Alexandria, VA).

CHARLES LORING BRACE
(1826–1890)

Founder and Leader of the Children's Aid Society

INTRODUCTION

Charles Loring Brace wrote, "As Christian men, we cannot look upon this great multitude of unhappy, deserted, and degraded boys and girls without feeling our responsibility to God for them. We remember that they have the same capacities, the same need of kind and good influences, and the same Immortality as the little ones in our own homes" (Brace 1967, 91). Brace became one of the most prominent child welfare reformers of the nineteenth century because of his extensive use of "orphan trains," which sent destitute New York City children to new homes in the American West. It is estimated that throughout Brace's thirty-seven-year career as executive secretary of the Children's Aid Society, his system of workshops, lodging houses, industrial schools, and orphan trains touched the lives of more than 300,000 boys and girls.

EARLY YEARS AND EDUCATION

Charles Loring Brace was born on June 19, 1826, to John and Lucy (Porter) Brace, a prominent Connecticut family. When he was seven, his father, a minister, became principal of a girl's seminary school in Hartford (the first of its kind in the United States and founded by John Brace's aunts). John Brace tutored his son in history and the classics from an early age and Charles Brace was ready for college work by his fourteenth birthday. The death of his mother put off his educational plans for two more years, but he entered Yale College in 1842.

After graduating from Yale in 1846, Brace studied theology at both Yale and Union Theological Seminary in New York City. Unsure whether the ministry was his life's calling, he took a year off to travel and study in Europe. During his time abroad, two experiences set him upon a philanthropic path. Of all the people he met during his travels, Brace admired the Germans above all others. In his book *Home Life in Germany* (1853), Brace wrote glowingly of the strong family bonds he observed in German families. "It has seemed to me that in this universal greed for money, in this clangor and whirl of American life . . . and in the little heed given to quiet home enjoyment . . . a voice from those calm, genial old German homes might be of good to us" (Brace 1894, 149). His stay in Hungary in 1851 solidified his desire to work among the poor. The occupying Austrians accused him of carrying subversive material linked to a well-known Hungarian revolutionary and subsequently arrested him. During Brace's three-month imprisonment, he lived side by side with what he described as all sorts of men. Shortly after his release, he wrote to a friend, "I must, till I die, feel for the oppressed, like one who has shared their dungeons with them" (Brace 1894, 147).

When Brace returned to New York City, he was appalled by what he viewed as rampant materialism and the disintegration of family life. Newly arrived immigrants (mostly Germans and Irish Catholics) settled in already densely populated neighborhoods and lived in overcrowded tenement houses. The lack of available work also meant many of the immigrants lived in abject poverty. Not surprisingly, these hardships took a toll on family life. Unable to feed and clothe their children, it was not uncommon for parents to send their children out onto the streets to fend for themselves or to surrender them to an orphan asylum or house of refuge. With large numbers of vagrant children roaming the streets, juvenile crime was rampant. An

1849 report on crime, authored by the New York City chief of police, cited 10,000 youngsters living on the streets. Furthermore, the warden of the city prison estimated that nearly half of those imprisoned for petty crimes in 1849 were under the age of twenty-one and called "for the adoption of some measure, which shall stay the progress of these cadets of crime" (Children's Aid Society 1971, 4–5).

CAREER HIGHLIGHTS AND MAJOR PHILANTHROPIC CONTRIBUTIONS

Confident that a life of service to the poor was the direction he should embrace, Brace threw himself into the work of a city missionary. He began working at the Five Points Mission (located in a slum neighborhood of New York City) and made frequent visits to Blackwell's Island, which housed the city-run prison, almshouse, hospital, and asylum. What Brace witnessed of human suffering at Five Points and Blackwell's Island profoundly moved him.

During this period, Brace came to the conclusion that working with adults—already beaten down by a lifetime of poverty and vice—was futile. Rather than feel pity or distress over their plight, he came to view poverty as the result of a defective moral character. All attempts at helping humankind were futile unless they touched upon "the habits of life and the inner forces which form character" (Brace, 1967, 22–23). Much better, Brace believed, to develop good character at an early age, so he turned his attention to helping neglected street children.

In the mid-1800s, destitute children typically became the wards of orphanages or houses of refuge run by municipalities or religious institutions. However, Brace believed these institutions produced children who were passive and dependent—two traits at odds with his ideal of a strong, self-reliant child. While he clearly understood the importance of the family in shaping a child's character, he also believed that slum families could be detrimental to their children's moral development. Even more radical, he asserted that poor mothers could not be inherently depended upon to provide a nurturing family life. The only solution, Brace wrote, was to permanently separate children from their parents and place them in a healthier environment. In doing so, Brace believed that any bad traits would die out in four generations.

Unlike many of his contemporaries, Brace admired the positive attributes (resourcefulness, tenacity, and quick intelligence) exhibited by street children and felt a particularly close affinity for newsboys. In fact, Brace's rather romantic descriptions sparked America's imagination, giving rise to several popular novels of the day, including Horatio Alger's *Ragged Dick*. Rather than institutionalize these young "street Arabs," or "street rats," as vagrant children were often called, Brace argued that it would be much more effective to channel the boys' admirable traits into more socially acceptable avenues.

Brace also recognized the immediate and future social problems associated with having so many homeless children. He later wrote in *The Dangerous Classes of New York* (1872) that the multitudes of "ignorant, untrained, passionate, irreligious boys and young men" would eventually grow up to become a threat to social order (Brace 1967, 28–29, 92). Furthermore, Brace believed that the traditional religious-based methods of dealing with the poor (such as holding prayer meetings) were ineffective when dealing with such a large "ruffian class." He called for the formation of one association in each large city whose sole purpose would be to work toward improving the lives of vagrant and neglected children. Consequently, Brace founded the Children's Aid Society in 1853. He became the organization's secretary and held that position until his death in 1890. Brace's methods were practical and straightforward: (1) get boys and girls off the streets by creating workshops and industrial schools where they could learn a useful trade; (2) provide lodging houses and hot meals; and (3) take the children out of the city (whenever possible) and send them to families in the labor-starved West.

While the first efforts of the Children's Aid Society focused on providing food, shelter, and education as well as training for boys and girls in poor city neighborhoods, Brace later devised a system to transport children—mostly boys—by rail to new lives in rural America. Brace's "placing-out" program had been practiced in various forms in Europe and in colonial America but represented a radical departure from the practice of the day: placing needy children in orphanages. Indeed, Brace largely derived his success from the fact that his program, unlike indentured servitude (which involved a binding contract), based itself upon a voluntary arrangement: both the host family and the placed child were free to end the agreement at any time. It is estimated that by the mid-1890s, some 85,000 children had been placed in new homes. Most of these children were sent to Michigan, Illinois, Indiana, Ohio, Kansas, Iowa, Texas, and Nebraska; but the first children were actually placed in the mid-Atlantic and New England states.

Although Brace's placing-out system to the American West became popularly known as "orphan trains," many of these children were not orphans. In 1873, the Children's Aid Society placed, for example, some 3,000 children and 40 percent had one or both parents living. In their annual reports, the Children's Aid Society boasted of the success of their placing-out system and a number of the orphan train riders did achieve much success in life. A 1917 annual report stated that its alumni included two governors, two district attorneys, two sheriffs, two mayors, a justice of the supreme court, two college professors, twenty-four clergymen, and ninety-seven teachers.

Nonetheless, Brace's orphan trains were controversial from the beginning. Advocates of institutionalized care charged the Children's Aid Society with ignoring children's basic needs for stability and the familiar. Alternatively, Catholic Americans accused the Children's Aid Society of placing Catholic children with Protestant families and started their own placing-out program. Furthermore, some critics also found it ironic that

Brace, who clearly understood the powerful influence of parents in shaping a child's character, took the extreme view that the poor might actually "poison" their children.

CONCLUSION

Criticism of orphan trains continued to grow over time. With allegations of kidnapping and abuse, some people criticized the Children's Aid Society for not taking more care in screening families and for not following up once the children were placed. At a National Prison Conference in 1876, Western members complained that the Society's street children were "crowding the Western prisons and reformatories" (Brace 1894, 347). Although Brace admitted that the older boys could be problematic, he argued that these instances were rare. Placing-out continued to fall out of favor and ceased entirely by 1930. Many Western states put into place legislation restricting or even banning the placement of children from out of state. Labor demands in the West also subsided and more restrictive child labor laws were passed, education became compulsory, and a new wave of philanthropic organizations, such as **Jane Addams**'s Hull-House (1889), focused on saving children by supporting the family.

Nonetheless, Brace's highly visible role with the Children's Aid Society made him a prominent national and international authority on children's issues and an influence upon numerous children's lives. Although most commonly associated with the orphan trains, the Children's Aid Society, under Brace's leadership, also established the first industrial schools, nutrition programs, visiting nurses service, free dental clinics, day schools for handicapped children, and the forerunners of foster care, kindergarten, and fresh air vacations. Brace died on August 11, 1890, in Campfer, Switzerland, but his son, also named Charles Loring Brace, became the next executive secretary of the Children's Aid Society and held that post until his retirement in 1928. Today, the Children's Aid Society represents one of the oldest and largest child welfare agencies in the country.

Diane L. Schaefer

FURTHER READING

Boyer, Paul. *Urban Masses and Moral Order in America, 1820–1920.* Cambridge, MA: Harvard University Press, 1978.

Brace, Charles Loring. *The Dangerous Classes of New York, and Twenty Years' Work among Them.* [1872], reprinted from the third edition (1880). Montclair, NJ: Patterson Smith, 1967.

Brace, Emma, ed. *The Life and Letters of Charles Loring Brace.* New York: Scribner, 1894.

Children's Aid Society. *Annual Reports of the Children's Aid Society,* Nos. 1–10, Feb. 1854– Feb. 1863. New York: Arno Press & the New York Times, 1971.

Holt, Marilyn. *The Orphan Trains: Placing Out in America.* Lincoln: University of Nebraska Press, 1992.

Patrick, Michael, and Evelyn Goodrich Trickel. *Orphan Trains to Missouri.* Columbia: University of Missouri Press, 1997.

Wheeler, Leslie. "The Orphan Trains." *American History Illustrated* 18 (8), 1983, 10–23.

PAPERS

Charles Loring Brace's papers are primarily located in the Special Collections Manuscript Division of the New York Public Library. A small collection of his papers can be found at Yale University (New Haven, CT) and Duke University (Durham, NC).

ROBERT SOMERS BROOKINGS
(1850–1932)

Entrepreneur, Government Administrator, and Founder of the Brookings Institution

INTRODUCTION

Writing to the dean of the Washington University Law School shortly after the stock market crash of 1929, Robert S. Brookings, a man of great wealth and social vision, warned that "our democratic government through the ever-widening influence of our financial groups in and out of Wall Street, have, through the adoption of corporation laws, placed the great bulk of the people in a state of economic servitude" (Hagedorn 1936, 310). Brookings, as his contemporaries knew, was neither a profound nor an original thinker, but his writings conveyed the excitement of a man who saw the possibilities of building a better world. Those who knew him described him as a somewhat eccentric, talkative entrepreneur. Above all else, though, Brookings was a builder. The St. Louis businessman was chancellor of Washington University in St. Louis, the cochairman of the War Industries Board, and the founder of the Brookings Institution.

His reform proposals were specific, to the point, and eschewed elaborate theoretical discussion. At the core of Brookings thought was a belief that more (and "wiser") government intervention in the economy would benefit all classes. Critical to his belief in an activist federal government was a new vision concerning the role of social scientists, especially economists, in bringing expertise to government. It was this vision that led him to found the Brookings Institution, the first "think tank" in the United States, in 1927.

EARLY YEARS AND EDUCATION

Brookings was born in Cecil County, Maryland, the son of Richard Brookings, a physician, and Mary Carter. When Robert Brookings was three, his father died. Subsequently, his mother moved the family to Baltimore, where she married Henry Reynolds, a carpenter. In the winter of 1866, at the age of seventeen, Robert Brookings moved to St. Louis, Missouri, a city enjoying newfound prosperity in the aftermath of the Civil War

A c. 1920 portrait of Robert Somers Brookings. Library of Congress; LC-USZ62-124529.

and the opening of the West. Upon arriving in St. Louis, he immediately enrolled in an accounting course at the local business school. Then, he joined his older brother Harry to work for Cupples and Company, a dry goods firm, which conducted an impressive woodenware business in the new western market between the Mississippi River and the Pacific. The founder of the company, Samuel Cupples, perhaps because he was without children of his own, took a quick liking to the tall, good-looking, gregarious but temperate Robert S. Brookings, who neither smoked nor drank. Cupples soon promoted the young man from bookkeeper to the firm's traveling salesman.

CAREER HIGHLIGHTS

Traveling throughout the West, Brookings spent the next four years on the road, coming home only one month each year. Competition in the wholesale woodenware business

was particularly fierce in these years, as Chicago and St. Louis fought for control of the market. Within four years, Brookings had built Cupples and Company into the dominant outlet for clothespins, bowls, kitchen utensils, rolling pins, ropes and twine, and a variety of other items found in late-nineteenth-century grocery stores. Store owners were won over by the outgoing, serious young salesman who read Plutarch's *Lives* in his spare time, had taught himself German (mostly to talk to his customers), and played the fiddle on request. Thus, when the twenty-one-year-old salesman threatened to leave Cupples to start a business with his brother, Cupples quickly offered the two brothers an equal partnership. Later Brookings would say, "I went to work for Samuel Cupples at seventeen. Four years later, Mr. Cupples became my partner" (Hagedorn 1936, 153). Under Brookings' direction, the firm—over the next decade—established offices in all the major distributing centers between New York City and San Francisco.

Throughout these years, while Brookings was building his business, he continued to seek self-improvement. He took instructions under an elderly matron, prominent in St. Louis society, to refine his tastes in art and music; in the appreciation of fine furniture, silver, china, linen, and rugs; and in the social graces of a young gentleman. Still, after ten years in St. Louis, he still spoke a rough Maryland vernacular and was given to saying, "You was." Nonetheless, in the summer of 1884, Brookings astounded St. Louis society by taking leave of business to travel to Berlin, where he hoped to begin a new life as a concert violinist. Here, he became a friend of Nicholas Murray Butler, then a twenty-two-year old student and later president of Columbia University. Through Butler, Brookings was given an audition with Joseph Joachim, Germany's best-known musician, who, after listening to Brookings perform, pronounced his talents as those of a good amateur. A disappointed Brookings returned to America and threw himself into business. He built Cupples into a major business enterprise, but remained dissatisfied. In 1895, at the age of forty-seven, Brookings retired to devote himself exclusively to philanthropy.

MAJOR PHILANTHROPIC CONTRIBUTIONS

In 1896, at the suggestion of Samuel Cupples, Brookings was appointed president of Washington College, a small school occupying a single building in downtown St. Louis. Brookings devoted himself unsparingly to transforming the school into a first-class institution, Washington University. He personally selected and purchased a site outside of St. Louis (in Forest Park) to build a new campus, which would be completed in 1906.

To further ensure its financial success, he and Samuel Cupples donated their interest in Cupples Station (a state of the art transportation terminal) to the new Washington University. Furthermore, he raised a substantial endowment from leading St. Louis businessmen, including Cupples, William K. Bixby (president of the American Car and Foundry Company), Edward Mallinckrodt (founder of the National Ammonia Company), attorney Charles Nagal, and brewer Adolphus Busch. At the same time, Brookings funded the construction of an administration building, while Cupples did the same for an engineering building. Additional support came from the St. Louis World's Fair committee, which agreed in 1904 to build a library, stadium, and gymnasium for the university in exchange for use of university property during the fair. As chair of the board of trustees, Brookings also played a key role in devising a new curriculum and hiring new faculty. After a 1907 report by Abraham Flexner, commissioned by the Carnegie Foundation for the Advancement of Teaching to survey medical education in the United States, rated the medical school at Washington University as mediocre, Brookings also oversaw the construction of Barnes Hospital and Children's Hospital in 1913. Funds for its construction came from leading citizens of St. Louis, while the Carnegie Foundation provided additional funding for the project.

Through his work with the Carnegie Foundation, he met **Andrew Carnegie**. At Carnegie's invitation, he became a founding member of the Carnegie Corporation and a trustee of the Carnegie Peace Foundation in 1910. Also at Carnegie's instigation, he became a trustee for the Smithsonian Institution, an active participant in the National Civil Federation, and a consultant to President Taft's Commission on Economy and Efficiency to promote the creation of a national budget system. Thus, Brookings was a natural choice when Jerome Greene, a Rockefeller Foundation associate, asked him to become a founding trustee for the Institute for Government Research (IGR) in 1916. The IGR was established primarily as a lobbying effort to bring "efficiency and economy" to government through the enactment of a national budget system. Reformers hoped that the creation of a national nonpartisan research center such as the IGR would provide an institutional base to nonpartisan expertise in government.

In 1916, President Woodrow Wilson selected Brookings to become a member of the War Industries Board, a federal agency established to set industrial priorities, prices and wages, and the allocation of resources for the defense effort during World War I. From this experience, Brookings learned the importance of gathering reliable information in making managerial decisions and the important role economists and statisticians played in gathering this information. This vision led Brookings to propose the founding of the Institute of Economics (IE) and a graduate school as sister organizations of the Institute for Government Research. The purpose of these new organizations was to collect objective economic data, to investigate economic problems, to evaluate current economic policy, and to develop a cadre of scientifically trained professionals to enter government. The Carnegie Corporation offered a five-year grant of $200,000 to seed the new Economics Institute, under Harold G. Moulton, a brilliant economist at the University of Chicago. In 1927, Brookings, disappointed in the training aspect of the program, disbanded the graduate school and merged the Institute for Government Research and the Institute of Economics into a single organization, the Brookings Institution. To complete this merger, Brookings raised $75,000 from friends. Brookings selected Moulton to become the institution's first president, a position he would hold until 1952.

Although Brookings deferred to Moulton on matters of economics, Moulton, for his part, felt Brookings' ignorance of economics was appalling and did not hesitate to tell him so. Yet, in many ways Brookings, because of his lack of formal training in economics, maintained a broad vision for reforming the world. He often expressed his concern that the institution was not moving fast enough in devising practical economic programs. Moulton and his staff of professionally trained economists knew the limits of reform in a world of scarcity: to give to one group meant to take away from another. The world of the economist was a world of trade-offs.

Contrary to the outlook of the professional economist, Brookings became increasingly more reform-minded as he grew older. Following two severe heart attacks, a new world seemed to open for Brookings. On June 19, 1927, he married Isabel January, the daughter of a longtime St. Louis friend and a woman over thirty years his junior. His marriage seemed to reawaken his creative instincts. At the age of seventy-five, Brookings published his first book, *Industrial Ownership: Its Economic and Social Consequences.* In the next five years, he published half a dozen pamphlets and two other books.

In his writings, Brookings maintained that the evolution of the corporation in modern capitalism was inevitable and for the best, but he believed that some corporate practices continued to hurt the public, particularly the laboring classes. He urged the enactment of a federal incorporation act that would confer upon a governmental body the power to prevent corporate abuse. He argued that this government agency should be given access to corporate books, which he insisted be open. He also spoke in favor of agricultural cooperatives, federal unemployment insurance, and a European trading union. With the onset of the Great Depression in 1929, Brookings came to believe that inequality of wealth remained the major problem confronting the nation.

CONCLUSION

When Robert Brookings died in the autumn of 1932, he left behind a legacy of building three major institutions: Washington University, Barnes Hospital, and the Brookings Institution. In building these institutions, he shared with other philanthropists of his day, including his close friend Andrew Carnegie, a desire to create. These men prided themselves on being architects of a new age. In this way, capitalists such as Brookings and Carnegie entertained bold dreams for American society. The founding of a nonpartisan economic institute, located in the nation's capital, marked the culmination of Brooking's efforts to bring harmony to the world. The institution manifested an activist faith—accepted by progressive businessmen of the day—that the world could be reordered according to human desires. Yet if these capitalists—such as Carnegie, **John D. Rockefeller, Sr.**, and Brookings—reflected the optimism of an age, they were also people who stood as unique individuals within the broad sweep of history.

Their optimism for a better world contributed much to reform in the first half of the twentieth century. Nonetheless, Brookings' faith in nonpartisan expertise displayed an overconfidence typical of the age. The development of the modern state created new opportunities for social scientists to play roles in the policy and political process. As a result, the nonpartisan ideal would be eroded as ideological commitment and, often, partisan linkage became a prominent feature of social science expertise. This became evident in the proliferation of think tanks representing various ideological persuasions in Washington, DC following World War II. As a result, tension was created between advocacy and the claim of scientific objectivity in social science research. The proliferation of think tanks marshaled expert against expert, testing the credibility of each, even while enriching the information environment in which policy discourse occurs and decisions are made.

Furthermore, because of his own social background, Brookings articulated keen insights into the imperfections of industrial capitalism, the social disparities between classes, and the conflict between labor and capital. Yet, even while he benefitted from this economic system and sought to make a better world through his philanthropic endeavors, Brookings placed too much faith in an activist federal government to solve social problems. At the same time, he failed to see that the marketplace, too, offered solutions to many social problems by broadly extending wealth in society, a necessary foundation for the American democracy that he sought to reform.

Donald T. Critchlow

FURTHER READING

Brookings, Robert S. *Industrial Ownership: Its Economic and Social Significance.* New York: Macmillan, 1925.

Critchlow, Donald T. *The Brookings Institution, 1916–1952: Expertise and the Public Interest in a Democratic Society.* DeKalb: Northern Illinois University Press, 1985.

Hagedorn, Hermann. *Brookings: A Biography.* New York: Macmillan, 1936.

Smith, James Allen. *The Idea Brokers: Think Tanks and the Rise of the New Policy Elite.* New York: Free Press, 1991.

PAPERS

A small collection of Robert Brookings' correspondence can be found in the Chancellor Files, Washington University (St. Louis, MO), and the Brookings Institution Archives (Washington, DC).

C

ANDREW CARNEGIE
(1835–1919)

Industrialist, Author of "The Gospel of Wealth," and Patron Saint of Public Libraries

INTRODUCTION

"The man who dies thus rich dies disgraced" (Wall 1992, 41). Andrew Carnegie wrote these words in an 1868 memorandum to himself and tried to stay true to this guide through most of his life. When most people hear the name Carnegie, they think of the steel empire that he built in the later nineteenth century as well as the business practices that propelled him to the top. Still, Carnegie is also known for his philanthropies, particularly his creation of public libraries. Indeed, he donated over $56,000,000 for the construction of 2,509 library buildings in the English-speaking world. Although he authored classic works on philanthropy, Carnegie is not, however, known as a prolific writer. Still, he authored eight books, sixty-three articles, and had ten of his major speeches published in pamphlet form from 1882 until 1916.

EARLY YEARS AND EDUCATION

Andrew Carnegie was born on November 25, 1835, in Dunfermline, Scotland. Andrew's father was a weaver in a town that had fallen on hard times because of the industrialization of the textile industry. The weavers put their faith in a political movement called Chartism, of which his father Will Carnegie was a leader. The movement was rejected by Parliament and died out around the same time (1848) that the Carnegie family emigrated to America, ending young Andrew Carnegie's formal education at the age of twelve. They settled in the Pittsburgh area, the place where Andrew Carnegie was determined to bring the good life to his family. Upon the death of Andrew's father in 1855, the responsibility for his mother and younger brother, Tom, motivated him further to succeed.

Carnegie, at thirteen, obtained his first job as a bobbin boy for $1.20 per week. During the remainder of his youth, Carnegie pursued self-education by studying businessmen and

Andrew Carnegie, c. 1913. Library of Congress; LC-USZ62-101767.

their practices as well as reading voraciously from the library of Colonel James Anderson, who opened his library each Saturday afternoon to working boys of the area. After a year of work, he became a messenger boy for a telegraph company. He subsequently learned the art of telegraphy and met important people in industrial Pittsburgh, including Thomas Scott, a superintendent of the Pennsylvania Railroad. Subsequently, Scott hired him as his private secretary. Eventually, Carnegie became a superintendent of the Pittsburgh Division upon the promotion of his predecessor.

CAREER HIGHLIGHTS

From 1853 to 1865, Carnegie explored a wide area of business interests. In 1865, he forged a partnership, the Union Iron Mills, which was the beginning of his dominance in the steel industry. Carnegie was often viewed as ruthless, and the bloody battle at his Homestead plant in 1892 has become a sym-

bol of owners' injustices against labor organizations. In 1901, he sold Carnegie Steel Company to J.P. Morgan for nearly $5 million. Carnegie's climb to fame and fortune paralleled America's transformation from an agricultural society to an industrial power.

By 1868, at age thirty-three, Carnegie was already worth $480 million (a multimillionaire in today's terms). It is during this time that he wrote a letter in which he told himself he would quit working in two years and pursue a life of educational advancement and good works. "Man must have an idol—the amassing of wealth is one of the worst species of idolatry—no idol more debasing than the worship of money," he wrote (Wall 1992, 42). Nonetheless, it was not until 1889 that he formally declared to the world his philosophy of wealth through an essay entitled "Wealth" in the June 1889 issue of the *North American Review*. He followed this piece with a second essay in December 1889, where he detailed the best fields for philanthropy. The essay was picked up by the British press and retitled "The Gospel of Wealth," by which it is most often referred.

Nine years earlier (1880), forty-five-year-old Carnegie began courting Louise Whitfield, who was twenty-three years old. Carnegie's mother, Margaret Carnegie, was the main obstacle to the relationship. She was by all accounts a controlling person. She shared a suite in New York with her son and accompanied him almost everywhere, including many business meetings. Consequently, the couple only made their engagement public after Margaret Carnegie's death in 1886. On April 22, 1887, they wed in a very private ceremony. Ten years later, their only child, Margaret (named after Andrew's mother), was born on March 30, 1887.

MAJOR PHILANTHROPIC CONTRIBUTIONS

One cannot mention Carnegie's philanthropy without first thinking of public libraries. Indeed, he never forgot his childhood experience when he was unable to pay a subscription fee of $2 to borrow books from the local "public" library; he soon found out that public did not necessarily mean free. Fortunately, Colonel James Anderson opened up his library to working boys and men in Pittsburgh and young Carnegie would spend his Saturday afternoons there in his pursuit of self-education. These experiences led to Carnegie's determination to make free libraries available to all because he felt they were the best vehicles to afford an opportunity for popular education, which was essential to the survival of democratic and capitalist society.

Beginning in 1881, when Carnegie made his first gift for a library in Dunfermline, Scotland, he used much of his personal fortune to establish 1,681 public libraries in the United States and 828 in other parts of the English-speaking world. Due to this generosity, Carnegie has been credited by some as fostering the greatest incentive to the public library development movement in the United States and was labeled the "Patron Saint of Libraries." His detractors, however, claimed that he built libraries as monuments to himself and as a way to counterbalance his negative image among labor unions. Others argued that he built "bookless" libraries and thus was only furthering his own ends. However, he leveraged—in most cases—his gifts by requiring the towns to agree to pass a tax to operate the library, including buying books.

Carnegie is also often credited as a father of scientific philanthropy, creating "ladders upon which the aspiring can rise" (Carnegie, 1992, 11). His 1889 essays laid out his "Gospel of Wealth," which included three main arguments. First, do not spoil your heirs by leaving them vast amounts of money. Second, do your giving during your lifetime because you possess the knowledge to make money and are consequently the most able to give it away wisely. In fact, Carnegie was in favor of high estate taxes or "death duties" to insure society would benefit from one's wealth accumulation if the holder was unsuccessful in giving it away during his or her lifetime. Third, help those who are willing to help themselves. "It were better for mankind that the millions of the

rich were thrown into the sea than spent as to encourage the slothful, the drunken, the unworthy" (Burlingame 1992, 10). Carnegie also singled out the seven "wisest fields" of philanthropy which, in order of importance, were: universities, free libraries, hospitals, parks, concert or meeting halls, swimming baths, and church building. His very first endowment was in fact one to support the Carnegie Institute at Pittsburgh, which became Carnegie Mellon University. Carnegie believed that American private universities represented a worthwhile educational model because they were under the direction of a board of trustees often made up of successful businessmen of the day. Shortly after, in 1901, Carnegie created the Carnegie Trust for the Universities of Scotland followed by a Carnegie Dunfermline Trust, which has served to be much like the modern community foundation of today. With these two benefactions established, Carnegie turned his attention back to the United States and the rest of the world.

He initially wanted to establish a national university in Washington, DC. However, this plan did not work out and he finally settled on the establishment of the Carnegie Institution of Washington, which would help build knowledge for the benefit of all universities. By 1911, he had given the Carnegie Institution over $25 million for its endowment. Many colleges and universities also sought support from Carnegie but most were unsuccessful. Carnegie believed they already had enough and were not using their resources in the best manner. However, he was taken with the need for pensions for teachers. In 1905, he endowed the Carnegie Teachers Pension Fund with $10 million. Within a year, he received a national charter and the name was changed to the Carnegie Foundation for the Advancement of Teaching. He also granted an additional $5 million to provide pension funds for state universities. This fund grew into what is now known as TIAA-CREF.

The other major philanthropic effort Carnegie undertook was peace. It is not surprising that his pacifist roots, learned by all good Chartists in Scotland, would someday find an outlet in his philanthropy. Between the years 1901 and 1910, Carnegie endowed four funds for peace—including the Hero Fund and the Carnegie Endowment for International Peace—as well as supporting three major building projects for peace, the most challenging being the Hague Peace Palace.

CONCLUSION

After ten years as a full-time philanthropist, Carnegie was getting discouraged. No matter how fast he gave away his fortune, the value of his bonds continued to grow. By the beginning of 1911, he had given away more than $180 million but he still had about the same amount remaining. To not die in disgrace, Carnegie created the Carnegie Corporation of New York in 1911 and transferred the bulk of his remaining fortune, $125 million, for the diffusion and advancement of knowledge. In compliance with his own gospel, Carnegie gave away 90 percent of his wealth during his lifetime, but was unable to oversee its management.

Dwight F. Burlingame

FURTHER READING

Bobinski, George S. *Carnegie Libraries: Their History and Impact on American Public Library Development.* Chicago: American Library Association, 1969.

Carnegie, Andrew. *Autobiography of Andrew Carnegie.* Boston: Houghton Mifflin, 1920.

———. "The Gospel of Wealth." In *The Responsibilities of Wealth*, ed. Dwight F. Burlingame. Bloomington: Indiana University Press, 1992, 1–31.

Hacker, Louis M. *The World of Andrew Carnegie: 1865–1901.* Philadelphia: J.B. Lippincott, 1968.

Hendrick, Burton J. *The Life of Andrew Carnegie, I and II.* New York: Doubleday, Doran, 1932.

Hendrick, Burton J., and Daniel Henderson. *Louise Whitfield Carnegie: The Life of Mrs. Andrew Carnegie.* New York: Hastings House, 1950.

Livesay, Harold C. *Andrew Carnegie and the Rise of Big Business.* Boston: Little, Brown & Company, 1975.

Wall, Joseph Frazier. *Andrew Carnegie.* New York: Oxford University Press, 1970.

———, ed. *The Andrew Carnegie Reader.* Pittsburgh: University of Pittsburgh Press, 1992.

PAPERS

The manuscript divisions of the New York Public Library and of the Library of Congress house the major collections of Andrew Carnegie papers.

CESAR ESTRADA CHAVEZ
(1927–1993)

Founder of the National Farm Workers Association and Labor Reformer

INTRODUCTION

"I am convinced that the truest act of courage, the strongest act of manliness, is to sacrifice ourselves for others in a totally nonviolent struggle for justice. To be a man is to suffer for others. God help us to be men!" remarked community activist and organizer Cesar Estrada Chavez (Griswold and Garcia 1995, 76). Cesar Chavez dedicated his life to the improvement of working conditions for migrant farm workers in America. Although he was largely involved with Latino and His-panic workers, he advocated for the rights of farm workers everywhere. Chavez waged fights to restore the pride and dignity of the farm workers by demanding safer working conditions and their right to unionize. All the while, Chavez advocated nonviolent reform tactics such as pickets and boycotts.

EARLY YEARS AND EDUCATION

Chavez was born on March 31, 1927, in a small town outside of Yuma, Arizona to parents Juana Estrada and Librado Chavez.

As a child, Chavez attended grade school but his formal education ended after he graduated from the eighth grade in 1942. Chavez's formal education took place in many schools, due to the frequent relocation of his family. Even though some of the schools Chavez attended were integrated, most were not. At school, Chavez endured countless racist remarks and was not allowed to speak his first language, Spanish. In fact, students were often punished for speaking Spanish while at school. After the eighth grade, Chavez became a farm worker to help support his family. Even though he was unable to attend school, education was one of Chavez's many passions, feeding his inquisitive mind as an ardent reader.

During his childhood, Chavez encountered injustices that would drive him to pick up the cause of migrant farm workers, and, more broadly, Hispanic civil rights. Chavez's father, Librado Chavez, was a moderately successful Mexican-American businessman who ran—at different times—a store and a pool hall in the Yuma area. Librado was trying to purchase a small farm, but lacked some of the capital. He was advised (by a deceitful lawyer) to take out a loan for the property. Librado was unable to pay the loan, so he laid out a work agreement with the landowner in exchange for the property. In spite of the work agreement, the land was repossessed and sold back to the original owner. The injustice incurred by his family was one of the formative events leading Chavez to dedicate his life to a fight for social justice. After losing their land and assets, the Chavez family resorted to migrant farming, traveling through California, working on various farms, and living with the harsh conditions of the camps.

Chavez joined the U.S. Navy in 1944, but before leaving was arrested for sitting in the "whites only" section of a movie theater. During his time in the service, Chavez realized that prejudice and discrimination exist for many groups, not just Hispanics. Chavez was in the Navy for two years, returning home in 1946 to resume his life as a farm worker. In 1948, Chavez married Helen

Fabela and settled in Delano, California. Chavez and Fabela had eight children. During this time, Chavez continued with farm work and also took a job with a lumber company.

As a passionate reader and advocate of education, Chavez began studying the social teachings of the Catholic Church. A devout Catholic, Chavez's religion was a source of strength and direction throughout his life. In 1952, Fred Ross recruited social justice-minded Chavez to the Community Service Organization (CSO), an organization founded by well-known community organizer Saul Alinsky. This was the beginning of a ten-year working relationship between Ross and Chavez. The CSO was a community action group that focused on voter registration and citizenship establishment as well as other calls for community and political action.

CAREER HIGHLIGHTS AND MAJOR PHILANTHROPIC CONTRIBUTIONS

Chavez subsequently founded the National Farm Workers Association (NFWA) in 1962, later known as the UFW, with the slogan "Viva la Causa!" The NFWA provided members with burial insurance and a credit union. Chavez was driven by the civil rights movement to promote the equality of his people racially and economically. He sought reforms for wage contracts, improvements of living quarters (including more reasonable rent) provided by the growers, the use of child labor, and civil rights. Consequently, Chavez led the NFWA in countless strikes and boycotts. It was often difficult for Chavez to organize farm workers because they were highly mobile and often in great need of money to provide for their families—but he persevered.

The NFWA began its fight against grape growers in the Delano, California area, demanding wage increases and better working conditions, in 1965. The NFWA, along with Filipino farm workers and the Agricultural Workers Organizing Committee (AWOC), agreed to strike against the grape growers

Ceasar Chavez speaking during a Los Angeles news conference in March 1989. AP Photo/Alan Greth.

when they refused to grant the modest changes proposed by the two organizations. The strike encompassed large farms and was effective in changing California's grape industry. The strike spread throughout the state and eventually became a national movement. As part of the union's nonviolent tactics, Chavez led a march from Delano to Sacramento, the state capital, in 1966. Before the strikers reached Sacramento, Chavez was able to reach an agreement for wage increases and improved working conditions with one grape grower, the Schenley Corporation. This agreement was a historical marker for farm workers' rights because it was the first signed farm labor agreement. Shortly after this strike, the AWOC and the NFWA would merge to become the United Farm Workers (UFW) and, consequently, part of the AFL-CIO. The union's fight against California grape growers became so powerful that Americans boycotted grapes nationwide, forcing most grape growers to sign contracts with the newly formed UFW by the end of 1970.

After the grape growers undermined the renegotiation of contracts in 1973, Chavez called for another nationwide boycott. This consumer boycott was so successful that growers backed the Agricultural Labor Relations Act (1975), a collective bargaining law under which workers receive such benefits as higher wages and health coverage. By the early 1980s, California governors, who were hostile to its measures, curtailed the legislation's effectiveness.

As evidenced by the grape growers boycott, Chavez gained much support for his cause during the 1960s and 1970s. He and the UFW were supported by thousands of farm workers, clergy members, celebrities, and prominent political and civil rights leaders such as Senator Robert Kennedy and Dr. **Martin Luther King, Jr**. Dedicated to the use of nonviolent tactics, Chavez admired Gandhi and read books about him to understand what was entailed in fasting, and to glean other words of wisdom. Chavez ultimately fasted multiple times, but his most famous fast, lasting twenty-five days, was in 1968. During those twenty-five days, farm workers camped out to show their support. Chavez's fast was also a remarkably spiritual event, and he attended mass daily with farm workers in a demonstration of solidarity. During the fast, Chavez was able to talk to workers and encourage them to work together and educate themselves so they could fight for better living and working conditions. Chavez also stressed unity between the Mexican and Filipino farm workers. On the twenty-fifth day of the fast, by Chavez's invitation, Senator Robert Kennedy traveled to California and Chavez finally broke his fast.

Also in 1968, the UFW began researching the dangers of pesticides after health complaints by workers. Pesticides can cause skin rashes and respiratory infections as well as other ailments that victimize farm workers. Indeed, women and children are often victimized through the use of pesticides because the fetus is often exposed to the dangerous (sometimes cancerous) chemicals. Children are even further victimized because they often have to go to the fields with their mothers due to the lack of child care facilities. Subsequently, Chavez campaigned against the use of deadly pesticides in fields where the farm workers were working. To gain momentum for UFW boycotts, Chavez also emphasized the dangers pesticide residue posed to consumers. In addition to the boycotts, Chavez fasted on water for thirty-six days in 1988, known as the Fast for Life, to protest the use of pesticides.

CONCLUSION

Chavez remained active in labor reform efforts until his untimely death. In April 1993, Chavez was in Yuma, Arizona, assisting farm workers in their boycott against Bruce Church Inc., a lettuce and vegetable producer. Quite unexpectedly, Chavez died on April 23, 1993, near Yuma. During funeral services for Chavez, mourners (an estimated 40,000) marched behind his casket in Delano. On August 8, 1994, President William Clinton posthumously honored Chavez with the Medal of Freedom.

Amelia Clark

FURTHER READING

Ferris, Susan, and Ricardo Sandoval. *The Fight in the Fields: Cesar Chavez and the Farmworkers Movement.* New York: Harcourt Brace & Company, 1997.

Griswold, Richard del Castillo, and Richard A. Garcia. *Cesar Chavez: A Triumph of Spirit.* Norman and London: University of Oklahoma Press, 1995.

Ross, Fred. *Cesar Chavez at the Beginning: Conquering Goliath.* Keene, CA: El Grafico Press Book, United Farm Workers, 1989.

PAPERS

Cesar Chavez's papers are located at the Cesar Chavez Collection, Archives of Labor and Urban Affairs, Walter P. Reuther Library, Wayne State University (Detroit, MI).

PETER COOPER
(1791–1883)

Inventor and Founder of Cooper Union

INTRODUCTION

"While I have always recognized that the object of business is to make money in an honorable manner, I have endeavored to remember that the object of life is to do good" (Curti and Nash 1965, 76). With this simple statement, Peter Cooper summarized the philosophy of life that led him to donate a substantial portion of his fortune to philanthropy. Blessed with inventive genius, Cooper became a giant in the glue industry, designed and built the first steam locomotive in America, and used his philanthropy to make a lasting mark upon higher education.

EARLY YEARS AND EDUCATION

There was little about Peter Cooper's background to suggest that he would become a captain of industry, much less a philanthropist and one of the pioneers of American higher education. Born on February 12, 1791, Peter Cooper was the fifth of nine children born to John and Margaret Campbell Cooper. Although he was born in New York City, Cooper grew up mostly around Peekskill, New York, where his father moved the family when Peter was three. Cooper spent most of his childhood hunting, fishing, and helping his father with his various attempts to establish a business. As a result, Peter had less than a year of formal

Peter Cooper. Courtersy of The Cooper Union.

education, an inadequacy that would haunt him throughout his adult life.

Returning to the city of his birth at the age of seventeen, Cooper apprenticed himself to John Woodward, a leading coach builder. So diligently did Cooper attend to his duties that Woodward voluntarily doubled his pay at the end of the third year of his apprenticeship and raised it again in the fourth year. It was during this apprenticeship that Cooper created his first commercial invention: a device for mortising the hubs of carriages, a process previously done by hand.

When the apprenticeship was over, Cooper's mentor offered to lend him the money to set himself up in the coach-building business. Cooper, however, had a lifelong fear of debt (perhaps because of his father's long struggle with insolvency) and declined the offer. He moved instead to Hempstead, Long Island, where he went to work for a manufacturer of cloth-shearing machines. Seeing the potential for improving the product, Cooper bought the New York rights to the machine, which he perfected and patented as a new cloth-shearing machine. He then began manufacturing it on a full-time

basis and continued in this business until profits declined after the War of 1812. Thereafter, he went into the grocery business, first with his brother-in-law, then on his own. While in Hempstead, Cooper also met Sarah Bedell, whom he married on December 18, 1813. The couple were married for fifty-seven years and had six children.

CAREER HIGHLIGHTS

Cooper left the grocery business in 1821 and purchased a glue factory in New York City. It was this business that laid the foundation for Cooper's wealth. Cooper produced the first bonding agent in America of sufficient commercial quality to compete with the more expensive imports from France and Great Britain. With his success in glue, Cooper expanded his product line to gelatin and isinglass (a substance used in various products, including printer's ink, jelly, candy, and soup).

As the result of a business deal gone sour, Cooper also played a pivotal role in the history of American railroading. In the 1820s, the city of Baltimore, Maryland was trying to establish itself as a major East Coast port, capable of competing with Boston, New York, and Philadelphia for the overseas shipping trade. Its hopes were pinned on the Baltimore & Ohio Railroad, which would link the harbor to the country's interior. In anticipation of this development, Cooper joined with two other businessmen in a substantial investment in property on the Baltimore harborfront. Cooper would later learn that he was the only one of the three who had actually put money into the deal—money he stood to lose when it looked as if the railroad might fail.

The crisis unfolded when word came from the British manufacturer of steam locomotives that its engine could not pull the steep grade and navigate the narrow curves that it would encounter west of Baltimore (at Ellicott's Mills). Just as it appeared that all was lost, Cooper went to the directors of the B&O Railroad with a proposal that he be allowed to design and build a steam engine suitable for pulling a train over American terrain. With little to lose, the directors granted him permission and Cooper created an engine he nicknamed, due to its small size, the "Tom Thumb." The Tom Thumb gave an impressive account of itself on its trial run in August 1830. In addition to the six men who stood on the engine platform, the Tom Thumb pulled a car with another thirty-six people aboard from Baltimore to Ellicott's Mills and back again.

With a productive B&O Railroad and his investment in the Baltimore harbor front secured, Cooper returned to New York, his family, the glue factory, a growing involvement in the iron industry, and other interests. Cooper became involved in civic affairs as an assistant alderman for the city (first elected to this position in 1828) and chaired the water committee, which oversaw the development of a new reservoir for the growing city. During his career on the Board of Aldermen, Cooper supported the establishment of professional police and fire protection services. Despite his own lack of schooling, Cooper was also actively engaged in efforts to make educational opportunities widely available to the children of New York. He became a trustee of the Free School Society in 1838 and served a two-year term as vice president of the Board of Education after it was formed.

MAJOR PHILANTHROPIC CONTRIBUTIONS

Indeed, it was in the field of education that Cooper would make one of his most lasting marks upon the world. For three decades, as Cooper worked to establish himself as a leader in business and industry, he nurtured a dream of what he would do with the wealth he was accumulating. The dream—which came to fruition in 1859 with the opening of the Cooper Union—first began to germinate around 1828, after he heard a friend's account of the practical education offered, without charge, to young Frenchmen at the École Polytèchnique in Paris. Recalling his own experience, Cooper reflected:

> How glad I would have been, if I could have found such an institution in my youth in [New York City], with its doors open to give instruction at night, the only time that I could command for study. And I then reflected at the fact that there must be a great many young men in this country, situated as I was, who thirsted for the knowledge they could not reach, and would gladly avail themselves of opportunities which they had no money to procure. (Curti and Nash 1965, 76)

At an initial cost of more than $600,000, Cooper built the school of his dreams, based upon his belief in entrepreneurship and pragmatism, in downtown New York City. When the original six-story structure was completed, he turned the school over to a board of trustees "to be forever devoted to the advancement of science and art, in their application to the varied and useful purposes of life" (Curti and Nash 1965, 76–77). In addition to the fact that all of its services were free to the public, the Cooper Union made itself accessible to the working class by offering night classes, public lectures and concerts, and an excellent library. Moreover, there were no distinctions of class, creed, race, or sex among its beneficiaries. Despite some people predicting Cooper's dream would prove to be folly, the public loved it. Over 1,000 students registered, filling its courses to capacity on opening day. Today, the Cooper Union for the Advancement of Science and Art is the only private college in the United States dedicated exclusively to preparing students for the professions of architecture, art, and engineering and providing full-tuition scholarships for its students.

Cooper's example provided **Andrew Carnegie** with a powerful illustration of his argument that the rich should view themselves as trustees of wealth and should attend to its administration during their lifetimes. In his 1889 treatise "The Gospel of Wealth," Carnegie cited Peter Cooper and his genius in creating the Cooper Union as a prime example of the useful purposes to which a rich man, who had been creative and industrious in accumulating great resources, might deploy wealth if he—not his heirs—decided on its best use. The influence of Peter Cooper's legacy on Carnegie's own philanthropy was confirmed again in 1902, when the steel magnate gave $600,000 to the Cooper Union's endowment.

CONCLUSION

Inventor, industrialist, and civic leader, Peter Cooper accomplished much during his lifetime. Still, he derived great satisfaction from the product of his philanthropic vision, a prominent full-tuition scholarship college in New York City. To this day, few philanthropists have been bold enough to conceive of, let alone establish, an undergraduate educational institution that would be free to all its students. Moreover, Cooper's actions put him on a continuum that connected him to the self-help philanthropic tradition of such past figures as **Benjamin Thompson** (Count Rumford) and such future figures as Andrew Carnegie and **Josephine Shaw Lowell**.

Richard W. Trollinger

FURTHER READING

Carnegie, Andrew. "The Gospel of Wealth." In *The Responsibilities of Wealth*, ed. Dwight F. Burlingame. Bloomington: Indiana University Press, 1992, 1–31.

Curti, Merle, and Roderick Nash. *Philanthropy in the Shaping of American Higher Education*. New Brunswick, NJ: Rutgers University Press, 1965.

Lach, E. L. "Peter Cooper." In *American National Biography*, vol. 5, ed. J.A. Garraty and M.C. Carnes. New York: Oxford University Press, 1999, 454–455.

Nevins, Allen. *Abram S. Hewitt: With Some Account of Peter Cooper*. New York: Octagon Books, 1967 [1935].

Raymond, Rossiter W. *Peter Cooper*. Freeport, NY: Books for Libraries Press, 1972.

PAPERS

Peter Cooper's papers are located in the Special Collections Division of the Cooper Union Library in New York City.

PAUL CUFFE (1759–1817)
and JAMES FORTEN (1766–1842)

African-American Entrepreneurs and Advocates of African Philanthropy

INTRODUCTION

"I am of the African race," wrote Paul Cuffe in justifying a visit to Sierra Leone because "I feel myself interested for them" (Thomas 1988, 40). In contrast, James Forten focused upon African descendants in America, but for a period of time both American maritime merchants joined their considerable influence to further a philanthropic scheme for African descendants on both sides of the Atlantic Ocean. Cuffe, the black Yankee shipping merchant, Sierra Leone landholder, and model for British philanthropists, contrasted with Forten, Philadelphia's established black business mentor, spokesman for the city's free population, and published antislavery advocate. Eventually, these likeminded entrepreneurs would be known to advocate solutions that would appear to be oceans apart.

EARLY YEARS AND EDUCATION

James Forten was born to free parents Thomas and Sarah Forten. Thomas Forten was employed at the Philadelphia sail loft of Robert Bridges. Formal education, a rarity for late-eighteenth-century Americans, became available to seven-year-old James Forten at Quaker **Anthony Benezet**'s school for African children. The Quaker school was located in Philadelphia, the second largest urban center within the British empire in 1773. Forten received instructions in reading and writing within a supportive Quaker environment: neither he nor any African descendant would overlook the pervading pacifist and antislavery philosophy of the Society of Friends (Quakers). Notably, Benezet's writings included an uncompromising condemnation of slave trading along the West African Guinea coast and an attack upon slavery within the British colonies. Later, Forten would also author similar antislavery attacks.

Paul Cuffe, Forten's senior by seven years, was the seventh of ten children to Coffe Slocum, an Ashanti enslaved to Ebenezer Slocum until he purchased his freedom in 1742, and Ruth Moses a member of the indigenous Wampanoag people living in the vicinity of the Massachusetts Bay colony. Cuffe only boasted of two weeks' formal education, which comprised navigational training. The family lived a seafaring life of farming, fishing, and coasting along Massachusetts' Buzzards Bay. Thus, Paul Cuffe developed sailing, boat building, and farming skills. Living first on secluded Cuttyhunk Island and then within Martha's Vineyard's Native American stronghold of Chilmark, the growing family personified Puritan and Quaker ethics. Not long before dying, patriarch Coffe Slocum crudely but boldly recorded those values in a ledger: "Care Dare Ere Fear Give . . . good Do good all Do good to All . . . Give Give Give . . . Good Do Good at all time" (Thomas 1988, 6).

CAREER HIGHLIGHTS

Cuffe and Forten led parallel lives as they established themselves in their respective careers. Prior to the American Revolution, both men lost their fathers within a year of one another and then, while sailing aboard American vessels, each was captured and incarcerated in a British prison. Unlike the young Forten, a fourteen-year-old powder boy who narrowly escaped being enslaved in the West Indies, the youthful Cuffe returned home from jail to commence blockade running to Nantucket Island. By the end of the American Revolution, each embarked upon a different maritime enterprise to achieve upward mobility in white America.

Forten's maritime business stayed ashore. After the war, he sailed as a deckhand to Liverpool, England, the country's most notorious slave-trading port. There, along the docks, he witnessed incoming slavers and heard firsthand about Britain's most notable critics of the slave trade, such as Granville Sharp, Thomas Clarkson, and William Wilberforce. Back home, like his father, Forten became employed at the respected Robert Bridges sail-making business. In a few short years he rose to become foreman and then, at the age of thirty-two, the sole owner. Soon, the Forten Sail Loft had become the most prosperous loft in the city and was known for outfitting any vessel but a slaver. The firm's lofty reputation for its meticulous preparation of canvass, innovative sail-handling devices, and industrious multiracial employees assured clients. Eventually, the firm would earn Forten $100,000. Forten married Charlotte Vandine in 1805; they subsequently raised eight children. After getting married, Forten moved from Shippen Street to a spacious home on Lombard. By that stage, he was vestryman at St. Thomas African Episcopal Church.

In contrast to Forten's land-based business, Cuffe's career took him to sea. Following the American Revolution, his family business began along Massachusetts' Buzzards Bay. During the early years, the business included his wife, Alice Pequit (married in 1783), and their seven children, as well as his sister Mary Cuffe's family of twelve (eight males) fathered by Pequot native Michael Wainer. This African-Pequot extended family, whose males became boat builders, whalers, and coastal traders, and whose females farmed and often married seafarers, was identified in the press as "black." Prominent underwriters for the Cuffe enterprise included New Bedford Quaker William Rotch, Jr., who upon Cuffe's death would become his trustee, and Quaker James Brian of Wilmington, Delaware.

By 1798, when Forten owned the sail loft, Cuffe had frequently entered Philadelphia, known also as the Quaker City due to its preponderance of Quakers. At the time, Cuffe's favorite vessel, schooner *Ranger*, was just completing two roundtrips to Vienna, Maryland, a Chesapeake Bay community that had unsuccessfully blocked the vessel's entrance into port for fear the ship's company might liberate the region's slaves. Return visits to Vienna netted the Cuffe business in excess of $2,000.

Around 1806, Westport, Massachusetts workers laid the keel for the 269-ton ship *Alpha* and planned construction of another vessel, brig *Traveller*. Unknowingly, the *Alpha*'s maiden voyage would coincide with efforts by international philanthropists to counteract arguments of African inferiority. With Cuffe's hallmark black crew, Cuffe conducted business at Friend James Brian's Wilmington docks and at Georgia's slave trading port of Savannah before sailing on to the Baltic ports of Goteborg, Sweden, and Elsinore, Denmark. After a rough passage, the ship reentered Philadelphia crowded with passengers, including a Swedish apprentice indentured to Cuffe. With his growing success, Quaker Ann Emlen Mifflin of New Bedford concluded, "He is a man whom I suppose to be worth 20,000 dollars, of more extensive credit & reputation than any other in the township" (Thomas 1988, 26). Simultaneously, the Royal African Institution in London published "Memoirs of an African Captain" to discredit theories of African inferiority. The work made its case by citing the careers of two Americans, Paul Cuffe and James Forten.

MAJOR PHILANTHROPIC CONTRIBUTIONS

Cuffe's early activism suggested the dual benefits of voluntary action for communal as well as personal benefit. During the American Revolution, his African-Indian family was unable to pay taxes, so in 1780 he and oldest brother John Cuffe skillfully crafted a petition—reminiscent of the Declaration of Independence—to the Massachusetts General Court. The seven petitioners argued that they had been deprived of the right to elect "those that tax us . . . , against a familiar Exception of Power . . . too well known to need a Recital at this place" (Thomas 1988, 11). The group further appealed as destitute persons chiefly of African extraction. Turning to local selectmen, the Cuffes also advocated that free Negroes and mulattoes should have the same commercial privileges as whites.

James Forten's first voluntary action venture was, like Cuffe's, a collective effort. In 1801, with coauthors likely to have included African clergymen Rev. Richard Allen and Rev. Absalom Jones, Forten and associates focused on slavery. Their concerns addressed a national problem as important to Forten Sail Loft employees as those Africans kidnapped on city streets. Addressed to the United States Congress, this document represented "700,000 Blacks in slavery in these states" and pleaded for the political body to "revise the Fugitive Slave Act and the laws relating to the slave trade" (Douty 1968, 93). Congressmen feared the potentially disruptive consequences of such antislavery sentiments, which challenged the nation's legal claim to rightfully arrest and return fugitive slaves. Thus, they voted 84–1 against the petition. To their lone defender, George Thatcher of Massachusetts, Forten wrote: "Africans and descendants of that unhappy race thank you for the philanthropic zeal with which you defended our cause. . . . Unprejudiced persons, who read the documents in our possession, will acknowledge that we are miserable" (Purvis 1842, 13).

In contrast, Cuffe took his activism into Africa's slave-trading waters. For years, he had been concerned about Sierra Leone, the British asylum for Africans who had been seized upon the high seas while en route to a life of slavery in the New World. Cuffe wondered how he could help the Sierra Leone colony. Two influences motivated Cuffe's subsequent efforts: his admission into the Society of Friends—a rarity for an African descendant—and imploring sentiments from members of the Royal African Institution, who were charged with maintaining the British colony. Royal African Institution letters also assured him that a visit to Sierra Leone would receive adequate remuneration in the way of commercial privileges. The frugal black Yankee did not intend to sail there on a mercy mission at his own expense, but he was in for a surprise.

From Philadelphia's wharfs, Cuffe departed aboard the brig *Traveller*. He spent two months at Freetown, the colonial capital of Sierra Leone, and then sailed on to London where he privately disclosed that a colonial merchant monopoly was inhibiting profit making by industrious black merchants. Cuffe also resolved to promote a triangular African traffic of legitimate commerce, as opposed to the continuing traffic in slaves, between America, England, and Sierra Leone. Plus, the shipping would become a means for a few black Americans to emigrate to Sierra Leone. Back in the colony, he firmed up his plan by purchasing a home for himself in Freetown and then turned homeward. Thereafter, Cuffe became convinced that such an African plan would require considerable expense. No records tell us his losses, but he complained about his considerable costs and the effects of the local monopoly upon him. Henceforth, he concluded that American blacks must collectively aid their brethren in Africa.

To complicate such an effort, America's war against England, the War of 1812, was about to begin. Amidst the impending conflict, both black and white Philadelphians warmly welcomed news from their African expert. Cuffe proceeded to sell his African plan among the city's poor, the disenfranchised, petty merchants, churchmen, the city's clergy (such as Absalom Jones and Richard Allen), and especially to fellow merchant and friend James Forten. In Philadelphia, as well as other cities such as Baltimore, New York, and Boston, urban African Americans approved of Cuffe's plan by establishing

black American versions of the Royal African Institution. These African institutions would foster transatlantic correspondence and mutual aid between fellow Africans.

For the next few years, Forten, president of the local African institution, reverted to pressing domestic issues. He prepared a publication entitled "Series of Letters by a Man of Color." These letters, which would receive wide distribution, attacked proposed Pennsylvania legislation bound to require all blacks to register within the first twenty-four hours of entering the state. Forten contrasted the legislation against the state's constitution, which had earlier declared equality: "All Men are born equally free and Independent, and have certain inherent and indefensible rights, among which are those of enjoying life and liberty" (Newman 2000, 227). As the War of 1812 wore on, Forten also mobilized brethren to help defend Philadelphia should the British attack.

For once confined to home, Cuffe turned his attention to community needs. For some time the Westport Monthly Meeting House had needed considerable repairs. Merchants, shipbuilders, and families turned their attention to erecting a new structure. An auction raised a hefty $204. With a final cost of $1,200, the black Quaker contributed $577.97 toward the meeting house. Cuffe also attended to the maintenance of and teacher's salary for what neighbors affectionately termed "Cuff's School" (Thomas, 1988, 21). Since his neighbors some years earlier had refused to join him in providing a school, Cuffe built his own school for extended family members and community children on his own property. This school became the area's first public school.

Still, thoughts of Africa were never far away. Forten remained convinced of their plan to bond brethren together from both continents. African institution members from Baltimore to Boston corresponded about devising a transatlantic black trading network, constructing a suitable 200-ton vessel, reporting illegal American slavers, and gathering names of would-be settlers. In early 1815, Forten assured Cuffe that he would raise the issue of "building a ship for the African trade" among institution members (Thomas 1988, 92).

Nonetheless, advocating such African philanthropy had its perils in a slave-holding culture, suggesting an ominous foreshadowing of things to come. During the War of 1812, Cuffe sent a petition to Congress requesting permission to enter Sierra Leone on humanitarian grounds, but to do so required a trading license with the British colony. On his ship, he also planned to carry a few immigrants. The ensuing congressional debate, reprinted verbatim in national papers, netted both good and bad press. While the consequences may have made Cuffe a household word, proslavery congressmen were reported as supporting the proposed African scheme simply because "the emigration of free blacks [was] a part of our population which we could well spare"(Thomas 1988, 90). Ultimately, the measure was denied.

As the War of 1812 concluded, few foresaw the potential danger of interlocking proslavery and proemigration arguments upon Cuffe and Forten's plan. Nor could they have foreseen—given the optimism surrounding this first emigration voyage—how the black urbanites, particularly in Philadelphia, might play a key role. Families from Boston, Bridgeport, New York, Philadelphia, and Baltimore inquired about passage to Africa. In fact, Cuffe and Forten fielded dozens of questions. The media suitably announced the story: "VOYAGE TO AFRICA," proclaimed Philadelphia's *Paulson's American Daily Advertiser* on September 20, 1815. The insertion announced that persons who wished to emigrate should contact the local African institution or the black captain Paul Cuffe aboard his brig *Traveller* at the city wharf. The announcement was "Signed on behalf of the African Institution of Philadelphia. James Forten, Pres't, Russell Parrott, sec'ry."

This voyage to Africa, no longer dependent upon an American license, successfully carried thirty-eight persons who wished to leave America. According to documents Cuffe brought back and displayed before the public, the settlers were all well received. Newspapers reprinted records from the colony, sometimes excerpting minutes from the New York African Institution, which included copies of official correspondence from black settlers and from the governor's council. Other more lengthy and positive publicity appeared, such as "Our Black Countrymen in Sierra Leone." Privately, Cuffe was more circumspect. He had rightfully returned to "the great family of Africa . . . in our region [who] ought not to be neglected" and the total costs for the recent voyage had cost him $8,000 (Thomas 1988, 104). He knew he could not repeat the enormous financial losses arising from carrying settlers.

Optimism over Cuffe's voyage also reigned in the U.S. capital, but for different reasons. By mid-December 1816, self-proclaimed white philanthropists and prominent clergy as well as slave-holding congressmen and senators convened a new society in the chambers of the House of Representatives. It was to bear the title "The American Society for the Colonization of Free People of Color," later called the American Colonization Society. Cuffe, the black emigrationist, welcomed these humanitarians to his side.

Cuffe and Forten's plan to maintain a legitimate triangular African traffic and emigration voyages began to unravel as the media reported the substance of the proceedings in the nation's capital. These developments set in motion a gradual process of disengaging the city's black leadership from any ties with the American Colonization Society. At this point, Cuffe, writing from the confines of his Westport home, counseled patience to his Philadelphia friends.

Daily confronted with inflammatory stories and protests arising on the street, Forten and Russell Parrott summoned members of the city's African institution to Richard Allen's African Methodist Church on January 6, 1817. The tumultuous gathering of free persons led to four resolutions, each condemning the American Colonization Society. Members angrily condemned the society that boasted an untenable credo: free blacks "are a dangerous and useless part of our community" (Purvis 1842, 15). Leaders agreed to sign the resolutions, but they remained hopeful (with Paul Cuffe) that the new society might somehow benefit black brethren. By the early summer, Cuffe's health was rapidly deteriorating and Forten's hope was fading. On August 10, African institution members unanimously declared that the colonization scam was but a manipulative slaveholder's society. Cuffe died three weeks later, and with him went the shared philanthropic plan that linked together the pan-African destinies of brethren across the Atlantic.

James Forten, who survived his partner and friend by twenty-five years, focused his future efforts on the evils of slavery in America. Within time, he joined others pointing to the implicit dangers the colonization society might have upon the perpetuation of slavery. In the years ahead, he cofounded the American Anti-Slavery Society, Philadelphia's first African Masonic Lodge, presided over the American Moral Reform Society, and contributed writings to *The Colored American* and *The Herald of Freedom*. He subscribed to, donated to, and often published in the first black newspaper, *Freedom's Journal*, which carried Cuffe's biography in an early issue.

In 1830, Forten addressed a budding Boston reformer, William Lloyd Garrison, who would later become one of the nation's most articulate white radical abolitionist reformers: "I am extremely happy to hear you are about publishing a paper in Boston. I hope your efforts may not be in vain, and may *The Liberator* be the means of exposing, more and more, the odious system of slavery" (Newman 2000, 230–231). Forten generously contributed to Garrison's *Liberator* and provided volatile black activist writings for Garrison's salvo against the American Colonization Society, *Thoughts on Colonization*. A few years later, the aging philanthropist returned to black brethren injustices. With Robert Purvis, he compiled the sensational "Appeal of Forty Thousand Citizens" that unsuccessfully challenged the state's right to withdraw suffrage from blacks that

were now free. James Forten's public action and public giving only ceased with his death in 1842.

CONCLUSION

James Forten and Paul Cuffe represent a reliable portrayal of philanthropic activity among American black leadership at the turn of the nineteenth century. In both cases, existing records do not adequately list their financial donations to causes in which they were engaged. If Cuffe, who died in 1817 with an estate of $20,000, expended an excess of $8,000 upon settling thirty-eight persons in Sierra Leone, did the same proportion of giving apply to Forten, who died in 1842 with an estate of $100,000? One may never know.

Evidence does suggest that Cuffe and Forten were individuals whose lives interlocked along Philadelphia's docks and streets and within homes and commercial establishments. Indeed, their dreams and visions for fellow Africans found commonality among persons of diverse cultures and from three continents. Their mercantile-philanthropic teamwork exceeded the sum of their individual parts, which blended Cuffe and Forten's priorities, the Atlantic slave trade and American slavery, respectively. Both men became precursors for those that followed. Eventually, the American Colonization Society, a body more dedicated to white American priorities than African advancement, would colonize less than 10,000 persons (who would establish Liberia in 1847). Meanwhile, black abolitionists would maintain the tradition of condemning slavery until the Civil War.

Lamont D. Thomas

FURTHER READING

Douty, Esther. *Forten, the Sailmaker: Pioneer Champion of Negro Rights*. Chicago: Rand McNally, 1968.

Newman, Richard. "Not the Only Story in 'Amistad'; The Fictional Joadson and the Real James

Forten." *Pennsylvania History* 67, no. 2, Spring 2000, 218–239.

Purvis, Robert. *Remarks on the Life and Character of James Forten, Delivered at Bethel Church, March 30, 1842*. Philadelphia: Merrihew & Thompson, 1842.

Thomas, Lamont D. *Paul Cuffe, Black Entrepreneur and Pan-African*. Urbana: University of Illinois Press, 1988.

Wiggins, Rosalind C. *Captain Paul Cuffe's Logs and Letters, 1808–1817*. Washington, DC: Howard University Press, 1996.

Winch, Julie. *Philadelphia's Black Elite: Activism, Accommodation, and the Struggle for Autonomy, 1787–1848*. Philadelphia: Temple University Press, 1988.

PAPERS

The core of Paul Cuffe's papers is in the New Bedford Free Public Library (New Bedford, MA) and is available on microfilm. Contemporary media, during his day, also offer abundant evidence. Other material is scattered in private and public repositories such as the New York Historical Society (New York City), Cox-Parrish-Wharton Collection, Historical Society of Pennsylvania (Philadelphia, PA), and the National Archives (Washington, DC).

James Forten left no documents or papers. For other related papers, see the Cox-Parrish-Wharton Collection, Historical Society of Pennsylvania (Philadelphia, PA). The bulk of primary material on Forten originates from contemporary media and government documents, some of which are available in edited works such as Herbert S. Aptheker's *A Documentary History of the Negro People in the United States*, vol. 1 (New York: Citadel Press, 1968).

D

DOROTHY DAY
(1897–1980)

Founder of the Catholic Worker Movement

INTRODUCTION

"The most significant thing about *The Catholic Worker* is poverty, some say. The most significant thing is community, others say. . . . But the final word is love" (Day 1952, 285). With these words, Dorothy Day defined the Catholic Worker movement. In March 2000, the Vatican announced that Dorothy Day, cofounder (with Peter Maurin) of the Catholic Worker movement, would be considered for sainthood. Day, who converted to Catholicism in her thirties, was, during her lifetime, an avowed socialist and anarchist; an accomplished writer who counted Hart Crane, Diego Rivera, and Eugene O'Neill as friends; and an activist who fearlessly risked arrest to protest for her beliefs. Her earlier life was also marked by an abortion, a common-law marriage, and a child out of wedlock. However, her dedication to those who have been marginalized by society, her own voluntary poverty, and her strong faith make her an important figure in American philanthropy.

EARLY YEARS AND EDUCATION

Dorothy Day was born on November 8, 1897, in Brooklyn, New York, one of four children. Her father was a newspaper journalist whose job took the family to cities across the country. One such stop was San Francisco, where the family endured the great earthquake of 1906. It was this calamity that exposed the young Day to her first real remembrance of generosity. While her family suffered some material losses in the earthquake, others fared far worse, and her family, along with others less affected, shared all they had with those who lost everything. The enormity of the disaster coupled with the human outpouring of help impressed Day indelibly.

Because the publication that employed her father was destroyed, the Day family left San Francisco soon after the earthquake and settled in Chicago, where Dorothy Day would spend the remainder of her childhood. As a journalist, her father witnessed much of the harshness and violence of the world. These

Dorothy Day, publisher of *The Catholic Worker*, c. 1960. AP Photo.

experiences, combined with his own introversion, insured that his daughter would lead a sheltered life. For example, she could only read classic literature in the home. While her family was not especially religious, Day and her family did attend an Episcopalian church. Living in Chicago, however, she saw the wide chasm between the wealthy and the poor and was deeply moved by the pain and powerlessness of those who lacked resources.

After high school graduation, Day attended the University of Illinois at Urbana on a full scholarship and dedicated her time to general studies to receive the broadest education possible. As a college student, she endured major financial struggles, which allowed her to personally identify with the poor. Observant of the stark differences between the social classes in Urbana and in American society at large, Day immersed herself in the writings of Upton Sinclair, Jack London, and other authors who shared her outrage. Consequently, she joined the Socialist party because she believed that group best represented the needs of the masses.

While studying at the university, Day also worked odd jobs to purchase books and sustain her writing, which consisted of selling the occasional column to small newspapers. Because her writings often critiqued the structure of society's classes, she routinely experienced problems selling her work for publication. She intentionally lived a solitary life and, more often than not, had no money to eat properly. During this immersion into socialism, Day rejected organized religion because she could not relate her concept of faith with conventional denominations and their beliefs. Her belief in a higher power, however, was sustained through the readings of Russian authors such as Fyodor Dostoevsky and Leo Tolstoy. After two years in Illinois, her family again relocated, this time to New York City, and Day, ready for a change, followed them.

In New York City, she found work writing for left-wing publications, *The Call* and then *The Masses*. Soon after the closing of *The Masses*, she was arrested and jailed for the first time. Participating in a 1917 suffragist protest in Washington, DC, Day was actually arrested several times during the multiday event. Day and the other protesters received various jail sentences and—instead of being held in a city jail (appropriate for lesser crimes)—were sent to Occoquan, an institution usually reserved for more severe criminal behavior. In addition, they were treated roughly, confined to inordinately small cells, and kept from exercise and audible conversation. To demonstrate their outrage at being incarcerated at Occoquan, the women began a thirty-day hunger strike. While dismissed at first, the women tenaciously fasted, and their story received coverage by the media. It was during the darkest days of the hunger strike that Day turned to the Bible for relief and found solace in the Psalms. Finally, after ten days of negative publicity, the jail officials relented, and the women were moved to a more accommodating city jail.

After a relationship with newspaperman Lionel Moise, which ended soon after Day became pregnant in 1919, she had an abortion. Afterward she wrote the autobiographical *The Eleventh Virgin* (1924) and undertook a variety of other jobs. Day also met and fell in love with English biologist Forster Battingham in 1924, and their relationship became a common-law marriage. The two shared a hunger for knowledge and held similar political views. Indeed, both were anarchists, seeing the best political order as the abolition of the state and the free associations of individuals and groups. Day, however, began to feel increasingly drawn to the Catholic Church. After her arrest for the suffragist protest, her interest in the church began during a short stint as a nurse.

While in nursing training, she was befriended by a Catholic nurse. Subsequently, Day attended mass with her friend and began to see parallels with her radicalism and the social teachings of the Church. As a radical, she associated and identified with the masses, and the Catholic Church, to her, was the church of the masses. W.H. Locke Anderson, an author who has studied Day and her politics, observes that "religion and revolutionary politics share a vision of transcendence, of victory over the 'forces of darkness,' of meaning that extends beyond one's own immediate life, and therefore in one sense or another, a life beyond death" (Anderson 1996, 22).

However, Day was disturbed by what she viewed as a paradoxical Catholic Church: it was an agent for change in the lives of the poor, yet was extremely wealthy—in property and money—and rarely delved into its own resources to help its members—relying on individuals to contribute to causes rather than expend resources it possessed. Despite these tensions, she was ultimately drawn by the tradition of the Church. As her interest in the church and her inner faith grew, she became increasingly aware that her relationship with Battingham would end. He saw all religion, especially Catholicism, as being for the weak, and, moreover, the Church would not tolerate their common-law marriage. Around the same time, Day became pregnant and was certain she wanted her child (Tamar Theresa, born March 3, 1927) to be baptized in the Church. With the birth of her child and her eventual conversion to Catholicism, her relationship with Battingham concluded.

CAREER HIGHLIGHTS AND MAJOR PHILANTHROPIC CONTRIBUTIONS

Soon after her conversion in 1927, the world plunged into the Great Depression and Day was again conflicted by her radicalism and her newly found faith. It seemed to her that many of those most negatively affected by the economic depression were Catholics, but the Church was providing no leadership in tending to the needs of the unemployed and those suffering in poverty. When told of the charity of many Catholic institutions, Day was not impressed because she believed charity was not a virtue. Instead of charity, Day felt the Church needed to address the causes of poverty, not just treat the effects. After covering the Hunger March in Washington, DC for *The Commonweal*, a Catholic publication, Day met Peter Maurin. Together, they would create a movement to provide assistance to those suffering from poverty and who were physically, emotionally, and spiritually neglected.

Maurin heard of Day through her reputation as a writer and came to her home believing the two of them shared common beliefs. One of twenty-three children, he was a French scholar and a deeply committed Catholic. Twenty years older than Dorothy, he shared her love for the masses and saw industrialization and bureaucratization as ultimately dehumanizing. Maurin, moreover, saw the virtue of manual labor and believed that one should produce all that one needs. He also felt that every person was his brother and ritually gave away anything that he owned. Poverty, he felt, liberated him from the bondage of materialism. He strongly believed that "we are our brother's keeper, and the unit of society is the family; that we must have a sense of personal responsibility to take care of our own, and our neighbor, at a personal sacrifice" (Day 1952, 179).

In May 1933, Day and Maurin began publishing *The Catholic Worker*, a publication dedicated to raising awareness of poverty, racism, and labor practices. The paper sold for one penny a copy to insure that cost did not deter readers from purchasing it (the paper still sells for this same price more than sixty-seven years later) and began with an initial run of 2,500 copies. By the end of 1933, circulation rose to 100,000 and reached its peak of 150,000 by 1936.

Day and Maurin, in response to the continuing economic depression, began to open houses of hospitality, also known as Catholic Worker houses, to provide food and, where possible, shelter for those in need. In her autobiography *The Long Loneliness*, Day stated, "Every one of us who was attracted to the poor had a sense of guilt, or responsibility, a feeling that in some way we were living on the labor of others. The fact that we were born in a certain environment, were enabled to go to school . . . all these things marked us as the privileged in a way" (Day 1952, 204). For Day, those who avoided poverty and lived a life of privilege had a responsibility to comfort those in need. True to her vision, college students often volunteered at houses of hospitality, located in storefronts or other appropriate gathering places, and took the idea of the Catholic Worker with them to their hometowns after graduation. Soon, the Catholic Worker movement spread throughout the United States and eventually to England and Australia. Many overseas houses published their own newspapers as well. Today, many of these houses of hospitality remain in existence, and while some still publish newspapers, other Catholic Worker houses have turned to the Internet as a way to communicate their beliefs.

To Day and Maurin, voluntary poverty was a vital component in the Catholic Worker movement. John Cort, an early member of the movement, remembers that Day asserted that voluntary poverty allowed one to obtain a closer connection to, and understanding of, individuals in need. In a 1930s issue of *The Catholic Worker*, Day wrote, "We are willing to clothe ourselves in donations of clothes that come in; we are willing to eat the plainest and most meager of meals and to endure cold rooms and lack of privacy. . . . And we feel that the work gains by it" (Cort 1980, 361). Whether Day was living in houses of hospitality—working along with other volunteers to meet the needs of the dispossessed—or traveling the country for speaking engagements, she continually maintained a materially poor lifestyle.

Pacifism was also a strong theme in the Catholic Worker movement and in Day's personal ideology. On this issue, as in others, Day did not fear arrest or other serious consequence to make her point. Strict adherence to pacifism during World War II meant she wrote against American involvement in *The Catholic Worker* newspaper—an unpopular stance that cost her and her newspaper support. In 1957, she led a protest against the Civil Defense Act, a law that forced citizens to take shelter during air raid tests. Knowing that no shelter can exist in a nuclear war, Day led the protest to voice her pacifist views and was jailed at the age of sixty. Day and others continued protesting, ultimately forcing an end to the air raids.

CONCLUSION

Day served the poor until her death at the age of eighty-three. Throughout her leadership of the Catholic Worker movement, she demonstrated a willingness to risk her own freedom and to sacrifice personal comfort to fight for ideals. Her legacy survives in the many Catholic Worker houses, farms, and publications that serve and advocate for the poor and marginalized. Moreover, Day certainly spurred others to join reform efforts beyond the Catholic Worker movement.

Michael P. Grzesiak

FURTHER READING

Anderson, W.H. Locke. "Living as Though the Truth Were True: Dorothy Day and *The Catholic Worker.*" *Monthly Review*, (March 1, 1996, 19–24.

Buckley, Gail Lumet. "The Far Right Thought Dorothy Day Was a Communist; the Far Left Thought She Was a Tool of the Vatican. In Reality, She Had No 'Extremes.' " *America*, February 14, 1998, 5.

Cort, John C. "My Life at the Catholic Worker." *Commonweal*, June 20, 1980, 361–367.

Coy, Patrick G., ed. *A Revolution of the Heart: Essays on the Catholic Worker*. Philadelphia: Temple University Press, 1988.

Day, Dorothy. *By Little and By Little: The Selected Writing of Dorothy Day*. Robert Ellsberg, ed. New York: Knopf, 1983.

———. *The Eleventh Virgin*. New York: A & Co. Boni, 1924.

———. *The Long Loneliness*. San Francisco: HarperSanFrancisco, 1952, 1997.

Miller, William D. *All Is Grace: The Spirituality of Dorothy Day*. Garden City, NY: Doubleday, 1987.

———. *Dorothy Day: A Biography*. San Francisco: Harper & Row, 1982.

———. *A Harsh and Dreadful Love: Dorothy Day and the Catholic Worker Movement*. New York: Liveright, 1973.

Piehl, Mel. *Breaking Bread: The Catholic Worker and the Origin of Catholic Radicalism in America*. Philadelphia: Temple University Press, 1982.

Roberts, Nancy L. *Dorothy Day and the Catholic Worker*. Albany: State University of New York Press, 1984.

PAPERS

Dorothy Day's papers as well as papers of the Catholic Worker movement are located in the Department of Special Collections and University Archives, Marquette University (Milwaukee, WI).

DAYTON FAMILY

George Draper Dayton (1857–1938)

Banker, Tither, and Founder of the Dayton Company (Datyon's) and the Dayton Foundation

Kenneth Nelson Dayton (1922–   )

CEO of Dayton Hudson Corporation, Corporate Philanthropist, and Promoter of the Social Responsibility of Business and the "Stages of Giving"

Donald Chadwick Dayton (1912–1989)

CEO of Dayton Corporation, Corporate Philanthropist, Founder of the Sister Kenny Institute

Bruce Bliss Dayton (1918–)

CEO of Dayton Hudson Corporation, Corporate Philanthropist, Art Collector, and Major Benefactor of the Minneapolis Institute of Art

Wallace Corliss Dayton (1921–)

Dayton Corporation Executive, Corporate Philanthropist, Environmentalist, and Conservationist

Douglas Dayton (1924–)

Dayton Corporation Executive, Corporate Philanthropist, and Community Benefactor

INTRODUCTION

In 1921, George Draper Dayton, the founder of a Minneapolis-based retail empire, received a letter from a minister named Charles Bronson. Since seminary, Bronson had received charitable support from George Dayton and he expressed his appreciation by writing "most men spend all their time making money. You evidentially spend not a little in thinking how to give it away" (Dayton and Green 1997, 433). George Dayton subsequently shared a copy of Bronson's letter with his children and added, "I can truly say to you, my children, that nothing brings as much pleasure to your father and mother as the doing something for others. Our hope is that our children will catch the spirit of it and find great pleasure in their passing on to others some of the good things which God has brought to them" (Dayton and Green 1997, 433). True to his wish, George Dayton's descendants caught his philanthropic spirit and became important philanthropists.

As for a specific approach to giving, George Dayton promoted tithing because he believed it caused one to deliberately plan and budget one's annual philanthropy. In a business tithing fashion, five of George Dayton's grandsons followed their grandfather's teachings. In 1946, these five Dayton brothers established a Dayton Company (Dayton's) policy of annually giving 5 percent of the corporation's pretax profits to charity, which was the maximum amount deductible under the federal tax code. Kenneth Nelson

Dayton, who would become one of the most prominent Dayton grandsons as well as the head of the reconstituted Dayton Hudson Corporation, would even give public speeches promoting corporate philanthropy and the "five percent solution" (Dayton 1980, 619). In a 1980 address in Houston, Kenneth Dayton stated, "At Dayton Hudson we're convinced that corporate philanthropy—combined with a comprehensive program of community involvement—is not only good for our city, it's good for our business and it's good for the free enterprise system" (Dayton 1980, 619). Ultimately, the Dayton Hudson Corporation would not only become a corporate philanthropy leader but also illustrate the value of such giving when it faced a hostile takeover.

GEORGE DRAPER DAYTON

George Draper Dayton was born in Clifton Springs, New York on March 6, 1857, but his family soon made their permanent home in Geneva, New York. The son of David Day Dayton, M.D., and Caroline Wesley Draper Dayton, he was raised in a deeply religious home. Caroline Dayton came from a long line of Methodist ministers and David Dayton was an elder of the First Presbyterian Church of Geneva. Since his father was a Presbyterian, George Dayton became a Presbyterian as well. As a child, however, he attended the Presbyterian Church and participated in Methodist prayer and class

George Draper Dayton in 1934. Photo by Lee Brothers, Minnesota Historical Society.

DAYTON'S STORE AND THE DAYTON COMPANY

In 1881, central New York investors, who held mortgages in the rural Worthington, Minnesota area, asked twenty-four-year-old George Dayton to evaluate their investments. He reported back with deep concerns and was finally convinced to move to Worthington, take over the Bank of Worthington, and fix the problems. Lacking commercial bank experience, George Dayton proved himself an excellent banker as well as a realtor. By 1900, George Dayton's Minnesota Loan and Investment Company—started in 1884 to focus exclusively on realty business—possessed assets of $1,172,829.

Eight years earlier, George Dayton began to diversify his land holdings by buying urban as well as rural property, including properties in the Minneapolis area. In 1902, his large amount of investments in the Minneapolis area forced him to relocate there. That same year, George Dayton became a silent partner in Goodfellow's Dry Goods, which opened in a six-floor building constructed on his property at the corner of Nicollet Mall and Seventh Street. After his partners proved less adept at running the store, George Dayton bought them out and he and his son Draper found themselves in the retail business.

In the following years, George and Draper Dayton greatly expanded the size and offerings (including art parlors and tea rooms) of the renamed Dayton's store. They also reached all types of consumers by offering low-price and middle- and upper-price floors. In 1911, Nelson Dayton joined the store and George Dayton sold a third of the store (the Dayton Company) to each son, left active management, and focused on real estate.

The Dayton brothers kept Dayton's prospering until Draper died in 1923. Thereafter, George Dayton (until his death in 1937) provided Nelson Dayton with some assistance as he ran the store. After Draper's death, Nelson Dayton also set forth Dayton's philosophy of service: "Capture the customers' imagination with an array of goods; Earn

meetings with his mother. With such an upbringing, George Dayton wished to embark on a career in the ministry.

However, George Dayton soon found himself developing a business career due to the onset of a depression (the panic of 1873). Responding to a businessman's plea for help, David Dayton offered a loan and an apprentice (George Dayton) for the businessman's coal and lumber yard. George Dayton subsequently earned enough money in salary and commissions to buy the coal and lumber yard before he was eighteen. After devoting day and night to the business, he collapsed from exhaustion in 1877. After a period of rest, he returned to business and later married Emma Willard Chadwick on December 17, 1878. The couple would have four children: David Draper, Caroline Ward, George Nelson, and Josephine.

A 1924 photo of Nelson Dayton and his children, the grandchildren of George Draper Dayton. Photo by C.J. Hibbard, Minnesota Historical Society.

loyalty with generous merchandising policy; Provide incidental attractions and conveniences within Dayton's walls so customers do not wander to the doors of competitors" (Dayton and Green 1997, 302). This philosophy appeared to work as Dayton's continued to post sizable profits, even during the Great Depression. In 1936, the Dayton Company recorded sales of $16.4 million and profits of $1.1 million.

Nelson Dayton married Grace C. Bliss in 1912, and they raised five sons and a daughter: Donald Chadwick, Elizabeth, Bruce Bliss, Wallace Corliss, Kenneth Nelson, and Douglas James. In the 1940s, Nelson Dayton stopped managing the store but his five sons (the Dayton brothers) became the third generation of Daytons to manage the retail business, with Donald, Bruce, and Ken Dayton taking subsequent turns as president. Nelson Dayton subsequently died of cancer in 1950.

DAYTON HUDSON CORPORATION

Having developed successful department stores and a huge market share in the Twin Cities, the Dayton brothers considered growth options. From their 12-story and 1.3-million-square-foot store in Minneapolis, they expanded geographically and organizationally. In 1962, the Dayton brothers created the first Target store; this discount market venture would eventually become their company's most profitable division. Having become what *Business Week* called "the dominant store in the upper Middle West," Dayton's went public in 1967 (*Business Week* 1964, 70). Two years later, they merged with Detroit department retailer Hudson's and became the Dayton Hudson Corporation.

Continuing their acquisitions, Dayton Hudson bought Mervyn's California (1978) and Marshall Field & Co. (1990). Meanwhile, Dayton family members stopped managing the company when Kenneth Dayton retired in 1983. By 2000, Dayton Hudson Corporation had 1,200 stores in 44 states. On January 30, 2000, the corporation renamed itself the Target Corporation.

MAJOR PHILANTHROPIC CONTRIBUTIONS

George Draper Dayton

Long before any Daytons possessed great wealth, George Dayton engaged in charitable giving. George Dayton's philanthropy sprang from a religious life that involved praying and reading the Bible daily, attending church regularly, and never opening Dayton's on the Sabbath. He strongly believed in the Bible's instruction to tithe (give one-tenth of one's income to God) because "tithing is putting evangelism into action" (Dayton and Green 1997, 416). Thus, he even tithed when he was only making a few hundred dollars a year or was experiencing bad times. George Dayton also carefully traced and annually budgeted his giving. He argued, "Many people . . . really think they are generous because they have no record and guess their donations bulk larger than they do. Right here is one splendid benefit of tithing" (Dayton and Green 1997, 416). In later years, feeling that many ministers neglected their responsibility to promote tithing, he even became a tithing advocate. In speeches such as "Tithing and Stewardship," he strongly encouraged ministers to preach repeatedly on tithing.

George Dayton also believed 10 percent should only be a starting point for one's giving. As one developed as a donor, one would see that 10 percent was not enough. In fact, records show George Dayton gave away 40 percent of his income around the age of thirty. No matter how much he gave, he also recognized the value of challenge or matching gifts and often offered a donation or a further donation if the charitable institution could match the gift with an additional amount.

To honor his parents, who had inspired his giving, George Dayton began to make plans to establish a charitable foundation in 1909. Nine years later, with approximately a $900,000 endowment, he created the Dayton Foundation, whose articles of incorporation set forth an extremely broad purpose:

"to aid in promoting the welfare of mankind anywhere in the world" (Dayton and Green 1997, 430). George and Emma Dayton made their four children incorporators and trustees as a way to reinforce the value of giving within their family. Even after the creation of the foundation, George Dayton gave personally as well as through the foundation. Although his philanthropy included nonreligious groups, George Dayton's beneficiaries tended to represent a variety of religious activities: foreign missionaries, churches, ministers, and Macalester College (established as a Presbyterian school). During the last three decades of his life, for instance, he annually read numerous inspirational volumes, selected the best two or three books, and sent copies to thousands of clergy. The Dayton Foundation's articles of incorporation also required that 25 percent of its income—over five years—be distributed to Protestant missions. Before the company went public, a quarter of the Dayton Foundation's assets went to the Minneapolis Foundation and for the benefit of the United Theological Seminary. In 1969, the Dayton Foundation merged into the Dayton Hudson Foundation.

Five Dayton Brothers

As the Dayton family's wealth grew, George Dayton worried about its effect on his descendants. However, his family proved ample bearers of his legacy. Accounts note that the Daytons gave a portion of their company profits to charity before the Dayton brothers, Donald, Bruce, Wallace, Kenneth, and Douglas Dayton, instituted the policy of giving 5 percent of their pretax profits to charity in 1946. At that time, Dayton's was the second corporation—after S&H Green Stamps—in the United States to institute such a giving policy.

This corporate philanthropy program began at a time when the concept of corporate giving was viewed as suspect and only those gifts that clearly illustrated a direct benefit, such as a community service that aided its employees, were generally accepted. In the *Smith v Barlow* case of 1953, the A.P. Smith Manufacturing Company was sued by a stockholder when it gave $1,000 to Princeton University. Describing corporations as citizens with social obligations, the New Jersey Supreme Court ruled for the A.P. Smith Manufacturing Company and, more significantly, removed the concept of direct benefit. Still, corporations generally ventured into philanthropy cautiously and very few gave anything close to 5 percent. By 1974, the Commission of Private Philanthropy and Public Needs (also known as the Filer Commission) stated that only 6 percent of corporations gave more than $500 and corporate givers averaged 0.85 percent of pretax profits.

As a family-owned corporation, Dayton's avoided stockholder complaints for many decades. When the corporation went public in the late 1960s, the Daytons made it clear to investors that they viewed the 5 percent philanthropy program as an important part of the company's long-term profitability. In justifying their corporate philanthropy to the public, the Dayton family members cited their social responsibility as well as the need to satisfy all their stakeholders. Referring to the company's social responsibility to engage in philanthropy, Kenneth Dayton stated, mimicking his grandfather's religious tenor, "I say it's immoral for a company to take profits out of the community—without putting something else back in!" (Dayton 1980, 620). The Daytons also subscribed to what is known in management circles as the stakeholder model; they argued that the health of a corporation—as well as the free enterprise system—revolves around careful attention to all its stakeholders: stockholders, customers, employees, and community. Moreover, Kenneth Dayton asserted that giving the maximum 5 percent distinguished them from other companies, which helped in recruiting new employees.

Viewing the health of their community as an indicator of the growth potential of their corporation, the Daytons expanded on this philosophy when they brought Wayne Thompson, Oakland, California's city manager, to Minneapolis in 1965 and made him head of the Dayton Foundation as well as a new Environmental Development Department. During his first day on the job, Donald Dayton charged him with "everything outside" of the "four walls" of the company. "I am convinced that our profitability as a company is as much reliant on the quality of life which exists there" (Matthews et al. 1985, 216). For numerous years, Thompson guided—along with the Dayton brothers—a Dayton Hudson Foundation that primarily contributed to two areas: social action and the arts. The Dayton Hudson Foundation focused on social action (such as youth development) to improve current community problems and the arts because they believed high-quality cultural institutions correlated with a higher standard of living for a community. Unlike many foundations, the Dayton Hudson Foundation also made long-term commitments to support an organization's operating costs.

With the Minneapolis Chamber of Commerce, Thompson also created the Five Percent Club (later renamed the Minnesota Keystone Program), which initially represented a group of twenty-six Minneapolis corporations that promised to give 5 percent of their pretax profits to charity. By 1996, 147 Minnesota corporations participated at the 5 percent level and 90 Minnesota corporations participated at the 2 percent level. While the Daytons fully supported the work of the Keystone Club, they also worked informally to develop a larger corporate giving culture by making new CEOs understand the value of corporate giving. Furthermore, Bruce and Kenneth Dayton served on the board of Honeywell and General Mills, respectively, and promoted greater charitable contributions at each. In 1994, the *Chronicle of Philanthropy* noted, for example, that Minneapolis possessed the highest per capita level of corporate contributions. No doubt, the Daytons deserve some credit for such a corporate philanthropy environment.

In 1987, the Dayton Hudson Corporation faced a hostile takeover bid from Robert and

Herbert Haft's Dart Group. In that year, the goodwill and social capital built up by decades of corporate philanthropy paid off in ways unimaginable to Dayton family members. On June 19, 1987, one day after the Dayton Hudson Corporation announced that it could be subject to a hostile takeover, the Dayton Hudson Foundation held a meeting with 500 community leaders. Quickly, a legion of charities as well as employees, customers, and other citizens lobbied for Dayton Hudson's cause. By June 24, the Minnesota governor called a special session and the legislature enacted anti-takeover laws to help the Dayton Hudson Corporation on June 25. Despite a victory celebration at Dayton Hudson's, the Hafts started another takeover attempt—this time they even promised to keep the company's 5 percent giving program—but this effort ultimately collapsed due to the stock market crash of October 1987. Nonetheless, it is clear that the Dayton Hudson Corporation would not have survived the first takeover attempt without the sizable goodwill generated by their long-standing commitment to corporate philanthropy.

Outside the walls of the company, Daytons also adhered to their grandfather's tradition of charitable giving, but their major benefactions seemed more secular. George Draper Dayton's sons, Draper and Kenneth Nelson Dayton, were active in such groups as the Minneapolis Symphony Orchestra, the Minneapolis Public Library, and the Westminster Presbyterian Church. Nelson Dayton's sons followed their forebears' examples. Among other groups, Douglas Dayton supported the YMCA and Donald Chadwick Dayton supported the United Way. Experiencing polio as a child, Donald Dayton also founded the Sister Kenny Institute, which offered rehabilitation to people with polio and other disabilities. In 1968, Wallace Corliss Dayton left the family business to devote himself to environmental and conservation causes. He founded a Minnesota lobbying group called Project Environment and served on the national board of such groups as the Nature Conservancy, Sierra Club, and Audubon Society. Meanwhile, Bruce Bliss Dayton became the

art patron of Minneapolis. Joining the board of the Minneapolis Institute of Art at the age of twenty-three, Bruce Dayton has served on the board for over fifty years while buying and donating art to the museum. His sizable donations of art (including works by Rembrandt, Matisse, and Picasso) and money made long-time art museum executive Edmund Pillsbury remark, "Bruce Dayton is to Minneapolis what **Paul Mellon** has been to the National Gallery of Art: a man of taste and great generosity with a strong commitment to public service" (Abbe 1992, 1E).

Of Nelson Dayton's five sons, Kenneth Dayton, who has stridently promoted corporate philanthropy, may be the most significant philanthropist of his generation. Kenneth Dayton married Julia Davis Winton on June 12, 1953, and raised two children with her: Judson McDonald and Duncan Nelson. Kenneth and Julia Dayton have substantially supported the Minnesota Orchestra and Walker Art Center and have given away over $100 million (some gifts coming from their Oak Leaf Foundation). Kenneth Dayton's philanthropic biography also mirrors and furthers his grandfather's philanthropic legacy. After the publication of Claude Rosenberg's *Wealthy and Wise*, he and Joe Selvaggio started the One Percent Club in 1997. This group comprised people who promise to give 1 percent of their net worth to charity each year. By 1998, 110 Minnesotans had joined the club. That same year, Kenneth Dayton announced that he was capping his wealth and urged other wealthy individuals to locate themselves on his "The Stages of Giving" and make progress toward the next stage of giving. Noting that he started as a tither and carefully tracked his giving since 1945, Kenneth Dayton identified nine stages of giving developed with his wife:

- *Minimal Response.* [G]iving because we were asked and only because we were asked.
- *Involvement and Interest.* As soon as one becomes involved as a volunteer in a nonprofit organization . . . giving . . . becomes [more] meaningful.

- *As Much As Possible.* Giving [this amount] requires a plan and a budget.
- *Maximum Allowable.* For most of the last thirty years or so we [gave] . . . the [m]aximum [a]llowable by the IRS. [This policy] was a marvelous discipline . . . it gave us an open-to-give budget.
- *Beyond the Max.* No longer would we let the IRS tell us how much (or how little) we could give. . . . [however], we no longer had . . . [a] benchmark . . . we, therefore, needed to invent one.
- *Percentage of Wealth.* Until we started to measure our giving against our wealth, we did not fully realize how much we could give away and still live very comfortably.
- *Capping Wealth.* Giving each year a percent of one's wealth forces one to start thinking about the relative importance of increasing giving vs. increasing wealth.
- *Reducing the Cap.* We can visualize the possibility of doing so as we get older . . . we cannot say . . . whether we will ever have the courage.
- *Bequests.* [Having given our heirs enough assets], we are able to leave almost all our assets [to charities]. (Dayton 1999, 2–6)

Kenneth Dayton acknowledges that he is presently in the seventh stage but is contemplating the final two stages. Ideally, and in **Andrew Carnegie**-esque fashion, he wants to come as close as possible to giving all his money away before he dies. Similar to his grandfather, he encourages wealthy colleagues to recognize that philanthropy "should command the same kind of dedication and energy that accumulating wealth does" (Dayton 1999, 6). Few wealthy Americans followed such objectives 100 years ago and time will only tell how successful Kenneth Dayton—and groups such as the One Percent Club—will be in recruiting others to a modern-day "Gospel of Wealth."

CONCLUSION

In 1933, George Draper Dayton shared his values with his family through a privately published autobiography. In 1997, grandson Bruce Dayton—possibly to reinforce family values—privately published a biography of George Dayton, including a chapter on philanthropy. In the twentieth century, Dayton family members clearly upheld the legacy of the man who started a retail empire but also encouraged all to carefully plan their philanthropy and make substantial gifts. Like his grandfather, Kenneth Dayton promotes a philosophy of giving and ensures his actions follow his beliefs. Moreover, George Dayton's grandsons made his company into a corporate philanthropy leader. The company's giving program is recognized for benefiting numerous communities, probably playing a part in Minnesota's high quality-of-life indicators, and clearly illustrating the value of such philanthropy.

Robert T. Grimm, Jr.

FURTHER READING

Abbe, Mary. "A Gentleman Collector: Museum Has Celebration for Dayton Who Helped Stock It." *Star Tribune*, May 16, 1992, 1E.

Bockelman, Wilfred. "The Contribution of the Daytons." In *Culture of Corporate Citizenship: Minnesota's Business Legacy for the Global Future.* Lakeville, MN: Galde Press, 2000, 33–45.

Dayton, Bruce B., and Ellen B. Green. *George Draper Dayton: A Man of Parts.* Minneapolis: Privately printed, 1997.

Dayton, George Draper. *An Autobiography.* Privately printed, 1933, 1934.

Dayton, Kenneth N. "The Case for Corporate Philanthropy" [June 25, 1980]. In *Vital Speeches of the Day*, vol. 46. New York: City News Publishing Company, August 1, 1980, 619–622.

———. *The Stages of Giving.* Washington, DC: Independent Sector, 1999.

Inskip, Leonard. "Dayton Hudson Corp. Celebrates 50 Years of Charitable Giving." *Star Tribune*, June 18, 1996, 15A.

Mathews, John B., Kenneth E. Goodpaster, and Laura L. Nash. "Dayton Hudson Corporation." In *Policies and Persons: A Casebook in Business Ethics.* New York: McGraw-Hill, 1985, 212–231.

———. "Dayton Hudson Corporation: Conscience and Control." In *Policies and Persons: A Casebook in Business Ethics.* New York: McGraw-Hill, 1991, 256–284.

"The Midwest's Charitable Advantage." *Chronicle of Philanthropy*, February 22, 1996, 1+.

Pratt, Jon. "The Case of Minnesota: Institutionalizing Public Spirit." In *Philanthropy and the Nonprofit Sector in a Changing America*, ed.

Charles T. Clotfelter and Thomas Ehrlich. Bloomington and Indianapolis: Indiana University Press, 1999, 293–314.

"Retail Empire Reaches across the Prairie." *Business Week*, March 7, 1964, 70.

Shannon, James. "Dayton Hudson Reaps Benefits of Its Good Image." *Star Tribune*, July 5, 1987, 19A.

PAPERS

George Draper Dayton's papers are located at the Division of Archives and Manuscripts, Minnesota Historical Society (St. Paul, MN). The papers of other family members have not been deposited in an archive.

DOROTHEA LYNDE DIX
(1802–1887)

Campaigner for Mental Hospitals

INTRODUCTION

"I am the Hope of the poor crazed beings who pine in the cells, and stalls, and cages. . . . I am the Revelation of hundreds of wailing, suffering creatures" (Gollaher 1995, 250). So declared Dorothea Lynde Dix, as she campaigned for state-supported hospitals where mentally disabled men and women would be cared for humanely rather than left to burden their relatives, to wander about homeless, or to suffer cruelty and neglect as inmates of jails and poorhouses. After an unhappy childhood, Dix achieved success both as a teacher and as an author. Then, in her late thirties, she discovered the philanthropic cause that would occupy the remainder of her active life.

EARLY YEARS AND EDUCATION

Born in Hampden, Maine, on April 4, 1802, Dorothea Dix was the first of three children by Joseph and Mary Bigelow Dix. Although he was the son of a wealthy physician, Joseph Dix squandered his opportunities. More interested in religious zealotry than in making a living, he neglected his impoverished family. Mary Dix appears to have been equally feckless. For the rest of her life, Dorothea Dix would seek to distance herself from her miserable childhood by making her way in the world on her own and with an iron will.

Dorothea Dix seated on Lookout Mountain in Tennessee. By permission of the Houghton Library, Harvard Univeristy.

As a teenager, Dix went to live with her paternal grandmother in Boston. There she made a determined effort to educate herself and to find a meaningful role in life. She became a firm adherent of the Unitarian church, which preached individual enlightenment and social uplift rather than dogmatic doctrines. Dix opened a school in which her high standards and harsh discipline appealed less to her pupils than to their parents. She also embarked upon a writing career, producing religious and instructional works. Her first book, *Conversations on Common Things* (1824), a curious compendium of information intended for use by teachers, went through many editions.

Despite her accomplishments, Dix was not content. Although she did not lack male admirers, she seems to have sensed that her ambitions could not be satisfied within the confines of marriage and motherhood. Concentrating on work, she drove herself unmercifully and fell ill as a result. In the spring of 1836, her friends became so concerned about her condition that they persuaded her to sail for England, in the hope that a trip abroad would restore her health. When she arrived in Liverpool, she was received into the household of William Rathbone, a fellow Unitarian who was also a prominent politician, reformer, and philanthropist. Staying over a year as a guest of the Rathbones, Dix slowly regained her physical and mental equilibrium. She also became acquainted with British reform activities, including parliamentary investigations of the care of the insane.

Upon returning to Boston, Dix resumed her quest for a vocation that would fulfill her hunger for personal accomplishment and service to humanity. She believed that life "cannot be granted to any, but for some wise and good end. What that end be, it is ours diligently to inquire" (Brown 1998, 76). An inheritance from her grandmother, who had died while she was abroad, together with royalties from her writings, had made Dix financially independent. Now, she could look beyond the horizons of teaching and writing, toward greater things.

CAREER HIGHLIGHTS

At the urging of **Samuel Gridley Howe**, a reform-minded member of the Massachusetts legislature, Dix began inquiring into the condition of the insane. She took up the task with her accustomed vigor, visiting jails and poorhouses throughout the state in the summer of 1842. In one week alone, she covered thirty-five towns. She then prepared and submitted to the state legislature a memorial in which she described vividly the horrible conditions endured by the disturbed men and women whom she had seen in "*cages, closets, cellars, stalls, pens! Chained, naked, beaten with rods, and lashed* into obedience!" (Lightner 1999, 3). Her memorial was instrumental in persuading the legislature to appropriate funds to enlarge the existing state mental hospital at Worcester.

Elated by her first victory, Dix extended her crusade far beyond the borders of Massachusetts. In state after state, she gathered evidence on the plight of the mentally ill, wrote a memorial, and then lobbied the legislature to create a new hospital or enlarge an existing one. By 1845, she had traveled 10,000 miles and had visited 18 prisons, 300 jails, and 500 poorhouses and other institutions. By 1848, she had logged more than 60,000 miles and had carried her campaign to most parts of the United States and Canada.

Dix then turned her attention to the national government. Granted work space in the Capitol building itself, she lobbied Congress to transfer 10 million acres of public lands to the states to provide them with a perpetual source of support for their mental hospitals. After years of struggle, her bill passed both the House and the Senate but was vetoed by President Franklin Pierce in 1854. In a particularly notable veto message, Pierce stated his objections, particularly his belief that the bill would make the federal government responsible for the social welfare of its citizens:

> It cannot be questioned, that if Congress have the power to make provision for the indigent insane . . . it has the same power to provide for the indigent who are not insane, and thus to transfer to the federal government the charge of all the poor in all the States . . . to assume all the duty . . . which

is now discharged by the States themselves, or by corporate institutions, or private endowments, existing under the legislation of the States. . . . I readily . . . acknowledge the duty incumbent on us all . . . to provide for those who . . . are subject to want, and to disease of body or mind; but I cannot find any authority in the Constitution for making the federal government the great almoner of public charity throughout the United States. (U.S. President 1854, 2–3)

With this veto, the federal government largely left social welfare to the responsibility of states, local governments, and private charities until the Great Depression.

After Pierce's veto, Dix went to Europe, visited hospitals everywhere from France to Turkey, and won improved facilities for the insane in Scotland, Jersey, and the Vatican. Returning to the United States in the fall of 1856, she resumed her work in the states. At the outbreak of the Civil War, she volunteered her unpaid services as Superintendent of Women Nurses, the first woman ever to wield executive authority in the federal government. She encountered resistance both from some of her nurses, who resented the unbending moral code of "Dragon Dix," and from a host of army doctors and government bureaucrats, who eventually succeeded in wresting power from the woman one of them called a "philanthropic lunatic."

After the war, Dix again took up her work on behalf of the insane, until the ravages of age, chronic lung disease, malaria, and circulatory problems at last ended her travels. On a visit to the New Jersey State Lunatic Asylum in 1881, she found herself too weak to move on. The asylum set aside a small suite of rooms for her use, and there she remained until her death on July 17, 1887. Dix yielded only slowly to her infirmities, because, she said, "even lying on my bed I can still do something" (Gollaher 1995, 447).

MAJOR PHILANTHROPIC CONTRIBUTIONS

Modern scholarship has modified the romantic image of Dorothea Dix as the woman who single-handedly created America's mental hospitals and delivered the insane from misery and chains. In fact, nearly everywhere she went, Dix did not begin a new movement but rather came to the aid of local reformers already working for the cause. A dozen public hospitals for the insane already existed before Dix began her crusade. Moreover, even in her own lifetime many of her hospitals became hopelessly overcrowded and failed utterly to provide the quick and permanent cures that Dix had expected. It must also be said that Dix had no sympathy for the two greatest reform movements of her time: the abolitionist crusade against slavery, and the struggle for women's rights. Yet there can be no question that she made an enormous difference. For thousands of mentally ill men and women, hospital care was far better than any available alternative, and no one did more than Dix to create and sustain mental hospitals. She was constantly bombarded with pleas that only her presence could secure the passage of funding bills. Time and again, local activists declared that victory had been achieved as a direct consequence of her personal intervention.

Besides campaigning for mental hospitals, Dix indulged in countless acts of charity, from obtaining lifeboats for Sable Island to personally nursing William Seward after he was grievously wounded in the Abraham Lincoln assassination plot. Dix also encouraged others to follow her example. From both Dix and those inspired by her, the state hospitals received a constant stream of books, pictures, and other gifts. Dix insisted that no one was too rich or too poor to help others. She persuaded a skinflint Rhode Island businessman to donate $40,000 toward the cost of an asylum in that state, and she urged the boys living in the Illinois Institution for the Deaf and Dumb to plant a flower garden at the nearby home for the blind.

CONCLUSION

While admitting that she possessed "an exhaustless fund of compassion" for individual human beings, Dix denied that she was a philanthropist on the grounds that she had no love of humanity in general. She was motivated, she said, by "a certain sort of obstinacy that some people make the blunder of calling zeal; and yet the greater blunder of naming . . . philanthropy" (Gollaher 1995, 349). In her own eyes, Dix served merely as an instrument of divine purpose. "I *seek* no work," she said, "but the will of God is made clear to me as I walk in the devious roads of this world" (Brown 1998, 230).

For four decades, Dix wandered the earth in selfless devotion to the insane. "As my own discomforts have increased," she once wrote, "my conviction of the necessity to search into the wants of the friendless and afflicted has deepened—if I am cold they are colder—if I am weary they are distressed—if I am alone they are abandoned, and cast out" (Gollaher 1995, 376). Her whole life reflected her credo: "We are not sent into this world merely to enjoy the loveliness therein, nor to sit us down in passing ease. No, we are sent here for action—for constant action" (Brown 1998, 41).

David L. Lightner

FURTHER READING

Brown, Thomas J. *Dorothea Dix: New England Reformer.* Cambridge, MA: Harvard University Press, 1998.

Dix, Dorothea. *Conversations on Common Things, or, Guide to Knowledge: With Questions for the Use of Schools.* Boston: Munroe and Francis, 1824.

Gollaher, David. *Voice for the Mad: The Life of Dorothea Dix.* New York: Free Press, 1995.

Lightner, David L. *Asylum, Prison, and Poorhouse: The Writings and Reform Work of Dorothea Dix in Illinois.* Carbondale: Southern Illinois University Press, 1999.

Marshall, Helen E. *Dorothea Dix: Forgotten Samaritan.* Chapel Hill: University of North Carolina Press, 1937.

Tiffany, Francis. *Life of Dorothea Lynde Dix.* Boston: Houghton, Mifflin & Co., 1890.

U.S. President. Veto. 1854. "An Act Making a Grant of Public Lands to the Several States for the Benefit of Indigent Insane Persons." *Executive Documents,* 1–9.

PAPERS

Dorothea Lynde Dix's papers are located in the Houghton Library, Harvard University (Cambridge, MA).

KATHARINE DREXEL
(1858–1955)

American Founder of the Sisters of the Blessed Sacrament for Indians and Colored People, Patron of Catholic Schools and Missions to Native and African Americans, and Roman Catholic Saint

INTRODUCTION

"Freely have you received; freely give." These words, from the tenth chapter of the Gospel of Matthew, were given to Katharine Drexel in a vision of the Madonna of San Marco in 1883 and summarized her dedication to giving all that she had for the benefit of others. Vowed to poverty and simplicity in her own life, this "millionaire nun," as she was sometimes called, distributed some $20 million to feed, clothe, educate, and save the souls of Native and African-American children.

EARLY YEARS AND EDUCATION

Katharine Drexel was born into a prominent Philadelphia family. Her father, Francis Anthony Drexel, was a banker and business partner of J.P. Morgan. The family business eventually evolved into the Wall Street firm of Drexel Burnham Lambert. Katharine Drexel and her two sisters were educated by private tutors and enjoyed frequent trips to Europe and the American West. Although able to live lives of luxury and privilege, the Drexels were also a devout and pious Cath-

An undated photo of Mother Katharine Drexel, who was beatified by Pope John Paul II in November 1988. AP Photo.

olic family: grateful for the love of God and the many blessings bestowed upon them, while also conscious of their philanthropic obligations. The Drexel children watched and learned as their elders prayed, received the sacraments of the church, and gave generously to churches, hospitals, schools, missions, and asylums.

While her mother, Hannah J. Langstroth Drexel, died a month after her birth, Katharine Drexel's stepmother, Emma Drexel, was a powerful philanthropic role model. Twice a week, Emma Drexel, along with Katharine and her two sisters, distributed clothes, food, and rent money to Philadelphia's poor from the back door of the family home. It is thought that Emma Drexel gave well over $20,000 a year in this manner. While Katharine and her sisters accompanied their fa-

ther on trips abroad, Emma Drexel generally remained at home to look after her many charitable projects.

Meanwhile her father, who was known to spend an hour each evening in private prayer, generously supported the work of missionary priests abroad. Consequently, Katharine Drexel's life and work can only be understood within the context of religious devotion, a love of God, and a love for others—regardless of ethnicity, race, or cultural background. Indeed, she wrote, "Let us give ourselves to real pure love. . . . The renewal which I seek and which we all seek is a work of love and can be accomplished by love alone" (Duffy 1966, 397).

Meanwhile, Rev. James O'Connor, a longtime spiritual advisor who became Bishop of Omaha, also influenced Drexel's religious and philanthropic formation. O'Connor, for example, wrote Drexel letters about social and economic problems experienced by Native Americans. Until his own death in 1890, O'Connor even guided many of Drexel's early philanthropic initiatives among Native Americans. On a trip to the American West in 1884, Drexel saw the miserable conditions in which Native Americans were forced to live, which motivated her to find solutions to their problems. During a private audience with Pope Leo XIII in 1887, she asked him to send missionaries to the American Indians. The Pope challenged her to become a missionary. During this same period, she began to support her sister, Louise Drexel, in her efforts to fund boarding schools and missions to African-American children. Katharine Drexel's sisters soon followed the traditional path of marriage and social leadership but her own career was about to take a very different turn.

CAREER HIGHLIGHTS AND MAJOR PHILANTHROPIC CONTRIBUTIONS

In 1885, Francis Drexel died, leaving for his three daughters a trust worth $15 million (about $250 million in today's dollars). Meanwhile, Katharine Drexel shocked her friends by indicating a desire to leave her life of privilege and live as a nun. In fact, Bishop

O'Connor, and others, advised her to approach such a decision with much caution and deliberation. Over the next few years, she clarified and articulated her desire to combine a religious vocation with her aspiration to aid and evangelize Native Americans. In 1889, she began her religious training with the Sisters of Mercy in Pittsburgh and made her vows in February 1891. In that same year, with the support of her family and spiritual advisers, she founded the Sisters of the Blessed Sacrament for Indians and Colored People (S.B.S.), to whose work of education and evangelization she dedicated herself and all she possessed.

One of the congregation's first missions, St. Catherine's Boarding School for Pueblo Indians, Santa Fe, New Mexico, was founded in 1894. The following year, St. Emma Military Academy, a vocational school for African-American boys, was opened at Rock Castle, Virginia, and the nearby St. Francis de Sales School for Girls opened in 1899. By 1903, additional schools had opened in Arizona and Tennessee. Xavier, a coeducational secondary school for black children, was founded in New Orleans, Louisiana in 1915. With an initial enrollment of 47 students, it became Xavier University of Louisiana in 1925. By 1936, the enrollment had jumped to 829. It remains the country's only predominantly black Catholic university. In these early years, the Sisters of the Blessed Sacrament schools stressed both religious formation and practical skills. Boys were taught agricultural skills, such as farming, equipment maintenance, cannery management, and accounting, as well as blacksmithing, iron working, printing, carpentry, and masonry. At the same time, girls were taught such skills as homemaking, needlecraft, sewing, and nursing.

One can hardly overstate the impact of Drexel's work. At a time when most white Americans were indifferent, or even hostile, toward minorities, Drexel and the Sisters of the Blessed Sacrament were determined to tear down the barriers of racism and civil inequality, which were so much a part of American society during the first half of the

twentieth century. Indeed, some communities were so hostile to the education of minorities that the Catholic congregation was often forced to resort to third parties, also known as "straw buyers," to purchase land and materials for the schools. Yet, in spite of such opposition, some sixty schools were established in the West, Midwest, and South during Drexel's lifetime. Meanwhile, missions in Alaska, Canada, and Africa also received generous support. Consequently, tens of thousands of African-American and Native-American children were given the tools with which to lift themselves out of poverty and to become contributing members of their communities. Since 1927, Xavier University alone accounts for one-quarter of the black pharmacists practicing in the United States. The alumni lists of Sisters of the Blessed Sacrament schools include such notables as Alexis Herman (first African-American U.S. Secretary of Labor), Marie McDemmond (first female president of Norfolk State University), and singers Maria Salas Marino (jazz) and Annabelle Bernard (opera).

CONCLUSION

Since none of the three Drexel sisters left an heir, Francis Drexel's will stipulated that the trust's principal be divided among several specified charities. Given that the Sisters of the Blessed Sacrament community had not been founded until after his death, they were not eligible to receive any of these funds. Aware of the community's dependence on her money, Katharine Drexel's financial advisers recommended that some of her income be set aside for future needs. However, Drexel's response was indicative of her conviction that the community's charitable work was based on love and faith. "I feel that if we use all our money for the salvation of the souls who need us, God will bless our congregation [Sisters of the Blessed Sacrament] more than He would if, with worldly prudence, we were to store away immense sums to support our present institutions and ourselves" (Burton 1957, 181). Indeed, the Sisters of the Blessed Sacrament continues to be supported, just as Drexel had foretold.

By 1934, Drexel's health was clearly in decline, which forced her to give up the visits she routinely made to the congregation's various schools and convents. In 1937, by canon law (church laws), her term as Superior General ended. Her last significant outing occurred in 1939, when she received an honorary doctorate from Catholic University. Although she was forced to give up the day-to-day running of the community, Drexel remained its inspiration and soul. She also continued to receive many visitors: bishops of dioceses in which the congregation had founded its schools, Papal representatives, friends, and family. Increasingly, however, her "work" centered around prayer, the contemplative vocation for which she had always longed, and in the adoration of the Blessed Sacrament, to which she had dedicated her order from the beginning. Drexel died on March 3, 1955. At the time of her death, the Sisters of the Blessed Sacrament congregation numbered 511 professed members in 51 convents (located in 22 states and the District of Columbia). The Catholic Church canonized Drexel as a saint on October 1, 2000.

Joseph C. Harmon

FURTHER READING

Baldwin, Lou. "Giving It All: Mother Katharine Drexel's Habit of Charity," *Philanthropy* 13, March–April 1999, 13–15.

Burton, Katharine. *The Golden Door: The Life of Katharine Drexel.* New York: P.J. Kenedy & Sons, 1957.

Duffy, Consuela Maria. *Katharine Drexel: A Biography.* Philadelphia: Reilly Co., 1966.

Ellis, John Tracy, ed. "Mother Katharine Drexel Drafts the Constitutions of Her Congregation, May 25, 1907." *Documents of American Catholic History*, vol. 2. Wilmington, DE: M. Glazier, 1987, 574–576.

Tarry, Ellen. *Katharine Drexel: Friend of the Oppressed.* Nashville, TN: Winston-Derek, 1990.

PAPERS

Katharine Drexel's papers can be found in the congregation's archives at the Sisters of the Blessed Sacrament motherhouse (Bensalem, PA), but other papers, largely the records of the order she founded but also letters to and from Drexel, are at the Library of Congress (Washington, DC).

E

GEORGE EASTMAN
(1854–1932)

*Inventor, Local Benefactor, and Founder of the Eastman Kodak Company, the Eastman
School of Music, and the School of Medicine and Dentistry of the University of Rochester*

INTRODUCTION

"What you do in your working hours determines what you have. What you do in your leisure hours determines what you are" (Brayer 1996, 346). George Eastman's rationale for founding the Eastman School of Music could also refer to his stimulus for other charitable gifts. The self-education he conducted, after working hours as a young man, surely motivated his enormous gifts to education in later life. Eastman translated his personal passions into philanthropic ventures that significantly benefited and shaped his hometown of Rochester, New York, but also assisted those outside of Rochester.

EARLY YEARS AND EDUCATION

Born on July 12, 1854, in Waterville, New York, George Eastman was the youngest child and only son of George Washington and Maria Kilbourn Eastman. The family ran a thirty-acre nursery of roses and fruit trees in Waterville and G.W. Eastman commuted 130 miles west to Rochester, New York to attend to his other business, the Eastman Commercial College. Founded in 1842, this groundbreaking school, as George Eastman wrote, was "the first commercial school in which the scholars were actually carried through the regular business transactions . . . by means of dummy banks, warehouses and factories" (Brayer 1996, 38). In 1860, the family sold the nursery and moved to Rochester. Two years later, his father died, leaving a widow with three young children and little money for support. Consequently, Maria Eastman operated a boardinghouse.

For seven years, young George Eastman attended public and private schools in Rochester. In 1868, his older sister, Ellen Maria Eastman, married; that same year, George Eastman quit school to help support the remaining family. Emma Kate Eastman, his invalid sister, died in 1870. George Eastman

George Eastman in Rochester, New York, in 1921. AP Photo.

remained close to his mother until her death in 1907 and never married.

Eastman first worked at menial tasks for two insurance agencies, but rose to writing policies. At age nineteen, he became a bank clerk but his sideline photographic materials business demanded full attention by 1881. Despite leaving school at thirteen, young Eastman continued self-education through reading encyclopedias at the neighborhood bookstore and learning enough French and German to read the photographic literature in those languages.

CAREER HIGHLIGHTS

In the fall of 1877, Eastman took up wet-plate collodion photography as a hobby and immediately began to simplify the cumbersome process for his own purposes. He produced his own dry plates, tinkered with emulsions, corresponded with other amateurs, and, in 1878, entered the literature of photography with a brief article in the *British Journal of Photography.* In 1879, he invented

a machine to coat dry plates and took that plate coater to London to patent and license it. The following year, he opened the Eastman Dry Plate Co. in Rochester and obtained a U.S. patent for the plate coater. In 1881, Eastman gained an investor and partner: neighbor Henry Strong became president of the company, a position he held until his death in 1919, while Eastman remained the hands-on treasurer and general manager.

Eastman manufactured cameras, paper, and dry plates while struggling to replace heavy, breakable, single-glass negatives with a roll of transparent, flexible film that held many exposures. In 1884, with second partner William H. Walker, the Eastman Dry Plate and Film Co. constructed a roll holder that attached to existing cameras. Unable to produce a suitable transparent film, Eastman marketed the roll holder with inferior paper-backed stripping film. Unsuccessful with professional photographers, Eastman began to think about creating a whole new category of photographers—everyone.

He attached the roll holder to the hand-held Eastman Detective Camera in 1886, but design flaws led him to destroy the lot of cameras. In 1888, however, Eastman incorporated the roll holder inside another camera of his own design, which he called the Kodak. Marketed for $25 with a roll of paper-backed American film, it captured the fancy of complete novices who could afford the price. Indeed, he had begun to create a world of amateur snapshooters. Each year better, smaller, and cheaper camera models appeared until 1900, when the $1 Brownie, which took a 15-cent roll of film, made photography truly available to everyone.

In 1889, Eastman successfully marketed transparent film and Thomas Edison obtained a sample for his prototype motion picture machine. After movies were projected in theaters in 1895, Eastman sold miles of photographic film. By 1900, he had built the largest photographic materials business in the world. Thereafter, he investigated and marketed color photography and nonflammable film, started an early industrial research laboratory (1912), and developed innovative employee benefit programs. When key employees wanted to go elsewhere or refused to move to provincial Rochester, Eastman set up perks and rewards to keep them. Upon refinancing the company himself, netting a $1 million profit, he also distributed one-third to employees "not as a gift but as extra pay for good work" (Brayer 1996, 178). The bonus was institutionalized in 1912 as an annual wage dividend and supplemented throughout Eastman's life and beyond by an array of employee benefit programs unsurpassed in American industry.

In the twentieth century, Eastman often found himself in the courts. Fierce competition with older photographic companies led to patent litigation and antitrust investigations developed because Kodak produced 90 percent of the world's film. In 1925, Eastman retired from active participation in the Eastman Kodak Company. After enduring health problems, he committed suicide in 1932.

MAJOR PHILANTHROPIC CONTRIBUTIONS

The foundation of Eastman's philanthropic philosophy was pragmatism and personal appeal. Trained technicians were so important to his business that as early as 1886, when he paid himself a salary of $60 a week, he made a $50 contribution to Mechanics Institute (now the Rochester Institute of Technology) and urged his partners to do likewise. In 1890, he became a major fund-raiser for Mechanics Institute and the Rochester Orphan Asylum (his mother's favorite charity). By 1900, he was president of both boards and constructing significant buildings for the two institutions. The son of abolitionists, Eastman began supporting African-American education after receiving a copy of **Booker T. Washington**'s *Up from Slavery* in 1902. He supported Tuskegee Institute (now University) and Hampton Institute (University) and even helped build, equip, and staff an elementary "Eastman School" for black children near his North Carolina farm in 1919.

Eastman's efforts to groom the Mechanics Institute as a training school for Kodak employees failed, in his opinion, because of poor management. In the 1890s, he began hiring chemical and mechanical engineer graduates of the Massachusetts Institute of Technology (MIT). His heavy reliance on "the good stock of material" coming to Kodak from MIT led him to seek out the president, Richard Maclaurin, to determine how to assure that the supply of technicians continued (Brayer 1996, 185). By 1912, he was building a new Cambridge, Massachusetts campus for MIT as an anonymous donor; the benefactor of this gift was merely known as "Mr. Smith." In 1929, he added the Eastman Laboratories building to MIT.

Although he wanted his name on his company and its products, as a philanthropist Eastman shunned personal publicity, preferring to work behind the scenes when possible. "The fun is in the game rather than the mostly unintelligent holler about it," he said (Brayer 1996, 365). Thus, the dental dispensary he created was not renamed the Eastman Dental Center until after his death and the names he originally chose for the Eastman Theatre and School of Music were the Academy of Motion Pictures and the Academy of Music. He insisted on and achieved anonymity in his gifts to individuals but with institutions, it was only at MIT that the name of the donor was withheld for eight years.

Eastman's concern about preventive dentistry for children had a personal—his own poor teeth and receding gums led to dentures at an early age—as well as a community service component. The Rochester Dental Society started the first free clinic in the country in 1901, but soon closed it for lack of funding. In 1904, colleague and fellow-philanthropist Henry Lomb (of Bausch and Lomb Optical Company) funded a clinic in a public school and persuaded Eastman and William Bausch to finance a clinic in another school. By 1909, Eastman was one of ten Rochester businessmen supporting a central clinic. In 1914, he visited the new Forsyth Dental Infirmary in Boston. Within the year, he offered to build, equip, and staff a complete Rochester Dental Dispensary. Eastman later established clinics in five European capitals—London, Paris, Brussels, Rome, and Stockholm—where Kodak employees were concentrated. All but the Brussels clinic continues today. In 1920, when **Rockefeller** philanthropic interests, led by Abraham Flexner, proposed that he establish a medical school—modeled after Johns Hopkins University—at the University of Rochester, he readily agreed to expand his health care interests. He and Henry Strong's family also founded the Strong Memorial Hospital and that complex continues as the region's largest and most complete medical center.

Eastman began collecting art in Europe in the 1890s. He had the only old master collection in Rochester and, in 1932, bequeathed fifty-five paintings and prints to the Memorial Art Gallery of the University of Rochester—where they continue to be on view. For his community, he also purchased the land for Cobbs Hill and Durand Eastman Parks. Furthermore, Eastman's early interest in technical education gradually widened to include liberal arts, education for minorities, and women's education—particularly at the University of Rochester. He eventually donated $51 million—half of his worth—to the university.

Eastman's interest in Rochester was partly to make the city a "better place for the community to work and live in. This means health, enjoyment, artistic development" (Brayer 1996, 363). He was frustrated, however, by the countless appeals from local charities that daily crossed his desk and hired a woman to screen and recommend those that were credible. Meanwhile, federated fund-raising campaigns—an effort to raise funds for numerous charities through one fund-raising campaign—had begun in places such as Denver and Cleveland, which dovetailed into war chest campaigns. Many communities, including Rochester, were combining Liberty Loan and Red Cross drives into one war chest that collected and allocated contributions. Patriotism led Eastman to head the local Red Cross and war

chest campaigns during World War I. At war's end, Eastman saw the value of continuing this fund-raising system: one annual appeal for all local charities and experts deciding the percentage of "chest" contributions that would go to each charity. Local legend has it that Eastman coined the term "Community Chest" (since renamed United Way) and its slogan "Suppose Nobody Gave" much as he coined "You Press the Button, We Do the Rest" thirty years earlier.

His failed attempt to play the flute as a teenager, led Eastman to become an educated music "listener." Beginning in the 1890s, he planned musical marathons for himself and friends in New York and London: six operas or symphonic concerts in as many days. He even installed two theater organs in his Rochester home. He also supported local orchestras, bands, and choral societies. Further, he paid for the education and a Stradivarius for the prodigy violinist David Hochstein, and bought musical instruments for the Rochester public schools so that children had a chance to play an instrument as well as have their teeth cleaned at his Rochester Dental Dispensary. He planned to bequeath Eastman House, his fifty-room mansion, to the University of Rochester for a music conservatory, but then decided to "see the action in my lifetime" by hatching an unparalleled scheme to "train" other listeners and bring music beyond compare to Rochester (Brayer 1996, 346).

In 1918, he bought and donated the financially strapped Institute of Musical Art to the University of Rochester and demolished the nineteenth-century building that housed it. In fact, he demolished most of a city block to build an enormous and unusual complex that was eventually named the Eastman Theatre and School of Music. The Eastman School was a conservatory for training performers and teachers. Eastman even imported dozens of musicians from England and Europe, especially those fleeing the Russian Revolution. These immigrants joined Rochester musicians at the Eastman School and in community teaching positions while also performing with the Rochester Philharmonic Orchestra, which Eastman founded in 1923.

Since Eastman possessed a passion for film, the 3,500-seat Eastman Theatre, which adjoins the music school, was built to show silent movies. The films were accompanied by an enormous organ sometimes played by Eastman's personal organist and by a pit orchestra of fifty players drawn from the Rochester Philharmonic Orchestra. One evening a week, the Rochester Philharmonic Orchestra played a strictly classical music concert. The arrangement of films accompanied by live music did not survive the advent of talking motion pictures. However, the Rochester Philharmonic Orchestra still performs in the theater and the music school often leads the list when "best" music schools in the country are named.

CONCLUSION

Eastman preferred to work anonymously or behind the scenes, what the *New York Times* called "philanthropy under a bushel" (Brayer 1996, 346, 364). Since Eastman believed in "seeing the action in [his] own lifetime," he also distributed his $100 million fortune rather than creating a foundation that would allocate it posthumously (Brayer 1996, 346). Despite a myriad of charitable gifts, Eastman considered his major contribution to be the company he founded, which provided thousands of jobs for people worldwide. Along these lines, he can be seen as a local and corporate philanthropist who gave to enrich the communities that were home to his company and employees as well as the institutions (such as MIT) that would produce individuals that could improve his company. Nonetheless, his philanthropic efforts reached far beyond the local communities inhabited by Eastman and his employees.

Elizabeth Brayer

FURTHER READING

Ackerman, Carl. *George Eastman*. Boston: Houghton Mifflin, 1930.

Brayer, Elizabeth. *George Eastman: A Biography*. Baltimore: Johns Hopkins University Press, 1996.

Coe, Brian. *George Eastman and the Early Photographers*. London: Priority Press, 1973.

Collins, Douglas. *The Story of Kodak*. New York: Harry M. Abrams, 1990.

Jenkins, Reese. *Images and Enterprise: Technology and the American Photographic Industry, 1839–1925*. Baltimore: Johns Hopkins University Press, 1975.

Solbert, Oscar N. "George Eastman." *Image: The Journal of Photography of the George Eastman House, Inc.* 2, no. 8, November 1953, 49–56.

Taft, Robert. *Photography and the American Scene, 1839–1889*. New York: Macmillan, 1938.

Whipple, George. *George Eastman Picture Story of an Out-of-Doors Man*. Rochester, NY: Eastman Kodak Company, 1957.

PAPERS

George Eastman's papers are located in the George Eastman Study Center at George Eastman House (Rochester, NY) and the Department of Rare Books and Special Collections, Rush Rhees Library, University of Rochester (Rochester, NY).

F

HENRY FORD (1863–1947)
and EDSEL FORD (1893–1943)

Industrialists and Founders of the Ford Foundation

INTRODUCTION

"I believe in living wages—I do not believe in charity. I believe we should all be producers. Organized charity and schools of philanthropy and the whole idea of 'giving' to the poor are on the wrong track. They don't produce anything" (Greenleaf 1964, 15). These words revealed the essentially contradictory nature of Henry Ford, for the man who hated philanthropy became one of the greatest benefactors in U.S. history, both as a generous individual giver and as a founder (with his son Edsel), of the private foundation that was, for most of the twentieth century, the nation's largest. Between them, Henry and Edsel Ford left indelible marks on fields as disparate as hospitals, museums, public education, housing, historical preservation, and polar exploration.

In everything Henry Ford did, however, dualities came to the fore. He was not only the philanthropist who hated philanthropy; he was also the industrialist who revered the preindustrial era; the anti-intellectual whose

company had a sociological department; the virulent anti-Semite who provided workplace and social opportunities for African Americans; and the great historical museum builder who proclaimed that "history is more or less bunk" (Greenleaf 1964, 96). Yet out of this welter of contradictions arose a record of philanthropic achievement that is at once broad in scope and daunting in ambition.

HENRY FORD

Early Years and Education

Henry Ford was born on July 30, 1863, in Dearborn, Michigan, the son of William and Mary Litogot Ford. William Ford was a farmer, and he cherished the hope that his son would take up this vocation, but Henry Ford detested farming as much as he loved mechanical devices of all kinds. He attended the Scotch Settlement School in Dearborn regularly until 1876 and irregularly thereafter.

Henry Ford with his wife, Clara Bryant, and their son, Edsel, at Greenfield Village in Dearborn, Michigan, July 1942. AP Photo.

Henry Ford's first jobs did not mark him as a man of great promise. He lost his first position, as an apprentice at the Michigan Car Company Works, after six days of employment. He went on to become a roustabout in a brass factory and a repairman for Westinghouse. In 1884–1885, he attended Goldsmith's Bryant & Stratton Business University located in Detroit. There followed a series of abortive occupations: engine repairman, furniture manufacturer, and sawmill operator. Finally, in 1891, Ford signed on with the five-year-old Edison Illuminating Company, one of Detroit's electric power concerns. Here, he found work congenial to his interests, and for the first time in his life, he stuck with a job for longer than a few months.

It was well that Ford found a job that interested him, for he had found a woman who loved him. Ford met Clara Bryant, a Dearborn native, at a New Year's Day dance in 1885. They married on April 11, 1887, and lived at first with the bride's parents. When Henry found work at the Edison Illuminat-

ing Company, the couple moved—in a hay wagon—to a small house on John R. Street in Detroit. It was here that their only child, Edsel, was born on November 6, 1893.

Career Highlights

Ironically enough, the man who spectacularly succeeded in putting the world on wheels consistently failed at his early mechanical ventures. He constructed a steam engine that ran for forty feet before falling apart. He built engines that would not start at all. Ford, however, had a cheerful optimism in the face of failure and he continued to tinker contentedly in his spare time. Late in 1893, the Fords moved to property at 58 Bagley Street in Detroit, which had a shed in back that became his headquarters for experimentation with gasoline-powered engines. Some time in the spring of 1896—accounts vary from April 2 to June 6—Ford finally hit the mechanical jackpot. He had built from scratch (buying only the batteries) an open-seated vehicle he called a quadricycle, powered by an internal combustion engine, and it was finally ready for a test drive. To Ford's chagrin, he had built it too big to fit through the door of the shed, so it was necessary to literally knock down part of the wall. The destruction was vindicated when Ford rode around the block and into history.

Riding into business proved more challenging. It took Ford more than two years to round up financial backers, but he formed the Detroit Automobile Company on August 5, 1899 (and ten days later resigned from the Edison Illuminating Company). Once again, Ford tasted failure. His new company produced a delivery truck that broke down constantly, and three different models of ponderous and unreliable cars. By February 7, 1901, having burned through nearly $100,000 in capital, Ford and his backers closed the company. A second attempt to create an automobile manufacturing company fared no better.

Undaunted, Ford, with two partners and nine stockholders, established the Ford Motor Company on June 15, 1903. The new enterprise had a clear mission statement supplied by Ford: "I will build a motorcar for the multitude. It shall be large enough for the family, but small enough for the unskilled individual to operate easily and care for and it shall be light in weight that it may be economical in maintenance" (Olson 1963, 186). The company came close to realizing this goal when it introduced the Model A later in 1903, and achieved it when it rolled out the Model T in 1908.

Durable, dependable, and economical, the Model T became "America's Jitney," for by 1918, half of all cars in the United States were Model T's. To meet the demand for the "T," Ford built a large plant in Highland Park, Michigan in 1910, and instituted a continuously moving assembly line at that plant three years later. The efficiencies made possible by this innovation slashed the cost per vehicle, and by 1915, Ford had fulfilled his vow to "build a motorcar for the multitude."

In 1917, he began construction of the world's largest industrial complex along the Rouge River in Dearborn. By the time it was finished in 1921, "the Rouge" covered more than 6,950,000 square feet and all of the steps in automobile production—from refining raw materials to the final assembly of the car—took place under its cavernous roof. In that year, the Ford Motor Company commanded a near monopolistic 55% of the U.S. market for automobiles. But Ford did not stop there. He plunged into other businesses, including manufacturing of tractors and aircraft, radio broadcasting, farming, and, for a few years, even the operation of a small railroad.

The Ford Motor Company's dominance in the auto market, and its success in other markets, provided the wherewithal for Ford to become a generous and innovative employer. In 1914, he caused a sensation by announcing a profit-sharing plan with his employees and raised their wages to an unprecedented $5 per day. Many observers interpreted these decisions as acts of philanthropy, but Ford strenuously objected: "The only charity I know is paying people for what they do. . . . The very best charity is to help a man to a place where he will never need charity . . . we can give by developing. We cannot develop by giving" (Greenleaf 1964, 14).

Indeed, as these words make plain, Ford's philanthropy was not without a strong tinge of self-interest. During World War I, for example, he established a sociological department at the Ford Motor Company to deal with the problems of his employees and the communities in which he did business. The sociological department also served a paternalistic function, molding employees, on the job and even at home, along the lines that Ford found acceptable. In 1915, he outfitted the ship *Oscar II*, filled it with pacifist spokesmen, and sent it to Norway on a quixotic mission to end the Great War. The war, of course, was playing havoc with Ford's European markets. Three years later, he made an unsuccessful bid for the U.S. Senate. This came as a relief to those who feared that he sought political power to complement his industrial clout. When the war finally ended, Ford found himself, like many other Americans, disillusioned by the peace that followed. During the 1920s, he retreated from the humanitarianism that had distinguished him during the previous decade. Ford cut himself off from the world, working almost exclusively with a small clique of narrow-minded and visionless men who were derisively nicknamed the "Scavengers." Yet, paradoxically, even as his humanitarian impulses receded, his philanthropy blossomed.

Major Philanthropic Contributions

Ford's first significant benefaction, made in 1911, was the Valley Farm, an eighty-acre home for orphaned boys west of Dearborn. It operated for only a few years, but spurred his desire for giving on a grander scale. In 1915, after Clara Ford was overcharged (as Henry Ford believed) for a hospital stay, he took the lead in the establishment of Detroit's Henry Ford Hospital, which aimed to provide medical care at a reasonable charge based on actual costs. Ford contributed more than $14 million to the hospital during his lifetime and served as its first president, with Edsel Ford as vice president. The hospital had a checkered beginning, in terms of both fund-raising and administration, but it distinguished itself during the Depression by providing free medical service to tens of thousands of impoverished patients. Today, Ford's gift remains as part of the Henry Ford Health Care System.

Ford's love of his fellow human beings was uneven, as his notorious anti-Semitism bore witness. In his treatment of African Americans, however, Henry Ford far outshone his contemporaries. Decades before the Civil Rights Movement began, he opened the Ford line and its skilled trades to qualified African Americans. By the 1930s, 65% of all African Americans employed in Detroit industry were working at the Ford Motor Company and they received equal pay for equal work. Ford's concern for African Americans ran deeper than mere business interest, for it extended far beyond the factory

floor. In 1931, Inkster, Detroit's predominately African-American suburb, was ravaged by unemployment and poverty. Civic leaders asked the American Red Cross for help, but the Red Cross, drained by crises across the nation, appealed to the Ford Motor Company for assistance. From 1931 to 1941, the company poured nearly $1.7 million into the village, all of which was reimbursed by Ford's personal funds. At first, emergency assistance was provided, but gradually Inkster residents took the lead in projects to grow food, build housing, pave streets, and improve public health. By the end of the Ford intervention, Inkster was described as a haven from the worst effects of the Great Depression.

Ford also made it his business to improve the educational opportunities for African-American children on his Richmond Hill plantation, a winter home on the coastal plain of Southeastern Georgia. When he began his program in 1937, African-American residents were "served" by woefully inadequate schools. Ford constructed both a kindergarten and a consolidated school serving grades 1–11, with modern facilities and equipment, and teachers whose salaries he subsidized. To be sure, these schools were, like all in the South at that time, segregated, but Ford saw to it that their facilities were at least equal to those serving the district's white children.

The ruling passion of Henry Ford's last thirty years was the preservation of the past. Many commentators remarked on the irony of the situation, for Ford had done more than anyone else to transform the United States from an agrarian to an industrial society. Undeterred by the contradiction, Ford became interested in history in 1914, when he started a collection of *McGuffey's Readers*. His interest intensified in 1919, when he restored his family homestead in Dearborn to its original character, and it became virtually all-consuming in 1923, when Ford embarked upon his first major venture in historical preservation, the Wayside Inn, near South Sudbury, Massachusetts. The inn, immortalized in a poem by Henry Wadsworth Longfellow, dated to the seventeenth century, but by

1923 it was in imminent danger of demolition. Ford purchased it, rerouted a state highway to preserve it, refurbished it, and moved other historical structures from around New England to the site to create a small preservationist village. Ford spent nearly $15 million on the venture before deeding the entire village to a free-standing nonprofit corporation.

The Wayside Inn, as significant as it was, was but a rehearsal for Ford's philanthropic life work at the Edison Institute in Dearborn, consisting initially of Greenfield Village, the Edison Institute Museum, and the Edison Institute Schools. Ford lavished more time and money on the Edison Institute than on any of his other charities. He announced his intention to launch the Edison Institute in 1929, but had given his rationale for doing so as early as 1926. "We are trying to assemble a complete series of every article used or made in America from the days of the first settlers down to the present time. When we are through we shall have reproduced American life, and that is, I think, the best way of preserving at least part of our history and our tradition" (Greenleaf 1964, 93).

Ford had been a voracious collector of Americana for years before conceiving of the institute. Consequently, he quickly poured artifacts into the Edison Institute Museum until it was crammed with everything from scraps of linsey-woolsey (a coarse fabric made of linen or cotton and wool) to fully functioning locomotives. Ford moved every historical building that caught his fancy to Greenfield Village. His old Scotch Settlement Schoolhouse was moved there, as was an Illinois courthouse in which Abraham Lincoln had tried cases, and the Wright Brothers' Bicycle Shop. The centerpiece was a combination of a restoration and a recreation—because the originals had been in a derelict state—of the buildings at Menlo Park, New Jersey, where Thomas Edison had operated his first laboratory. The work was meticulous, down to the carting of seven freight car loads of New Jersey soil to Dearborn. The Edison Institute was dedicated on

October 21, 1929, with President **Herbert Hoover** officiating. The highlight of the ceremony, which also celebrated the fiftieth anniversary of Edison's invention of the incandescent light, was a nationwide blackout that ended after Thomas Edison re-enacted the lighting of the first bulb. Although light bulbs were allowed on the grounds of Greenfield Village, Henry Ford strictly forbade the admission of automobiles. It was not until the fiftieth anniversary of the Ford Motor Company in 1953 that the museum was renamed the Henry Ford Museum in honor of its founder, who had died six years prior.

EDSEL FORD

Edsel Ford was fated to live his entire life in the shadow of his famous father, for he predeceased Henry Ford by nearly four years. Edsel possessed a better education than his father, and also had a broader charitable vision. He did, however, share his father's admiration of self-reliance and animosity toward endowments. Still, Edsel Ford cherished a strong interest in the life of the mind that his father lacked, and displayed more concern for the well-being of the local community than did Henry Ford. Edsel Ford joined the Ford Motor Company after graduation from high school, becoming its secretary at age 21, its vice president at age 23, and its president at age 25. He entered into the realm of philanthropy just as rapidly. Edsel Ford was generous to several local causes, such as the precursor of the United Way in Detroit, which his father refused to support. During this time, he also married Eleanor Lowthian Clay on November 1, 1916. Within a few years, the couple produced four children: Henry Ford II (1917), Benson Ford (1919), Josephine Ford (1923), and William Clay Ford (1925).

Four benefactions made Edsel Ford's mark as a philanthropist. The first was the expedition of Commander Robert Byrd, which, on May 9, 1926, became the first to reach the North Pole by airplane. Edsel Ford was

Byrd's largest backer, and the Commander's plane was christened the *Josephine Ford* after Edsel Ford's only daughter. Edsel Ford continued to support Byrd as the latter undertook Antarctic expeditions in 1928–1929 and 1933–1934. Besides cash, he contributed Byrd's plane, a Ford Tri-Motor. In recognition of his assistance, a range of Antarctic Mountains was named in his honor.

The second philanthropic venture, for which Edsel Ford gained fame, was his support for the Detroit Institute of Arts. From 1921 until his death in 1943, Edsel Ford served as a trustee or member of the Founders Society, and was a generous donor of both cash and artwork to the museum's expanding collection. His greatest gift, that of twenty-seven fresco murals painted by Diego Rivera and interpreting industrial life in the United States, sparked enormous controversy soon after it was unveiled in March 1933. Rivera was a devoted Communist, and certain religious leaders in Detroit interpreted one of the twenty-seven panels, "Preventive Medicine," as a blasphemous lampoon of the Holy Family. The *Detroit News* editorialized that the frescos should be whitewashed, but Edsel Ford refused to bow to the anti-Rivera hysteria. The panels, happily unwhitewashed, remain today as one of the treasures of the Detroit Institute of Arts collection.

Edsel Ford's third philanthropic achievement was shared with his father and mother, for all of the Fords were deeply involved in the founding and operation of the Edison Institute. Edsel Ford was a donor to both Greenfield Village and the Edison Institute (Henry Ford) Museum, and he served ably and actively on the board. In fact, the Institute's evolution owed more to Edsel Ford's guidance than to Henry Ford until the former's death.

The fourth, and most far-reaching, of Edsel Ford's philanthropies was begun with little fanfare. In 1936, with a check for $25,000, Ford launched the Ford Foundation. In its early years, the Ford Foundation was relatively modest in size, and made gifts mainly in the Detroit area to charities favored by Henry and Edsel Ford. The deaths of Edsel Ford in 1943 and Henry Ford in 1947 dramatically changed this picture. Between the two of them, Henry and Edsel Ford had owned nearly all of the stock of the Ford Motor Company. They left about 10% of that stock to their heirs; the remaining 90% went to the Ford Foundation. This windfall made the Ford Foundation the largest and most influential charitable foundation in the United States, a position it was destined to hold for nearly the remainder of the twentieth century. Thus, the Ford Foundation carried on the Ford family tradition of philanthropy, albeit in new and often unexpected ways.

One of these unanticipated events was the departure of the foundation from Dearborn, Michigan. The trustees had decided to expand its scope of giving from Michigan-based to international and believed that Dearborn was too provincial a headquarters to support such global aspirations. The Ford Foundation accordingly moved to an estate in Pasadena, California and then to New York City.

Along with the physical moves came philosophical shifts. The Ford Foundation not only evolved from local to international grant making, but also evolved from essentially conservative to fundamentally liberal in its approach. By the 1960s, Ford Foundation grants were flowing largely to organizations that were on the progressive side of the center line of the U.S. political spectrum. This "march to the left" proved too much for Edsel's son, Henry Ford II, to tolerate. Early in 1977, Henry Ford II, who had served as CEO of the Ford Motor Company, departed from the Foundation's board after thirty-four years of service. In his letter of resignation, Ford expressed satisfaction with many of the foundation's accomplishments but criticized the foundation's lack of interest in free enterprise. As he put it, "I am just suggesting to the trustees and the staff that the system that makes the foundation possible very probably is worth preserving" (Nielsen, 1985 72). At least partly in response to such critiques, the Ford Foundation has to some extent moved back toward the center in its ideology, although it was still fair to describe it as a predominantly progressive institution at the close of the twentieth century.

CONCLUSION

Edsel Ford's premature passing—he was forty-nine when he died on May 26, 1943—cut short a philanthropic career that, although constrained by his father's presence, was nonetheless highly impressive. Henry Ford lived on until 1947, more than fifty years after he had first driven his quadricycle out of the shed on Bagley Street. He died on April 7, fittingly enough in Dearborn at his Fair Lane estate.

Both Henry Ford and his son Edsel believed in a brand of philanthropy that focused on providing a hand up rather than a hand out. They offered these hands up on a massive scale: From 1917 to 1943, nearly one-third of Henry Ford's net taxable income went to charities. There was a final irony in their philanthropic lives: two men who had always despised endowments created, in the Ford Foundation, one of the world's largest charitable endowments, valued at more than $10 billion by the beginning of the twenty-first century. Whether they liked the title or not, Henry and Edsel Ford both certainly earned the sobriquet of "philanthropist."

Joel J. Orosz

FURTHER READING

Bryan, Ford R. *Beyond the Model T: The Other Ventures of Henry Ford.* Detroit: Wayne State University Press, 1990.

Collier, Peter, and David Horowitz. *The Fords: An American Epic.* New York: Summit Books, 1987.

Greenleaf, William. *From These Beginnings: The Early Philanthropies of Henry and Edsel Ford, 1911–1936.* Detroit: Wayne State University Press, 1964.

Herndon, Booton. *Ford: An Unconventional Biography of the Men and Their Times.* New York: Weybright and Talley, 1969.

Jardin, Anne. *The First Henry Ford: A Study in Personality and Business Leadership.* Cambridge, MA: MIT Press, 1970.

Lacey, Robert. *Ford: The Men and the Machine.* New York: Little Brown, 1986.

Macdonald, Dwight. *The Ford Foundation: The Men and the Millions.* New York: Reynal & Company, 1956.

Nevins, Allan, and Frank Ernest Hill. *Ford.* 3 vols. New York: Scribner, 1954–1963.

Nielsen, Waldemar A. *The Golden Donors: A New Anatomy of the Great Foundations.* New York: E.P. Dutton, 1985.

Olson, Sidney. *Young Henry Ford: A Picture History of the First Forty Years.* Detroit: Wayne State University Press, 1963.

Rae, John B., ed. *Henry Ford.* Englewood Cliffs, NJ: Prentice-Hall, 1969.

PAPERS

Henry Ford and Edsel Ford's papers are located in the archives of the Edison Institute (Henry Ford Museum and Greenfield Village) in Dearborn, Michigan.

ACKNOWLEDGMENTS

The author is indebted to Steven K. Hamp, president of the Edison Institute (Henry Ford Museum and Greenfield Village), who reviewed this paper and made many helpful comments.

JAMES FORTEN. *See* **Paul Cuffe and James Forten.**

BENJAMIN FRANKLIN
(1706–1790)

Printer, Author, Scientist, Diplomat, and Promoter of Collective Voluntary Action and Associational Life

INTRODUCTION

"Do you think of any thing at present, in which the Junto may be serviceable to *mankind*? to their country, to their friends, or to themselves?" (Labaree et al. 1959-, I:257). This question became one of standing queries addressed at every meeting of the voluntary association Benjamin Franklin founded, the Junto Club. Led by Franklin, this club became the catalyst for numerous civic improvements in Philadelphia and beyond. Based upon his desire to produce "good works," Franklin's life repeatedly demonstrated the value of collective voluntary action (such as a community effort to raise money and establish a school) and associational life (such as participation in clubs). In appealing for the creation of a hospital in Philadelphia, Franklin succinctly defined his philanthropic philosophy by writing, "But the Good particular Men may do separately, in relieving the Sick, is small, compared with what they may do collectively, or by a joint Endeavor and Interest" (Franklin 1987, 363). Although Franklin is recognized today as one of America's founding fathers, his promotion of collective voluntary action and associational life is rarely recognized. Nonetheless, Franklin could be considered one of the founding fathers of American philanthropy.

EARLY YEARS AND EDUCATION

In 1706, Benjamin Franklin became the tenth son of Josiah Franklin and the eighth child from his father's union with Abiah Folger. Disapproving of the Anglican Church and hoping for economic advancement, Josiah Franklin, who had seven children from a

A portrait of Benjamin Franklin painted by Charles Wilson Peale in 1787. Library of Congress; LC-USZ62-101098.

previous marriage, left England and moved to America in 1683. Settling in Boston, he started a soap and candle shop. Born into a family of artisans and farmers, Benjamin Franklin was singled out for the ministry (his Puritan father's male tithe to the lord). He received reading instruction at home and a small amount of formal schooling while other brothers were trained in trades. Although young Benjamin demonstrated intellectual interest and aptitude, his family could not afford further formal schooling. At twelve, he became an apprentice at his brother James's printing business. For the next few years, he devoted spare hours to reading and writing, even skipping church on Sunday because his self-improvement required it. In their *New England Courant*, Benjamin and James published satires about religion, which ultimately caused the General Court, in 1723, to prohibit James from printing in Boston. The same year, Benjamin left Boston in pursuit of printing opportunities elsewhere.

CAREER HIGHLIGHTS

In October 1723, Franklin arrived in Philadelphia and sought to open a print shop in the leading city of the recently established Pennsylvania colony. After experiencing some setbacks and working for a while in London, he ran his own print business and newspaper at the age of twenty-four. Soon, he became famous for his *Poor Richard's Almanac* as well as his widely read newspaper *The Pennsylvania Gazette*. Meanwhile, in 1730, Franklin entered into a common-law union with Deborah Reed (whose husband John Rogers abandoned her in 1725). The couple had two children, Francis Folger and Sarah Franklin, and Franklin also fathered one illegitimate child, William Franklin.

Having achieved sufficient wealth, forty-two-year-old Franklin retired from running his businesses and devoted himself full time to science. An Enlightenment disciple, Franklin believed one could make useful discoveries and inventions through careful reasoning and scientific investigations. During a trip to England in 1724–1726, the country's Enlightenment atmosphere stimulated young Franklin; he heard of the illustrious scientist Isaac Newton and met scientists who were members of the prestigious Royal Society. After Franklin returned to America, scientific interests continually demanded a larger part of his life until he largely focused on scientific work from 1743 to 1753. Perhaps most famous for his work in the area of electricity, Franklin hypothesized and proved that lightning was electricity. Among others, he also created the concept of positive and negative electricity as well as the practical lightning rod, which protected buildings from lightning. Hailed for his work, Franklin even received a medal and membership in the Royal Society. During his life, Franklin's inventions also included bifocal eyeglasses and the Franklin Stove (improving home heating efficiency).

In 1751, Philadelphia elected celebrated Benjamin Franklin to the Pennsylvania Assembly, eventually setting him on a course to become a founder of the United States. Though not challenging America's relationship with England at the time, he proposed intercolonial cooperation for such matters as defense in his Albany Plan of the Union (1754). Nonetheless, his fellow colonists were not yet able to accept such a concept. Three years latter, he sailed to England to present Parliament with a grievance from the Pennsylvania Assembly. Returning to America in 1762, Franklin entered the continent near the close of the French and Indian War and the start of numerous acts and events that would lead to the American Revolution. After returning to England in December 1764, Franklin subsequently lobbied for the repeal of the Stamp Tax by testifying before Parliament and wrote tracts against the Tea Act. In 1775, he returned to Philadelphia and was elected to the Second Continental Congress; Franklin offered Thomas Jefferson suggestions for and later signed the Declaration of Independence. Thereafter, he served as a diplomat to France and worked to secure that country's valuable support during the Revolutionary War. In 1787, Franklin aided America once more by participating in the Constitutional Convention.

MAJOR PHILANTHROPIC CONTRIBUTIONS

Numerous influences caused Franklin to form a club of bright acquaintances who initially met at a tavern on Friday nights. Nonetheless, two works undoubtedly spurred this action. Englishman Daniel Defoe's *An Essay on Several Projects* (1697) advocated a public spirit that used Enlightenment reasoning to develop useful civic improvements and practical solutions to social problems. These ideas certainly appealed to Franklin's sensibilities; he likewise scorned individual charity relief as wasteful and fleeting, but valued civic projects, such as schools and improved roads, for their permanent benefits. Franklin also found much of value in Minister **Cotton Mather**'s *Bonifacius: An Essay upon the Good* (1710). Intended solely for reborn Christians, Mather's work promoted the value of good works and offered advice on charitable endeavors. Moreover, Mather created neighborhood benefit societies (one for each church) and some of his societies' standing inquires bore much resemblance to the standing inquiries Franklin later adopted for the Junto Club. Although Franklin was a professed deist for a while and never became a reborn Christian, he still viewed God as an important source for human morality and interpreted Mather in his own way. Thus, Franklin developed a philanthropic philosophy that viewed a virtuous person as one who performed practical and secular good works, specifically acts of collective or community benefit.

When the Junto Club (known initially as the Club of the Leather Aprons) began in 1727, Franklin formed this mutual benefit society with men who represented numerous trades, such as printers, clerks, and shoemakers. In examining the standing inquiries later adopted for the club, one can see that its purview included both private and public purposes. Besides providing an entertaining evening of conversation, the club provided its members with self-improvement opportunities by sharing business tips and social connections. Franklin also created an intellectual roundtable atmosphere in which members discussed a wide variety of literature and ideas, ranging from science to history. While such sessions advanced the knowledge of its members, Franklin also ensured that members suggested, debated, and acted on proposals that would benefit their community.

Living in a rapidly growing colonial city and in an era of weak government, Franklin and his club colleagues subsequently worked to implement many community improvement projects. In pursuing these improvements, Franklin promoted their reform ideas in print but also raised funds for and donated to the project. Given Franklin's love of and desire for books, it is not surprising that the club initially pooled their own books and then made plans for a circulating library in 1731. Indeed, the Library Company of Philadelphia became the first American subscription library. In subsequent years, the club's activities probably touched the lives of all of their neighbors. For instance, the club helped bring about paved roads and a volunteer fire department known as the Union Fire Company (1736) as well as systems of municipal policing (1745) and street lighting.

In 1751, Franklin innovatively worked to establish a city hospital by getting the Pennsylvania Assembly to agree to match private contributions if they reached a certain level. Pioneering the matching grant concept, Franklin fund-raised by noting to prospective donors that "the conditional Promise of the Law" was "an additional Motive to give, since every Man's donation would be doubled" (Franklin 1964, 201). This public-private partnership motivated private giving and the Pennsylvania Hospital opened in 1752.

Around this time, Franklin also worked on plans for an institution that would educate youth. The Philadelphia Academy, which became the University of Pennsylvania, began in 1751. While the academy's training exhibited some of Franklin's preference for utility, his American Philosophical Society prominently displayed such values. Founded in 1744, this association represented the first scientific society in America and remains in existence today. Influenced by the Royal Society and correspondences with fellow American and British scientists, Franklin's 1743 proposal for the association expressed his wish to connect the American colonies into a scientific exchange that would produce practical benefits to the public, such as new cures for diseases and labor-saving inventions. He remained involved in society activity for the rest of his life.

Although a slave owner, Franklin's views on African Americans and slavery changed during the course of his life. Influenced by his friend **Anthony Benezet**, among others, Franklin ultimately became an abolitionist. The Associates of Dr. Bray, an English charity that wished to educate and Christianize Africans in colonial America, even consulted with Franklin about future charitable endeavors in 1757. Franklin advised them to establish a school for African-American boys and girls in Philadelphia (opened in 1758) and even remained a caretaker of the school after the American Revolution. Participating in one final voluntary association, Franklin became president of the reorganized Pennsylvania Society for Promoting the Abolition of Slavery in 1787 and authored petitions on the society's behalf.

Franklin is rightly praised for the philanthropic accomplishments achieved throughout his lifetime, but his final charitable acts have received mixed reviews. Franklin's last will and testament assigned several old and small debts to the Pennsylvania Hospital. Unfortunately, the hospital found the debts too difficult to collect. In the June 23, 1789 codicil to his will, Franklin laid out one final civic improvement project. By providing 1,000 pounds each to Boston and Philadelphia, fund trustees in each city would lend out loans, at 5 percent interest, to married apprentices who were under the age of twenty-five and known to be of good character. Remembering the value of such a loan in his youth, Franklin wrote in the codicil that he wanted "to be useful even after my death" by "forming and advancing other young men" (Franklin 1907, 503). Through compound interest, Franklin calculated the fund amount achieved at different intervals and set forth instructions for expending large portions of the funds after 100 years and loaning out the rest for 100 more years. In 200 years, Franklin wished to turn over each fund to its city and state (broken down roughly one-fourth to the city and three-fourths to the state).

However, Franklin could not anticipate the changes in American society, which caused the decline of apprentices and, as a result, slowed the projected growth of his funds. The Philadelphia fund, for instance, found itself unable to make a single loan during some decades and went to court on numerous occasions to change the loan qualifications.

Thus, some notable philanthropists came to view and cite Franklin's final actions as exemplifying poor philanthropy. Addressing the dangers of perpetual endowments or so-called "dead hand" philanthropy, **Julius Rosenwald**'s "Principles of Public Giving" (1929) discussed Franklin's gift in some length and noted that even such a great founding father could not predict the future. Meanwhile, knowledge of charitable trusts such as Franklin's spurred **Frederick Goff** to develop the community foundation concept in 1914.

Even though Franklin's fund did not provide as many good works as he imagined, it did offer public benefits. After 100 years and then 14 years of litigation over the use of some of its principal, a large portion of the Philadelphia fund was given to the Franklin Institute (a science and technology center) and the Boston fund, and **Andrew Carnegie** created a technical school called the Franklin Union. In 1990, 200 years after his death, the city of Philadelphia decided to maintain the current principal of its portion of the Philadelphia fund ($520,000) and offer the interest as financial aid for high school graduates who want to study trades and crafts. With a principal of $4.5 million, the final disbursement of the Boston fund ended up in a Massachusetts Supreme Court case before three-fourths went to the state of Massachusetts and one-fourth to Boston.

CONCLUSION

Benjamin Franklin's appealing "rags to riches" life and the enduring popularity of *The Autobiography of Benjamin Franklin* (published after his death) helped make him an American legend. Indeed, he became a kind of mythic figure whose life defined the word "American" and whose autobiography became required reading for American youth. By demonstrating the value of collective voluntary action and associational life, Franklin's "good works" surely inspired other Americans to engage in such activities.

Robert T. Grimm, Jr.

FURTHER READING

Brands, H.W. *The First American: The Life and Times of Benjamin Franklin*. New York: Doubleday, 2000.

Franklin, Benjamin. *The Autobiography of Benjamin Franklin*. Leonard W. Labaree et al. eds. New Haven, CT: Yale University Press, 1964.

———. "Franklin's Last Will and Testament" and "Codicil." In *The Writings of Benjamin Franklin*, vol. 10, ed. Albert Henry Smyth. New York: Macmillan, 1907, 493–510.

———. *Writings*. J.A. Leo Lemay, ed. New York: Library of America, 1987.

Jennings, Francis. *Benjamin Franklin: Politician*. New York: W.W. Norton, 1996.

Labaree, Leonard W., et al., eds. *The Papers of Benjamin Franklin*, vols. 1–. New Haven, CT: Yale University Press, 1959-.

Van Horne, John C. "Collective Benevolence and the Common Good in Franklin's Philanthropy." In *Reappraising Benjamin Franklin: A Bicentennial Perspective*, ed. J.A. Leo Lemay. Newark: University of Delaware Press, 1993, 425–440.

Wright, Esmond. *Franklin of Philadelphia*. Cambridge, MA: Harvard University Press, 1986.

PAPERS

Benjamin Franklin's papers are located at the American Antiquarian Society (Worcester, MA), the Historical Society of Pennsylvania (Philadelphia, PA), and the Library of Congress (Washington, DC).

G

HECTOR PEREZ GARCIA
(1914–1996)

Civil Rights Leader and Founder of the American G.I. Forum

INTRODUCTION

"Education is our freedom, and freedom should be everybody's business." These are the words that served as a motto for Hector Garcia, a man who fought for equality and defended the right of all people to become educated. These values imbued his professional life and fueled his desire to help his fellow Mexican Americans make a better life. While much of his work began in Texas, Dr. Hector, as his friends knew him, had an impact that reached far beyond the Longhorn state. He founded the American G.I. Forum, which originally addressed veteran health and benefit issues under the American G.I. Bill, but expanded to address civil rights, housing, poll taxation, and other social services across the country. His conviction that people have equal rights under our country's laws and Constitution propelled his activities toward equality in education, in human rights activism, and in fighting for veterans' rights.

EARLY YEARS AND EDUCATION

Hector Perez Garcia was born in the village of Llera, Tamaulipas, Mexico on January 16, 1914. At the age of four, Mexican-born Garcia moved with his family to Mercedes, Texas, fleeing the chaos of the Mexican Revolution. Many Mexican-American families worked in the agricultural fields and the Garcias were no different. What did set them apart was Garcia's parents, in particular his father, a stern disciplinarian, who taught all of his children to value education. The elder Garcia, a college professor by training, supplemented the family's income with a *barrio tienda*—neighborhood store—where all the family worked. In an era where Mexican-American Texans—*Tejanos*—only achieved a third-grade education on average, Jose Garcia and Faustina Perez Garcia raised six children who attended medical school and became doctors. Hector Garcia attended the University of Texas for his undergraduate studies, receiving his B.A. in 1936. He subsequently enrolled in the University of Texas

Hector Perez Garcia. Dr. Hector P. Garcia Papers, Special Collections and Archives, Texas A & M University—Corpus Christi, Bell Library.

Medical School at Galveston, graduating in 1940 just before the United States' entry into World War II.

Garcia performed his general internship and surgical residency at Creighton University's St. Joseph's Hospital in Omaha, Nebraska. World War II took Garcia from the Midwest to Italy. Garcia joined the Army as an infantry officer and served as a combat engineer; later, he became an Army doctor when his superiors became aware of his education and experience. At the age of thirty, Captain Garcia met Wanda Fusillo and they married after a three-month courtship.

CAREER HIGHLIGHTS AND MAJOR PHILANTHROPIC CONTRIBUTIONS

During his service, the Army awarded Garcia a Bronze Star medal with six battle stars. Upon returning from the war, Garcia opened a medical office in Corpus Christi. His practice floundered at the beginning, but was kick-started by some contractual work Garcia received from the Veterans Administration. As a result, in addition to his family practice, Garcia also helped veterans in the region. Many of the returning soldiers were Latino and he heard the problems they were facing,

such as deprivation of medical services due to segregated hospital wards and doctors who refused to treat them. Consequently, Garcia founded the American G.I. Forum in 1948 to organize Latino veterans so they could receive benefits owed to them for fighting their country's war.

Events a year later launched the American G.I. Forum's national profile. The actions of a funeral home in Three Rivers, Texas spurred a local controversy, which quickly reached international awareness. A veteran, Army Private Felix Longoria, was scheduled to be reinterred at home after having died three years earlier during a volunteer mission in the Philippines. However, when his family went to bury him at the only local chapel, the funeral director refused to allow him to be given services because the local white community "would not stand for it," as Garcia later recalled (del Olmo 1996, 5). After hearing about the American G.I. Forum, Longoria's widow contacted Garcia and asked for his help. After Garcia unsuccessfully approached the funeral home, which offered to bury Private Longoria in a portion of the cemetery segregated by barbed wire, he turned to the state press and congressional leaders to plead his case. He presented Private Longoria as an American hero and argued that he should receive a funeral fitting his sacrifice: giving one's life to one's country. The story was covered internationally and raised the awareness of then-Senator Lyndon Baines Johnson. With the support of Johnson, Private Longoria was eventually buried at Arlington National Cemetery. The devastating Longoria situation convinced Garcia that the American G.I. Forum needed to take up the rights of Latinos generally. His wife, Wanda Garcia, was later quoted as saying, "In Italy and many European countries that I have visited, the word 'America' is always associated with liberty, equality and the freedom of opportunity. . . . I was dumbfounded at the attitudes displayed towards the Mexican people [in Texas]" (Avila 1996, 18). It was the oppression faced by *Tejanos* in his home state that inspired Hector Garcia.

As a result of these incidents, the American G.I. Forum expanded its original mission, going beyond health and veterans' benefits to address education, housing, poll taxation, and other social issues. Garcia fought hard to change the systemic segregation in Texas. Medical care offered to *Tejanos* was separate and inferior to that given to whites. In addition, education opportunities were tainted by rampant prejudice. Garcia often recounted that a former teacher had told him that no Mexican in his class would ever get an "A." Rather than accept defeat, he recruited associates and fought for *Tejano* rights using the legal system. Additionally, he fought to abolish the long-standing poll tax in Texas. By 1950, Garcia was the most prominent Hispanic civil rights leader in the nation.

Under the auspices of the American G.I. Forum, lawyers promoted the rights of Latinos to receive fair trials by juries of their peers. In *Hernandez v. The State of Texas* (1954), a case that went to the U.S. Supreme Court, the Court unanimously decided that Hernandez, a *Tejano* farm worker, had received an unfair trial because Mexican Americans were systematically removed from grand jury selection. Around the same time as the *Hernandez* case, Garcia took up the cause of educational equal-

ity. Garcia fought the English-only movement as "nothing but racism, designed to make Hispanics look inferior for speaking Spanish" (Flynn 1987). He believed that bilingualism and biculturalism made the United States stronger by increasing Americans' ability to interact internationally. He also was a passionate champion of bilingual education because it could contribute to improved commerce and relations with Latin American countries. In addition, Garcia was fond of saying that *Tejanos* "were never immigrants and are 'as American as the heirs of the Mayflower'" (Flynn 1987).

Garcia also supported a pivotal desegregation case, *Delgado v. Bastrop ISD* (1948), which began to shake the foundation of overt educational bigotry. This case was crucial in changing the way that Mexican Americans were treated under Texas law. According to the 1950 U.S. census, the average school level completed by persons with Spanish surnames and aged over twenty-five was between second and third grade. In sharp contrast, white Americans averaged between a ninth- and tenth-grade education. During this era, moreover, around 27 percent of adults with Spanish last names had never attended school. It took Garcia over ten years to permanently end the segregation of Mexican Americans in Texas public schools. This civil rights journey started with the *Delgado* case, which made separate education of Hispanic children illegal. Despite this pivotal decision to end segregation, the majority of school districts ignored the law. In a partnership he formed between the American G.I. Forum and the League of United Latin American Citizens (LULAC), he was able to reach his goal in the 1957 case, *Hernandez v. Consolidated ISD*, which finally ended segregation in the Texas public school system.

His friend Lyndon Baines Johnson, who later became president of the United States, recognized the leadership that Garcia provided in bringing these cases to court. Thus, President Johnson appointed Garcia to serve on the U.S. Commission on Civil Rights in 1968. President Johnson also appointed Garcia as U.S. alternate ambassador to the United Nations in the late 1960s. Later, in the mid-1970s, President Jimmy Carter appointed Garcia to the U.S. Circuit Judge Nominating Commission for the Western Fifth Circuit Panel. A decade later, Garcia became only one of three Hispanics to receive the Medal of Freedom in the twentieth century. President Ronald Reagan conferred this most prestigious civilian honor upon him in 1984.

CONCLUSION

Hector Garcia continued to serve as a spokesperson for the Hispanic communities of the nation until his death on July 26, 1996. Dr. Xico Garcia, Garcia's brother, eulogized him as a warrior and a man of peace as well as an individual who believed that everyone should be treated equally. President William Jefferson Clinton was among those who also spoke at his funeral.

In 1998, in honor of Garcia, the U.S. Congress chartered the American G.I. Forum, recognizing him posthumously and placing the organization among other great veteran associations such as the American Legion. He also received the highest honor from the Mexican government—the Aztec Eagle—in that same year. The Texas legislature enacted Senate Bill 419 effective September 1, 1999, creating Dr. Hector P. Garcia Day every January 17. The G.I. Forum, now headquartered in Denver, Colorado, has a membership exceeding 160,000 individuals in twenty-four states and Puerto Rico. It still uses its founder's motto as its own: "Education is our freedom, and freedom should be everybody's business."

Susan Haber

FURTHER READING

Avila, Alex. "Freedom Fighter." *Hispanic*, January/February 1996, 18.

del Olmo, Frank. "Perspective on Latinos: A Veteran's Cause Paved the Way." *Los Angeles Times*, September 22, 1996, Part M, 5.

Flynn, Ken. "Founder of Hispanic Veterans Organization Decries 'English Only.'" UPI, June 23, 1987.

Harris, Joyce Saenz. "Hector P. Garcia: When It's Time to Pull Some Strings, They Call Him 'Dr. Hector;' Civil Rights Leader and Founder of the American G.I. Forum." *Dallas Morning News*, August 19, 1990, 1E.

Miller, Lauraine. "Many Eulogize Garcia as a 'Freedom Fighter.'" *Houston Chronicle*, July 31, 1996, A15.

PAPERS

Hector Perez Garcia's papers are located at the Mary and Jeff Bell Library, Special Collections and Archives Department, Texas A&M University–Corpus Christi (Corpus Christi, TX).

MARY ELIZABETH GARRETT
(1853–1915)

Benefactor of the Bryn Mawr School for Girls, the Johns Hopkins University School of Medicine, Bryn Mawr College, and the National American Woman Suffrage Association

INTRODUCTION

"[O]pportunities for research, investigation and teaching of Medical Science in its various branches shall be open to women" (*The Last Will and Testament of Mary Elizabeth Garrett* 1908, 13). These words exhibit the feminist philosophy that directed Mary Elizabeth Garrett's philanthropy. A reticent woman, Garrett never sought personal recognition through her philanthropy but became one of the first American women of independent wealth to use her fortune to promote social change. The gifts that she made over a century ago have had long and enduring value. Garrett primarily used her fortune to provide new educational and cultural opportunities for women but also gen-

Mary Elizabeth Garrett, whose 1893 gift made possible the opening of The Johns Hopkins School of Medicine. The Alan Mason Chesney Medical Archives of The Johns Hopkins Medical Institutions.

erously bestowed funding and staunch personal support to the women's suffrage movement and to causes that advocated financial and political independence for women.

Garrett achieved great successes in practicing what is sometimes termed "coercive philanthropy." Since she wanted to be certain that her money would be spent for what she intended, she would frequently attach conditions to her gifts. In these conditions, she would specify what she wanted to accomplish with her funding and that the funding would be revoked if her conditions were not met. Only after negotiating her desired conditions would she release the funding. Then, Garrett would monitor the project being supported to assure that her stipulations were being met. Through her persistence and stewardship, she raised the quality of education for

women and helped them to surmount societal and political barriers.

EARLY YEARS AND EDUCATION

Born in 1853, Mary Elizabeth Garrett was the daughter of John Work Garrett and Rachel Anne Harrison Garrett and the sister of Henry Stouffer Garrett, Robert Garrett, and T. Harrison Garrett. Mary Elizabeth inherited her fortune and also acumen for finance from her father, titan of the Baltimore and Ohio Railroad. Having been especially close to her father as an only daughter, she became his most trusted confidante in both family and business matters. In early adulthood, she served as John Work Garrett's secretary and in that capacity helped him with his correspondence and attended business meetings with him—a most unusual opportunity for a young woman of her station. Information about Garrett's educational background is limited; she studied mainly with private tutors and gained a rich cultural education through travels abroad with her parents. On these trips, she had occasion to meet well-known authors and artists, visit museums and galleries, and attend concerts, plays, and other cultural events. Through her tutoring and her rarified cultural education, she developed a broad knowledge and great love of literature and the arts.

Garrett's commitment to helping women better their lives began even before she received her inheritance. As a young woman, Garrett contributed her time and energies to the Woman's Industrial Exchange movement—a nationwide effort to help women of limited means earn money through the sale of their wares, which included baked goods and hand-sewn items ranging from children's clothing to table linens. In 1880, she helped launch the Woman's Industrial Exchange of Baltimore as a founding director.

In her youth, as she gained more independence, she became acquainted with a lively group of young women in Baltimore. This circle included M. Carey Thomas, Mary Mackall Gwinn, Elizabeth T. King, and Julia R. Rogers—each of whom had been reared in privileged circumstances. Thomas had the most powerful personality and the most progressive ideas. In her Quaker upbringing, she was exposed to more free thinking than the others. Garrett was the richest member of the group and the most culturally sophisticated. They gathered often to socialize and to ponder lofty intellectual and social issues. Since they frequently met on Friday evenings, they informally named their circle the Friday Evening in 1878. This was a heady group, brimming with high ideals for education, social change, and the desire to perform good works.

The example of philanthropist Johns Hopkins may well have made a strong impression upon the Friday Evening members. A wealthy Quaker merchant, Hopkins declared his moral obligation was to use his wealth to serve humanity. Thus, he incorporated a university and a hospital that were to bear his name. In 1873, he died, leaving his fortune to develop these two institutions. Hopkins had selected leading citizens, many of whom were Quakers, to serve as trustees of these institutions and instructed them to develop the best possible institutions of their kind. In 1876, the Johns Hopkins University opened. Thirteen years later, the Johns Hopkins Hospital and the Johns Hopkins Hospital School of Nursing commenced operations. Each of the fathers of the women who composed the Friday Evening group served terms as trustees for Hopkins. As these young women were growing up, they were undoubtedly exposed to much discussion about the planning and development of this hospital and university.

CAREER HIGHLIGHTS AND MAJOR PHILANTHROPIC CONTRIBUTIONS

Upon the death of her father in 1884, Garrett inherited great wealth and gained the freedom to pursue an independent life. Soon thereafter, she embarked upon her course of philanthropy. Her first major funding endeavor was to help establish the Bryn Mawr School for Girls in Baltimore. She and her Friday Evening friends, who decried the limited educational resources for young women in Baltimore, determined to change this lamentable situation. Their goal was to provide a comprehensive and high-quality college-preparatory education for young women. Initially, they met informally for planning sessions and later formally constituted themselves as the school's board of governance.

The Bryn Mawr School for Girls officially opened in temporary quarters on September 21, 1885. At the time the five friends were engaged in planning the Baltimore School, M. Carey Thomas served as dean of Bryn Mawr College. The women chose to name the school after Bryn Mawr College because the women's college was a symbol of excellence and the trustees of Bryn Mawr College gave their permission to use the college's name. Garrett gave $400,000 for the construction of new facilities and became deeply involved in overseeing every step of the building process. The new building, completed in 1889, received great acclaim throughout the country as one of the finest facilities of its kind, equipped to nurture both the intellectual and physical growth of young women. Included in this school were state-of-the-art science laboratories, art studios, and physical education facilities such as a gymnasium, swimming pool, and tennis courts.

Emboldened by successfully establishing the Bryn Mawr School, Garrett next focused upon the new bastion of male education in Baltimore, the Johns Hopkins University. In 1877, shortly after the university had opened, President Daniel C. Gilman and the trustees rejected M. Carey Thomas's application for admission. They were resolute in their stand that no woman be admitted. In 1887, Garrett reopened the issue of coeducation. She offered the president and trustees of the university a donation of $35,000 annually to establish a coeducational school of science. Even with the promise of substantial funding, the president and trustees refused her offer because they still steadfastly opposed coeducation. Spurned but not defeated, Garrett and her indomitable friends soon rallied to another cause for coeducation at Johns Hopkins University.

Learning that the university had financial difficulties and would not be able to open the proposed school of medicine when the hospital was to commence operations in May 1889, the women quickly seized upon the opportunity presented by these circumstances. M. Carey Thomas, representing the group, met with President Gilman in December 1888 to present a proposition for funding the school of medicine. In the intervening years since Gilman and the trustees had rejected her application for admission, Thomas had pursued graduate studies abroad. In 1882, she received a doctorate from the University of Zurich. Subsequently, she became Professor of English and Dean of Bryn Mawr College in 1884. Now an eminent professional woman with a new purpose, Thomas stated that she, Garrett, and the three other friends from the Friday evening group were prepared to launch a campaign to raise the $100,000 needed to endow the school, provided women were admitted on equal terms as men.

On May 2, 1890, these five friends officially formed the Women's Fund Committee and quickly set up branches across the country. They chose nationally prominent women to chair the various regional groups, thus giving the campaign a stamp of major significance. Politically astute, they selected major luminaries of society and trailblazers for social change. Some of the well-known women who joined the committee and made financial contributions as well included: Caroline Harrison, wife of Benjamin Harrison, the sitting president; **Jane Stanford**, wife of **Leland Stanford**, founder of Stanford University and U.S. Senator; Bertha Palmer, the queen of Chicago society, whose husband Potter Palmer, had built the Palmer House Hotel; Louisa Adams, wife of President John Quincy Adams; Julia Ward Howe, the abolitionist who wrote "The Battle Hymn of the Republic"; Alice Longfellow, daughter of the poet Henry Wadsworth Longfellow; Sarah Orne Jewett, who featured strong and independent women in her novels; physician Mary Putnam Jacobi, organizer of the Association for the Advancement of Medical Education for Women; and pioneer women physicians Emily Blackwell and Marie Zakrzwska.

By the autumn of 1890, the Women's Fund Committee had raised the requisite $100,000 and was able to make a formal offer to the university. Nearly 700 subscribers contributed $52,212.50 and Garrett made up the needed $47,787.50 from her personal fortune. The trustees voted on a resolution to accept the gift and stated that it would be invested as the Women's Medical School Fund, but the school could not be opened until they obtained contributions that totaled $500,000. Neither the university nor the Women's Fund Committee was successful in raising this amount.

Once again, Garrett stepped into the breach and salvaged the situation with her philanthropy. She made a gift of $306,977 to bring the endowment of the school of medicine to the requisite $500,000. Thus, with her earlier gift of $47,787.50, she contributed a total of $354,764.50, which in today's currency would be worth approximately $6.5 million. Of her stipulations, the following three brought about the greatest transformation in American medical education:

- That women be admitted to the school on equal terms as men and have the same privileges accorded to male students;
- That the school of medicine be a graduate school with a four-year program for a Doctor of Medicine degree;
- That criteria for admission require that all applicants hold a bachelor's degree and a transcript showing that they have successfully completed courses in physics, chemistry and biology, and have a good reading knowledge of French and German (Chesney 1943, 298–301).

Garrett concluded her stipulations with the following proviso, "That in the event of any violation of any or all of the aforesaid stipulations the said sum of $306,977 shall revert to me, or such person or persons, institution or institutions, as I by testament or otherwise may hereafter appoint" (Chesney 1943,

300). Persuading the reluctant trustees and medical faculty to accept her gift with its conditions was a major feat for Garrett. Thanks to the influence of her father, Garrett was a firm and persistent negotiator. She was also fortunate to have had the strong support of several key trustees. These men used their best diplomatic skills and worked behind the scenes to persuade their balking colleagues to accept the funding and the conditions that Garrett stipulated. In October 1893, after the faculty and trustees finally agreed to her stipulations, the Johns Hopkins University School of Medicine opened and enrolled its first class of students.

To understand the importance of Garrett's stipulations, it is necessary to know about the deplorable condition of most American medical schools in the late nineteenth century. These schools were largely diploma mills that promoted apprenticeship as the principal mode of learning. They had few, if any, requirements for admission and very limited medical training. Their curricula essentially ignored the emerging role of science in the study of medicine and the need to incorporate research and new scientific knowledge into the course of study. American students wanting to obtain the best possible medical education had to journey to European universities and research institutes, which offered lecture and laboratory courses with the latest scientific findings. Thus, Garrett's gift, with its goal-oriented stipulations, helped to transform medical education in America by spearheading a movement to provide equal opportunities for women and by elevating the overall standards for medical education.

After completing her good works at Johns Hopkins, Garrett went on to become involved in the suffragist movement and drew upon her fortune to provide business and educational opportunities for women in all walks of life. Through her work with the National American Woman Suffrage Association, she became dedicated to Susan B. Anthony and did much to support her causes. In 1906, Garrett generously hosted several events for the National American Woman Suffrage Association when it met in Baltimore. She also chaired a committee to raise funding for the association. Since Anthony requested a total of $12,000 per year for a period of five years, Garrett embarked on the fund-raising campaign in February 1907. By May of that year, she raised a total of $60,000 (personally contributing $2,500).

Over a thirty-year period from the 1880s until her death in 1915, Garrett made many generous contributions to Bryn Mawr College. These gifts included fellowships, scholarships, books, artwork, scientific equipment, and many more items to enhance the life of the college. She even helped to cover deficits in the college's budget on several occasions. In another instance of coercive philanthropy, Garrett helped to secure M. Carey Thomas's appointment as president by promising to donate $10,000 annually to Bryn Mawr if Thomas became its president. In 1896, Garrett contributed $100,000 to renovate the Deanery, the official residence of the president, M. Carey Thomas.

CONCLUSION

Troubled with fragile health throughout her life, Garrett died of leukemia at the age of sixty-two. In her last will and testament, Garrett affirms her ongoing commitment to higher education for women through her bequest to M. Carey Thomas. She stated that "the said M. Carey Thomas and myself have been closely associated in our work for the higher education of women and I am confident that an appropriate and wise use will be made of my gift to her" (*Last Will and Testament of Mary Elizabeth Garrett* 1908, 14). Whereas she left the bulk of her estate to Thomas, she also made generous bequests to the educational institutions she helped in her lifetime. Clearly, she left a remarkable legacy of personal philanthropy. The educational institutions that she supported, the Bryn Mawr School, the Johns Hopkins University School of Medicine, and the Bryn Mawr College, have grown and thrived over the past century, becoming major centers of educational excellence. Meanwhile, the women's suffrage cause, which she so ardently supported, has been achieved.

Nancy McCall and Elizabeth M. Peterson

FURTHER READING

Beirne, Rosamond Randall. *Let's Pick the Daisies: The History of the Bryn Mawr School, 1885–1967.* Baltimore: Bryn Mawr School, 1970.

Chesney, Alan Mason. *The Johns Hopkins Hospital and the Johns Hopkins University School of Medicine, A Chronicle,* vol. 1. Baltimore: Johns Hopkins Press, 1943.

Finch, Edith. *Carey Thomas of Bryn Mawr.* New York and London: Harper & Brothers, 1947.

Garrett, Mary Elizabeth. *Last Will and Testament.* February 27, 1908.

Horowitz, Helen Lefkowitz. *The Power and Passion of M. Carey Thomas.* New York: Alfred A. Knopf, 1994.

McCall, Nancy. "Mary Elizabeth Garrett, Founding Benefactor of the School of Medicine." *Johns Hopkins Gazette* 30, no. 21, 2001, 8–9

———. "The Savvy Strategies of the First Campaign for Hopkins Medicine." *Hopkins Medical News* 8, no. 4, 1984, 2–5.

Sander, Kathleen Waters. "Trailblazer for Women Doctors." *Baltimore Sun,* March 4, 2001, 1C, 4C.

Thomas, M. Carey. "Mary Elizabeth Garrett." In *Maryland Women,* ed. Margie H. Luckett, Baltimore: Margie H. Luckett, Publisher, 1931, 151–153.

West, Lucy Fisher, ed. *The Papers of M. Carey Thomas in the Bryn Mawr College Archives: Reel Guide and Index to the Microfilm Collection.* Woodbridge, CT: Research Publications International, 1982.

PAPERS

Correspondence of Mary Elizabeth Garrett may be found in the following repositories: the Bryn Mawr College Archives (Bryn Mawr, PA); the Bryn Mawr School Archives (Baltimore, MD), the Alan Mason Chesney Medical Archives of the Johns Hopkins Medical Institutions (Baltimore, MD); Special Collections, the Milton S. Eisenhower Library of the Johns Hopkins University (Baltimore, MD); and the Manuscripts Division of the Library of Congress (Washington, DC).

WILLIAM H. (BILL) GATES III
(1955–   )

Founder of Microsoft and the Bill & Melinda Gates Foundation

INTRODUCTION

"As there is progress, which is partly advances in technology, in a certain sense the world gets richer. That is, the things we do that use a lot of resources and time can be done more efficiently. So people wonder, 'Will there be jobs? Will there be things to do?' Until we are educating every kid in a fantastic way, until every inner city is cleaned up, there is no shortage of things to do" (Rensin 1994, 28). In a way, this statement by William H. (Bill) Gates aptly describes his life—a commitment to the advancement of computer technology, and a dedication to distributing the wealth that he accumulates through his work.

Displaying an aptitude for mathematics at an early age, Bill Gates focused this talent on computer technology. When the computer field was still in its infancy, he began to write computer programs with his friend, Paul Allen, at age thirteen. His talent for computer programming, as well as his friendship with Paul Allen, continued throughout high school and his years at Harvard University, but no one could have predicted the success that the two friends would achieve in the field. After delivering a successful computer language for the first microcomputer, they founded their own company, Microsoft. Subsequently, Microsoft became a major innovator in the field of computer technology. By the end of the twentieth century, Microsoft's computer operating system, Windows, ran

85 percent of the world's computers. This amazing success also made Bill Gates the wealthiest person in the world and potentially an important philanthropist.

EARLY YEARS AND EDUCATION

Born in Seattle, Washington, on October 28, 1955, William H. (Bill) Gates III was the second of three children. His parents, Mary and William H. Gates II, were prominent members of the Seattle community. His father enjoyed a successful legal practice in the area. His mother, a former schoolteacher, came to focus her efforts on the philanthropic field. In addition to serving on several charitable boards, Mary Gates served as a University of Washington regent and chairwoman of United Way International. So it could be said that Gates learned, at an early age, the importance of philanthropy.

From an early age, Gates also showed an enormous talent for mathematics. Growing up in Seattle, he attended public elementary school. After a rebellious period in Gates's young life, his parents made a decision that would set his successful future in motion. At the age of twelve, Gates enrolled in Lakeside School, an academically rigorous private school in Seattle. At Lakeside School, he discovered computers and met Paul Allen, the future cofounder of the Microsoft Corporation. At the time, computer technology was in the early stages of development, and the computers themselves were quite large and managed only by scientists. Still, Gates and a few friends from Lakeside worked to learn as much as they could about computer technology. By the eighth grade, Gates had written his first successful computer program. Thereafter, Allen and Gates strove to work on more complex computer calculations. They wrote, for example, a class scheduling program for the school. A while later, the two formed their first company, Traf-O-Data, to analyze traffic data for the city. An amazing feat by any standard, Gates and Allen were making money with their computer aptitude while they were still in high school.

Foreshadowing future events, Gates took some time off from his senior year of high school to work on a computer project with a local company. Nonetheless, he did not think that the computer field would end up as his career. After graduating from Lakeside School, he chose to attend Harvard University with full intentions of following in his father's footsteps and becoming a lawyer. While at Harvard University, Gates continued to have an interest in computers, but did not make it his main focus until a fateful day in December 1974 when his friend Paul Allen showed him an article in *Popular Mechanics* about the first microcomputer (one that could be built at home), called the MITS Altair. As Gates remembered, "Here was someone making a computer around this chip in exactly the way that Paul had talked to me, and we'd thought about what kind of software could be done for it, and it was happening without us" (Allison 1993, 9). After contacting the company, Gates and Allen wrote a version of the BASIC computer language for the microcomputer, which Allen delivered to the company's headquarters in Albuquerque, New Mexico. When the computer language became a success, Gates, though only in his junior year of college, decided to take a leave of absence and join Allen in Albuquerque. There, the two formed the now famous company, Microsoft, in 1975. Due to Gates's business savvy, Microsoft worked on a completely contractual basis, enabling the company to provide programming software for many different companies during a very volatile time in the growing computer industry. As Microsoft was experiencing growing pains in Albuquerque, such as having trouble finding quality programming personnel, Gates and Allen decided to move their company to their hometown of Seattle in 1979. The following year, Microsoft, and the computer industry as a whole, experienced a major milestone, when IBM requested an operating system for its first personal computer. When IBM's personal computer was introduced in 1981 with Microsoft's system, MS-DOS, it proved an instant success.

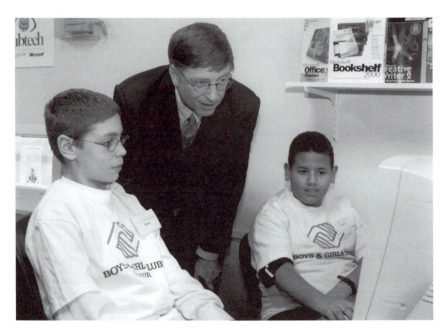

Bill Gates speaks to two children in a computer lab in New York, December 2000. AP Photo/Jeff Christensen, Pool.

CAREER HIGHLIGHTS

With Microsoft firmly planted as a vital part of the computer industry, the subsequent years were extremely successful. The company continued to focus on computer software, expanding on the success it had experienced with MS-DOS. Recognizing the future of personal computers, Gates wanted to continue to create systems that could be easily utilized by the consumers. Applications such as Microsoft Word and Excel were introduced, and later packaged with other applications when Microsoft debuted its Windows operating system. Partly as a way to gain greater exposure for the advances that it had made in the computer industry, Gates decided to go public with his company in 1986. Practically overnight, Gates became a billionaire. The same week that Microsoft went public, the company moved into its new corporate campus in nearby Redmond, Washington.

Microsoft continued to stay on the cutting edge with its software. By 1993, Windows was selling a million copies per month. A later version, Windows 95 (introduced in August 1995), sold 7 million copies during the first six weeks that it was available. Despite incredible success, Microsoft experienced a major setback when it came under investigation by the U.S. government during the 1990s, beginning with the Federal Trade Commission and then continuing to the Department of Justice. Ironically, the success that Microsoft achieved by going public and receiving greater exposure also brought on the scrutiny of these agencies and charges of antitrust violations.

Meanwhile, Gates met his future wife, Melinda French, when she was a marketing executive for Microsoft. The couple married on January 1, 1994. By the end of the 1990s, they had two children: Jennifer (1996) and Rory (1999).

MAJOR PHILANTHROPIC CONTRIBUTIONS

From his incredible success in the computer industry, Bill Gates became the wealthiest person in the world, with assets of more than $60 billion. Still, the software innovator asserts that he is not interested in his growing wealth as much as he is interested in the future of computer technology as well as the future of his philanthropic interests. "Certainly, my wealth is a mixed blessing. Things like the Gates Library Foundation, where Melinda and I make sure that anyone who goes to a library can get hooked up to the Internet, things like that are the positive side. What wealth means in terms of people's over-interest and overfocus on me personally is the bad side. . . . If they want to put in the consent decree that I'm going to give away 95% of my wealth, I'd be glad to sign that" (Schlender 1998, 158).

Though he learned the importance of philanthropy from his mother, Bill Gates's first official venture into the realm of philanthropy occurred in 1994, when he founded the William H. Gates Foundation. In a philanthropic outlook similar to that of the **Rockefeller** family and **Jane Addams**, the William H. Gates Foundation focused its efforts on health issues in developing Third World countries. Three years later, Gates founded the Gates Library Foundation, which he later renamed the Gates Learning Foundation. In a distinctly **Andrew Carnegie** fashion, this foundation forms partnerships with public libraries throughout North America to provide access to personal computers and digital information as general educational assistance. In 1999, Gates and his wife decided to merge the foundations into the Bill & Melinda Gates Foundation, creating the most richly endowed philanthropic organization in the world, with assets of more than $22 billion. Still largely focused on his business affairs, Bill Gates's father became cochairman of this foundation.

The main concentration of the Bill & Melinda Gates Foundation is the health care field, a continuation of the original foundation Gates formed. An excellent example of this commitment was the grant of $750 million, over five years, to the Global Alliance for Vaccines and Immunization. Still, this field is not the only area receiving large grants from the Bill & Melinda Gates Foundation. The foundation has committed $200 million to fund technology progress, such as computers with Internet access and technology training, to public libraries across North America, with a focus on serving lower-income areas. Another example of the foundation's commitment to education can be seen by its dedication of $1 billion, over twenty years, to the Gates Millennium Scholars scholarship program, offering college scholarships to promising low-income students.

Following in **George Eastman**'s charitable tradition, the final major focus for the Bill & Melinda Gates Foundation is its founders' home: the Pacific Northwest. The foundation is dedicated to supporting a wide range of projects and programs in the Pacific Northwest, especially those that focus on needy children and their families. For instance, the foundation provided a $40 million grant to establish the Sound Families Program, which will utilize the grant to build transitional housing for homeless families and expand support services available to them in three counties in the state of Washington.

CONCLUSION

The incredible success of Microsoft made Gates the wealthiest person in the world, and he has utilized that wealth to create a foundation that was also the richest in the world before he reached the age of forty-five. Given his young age and tremendous wealth, he certainly possesses the potential to become a notable American philanthropist.

Heather E. Harmless

FURTHER READING

Allison, David. "Transcript of a Video History with Mr. William 'Bill' Gates." 1993 Price Waterhouse Leadership Award for Lifetime Achievement, ComputerWorld Smithsonian Awards.

Cabrera, Luis. "Gates, Allen Philanthropy Differs." *Seattle Times*, November 19, 2000, B6.

Corcoran, Elizabeth. "Gates Unplugged: Weary of Legal Battles, Pulled by His Family, Confident in His Lieutenant—Bill Gates Can Imagine Himself Quitting His Job." *Forbes*, December 13, 1999, 76–78.

Cowley, Geoffrey. "Bill's Biggest Bet Yet." *Newsweek*, February, 4, 2002, 44–52.

Dickinson, Joan D. *Bill Gates, Billionaire Computer Genius.* Springfield, NJ: Enslow Publishers, 1997.

Gates, Bill. *Bill Gates Speaks: Wisdom from the World's Greatest Entrepreneur.* Compiled by Janet C. Lowe. New York: John Wiley & Sons, 1998.

Gates, Bill, with Collins Hemingway. *Business @ the Speed of Thought: Succeeding in the Digital Age.* New York: Warner Books, 2000.

Gates, Bill, with Peter Rinearson and Nathan Myhrvold. *The Road Ahead.* New York: Penguin Books, 1996.

Gatlin, Jonathan. *Bill Gates: The Path to the Future.* New York: Avon Books, 1999.

Greenfeld, Karl. "Giving Billions Isn't Easy." *Time*, July 24, 2000, 52–53.

Greenfeld, Karl Taro, et al. "A New Way of Giving." *Time*, July 24, 2000, 48–51.

Kennedy, Mike. "Found Money." *American School & University*, June 2000, 16–22.

Rensin, David. "Playboy Interview: Bill Gates." *Playboy*, July 1, 1994, 55.

Schlender, Brent. "An Interview with Gates: In the Heat of Antitrust Negotiations, Gates Took Time for a Two-Hour Interview in Which He Explained Why He Finds Dealing with the Government So Frustrating." *Fortune*, June 8, 1998, 150–158.

Stross, Randall E. "Bill Gates: Richest American Ever and You Thought Rockefeller Had Money." *Fortune*, August 4, 1997, 38–40.

Verhovek, Sam Howe. "Elder Bill Gates Takes on the Role of Philanthropist." *New York Times*, September 12, 1999, 1A.

PAPERS

William H. Gates III's papers have not been deposited in an archive.

STEPHEN GIRARD
(1750–1831)

Merchant, Misunderstood Republican Idealist, Donor of a Landmark Bequest, and Founder of Girard College

INTRODUCTION

Stephen Girard believed "labor is the price of life, its happiness, its everything; to rest is to rust; every man should labour to the last hour of his ability" (Minnigerode 1927, 29). During his life, but even more so after his death, people criticized Girard for the harshness of his demanding rationality, his atheism, and his seeming love of property more than people. Yet, this man, who became one of the wealthiest Americans of any period in the nation's history, donated much of his time and nearly all of his money to alleviating suffering and encouraging human potential. Ironically, the immigrant Girard embraced the values of the American self-made man ideal more strongly than most of his adopted countrymen, and his devotion to those values in life and death contributed to his unpopularity.

EARLY YEARS AND EDUCATION

Stephen Girard's father served as a French naval officer in the War of the Austrian Succession (1740–1748). After the war, he returned to his wife in the Bordeaux region of France to operate a prosperous shipping business and raise a family. Stephen Girard, the second of ten children, was born on May 20, 1750.

Girard spent much of his youth at the shipyards and developed an early interest in navigation. At age fourteen, expressing a desire to escape the limited opportunities he perceived among family and friends in Bordeaux, he convinced his father to let him sign on as a cabin boy on one of Girard's merchant ships. His desire for even greater freedom resulted in a rift with his father, and he was entirely on his own by age sixteen. By the early 1770s, Girard had his master's li-

Portrait of Stephen Girard, founder of Girard College, by Bass Otis. Courtesy of Girard College, Philadelphia, PA.

cense and was responsible for large cargoes on transatlantic voyages. In the mid-eighteenth century, merchant sailors most frequently assumed responsibility to obtain the best prices for the goods they carried. Commissions or other forms of incentive pay encouraged them to shop the cargo to the highest bidder. On the downside, they also assumed responsibility for losses. In 1774, Girard had to sell his cargo for a huge loss in the French Caribbean island of St. Dominique. Fearful of imprisonment for debt if he returned to France, he became a sailor on a boat to Britain's American colonies. Disgraced, penniless, and cut off from his family, the twenty-four-year-old Girard disembarked in New York, eager to earn enough money to pay off his creditors and return to his previous business.

Revolutionary fervor enveloped New York in 1774. Merchants chafed at the restrictions and duties that England imposed upon colonial shipping. The times were ripe for a daring sea captain to profit from the circumstances. Girard never lacked courage and began smuggling ventures. By the time the British imposed a wartime blockade, Girard was an adept blockade-runner and privateer. Operating out of Philadelphia, he attacked the King's merchant ships and sold their cargo in America and the Caribbean. By 1777, he had paid off most of his debts and amassed enough money to offer a comfortable lifestyle to Mary Lumm. Tired of the libertine life of a sailor and in love with Lumm, he purchased a home in Mount Holly, New Jersey, became an American citizen in 1779, established a reputable shipping business that allowed him to stay home, and enjoyed a few happy years.

Unfortunately, Stephen and Mary Girard were unable to conceive children, a fact that threw Mary Girard into deep despair. Diagnosed with mental illness, she was institutionalized in 1785. She recovered sufficiently to return home in the late 1780s, surprisingly giving birth to a daughter in 1791. It appeared, momentarily, that Stephen Girard would enjoy the family life he sought after all. Yet, the baby girl died in her first year of life. Mary Girard broke down completely, returned to the institution, and spent the rest of her life, until 1815, in near isolation.

CAREER HIGHLIGHTS

By 1782, Girard's younger brother, Jean, had established business operations in St. Dominique. Subsequently, the brothers started a new company, combining their skills and businesses. As an agent, Jean Girard's job was to obtain the best prices for shipped goods. He also had built large warehouses in St. Dominique, allowing him to store nonperishable goods until market prices rose. The integration of Jean Girard's shipping agent business with Stephen Girard's merchant shipping business provided an innovative solution to many of the business risks inherent in transatlantic shipping during that era. With his younger brother assuming full control over market sales, Girard was able to pay his captains straight wages on a trip-by-trip basis. Accordingly, Girard's captains, freed from the burdens of selling at the highest price, were motivated to travel quickly and unload at Jean Girard's direction. The brothers also began using the still somewhat unusual practice of insuring their cargoes against piracy, loss in a storm, and spoilage.

Girard ships sailed from the United States to Europe and the Caribbean with wheat, lumber, fish, spices, molasses, sugar, and coffee. Stephen Girard despised European proscriptions on free trade and frequently smuggled banned products into European ports, reaping huge profits in the process. However, Girard's trade in contraband cargoes frightened his brother. Consequently, the two separated in 1790. Nevertheless, Girard had built a fortune worth several million

dollars and owned a substantial fleet by the turn of the century.

At home, Girard maintained a decent library and was well read in Enlightenment philosophy and political theory. He supported Thomas Jefferson for the presidency in 1800 and contributed to Republican candidates throughout his life. The Republican (Democratic-Republican) Party embodied the liberal principles of legal equality, limited government, and free trade at home and in international commerce. Its politics contrasted with those of the Federalist Party, which favored a more classic republicanism in which a government of elected elites used the powers of the state to serve social needs. Girard's personal relationships evinced his devotion to Enlightenment reason. He considered merit, not need, the basis for all business dealings, even when it came to paying his house staff. A contract was a bargain between two free and equal parties, and he could not be expected, merely because of his relative wealth, to make bad bargains to compensate for another's needs. In addition, he did not recognize biblical truths and considered much of Christian ethics to be only a rationalization of weakness. As a self-made man, he expected others to exert the effort necessary for their own success. He called work "the only pleasure I have on this globe" and believed women, as well as men, capable of labor and useful roles in society (Minnigerode 1927, 15). In fact, he paid for all of his nieces to attend school when their own parents refused to do so.

However, Girard recognized that some were not able to secure their own places in the world, and to them he devoted tremendous time and money. He deplored the plight of the many orphaned children in America's growing cities and always offered a warm hand and open home to stray dogs and injured birds. Girard even put stray dogs aboard his ships to provide homes to those he could not house himself. He worked to increase awareness of animal cruelty, especially toward horses, in an age when little attention was paid to such matters.

The success of Girard's shipping business gave him the financial opportunity to diversify. In the early 1800s, Girard owned extensive property in Philadelphia, coal mines, and a stake in potential railroads; but his greatest venture outside of shipping was banking. By 1812, even Republicans such as President James Madison recognized the need for a modernized banking system. Yet, more radical Republicans resented any government involvement in the private economy. In 1812, the Pennsylvania legislature refused to charter the then-defunct Bank of the United States. Girard bought the bank building, reopened it as a private bank, and, using 1 million dollars of his own funds, increased the bank's assets to $2.5 million. Given its size, Girard's bank was able to compete with any American bank. During the War of 1812, he underwrote a loan of $16 million to the United States when the American people failed to subscribe to war bonds. By the early 1820s, some estimate Stephen Girard's financial holdings to have been in excess of $40 million—an immense fortune at that time.

MAJOR PHILANTHROPIC CONTRIBUTIONS

Surprisingly, in the case of a man as successful and influential as Girard, he is remembered nearly 200 years later primarily for the will he left at his death. Yet, that controversial will was but the final act in a long series of philanthropic activities. Girard joined the Masonic Order and donated time and money to its charitable causes. During his lifetime, he actually supported numerous other charitable groups, such as the Society for the Relief of Distressed Masters of Ships and Their Widows, the Public School Fund of Philadelphia, the Pennsylvania Institution for the Deaf and Dumb, and the Orphan Society.

When Philadelphia suffered from terrible yellow fever epidemics in 1793, 1797, 1798, 1802, and 1820, Girard became a pivotal figure. Doctors of the time seemed powerless to stem the spread of the disease, prescribing explosions of gunpowder in town squares and the bleeding of patients. Infected sufferers were scorned and sometimes driven out of town. Philadelphia purchased an old mansion on the city's outskirts on Bush Hill to house yellow fever "patients," who were ensconced there while they waited to die. Girard, who visited Bush Hill for the first time in September 1793, found this "solution" unacceptable. It seemed at once to exacerbate fears of residents and visitors and to relinquish control over life and death to some power that man did not understand. Girard donated money to improve the provisions of the makeshift Bush Hill Hospital and spent countless days there tending to the patients and the business needs of the facility. While many other men of means left the city, Girard actually bathed and cared for the victims.

By far, his greatest charitable concern was the orphans who roamed the city streets, stealing, begging, and prostituting themselves while subject to the taunts and blows of passersby. In Philadelphia, as in other major American cities in the early 1800s, high numbers of orphans and abandoned children resulted from the deaths of parents in childbirth or epidemics as well as the unprecedented rise in "illegitimate" births, which coincided with the decline in Christian morality and the rise of liberalism in early nationhood. As early as 1810, Girard conceived of founding a large boarding school to shelter and educate these children.

In 1826, at the age of seventy-six, Girard began to work on his will. He procured the services of well-known and respected attorney Horace Binney. In the document developed with Binney, Girard's basic conceptions for the school were outlined and his intent to have it serve liberal secular goals was clearly articulated. Yet, Girard continued to refine his plans, further developing his intentions in a redraft of his will.

Girard's will left $140,000 to various relatives, provided for the lifetime support of a one-time slave and long-term housekeeper, and distributed about $1 million among the various charities that he had supported during his life. The bulk of his estate, approximately $7 million, he donated to the city of Philadelphia to found a "college for poor white male orphans" (*Vidal, Girard, et al. v. Philadelphia*, 43 U.S. 126 [1844]). Reflecting Girard's adherence to the liberal philosophical doctrines of the Enlightenment, he prescribed that the school's instructors be chosen on merit to teach their practical knowledge of geography, grammar, reading, writing, mathematics, astronomy, and experimental philosophy.

Contrasting his desired educational methods with those provided in church-affiliated schools, courses in religion and ethics were absent from this curriculum. Girard explained that religion was merely "a speculative question," and he desired the boys in attendance at school to be free from religious prejudice at an early age, so that later in life they may "adopt such religious tenets as mature reason may prefer" (*Vidal* 1844, 132). Through a liberal and practical curriculum, Girard clearly sought to encourage "a pure attachment to our Republican Institutions" and instill "from inclination and habit . . . a love of industry" (*Vidal* 1844, 131). Consistent with the threat perceived by many liberals of the time that evangelical Christians were leading the Second Great Awakening (a religious revival started in the 1790s) in an attempt to overthrow the American Revolution, Girard forbid any Christian influence in his new school: "No ecclesiastic, missionary, or minister of any sect whatsoever, shall ever hold or exercise any station or duty whatever in the said college: nor shall any [such] person ever be admitted for any purpose, or as a visitor, within the premises appropriated to the purposes of the said college" (*Vidal* 1844, 132).

The greatest financier of the early American republic died in December 1831. As Girard expected, his heirs challenged the will, using his expressions against religious teaching as a means to attack the document's validity. They hired the noted Daniel Webster to represent them and the case made its way to the U.S. Supreme Court in 1844. The great orator told the court that "public policy" required that the will be voided, as it was "derogatory to the Christian religion, contrary to sound morals, and [therefore] subversive of laws" (*Vidal* 1844, 197).

Justice Joseph Story's decision was an important legal pronouncement on the law of philanthropy in the United States. First, the Court confirmed that to receive property, the benefactor of a will must be a legal entity—that is, either a person or a corporation. Second, a corporation may take the public or private form, but either way is bound to act in strict accordance with the decedent's or testator's intent if it accedes to the funds. Third, the Court found the will not to be inconsistent with public policy and therefore the State (the City of Philadelphia) was able to take the bequest if it was willing to follow Girard's instructions for its use. In 1848, Girard College opened its doors. Today, Girard College continues as a private but full-scholarship K–12 boarding school, with a college-preparatory curriculum, for children of limited financial means.

CONCLUSION

In life and in death, Stephen Girard confronted the American people with the significance of their own ideological liberalism. Treating all people as equals, he was perceived by many as unkind and uncharitable for his refusal to condescend, as would a benign patriarch, to their needs. Embracing the law of contracts, he sought to assert his rights to use his wealth to serve his perception of social needs, encouraging equal opportunity without endorsing moral duty. In the Court's endorsement of this right, he established the power of private individuals to contribute to their conception of the social good even when it is in conflict with prevailing social policy. In America, that has consistently been the role and the definition of philanthropy.

Mark McGarvie

FURTHER READING

Abbott, Edith. *Some American Pioneers in Social Welfare.* New York: Russell & Russell, 1963, 66–87.

Adams, Donald R. *Finance and Enterprise in Early America: A Study of Stephen Girard's Bank, 1812–1831.* Philadelphia: University of Pennsylvania Press, 1978.

———. "Portfolio Management and Profitability in Early-Nineteenth-Century Banking." *Business History Review,* Spring 1978, 61–79.

Husband, Joseph. *Americans by Adoption.* Boston: Atlantic Monthly Press, 1920.

Keats, John. "Consider the Curious Legacy of Stephen Girard." *American Heritage,* Fall 1978, 38–47.

McMaster, John Bach. *The Life and Times of Stephen Girard, Mariner and Merchant.* Philadelphia: Lippincott, 1918.

Miller, David S. "The Polly: A Perspective on Merchant Stephen Girard." *Pennsylvania Magazine of History and Biography,* April 1988, 189–208.

Minnigerode, Meade. *Certain Rich Men.* New York: G.P. Putnam's Sons, 1927, 3–30.

Taylor, Michele Taillon. "Building for Democracy: Girard College, Educational and Architectural Ideology." Diss. University of Pennsylvania, 1997.

Vidal, Girard, et al. v. Philadelphia, 43 U.S. 126 (1844).

PAPERS

Stephen Girard's papers are located at Girard College (Philadelphia, PA) and in the Division of Archives and Manuscripts at the Pennsylvania Historical and Museum Commission (Harrisburg, PA).

FREDERICK HARRIS GOFF
(1858–1923)

Lawyer, Banker, and Founder of the Cleveland Foundation and the Community Foundation Concept

INTRODUCTION

Frederick Harris Goff stated, "I hope the time will come when the law will recognize that property belongs to the living and not the dead" (Hayes Papers, Folder 180). In 1914, Goff created the Cleveland Foundation and in so doing established the concept of the community trust. The impetus for this new grantmaking institution rested on his desire to free bequests from what Sir Arthur Hobhouse had characterized as the "dead hand" of the past, and to establish a permanent source of funding for programs and projects that would benefit his adopted city, Cleveland, Ohio.

EARLY LIFE AND EDUCATION

Goff was born on December 15, 1858, to Frederick C. and Catherine Brown Goff in Blackbury, Illinois. After moving to Evanston, Illinois for a short time, the family came to Cleveland in 1864, where his father served as the chief agent for an agricultural implements company. Other than stories pointing to his early assumption to positions of responsibility, little is known of Goff's early life. He reputedly rode to Cleveland in the boxcar with the family's prize possession, its horse, safeguarding it throughout the journey. At the age of ten or twelve, he signed on as a crew member on a Great Lakes sailing vessel. Later, he served as a transit man for a railroad survey party in the Cleveland area. Sometime in the early 1870s, while Goff was still in his teens, the Goff family moved to Kansas because of his father's ill health. Frederick Goff, however, soon returned to Cleveland, attending the Hudson Street School. In 1874, he went to Ann Arbor, Michigan, where he attended high school and then the

University of Michigan, graduating in 1881. Thereafter, he returned to Cleveland where he studied for the bar and was admitted in 1883 or 1884.

CAREER HIGHLIGHTS

Goff's rise in the legal profession was rapid. Initially, he worked as a law librarian, using the money he earned to pay off his college debt. His first professional association was as a partner with William F. Carr in the firm Carr and Goff. By 1890, he was a member of the firm of Estep, Dickey, Carr, and Goff. Six years later, he was a partner in the firm of Kline, Tolles, and Goff. Both firms were active in the practice of corporate and estate law, and Kline, Tolles, and Goff served as a counsel for **John D. Rockefeller, Sr.**'s Standard Oil Company.

Goff specialized in reorganization and financial problems. His abilities were such that Rockefeller reputedly asked him to assume charge of his legal affairs. Since the job would have entailed Goff's removal to New York, he declined, preferring to stay in Cleveland where his career flourished. By the early 1900s, he earned in excess of $100,000 a year.

The first major change in Goff's career occurred as a consequence of his residence in Glenville, then an upper-class suburb some five miles to the east of the center of Cleveland. In 1896, he had married Frances Southworth, whose family operated a major wholesale grocery firm, securing his position among the area's social elite. His neighbors prevailed upon him to enter political life, asking him to run for the mayor of Glenville. At that time, the suburb's major controversy centered on gambling at the Glenville Race Track. While the track and the adjacent Roadside Club attracted the cream of local society, there was a concern that the betting was improper. The issue also clouded the chances for Glenville's annexation to Cleveland.

When Goff ran for mayor, he was unequivocal in his promise to end betting despite the fact that some of his neighbors and wealthy friends found it central to their social lives. When he won the office in 1903, he did so, an action that eventually drove the track from the area but also set the stage for Glenville's annexation to Cleveland in 1908. Goff's straightforward, moral approach to the situation was indicative of almost every aspect of his career.

The mayoral campaign in Glenville took place at the same time that the city of Cleveland underwent a major progressive political transformation led by Tom L. Johnson, the city's mayor from 1901 to 1909. Johnson's brand of progressivism, which included advocacy of municipal ownership of utilities and public urban transit, challenged the city's elite, many of whom had a financial interest in private utilities and transportation. For seven years, Johnson pursued his "transit war" in an effort to create cheaper fares for residents. By 1906, Johnson's system, Municipal Traction Company, was competing with the major privately held system, the Cleveland Railway Company. The result was not reform, but bankruptcy. Both Johnson and the owners of the Cleveland Railway Company found themselves in Federal District Court with Johnson appointed as receiver for his company and Frederick Goff for the private lines.

Johnson and Goff had every reason to dislike one another, the former viewed as a radical reformer and the latter as a "representative of vested interests" (Howard 1963, 3). Yet, to Johnson's surprise, he found Goff to be flexible and open to his ideas of affordable transit. The plan they worked out with Federal Judge Robert Tayler called for the city to control the transit lines, but lease them back to a private company with the guarantee of a 6 percent return. The plan worked for nearly three decades and Johnson and Goff became friends.

During the transit compromise, Goff made a major change in his career, leaving the practice of law for banking. In 1908, the directors of the Cleveland Trust Company asked him to become its first full-time president because his work on the transit problem had greatly impressed them. He accepted promptly, sacrificing approximately $75,000 a year as the bank position paid only $25,000.

MAJOR PHILANTHROPIC CONTRIBUTIONS

At the age of fifty, it is likely that Goff was looking for a change of pace. It is also probable that he knew the job with Cleveland Trust would allow him to test some theories he had concerning trusts and bequests. Under U.S. and British law, a deceased donor's expressed intent for a charitable bequest, even when that purpose became obsolete, could not be altered without incurring huge legal costs and sometimes decades of legal wrangling. As a lawyer, Goff had, for many years, known of and become concerned about trusts and bequests that were locked into antiquated or irrelevant purposes. He knew, for example, that **Benjamin Franklin**'s will established a trust to provide loans to apprentices and the trust remained long after apprentices ceased to exist. When he worked with the law firm representing John D. Rockefeller Sr., he undoubtedly became more aware of the issues pertaining to the efficient disposal of charitable donations.

His interests in these issues led him to read Sir Arthur Hobhouse's writings on the topic of bequests. In a book of Hobhouse's speeches entitled *The Dead Hand*, Goff marked off the following quotation: "The grip of the dead hand shall be shaken off absolutely and finally; in other words, that there shall always be a living and reasonable owner of property, to manage it according to the wants of mankind. This again must be a public tribunal charged with the duty of adjusting to new objects all foundations which have become pernicious and useless" (Howard 1963, 6). Goff became fixated on the matter of the "dead hand" (known as the legal doctrine of cy pres), so much so that he constantly talked about it with friends and family. Purportedly, one of his young daughters (he had three children, Fredericka, William S., and Frances) hesitated to climb a dark staircase at home for fear that the "dead hand would reach out and grab her" (Howard 1963, 7).

Goff first tested his theories at Cleveland Trust by making provisions for living trusts wherein donors could begin the disposition of their funds during their lifetime. Goff himself did so, seeing that his three children had sufficient funds to live well, but not an excess of money. He was intent that his children would prosper on their own merits. The living trust was one of many innovations Goff made at the bank. In the fifteen years that he served as its president, Cleveland Trust expanded from 15 branches, 70,000 depositors, and $30 million in assets to 52 branches, 397,000 depositors, and $176 million in assets. At the time of Goff's death in 1923, Cleveland Trust ranked as the nation's sixth largest bank.

The Cleveland Trust Bank became the platform on which Goff built his most lasting charitable legacy, the community foundation. While Goff, like many of his wealthy peers, donated personal funds to local charities and sat on the boards of organizations such as Hiram House Social Settlement, he worried about larger issues in philanthropy, such as the "dead hand" and the long-term rational use of charitable funds for the civic good.

Meanwhile, Goff's Cleveland was on its way to becoming the nation's fifth largest city and, during the first two decades of the twentieth century, possessed a reputation as one of the nation's most progressive cities. In fact, the creation or founding of the Federation for Charity and Philanthropy (which included Frances Goff as one of its fifteen founders and subsequently evolved into a community chest and then the United Way), the Cleveland City Club (a forum for the open discussion of political and social issues), and cultural organizations such as the Cleveland Orchestra and the Cleveland Museum of Art were hallmarks of Cleveland's growth into progressive urban maturity.

In 1914, Goff acted on his concerns about bequests and the needs of Cleveland when he created what might be considered the capstone of the city's progressive period, the Cleveland Foundation. The Cleveland Foundation was the nation's first community trust and one of only a dozen or so foundations in existence at that time (others included **Andrew Carnegie**'s Carnegie Corporation and

John D. Rockefeller Sr.'s General Education Board). The Cleveland Foundation combined two basic ideas. First, it allowed a number of bequests (large and small) to be pooled into a common fund administered by a single trustee, the Cleveland Trust Bank (in 1931 the foundation would change to a policy of multiple trustees), to meet general civic purposes. This plan had the merit of allowing individuals with even small estates to know that their bequests could be devoted to substantial endeavors. Second, an ongoing board of directors would administer the pooled funds. This operational feature was the "living hand" that allowed the foundation to continually redirect or redefine the needs it would fund. While the foundation would accept bequests that were designated toward a specific purpose within its general guidelines, the board had the power to modify the use of those funds when the purpose was no longer valid or viable.

Goff initially conceived of the foundation as being governed by trustees selected by the bank. The editor of a local newspaper, the *Cleveland Press*, suggested that publicly appointed members be a part of the decision-making board if Goff, indeed, wanted his creation to represent the community. Goff's wife also argued this point. Thus, Goff modified his concept to include three individuals appointed by public officials (including the city's mayor) on the foundation's five-person distribution committee.

The Cleveland Foundation, which was created on January 2, 1914, took several years to accumulate enough capital to begin distribution. In the interim, personal donations from Goff and from the Cleveland Trust Bank underwrote its activities. Chief among them were major surveys of community conditions—ranging from criminal justice to education. These surveys bore the stamp of rational progressive planning and of Goff's own insistence on doing things properly.

Goff quickly developed a national reputation. In the wake of the "Ludlow Massacre" at the Rockefeller-owned Colorado Fuel and Iron Company in 1915, for example, he was called to New York City to testify at federal hearings regarding charitable trusts and the possible manipulation of public opinion by those trusts. His answers to the sometimes hostile questions of labor lawyer Frank P. Walsh regarding the purposes of the Cleveland Foundation served only to build its reputation and, ultimately, to win Walsh over to his side.

CONCLUSION

Despite such national attention, Goff remained wedded to his adopted city, devoting much of the last nine years of his life to the foundation he had created and to investigating how it could help Cleveland. Moreover, his concept of the community trust was transcendent. After Goff's death on March 14, 1923, Ralph Hayes testified to this fact. Hayes had served as Goff's personal assistant at Cleveland Trust in the years after World War I and then gone on to become the first director of the New York Community Trust. In a speech given before the Cleveland City Club in 1926, Hayes noted that the Cleveland Foundation "would one day be deemed as Cleveland's most important contribution to the ideas of the world" (Tittle 1992, 24). Given the pervasiveness and influence of community foundations in early twenty-first century America, Hayes may well have been correct in his assessment of Frederick Goff's principal legacy.

John J. Grabowski

FURTHER READING

Frederick Harris Goff, A Memorial. Cleveland: Cleveland Trust Co., 1924.

Howard, Nathaniel R. *Trust for All Time: The Story of the Cleveland Foundation and the Community Trust Movement.* Cleveland: Cleveland Foundation, 1963.

Tittle, Diana. *Rebuilding Cleveland: The Cleveland Foundation and Its Evolving Urban Strategy.* Columbus: Ohio State University Press, 1992.

Van Tassel, David D., and John J. Grabowski, eds. *The Dictionary of Cleveland Biography.* Bloomington: Indiana University Press, 1996.

———. *The Encyclopedia of Cleveland History.* Bloomington: Indiana University Press, 1987.

PAPERS

A single body of Fredrick Harris Goff papers does not exist but material relating to and generated by Goff can be found in the Cleveland Foundation Records and the Ralph Hayes Papers at the Western Reserve Historical Society (Cleveland, OH).

PIERRE FRIST GOODRICH
(1894–1973)

Attorney, Entrepreneur, and Founder of the Liberty Fund

INTRODUCTION

If people are to attain their "full potential," wrote Pierre Frist Goodrich in 1961, "is it not clear and reasonable to say that there is a basic necessity for liberty?" This, he continued, "together with the known necessity for individual development in order to maintain liberty, makes it desirable to provide for research . . . so that the knowledge of the past and the present may be useful within the full capacity of individuals" (Goodrich 1961, 18). By establishing and carefully prescribing the operating philosophy of the Liberty Fund, Goodrich, a successful Indiana lawyer and businessman, created a program aimed at disseminating and discussing new and classical works on the concept of liberty, one that has been remarkably faithful to its donor's ideals for over a quarter-century.

Pierre Frist Goodrich. Courtesy of the Liberty Fund, Inc.

EARLY YEARS AND EDUCATION

Pierre Goodrich's life began in the small Western Indiana community of Winchester. Son of James and Cora Goodrich, he was a shy, quiet, studious boy who was not particularly athletic and attended public schools throughout the primary grades. During his early years, he learned to play the violin and became involved in a young men's dance troupe. Much of his childhood was spent under his mother's influence, as his father, together with his uncles, built a commercial empire. James Goodrich also served as the Indiana State Republican Party Chairman for nearly ten years, governor of Indiana from 1917 to 1921, and special advisor to Presidents Warren G. Harding, Calvin Coolidge, and **Herbert Hoover**.

From early on, Pierre Goodrich possessed a strong appetite for learning. According to one account, after his father had bought a new car, "Pierre methodically took the vehicle apart to see how it was built and then put it back together" (Starbuck 2001, 59). After graduation from Winchester High School, Goodrich attended Wabash College in Crawfordsville, Indiana. He graduated Phi Beta Kappa in 1916 with a bachelor's degree in humanities. He then matriculated to Harvard University Law School, where he attended one year before spending two years serving his country in World War I as a second lieutenant in the Army Quartermasters Corps. He went back to Harvard University and finished his law degree in 1920.

After graduation, Goodrich returned to Winchester and began to practice law, forming an association with John Macy under the firm name Macy and Goodrich. He also took part in his family's numerous business ventures. In 1923, Goodrich moved to Indianapolis and launched what some called "one of the most diversified careers in the city's history" (*Indianapolis Star* 1973, A1).

CAREER HIGHLIGHTS

In Indianapolis, Goodrich became a member of the firm Haynes and Mote, which became Mote and Goodrich after the 1923 death of Paul Haynes. Goodrich developed into one of the most well-respected corporate lawyers in Indiana and most of the law firm's business came from the Goodrich family companies. From the 1940s to 1960s, many of these companies experienced tremendous success, including Ayrshire Collieries Coal Corporation, Peoples Loan and Trust (a Winchester-based bank), the Indiana Telephone Corporation, City Securities, and Central Newspapers.

Goodrich regularly worked twelve-hour days, occasionally all day and night just to prove he possessed the fortitude. This work ethic, coupled with his keen intellect, played an important role in the success of the Goodrich business empire. He also instituted various business practices that are now commonplace among similar companies. For instance, at Peoples Bank and Trust, he initiated fee-based services long before any other bank considered the practice. At the Ayrshire Collieries Coal Corporation, he started the practice of reclaiming the stripmined coalfields, which was not required by state and federal law for another thirty years. In another farsighted act, Goodrich outlawed smoking in all of his office buildings in 1960.

In the mid-1940s, the success of the family-owned businesses allowed Goodrich to turn "decidedly intellectual and associational" (Starbuck 2001, 312). As he often told his long-time assistant Ruth E. Connolly, his "education did not really begin until after he left Harvard law school, because it was then that he became involved in the 'Great Books'" (personal communication with author, August 7, 2000). He subsequently became active in the Great Books Foundation, an organization founded by the University of Chicago's former president, Robert Maynard Hutchins, to promote reading and discussion of classical works by ordinary Americans. According to a rare magazine article about him, the wealthy Indianapolis lawyer "had suddenly taken to touring Indiana's small towns, sleeping in second-class hotels, eating in hamburger joints, rubbing elbows with plain folks—all this to get them to join groups to discuss the ideas of Aristotle, Plato, St. Thomas Aquinas, Shakespeare, John Locke, Rousseau and others" (Fraser 1948, 20). In the same period, he also began attending meetings of the Mont Pelerin Society (a group created by future Nobel Prize–winning economist F.A. Hayek), the Foundation for Economic Education, and the Institute of Humane Studies, each of which was established to advance the cause of economic and political liberty.

MAJOR PHILANTHROPIC CONTRIBUTIONS

Throughout his adult life, Goodrich was dedicated to several local nonprofit organizations. He was a long-time Wabash College trustee, founder of the Winchester Community Foundation, and supporter of local music and education charities. Still, he did not create his lasting legacy, the Liberty Fund, until 1960. The foundation, according to James Buchanan, Nobel Laureate (1986) in Economics, "is the permanent embodiment of Pierre Goodrich's faith in the power of ideas and his personal belief that ideas are more exciting and more important than things" (Starbuck 2001, xvi). The *Liberty Fund Basic Memorandum*, written by Goodrich, served as both a statement of his philosophy and a detailed operating manual for the foundation. In the 129-page document (which has never been published), Goodrich stated that he created the fund that "some hopeful contribution may be made to the preservation, restoration, and development of individual liberty through investigation, research, and educational activity" (Starbuck 2001, 414). The *Memorandum* went on to describe the qualities Goodrich desired in trustees and staff, how the fund's assets were to be managed, the way in which its programs were to be run, and, not least importantly, the knowledge those directing it should have to discharge their responsibilities faithfully.

Goodrich's guidance included a "Liberty Fund Book List," aimed, he wrote, at "giving some partial perspective of the cultural conversations and experiences which were a part of the background of the people who wrote the Declaration of Independence and the Constitution of the United States" (Goodrich 1961, 111). The titles amounted to a compendium of the classics of Western political thought. While he expected the Fund's trustees and staff to have read many of these books, he was under no illusion that they provided all the answers. To the contrary, he wrote, "This Book List should help in the sense of humility and awareness of the nature of the choice of imperfections by which decisions may be made in favor of liberty" (Goodrich 1961, 111).

During the 1960s and 1970s, the Liberty Fund primarily served as a grant-making foundation, underwriting seminars, publications, and organizations whose activities were consistent with its philosophy. However, before his death on October 25, 1973, Goodrich began to take steps to change the Liberty Fund to an operating foundation that would conduct its own programs. Due to tax obstacles (overcome with assistance from future Central Intelligence Agency chief William Casey), this change officially occurred after a three-year probationary transition period, which began in May 1975 and ended with the Internal Revenue Service granting it

operating-foundation status in March 1979.

The main focus of the Liberty Fund's activities is a series of conferences—currently, over 175 a year—that allow scholars from around the world to congregate, study, and discuss issues related to liberty. The conferences are based upon the great works and ideas of the past: recent topics have ranged from "Jefferson, Madison, and the Constitution of a Liberal Republic" to "Liberty in Melville's *Moby Dick*." Papers are presented and discussed in a Socratic manner that bears more than passing resemblance to the Great Books Foundation seminars that had made such a deep impression on Goodrich.

Over the years, an extraordinary group of scholars has led or participated in these symposia, often on multiple occasions. In addition to James Buchanan, these meeting have included historians Stephen Tonsor and Forrest McDonald, political theorists Ralph Lerner and Kenneth Minogue, and the economist Benjamin A. Rogge, a Wabash College professor who also served as a Liberty Fund trustee. While there is no way to gauge its impact with precision, the program's longevity alone—through more than two decades—has enabled it to leave a mark on the thinking, writing, and teaching of literally thousands of college and university professors, as well as their students.

The Liberty Fund's other major focus is more easily measurable and has perhaps been even more important: its publishing program. At a board meeting in August 1972, Henry Regnery, a Chicago publisher who featured the works of Hayek, Russell Kirk, and other conservatives and classical liberals, reported to Goodrich and his trustees that producing serious books was becoming financially difficult. He urged them to begin subsidizing the printing of six or ten "very high quality" titles each year.

From that recommendation has come a publication list of over 100 important books, including many that had previously been out of print or inaccessible, priced inexpensively, and printed and bound to be long-lasting. Among the best known are the definitive

Glasgow edition of Adam Smith's writings, David Hume's *History of England*, the collected works of James Buchanan, and influential volumes by Bernard Mandeville, Lord Acton, Michael Oakeshott, Bertrand de Jouvenel, and others. Just as some philanthropists direct their resources to preserving historical buildings, the Liberty Fund has devoted a portion of its funds to preserving classical texts—the very kinds, in fact, that Goodrich had placed on his "Book List."

With the death of his widow, Enid Goodrich, in 1996, the Liberty Fund received additional bequests, pushing its assets to nearly $300 million. This enabled it to expand its conference and publishing programs, as well as to make more grants through a new affiliate, the Pierre F. and Enid Goodrich Foundation. Rather than embark on new ventures, this foundation's work is governed by Goodrich's vision, as its guidelines stated: "Grant support should be confined to those known to the Directors . . . to be committed to the ideals of Liberty Fund, as discussed at length in . . . the *Liberty Fund Basic Memorandum*" (Pierre F. and Enid Goodrich Foundation 2000, 4).

CONCLUSION

"Pierre F. Goodrich was the most complicated man I have ever known," a Wabash College friend, Byron K. Trippet, has written (Trippet 1982, 182). That may have been true about his thinking or his business life, but with regard to his philanthropy, Goodrich was nothing if not single-minded. Moreover, what appeared to Trippet (and undoubtedly others) to be stinginess in giving, a desire for "elaborate continuing controls over whatever he did give," was perhaps instead a reflection of Goodrich's strong wish to see that his donations were used as he intended (Trippet 1982, 79).

Forty years after he wrote the *Basic Memorandum*, a quarter-century after his death,

and with only one of his original trustees still active, the Liberty Fund's continued adherence to Goodrich's intentions is remarkable. Moreover, it has done so with programs that still make important contributions to intellectual and public life, both in the United States and, increasingly, throughout the world.

To those who believe that foundations must change with the times to be effective, the Liberty Fund presents an example of one that has not done so, but has succeeded. Like the concept of liberty it champions, its history suggests that a donor's vision can be timeless and that faithfulness to it can result in much that is valuable.

W. David Lasater and Leslie Lenkowsky

FURTHER READING

Fraser, Hugh Russell. "Unlocking the Great Books." *Pathfinder*, February 25, 1948, 20–23.

Goodrich, Pierre F. *Liberty Fund Basic Memorandum*. Privately printed, 1961.

Liberty Fund. [Brochure]. Indianapolis, IN: Author, 2000.

Pierre F. and Enid Goodrich Foundation. [Brochure]. Indianapolis, IN: Author, 2000.

"Pierre Frist Goodrich." In *The National Cyclopaedia of American Biography*, vol. 59. New York: James T. White & Company, 1980, 206–207.

"Pierre F. Goodrich Dies; Business Executive Had Diversified Career." *Indianapolis Star*, October 26, 1973, A1.

Starbuck, Dane. *The Goodriches: An American Family*. Indianapolis: Liberty Fund, 2001.

Trippet, Byron K. *Wabash on My Mind*. Crawfordsville, IN: Wabash College, 1982.

PAPERS

Though not a complete collection, many of Pierre F. Goodrich's papers are located at the offices of the Liberty Fund (Indianapolis, IN).

ACKNOWLEDGMENTS

The authors of this entry owe a debt of gratitude to Dane Starbuck, who allowed them to review his unfinished manuscript on the Goodrich Family.

REBECCA GRATZ
(1781–1869)

Founder of American Jewish Women's Charitable Organizations and the First Jewish Sunday School

INTRODUCTION

"Nothing interests me like the development of young minds," Rebecca Gratz wrote to a friend in 1834 (Ashton 1997, 138). By organizing two charitable societies for women and two orphanages in her hometown of Philadelphia, Gratz aided many young people. Of all her charitable efforts, she felt that her "crowning glory" was the Hebrew Sunday School, the first such Jewish school in history, which she founded and served as both superintendent and teacher. Soon after launching her school in Philadelphia, Gratz advised Jewish women in other American cities and towns to establish similar schools in their communities. While most of her organizations continued to thrive until long after her death, her dedication and success made her the leading American Jewish woman of the nineteenth century.

EARLY YEARS AND EDUCATION

Although Gratz worked to aid the poor, her own family was quite wealthy. Michael and Barnard Gratz, her father and uncle, respectively, came to colonial Pennsylvania from Silesia in the 1750s, at a time when the colonial city of Philadelphia was growing rapidly. While working as merchant traders, shipping Pennsylvania's goods to ports along the east coast and the Caribbean, the Gratz brothers helped to put the local synagogue on a more secure footing by assisting in writing its charter and donating needed funds. Michael Gratz's children continued his businesses and formed new ones, such as insurance companies and banks, and used their wealth and influence to help establish many new educational, religious, charitable, and political organizations in Philadelphia.

Rebecca Gratz was a middle child, one of twelve born to Michael and Miriam (Simon) Gratz. Ten Gratz children survived to adulthood, and Rebecca Gratz's early years were spent in the noisy sociability of a large household. Like other families of their class, the Gratz children were taught at an early age to read the classic literature that was imported from England and to write polite letters. While still a girl, Rebecca Gratz formed a love for both literature and letter writing that lasted throughout her life. Few schools for girls existed when she was young, but she probably attended the Young Ladies Academy in Philadelphia when she was in her early teens. There, she studied literature, geography, chemistry, natural philosophy, some Christian teachings, and the republican political values shared by many Americans in the country's early years. From that experience, Gratz developed a sense of patriotism based on the political ideas of her era, acquired a sophisticated and literary letter-writing style, and learned to intelligently defend Judaism against Christian critics.

Gratz grew up seeing charitable activity as a way of life. In addition to his work with the Philadelphia synagogue, her father regularly sent funds to his family in Europe and to special charities in their community. In Lancaster, Gratz's maternal grandfather opened his home to all local Jews for religious services. Meanwhile, her mother was known for her nursing abilities and personal charity and led her daughters in more formal charitable endeavors that aided women and children. Rebecca Gratz's five brothers even helped establish three local libraries, an art school, a school for the deaf, and a college of Jewish

Rebecca Gratz. American Jewish Historical Society, Waltham, Massachusetts and New York, New York.

studies, while also leading their synagogue and donating to many different charitable societies in Philadelphia.

When she was nineteen years old, Gratz's life took a new direction as she learned to deal with personal losses. Her father suffered a stroke that left him, for a time, bedridden and unable to speak. Few hospitals existed in those years, and most medical care was received at home. Rebecca Gratz and her mother shared the many activities of nursing and caring for Michael Gratz, although the teenager found it agonizing. She felt guilty about her feelings and about not being more helpful to her mother. During her father's illness, Gratz's friends told her about their parties and romances while she stayed at home caring for her parent, providing emotional support to her mother, and learning a self-discipline that was new to her. That experience was the beginning of a new family

role for Rebecca Gratz, as she slowly took over her mother's place in serving as nurse to their large family. Gratz remained a family nurse for most of her life, and helped to deliver and care for the twenty-two children born to her three sisters who married. Three years after her father's stroke launched her into nursing, she was able to explain her philosophy of life, assuring friends that although "there are many kinds of trials in this life, an unsubdued spirit can overcome them all" (Ashton 1997, 51).

CAREER HIGHLIGHTS

By creating new voluntary associations, Rebecca Gratz devised a career for herself in an era when few women enjoyed such self-fulfillment. Early nineteenth-century America denied women equal access to education, to wage-labor, and if married, to own any wealth other than inherited land. Gratz never married and her single status allowed her to control the funds provided for her by her father and brothers and to use that money to launch charities and schools. Although she served on the boards of directors of all of her organizations, she never took the post of president. She preferred to be secretary. In that position, she could use her writing talent and abilities to further her causes, while earning praise for her moving appeals and clear descriptions of both needy cases and the accomplishments of her groups. She found friends and colleagues among Philadelphia's charitable women and among the women in her congregation, with whom she established several new charities for Jews. She also helped to raise several of her many nieces and nephews and took a personal interest in children aided by her organizations. Thus, Gratz's career provided her self-fulfillment, regular meetings with congenial friends and colleagues, a route to effect and improve her world, and the delights of children, but no income.

MAJOR PHILANTHROPIC CONTRIBUTIONS

It was with her mother, younger sister Rachel, and twenty other women that Gratz helped to organize a women's charitable society in 1801 (when she was only twenty years old). This association represented the first nonsectarian women's charitable organization in Philadelphia, and eight of its twenty-three founders were Jews. Called the Female Association for the Relief of Women in Reduced Circumstances, its purpose was to aid women whose households had lost their financial security in the economic turbulence that followed the American Revolution. Because the laws of that day did not allow a married woman to own money independently of her husband, the Female Association provided goods and resources to help such women care for their families and themselves with funds that would not go to pay their husband's debts. The charity insisted that recipients educate their children in an era when most poor children were sent out to work.

The Female Association also required their treasurer to be an unmarried woman. Gratz served as an officer of the organization for many years. There she learned about organizing and gained an understanding of poverty that remained with her throughout her life.

Fourteen years after establishing the Female Association, Gratz joined other Philadelphia women to organize the Philadelphia Orphan Asylum. Like the Female Association, the Philadelphia Orphan Asylum served all faiths. Gratz served as its secretary for many years, writing its charter, minutes, annual reports, and fund-raising letters. She loved writing these documents, and carried the same responsibilities in all of the agencies she founded.

A second tragedy struck the Gratz household in 1817, when Rebecca Gratz's older sister Sarah died after an illness of several months. By this time, both Gratz's mother and father had passed away. Sarah and Rebecca Gratz had run the family home where their three unmarried brothers also resided. Rebecca Gratz always felt that her older sister was the better nurse and housekeeper, and the person to whom she turned most often for emotional support in her personal life. Gratz mourned her sister's death deeply. To cope with that loss, she turned to her religion, and became even more concerned about the welfare of her congregation and the future of Judaism in America. By the end of the year, she organized an informal Hebrew school in her home for her many nieces and nephews (along with any adults). The instructor had applied for the position of rabbi at her synagogue but instead found work teaching for the Gratz family.

In the two years following her sister's death, Gratz spent much of her time among other women in her congregation. Then, in 1819, she organized some of those women to establish the first independent Jewish women's charitable society in the country, the Female Hebrew Benevolent Society. This society not only served all the Jews of Philadelphia and eastern Pennsylvania, but often received requests for aid from Jews as far away as Alabama and Kentucky. When Jewish women in New York City subsequently organized a similar organization, they adopted the same name and made Gratz an honorary member. Within twenty years, Jewish women in towns around the country had organized their own Female Hebrew Benevolent Societies.

Gratz and the Philadelphia society women had hoped to improve the city's meager Jewish educational resources. At that time, no formal Jewish school existed in that region. The best Hebrew readers in congregations would train boys for Bar Mitzvah, but nowhere were children formally trained in Jewish beliefs. Gratz turned to the Female Hebrew Benevolent Society women to establish a Jewish version of the Protestant Sunday schools that were springing up all over America, many of them headquartered in Philadelphia. Called the Hebrew Sunday School, it enrolled students for the first time in 1838. Gratz served as Hebrew Sunday School superintendent until late in her life. Two Jewish women, who ran a secular school in their home, joined her as its first faculty and wrote some of its early textbooks. She often turned to the rabbi of her synagogue for advice and for new textbooks, which he translated from German volumes available in Europe. Immediately, the Hebrew Sunday School was successful. Gratz soon sent lesson plans and advice to women in Charleston, South Carolina, and New York City who established similar schools there. The Philadelphia school continued to thrive throughout the nineteenth and twentieth centuries.

Gratz continued to provide direction to all her organizations even as she created new ones. Through her work on the Philadelphia Orphan Asylum, she knew that Jewish children who came under its care would be instructed in Christianity, rather than their own faith. Although the asylum opened its doors to all children, it was not nonsectarian and often refused to allow its children to be adopted by families whose religious beliefs the mostly Presbyterian Philadelphia Orphan Asylum board did not approve. Moreover, Presbyterian ministers regularly instructed the asylum's children and led them in Prot-

estant worship. By the 1840s, as Jewish immigration from central Europe increased and the numbers of poor and broken Jewish families in Philadelphia rose, Gratz began to argue for an establishment to care for the needy children of those families but a foster home was an expensive undertaking. Finally, the Jewish Foster Home and Orphan Asylum opened its doors in 1855. Gratz, then seventy-four years old, initially served only as an advisor. Soon, she was convinced to take on the role of vice president. Having earned a reputation for effective care and good management, she assured prospective donors that the organization would be run well.

CONCLUSION

Gratz transformed the landscape of Jewish life for women and children in early America. Her organizations provided instruction as well as material and financial aid for their recipients, and sociability and self-fulfillment for the many women who served in them. By refusing to take the presidency in any of her organizations, she encouraged many other women to take leadership roles and make the work their own. Although Gratz donated funds to these groups, she never solely supported any of them. Instead, she advised them on good financial management and helped the groups to gain the financial support of most other philanthropically minded individuals among the local Jewish community. By drawing others into the projects she led, she made them successful and responsive to community needs as she understood them. Through her published organizational reports, she convinced others that her organizations were crucial to the future of Jewish life in America. At the same time, she made herself a beloved figure. Philadelphians widely believed her to be the inspiration for the character of Rebecca of York in Sir Walter Scott's popular novel *Ivanhoe*. Like the fictional Rebecca, Gratz was seen as lovely, loyal to her family, and rumored to have refused to wed a non-Jew through devotion to her faith. Her labor on behalf of others made her the foremost Jewish American woman of the nineteenth century.

Dianne C. Ashton

FURTHER READING

Ashton, Dianne. *Rebecca Gratz: Women and Judaism in Antebellum America.* Detroit: Wayne State University Press, 1997.

———. "Souls Have No Sex: Philadelphia Jewish Women and the American Challenge." In *When Philadelphia Was the Capital of Jewish America,* ed. Murray Friedman. London: Associated University Presses, 1993, 34–57.

Rosenbloom, Joseph. "Rebecca Gratz and the Jewish Sunday School Movement in Philadelphia." *Publications of the American Jewish Historical Society,* 47, no. 2, 1958, 71–77.

PAPERS

Collections of letters by Rebecca Gratz are located in the American Jewish Archives (Cincinnati, OH), American Jewish Historical Society (Center for Jewish History, New York City), and American Philosophical Society (Philadelphia, PA).

GUGGENHEIM FAMILY

Meyer Guggenheim (1828–1905)

Founder of the Guggenheim Fortune

Daniel Guggenheim (1856–1930)

Industrialist and Founder of the Daniel and Florence Guggenheim Foundation and the Daniel Guggenheim Fund for the Promotion of Aeronautics

Solomon R. Guggenheim (1861–1949)

Industrialist and Founder of the Solomon R. Guggenheim Foundation and the Solomon R. Guggenheim Museum

Simon Guggenheim (1867–1941)

Industrialist and Founder of the John Simon Guggenheim Memorial Foundation

Harry Frank Guggenheim (1890–1971)

Cofounder of Newsday, *Founder of the Harry Frank Guggenheim Foundation, and President of the Solomon R. Guggenheim Museum*

Marguerite "Peggy" Guggenheim (1898–1979)

Art Collector and Patron

INTRODUCTION

During the first half of the twentieth century, the Guggenheim family comprised some of the period's most energetic philanthropists. Their interests ranged from abstract art to aviation, from literature to dentistry. Indeed, Guggenheim Fellowships aided most of the important authors who flourished between 1925 and 1975, while many modern painters were encouraged by

Solomon Guggenheim or his niece Peggy Guggenheim. Although the Guggenheim foundations are well known, the family remains obscure. Today, few connect the Guggenheims to copper as easily as they equate **Henry Ford** with cars or **Andrew Carnegie** with steel. Still, it is clear that Meyer Guggenheim had grand ambitions, which his children amply fulfilled. According to the anonymous author of a 1930 *Fortune* profile, Meyer Guggenheim said "not once, but many times, 'I have seven sons, and each of them will have a million dollars' " (*Fortune* 1930, 86).

MEYER GUGGENHEIM CREATES THE GUGGENHEIM FORTUNE

Meyer Guggenheim grew up in Langnau, a relatively poor area of western Switzerland, and emigrated to the United States in 1848 with his father, the first Simon Guggenheim. During the trip, Meyer Guggenheim also met his future wife, Barbara Meyers. In America, father and son roamed the streets of Philadelphia with a pushcart, hawking needles, lace, glue, and shoe polish. In the early 1860s, Meyer Guggenheim acquired the rights to a shoe polish that did not blacken customers' hands. He then used his wealth to buy lace factories in Switzerland. By 1872, these factories were sending a steady flow of profits to the United States. In the 1870s, Meyer Guggenheim was regularly making trips to Switzerland, taking many of his sons with him to add some European polish to their American educations.

Meyer Guggenheim began to diversify his investments and created (in partnership with his sons) M. Guggenheim's Sons in 1881. The partnership's first investment was to spend $5,000 for a 50% interest in two mines in Leadville, Colorado called the A.Y. and the Minnie. Few thought these flooded mines were profitable, but Meyer Guggenheim proved them wrong. When the mines were drained, they found them packed with silver. Meyer Guggenheim had become what

journalists of the day called a "Bonanza King" (O'Connor 1937, 57).

By 1889, the Guggenheim family was out of the lace business and went into mining fulltime as Philadelphia Mining and Smelting. In 1890, they acquired a concession in Monterey, Mexico, which proved to be a lucrative source of low-cost lead and silver. In 1899, Guggenheim's competitors formed American Smelting and Refining as a trust to which twenty-three competitors united—all except the Guggenheims. Between 1899 and 1900, American Smelting and the Guggenheims waged a bitter war against each other. In December 1900, the Guggenheims, for $45.2 million, purchased a majority interest in American Smelting, which became the cornerstone of the Guggenheim fortune. Later called ASARCO, American Smelting and Refining remained one of America's leading mining companies until it was bought out by Grupo Mexico in 1999.

In 1905, Meyer Guggenheim died. Unlike his children, he was not a great philanthropist, although he did give steadily to Jewish charities in Philadelphia, including the Hebrew Benevolent and Orphan Asylum, the Montefiore Home for Chronic Invalids, and the Mt. Sinai Hospital. Still, Meyer Guggenheim taught his children that wealth was something that could be used to better humanity. He was opposed to the notion that wealth creators should simply accumulate capital without putting it to good use. Financier Bernard Baruch, who frequently worked with the Guggenheims, recalled in his memoirs a story about someone who called on Meyer Guggenheim with a moneymaking idea. "See Mr. Guggenheim," the man said, "what wealth, what power that would give you!" Meyer Guggenheim stroked his muttonchop whiskers, and remarked, "*Und denn?*" (Baruch 1957, 193). The notion of putting wealth to good use, Baruch wrote, "was characteristic of all the Guggenheims. They believed a project had to do more than just make money. They showed the same breadth of interest in their philanthropies" (Baruch 1957, 193).

THE GUGGENHEIM FORTUNE IN THE TWENTIETH CENTURY

Meyer Guggenheim had seven sons who reached adulthood. Isaac Guggenheim showed no interest in the family enterprise. William Guggenheim and Benjamin Guggenheim both split from the remaining four brothers in about 1910, ensuring that their fortunes would be relatively small. William Guggenheim was a spendthrift who dissipated his inheritance on wild-eyed schemes and left a tiny legacy to four girlfriends, including a former Miss America and a former Miss Connecticut. In 1912, Benjamin Guggenheim sank with the *Titanic*.

The remaining four Guggenheim brothers—Daniel, Murray, Simon, and Solomon—were actively involved both in American Smelting and Refining, as well as M. Guggenheim's Sons and Guggenheim Exploration (or Guggenex), which conducted more speculative mining activities. The Guggenheims extended their exploration, opening successful mines in the Yukon, the Congo, Arizona, Utah, and Alaska. In 1916, they organized all their copper mines and Guggenheim Exploration into Kennecott Copper, a highly profitable enterprise. Their greatest coup was in Chile, where engineer Albert C. Burrage convinced the Guggenheims that he had found a massive source of low-grade copper ore. The Guggenheims investigated, and found that he had found 300 million tons of 3% ore in a region known as Chuquicasnata. In 1914, they founded Chile Exploration to conduct their mining operations in that nation. Using government surplus equipment from the construction of the Panama Canal, the Guggenheims found their Chilean operations quite lucrative, particularly as demand for the metal increased during World War I.

In 1922, the Guggenheims sold Chile Exploration to Anaconda for $70 million. At the time this sale ensured that the Guggenheims were one of the richest families in America. The *New York Times* estimated the family to be worth $200 million (O'Connor 1937, 422). "The **Rockefellers** have more wealth," a *Fortune* profile noted in 1930, and "Henry Ford is wealthier than any Guggenheim. "But," someone has said, "there is only one Henry Ford, and there are a lot of Guggenheims" (*Fortune* 1930, 88).

DANIEL GUGGENHEIM

The oldest member of the second generation of Guggenheims, Daniel Guggenheim was born on July 9, 1856, in Philadelphia. In 1873, he abandoned formal education and spent the remainder of his career working for various Guggenheim enterprises, capping his career by serving as chairman of the board of American Smelting and Refining from 1901 until his retirement in 1919. While pursuing business ventures, he married Florence Schloss in 1884 and the couple produced three children. Guggenheim biographer Harvey O'Connor notes that Daniel Guggenheim began his giving early. In 1906, after the San Francisco earthquake, he wired $50,000 to an Oakland, California bank, which was then sent around San Francisco by horse cart and used to help the unfortunate.

But until Daniel Guggenheim's retirement, Daniel, Murry, Simon, and Solomon Guggenheim did the Guggenheim family giving jointly. Encouraged by financier Jacob Schiff, they donated $50,000 in the 1905–1910 period to the Jewish Theological Seminary, and also donated $165,000 to the Mt. Sinai Hospital to endow a pavilion in honor of Barbara and Meyer Guggenheim. Acting on his own during this period, Daniel Guggenheim also tried to donate a statue of George Washington to Germany, in response to German Emperor Kaiser Wilhelm II's gift to America of a statue of Prussian ruler Frederick VIII. However, "German diplomats felt that the Guggenheims without warrant put themselves on a plane" with the Kaiser, and therefore rejected the gift (O'Connor 1937, 166).

After his retirement, Daniel Guggenheim decided to become a full-time philanthropist. Daniel Guggenheim's son, Harry Frank

Guggenheim, was an aviator in the U.S. Navy during World War I and returned to America eager to advance America's aviation efforts. In 1925, the younger Guggenheim attended a meeting of New York University engineering professors, where they asked if the Guggenheims would join a campaign to raise $500,000 to start a school of aeronautics. Harry Guggenheim decided this would not be a good idea, and offered to write a fund-raising letter instead. He went home and wrote the letter, which he gave to his father. The next day, Daniel Guggenheim told his son, "Well, Harry, I've thought about your letter and I've decided to endow the school myself" (Pendray and Serling 1982, 10).

In 1924, Daniel Guggenheim created the Daniel and Florence Guggenheim Foundation. During the donor's lifetime, this foundation primarily funded free band concerts in New York City but, in October 1925, Daniel Guggenheim announced that he would create a second fund for aeronautics. After meeting with President Calvin Coolidge and Secretary of Commerce **Herbert Hoover**, Guggenheim created the Daniel Guggenheim Fund for the Promotion of Aeronautics in January 1926. When the Daniel Guggenheim Fund was created, it was seen by the philanthropic world as "little more than a manifestation of technological exhibitionism" (Davis 1978, 254). When President Coolidge heard that someone was giving $2.5 million to make airplanes go faster, he said, "What's the use of getting there quicker if you haven't got anything better to say when you arrived?" (Davis 1978, 254).

The Daniel Guggenheim Fund lasted only four years; it was liquidated in February 1930, a few months before Daniel Guggenheim's death in New York City on September 28, 1930. Still, the fund had many achievements during its short life. It created the Daniel Guggenheim Committee on Aeronautical Meteorology to study ways in which airplanes flying in bad weather could be made safer. Under the committee's sponsorship, aviator Jimmy Doolittle became the first aviator to take off and land using instruments alone in 1928 (Pendray and Serling 1982, 13).

When Charles Lindbergh complained that there were relatively few landmarks when he flew the *Spirit of St. Louis* from California to New York in preparation for his landmark transatlantic flight in 1927, Harry Guggenheim decided to start a drive to have cities and towns mark their roofs to enable aviators to figure out where they were, enlisting the Post Office's help in persuading postmasters to mark roofs. Later on, civic groups such as the Kiwanis, Rotary, and Lions Clubs were also persuaded to help. Ford Motors even encouraged its dealers to help out. Everyone who had their roof marked received a certificate personally signed by Charles Lindbergh. By the close of 1929, more than 6,000 communities had added rooftop markings to their towns. "We hope that eventually no aviator need be lost in the United States because the communities of the country have failed to identify themselves," Harry F. Guggenheim observed in his book *The Seven Skies* (Guggenheim 1930, 110).

The Guggenheim Fund was also responsible for the creation of the first successful commercial air passenger service in the United States. In 1927, the fund held a conference on the potential of passenger aviation. Nearly everyone who attended believed that passenger aviation would not be successful without heavy subsidies. The fund then decided to find an entrepreneur willing to invest in a passenger airline that did not also carry airmail. They found Harris "Pop" Hanshue, whose firm held the mail contract between Los Angeles and Salt Lake City. The fund loaned Hanshue $180,000 to launch a "Model Airway" between Los Angeles and San Francisco. In addition, the fund spent $60,000 to upgrade air terminals in the two cities (including $2,000 for Cadillacs to shuttle them to and from the airport), and also helped choose the Fokker F-10s, which the fledgling airline used. On May 26, 1928, the Model Airway made its first run. The passengers, G. Edward Pendray observes, paid $50

Solomon R. Guggenheim. © The Solomon R. Guggenheim Foundation, New York.

for a three-hour flight (compared to eleven hours for railroads). They were treated to "thick, succulent sandwiches catered by the 'Pig 'n Whistle,' a well-known Los Angeles restaurant" as well as a cabin with mahogany walls and comfortable seats with plenty of leg room (Pendray and Serling 1982, 17). Thanks to a 99% flight safety record, Hanshue had repaid the Guggenheim loan by 1929. Commercial flights would not become routine until the 1930s, but Daniel Guggenheim's grants showed that passenger flights could be quite profitable.

SOLOMON R. GUGGENHEIM

Born in Philadelphia on February 2, 1861, Solomon R. Guggenheim did not become an important philanthropist until he was nearly eighty. He attended public schools in Philadelphia as well as the Concordia Institute, a private secondary school in Switzerland. He joined the family business in about 1880 and worked steadily for the firm for the rest of his life. He was originally in charge of the Guggenheims' Mexican smelters, and he also helped launch Guggenheim mines in Mexico and the Yukon.

In 1895, Solomon Guggenheim married Irene Rothschild, who introduced him to art collecting. For the next thirty years, Guggenheim was a conventional collector, specializing in Old Masters and early Renaissance paintings. But in 1927, Solomon Guggenheim, traveling in Paris, met Baroness Hildegarde (Hilla) Rebay von Ehrenweissen, whom he hired to paint his portrait. Rebay convinced Guggenheim that "nonobjective art" was supremely important, specifically the work of Russia's Wassily Kandinsky, Hungary's Laszlo Moholy-Nagy, and Poland's Rudolf Bauer. Solomon Guggenheim fell madly in love with Baroness Rebay, inviting her frequently to his South Carolina plantation and often sending her letters addressed to "Dearest Hillachen." The baroness maintained the relationship was platonic, and Guggenheim never divorced. Although the extent of their relationship is unclear, Hilla Rebay was Solomon Guggenheim's principal artistic adviser for the remainder of his life.

In 1937, the Solomon R. Guggenheim Foundation was created and began temporary exhibitions of "nonobjective art" in various cities. Many critics were highly confused by the exhibition, which combined work by Rebay's favorites as well as Piet Mondrian and Fernand Lèger accompanied by Johann Sebastian Bach recordings playing discreetly in the background. *New York Times* art critic Edward Alden Jewell described the exhibition as "a religious cult set to incidental music" (Lyon 1959). Another critic described one of the paintings in the exhibit as a "cross between a college pennant, a billiard table, London Bridge (falling down) and thirteen microbes, under a microscope" (O'Connor 1937, 477).

In 1939, Guggenheim had collected so many paintings that the exhibit rented space on East 54th Street in New York City. Still, the Solomon R. Guggenheim Collection of Non-Objective Art (as it was then called) needed a permanent home. So in 1943, Guggenheim commissioned architect Frank Lloyd Wright to design and construct a building. Guggenheim delegated all details about design and construction to Hilla Rebay, while retaining financial control of the project. Wright alternated between writing "Dear Hilla" with design questions and "My dear Mr. Guggenheim" whenever he needed a change in the contract or another payment. By 1944, Wright had constructed models showing the museum's distinctive upside-down circular pyramid design. Two years later, Wright had decided that the museum's distinctive continuous spiral staircase was the preferred way to house the collection's paintings, and was conducting tests to see how to ensure that the design would be architecturally sound. Guggenheim also acquired most of the land needed for the building but zon-

ing delays and Guggenheim's failing health ensured that the museum project would advance no farther during Guggenheim's lifetime. When Guggenheim died in New York City on November 3, 1949, Wright's museum was a pipe dream few expected would ever be built. It would take Harry Guggenheim a decade of energetic effort before the Guggenheim Museum would ever be completed.

SIMON GUGGENHEIM

Born in Philadelphia on December 30, 1867, Simon Guggenheim began his career by attending a trade school but decided to spend two years in Spain rather than going to college. He then went to Colorado, where he supervised Guggenheim operations in that state. Fluent in Spanish, he also assisted in the Guggenheim family's Mexican operations. In 1898, he married Olga Hirsch and fathered two children with her. In 1919, Simon Guggenheim succeeded his brother Daniel as chairman of the board of American Smelting and Refining, a position he retained until his death in New York City on November 2, 1941.

Simon Guggenheim was the only Guggenheim of his generation to be actively interested in politics. After two abortive attempts for political office, he was elected by the Colorado state legislature to the U.S. Senate in 1906 as a "Silver Republican," committed to having the U.S. government buy large quantities of silver. According to Guggenheim foundation historian Milton Lomask, Simon Guggenheim generally voted against expanding government, save for pork-barrel projects in Colorado and high tariffs (particularly in minerals). Indeed, political reporters delighted in calling Guggenheim "the most conservative man in the U.S. Senate" (Lomask 1964, 157).

Disliking daily combat in the political arena, Simon Guggenheim left the Senate, after his term was completed in 1913, and returned to American Smelting and Refining. There, his life resumed its placid course until 1922, when his eldest son, John Simon Guggenheim, died at age seventeen after complications from pneumonia. Like his brothers, Simon Guggenheim made occasional grants during his working life. In 1905, for example, he commemorated John Simon's birth by donating $60,000 to the Colorado School of Mines but he was not known for his charity. In 1910, Senator Thomas Martin of Virginia responded unfavorably to a constituent who asked if Simon Guggenheim would give money to a Virginia college. "Mr. Guggenheim does not, as far as I have been able to observe, take any broad view of educational or other public interests," Senator Martin wrote, "I do not think it will be possible to get any generosity for the cause of education from the Guggenheims" (Davis 1978, 255).

Thus, the creation of the John Simon Guggenheim Memorial Foundation in 1925 was unexpected. When Simon Guggenheim decided to start a foundation as a memorial to his son, he went to American Smelting and Refining general counsel Carroll Atwood Wilson for advice. Wilson recommended that two other men be Simon Guggenheim's advisers—Swarthmore College president Frank Ayledotte and Henry Allen Moe. Wilson, Ayledotte, and Moe were all Rhodes Scholars; Moe had just finished his Rhodes-funded years at Oxford University and was looking for work. Consequently, the three of them proposed an organization that was very Rhodes-like. By 1924, Ayledotte and Moe had created the basic plan of the Guggenheim Fellowships: competitive one-year grants, open to scholars in all fields who were between age twenty-five and thirty-five. Simon Guggenheim agreed to the plan, and endowed the John Simon Guggenheim Memorial Foundation with $3 million.

Although Simon Guggenheim remained president of his foundation until his death, the evidence suggests that Guggenheim declined to impose his will on the foundation. In a 1939 article in *Survey Graphic*, Guggenheim fellow Donald Culross Pettie reported that neither Simon Guggenheim nor his wife Olga Guggenheim "ever makes a suggestion for or against an applicant, or criticizes a decision of the governing committee. . . . He

has chosen to have no more influence than the elevator boy in the building" (Pettie 1939, 509). Moe was thus firmly in charge, and made sure that the foundation under his leadership was a freewheeling place.

Since no one had ever set up a foundation that gave money directly to individuals before, journalists thought the Guggenheim's role was to enable dilettantes to while away the hours in Parisian cafés. In 1931, for example, *New Yorker* cartoonist Carl Rose showed two youths lounging in a Left Bank cafe. "The Guggenheims will be awfully sore at me if I don't get down to writing pretty soon," the caption read (Lyon 1959, 9). Nonetheless, the new grantmaking program also received praise. "Imagine being granted a fellowship for a year of $2,500 or more," noted an unsigned article in *Survey*, "and getting the money right off with no strings or obligations attached. And imagine, further, that if the—whatever it is—warrants another year or two, getting the extension! It seems a veritable El Dorado for the gifted" (*Survey* 1930, 539).

Still, some intellectuals thought the Guggenheim Foundation would be more useful if they controlled it. According to Guggenheim Foundation president Gordon Ray, shortly after the foundation was created in 1925, Ezra Pound wrote to Simon Guggenheim, stating that "your endowment represents a new phase . . . You really want the goods delivered." He proposed that the foundation give long-term grants (ranging from five years to a lifetime) to composer George Antheil, poets T.S. Eliot, Marianne Moore, William Carlos Williams, novelist Wyndham Lewis—and, Ray reports, "by implication himself" (Ray 1979, xxiii). Pound's proposals were ignored, and, according to Ray, "within a few years Pound's occasional letters became as abusive as those that he customarily wrote to other American cultural institutions" (Ray 1979, xxiii). Antheil and Moore, however, did become Guggenheim Fellows (Eliot, Lewis, and Williams never applied).

By 1939, there were so many articles about how the Guggenheim Foundation supported idleness that Henry Allen Moe had put them into a fat album, but Moe was quietly ensuring that the Guggenheim Foundation had a good track record. Moe liked to say that his goal was to give a "grubstake" to the best young minds in America, to give them a chance to show what they could do. "The Guggenheim Foundation grants fellowships to the academic outlaws," he said in a 1941 address to the University of Michigan, "to the poets and novelists, the painters, sculptors, and photographers, and other two-gun men" (Lomask 1964, 159). In 1945, Moe told the American Academy of Arts and Sciences that his goal was "to look at a field and know that practically everyone of significance, in say the twenty-five to fifty-year age range, in it has the Foundation's assistance and that there is not, on the other hand, a high percentage of duds in the field who have had our assistance" (Lomask 1964, 161).

Moe's goal was lofty, but it was achieved. Most of the important painters, composers, and novelists of the era received Guggenheim Fellowships, as did many of the scientists. There were some important artists who were rejected for Guggenheim Fellowships, most notably Henry Miller, who was so disgruntled that he wrote a book, *The Air-Conditioned Nightmare* (1941), combining descriptions of his travels with periodic rants against the Guggenheim Foundation. On at least one occasion, a Guggenheim Fellowship was given to a writer who used the money to attack Guggenheim businesses. In 1931, journalist Carleton Beals used his fellowship to write *The Crime of Cuba*, which included lengthy sections denouncing Harry Guggenheim's control of Cuban copper mines. If Simon Guggenheim made any objections to the book, he never made them public.

HARRY FRANK GUGGENHEIM

Harry Guggenheim, son of Daniel Guggenheim, was the most energetic member of the third generation of Guggenheims. Born in West End, New Jersey, on August 23, 1890, Harry Guggenheim briefly attended Yale University, dropping out to assist his father in running Guggenheim's Mexican operations. In 1910, he returned to school at Pembroke College, Cambridge University, where he earned a bachelor's degree in 1913 and a master's degree in 1918. He also served as a lieutenant in World War I and a captain during World War II. As he was fairly active in Republican politics, President Herbert Hoover rewarded Guggenheim's efforts in the 1928 presidential contest by naming him ambassador to Cuba, a position he held between 1929 and 1933.

In 1939, after two divorces and three children, Harry Guggenheim married Alicia Patterson, daughter of *New York Daily News* founder Joseph Medill Patterson. The couple would not have any children during their marriage. In 1940, Guggenheim purchased a small newspaper in Nassau County, New York, for $50,000, and turned it into *Newsday*. Alicia Patterson became publisher, a position she held until her death in 1963 at age fifty-seven. In 1946, using funds from her father's estate, she purchased a 49 percent share of the newspaper. The political differences between Patterson and Guggenheim became particularly vitriolic. After the newspaper endorsed Democrat Adlai Stevenson in 1956, Patterson temporarily resigned as publisher because Harry Guggenheim attempted to use his majority control of the newspaper to force an editorial endorsement of Republican President Dwight D. Eisenhower's re-election bid. In 1960, *Newsday* endorsed Democrat John F. Kennedy, but the op-ed page featured a Harry Guggenheim column endorsing Republican Richard Nixon.

In 1963, Alicia Patterson died, and Harry Guggenheim purchased her minority interest. Much of the funds for the purchase were used to create the Alicia Patterson Fund, which provides fellowships for journalists working on book projects. Guggenheim briefly became publisher for a few years, but finally sold the newspaper to Times Mirror in 1970 for $70 million, shortly before his death in Sands Point, New York, on January 22, 1971. Some of the funds from the *News-*

day sale were used to endow the Harry Frank Guggenheim Foundation, which subsidizes projects designed to prevent violence.

As a philanthropist, Harry Guggenheim continued and completed the philanthropic projects of his father Daniel and his uncle Solomon. He became president of the Daniel and Florence Guggenheim Foundation in 1930, and also became president of the Solomon R. Guggenheim Foundation in 1949. As noted, Harry Guggenheim was principally responsible for his father's interest in aviation, and the Daniel Guggenheim Fund for the Promotion of Aeronautics can be regarded as the joint philanthropic project of Daniel and Harry Guggenheim.

In 1929, Charles Lindbergh (who wrote his memoir *We* at Harry Guggenheim's Long Island estate) advised his patron to fund the work of rocket scientist Robert H. Goddard. Though the initial grants to Goddard were made before Daniel Guggenheim's death, they were largely given while Harry Guggenheim had control of his father's foundation. Thanks to Daniel and Florence Guggenheim Foundation grants, Goddard's pioneering research laid the foundation for American space travel. In addition, Guggenheim grants also helped subsidize fellowships at most of the leading aeronautical engineering schools, and also helped start the Jet Propulsion Center at the California Institute of Technology, which later became the Jet Propulsion Laboratory. By the 1950s, "virtually all of America's senior aerospace engineers were graduates of Guggenheim-sponsored schools" (Davis 1978, 349). The foundation also awarded the Guggenheim Medal, an annual prize given to the individual who has done the most to advance aviation.

Harry Guggenheim also ensured completion of the Guggenheim Museum. When Solomon R. Guggenheim died in 1949, museum construction had not begun. Probate on Solomon Guggenheim's will was not completed until 1952 and the New York City Department of Housing and Building inspectors, who claimed that Wright's plans violated thirty-two clauses of the New York

City housing code, created more delays. Consequently, construction did not begin until March 1956 and the museum was finally opened in October 1959.

While shepherding construction, Harry Guggenheim also settled a fractious dispute between Hilla Rebay and him. In 1952, Harry Guggenheim ousted Rebay as museum director. Then, he changed the name of the institution from the Solomon R. Guggenheim Museum of Non-Objective Art to its current title, the Solomon R. Guggenheim Museum. After James Johnson Sweeney was appointed to be Hilla Rebay's successor, Guggenheim gave him a free hand to manage the collection while he concentrated on completing the construction of the building. When Rebay left, she took dozens of paintings with her, which she said were hers and the museum said were lent to her by Solomon R. Guggenheim. When Rebay died in 1967, Harry Guggenheim arranged for the museum to purchase these paintings, restoring them to the collection. In 1970, when he was dying, Harry Guggenheim completed one final negotiation; he persuaded his cousin, Peggy Guggenheim, to leave her paintings to the Guggenheim Museum upon her death.

MARGUERITE "PEGGY" GUGGENHEIM

Born Marguerite Guggenheim in New York City on August 26, 1898, Peggy Guggenheim changed her name when she was a teenager. Aside from a brief stint at the private Jacoby School, she was educated at home and did not attend college. Peggy Guggenheim was the daughter of Benjamin Guggenheim, who split with his brothers before they made the discoveries that lifted the Guggenheims into the ranks of the great American fortunes. Thus, when she received her estate upon turning twenty-one in 1919, she was only worth $450,000. Despite this relatively small sum for a Guggenheim, she became one of the greatest patrons of twentieth-century art.

In 1922, Peggy Guggenheim went to

Marguerite "Peggy" Guggenheim in the late 1930s. Courtesy of Julia and Karole Vail.

Paris, where she rapidly became acquainted with the circle of American expatriates. She met—and then married (1922)—Laurence Vail, with whom she had two children. After their divorce, she drifted for some years. In 1937, she found her vocation in the art world. She studied with French painter Marcel Duchamp, who advised her on what artists were worth collecting, and gave her introductions to the important French artists of the day. She was also fortunate to be buying modern art in the late 1930s, when the Great Depression and the rumors of war caused prices to be extraordinarily low. Her purchases, including masterworks by Fernand Léger, René Magritte, and Georges Braque, cost about $250,000, for a collection that her biographer, Josephine Bograd Weld, estimates was worth $40 million on her death in 1979. "You know," Peggy Guggenheim told Weld, "I didn't realize then that I was buying things cheap because of the war, and

everyone since then has accused me of taking advantage of the situation, but I didn't even realize it. I didn't know anything about the prices of things. I just paid what people told me" (Weld 1986, 196–197).

In 1938, Peggy Guggenheim opened an art gallery in London, which she called "Guggenheim Jeune," which featured most of the important abstract and surrealist artists of her time, including Hans Arp, Henry Moore, and Alexander Calder. She also began to represent Wassily Kandinsky. When she tried to sell her uncle a Kandinsky painting, she received a rebuke from Hilla Rebay, who wrote that "it is extremely distasteful at this moment, when the name of Guggenheim stands for an ideal in art, to see it used for commerce so as to give the wrong impression, as if this great philanthropic work was intended to be a useful boost to some small shop. . . . through our work and experience . . . Guggenheim became known for great art and it is very poor taste indeed to . . . cheapen it to a profit" (Guggenheim 1979, 171). In 1939, Guggenheim returned to Paris, where she continued to buy modern art even as the Germans occupied France. In 1941, she escaped for New York with several hundred paintings, her former husband Laurence Vail, her two children, and painter Max Ernst, whom she later married and divorced.

By 1942, Peggy Guggenheim had reestablished her art dealership in New York, calling it Art of This Century, which combined Guggenheim's collection with a sales gallery. Everything about the gallery was cutting-edge; one room was the Surrealist Gallery, where paintings were unframed, and hung on cantilevers that some thought looked like baseball bats. Another was the Kinetic Gallery, where patrons looked at works by Duchamp and André Breton through peepholes and at odd angles. Still, her most important role was to nurture a younger generation of American artists. In part, the Art of This Century was a place for young artists to network. "Art of This Century was a meeting place," notes critic Philip Rylands, "one of those hang-outs that become retrospectively sanctified by the avant-garde ambience" (Rylands, 1998, 11). The most important artist of this group was Jackson Pollock, whom Guggenheim championed through early commissions and by staging his first one-man exhibition in 1943.

In 1947, Peggy Guggenheim returned to Europe with her paintings, settling in Italy for the remainder of her life. She exhibited many of these works at the 1948 Venice Biennale, where she introduced many of the American Abstract Expressionists (notably Pollock and Robert Motherwell) to Europe. She then retired as a dealer, although she continued collecting for another thirty years. Peggy Guggenheim died in Padua, Italy, on December 23, 1979. Her collection and her Italian mansion were acquired by the Solomon R. Guggenheim Museum in 1974 (the first of the Guggenheim Museum's many branches).

CONCLUSION

Harvey O'Connor concluded his critical look at the Guggenheim fortune with a chapter on Guggenheim family philanthropy. "For a Lord's tithe of their fortune the Guggenheims had made a remarkable bargain in public esteem," O'Connor wrote. "**John D. Rockefeller [Sr.]** had to spend millions to wash away the blots on his escutcheon; Carnegie distributed practically everything to erase from public scrutiny the picture of a shrewd, ruthless little steelmaster. The Guggenheim brothers had achieved the same result for much less, and they basked, in their declining years, in the warm glow of public praise" (O'Connor, 1937, 435). As the generations have passed, it is increasingly clear that the Guggenheims are known for their philanthropy rather than their fortune. In their lifetime, the Guggenheim brothers also avoided controversy. Since their wealth was created in remote and inaccessible parts of the globe, they were far less likely to attract press scrutiny.

As philanthropists, the Guggenheims were innovators, in that they found areas of patronage neglected by other foundations. The John Simon Guggenheim Memorial Foundation invented the idea of awarding fellowships to individuals; all other fellowships of this type, including the MacArthur Fellows today, derive their shape and scope from the forms devised by Simon Guggenheim and his associates in 1925. Although the Guggenheim Foundation was less successful in spotting rising talent after 1945, it was certainly successful in aiding the most important novelists, painters, composers, and scientists who flourished between 1925 and 1945.

Other contributions by the Guggenheim family were equally important. Daniel Guggenheim's support of aviation in 1926–1930 helped to jump-start the passenger aviation industry. Both Peggy and Solomon Guggenheim, in somewhat competing ways, were active patrons of modern art. Meanwhile, Harry Guggenheim deserves credit for continuing his father's support of Robert H.

Goddard and for ensuring completion of the Solomon R. Guggenheim Museum.

All in all, the Guggenheims were among the greatest donors of the twentieth century. No other philanthropic family had as broad a range of interest as the Guggenheims had, and few did as much to help American artists and scientists.

Martin Morse Wooster

FURTHER READING

Baruch, Bernard. *My Own Story.* New York: Henry Holt, 1957.

Beals, Carleton. *The Crime of Cuba.* Philadelphia: J.B. Lippincott, 1933.

Davis, John H. *The Guggenheims: An American Epic.* New York: Morrow, 1978.

Guggenheim, Harry. *The Seven Skies.* New York: Putnam, 1930.

Guggenheim, Peggy. *Out of This Century: Confessions of an Art Addict.* New York: Universe Books, 1979.

"The Guggenheims." *Fortune,* May 1930, 72–76.

Holbrook, Stewart H. *The Age of the Moguls.* Garden City, NY: Doubleday, 1953.

Lomask, Milton. *Seed Money: The Guggenheim Story.* New York: Farrar, Straus, 1964.

Lyon, Peter. "The Adventurous Angels." *Horizon,* May 1959, 4–11.

Miller, Henry. *The Air-Conditioned Nightmare.* New York: New Directions, 1970 [1945].

O'Connor, Harvey. *The Guggenheims: The Making of an American Dynasty.* New York: Covici-Friede, 1937.

"One Way of Getting Over." *Survey,* February 1, 1930, 539.

Pettie, Donald Culross. "Grubstaking the Best Folks." *Survey Graphic,* August 1939, 508–509.

Pendray, G. Edward, ed., revised by Robert J. Serling. *Daniel Guggenheim: The Man and the Medal.* New York: Guggenheim Medal Board of Award of the United Engineering Trustees, 1982.

Pfeiffer, Bruce Brooks, ed. *Frank Lloyd Wright: The Guggenheim Correspondence.* Carbondale: Southern Illinois University Press, 1986.

Ray, Gordon. "Report of the President." In *Reports of the President and the Treasurer, 1978.* New York: John Simon Guggenheim Memorial Foundation, 1979.

Rylands, Philip. "Peggy Guggenheim and Art of This Century." In *Art of This Century: The Women.* New York: Solomon R. Guggenheim Museum, 1998, 9–15.

Straus, Dorothea. *Palaces and Prisons.* Boston: Houghton Mifflin, 1976

Weld, Jacqueline Bograd. *Peggy: The Wayward Guggenheim.* New York: Dutton, 1986.

Wooster, Martin Morse. "The Guggenheim Foundation's Slide towards Irrelevance." *Foundation Watch,* March 1997.

PAPERS

The papers of Harry Frank Guggenheim and the Daniel Guggenheim Fund for the Promotion of Aeronautics are in the Library of Congress (Washington, DC). The papers of Peggy Guggenheim and Solomon R. Guggenheim are in the Solomon R. Guggenheim Museum (New York City). Some additional papers relating to the construction of the Guggenheim Museum are in the Frank Lloyd Wright archives in Taliesin West (Scottsdale, AZ).

H

HENRY LEE HIGGINSON
(1834–1919)

Banker and Founder of the Boston Symphony Orchestra

INTRODUCTION

During the summer of 1898, Civil War veteran Henry Lee Higginson complained to Henry Cabot Lodge of his inability to participate in the American war against Spain. "Here I sit in the dude club" but "long to go into service" (Meyerhuber 1974, 182). This aching for glory symbolizes Higginson's frustrating life, one often fraught with lost opportunities. He wanted a Harvard University education but failing eyesight forced him to leave school midway through his freshman year. A few years later, he pursued a career as a concert pianist but a minor arm injury, which was magnified by poor medical treatment into a severe condition, abruptly ended that dream. During the Civil War, he joined the Union Army but never participated in a major battle or achieved the military fame he desired. Despite numerous setbacks, Higginson made an invaluable contribution to the American art world by founding the first per-

manent symphony in the United States, the Boston Symphony Orchestra.

EARLY LIFE AND EDUCATION

In 1834, Henry Lee Higginson was born to George Perkins Higginson and Mary Cabot Lee. George Higginson worked as a commission merchant in New York City but moved the family to Boston in 1837 after some financial setbacks. Here, George Higginson attempted to rebuild his business.

Although he proved to be a fair student, Henry Higginson exemplified dedication and industry. He did not shy away from hard work and spent his summers picking fruit on farms in Watertown, Newton, and West Cambridge, all near Boston. In 1851, Higginson entered Harvard University. Unfortunately, he developed a vision problem that forced him to drop out of school. After withdrawing, he departed for Europe, spending the better part of two years on a walking tour and expanding a passing interest in music by studying the piano during a stay in Dresden, Germany in November 1852. "My desire [to study music] has only increased very much since I've been abroad," wrote Higginson to his father. "I shall certainly study it with a master, if I have the eyes, and if not, at least I can play somewhat, and amuse my otherwise idle hours" (Perry 1921, 52).

After returning home, he followed his father's wishes and began a clerkship in a Boston merchant's office. For twenty months, he struggled in this position. Eventually, George Higginson recognized his son's travails. Consequently, Henry Higginson returned to Europe in 1856 and hoped to expand on his love of music by developing a career as a concert pianist and composer. Once again, a physical injury, this time to an arm (caused by a poorly executed "bleeding" of his left arm during the treatment of what may have been a migraine headache), kept him from realizing his aspirations. The injury even forced him to step away from active participation in music.

In 1860, he returned to Boston and attempted to start a private business as a wine merchant. When the Civil War erupted in 1861, Higginson enlisted and began a military career that held promise but he again endured missed opportunities and unfortunate events. In the end, he attained the rank of major, but illness and unlucky postings kept him from the fields of glory he desired. In his only major engagement, a minor conflict in Virginia, he earned a lifetime scar on his cheek from a saber blow inflicted by Confederate General Thomas Rosser.

Higginson's early life and track record of personal and professional setbacks culminated in a disastrous attempt to operate a Georgia cotton plantation with recently freed slaves as paid laborers. In this enterprise, Higginson and his Boston-based partners lost more than $90,000, a gigantic sum for that era, before selling the business.

CAREER HIGHLIGHTS

During a long convalescence following his wounding in the fall of 1862, Higginson courted the daughter of another prominent Boston family. Ida Agassiz subsequently married Higginson in December 1863. The couple would have one son.

With a history of business performance that ranged from mediocre to dismal, Higginson became an employee of Lee, Higginson and Company, one of Boston's premier banking firms (headed by his father, an uncle, and his brother), in 1868. Though Higginson never desired to be a banker, biographers believe that his reputation for honesty and personal attention brought him the achievement he had so widely sought. Over the next five years, Higginson gained significant wealth. Possessing a fortune estimated at $750,000–$1 million, he looked to his past and tried to use his newfound success to achieve past dreams.

MAJOR PHILANTHROPIC CONTRIBUTIONS

In 1873, Higginson renewed his interest in music when he represented Massachusetts as an honorary commissioner in the Vienna Exposition in Austria, an event that brought together some of the finest musical and theatrical talent in the world. At this event, he resumed acquaintances with former teachers and other musicians and began to formulate plans to bring a permanent world-class symphony to Boston.

Eight years later (1881), Higginson launched the symphony project. The idea to form the symphony first came to Higginson during his student days in Vienna. However, his many business struggles and the interruption caused by his Civil War service forced the postponement of his dream. It was not until he prospered in business that he felt stable enough to carry forward his vision. Under the direction of some of the leading conductors in the world (such as Wilhelm Gericke, Arthur Nikisch, and Karl Muck), the Boston Symphony became the leading organization of its type in America and received worldwide praise. Acting as its sole underwriter over four decades, Higginson donated nearly $1 million during his long association with the symphony.

His successful plan for a symphony was simple: leave the business affairs of the symphony to an able manager and the choice and care of the music and musicians to the conductor. Higginson summarized his own role in the venture this way: "to pay the bills, to be satisfied with nothing short of perfection, and always to remember that we were seeking high art and not money: art came first, then the good of the public, and the money must be an after consideration" (Perry 1921, 93). Higginson's symphony also followed the elite cultural philanthropy pattern of fellow Bostonian **John Lowell Jr.** and his Lowell Institute. Higginson's wealth and elite status allowed the symphony to drastically overshadow other musical associations (proprietary or nonproprietary) in the city.

Besides the symphony, Higginson made significant contributions to Harvard University. He donated, for instance, property for the medical and business schools and art to the university's Museum of Fine Arts. In addition, he created the Harvard Student Union and Soldiers Field. In the latter gift, Higginson honored six friends who died in the Civil War but also provided the athletic field because he believed the competitive drive of sports would properly shape the character of future leaders.

CONCLUSION

Despite numerous misfortunes, frustrations, and unfulfilled dreams, Higginson significantly advanced American music through his philanthropy. In his address to the members of the Boston Symphony Orchestra on April 27, 1914, Higginson happily concluded, "Ever since boyhood I have longed to have a part in some good work which would have a lasting mark in the world. Today we have a noble orchestra—the work of our hands—which gives joy and comfort to many people" (Perry 1921, 296).

Douglas Czajkowski

FURTHER READING

Higginson, Henry Lee. "Charles Russell Lowell." In *Harvard Memorial Biographies*. Cambridge, MA: Sever & Francis, 1866.

Katz, Irving. "Henry Lee Higginson vs. Louis Dembitz Brandeis: A Collision between Tradition and Reform." *New England Quarterly* 41 (1), 1968, 67–81.

Meyerhuber, Carl I., Jr. "Henry Lee Higginson and the New Imperialism." *Mid America* 56 (3), 1974, 182–199.

Perry, Bliss. *Life and Letters of Henry Lee Higginson.* Boston: Atlantic Monthly Press, 1921.

Taylor, Jason. "Building the Thoreau Institute." *The Concord Saunterer*, 6, 1998, 6–24.

PAPERS

Henry Lee Higginson's papers are located in the Manuscript Division, Baker Library, Harvard Business School (Boston, MA).

IMA HOGG
(1882–1975)

Arts Patron, Historic Preservationist, and Founder of the Hogg Foundation for Mental Health

INTRODUCTION

"As the physical needs of the state are being fulfilled," Ima Hogg once said, "we need to think more about the things that make life worth living, the nourishing of the spirit" (Bernhard 1996, 3). Her own contributions to that nourishment were many. She founded the Houston Symphony and created a major museum of American decorative arts. She also established the Houston Child Guidance Clinic and the Hogg Foundation for Mental Health. For most of her long life, the daughter of Texas Governor James Stephen Hogg devoted herself to projects that made "life worth living."

EARLY YEARS AND EDUCATION

Folklore has it that Governor James Stephen Hogg had three children, and their names were Ima, Ura, and Hesa. That story is widely believed, but only the name Ima Hogg is factual. Ima Hogg was born July 10, 1882, in the small town of Mineola, Texas. She spent much of her early life in Austin, Texas, where her father was governor from 1891 to 1895. She had an older brother, Will, and two younger brothers, Mike and Tom. Her mother, Sallie Stinson Hogg, died when Ima was thirteen. Subsequently, Ima Hogg was sent to boarding school at the Coronal Institute near San Marcos, and then enrolled in the University of Texas at Austin in 1899. After two years there, she went to New York City to study piano. In the summers, she lived at Varner Plantation near West Columbia, Texas, which her father had bought in 1901.

In 1905, James Stephen Hogg became ill. Thereafter, his daughter served as his nurse and constant companion until his death from a heart attack in 1906. A year later, Ima Hogg left for Europe to continue her piano studies in Vienna and Berlin. She returned to Houston in 1909, abandoning the notion of a career as a concert pianist. Instead, she taught piano to a few students, and began the first of her many philanthropic ventures. Meanwhile, the Hogg family fortunes grew rapidly as oil was discovered on their West Columbia property in 1919. Governor Hogg had instilled in his children a strong sense of public duty, and they had the financial means to engage in a myriad of philanthropic projects by the 1920s.

CAREER HIGHLIGHTS AND MAJOR PHILANTHROPIC CONTRIBUTIONS

In the summer of 1913, with Julian Paul Blitz (a Belgian cellist living in Houston), Ima Hogg organized the first concert of what would become the Houston Symphony Orchestra. Since New York City's Philharmonic had been founded in 1842 and the Philadelphia Orchestra in 1900, Hogg felt that Houston needed to join those ranks. After that first summer concert, she and others planned a season of three concerts during the winter of 1913–1914. Hogg saw to it that 138 guarantors pledged $25 each. She was also the Symphony Board's first vice-president, and took on the presidency of the Board in 1917. She served in this capacity until 1921, and again from 1946 to 1956. In addition, Hogg founded the Women's Committee, engineered fund-raising campaigns, and maneuvered behind the scenes to secure the best possible artistic and financial leadership. Her dedication is commemorated by the annual Houston Symphony Ima Hogg National Young Artist Competition, which draws young musicians from all over the world.

In 1929, Ima Hogg founded the Houston Child Guidance Clinic, a center for the study and care of mentally disturbed or "difficult" children. Part of her concern for such children came from her own experience. Eight-year-old Tom Hogg, the youngest of the Hogg children, went through a traumatic period of adjustment after his mother's death. He did not do well in school, and his habitual restlessness and extravagance worried his siblings. Indeed, Ima Hogg believed that an institution such as the Child Guidance Clinic could have helped Tom Hogg. As a young girl, Ima Hogg also heard her father frequently speak about the importance of children, family, and community. Having accompanied him on visits to state schools, prisons, and asylums, she further saw the conditions of society's underprivileged. Thus, she made her clinic open to people of all races and income levels. Some forty years

Ima Hogg. Courtesy of the Museum of Fine Arts, Houston.

later, Ima Hogg declared that, of all her many projects, the Child Guidance Clinic had given her the most satisfaction. In 1992, it merged with the DePelchin Children's Center.

In 1930, after Will Hogg's death, Ima Hogg and her brother Mike began planning for a unique institution: the Hogg Foundation for Mental Hygiene. Suffering from periodic bouts of mental depression, Ima Hogg believed in the importance of educating the public about mental health. In fact, Ima and Will Hogg had often discussed ways to improve mental health care, so they devised a plan that would use Will Hogg's bequest as well as funds from their own estates. The Hogg Foundation, a private organization, affiliated with and administered by a public institution (University of Texas), was to provide mental health services and education to communities all over Texas. In 1939, as the Great Depression was ending, the foundation was established. Its purpose was, as Ima Hogg put it, "educating people in the art of better living" (Kirkland 2001, 446). Bringing together mental health professionals and local groups to work towards community goals, the Hogg Foundation for Mental Hygiene was one of the first of its kind. Sixty years after its establishment, this blend of public and private efforts in mental health activities has helped to shape state policies, such as the enactment of Texas's first Mental Health Code in 1965, as well as create or fund private organizations. In 1996, for example, the Foundation helped to organize the Greater Houston Collaborative for Children, a group of over two dozen agencies for children's services. Meanwhile, Ima Hogg also established the Ima Hogg Foundation (1964) to fund children's mental health activities in Harris County. The Ima

Hogg Foundation, like the larger Hogg Foundation, was to be administered by the University of Texas. At the end of the twentieth century, the Hogg Foundation for Mental Health and Ima Hogg Foundation had a combined endowment of over $125 million.

In 1943, Hogg, then in her sixties, entered the public sphere, winning an election to the Houston Board of Education and serving until 1949. In an editorial supporting her candidacy, the *Houston Post* wrote, "Miss Hogg is no politician, and all her talents and efforts during her lifetime have been devoted to unselfish, public-spirited work for the betterment of social conditions or for the improvement and enrichment of life for others" (Bernhard 1996, 90). When she won the election, Ima Hogg established a visiting-teacher program for emotionally disturbed children who could not fit into the routine of daily public school classes. She labored to create a painting-to-music program in art classes, and she saw to it that the then-segregated Houston school system provided art instruction for African American as well as white students. Using her influence with the Houston Symphony, she also established a series of special free concerts for school children. She further worked to equalize the salary scales for teachers, regardless of race or gender.

In the 1940s, while she served on the School Board, Hogg continued her involvement with the Houston Child Guidance Clinic, the Hogg Foundation, and the Houston Symphony. A woman of formidable energy, she was also an active member of civic organizations ranging from the Houston Community Chest to the River Oaks Garden Club to the League of Women Voters. In 1956, she helped to found the Harris County Heritage and Conservation Society, beginning a historic preservation project that resulted in Sam Houston Park: a collection of antebellum and Victorian houses on a grassy slope at the edge of downtown Houston.

Appointed a member of the Texas State Historical Survey Committee in 1953, Hogg continued her interest in historic preservation and undertook a series of preservation projects from the 1950s to the end of her life. Some of her fascination with antiques and preserving the past came from her childhood memories of life in the historic Texas Governor's Mansion (built in 1855). Her first venture was the restoration of the Hogg family home near West Columbia, Texas, on the site of the historic old Varner Plantation. The spot was rich in Texas history, having been one of the original land grants issued to settlers in the 1820s. After restoring the antebellum plantation house and grounds, she donated them to the state of Texas as Varner-Hogg State Park.

Since the 1920s, Hogg studied and collected early American art and furniture. As the years passed, her collection grew. In 1966, she presented the furnishings and the gracious home that housed them to the Museum of Fine Arts, Houston. Bayou Bend, the twenty-two-room mansion the family had built in 1927, is situated on the banks of Buffalo Bayou and surrounded by fourteen acres of gardens at the edge of Houston's prestigious River Oaks neighborhood. Now the American Decorative Arts Wing of the Museum of Fine Arts, Bayou Bend houses one of the major collections of early American furniture and decorative arts west of the Mississippi.

Between the dedication of Varner-Hogg Park in 1958 and the opening of Bayou Bend in 1966, Hogg found time to restore a number of other historic properties and to serve on two national committees. In 1960, she was appointed by President Dwight Eisenhower to serve on a committee for the planning of the National Cultural Center (now Kennedy Center) in the nation's capital. In 1962, at the request of Jacqueline Kennedy, Hogg served on an advisory committee to aid in the search for historic furnishings for the White House. Meanwhile, in 1963, she began her most ambitious restoration project yet: a collection of century-old buildings— an inn, a barn, and some old cabins—near the town of Winedale (about eighty miles from Houston). When these were restored to her demanding standards, she presented them to the University of Texas as an endowed center for the study of Texas architecture, arts, and letters, as well as the ethnic history of the state.

CONCLUSION

Well into her eighties, Hogg showed few signs of slowing her busy schedule, but that schedule was increasingly filled with appearances to accept awards. In 1968, she was the first recipient of the University of Texas Santa Rita Award, given to individuals who have assisted the advancement of the university and the cause of higher education. In 1969, along with Lady Bird Johnson and Oveta Culp Hobby, Hogg was one of only three women selected as members of the Academy of Texas, an organization created to honor persons who "enrich, enlarge, or enlighten" knowledge in any field. That same year, she also received an award from the American Association of State and Local History for her work in historic preservation. In 1971, when Ima Hogg was eighty-nine years old, Southwestern University gave her an honorary doctorate in fine arts. In 1972, the National Society of Interior Designers presented

her with its Thomas Jefferson Award for outstanding contributions to America's cultural heritage. She died in 1975, while vacationing in London.

Ima Hogg, a talented pianist, chose to devote her talents to enriching the lives of others. For her patronage of the arts, her work to preserve the past, and her dedicated efforts on behalf of mental health, she will long be remembered in Texas and elsewhere.

Virginia Bernhard

FURTHER READING

Bernhard, Virginia. *Ima Hogg: The Governor's Daughter*. St. James, NY: Brandywine Press, 1996.

Iscoe, Louise. *Ima Hogg: First Lady of Texas*. Austin, TX: Hogg Foundation for Mental Health, 1976.

Kirkland, Kate. "A Wholesome Life: Ima Hogg's Vision for Mental Health Care." *Southwestern Historical Quarterly* 104, no. 3, January 2001, 416–447.

Warren, David. "Ima Hogg, Collector." *Antiques*, January 1982, 228–243.

PAPERS

Ima Hogg's papers are located at the Barker Texas History Center, the University of Texas at Austin.

HERBERT CLARK HOOVER
(1874–1964)

Engineer, President, Statesman, and Humanitarian

INTRODUCTION

In an autobiographical statement written sometime after World War I, Herbert Hoover declared: "There is little importance to men's lives except the accomplishment they leave to posterity. . . . When all is said and done . . . accomplishment is all that counts" (Pre-Commerce Papers, Subject File, "Information for Biographers," Herbert Hoover Presidential Library). For Hoover, the most accurately measured form of accomplishment was "the origination or administration of

tangible institutions or constructive works" (ibid.). True to his philosophy, he spent most of his adult life creating and administering such institutions. The result was a career of extraordinary philanthropic attainment.

EARLY YEARS AND EDUCATION

Herbert Hoover was born in West Branch, Iowa, on August 10, 1874, the second child of Jesse and Hulda Minthorn Hoover. His father was a blacksmith and his mother was

Herbert Hoover delivers a radio address during the presidential campaign of 1928. Bettmann/CORBIS.

an active Quaker. Before Hoover was ten years old, both of his parents died. When he was eleven, he was sent to Oregon to live with an uncle who had just become superintendent of a Quaker academy. During the next six years, Hoover received essentially a middle school education and then worked for his uncle's land settlement company.

In 1891, after taking entrance examinations and some special tutoring, Hoover was admitted to Stanford University, then opening its doors for the first time. For the impecunious orphan, it was a perfect match. In 1895, he graduated with a degree in geology and an unquenchable feeling of gratitude for the opportunity that his alma mater had given him. In 1899, he married Lou Henry of the Stanford class of 1898. They were married nearly forty-five years and had two sons.

CAREER HIGHLIGHTS AND MAJOR PHILANTHROPIC CONTRIBUTIONS

After graduating from Stanford, Hoover embarked upon a career as an international mining engineer based eventually in London. His rise to prominence was meteoric. By his late thirties, he was earning $100,000 a year. By 1914, at the age of forty, he was at the pinnacle of his profession, with business interests on every continent except Antarctica.

"If a man has not made a fortune by 40 he is not worth much," the resourceful, young engineer liked to say (Nash 1983–1996, I: 384). As worldly success increasingly favored him, Hoover grew restless. He told friends that he wanted to "stop making money" and "get into the big game" of public service back in the United States. "Just making money isn't enough," he confessed (Nash 1983–1996, I: 510, 513). Having done well, he now yearned for a more altruistic vocation. Several factors reinforced his longings: the childhood admonitions of his Quaker relatives that he should live usefully; his code of engineering professionalism, with its emphasis on unselfishness and constructive work; and, above all, the "Stanford spirit" of practical idealism that he had absorbed so deeply as a college student.

It was World War I that brought Hoover's dreams into focus and catapulted him onto the "slippery road of public life" (Hoover 1951–1952, I: 148). When the war broke out in Europe in August 1914, he was still living in London. Within a few months, as the armies of contending nations bogged down in bloody stalemate, Hoover founded and directed an institution of volunteers called the Commission for Relief in Belgium (CRB). As a neutral venture respected by the European belligerents, the CRB acquired, delivered, and distributed food to more than

9,000,000 desperate Belgian and French civilians caught between a German army of occupation and a British naval blockade. What appeared at first to be a brief, emergency rescue operation evolved rapidly into a gigantic humanitarian enterprise without precedent in world history. By the time it ceased operations in 1919, the CRB had spent nearly a billion dollars in governmental and private funds and had created a humanitarian hero in Hoover. It had also served as a pioneering embodiment of a new force in twentieth-century politics: American altruism in the form of humanitarian relief missions and foreign aid programs.

Hoover took no pay for his full-time service as chairman of the CRB, nor for his numerous other benevolent undertakings in later years. Nor did he return to his mining interests, although a stupendous war-generated fortune could have been his reward. "Let the fortune go to hell," he remarked in October 1914 as he launched the Commission for Relief in Belgium (Nash 1983–1996, II: 33). When, four years later, he sold the last and largest of his mining investments, the sum he received (perhaps $2.5 million) was sufficient to sustain a career in public service for as long as he wished.

Clearly he now desired such a life. Shortly after the United States entered World War I in 1917, President Woodrow Wilson appointed Hoover as Food Administrator, a governmental post in which he served with distinction. Five days after the war ended in 1918, he returned to Europe at the president's direction to organize food relief for suffering millions, facilitate economic recovery, and arrest the outbreak of revolutionary chaos in central Europe. His institutional instrument was the American Relief Administration (ARA), created by executive order in early 1919 and funded by a $100 million Congressional appropriation. For several grueling months Hoover (as the ARA's Director-General) and his volunteer staff raced to prevent famine and catastrophe. It was a herculean undertaking, entailing (among much else) the distribution of more than 4 million tons of food and supplies in more than twenty countries.

In mid-1919, Hoover's European philanthropic endeavors entered a new phase. The ARA became a private agency known as the American Relief Administration European Children's Fund, with Hoover and his team at the helm. In the early 1920s, the New York–based organization provided food for as many as 3 million undernourished European children daily. To finance this work, Hoover, in late 1920, initiated an unprecedented $33 million fund appeal in the United States under the auspices of a consortium of American philanthropic groups known as the European Relief Council. The campaign yielded nearly $30 million during a severe recession—a tribute to Hoover's immense prestige and administrative talent.

Then, in 1921–1923, at the request of the Communist authorities in Soviet Russia, Hoover's ARA organized a relief program for victims of a terrible famine in the Volga River region. With the help of private giving and a $20 million Congressional appropriation, Hoover and his colleagues delivered more than 768,000 metric tons of supplies to the stricken population. At its height the ARA operation in Russia fed more than 10 million people a day.

All in all, between 1914 and 1923 more than 83 million people in Europe and the Near East received humanitarian food allotments for which Hoover and his associates were at least partly responsible. This number is probably a conservative estimate. Of Hoover, it can confidently be said that he was responsible for saving more lives than any other person in history.

From 1921 to 1928, Hoover served as Secretary of Commerce under Presidents Warren G. Harding and Calvin Coolidge. Throughout his tenure, his concern for social betterment did not abate. He served as president of the American Child Health Association, authored the Child's Bill of Rights, and spearheaded the Better Homes in America movement. He chaired the CRB Educational Foundation (later renamed the Belgian American Educational Foundation), still another outpost in his expanding empire of philanthropy.

In 1927, President Coolidge asked Hoover to oversee the federal government's response to the Mississippi River flood, the gravest natural disaster in American history. His highly publicized efforts—including a successful $15 million fund drive for the Red Cross—further enhanced his reputation. This experience also confirmed his faith in voluntary, decentralized, and largely nongovernmental approaches to relief. Unlike Europeans (Hoover appeared to believe), Americans possessed the necessary initiative, generosity, financial resources, organizational skills, and community infrastructure to care for one another without the intervention of a bureaucratic, centralized state.

Acclaimed as the Great Humanitarian and Master of Emergencies, Hoover was elected President of the United States in 1928. Only a few months after his inauguration, the stock market crash of 1929 signaled the onset of the Great Depression. As the nation's economic troubles deepened and overwhelmed his presidency, more and more Americans clamored for the savior of Europe to initiate direct federal relief to his own people. Hoover forcefully refused. Direct relief to individuals from the federal government, he prophesied, "would bring an inevitable train of corruption and waste such as our nation had never witnessed" (Hoover 1951–1952, III: 54). Instead, in 1930, he established the President's Emergency Committee for Employment (PECE), which surveyed and coordinated relief measures at the state and municipal levels. This was followed in 1931 by the President's Organization on Unemployment Relief (POUR) and a national appeal for funds for private charitable organizations.

Although increasingly pilloried as a callous reactionary, Hoover stoutly insisted that his elaborate relief apparatus was "effectively preventing any hunger or cold" (Hoover 1951–1952, III: 155). Indeed, he never conceded otherwise. Toward the end of his term in office, he did agree to $300 million in federal relief assistance to state governments, but only in the form of loans. He never acquiesced in direct federal outlays to private citizens. That, he believed, would be a certain recipe for fiscal extravagance and abuse of power. Defeated for reelection in 1932 by Franklin Roosevelt, Hoover watched with dismay as Roosevelt launched a New Deal that directly provided federal relief funds to millions of Americans. To Hoover, the New Deal's record in this area only confirmed his dire forebodings. Citing election scandals in Kentucky and elsewhere, he accused New Dealers of blatantly using federal relief money to buy and coerce the votes of relief recipients. He also charged the Roosevelt administration with building a wasteful, politicized relief bureaucracy centered in Washington. In Hoover's view, the result was moral degradation of the citizenry and massive corruption of the political process.

With the advent of World War II, Hoover sought new outlets for his philanthropic impulses. In 1939, he founded the Commission for Polish Relief and the Finnish Relief Fund to aid the latest victims of war and totalitarianism abroad. In 1940, eager to replicate his Belgian relief success in World War I, he organized the National Committee on Food for the Small Democracies. Hoover hoped that his committee could funnel food, under safeguards, to the suffering civilian populations of Nazi-occupied Belgium, Holland, Norway, and Poland, as well as Finland. The opposition of Winston Churchill and the Roosevelt administration stymied his plans. In 1946, as the threat of a postwar famine imperiled millions around the world, President Truman enlisted Hoover to conduct a survey of global food supplies and requirements. The elderly humanitarian promptly visited more than thirty countries and made valuable recommendations to his government.

As he grew older, Hoover's benevolence increasingly focused on charitable institutions in the United States. Between 1936 and 1964, he chaired the board of directors of the Boys Clubs of America. As always, he was no figurehead. Under his leadership, more than 500 new Boys Clubs were established.

During this same period, he devoted himself strenuously to the improvement of Stanford University, on whose board of trustees he served for nearly fifty years. By the time of his death, no person, other than the university's founders **Leland and Jane Stanford**, had done as much for his alma mater. Above all, he labored tirelessly to strengthen the Hoover Institution on War, Revolution and Peace, which he had founded at Stanford with his own funds in 1919. In fact, he came to believe that the Hoover Institution—an incomparable archive of documentation on twentieth-century history—was the greatest single achievement of his life.

Hoover practiced the philanthropic virtues that he professed. As President, he declined to spend any of his salary on himself. Instead, he gave it away to charities or as income supplements to his associates. During their long marriage, he and his wife extended charitable assistance to countless needy recipients, usually anonymously and through surrogates. In the 1930s, Hoover's brother (who sometimes acted as an agent in these transactions) concluded that Hoover had given away more than half of his business profits for benevolent purposes. Characteristically, however, Hoover concealed most of his benefactions, with the result that their full extent may never be known.

CONCLUSION

Hoover believed that the building of "tangible institutions" was the highest form of human endeavor. In such "constructive works" as the Commission for Relief in Belgium and the Hoover Institution, he forged a remarkable philanthropic legacy. Still, as Ralph Waldo Emerson observed in "Self-Reliance," "An institution is but the lengthened shadow of one man." Of no one is this truer than Herbert Hoover, the humanitarian who saved more lives than any other person in history.

George H. Nash

FURTHER READING

Burner, David. *Herbert Hoover: A Public Life.* New York: Alfred A. Knopf, 1979.

Hoover, Herbert. *An American Epic.* 4 vols. Chicago: Henry Regnery, 1959–1964.

———. *The Memoirs of Herbert Hoover.* 3 vols. New York: Macmillan, 1951–1952.

Nash, George H. *Herbert Hoover and Stanford University.* Stanford, CA: Hoover Institution Press, 1988.

———. *The Life of Herbert Hoover.* 3 vols. New York: W.W. Norton & Company, 1983–1996.

PAPERS

The principal repository for Herbert Hoover's papers is the Herbert Hoover Presidential Library (West Branch, IA). Some of Hoover's papers, as well as the records of his relief organizations, are at the Hoover Institution on War, Revolution and Peace at Stanford University (Palo Alto, CA).

SAMUEL GRIDLEY HOWE
(1801–1876)

Educator of the Blind, Opponent of Slavery, and Social Reformer

INTRODUCTION

"There never was and never will be a reformer, a man ahead of his generation, who had not a host of difficulties and enemies to encounter," wrote Samuel Howe to Horace Mann on October 9, 1844 (Howe Family Papers, Houghton Library, Harvard University). Dr. Samuel Gridley Howe founded special education in the United States and worked against ignorance, slavery, disability, and discrimination. Howe was director of the Perkins Institution and Massachusetts Asylum for the Blind from 1831 to 1876, and he cofounded and headed the first American residential school for mentally retarded youth in 1848 with Walter Fernal. Howe also became a school committeeman for the city of Boston, a state legislator and lobbyist in Massachusetts for better treatment of the insane, and an activist in a drive for prison reform. He further developed printing methods for the blind and means of communication for the deaf. Over the last quarter-century of his life, Howe was an opponent of the Fugitive Slave Law, a fierce campaigner against the extension of slavery into Kansas, and a member of the U.S. Sanitary Commission as well as the Freedmen's Inquiry Commission during the Civil War. Many of these undertakings brought him into conflict with elected officials, established traditions, and hallowed institutions.

EARLY YEARS AND EDUCATION

Howe was born in Boston, Massachusetts. His father was a rope maker, and, according to family legend, one of his ancestors was involved in the Boston tea party and another in the fortification of Bunker Hill. Howe attended Boston Latin School and Brown University, but only became serious about his studies when he entered the medical school at Harvard University. Graduating in 1824, he had doubts about his future as a physician because he did not wish merely to acquire wealth and admiration as a society doctor.

One of the major influences in Howe's early life was his service to the Greek Revolution. In 1821, the Greeks rose against the Ottoman Empire. Their cause became especially popular in London and Boston, where philhellenic societies were formed. In 1825 and 1828, Howe lived in Greece. He witnessed civil war, political corruption, disease, poverty, brutality, and starvation. He returned with improved medical skills and was eventually decorated by the King of Greece with a chivalric order. Afterward, Howe experienced years of uncertainty until a college friend, Dr. John Fisher, offered Howe the directorship of a school for the blind. When

Howe accepted the position, his life and the education of people with disabilities in the United States and the world were transformed.

CAREER HIGHLIGHTS AND PHILANTHROPIC CONTRIBUTIONS

Throughout the remainder of his life and philanthropic activity, "Chev," as his family and friends referred to Howe, evolved into an effective educator and tireless reformer, but often an irascible collaborator. In April 1833, Thomas Perkins, inspired by Howe's pupils' appearance before the Massachusetts legislature, made a grant of $50,000 and donated his mansion in return for having his name affixed to the "Blind Asylum." Howe campaigned throughout the country to interest other states in establishing schools similar to the Perkins Institute.

In 1837, Howe met the deaf-blind Vermont farm girl Laura Bridgman, whose education earned Howe worldwide fame. Howe was able to "reach" this predecessor of the more famous Helen Keller. Under his direction, she learned to speak, read, write, perform household tasks, and care for herself. The instructive techniques, which Howe developed, became the foundation for teaching generations of deaf-blind children. Thus, Laura Bridgman inspired students and teachers alike. The general curriculum, designed by Howe, emphasized mechanical skills, academic subjects, music, and exercise aimed at promoting self-reliance.

Between 1844 and 1845, Horace Mann and Howe extended their drive for educational reform from the state to the local level. From his post on the Board of Education for the Commonwealth of Massachusetts, Mann pressed for the establishment of teachers' colleges, which Howe, as a state legislator, helped to fund. Thereafter, in 1845, as a member of the Boston School Committee, Howe argued for better textbooks, higher standards for reading and writing, and the abolition of corporal punishment.

Back in 1832, while traveling in Europe to learn about existing facilities for the blind,

Howe landed in prison. Prussian officials accused him of assisting refugees who had fled the Polish Revolution of 1831 against the Russian Tsar. Plunging into despair at this confinement, Howe may have developed an interest in prison reform, which subsequently led him to join forces with Charles Sumner. The two men favored the Philadelphia system, according to which prisoners would remain in solitary confinement where they could benefit from the concentrated influence of guards rather than the harmful effects of exposure to other criminals. Eventually, Howe would even become averse to capital punishment. Despite many bitter debates on these subjects, the Sumner-Howe partnership neither ended capital punishment nor changed the prison system in Massachusetts.

Often politically frustrated, Howe would resist the government. The two most noteworthy issues over which he rebelled against state authority were military recruitment and slavery. In fact, he saw these two issues as related. Inspired by an altercation with an Italian soldier, Howe denounced what government does to the characters of its men at arms: "I never see a soldier that I do not think of the awful responsibility which rests upon those who make of a man a machine; of one who might have been a kind husband, father and friend, a selfish, lonely, heartless stalk" (Richards 1909, 153). Two years later, reciting nearly the same litany of condemnations, he portrayed slavery as the most frightening example of human degradation. To Howe, when the master took possession of another human being, he deprived the slave of much more than freedom. He believed the slave lost his very humanity: all chance of realizing his potential and improving his own life.

As the Civil War approached, Howe would become more suspicious of government. He never would deny the state's capacity to act morally, only the will of its officials to do so. He consistently opposed legislation that required the return of persons who had escaped slavery by fleeing to the North. Moreover, at the risk of his own freedom, Howe supplied weapons to those who were forcibly resisting the extension of slavery into Kansas. At one point, during the 1850s, Howe had to evade a warrant for his arrest by hiding in Canada.

Howe's philosophy of life was close to that of the Transcendentalists, who were his friends and contemporaries. Transcendentalists believed human beings were, by their very nature, worthy of respect, entitled to the greatest individual freedom, and capable of assuming responsibility for their own improvement. They had been put in the world by a generous god who did not wish humanity to be chained by oppressive government, bound to obsolete traditions, or stifled by the cruelty of fellow creatures. From this philosophy sprouted each of Howe's cherished convictions: that individuals possessed a fundamental and sacred integrity, a basic equality, and a right to develop freely and morally those gifts with which Providence endowed them. These precepts accompanied Howe through the whole spectrum of his philanthropic activities. For example, his advocacy for the blind rested on the conviction that they were the equals of the sighted: " 'We are beings like you,' say they, 'We have the same organization, and the same feelings, if not the same powers,—and do not bow us still lower by the humiliating debt of charity . . . teach us to do something to cheer the dark blank of our existence; give us something to occupy our thought, and our hands, and enable us to be less dependent on charity' " (Samuel Gridley Howe 1833, 178).

Exposing abuses to which the insane were subjected, Howe wrote in like phrases: "be it remembered, even the insane do not lose their self-esteem, and this is often sadly wounded by the necessary herding together in public establishments" (Samuel Gridley Howe 1843, 180). He acted upon this conviction in two principal ways. With Walter Fernald, Howe pioneered the treatment of mentally retarded children. As a state legislator, Howe helped to enact **Dorothea Dix**'s recommendations on care for the mentally ill.

In his private as well as his public life, talented people surrounded Samuel Gridley Howe. In 1843, he married Julia Ward. Julia

Ward Howe managed an often-chaotic household, which intersected with the Perkins School. After Howe's death, she established herself as a gifted poet, biographer, memoirist, and world-renowned advocate for women's rights. The couple also had four children. Their daughter, Laura Howe Richards, won a Pulitzer Prize for her biography of Julia Ward Howe.

CONCLUSION

Samuel Gridley Howe believed that whoever relegated the blind to charity, the insane to crowded and unsanitary quarters, young men to soldiering, and African Americans to slavery was guilty of the most immoral behavior. The cardinal civic sin was to deny equality, self-esteem, and intellectual potential. For Howe, philanthropic reform entailed the wish to be useful to other human beings, a visionary sense of the future, an incessant pursuit of social needs, compassion for the victim, and confidence in the efficacy of hard work. Like his collaborators, Howe was variously guided by his loyalty to the moral capacity of the state, rebelliousness when faced by its indifference to suffering, and resistance to the obstacles threatening the individual's innate dignity. This innovator knew how to mobilize public and private sentiment, how to make personal sacrifices, but not how to submit to limitations.

Howe believed that human beings were fundamentally equal not only before the law, but in terms of their basic integrity. He was, as perhaps each reformer must be, a man more progressive than his era. Crucial to Howe's success was not being too progressive for his age: his optimism, his clear sense as to what constituted virtue, possibly his whole approach to life was something shared, at least in part, with his historic period.

Nicholas S. Racheotes

FURTHER READING

Freeberg, Ernest. *The Education of Laura Bridgman: The First Deaf and Blind Person to Learn Language.* Cambridge, MA: Harvard University Press, 2001.

Gitter, Elisabeth. *The Imprisoned Guest: Samuel Howe and Laura Bridgman, the Original Deaf-Blind Girl.* New York: Farrar Straus Giroux, 2001.

Howe, Julia Ward. *Memoir of Dr. Samuel Gridley Howe with Other Memorial Tributes.* Boston: A.J. Wright, 1876.

———. *Reminiscences.* Boston: Houghton, Mifflin & Company, 1899.

Howe, Samuel Gridley. "Education of the Blind." *New England Magazine*, March 1833, 177–187.

———. "Insanity in Massachusetts." *North American Review*, January 1843, 171–192.

Meltzer, Milton. *A Light in the Dark: The Life of Samuel Gridley Howe.* New York: Thomas Y. Crowell, 1964.

Parrington, Vernon L. *Main Currents in American Thought: An Interpretation of American Literature from the Beginnings to 1920.* 3 vols. New York: Harcourt, Brace & Company, 1927. (See volume 2; *The Romantic Revolution in America, 1800–1860*).

Racheotes, Nicholas S. "Boston's Knight Errant: Samuel Gridley Howe (1801–1876)." *New England Journal of History*, Winter 1998–1999, 22–36.

Richards, Laura E. *Samuel Gridley Howe.* New York: D. Appleton-Century, 1935.

———, ed. *The Letters and Journals of Samuel Gridley Howe, the Greek Revolution.* Boston: D. Estes, 1906.

———, ed. *Letters and Journals of Samuel Gridley Howe, Servant of Humanity.* Boston: D. Estes, 1909.

Sanborn, Franklin Benjamin. "Dr. Samuel Gridley Howe, the Philanthropist." In *American Reformers*, ed. Carlos Martyn. New York: Funk & Wagnalls, 1891.

Schwartz, Harold S. *Samuel Gridley Howe Social Reformer, 1801–1876.* Cambridge, MA: Harvard University Press, 1956.

Tyler, Alice F. *Freedom's Ferment.* Minneapolis: University of Minnesota Press, 1944.

Wilkie, Katherine E., and Elizabeth K. Moseley. *Teacher of the Blind: Samuel Gridley Howe.* New York: Julian Messner, 1965.

PAPERS

The Samuel Gridley Howe papers on the administration of the Perkins School for the Blind are available at the Perkins School for the Blind (Watertown, MA); the Howe family papers are at the Houghton Library, Harvard University (Cambridge, MA); some other material can be found in the Horace Mann papers at the Massachusetts Historical Society (Boston, MA).

J

HELEN MARIA (FISKE) HUNT JACKSON
(1830–1885)

Author and Native American Rights Activist

INTRODUCTION

"My object . . . has been simply to show our causes for national shame in the matter of our treatment of the Indians. It is a shame, which the American nation ought not to lie under, for the American people, as a people, are not at heart unjust" (Jackson 1995, 7). With relentless passion and energy, Helen Hunt Jackson fought to reform government policies toward Native Americans. Indeed, the struggle for the legal and property rights of the Native American Indians consumed the last six years of her life. She utilized her literary talents, advocacy abilities, and social and political connections to bring the unfair treatment of native people to national awareness. Jackson is best known for *A Century of Dishonor*, a documentary account of government abuses toward the Indians, and for *Ramona*, her romantic novel of the tragic story of the Mission Indians of California. Still, her efforts paved the way for legislative measures enacted well after her death, including the granting of full citizenship to Native Americans in 1925.

EARLY YEARS AND EDUCATION

Born in 1830, Helen Maria Fiske was the daughter of a minister trained at Dartmouth College and serving on the faculty of Amherst College (Massachusetts). A childhood neighbor and lifelong friend of Emily Dickinson, she grew up in the literary and academic worlds of Amherst; Newport, Rhode Island; New York City; and Boston. At twenty-two, she married Edward B. Hunt, an army engineer. Subsequently, she gave birth to two sons, neither of whom survived to adulthood. During the Civil War, she also lost her husband, who died while testing a submarine of his own design.

Following these personal tragedies, and on the advice of her friend Emily Dickinson, she turned to writing poetry and prose at the age of thirty-five. Writing under a variety of pseudonyms, she became a popular success while

Helen Hunt Jackson. Special Collections, Tutt Library, Colorado College, Colorado Springs, Colorado.

also being considered by many literary contemporaries to be an author of merit. Ralph Waldo Emerson, in the preface to his anthology *Parnassus* (1874), praised her as the best female poet in the United States. Her circle of friends included some of the most prominent literary, journalistic, and political luminaries of her time, valuable connections for her later efforts. In 1875, she married William Sharpless Jackson, a Colorado banker and railroad promoter, and for four years lived a life of comfort.

CAREER HIGHLIGHTS AND MAJOR PHILANTHROPIC CONTRIBUTIONS

Planning to attend the seventieth birthday celebration of Oliver Wendell Holmes, Helen Hunt Jackson arrived in Boston during the fall of 1879. During this visit, she was invited to a lecture given by Standing Bear, the chief of the Ponca tribe of Nebraska. Due

to a bureaucratic error, the Ponca Indians had been forcibly removed from their Nebraska homeland and placed in a desolate Indian territory in Oklahoma. Standing Bear, honoring the deathbed wish of his son to be buried in the place of his birth, had returned to Nebraska and was subsequently arrested for leaving the Oklahoma reservation. Denied the right to sue in court, Standing Bear's plight was noted by the *Omaha Herald*'s assistant editor, Thomas Henry Tibbles. Partly due to the advocacy and publicity generated by Tibbles, the Nebraska District Court eventually declared the Indian a "legal person" with the right of habeas corpus. Tibbles then devoted himself to helping the Ponca Indians recover their lands and to having the legal status of the Indians determined by the Supreme Court. To raise awareness and money for this effort, Tibbles organized a six-month lecture tour featuring Standing Bear and two Omaha Indians,

Francis La Flesche and his sister, Susette La Flesche (known as "Bright Eyes").

Jackson was in the audience of influential Bostonians who heard the story of Standing Bear. That audience also included such distinguished individuals as Henry Wadsworth Longfellow and Massachusetts Senator Henry L. Dawes (who in 1887 would sponsor the Dawes Act granting the right for private land allotment to Native Americans). Jackson was outraged by the treatment of Standing Bear and was moved to write a letter about the Ponca's dilemma for a New York City newspaper. At age forty-nine, Helen Hunt Jackson began the crusade that was to consume the remainder of her life.

Over the next year, Jackson relentlessly wrote letters to newspapers and magazines throughout the country, detailing various instances of ill treatment toward Native Americans. Her accusations of government mismanagement of the Ute Indians in Colorado prompted a heated exchange with a Denver editor and eventually caused a response from Secretary of the Interior Carl Schurz. The letters between Jackson and Schurz (whom Jackson referred to as a "blockhead") became noteworthy through their publication in Boston and New York City newspapers and prompted editorial support of Jackson and the condemnation of government policies. Indeed, Jackson did not hesitate to use her influence with editorial acquaintances and high-placed friends to have her letters and articles reprinted and kept in front of the public.

Jackson's extensive research for these letters provided a significant chronicle of government mistreatment of Native Americans. For seven months, Helen Hunt Jackson immersed herself in the Astor Library in New York, researching the abuses and injustices to Native Americans by the United States government. Her in-depth documentation of broken treaties, misappropriated funds, and government mismanagement of seven Indian tribes developed into a book, *A Century of Dishonor*, in 1881. Portraying the Native Americans as victims of government abuse, she countered the contemporary depiction of

Native Americans as savages, a widespread image in the aftermath of the 1876 massacre of General George Custer's troops at Little Bighorn. To ensure her catalog of government atrocities came to the attention of those with influence, Jackson had copies of *A Century of Dishonor* sent, at her own expense, to every member of Congress.

In the fall of 1882, *Century Magazine* commissioned Jackson to write a series of travel sketches on California, including one on the Spanish missions and their surrounding communities. Over the next six months, she traveled throughout California and became intimately aware of the pitiable conditions of the various tribes living around the former Spanish Mission towns—known collectively as the Mission Indians. She wrote to the current Secretary of the Interior Henry Teller outlining the illegal appropriation of tribal lands by white settlers and government agents. Teller responded by asking her to undertake an official visit to the Mission Indians on behalf of the federal government, specifically to locate suitable lands for permanent reservations.

In February 1883, Jackson visited the various Mission Indian sites, accompanied by a friend, Abbot Kinney, who shared Jackson's sympathies for the Mission Indians. Kinney proved to be a valuable partner as he spoke Spanish and was familiar with the California land laws. Their extensive travels uncovered numerous instances of abuses, particularly of the Mission Indians being deprived of their lands and displaced to desolate areas, threatening their lives. At times, the federal government sanctioned this displacement, and at other times, government agents condoned such behavior by ignoring the illegal seizure of fertile Indian lands by white settlers. The poverty and desolation caused by these actions deeply angered Jackson and prompted a burst of letters and accusations against the offending agents and policies. Her official fifty-six-page "Report on the Conditions and Needs of the Mission Indians of California" outlined eleven specific recommendations for reform, including provision for Indian ownership of land parcels. These recommendations formed a basis for future congressional legislation.

Despite the increased governmental and journalistic attention to Jackson's writings, the general public remained relatively unmoved by injustices against Native Americans. To gain greater popular awareness, Jackson embarked upon her final, and most successful, literary legacy. In the fall of 1883, Jackson began writing a story she felt would move public sentiment for the Indian cause in a way her previous writings had not. Piecing together several true stories she had gathered during her travels among the Mission Indians, she composed the story of *Ramona*.

Ramona is the tale of a beautiful maiden, part Indian and part Spanish, and her ill-fated love for a handsome Mission Indian man. Their idealized romance and marriage fall victim to the greed of American settlers. In the end, Ramona experiences the death of her child and her beloved husband. Published in the spring of 1884, *Ramona* was received by the public more as a romance than a political statement. Despite respectable initial sales, Jackson died a year later feeling proud of her efforts but concerned that she had largely failed in her attempts to reform American attitudes toward the Indians. In the years after her death, however, *Ramona* became one of the most popular novels of the late nineteenth and early twentieth centuries, going through more than 300 printings and inspiring several movies and a popular song. But more important, it also served as a powerful symbol for future Indian reform movements.

CONCLUSION

Jackson did not typify women reformers of the late nineteenth century. Her crusade to reform Americans' treatment of the Indians began relatively late in life and, with the exception of a mild interest in the abolition of slavery, she was never active in any of the various organized social reform movements. Still, Jackson exemplified what a single person can achieve in a relatively short period of time. For six years, she devoted all of her talents, resources, and efforts to Native American rights. Clearly, she alerted the public and government officials to the woeful treatment of Native Americans.

Jackson's public battles against government leaders and her literary achievements also served as vital rallying points for the organized reform efforts of the Women's National Indian Association and the Indian Rights Association and were an impetus for future legislative reforms. Over the next fifty years, her efforts proved to be a catalyst and model for those who continued the struggle for legal rights and citizenship for Native Americans.

Al Lyons

FURTHER READING

Jackson, Helen Hunt. *A Century of Dishonor: A Sketch of the United States Government's Dealings with Some of the Indian Tribes.* Norman: University of Oklahoma Press, 1995 [1881].

———. *Ramona.* New York: Signet Classic, 1988 [1884].

Mathes, Valerie Sherer. *Helen Hunt Jackson and Her Indian Reform Legacy.* Norman: University of Oklahoma Press, 1997.

———, ed. *The Indian Reform Letters of Helen Hunt Jackson, 1879–1885.* Norman: University of Oklahoma Press, 1998.

PAPERS

Helen Hunt Jackson's papers are located in the Charles Leaming Tutt Library, Colorado College (Colorado Springs, CO), and in the Jones Library (Amherst, MA).

K

ROBERT KEAYNE
(1595–1656)

Puritan Merchant and Donor of an Early American Bequest

INTRODUCTION

"My aim in all these things proposed is for the general good of the town"(Keayne 1970, 17). Thus, Robert Keayne, Boston's wealthiest merchant during the first three decades since its founding, declared, in his last will and testament, the intention motivating the legacies he apportioned to his community. Despite the humiliating sting of having been publicly censured, "not justly but by misconstruction"(Keayne 1970, 59), fourteen years earlier for selling his merchandise at inflated prices, and despite the "unchristian, uncharitable, and unjust reproaches and slanders" (Keayne 1970, 46) with which self-serving enemies vilified his reputation and incited public enmity against him, Keayne steadfastly conforms to the Puritan religion's imperative that those blessed by God with large estates are obligated to bestow part of it for public and charitable purposes. In his will, Keayne repays the community's "unkind and un-

neighborly discourtesies" with the Christian charity he himself was denied (Keayne 1970, 17).

EARLY YEARS AND EDUCATION

Robert Keayne's early years in England unfurled in a steady rise from obscurity to economic success and social respectability. Born to the butcher John Keayne in 1595 at Windsor, he was bound as an apprentice to a London merchant for a period of ten years at the age of ten. Evidently displaying enterprise and acumen, he was shortly admitted as a member of the Merchant Tailors Company after his apprenticeship ended on April 17, 1615. Two years later, on June 18, 1617, Keayne, then living in Cornhill, London, married Anne Mansfield, daughter of Sir John Mansfield, a fortunate connection for a young merchant seeking to gild his rising economic star with the luster of social station. Keayne's steady march to economic and social advancement culminated in 1623 when he was granted the honorific title of "gentleman" and admitted to the Honourable Artillery Company of London. At the age of twenty-eight, Robert Keayne had arrived.

Keayne's ascending financial condition, and the prospect of improving upon it, probably turned his attention to New England. In 1623, he became an "adventurer" in the Plymouth Colony Settlement. However, having seen no appreciable return on his investment, Keayne sold his rights in the undertaking to the settlers in 1627. By the early 1630s, he had shifted the focus of his New England adventuring to the Massachusetts Bay Company, which had established its plantation in 1630. Keayne made an initial investment of £100 in the company. In 1634, when the supply of ready currency ran dangerously low, he sent additional funds in response to a plea from the Massachusetts Bay Colony's General Court.

Sometime during the early months of 1635, Keayne, most likely motivated by a combination of commercial and religious motives, decided to cut his ties to his homeland, uproot his family, and start life anew in America. According to Thomas Dudley, an original settler of the Massachusetts Bay Colony and four times its governor, New England offered the possibility of mutually entailed religious and commercial enterprise: "If any godly men, out of religious ends, will come over to help us in the good work we are about, I think they cannot dispose of themselves nor their estates more to God's glory and the furtherance of their own reckoning" (Dudley 1846, 324). For Keayne, both Puritan and merchant, the image of the Massachusetts Bay Colony materialized as a place where "religion and profit jump together" (Winslow 1844, 372). Accordingly, on July 17, 1635, Keayne, with wife Anne and son Benjamin, set sail for America and arrived nearly three months later on October 8. He quickly established himself as a retailer of imported merchandise and immersed himself in town and colony affairs.

CAREER HIGHLIGHTS

With his business and financial acumen, and the military expertise he had acquired as a member of the Honourable Artillery Company of London, colonists called upon Keayne to serve in numerous civic functions. By September 1636, he was elected to the office of selectman. Between 1638 and 1649, he was reelected selectman four times, chosen as a representative to the General Court eight times, and named surveyor of highways. On November 20, 1637, the General Court, fearing an armed uprising by the religiously radical followers of Anne Hutchinson, requested that Keayne take possession of their weapons and store them at his residence. During the following year and a half, Keayne served on various committees charged with conducting civic affairs. During this period, Keayne also founded the Ancient and Honorable Artillery Company of Massachusetts and secured its charter on March 13, 1638. The following June, he was certified as the Company's first captain. One year later, the General Court rewarded Keayne's service to the colony, both before and after his emigration, with a grant of 400 acres of land.

Despite the sunny sky that smiled down upon his first four years in Boston, ominously dark clouds had begun to gather. Amid his flurry of civic activity, Keayne also pursued his commercial interests with equal ardor. Raging inflation beset the colony throughout the 1630s. The lack of sufficient provisions and manufactured goods caused prices to skyrocket, and the constant influx of new immigrants only served to widen the gap between supply and demand. As a retailer of imported goods, Keayne found himself uniquely positioned to benefit from the prevailing market forces, selling desperately needed goods at the inflated prices that high demand and low supply induced.

Given such economic conditions, and a reputation for avaricious business practices in Old England, it was inevitable that his efforts to capitalize on inflationary trends would provoke a swelling wave of communal resentment. This sentiment crested on November 9, 1639, when the General Court charged Keayne with selling his merchandise at extortionate prices. He admitted his guilt and was fined. In Puritan New England, however, excessive profiteering was considered not only a civil crime but also a sin. Thus, two weeks after his appearance before the Court, Keayne submitted to a public examination and eventual censure by his church. Only another confession of guilt enabled him to avoid excommunication. Fourteen years later, as he sat down to write his last will and testament, the memory of public disgrace still haunted Keayne to such an extent that the document metamorphosed into a five-month-long, 51,000-word endeavor "to leave a testimony of my innocency . . . to the world behind me" (Keayne 1970, 61).

Keayne vigorously maintained that the accusations against him were unfounded, a web of lies spun from prejudicial narrow-mindedness and a maliciously gross misrepresentation of the facts. His admission of guilt was both a pragmatic concession to the political and social animosity directed against him and a devout acknowledgement of God's providential sanction for his general state of human sinfulness—not an acquiescence to the specific crime imputed against him. Keayne's allegation of unjust treatment earned a measure of credence several years later while he was attending a meeting of the Massachusetts Bay Colony elders. **John Winthrop** told Keayne he had long been troubled by the General Court's actions against him and had decided to petition the Court to recall its censure of him—a decision the other elders in attendance approved. Winthrop died, however, before he could execute his intention.

Throughout the 1640s, Keayne reclaimed his reputation through tireless involvement in civic activities. In 1649, he was allotted 1,074 acres of land in the northern interior in appreciation for his community service. At its October 1651 session, the General Court appointed Keayne to the prestigious Board of Commissioners. Eight months later, however, his return to colonial prominence ground to a halt when he was found guilty of public drunkenness by the Court. Keayne resigned his commissioner's post and retreated to his 314-acre farm at Rumney Marsh, where he began writing the will he hoped would vindicate his reputation.

MAJOR PHILANTHROPIC CONTRIBUTIONS

The Puritan economic ethic demanded both frugality and liberality in administering one's estate. Wealth must be prudently managed to maintain both self and family but, at the same time, the welfare of the community required "a cheerful distribution of the things we have" (Willard 1969, 710). Charity effectually prevented material striving from degenerating into covetousness. In his will, Keayne manifests his adherence to this ideal. After bequeathing two-thirds of his estate to his wife Anne and son Benjamin, he reserved the remaining third for his own disposing. As testimonies of his affection, he left £300 to his granddaughter Hannah and smaller amounts to various relatives, friends, ministers, and widows. As for the remainder, he directed it toward the community, desiring to answer its "unkindness" toward him "with kindness" (Keayne 1970, 17).

With an eye toward Boston's continued commercial vitality and military security, Keayne bequeathed £300 toward the construction of a water conduit and a community center complete with a market area, granary, library, armory, and conference rooms. Should the town elders conduct deliberations in the community center, he specified £4 a year, for a period of ten years, to furnish them with food and drink. The Artillery Company Keayne founded and first captained received £10 for weaponry and two cows as constant stock, the yearly profit of which should be used to purchase powder and bullets.

Concern for the poor, however, motivated most of Keayne's gifts. Beginning in England, he had over the years maintained a charitable fund for the poor, contributing to it one penny out of every shilling he earned through trade and retailing. He left half of its £120 total to the Boston free school to aid indigent students and the other half to his church to aid its most needy members. Keayne's largest gift went to Harvard College. Either as a primary or secondary legatee, the college eventually received over £500, specifically intended by Keayne to defray the expenses of "poor and hopeful scholars" (Keayne 1970, 23). Today, income from that bequest is still being paid to Harvard University.

CONCLUSION

The Puritan economic ethic required strict attention to the line between "covetous affection" for worldly goods and "diligent zeal" in pursuing one's calling (Foster 1971, 122). Through one of earliest bequests in America, Keayne would have readers of his will see that he observed that line, and that prudence, charity, mercy, and the collective interests of the public governed the conduct of his business in New England.

Jerome DeNuccio

FURTHER READING

Dudley, Thomas. "Dudley's Letter to the Countess of Lincoln." [London:1631]. In *Chronicles of the First Planters of Massachusetts Bay, from 1623 to 1636*, ed. Alexander Young. Boston: Little Brown, 1846, 303–341.

Foster, Stephen. *Their Solitary Way: The Puritan Social Ethic in the First Century of Settlement in New England*. New Haven, CT: Yale University Press, 1971.

Keayne, Robert. *The Apologia of Robert Keayne*. Bernard Bailyn, ed. Gloucester, MA: Peter Smith, 1970.

Roberts, Oliver A. *History of the Ancient and Honorable Artillery Company of Massachusetts*, vol. 1. Boston: Alfred Mudge, 1895.

Willard, Samuel. *The Compleat Body of Divinity*. 1726. Facsimile Reprint. New York: Johnson Reprint Corporation, 1969.

Winslow, Edward. "Good News from New England." [London: 1624]. In *Chronicles of the Pilgrim Fathers of the Colony of Plymouth from 1602 to 1625*, ed. Alexander Young. Boston: Little Brown, 1844, 270–375.

PAPERS

A handwritten transcription of Keayne's will appears in volume 1 of the *Records of Suffolk County* and is located at the Boston Public Library. A printed version appears in volume 10 of the *Boston Record Commissioners Report* (1886) and is also located at the Boston Public Library. Between 1638 and 1646, Keayne compiled three books, totaling some 1,500 pages, containing abstracts of and notes and commentary on scriptural passages and on sermons preached by such preeminent Massachusetts Bay Colony ministers as John Wilson, John Cotton, Thomas Shepard, and John Davenport. Only two of these books remain: the first, located at the library of the Massachusetts Historical Society (Boston, MA), and the third, located at the library of the Rhode Island Historical Society (Providence, RI).

FLORENCE KELLEY
(1859–1932)

General Secretary of the National Consumers League and Social Reformer

INTRODUCTION

" 'Why are seals, bears, reindeer, fish, wild game in the national parks, buffalo, migratory birds, all found suitable for federal protection; but not the children of our race and their mothers?' " (Chambers 1963, 51). These words, spoken by Florence Kelley, convey her deep passion for social change on behalf of women and children. Kelley, a contemporary of **Jane Addams** and a leader of the Settlement House and Progressive Movements, worked tirelessly to end the exploitation of working women and children— effectively bringing about social change when women were denied the right to vote. Kelley's lifelong crusade to bring a voice to the disenfranchised included roles as the General Secretary of the National Consumers League, Vice President of the National Women's Suffrage Association, and a founder of the National Child Labor Commission, National Association for the Advancement of Colored People, and Women's International League for Peace and Freedom.

EARLY YEARS AND EDUCATION

Born in Philadelphia, Pennsylvania, in 1859, Florence Kelley was the third child of William D. Kelley, a self-educated lawyer and judge, and Caroline Bartram Bonsall, an orphan raised in a Quaker household. It is no surprise that Florence Kelley became a social reformer. From an early age, William Kelley shared his progressive views with his daughter. He opposed slavery, supported suffrage for women, and became appalled at the working conditions endured by children of the working class. Florence Kelley also suffered, along with her mother, as five of her eight siblings (all sisters) died as infants or young children. In addition, her Aunt Sarah, a Quaker, refused to use cotton or sugar because they were produced by slave labor. These early family influences contributed to Florence Kelley's sensitivity to social injustice, infant mortality, and labor conditions.

Because of childhood illnesses, Kelley received her early schooling at home. A voracious reader, she spent much of her time in her father's library. With her father's encouragement, she attended Cornell University from 1876 to 1882, spending three of those years at home recovering from an illness but graduating with a bachelor's degree in 1882. Kelley's senior thesis, entitled "Some Changes in the Legal Status of Children," even demonstrated her early interest in child labor reform. Denied entrance to the University of Pennsylvania for graduate studies because she was a woman, Kelley enrolled in Zurich Polytechnicum (Switzerland) in 1883 after a chance meeting with an old friend from Cornell, M. Carey Thomas, who re-

ceived a Ph.D. from the University of Zurich (the first European university open to women). Kelley studied economics and law in Zurich, but did not receive a degree.

While in Switzerland, Kelley met an international collection of students excited by socialism. She also became intrigued by socialism and believed it offered explanations and possible solutions to the problems of working women and children and racial inequities. As a new convert to socialism, Florence Kelley translated Freidrich Engels' *The Condition of the Working Class in England in 1844* to English in 1887, and subsequently translated and published a Karl Marx speech on free trade the following year. In Zurich, she also met and married Lazare Wischnewetsky, a Russian medical student, in 1884. The couple traveled to the United States in 1886 and settled in New York City with their young son. Plagued by heavy debt and a troubled marriage, Kelley moved to Illinois with her three children (Margaret, Nicholas, and John Bartram) in 1891. Subsequently, she obtained a divorce, reverted to using her maiden name, and began a professional career—all quite out of the ordinary for a woman of her day.

CAREER HIGHLIGHTS AND MAJOR PHILANTHROPIC CONTRIBUTIONS

Based on her life experiences, Florence Kelley arrived in Illinois with a well-developed theoretical framework for social reform. Indeed, it is no surprise that she landed on the doorstep of Jane Addams's Hull-House in 1891, quickly aligned with its founder, and was welcomed into Hull-House's inner circle. During her early professional years in Chicago, Kelley gained extensive field research experience. Later in her career, Kelley used the information and methods gained through fieldwork to become an effective activist, working with multiple advocacy organizations and the legal system to bring about social change.

In 1892, Kelley was hired by the Illinois Bureau of Labor Statistics to investigate the sweatshop system in the garment industry;

Florence Kelley, the General Secretary of the National Consumers League. Library of Congress; Lot 13306 (G).

that same year she also assisted the Federal Commissioner of Labor, Carroll D. Wright, with a survey of city slums in Chicago. The findings from these early endeavors gave Kelley, and indeed the other residents of Hull-House, an overview of the deplorable labor conditions and sweatshop practices in Chicago. Kelley found disorder and instability throughout the sweatshop system as well as squalor and filth, foul sanitary arrangements, poor wages, and long hours. Kelley was appalled to find children, some as young as three, working in the sweatshops. By 1893, the Illinois legislature—with Kelley's influence—passed a factory act limiting the hours of work for women, prohibiting child labor, and controlling tenement sweatshops. In 1895, Kelley sadly watched this law declared unconstitutional by the Illinois State Supreme Court.

In 1893, progressive Illinois Governor John Altgeld appointed Kelley chief factory inspector (the first woman in this position), complete with a staff of twelve and a $12,000 budget. This work was dangerous—exposed to disease and resistance in the course of the work—but Kelley developed methods for detailed scientific studies of factory conditions. She also reported her findings by combining moral zeal with scientific facts, which produced reports of great appeal to the public. Although her reports were thorough and skillfully written, Kelley became frustrated by the difficulty of prosecuting law violators. Consequently, she earned a law degree from Northwestern University in 1894. In 1895, Kelley, along with Hull-House colleagues, published a landmark work, *Hull-House Maps and Papers*, which statistically documented the needs and problems of an urban immigrant community. She also continued in her work as a factory inspector until her dismissal by Altgeld's successor in 1897. She remained in Chicago for two more years and worked at Chicago's John Crerar Library by night—to support her family—while continuing her activism, writing, and speaking by day.

In 1899, Kelley moved her family to New York City, where she accepted the position of general secretary of the newly formed National Consumers League, an organization devoted to using consumer pressure as a means to bring about safe and humane manufacturing practices and proper working conditions. Kelley viewed consumer action as a powerful new tool to enhance social change legislation. With great savvy, she instituted several techniques to demonstrate consumer power, including public education and publicity campaigns, consumer boycotts of sweatshop-produced clothes, and clothing labels to ensure safe manufacturing practices and fair labor standards. Most notably, the National Consumers League instituted the white label campaign. Employers received the white-label if their labor practices met National Consumers League's standards in terms of fairness and safety. The National Consumers League also encouraged consumers to support the white label and to boycott those who failed to meet National Consumers League standards. Throughout the twentieth century, the National Consumers League became instrumental in obtaining federal meat inspection laws, workplace safety standards, and unemployment compensation.

At this phase of her career, Kelley also began to look toward organizations and coalitions to effect legal and social change. In the early 1900s, she helped found the National Child Labor Commission, the National Association for the Advancement of Colored People (NAACP), and the Women's International League for Peace and Freedom. She worked wholeheartedly to support women's suffrage, serving as the vice president of the National Women's Suffrage Association.

Throughout Kelley's career, extensive field studies of social conditions, such as *Hull-*

House Maps and Papers, and the use of scientific data and evidence collection as a basis for legal change remained the hallmark of her reform work. Perhaps the most famous use of her studies came in the precedent-setting U.S. Supreme Court ruling *Muller v. Oregon* (1908). This case established the legality of the ten-hour workday for women. Kelley and her friend Louis Brandeis (later named a Supreme Court justice) made legal history by using scientific social data in their arguments before the court.

CONCLUSION

Kelley was not a woman of financial means. In fact, she lived most of her life in the shadow of her former husband's debt. Still, Kelley's greatest philanthropic legacy is her unflagging zeal and lifetime commitment to bring justice to those oppressed by the excesses of capitalism, women and children in particular. Kelley endured many disappointing setbacks, both personal and professional, but made important contributions to social reform and the newly evolving field of social work. Indeed, she became an effective spokesperson for reform by introducing scientific data collection as a basis for quantifying social problems. Based on factual data, Kelley argued that any strategy for social change could not be limited to simple remediation after the fact: approaches to prevent social ills must be incorporated into any plan. Consequently, she successfully pushed for reforms such as minimum wage and hour requirements as well as workplace safety and accountability. Kelley also developed creative, yet concrete, solutions to address social evils; launching campaigns still in common use today—consumer boycotts, informational labeling, and promotions to educate the public.

Kymberly A. Mulhern

FURTHER READING

Chambers, Clarke A. *Seedtime of Reform: American Social Service and Social Action, 1918–1932.*

Minneapolis: University of Minnesota Press, 1963.

Goldmark, Josephine. *Impatient Crusader.* Urbana: University of Illinois Press, 1953.

Hartley, Elizabeth Kennedy. "Social Work and Social Reform: Selected Women Social Workers and Child Welfare Reforms, 1877–1932." Thesis (D.W.S.). University of Pennsylvania, 1985.

Sklar, Kathryn Kish. *Florence Kelley and the Nation's Work.* New Haven, CT: Yale University Press, 1995.

PAPERS

Florence Kelley's letters are included in the Kelley Family Papers at Columbia University (New York City) and in the papers of the National Consumers League in the Library of Congress (Washington, DC).

WILL KEITH KELLOGG
(1860–1951)

Cereal Manufacturer and Founder of the W.K. Kellogg Foundation

INTRODUCTION

"I know how to invest my money. I'll invest it in people" (Powell 1956, 303). With characteristic brevity, Will Keith Kellogg described his motivation for dedicating virtually all of the fortune he made as a manufacturer of ready-to-eat breakfast cereals to the private foundation that bears his name. Kellogg lived three distinct lives; until age 46, he toiled as the business manager of the Battle Creek Sanitarium; from age 46 to 70, he founded and built the Kellogg Company; and from 70 until his death at age 91, while still actively engaged in corporate affairs, his priority shifted to his philanthropic interests.

EARLY YEARS AND EDUCATION

Born on April 7, 1860, to John Preston Kellogg and Ann Janette Stanley Kellogg, he was christened "Willie Keith Kellogg," but he detested his first name, and legally changed it to "Will" in 1898. His father was a farmer and broom manufacturer who was also a prominent member of the Seventh Day Adventist Church. In 1854, John Preston Kellogg was part of a consortium that persuaded the Adventist Elders to relocate the church's headquarters to Battle Creek, Michigan. This achievement would profoundly affect the career of two of his sons, Will and his older brother, John Harvey Kellogg.

Will Kellogg received little formal education, becoming an apprentice broom maker at age 11, and leaving school entirely to become a salesman for his father at age 14. Four years later, he briefly directed a broom factory owned by Adventist Elders in Dallas, Texas. He returned to Battle Creek to marry Ella "Puss" Davis on November 3, 1880. Their union produced five children, three of whom survived to adulthood: Karl Kellogg, John Leonard Kellogg, and Beth Kellogg Williamson. Ella Kellogg was never in robust health, and died in 1912. In the year of his marriage, Will Kellogg also completed his formal education, graduating from a three-month course of study at Parsons Business College in nearby Kalamazoo.

CAREER HIGHLIGHTS

On September 5, 1866, the Adventist Church founded the Western Health Reform Institute in Battle Creek, a spa that emphasized water treatments for illnesses. The Institute was later renamed the "Battle Creek Sanatorium." It remained a modest operation until 1876, when John Harvey Kellogg, a newly minted M.D. from Bellevue Hospital in New York City, returned to Battle Creek

A rare informal photograph of W.K. Kellogg vacationing at his summer home at Gull Lake, Michigan, in the late 1920s. Courtesy of the W.K. Kellogg Foundation.

to take its helm. A born promoter as well as a skilled physician, Dr. Kellogg quickly rechristened the "Sanatorium" as the "Sanitarium." The doctor not only coined a word in doing so, he also served notice that he would run the Sanitarium according to scientific principles of sanitation and a healthy lifestyle. He aggressively marketed, through books and lectures, his theory of "biologic living," which mixed Adventist doctrines of abstention from alcohol and tobacco and adherence to a strict vegetarian diet with his own beliefs in exercise, fresh air, innovative electrical cures, and a clean colon. Dr. Kellogg's combination of religion, medicine, and showmanship made the "San" into one of the nation's preeminent health spas, which attracted presidents, industrialists, and celebrities, as well as a broad clientele seeking its medical, surgical, and therapeutic services.

In April 1880, John Kellogg hired his brother Will as his assistant. From the start, the relationship was a difficult one; John piled duties upon his younger brother—ranging from serving as business manager to tracking down missing patients—until Will's typical work week was 100 or more hours. In return, Dr. Kellogg offered rock-bottom wages, small pay increases at infrequent intervals, and a host of indignities (for example, Will had to wait ten years to get even a small office). One of Will's manifold duties was to help his brother with food experiments that would enliven the bland vegetarian fare of the San's dining room. The wretched flavor of the San's food was a universal complaint among its patients and the cause of frequent "escapes" to nearby eateries, which offered meat dishes. To forestall these nocturnal ramblings, the Kellogg brothers created meat substitutes, which did not prove palatable to patients, and peanut butter, which did. In the late 1880s, the brothers established the Sanitas Food Company to market their culinary innovations, but conflict again erupted. Not only did John insist on retaining three-quarters of the venture's profits, he strictly limited the marketing of the products to current and former patients of the San. Will wanted a wide marketing of their products, but his older brother believed that aggressive advertising would not square with his medical ethics.

In 1894, the Kellogg brothers perfected the process for flaking grains; their first successful product was a wheat flake called "Granose." The flaked cereals proved an immense hit among the San's current and former patients, and Will once again pressed his brother to market them to the general public. The doctor adamantly reiterated his refusal. Later in 1894, however, a discharged Sanitarium patient named C.W. Post established a cereal company in Battle Creek. The Kellogg brothers grumbled that Post had stolen their process; Post roundly denied the charge, but everyone agreed that Post's products—Postum, a coffee substitute, and Grapenuts cereal—were rapidly making him a wealthy man. Will Kellogg chafed in genteel poverty while watching Post become a millionaire by—quite literally—eating the Kellogg brothers' breakfast.

In 1899, Will convinced his brother to organize the Sanitas Nut Food Company, and thought he had his brother's concurrence in building a large modern factory for the new enterprise. Upon its completion, however, John refused to pay for its construction. Consequently, Will left his brother's employ in 1901. Within a few months, however, the San burned to the ground, and Will, who regarded this institution as a part of his life's work, returned to supervise its rebuilding.

As the new San rose from the ashes of the old, Battle Creek was experiencing a cereal boom. From 1902 to 1904, the success of the Postum Company inspired a host of imitators; in all, some forty-two companies would attempt to purvey flaked grains in what was already being called the "cereal city." The Sanitas entry into this frenzied market was "Toasted Corn Flakes," introduced in 1903, but John Kellogg still placed restrictions upon the marketing of this popular product. Finally, after more than twenty-five years of conflicts, the brothers parted company for good; Will left his brother's employ and he established the Battle Creek Toasted Corn Flake Company on February 19, 1906. Less than six months later, the new company's factory burned to the ground. W.K. Kellogg—as he was increasingly being called—cobbled together financing to start again. Soon, a renamed Kellogg Toasted Corn Flake Company was in full operation.

Kellogg grew his business by masterful and audacious advertising and creative promotions. One campaign urged housewives to wink at their grocer; those brave enough to do so received a free sample of Toasted Corn Flakes. Another ad pleaded with consumers *not* to buy corn flakes, because the company could not keep up with the growing demand. So great was Kellogg's faith in the power of marketing that he doubled his ad budget at the beginning of the Great Depression.

Kellogg's marketing acumen paid handsome dividends in terms of sales. By the early 1920s, he could claim to be one of the richest men in the United States. This success, however, came at a high personal cost. From 1910 to 1920, W.K. Kellogg and his older brother squared off in a series of lawsuits and countersuits over the ownership of the flaking process and of the Kellogg Company itself. W.K. Kellogg emerged triumphant, but permanently estranged from his brother. He had similarly contentious relationships with his own children. John Leonard Kellogg came to work for his father in 1908, rising to the company presidency. Nonetheless, father and son clashed over a number of issues, and W.K. bought out his son in 1925. In the early 1930s, W.K. Kellogg brought John Leonard's son, John Leonard Kellogg Jr., into the company. W.K. Kellogg pushed his grandson too hard, promoting him to vice president before he was ready. When the young man could not handle the heavy responsibilities, W.K. Kellogg first demoted him, then fired him, and eventually brought suit against him for allegedly appropriating Kellogg Company trade secrets. Shortly thereafter, John Kellogg Jr. took his own life.

MAJOR PHILANTHROPIC CONTRIBUTIONS

W.K. Kellogg was philanthropic long before he earned a fortune. As the San's business manager, he regularly forgave the debts of patients who could not afford the treatment they received. In business, he offered his employees generous benefits. During the depths of the Great Depression, he added a fourth shift to his factory expressly to hire unemployed workers (although this reduced the hours of all shifts from eight to six, he still paid all employees for eight hours of work). The acquisition of wealth led him to increase the scale of his giving. Still, he felt overwhelmed by requests for assistance by 1925. In that year, he formed the Fellowship Corporation: an unendowed vehicle consisting of three friends who advised him on his philanthropy. Unsurprisingly, this corporation mainly made gifts in the Battle Creek area.

Two events, unrelated to each other and

separated by many years, propelled Kellogg to endow a private foundation. The first was a personal tragedy; his grandson Kenneth Williamson (son of his daughter Beth) tumbled from a second-story window in 1913. Kellogg was disturbed that, despite his great wealth, he could not find adequate medical care for his grandson in Battle Creek or elsewhere (although he partially recovered, Kenneth Williamson remained physically handicapped for the rest of his life). Then, in 1930, President **Herbert Hoover** invited Kellogg to be an observer at the White House Conference on Children and Youth. Kellogg returned from the conference determined to systematize his giving on behalf of children.

Accordingly, he established—later in 1930—the W.K. Kellogg Child Welfare Foundation. In a few months, he realized that the well-being of children depended upon many institutions and individuals: hospitals and housing, schools and social services, and cultural and recreational opportunities. With this insight, the Child Welfare Foundation was renamed the W.K. Kellogg Foundation at the end of 1930 and given the broad charter of improving the lives of young people. In its early years, Kellogg provided the budget for the foundation out of his personal funds. Indeed, he did not want to endow the foundation until he was satisfied that the foundation was proving itself useful. When he did endow it in 1935, however, he did so handsomely; eventually the W.K. Kellogg Foundation would receive virtually all of his ownership of the Kellogg Company: approximately 54% of its common stock.

In 1931, the new foundation launched a seventeen-year initiative called the Michigan Community Health Project. The project, focusing on seven counties in the south-central portion of the state's Lower Peninsula, consolidated rural schools, built modern hospital facilities, established county departments of public health, and launched the concept of outdoor education for elementary students. In 1942, while this project was still in full swing, the U.S. Department of State asked the foundation to begin programming

in Latin America to counter the growing threat of fascism in that region. In doing so, the foundation curiously became international in scope before it became national.

In the postwar period, under the able guidance of Dr. Emory Morris, the foundation expanded its programming to Europe, and distinguished itself in the United States by funding a comprehensive health agenda: medicine, dentistry, nursing, health services administration, public health, and the allied health fields. It also played a key role in the expansion of the U.S. network of community colleges as well as other forms of adult continuing education. The foundation grew to international prominence under the watchful eye of Kellogg, who served as chairman of the board of trustees into the 1940s, and took a keen interest in its activities until the end of his life. While Kellogg's role was active, it was rarely intrusive; he was usually content to leave its day-to-day management and governance in the hands of those whom he trusted.

Although Kellogg made a number of private gifts prior to establishing his foundation, he used the foundation as a vehicle for most of his personal giving after 1930. Still, his major personal benefactions included the presentation of a Bird Sanctuary and an experimental demonstration farm to Michigan State University in 1928–1929. Notable gifts through the foundation include the Ann J. Kellogg School (a pioneer in mainstreaming handicapped children) and the W.K. Kellogg Auditorium, both to the Battle Creek Public Schools, and his Arabian horse ranch in Pamona, California to the state, which has established the California Polytechnic University–Pamona on the site.

CONCLUSION

W.K. Kellogg passed away on October 6, 1951. Despite his many triumphs, he was thwarted in his last ambition, living a longer life span than his older brother. Although both reached their ninety-first birthdays, John Harvey Kellogg's life lasted a few weeks longer than his younger brother's. Nonetheless, W.K. Kellogg died satisfied that he had accomplished his desire to help people to help themselves. In the years after its founding, the W.K. Kellogg Foundation continually distinguished itself. While growing into one of the largest private American foundations by the end of the twentieth century, the foundation became a leader in funding areas such as health care, food systems and rural development, youth development, higher education, philanthropy and volunteerism, and leadership development. Certainly, he achieved his most important ambition, one that he articulated in a speech to veteran employees of the Kellogg Company in 1930: "It is my hope that the property that kind Providence has brought me may be helpful to many others, and that I may be found a faithful steward." (Powell 1956, 165).

Joel J. Orosz

FURTHER READING

Carson, Gerald. *Cornflake Crusade*. New York: Rinehart & Company, 1957.

Powell, Horace B. *The Original Has This Signature—W.K. Kellogg*. Englewood Cliffs, NJ: Prentice-Hall, 1956.

PAPERS

Will Keith Kellogg's papers are located in the archives of the W.K. Kellogg Foundation (Battle Creek, MI).

ACKNOWLEDGMENTS

The author is indebted to Dr. Russell G. Mawby, chairman emeritus, and Dr. William C. Richardson, president and chief executive officer of the W.K. Kellogg Foundation, both of whom reviewed this entry and made many helpful suggestions.

MARTIN LUTHER KING, JR.
(1929–1968)

Minister and Campaigner for Social Justice through Nonviolent Voluntary Action

INTRODUCTION

An eloquent champion of nonviolent direct action, Martin Luther King, Jr. was confident about the need to challenge the powerful. "Freedom is never voluntarily given by the oppressor," he wrote, "it must be demanded by the oppressed" (King 1964, 82). This approach inevitably made him a controversial figure during his tragically short career. FBI director J. Edgar Hoover even had King under constant surveillance as a dangerous subversive. Nonetheless, his Southern protest campaigns contributed to the ending of legal segregation and the protection of black voting rights. At the time of his murder in 1968, he was also campaigning for a guaranteed annual income to eliminate poverty and against America's continuing involvement in Vietnam in pursuit of what he called the "Beloved Community." With the establishment of a national public holiday in his honor in 1983, King eventually attained an unparalleled position among the handful of African Americans celebrated as major national heroes.

EARLY YEARS AND EDUCATION

In 1929, Martin Luther King, Jr. was born in Atlanta, Georgia. As the eldest son of Martin Luther King, Sr. and Alberta Williams King, he joined a family line of Baptist preachers that stretched back into slavery. From his father's example, he quickly learned that the church should be the natural hub of philanthropic efforts within the black community. Relatively affluent himself, he was inspired to dedicate his life to the disadvantaged. Entering Morehouse College at the age of fifteen, he wanted to be a doctor

Rev. Martin Luther King, Jr., speaking at a press conference in June 1964. Library of Congress; LC-USZ62-122985.

or a lawyer. Such secular career aspirations reflected the young King's doubts about the emotionalism of the black Baptist tradition. However, as public intellectuals, college president Benjamin Mays and other tutors offered alternate models of Christian ministry to King that married theological sophistication with social activism, encouraging him to seek ordination as his father's assistant in 1948.

He then entered Crozer Theological Seminary in Pennsylvania, where his reading of Reinhold Niebuhr tempered his Social Gospel instincts that stressed the application of Christianity to contemporary social problems. Set against the horrors of World War II as well as those of the African-American experience, Niebuhr's argument that the moral impulse might be cultivated in individuals but that immorality preyed easily on man en masse was highly persuasive. However,

family upbringing and the emphasis within Afro-Christianity on a personal relationship with a forgiving God predisposed King to believe in an ultimately benign universe, and he preferred the more optimistic theology of personalism: an outlook that strengthened his impulse for voluntary service since it stressed the innate, inalienable sacredness of each person and argued that positive social change could come from the accumulation of individual moral choices. It was also a potent foundation for King's later philosophy of nonviolence.

King subsequently decided to pursue a doctorate at Boston University under a leading personalist theologian, Edgar Brightman. As his doctoral studies neared completion, African-American university faculties and prestigious churches around the country courted King, who had recently married Coretta Scott, a black Alabaman who was studying music at the New England Conservatory. Since he could have chosen an easier life, his decision to become pastor at Dexter Avenue Church in Montgomery, Alabama, in 1954, despite his wife's misgivings, confirmed the extent to which King felt obliged to join the unfolding struggles for racial justice in his native South. Coretta King and eventually four children, Yolanda, Dexter, Martin III, and Bernice, would have to share the burden of King's dangerous public life.

CAREER HIGHLIGHTS AND MAJOR PHILANTHROPIC CONTRIBUTIONS

A succession of nonviolent protest campaigns defined King's public career (1955–1968). He truly entered history in December 1955 when he agreed, somewhat reluctantly, to head the Montgomery Improvement Association, a voluntary association founded to coordinate the boycott of segregated buses after the arrest of Rosa Parks. As the boycott continued throughout 1956, King's eloquent, charismatic leadership sustained black Montgomerians' morale and attracted national and international support. The national media publicized his calls for nonviolence in the face of white attacks, including the bombing of his home, which could easily have killed his wife and baby daughter.

From the outset, King referred to Mahatma Gandhi as an inspiration. However, American Gandhians, such as Bayard Rustin, discovered that the young leader of the Montgomery Improvement Association had little knowledge of Gandhi's philosophy. Nevertheless, as an act of noncooperation within an unjust system, the bus boycott was in the Gandhian tradition. In late 1956, the bus segregation in Montgomery ended. As the chief symbol of the boycott, King quickly became a race leader in the eyes of the national media. However, he did not substantially build on his boycott success until 1963. He founded the Southern Christian Leadership Conference (SCLC) in 1957 to develop a regional protest strategy, but his near-fatal stabbing in late 1958 inevitably slowed the

organization's development. The SCLC not only struggled to apply its nonviolent approach effectively during the late 1950s but also lagged behind other organizations during the sit-ins and freedom rides of 1960–1961.

King believed that nonviolence would ultimately produce the "Beloved Community" in which the Christian injunction to love your neighbor would ensure justice by compelling action. Although his imprisonment in Georgia, which stemmed from the Atlanta lunch-counter sit-ins, drew headlines during the 1960 presidential election, the young demonstrators of the Student Nonviolent Coordinating Committee (SNCC) seemed much more conspicuous exponents of nonviolent direct action. King refused their calls to join them on the freedom ride to Jackson, Mississippi in 1961, bolstering the impression that he was more talk than action. When King did go to jail in support of antisegregation protests in Albany, Georgia, he was wrongly persuaded to file bail after only a few days. In the summer of 1962, Albany's Sheriff Laurie Pritchett outmaneuvered King by realizing, seemingly before King himself, that nonviolence needed a crisis to create the political and economic pressure that forces concessions. Thus, Pritchett arranged for King to be anonymously bailed out rather than allowing him to attract publicity by his imprisonment. At the end of 1962, African Americans were questioning both King's leadership and his nonviolent approach.

Against this backdrop, King's decision to mount a sustained campaign in Birmingham, Alabama in 1963 was a desperate gamble. Designed to win the desegregation of facilities and employment in the downtown stores, the campaign anticipated that the extreme reaction of Birmingham's notorious police commissioner, Bull Connor, would force a "fence-sitting" Kennedy administration to intervene. Still, the campaign only fulfilled King's objective to "so dramatize the issue that it can no longer be ignored" when SCLC recruited hundreds of black schoolchildren to confront Bull Connor (King 1964, 81). Pictures of children confronting water cannons and attack dogs horrified the nation, creating the impetus for both local negotiations and a federal civil rights bill.

To rally bipartisan support for this bill, King spoke at the climax of the so-called March on Washington. His televised "I Have A Dream" speech, in which he spoke of "a dream deeply rooted in the American dream," confirmed his position as the pre-eminent advocate of racial integration (Washington 1986, 219). Nonetheless, his nonviolent approach and appeal to white liberals attracted criticism. The separatist Nation of Islam spokesman Malcolm X slammed King's position. "Real men don't put their children in the front line," he declared (McWhorter 2001, 442). He also challenged King's claim that nonviolence had appealed to white America's morality. Only when black Birminghamites fought back in late May, Malcolm X claimed, did the Kennedy administration intervene.

King orchestrated headline-grabbing non-violent demonstrations in the Florida resort of St. Augustine to ensure passage of the Civil Rights Act of 1964. Inspired by the award of the Nobel Peace Prize, he then used the same tactics in Selma, Alabama in 1965 to spotlight the denial of black voting rights in the Deep South. After the murder of a young black protester, SCLC organized a mass march from Selma to Alabama's state capital, Montgomery. When state police violently dispersed marchers on the outskirts of Selma, pressure for federal action grew as liberal sympathizers flocked to join the second march attempt. However, King's calculated use of protest to promote reform and his apparent courtship of the Johnson administration, which was rewarded by the passage of the Voting Rights Act, increasingly incensed black militants.

When black anger exploded in violent disturbances in the Watts district of Los Angeles in August 1965, it challenged King to develop nonviolent campaigns against ghetto poverty. He selected Chicago as his target in 1966, but his efforts faltered. Unable to meet rising expectations, King was still trying to organize black Chicagoans in June 1966 when violent disturbances erupted. Striving to generate the kind of creative tension that had forced concessions in earlier campaigns, King refocused his Chicago campaign on housing discrimination. Protest marches into all-white neighborhoods in August met a violent reaction from white residents. Increasingly, however, national audiences sympathized less with the demonstrators than with the police caught in the middle or with frightened white homeowners like themselves, and King's faith in the ultimate creativity of social tension was not shared. Simultaneously, SNCC leader Stokely Carmichael used a protest march in Mississippi to publicize his rejection of nonviolence and demand for "Black Power."

Although King opposed the racial separatism of black militants and their refusal to reject violence, his insistence that racial justice required a fundamental redistribution of economic resources and political power in America and his increasingly strident denunciation of American involvement in Vietnam alienated some SCLC supporters. Moderate black leaders rebuked King for his antiwar comments, which they believed damaged African Americans politically as Congress became more conservative. By the start of 1968, King was increasingly desperate to show that non-violent tactics could compel Congress to redirect resources away from militarism and toward a full-scale war against poverty. He planned to bring an army of the poor to Washington to engage in mass civil disobedience, believing that the dislocation it caused would create a national crisis. Colleagues, such as Jesse Jackson, questioned this strategy, and other advisers warned that any disorder would simply aggravate current reactionary political trends. Thus, when an ongoing industrial dispute drew King to Memphis in the spring of 1968, he was perceived to be a leader in decline. This impression deepened in late March when a march he was leading degenerated into rioting and looting. Seeking to restore his reputation, King returned to Memphis to lead a nonviolent march in early April. Before the march could take place, he was assassinated on April 4, 1968.

CONCLUSION

At the time of his death, King himself was deeply despondent and felt that he had failed to develop a program of nonviolent protest to address the deeply rooted problems of militarism, poverty, and discrimination. He was apt to say that the desegregation of public accommodations and restoration of voting rights had cost America nothing, but that now he was demanding changes that would require altered priorities and a redistribution of resources. However, the ending of the South's apartheid system was no meager achievement, and King's advocacy and use of nonviolence not only nurtured a positive climate for federal legislation, but also, just as importantly, instilled a new pride in African Americans.

Like Gandhi, King struggled to overcome the misperception that nonviolent direct action was passive and submissive. In part, this was due to his Christian rearticulation of Gandhi's assertion that nonviolence required that you love the oppressor and seek to change his heart. However, King's actual practice of nonviolence revealed that the key change came in the hearts of oppressed people, who realized that they could act against injustice and felt a new dignity as a result. In Montgomery, Birmingham, and Selma, King's tactics also created a compelling moral spectacle that forced a far larger audience of onlookers to review their complicity in the maintenance of an unjust system. His tactics also exploited a Cold War context that made successive presidents mindful that publicized racial injustice dented America's claim to be a champion of freedom.

Throughout his career, King was also convinced that African Americans could use their economic leverage, such as consumer boycotts, to attack discrimination. When he turned his attention to issues of ghetto poverty, this approach became a central strand of his efforts to promote not just employment opportunities but broader patterns of positive investment and empowerment. In his calls to end the war in Vietnam, he urged America "to get on the right side of the world revolution" and declared that the real choice was between "nonviolent coexistence or violent co-annihilation" (Washington 1986, 240, 243). Weapons of mass destruction were intrinsically immoral from a personalist theological standpoint since they ignored the "God" in every person and they were also socially self-destructive since they reinforced the treatment of people as things and expended resources that might otherwise be used to help those in need. King rejected violence on pragmatic as well as principled grounds, but more importantly he embraced dedicated voluntary action. He believed that a man had not found anything to live for until he found something for which he was prepared to die.

Peter J. Ling

FURTHER READING

Branch, Taylor. *Parting the Waters: America in the King Years, 1954–63.* New York: Simon & Schuster, 1988.

———. *Pillar of Fire: America in the King Years, 1963–1965.* New York: Simon & Schuster, 1998.

Carson, Clayborne, ed. *The Autobiography of Martin Luther King, Jr.* New York: Warner Books, 1998.

Garrow, David. *Bearing the Cross: Martin Luther King, Jr. and the Southern Christian Leadership Conference.* London: Jonathan Cape, 1988.

King, Martin Luther, Jr. *Why We Can't Wait.* New York: Harper, 1964.

McWhorter, Diane. *Carry Me Home: Birmingham, Alabama—The Climactic Battle of the Civil Rights Revolution.* New York: Simon & Schuster, 2001.

Washington, James M., ed. *A Testament of Hope: The Essential Writings of Martin Luther King, Jr.* New York: Harper & Row, 1986.

PAPERS

The chief repository of Martin Luther King, Jr.'s papers is currently the Martin Luther King Center for Nonviolent Social Change (Atlanta,

GA) although certain materials relating to his career prior to 1960 remain at Boston University (Boston, MA). The Martin Luther King, Jr. Papers Project, based at Stanford University, has so far published four volumes covering the period up to December 1958.

SEBASTIAN S. KRESGE
(1867–1966)

Retailing Pioneer and Founder of the Kresge Foundation

INTRODUCTION

Summing up his approach to philanthropy, Sebastian S. Kresge simply said, "I really want to leave the world a better place than I found it" (Garraty and Carnes 1999, 918). Kresge, referred to by family, friends, and colleagues simply as "S.S.," was born near Kresgeville, Pennsylvania. His parents were hard-working, poor farmers whose personal lifestyles instilled in their son core values including a devout belief in God, clean living characterized by abstinence from alcohol and smoking, charity toward others, hard work, and frugality. These values guided Sebastian Kresge's life: permeating his actions toward his family, employees, customers, as well as the causes that benefited from his considerable philanthropy. By the time Kresge died, he had created a billion dollar business and a billion dollar foundation. Indeed, he helped to make life better and to provide opportunities in business and philanthropy for thousands of Americans who would never know him personally.

Sebastian S. Kresge is photographed in his Detroit office in May 1957. © Bettmann/CORBIS.

EARLY YEARS AND EDUCATION

Early in life, Kresge learned the value of hard work. Indeed, he began doing chores on his family's farm when he was only five years old. His father and mother, Sebastian Kresge and Catherine Kunkle, were hard-working and financially stressed farmers. When he was eight years old, the family farm was seized and sold by the sheriff to satisfy a mortgage lien. At age fourteen, eager to pursue something other than farming, he decided to undertake a career in teaching. To pursue this goal, he needed to enter his uncle's Fairview Academy, the only school in the area capable of providing teacher education. Lacking the funds, Kresge persuaded his father to finance his education in return for his wages until the age of twenty-one. To meet his end of the bargain, he gave his parents his salary from his work at various local jobs and the $22 a month he earned when he began teaching at Gower School at age eighteen.

During this period of his life, the only funds he kept for himself were those generated by his beekeeping business, which he started when he was fourteen years old. He made money from it in its first year and from then on always had a cash reserve and some financial security. Kresge also loved beekeeping, because, as he would say later, "My bees always reminded me that hard work, thrift, sobriety, and an earnest struggle to live a Christian life are the first rungs of the ladder of success" (*New York Times* 1966, A1). Consequently, he continued beekeeping as a hobby into his adult life.

After graduating from Fairview Academy and teaching a term, he decided that his interest lay in business. So he took a $28-a-month job in a grocery store in Scranton, Pennsylvania. As his attraction to a business career grew, he decided to enroll in the Eastman's Business School in Poughkeepsie, New York. He completed the four-month course at the age of twenty-three and began to explore business opportunities.

CAREER HIGHLIGHTS

After a succession of jobs, including insurance and bookkeeping, Kresge accepted a two-year stint in a Scranton, Pennsylvania hardware store where he kept the books and worked as a salesman. It was here that Kresge would begin to cultivate his later-famous business acumen. Never wanting to be idle, he repaired and polished over twenty wood stoves in his free time. His employer thought the stoves were junk, but Kresge ended up selling every stove. This event impressed his employer, increased his salary from $28 to $40 a month, and symbolized Kresge's hands-on and enterprising behavior.

While working at the hardware store, Kresge met and befriended a prosperous tin salesman who convinced Kresge that an ambitious young man like himself would do well in the tin business. Taking a job on straight commission, he began a five-year career as a traveling tin and hardware salesman and became quite successful within two years. During his traveling salesman days, Kresge met three of his earliest mentors, S.H. Knox, John G. McCrorey (later called McCrory),

and Frank W. (later F.W.) Woolworth. All three men would later become some of the most successful chain store retailers. Their stores, their cash-transaction-only business methods, and the profitmaking power of their group purchasing techniques impressed Kresge.

Resolving to go into business for himself, he began to work even harder to save money for an investment stake. This goal was not as great a challenge for him as it might be for others. Frugality and saving were behaviors characteristic of his life. By age thirty, he had over $8,000 in savings. This was an especially large sum for 1896, when annual per capita income was estimated at less than $300. As a path toward starting his own venture, he tried to partner with F.W. Woolworth but was rebuffed. Soon thereafter, in exchange for Kresge's investment of $8,000, McCrorey took him on as a partner in a new retail business (a five-and-dime store) and agreed to train him as well. The retail operation was in Jamestown, New York, and Kresge began as the co-manager. Within two years, he earned enough money to buy out McCrorey and own his first store in Detroit. In thirteen short years (1899–1912), he built his company from one to eighty-five stores. In fact, his annual sales totaled $10 million and ranked second only to F.W. Woolworth in the dime store business. Considered an expert at choosing the best sites for stores as well as the mix of quality and low-cost retail goods, Kresge would later be considered one of the founding fathers of the chain store concept. When he died in 1966, Kresge owned 930 stores (including S.S. Kresge, K-Mart, and Jupiter Stores) in Canada and the United States, which employed over 42,000 people and generated over $1 billion in revenue.

Using principles that had guided him throughout his life, Kresge forged a corporate culture built on principles such as hands-on management, strict morality, progressive personnel policies, and close relationships with his employees. Well ahead of his time, he offered pensions, paid sick leave, paid holidays, and profit sharing. Kresge pointed with pride to the fact that many of his top managers were millionaires by 1925. Kresge also got to know his employees well and knew the names and family particulars of all his store managers. Often, Kresge even gave fatherly advice to a manager or employee. Devoted to family values at an early age, he also insisted that his mother's picture hang prominently in all of his stores.

Success in business was not always paralleled by success in personal matters. His first two marriages—controversial because the women were twenty-five years or more younger than him—ended with bitter divorces. In both cases, his stingy behavior was listed as a major reason for the divorce. Having acquired a habit of austere frugality as a child, he simply could not shake it, even for marriage. Kresge, for example, drove his cars until they were unreparable, wore shoes until he had to stuff them with paper to keep out the elements, and gave up golf because—though a multimillionaire—he could not tolerate losing golf balls. Still, he entered into a successful thirty-eight-year marriage to Clara K. Swaine (when she was 35 and he was 61) in 1928.

Similar to his zeal in frugality, Kresge vigorously opposed any consumption of alcohol because of his upbringing. He refused to donate to any church with a minister who used alcohol. Kresge also examined the prohibition stance of any political candidate before voting. In 1917, he supported the passage of the Eighteenth Amendment to the constitution, prohibiting alcohol consumption, out of personal beliefs as well as the belief that drinking could harm one's productivity and safety at work. Consequently, he also donated over one million dollars to prohibition efforts. Beyond his money, he recruited other business leaders to support the cause, and volunteered his time and talent on state prohibition committees in Pennsylvania and Michigan. Kresge even served on the Executive Committee of the National Anti-Saloon League, including two years as treasurer. Using the argument that drinking caused wasteful activity and drained the productivity of workers, he encouraged other business

leaders like **Andrew Carnegie**, J.L. Hudson, the **Rockefellers**, John Wanamaker, and Frank W. Woolworth to support prohibition efforts.

Ultimately, Kresge became disheartened by broad-scale efforts to repeal prohibition. In private correspondence, he revealed the dynamic tension between his personal belief about alcohol and his profit-making drive. He confided to others that his "dry" stand might be hurting his retail business because customers did not agree with his beliefs. In this instance, Kresge found that a prominent businessman's involvement in a social cause could hurt his bottom line. Disappointed by the lack of broad support from other businessmen and the public, Kresge was further devastated when one of his sons was arrested for smuggling champagne and whiskey into the United States. In 1933, the twenty-first Amendment repealed prohibition. Afterward, Kresge's zeal in this area waned and he turned more of his attention to his business and his major philanthropic endeavor, the Kresge Foundation.

MAJOR PHILANTHROPIC CONTRIBUTIONS

Though frugal in life, Kresge acted quite generously when it came to charitable efforts. He approached philanthropy with the same hands-on methods, Christian values, and strong work ethic that permeated all his other initiatives. In 1920, Kresge confided to fellow churchmen that he felt an obligation to help others. He felt that this obligation arose from the blessings of a favorable life and from a conviction that God expected no less of him. While he wanted to help others, Kresge remained a hard-nosed businessman. He studied the philanthropy field for a number of years, examining the charitable approaches of other wealthy men. He also sought the advice of close friends and colleagues. He did not just want to give money away, but give while retaining control of his gifts. After four years of study, he formed the Kresge Foundation with an initial contribution of $1.3 million.

True to his wish, he became involved in every aspect of his foundation's work. The foundation's policies favored—as they do today—grants that provided for the maintenance, expansion, or perpetuation of deserving existing organizations over grants that established new organizations or experimental projects. This policy was based upon Kresge's belief that there were more than enough other foundations focused on new and experimental charity ventures. From the start, he also promoted self-help and rewarded initiative because both concepts had served him well throughout his life. As a result, the Kresge Foundation required applicants to demonstrate that they had the resources to provide future yearly support and maintenance for the project once it was launched. Believing that America could not afford the secularization of its major charitable institutions (e.g., universities), Kresge also made gifts that would offset an organization's total reliance on tax money and subsequent secularization.

Kresge coupled these three fundamental tenets with his interests in education, religion, care of children, the elderly, health care and employment training for young people. The groups and issues he supported in 1924 are often the ones his foundation funds today. Examples of major beneficiaries include orphanages, the YMCA, Girls Scouts of America, Harvard University, Michigan State University–Kresge Art Museum, Notre Dame–Kresge Law Library, the Kresge Eye Institute for indigent eye patients, University of Michigan Medical School, and a program to help develop fund-raising programs at historically black colleges and universities.

CONCLUSION

Kresge's life was hallmarked by his promotion of values some might call conserva-

tive for lack of a better word. By the time he died in 1966, Kresge had contributed over $100 million to his foundation. Kresge's philanthropy reflected the same values that had served him well in life and business: generosity toward others, hard work, and hands-on management. His proficiency in philanthropy paralleled his business acumen. Kresge started his business with $8,000 in 1897 and had generated over $1 billion when he died seventy years later. He started the Kresge Foundation with $1.3 million and its assets grew to $1.9 billion in just over seventy years.

Michael Gerrity

FURTHER READING

The First Thirty Years: 1924–1953, The Kresge Foundation. Detroit, MI: Trustees of the Kresge Foundation, 1954, 1–46.

Furnas, J.C. *The Life and Times of the Late Demon Rum*. New York: G.P. Putnam's Sons, 1974, 308–310.

Garraty, John A., and Mark C. Carnes, eds. "Sebastian S. Kresge." *American National Biography*, vol. 24. New York: Oxford University Press, 1999, 917–919.

Lender, Mark E. "Sebastian S. Kresge." In *Dictionary of American Temperance Biography: From Temperance Reform to Alcohol Research, the 1600s to the 1980s*. Westport, CT: Greenwood Press, 1984, 282–283.

Pegram, Thomas R. *Battling Demon Rum: The Struggle for a Dry America, 1800–1933*. Chicago: Ivan R. Dee, 1998.

"S.S. Kresge Dead; Merchant Was 99." *New York Times*, October 18, 1966, A1.

PAPERS

Sebastian S. Kresge's papers as well as the annual reports of his company and foundation are located at the Bentley Historical Library at the University of Michigan (Ann Arbor, MI).

L

ELI LILLY
(1885–1977)

Pharmaceutical Company Executive and Cofounder of the Lilly Endowment

INTRODUCTION

Giving to "worthwhile charitable and educational objects . . . sounds easy," Eli Lilly advised his young daughter, Evie, in 1939, "but the 'catch' is that it takes lots of time and study to know what objects of that nature are worthwhile and what are not" (Madison 1989, 189). Eli Lilly spent lots of time and study seeking to give money in a responsible way. He developed intensely deep and broad charitable, educational, and cultural interests so that he was able to give primarily to people, institutions, and causes he knew personally.

EARLY YEARS AND EDUCATION

In 1885, Lilly was born in Indianapolis, Indiana. His grandfather, who founded the family pharmaceutical business in 1876, had been a Civil War officer and was often addressed as Colonel Eli Lilly. The Colonel's only son, Josiah K. Lilly, Sr., had two sons—the younger, Josiah K. Lilly, Jr., and the

older, Eli Lilly, addressed in later years as "Mr. Lilly" or "Mr. Eli" to distinguish him from his grandfather.

The three generations of Lilly men were very close. Young Eli Lilly developed a special affection for his grandfather, who instilled a love of history, including the Civil War, and a commitment to the city of Indianapolis. All four Lilly men contributed substantially to the growth of the family pharmaceutical business and to the family's philanthropy, but none more than "Mr. Eli."

Educated in the Indianapolis public schools, young Eli Lilly eagerly attended the Philadelphia College of Pharmacy. However, he later regretted his lack of a formal liberal arts education. Following graduation from pharmacy school in 1907, he entered the family business with a determination to prove himself.

CAREER HIGHLIGHTS

In his first years in the pharmaceutical company, Lilly pioneered techniques of time

Eli Lilly. Indiana Historical Society.

management and of systematic mass production. He was driven to reduce costs and increase production. Still, he made even more important contributions in moving the company toward scientific and research-based pharmaceuticals. The great breakthrough came in the early 1920s, when Lilly played a key role in several research and production collaborations that led to mass production of insulin. The medical and financial success of this new lifesaving drug was central to the evolution of Eli Lilly and Company from one of many small pharmaceutical companies, producing mostly ineffective medicines, to one of a handful of large firms in the industry producing scientifically based drugs.

Eli Lilly succeeded his father as president of the family-owned and managed corporation in 1932. He continued the push toward scientific research and development, including production of antibiotics in the 1940s. He also pioneered new employee relations programs that raised morale, including a refusal to lay off any worker during the Great Depression of the 1930s. Under his leadership, the company became known as one of the best places to work in central Indiana. Eli Lilly retired from the presidency in 1948 but

stayed closely involved in the business until shortly before his death in 1977.

MAJOR PHILANTHROPIC CONTRIBUTIONS

Despite his early business success, Eli Lilly approached middle age in the 1920s as an unhappy man. He was hard-driving, impatient, and prone to outbursts of temper. Employees feared him. At home, his marriage floundered.

In 1926, Lilly and his wife, Evelyn Fortune Lilly, who had married in 1907, divorced. His second marriage, to Ruth Allison in 1927, became one of great happiness. Still, the earlier unhappiness and especially the troubled life of his daughter Evie, who struggled with unhappy marriages and alcoholism, caused Lilly continued anguish. These family crises prompted him to reexamine his life. In an essay he wrote in 1934, he sought what he called "the proper outlook on life" (Madison 1989, 80). As deliberately as he had sought to produce insulin, Lilly now set out, he wrote, "to broaden and brighten his life and surroundings" (Madison 1989, 80). Soon, new personal interests tumbled forth. He began to read and to write, to educate himself in subjects not taught in pharmacy school. Furthermore, he sought friends who became tutors for his expanding interests.

At the center of Lilly's proper outlook was philanthropy. Lilly's philanthropy was personal, direct, and thoughtful. He wanted to give in ways that connected to his own growing interests and to concrete objectives. He wanted to know about the institutions and people who received his money. Thus, most of his giving was local, focused on Indianapolis and Indiana. In the 1930s and after, most donations also related to areas to which he had become passionately attached. These included history, archaeology, historic preservation, Chinese art, education, and religion. Among the objects of his philanthropy were the Indiana Historical Society, Historic Landmarks Foundation of Indiana, the Indianapolis Art Museum, private liberal arts colleges such as Wabash and Earlham, and his beloved Christ Church, all in Indiana;

Lilly came to know well each of these institutions and the people who headed them.

Some of Lilly's most personal philanthropy was quixotic. He gave millions of dollars in his quest to develop methods of character education. His hope of learning how to inculcate moral and spiritual values in children developed out of his regret over his daughter's unhappy life. The long years of effort in character education produced meager results. Some of his personal philanthropy brought him sorrow. A central institution in his life was Christ Church, the Episcopal church on the Circle in downtown Indianapolis. Lilly wrote its history and actively supported its liberal urban reformer, Paul Moore, when he arrived as dean in 1957. But the racial and social crises of the 1960s blew winds of change that were too liberal for Lilly: when a new dean and rector, Peter Lawson, pushed too hard for federal public housing and racial integration, Lilly, in great anger, withheld his attendance and his philanthropy.

Lilly's giving often took form in a check written from his personal funds. Usually, he demanded anonymity, out of his genuine modesty and his desire to reduce the many demands for help. He seldom set other conditions. His style of philanthropy deeply influenced the family foundation he cofounded. His idea for forming a foundation developed in the mid-1930s as profits from the pharmaceutical business accumulated and as income tax threatened. In 1937, Lilly urged his brother, J.K. Lilly, Jr., and their father, J.K. Lilly, Sr., to join him in forming the Lilly Endowment. Eli Lilly was its driving force and ran it for years from a single desk drawer. Its assets consisted almost entirely of Eli Lilly Company stock. The company's success in the middle decades of the twentieth century meant that it was one of the nation's wealthiest foundations by the 1960s.

Reflecting the family interests, the Lilly Endowment focused on three areas: education, religion, and community service. The family insisted that giving to medical and pharmaceutical areas be off limits. In the early 1960s, J.K. Lilly Jr. briefly moved the Lilly Endowment into conservative anticommunist, free market, and evangelical religious giving, causing foundation expert Wlademar A. Nielsen to charge that the Lilly Endowment "has now lost much of its good reputation in the swamps of the far Right" (Nielsen 1972, 171). Though socially and politically conservative, Eli Lilly himself was lukewarm toward or nonsupportive of these right-wing initiatives and soon moved the organization in broader directions following his brother's death in 1966. New board members came from outside the family and more sophisticated and professional staff arrived, though the three areas of education, religion, and community remained central foci. Even after the Lilly family stopped dominating the fund, Indiana and Indianapolis also continued to receive generous consideration.

CONCLUSION

Eli Lilly's memorial service at Christ Church in 1977 followed his wishes that there be no eulogies. He remained a modest man to the end. Only after his life ended did the extent of his personal philanthropy gradually become evident.

James H. Madison

FURTHER READING

Madison, James H. *Eli Lilly: A Life 1885–1977*. Indianapolis: Indiana Historical Society, 1989.
Nielsen, Waldemar A. *The Big Foundations*. New York: Columbia University Press, 1972.

PAPERS

Eli Lilly's papers are located at the Archives of Eli Lilly and Company in Indianapolis, Indiana, with smaller collections at the Glenn A. Black Laboratory of Archaeology at Indiana University (Bloomington, IN), and the Indiana Historical Society (Indianapolis).

JULIETTE "DAISY" GORDON LOW
(1860–1927)

Founder of the Girl Scouts of America

INTRODUCTION

"I've got something for the girls of Savannah, and all America, and all the world, and we're going to start it tonight!" (List 1960, 37). Juliette Gordon Low's enthusiasm and optimism created the American offshoot of the popular British Boy Scouts and Girl Guides. The Girl Scouts of America has grown since that 1912 call from eighteen eager Georgia girls to three million girls at the turn of the twenty-first century. Spurred on by the infectious spirit of the zealous Gordon Low, her earnest desire to be helpful in the world, and the certainty that girls could best grow into strong, useful women with the guidance of trained female leaders, Gordon Low dedicated the last fifteen years of her life and much of her fortune to the birth and successful growth of the Girl Scouts of America.

EARLY YEARS AND EDUCATION

Juliette Gordon's first five years were spent against the tumultuous backdrop of the Civil War that divided her family just as it did the country. Born in 1860 of a Yankee mother and a Southern father, Juliette, always called Daisy, would not know a truly stable family until she was nearly a teenager. Her father, William Gordon, a prosperous cotton broker, put aside his business and volunteered for the Confederate forces. Daisy Gordon, her two sisters, and her mother soldiered alone in their Savannah mansion until 1864 when, ahead of the Union forces, her mother Eleanor Kinzie Gordon whisked her daughters back to her home in Chicago. Reunited nearly a year later, the family suffered financial deprivations as they returned to Georgia and tried to recreate their lives.

Like many upper-class daughters of the South, Daisy Gordon attended private day schools for girls to augment the scripture study and decorum lessons taught by her mother. At age thirteen, she went to Stuart Hall, a boarding school for elite young women in Virginia. Her first philanthropic endeavor was the creation of a club called the Helpful Hands. Gordon gathered her friends into a sewing circle to make clothes for the less fortunate. The undertaking nearly failed, as she did not know how to sew. The effort, consistent with both the noblesse oblige implied by her social station and an already markedly serendipitous—some would call it eccentric—approach to life, was only moderately successful. She enjoyed her first tour of Europe that summer. In 1875, she transferred to Edge Hill, another Virginia boarding school. Two years later, at age seventeen, Gordon was sent to Charbonniers, a French finishing school in New York City, where she improved her language and literature skills, learned dancing and art appreciation, and attended museums and theaters. She cultivated a serious talent for painting and drawing, which would comfort her at troubling points in her life.

Daisy Gordon graduated after three years at Charbonniers, and made her debut in Savannah. Another trip to Europe culminated in a marriage proposal by an attractive, wealthy, but impulsive American named William Mackay Low (who was also from Savannah). At their 1886 wedding, a piece of good-luck rice lodged in her right ear. This freak accident caused an infection, which left her completely deaf in that ear. One year earlier, an earache in her left ear drove her to a doctor. She entreated the Savannah physician to use a new technique of injecting silver nitrate into her ear. It had a terrible result:

This 1924 photo shows Juliette Gordon Low and a group of Girl Scouts standing in the yard in Savannah, Georgia, where the first Girl Scouts met in 1912. AP Photo/ The Times of Northwest Indiana.

months of debility and significant hearing loss in her left ear. The two incidents left Daisy Gordon Low almost completely deaf.

She compensated for her deafness in distinctive ways. She was known to hear what she wanted to, and this meant that, as she drafted volunteers for her Girl Scouts, she never heard "no." Gordon Low also tended to speak first, dictating the conversational topic and making it easier for her to read lips and follow along. And, true to her ebullient personality, she never brooded on her disadvantage publicly.

CAREER HIGHLIGHTS AND MAJOR PHILANTHROPIC CONTRIBUTIONS

The Lows led a privileged life, traveling among their three homes in England, Scotland, and Savannah. They had friends among the English and Scottish nobility, and their pursuits reflected their status: such as fox hunting and opera. Alienated by her husband's big-game hunting and drinking, Gordon Low turned to art. She began drawing and painting in earnest, and added sculpture, wood carving, and metal forging to her repertoire. She also continued her childhood habit of assisting stray and wounded animals, and helped to alleviate the distress of less fortunate individuals in the villages near her. As the Lows grew more remote, she gladly agreed to help her mother establish a hospital in Savannah for wounded veterans of the Spanish American War in 1898.

Returning to England after the war, Gordon Low faced an alcoholic husband who confessed to a mistress and a desire for a divorce. She was devastated. Before the divorce was completed, William Low died in June 1905. Nevertheless, he left his estate to his mistress, forcing Daisy Gordon Low to sue, successfully, for her legal portion. She remained courageous throughout the humiliations, but it was not easy. She sought consolation in friends, travel, and sculpting. For ten years, she said she drifted, without any real purpose in life, until her 1910 meeting with General Sir Robert Baden-Powell.

Baden-Powell was a celebrated English

hero of the Boer War and famous for founding the Boy Scouts in 1907. Baden-Powell enlisted his sister, Agnes Baden-Powell, to help him form the Girl Guides, when, at his first call to form the group, 6,000 girls registered. Baden-Powell's idea for the Boy Scouts originated during the Siege of Mafeking (1899–1900). He deputized a band of boys and trained them to be messengers and lookouts. They were so enthusiastic that Baden-Powell thought other boys might respond similarly. He had not counted, however, on girls! The Girl Guides ably learned about nature and animal care and history, but true to their Edwardian-era beginnings, they also studied topics more in keeping with their gender: household and nursing skills, arts and crafts, personal hygiene.

Wooed by Baden-Powell's faith in her and frustrated by her apparent aimlessness in life, Daisy Gordon Low was eager to learn more about the Girl Guides. She found a kindred spirit in Baden-Powell, whose interests were as broad as hers. They shared a love of art and the outdoors, but mostly they were committed to making the world a better place. Working with children accomplished two purposes: it helped young people become good citizens, and their volunteerism assisted communities in need. Baden-Powell's encouragement spurred her to action. Gordon Low organized a Girl Guide troop near her home in Scotland. She enlisted some of her friends and they taught the local girls much more than the standard curriculum of knitting and knot tying. When Gordon Low found that their futures held either arduous factory labor or hardscrabble farm life, she sought to teach them self-sufficiency. Under Gordon Low's tutelage, the girls sheared their own sheep, carded and spun the wool, and handed it to their Girl Guide leader who had engineered a market in London. She also prompted them to raise chickens to sell to the wealthy hunters who visited seasonally.

Daisy Gordon Low then established two Girl Guide troops in poor sections of central London. Her belief was growing that guiding could serve many beneficial ends. Girls would be made more independent and self-aware. Their organized fun would include philanthropic endeavors in their own backyards, strengthening cross-generational and neighborhood ties. The outdoors emphasis in guiding promoted respect for nature and provided a necessary spiritual retreat. While guiding never undermined the prevalent social notion that women should be good wives and mothers—in fact, much guide training worked toward that end—Gordon Low's own experiences of being left so alone while married spurred her to emphasize activities that might provide solace against a similar storm in a girl's life.

Since Agnes Baden-Powell had the British Girl Guides well in hand, Gordon Low introduced guiding to the girls of the United States. On March 12, 1912, eighteen girls met at Gordon Low's home in Savannah and enrolled in two guiding troops. These girls had been meeting with a naturalist, Walter J. Hoxie, to learn about the outdoors and Gordon Low's cousin, Nina Anderson Pape, believed they would make a likely core for the American version of the Girl Guides. The eager girls scrutinized the British Girl Guide handbook and made it their own. They made a striking sight in their homemade blue uniforms. Soon six more troops were constituted locally and Gordon Low purchased some land for local hiking and camping trips, which she often led herself. Newspapers spread the story nationwide, and girls from all over the United States clamored to join.

The movement grew to include several troops of Girl Scouts begun independently by people inspired by Baden-Powell's organization. To unite all these endeavors under one umbrella, Gordon Low compromised on the name: her Girl Guides became Girl Scouts. She also worked tirelessly as a promoter. She established new troops and drafted local and state leadership. As Gordon Low traveled widely, she became wholly identified with her cause. She volunteered her time and energy, and was always creative in drawing attention to the Scouts. She financially underwrote the early movement, which became formalized in 1913 with the creation of a national headquarters in Washington, DC, and the adoption of *How Girls Can Help Their Country* (1913), the American scouting handbook adapted by Hoxie. The board of directors consisted of Gordon Low's friends, all elite women, including the First Lady, Ellen Axson Wilson. Gordon Low would convince all subsequent First Ladies to be honorary presidents of the Girl Scouts. By 1915, the Girl Scouts of America were incorporated under a national constitution and bylaws. That year, 5,000 girls were enjoying their scouting experiences and some attended the first annual scouting convention. The movement rapidly diversified: in 1917, African-American girls were joining and the first troop of girls with physical disabilities formed in New York City. The total number of scouts would grow to 50,000 by 1920, in part because of the visible role Girl Scouts played in World War I efforts. They assisted in hospitals and canteens, with war bond drives, victory gardens, and other programs, and volunteered extensively during the influenza epidemic.

In the decade following World War I, important changes occurred. Gordon Low resigned as president, happy to be free from administrative duties so that she could continue as a roving Girl Scouts ambassador in the United States and internationally. In tribute, Gordon Low's birthday, October 31, became Founder's Day, celebrated annually by Girl Scouts worldwide. She authored the new handbook, *Scouting for Girls*, and oversaw the modernization of the Girl Scouts magazine, *The American Girl*, in 1917. She also authorized training programs for scout leaders. She even helped with and appeared in the first Girl Scout film, *The Golden Eaglet*. Her continued close work with the Baden-Powells led to her involvement with the first International Conference of Girl Guides and Girl Scouts. From Scotland to England to America, Gordon Low watched how the good deeds of her Scouts wrought wonderful change in their communities and parallel personal growth in the girls. After the conference, she became zealous about the worldwide need for scouting and saw it as one more way to help secure international peace through understanding. The global arm of Girl Scouting has grown according to her desires. Over ten million girls currently participate in scouting or guiding in over 140 countries.

Gordon Low promoted Girl Scouting into the 1920s despite her own ill health. The deafness plagued her, but by 1923, she knew she battled the cancer that would eventually kill her. Always in uniform, she spoke in hundreds of cities, gave countless interviews, and wrote newspaper pieces to spread the word. In every new community, she met with women to choose leaders. While efforts to increase membership continued, so did the organizational work. The uniform color was changed from blue to khaki and the famous trefoil design was adopted. Fund-raising also became a priority after World War I had depleted her own savings.

CONCLUSION

After her death in Savannah on January 18, 1927, tributes poured in from all over the world, especially from the 200,000 American girls who knew her as their founder and mourned the absence of her lively spirit. Lord Baden-Powell keenly felt her loss and wrote this eulogy: "She gave the lead . . . [I]n that one greathearted woman . . . Scouting took its root and gained the widespread power for good it holds today among the girlhood of America" (List 1960, ix). Daisy Gordon Low's greatest legacy is the 43 million women who have gained strength, knowledge, skills, and new friends in Girl Scouting in the United States since its 1912 beginning. More difficult to measure is the extensive good their voluntary efforts in every field imaginable have done for their communities. Part of the Girl Scout Law is "to make the world a better place," which encapsulates Juliette Gordon Low's own reasons for becoming involved with the nascent movement.

Stacy A. Cordery

FURTHER READING

Choate, Anne Hyde, and Helen Ferris, eds. *Juliette Low and the Girl Scouts: The Story of an*

American Woman, 1860–1927. Garden City, NY: Doubleday, Doran & Company, 1928.

Kerr, Rose. *The Story of a Million Girls: Guiding and Girl Scouting Round the World.* London: Girl Guides Association, undated [1938?].

List, Ely. *Juliette Low and the Girl Scouts.* N.p.: Girl Scouts of the United States of America, 1960.

Lyon, Nancy. "Juliette Low: The Eccentric who Founded the Girl Scouts." *Ms. Magazine,* November 1981, 101–105.

Obituary. *New York Times,* January 19, 1927, 23.

Parker, Charlotte. "Juliette Magill Gordon Low." In *Dictionary of Georgia Biography,* vol. 2, eds. Kenneth Coleman and Charles Stephen Gurr. Athens: University of Georgia Press, 1983, 638–640.

Reynolds, Moira Davison. "Juliette Gordon Low, 1860–1927, Founder of Girl Scouts." In *Women Champions of Human Rights.* New York: McFarland & Company, 1991, 54–66.

Shultz, Gladys Denny, and Daisy Gordon Lawrence. *Lady from Savannah: The Life of Juliette Low.* Philadelphia: J.B. Lippincott, 1958.

Strickland, Charles E. "Juliette Low, the Girl Scouts, and the Role of American Women." In *Woman's Being, Woman's Place: Female Identity and Vocation in American History,* ed. Mary Kelley. Boston: G.K. Hall, 1979, 252–264.

PAPERS

Juliette Gordon Low's papers are located at the Juliette Gordon Low Girl Scout National Center (Savannah, GA), Juliette Gordon Low Collection, Girl Scouts of the U.S.A. National Headquarters (New York City), Gordon Family Papers, Georgia Historical Society (Savannah, GA), and Gordon Family Papers, Southern Historical Collection, University of North Carolina (Chapel Hill, NC).

JOHN LOWELL, JR.
(1799–1836)

Founder of the Lowell Institute

INTRODUCTION

"The idea of a foundation of this kind, on which, unconnected with any place of education, provision is made, in the midst of a large commercial population, for annual courses of instruction by public lectures, to be delivered gratuitously to all who choose to attend them, as far as it is practicable within our largest halls, is, I believe, original with Mr. Lowell," declaimed orator Edward Everett in 1839 (Everett 1840, 1). Indeed, John Lowell, Jr. drafted the testamentary provision that established the foundation—the Lowell Institute—with sufficient liberality to permit it to serve as a continuing source of innovation in public education.

EARLY YEARS AND EDUCATION

A member of the second generation of Boston's emergent Brahmin "caste," John Lowell, Jr. was the son of pioneer industrialist Francis Cabot Lowell. After receiving his earliest education in the Boston public schools, he was taken by his father to Europe and placed at the high school of Edinburgh. In 1813, at the age of fourteen, he entered Harvard College. Plagued with ill health, he left college after two years and entered his family's mercantile firm, sailing to India, the East Indies, and England.

CAREER HIGHLIGHTS

Returning from his voyages with "invigorated health," Lowell devoted himself to business and, in his leisure time, to book collecting, reading, and politics, serving on the Boston Common Council and in the Massachusetts state senate. In 1825, he married Georgina Margaret Amory. The 1820s and 1830s were a turbulent period in New England, marked by intense political and religious conflict between an insurgent popular democracy, which challenged economic and religious establishments, and an emergent capitalist elite, which, though almost invariably defeated at the polls, was learning to use its wealth to advance its political agenda through nonpolitical means. Conflict between the elite and the urban masses intensified in the 1820s; followers of popular evangelical ministers openly challenged elite-controlled institutions like Harvard College and the Boston Atheneum by using a variety of voluntary associations—young men's and mechanics societies, lyceums, debating clubs, and temperance groups. The continuing erosion of the elite's cultural authority was deeply troubling to Lowell and his contemporaries.

In 1830 and 1831, tragedy struck the Lowell household, with the deaths, within a few months of one another, of his wife and two children. Heartbroken, John Lowell retired from business and attempted to assuage his grief with travel, first to the Western states and subsequently to Europe, the Middle East, Africa, and Asia. Before departing for Europe in 1832, he wrote a will in which, according to his biographer, "he set aside a large portion of his ample property to be expended, forever, in the support . . . of lectures in the city of Boston" (Everett 1840, 29).

Over the course of the next four years, Lowell traveled through France, Holland, Belgium, Italy, Greece, Turkey, Armenia, Persia, and Egypt, down the Nile to Khartoum, through Ethiopia, and ultimately to India. Although the bequest providing for "the maintenance and support of public lectures, to be delivered in Boston, upon philosophy, natural history, the arts and sciences, or any of them, as the trustee shall, from time to time, deem expedient for the promotion of the moral, and intellectual, and physical instruction or education of the citizens of Boston" had been set forth before his departure from Boston, in a codicil to his will written "amidst the ruins of Thebes" and, subsequently, in letters written from Egypt, he further amplified his ideas about the trust (Everett 1840, 3). These instructions directed that religion be given an important

place among the lectures to be offered, along with topics that would contribute to the material prosperity of the region. Lowell concluded with the crucial directive that would give his trustees extraordinary discretion in how the money might be used. "After the establishment of these courses of lectures, should disposable funds remain, or, in process of time, be accumulated," Lowell wrote, "the trustee . . . may, also, from time to time, establish lectures on any subject that, in his opinion, the wants and taste of the age may demand" (Everett 1840, 5). Lowell died in Bombay on March 4, 1836. The first lecture supported by his trust was offered in December 1839.

MAJOR PHILANTHROPIC CONTRIBUTIONS

Although philanthropic gestures on this scale were a relative novelty in early nineteenth-century America, the idea of an elite institution providing popular lectures by eminent scientists and scholars was not. Having spent much of his youth in England, Lowell was undoubtedly familiar with the Royal Institution—an entity that sponsored basic scientific research and popular lectures and demonstrations. The Royal Institution had been founded in 1799 by expatriates **Benjamin Thompson** (Count Rumford) and Thomas Barnard, wealthy and influential Americans who, having sided with the British during the American Revolution, had taken up residence in London.

The trust—or Lowell Institute, as it came to be known—had a rather unusual mode of governance: a single trustee was empowered to appoint his successor and the new trustee must, in the language of Lowell's will, "always choose in preference to all others some male descendant of my grandfather, John Lowell, provided there be one who is competent to hold the office of trustee, and of the name of Lowell" (Everett 1840, 8). Despite this odd restriction (or perhaps because of it), the Lowell Institute proved to be an extraordinarily innovative philanthropic force.

Under its first trustee, the founder's

nephew John Amory Lowell, the Lowell Institute flourished. Lowell was both a man of extraordinary financial acumen and a man of high intellect. The list of Lowell lecturers during his tenure was a veritable pantheon of the most internationally celebrated figures in science, literature, political economy, philosophy, and theology, including Britain's most celebrated geologist Sir Charles Lyell, Swiss naturalist Louis Agassiz, and novelists Charles Dickens and William Makepeace Thackeray. The lectures were so immensely popular that crowds crushed the windows of the Old Corner Bookstore where the tickets were distributed and certain series had to be repeated by popular demand.

In the meantime, its capital, astutely managed by the well-connected Lowells, grew by leaps and bounds. By the 1960s, the $250,000 bequest had grown to more than $8 million. As its resources increased, the Lowell Institute broadened its activities. These grants included underwriting extension courses in a wide variety of subjects through the Massachusetts Institute of Technology (MIT); furnishing instruction in science to the teachers of the Boston public schools under the supervision of the Boston Society for Natural History; and providing lectures for workingmen on practical and scientific subjects through the Wells Memorial Workingmen's Institute. In 1872, working through MIT, the Institute established the Lowell School of Practical Design, which offered tuition-free instruction on techniques relating to the design and production of textiles. The Lowell Institute began its second century by funding the early development of public broadcasting through Boston radio (and later television) station WGBH. The productions it sponsored helped to transform educational broadcasting into a medium with a huge public audience.

CONCLUSION

The Lowell Institute set a pattern of elite cultural intervention that would recur later in the century, when investment banker **Henry Lee Higginson** established the Boston Symphony Orchestra. This nonprofit entity entered a rich and complex setting of voluntary and proprietary (for-profit) musical organizations, which served a broad public. Nonetheless, its substantial financial resources, combined with the prestige of its patrons, enabled it—within a few years—to virtually monopolize the top musical talent in the city, as well as bring an array of international stars to Boston audiences that fee-dependent organizations could not rival. Nonprofit museums had a similar impact, using their impressive financial resources and institutional connections to displace proprietary exhibitions of art and natural wonders that entertained the public with programs intended to elevate its aesthetic standards.

As enterprises like the Lowell Institute suggest, elite cultural philanthropy is paradoxical: on the one hand, it seeks to affirm the collective identity of elites through exclusion; on the other, to expand the elite's public influence, it must necessarily be inclusive and sensitive to demands in the cultural marketplace. The adaptability of the Lowell Institute over the past century and a half shows how skillfully these conflicting demands can be reconciled.

Peter Dobkin Hall

FURTHER READING

Bode, Carl. *The American Lyceum.* New York: Oxford University Press, 1956.

Brown, G.I. *Scientist, Soldier, Statesman, Spy— Count Rumford: The Extraordinary Life of a Scientific Genius.* Stroud, United Kingdom: Sutton Publishing, 2001.

Dalzell, Robert F. *Enterprising Elite: The Boston Associates and the World They Made.* Cambridge, MA: Harvard University Press, 1987.

Eliot, Samuel Atkins. "Charities of Boston." *North American Review* 71, July 1860, 149–165.

———. "Public and Private Charities of Boston." *North American Review* 56, July 1845, 135–159.

Everett, Edward. *A Memoir of Mr. John Lowell, Jun., Delivered at the Introduction to the Lectures on His Foundation in the Odeon, 31st December, 1839.* Boston: Charles C. Little & James Brown, 1840.

Gelfand, Mark I. *Trustee for a City: Ralph Lowell of Boston.* Boston: Northeastern University Press, 1998.

Greenslet, Ferris. *The Lowells and Their Seven Worlds.* Boston: Houghton Mifflin, 1946.

Smith, Harriette Knight. *The History of the Lowell Institute.* Boston: Lamson, Wolffe, 1898.

Story, Ronald. *The Forging of an Aristocracy: Harvard and Boston's Upper Class.* Middletown, CT: Wesleyan University Press, 1980.

Weeks, Edward. *The Lowells and Their Institute.* Boston: Little Brown, 1966.

PAPERS

John Lowell, Jr.'s papers are in the Massachusetts Historical Society (Boston, MA).

JOSEPHINE SHAW LOWELL
(1843–1905)

Philosopher and Architect of Organized Charity

INTRODUCTION

"Almsgiving and dolegiving are hurtful to those who receive them because they lead men to remit their own exertions and depend on others. . . . All charity must tend to raise the character and elevate the moral nature, and so improve the condition of those toward whom it is exercised" (Lowell 1971, 90, 94). Josephine Shaw Lowell was the most articulate spokesperson for the organized (or scientific) charity movement that dominated the American philanthropic scene in the late nineteenth century. In the statements above, she proclaimed one of its core beliefs: that giving material aid to the able-bodied poor was wrong because it encouraged dependency instead of self-reliance. Unlike most other proponents of organized charity, Lowell ardently supported the rights of workers. She thought that workers were underpaid, and that their unfairly small wages encouraged dependency and crime: "If the working people had all they ought to have, we should not have the paupers and criminals" (Stewart 1974, 358–359). Lowell was a sharp critic of charity that encouraged the dependency of the poor, who also took practical steps (for example, supporting the unionization of labor) that were designed to increase wages and hence to ensure the self-reliance of the poor.

EARLY YEARS AND EDUCATION

Josephine Shaw was the fourth of five children born to a wealthy couple in West Roxbury, Massachusetts (a suburb of Boston). Her father, Francis George Shaw, a merchant, retired from business at the age of thirty-two (a year before Josephine's birth) to become a gentleman farmer and to pursue his interest in social reform. Her parents were Unitarians, and their interest in social reform was kindled by the work of the Unitarian minister to the poor of Boston, **Joseph Tuckerman**. The Shaws frequently hosted eminent intellectual figures and reformers such as Ralph Waldo Emerson, Margaret Fuller, William Lloyd Garrison, and Harriet Beecher Stowe.

Sarah Shaw, Josephine Shaw's mother, suffered from an eye disease. Consequently, the Shaws moved to Staten Island (now part of New York City, then a rural suburb) in 1846 because it was home to an eminent eye doctor. From 1851 to 1855, the family lived in Europe, where Josephine Shaw learned to speak French, German, and Italian. When the family returned to Staten Island in 1855, Josephine Shaw attended a New York City school until she was seventeen, when she spent a year at a Boston finishing school. Neither Josephine Shaw nor any of her three sisters went to college. Before the twentieth century, it was unusual for the daughters of America's social elite to attend college.

The Shaws were prominent abolitionists, and they actively supported the Union cause during the Civil War. Robert Gould Shaw, Josephine Shaw's only brother, died in combat (as recounted in the movie *Glory* [1989]) as colonel of the black troops of the Fifty-fourth Massachusetts Regiment. The war also claimed the life of Josephine Shaw's husband, Charles Russell Lowell, a longtime family friend and the product of an equally celebrated (though much less wealthy) Massachusetts family. Charles and Josephine Lowell were married in October 1863, and he died in combat almost exactly a year later. Their daughter Carlotta Lowell was born a month after her father's death. Josephine Shaw Lowell spent the rest of her life as a widowed mother, never remarried, and dressed in black every day.

Lowell's philanthropic career began during the Civil War. In 1861, she, her mother, and all of her sisters joined the New York City Woman's Central Association of Relief for the Army and Navy of the United States, a branch of the U.S. Sanitary Commission. The Commission and the Woman's Central raised funds and provided volunteer labor to support the war effort. At war's end, Lowell continued her philanthropic labors, working for the National Freedmen's Relief Association of New York from 1866 until 1871. In that capacity, she oversaw the schooling of emancipated slaves in Virginia. Still, she is best known for her work with the urban poor of New York. She began this work when she became a full-time volunteer for the State Charities Aid Association (SCAA) of New York in 1871.

CAREER HIGHLIGHTS AND MAJOR PHILANTHROPIC CONTRIBUTIONS

As an SCAA volunteer, Lowell became familiar with the treatment of dependents in her county (Staten Island) and elsewhere in the state of New York. She wrote influential reports advocating improvements in the management of jails and almshouses; the placement of different sorts of dependents (for example, the able-bodied and the infirm)

in different institutions; and a work program for dependents who were neither mentally ill nor disabled. The reports were well received, and in 1876 Lowell was offered and accepted an unpaid government post: she served as one of eight commissioners (and as the first woman commissioner) of New York's State Board of Charities. Lowell's growing familiarity with poverty and the philanthropic response to it led her to take a leading role in the 1882 founding of the Charity Organization Society of the City of New York (COS).

Charity organization societies were established in most major American cities in the last quarter of the nineteenth century. The charity organization movement believed in what it called "scientific" charity: charity that was organized and efficient (avoiding duplication of efforts), and that treated the root causes of poverty, rather than seeking merely to relieve its symptoms. Its guiding assumption was that the poverty of the able-bodied was ordinarily a sign of character defects, such as a reluctance to work or a tendency to spend extravagantly. The movement sought to promote the self-help and self-reliance of the poor (by means of practical lessons conveyed to the poor by prosperous volunteer "friendly visitors"). Because it valued the self-reliance of the poor, the charity organization movement strongly opposed giving alms to the able-bodied poor, which was thought to encourage continued dependency.

In 1884, Lowell became the "leading philosopher" of the charity organization movement—having earlier become "the founder of its flagship organization"—when she published *Public Relief and Private Charity* (Waugh 1997, 54). This book was a brief and powerful statement of the rationale for organized charity, offering a "restatement of the principles upon which the Modern methods of Charity are founded" (Lowell 1971, Preface). In the volume, Lowell argued that poverty was "a wrong, an unnatural evil" that should be eradicated (Lowell 1971, 95). Still, she contended that the eradication of poverty would not be possible if one was to "give doles," which "often retard or entirely prevent the energetic action required on the part of the sufferers themselves to lift themselves out of their difficulties" (Lowell 1971, 95). Instead, Lowell believed that the best way to help the poor was to help them help themselves, by fostering their employment and by encouraging them to save. In keeping with these principles, the New York COS created institutions to help the poor find jobs and to enable them to deposit small sums for savings. In addition, they allowed the poor to borrow money at below-market interest rates.

In *Public Relief and Private Charity*, Lowell also observed—almost in passing—that "sober, industrious men and women are poor only because their wages are low" (Lowell 1971, 107). In this statement, Lowell recognized that good character by itself did not always relieve poverty: a sober and industrious person could nevertheless be poor, if he or she was paid very little for working. The full implications of that statement explain an important second aspect of Lowell's career. To reduce poverty, Lowell advocated not only teaching moral lessons to the poor but also taking steps to ensure that the poor were better and more fairly compensated for their labor. Lowell came to believe that more poverty was caused by unemployment and low wages (what are now called "structural" or economic factors) than by the moral defects of the poor (for example, the willing acceptance of dependency by able-bodied adults). Therefore, she was more concerned with increasing the wages of the 75,000 women in New York City who worked for starvation wages than to end the dependency of the 25,000 New Yorkers (many of whom were children) who did not support themselves at all.

Lowell took many steps that were intended to advance the interests of workers. She advocated the creation of labor unions as a means of improving wages and working conditions. In 1891, she established the Consumers' League of the City of New York, which mobilized public opinion against department stores that underpaid and badly treated their workers. And in the aftermath of the great industrial depression of 1893, she set up a committee that offered work relief to the unemployed, so that they could provide for their families without having to rely on doles.

CONCLUSION

Lowell died on October 12, 1905. In life, she fought for the rights of workers, while also fighting the dependency of those who could but did not work. In doing so, Lowell demonstrated that it is possible to combine two approaches to poverty that today are often thought to be incompatible: the moral and structural approaches. Advocates of the moral approach contend that the way to reduce poverty is through better (that is, more prudent and self-advancing) behavior on the part of the poor; advocates of the structural approach contend that the way to reduce poverty is through legislation and other social remedies designed to ease the lot of the poor.

Lowell's example suggests that these two approaches are not mutually exclusive, but can instead be adopted simultaneously. Through her support for labor unions and for work relief during times of high unemployment, Lowell did much that was designed to improve the material condition of poor people who worked and wanted to work (as well as their families). Still, she also insisted that poor people who could support themselves must try to do so, and must avoid unnecessary dependency. Lowell believed that the poor should aspire to self-reliance by laboring and that society was responsible for assisting their efforts to lift themselves out of poverty by ensuring that their labor received fair compensation. In contending that the best philanthropic work seeks to meet these twin responsibilities, Lowell set a standard that seems no less applicable today than it did in her lifetime.

Joel Schwartz

FURTHER READING

Lowell, Josephine Shaw. *Public Relief and Private Charity*. New York: Arno Press & the *New York Times*, 1971 [1884].

Schwartz, Joel. *Fighting Poverty with Virtue: Moral Reform and America's Urban Poor, 1825–2000*. Indianapolis: Indiana University Press, 2000.

Stewart, William Rhinelander. *The Philanthropic Work of Josephine Shaw Lowell Containing a Biographical Sketch of Her Life Together with a Selection of Her Public Papers and Private Letters*. Montclair, NJ: Patterson Smith, 1974 [1911].

Waugh, Joan. *Unsentimental Reformer: The Life of Josephine Shaw Lowell*. Cambridge, MA: Harvard University Press, 1997.

PAPERS

Some of Josephine Shaw Lowell's letters can be found in collections at the New York Historical Society (New York City), the Schlesinger Library at Radcliffe College (Cambridge, MA), the New York Public Library (New York City), and the Library of Congress (Washington, DC). The archives of the Charity Organization Society of the City of New York form part of the archives of the Community Service Society (the successor organization to the COS). These archives are located in the Rare Book and Manuscript Library of Columbia University (New York City).

MARY LYON
(1797–1849)

Educator, Missionary Advocate, and Founder of Mount Holyoke College

INTRODUCTION

"This institution is to be founded by the combined liberality of an enlarged benevolence, which seeks the greatest good on a large scale," Mary Lyon wrote in 1835 in an appeal for money to build Mount Holyoke Female Seminary (Porterfield 1997, 39). She praised those who contributed to the school for "advancing as fast as possible, the renovation of the whole human family" (Porterfield 1997, 39). Established in 1837 as the first publicly endowed institution of advanced learning for women in the United States, Mount Holyoke Female Seminary was the first American school where women of modest means could learn chemistry, physics, and geology as well as Latin, Greek, and theology. In addition to playing an important role in the history of women's higher education, Mount Holyoke functioned as a recruitment and training center for women missionaries and served as a model for schools established by missionaries in many parts of the world. Mount Holyoke and its satellite schools in Asia, Africa, and the Middle East reflected Mary Lyon's belief that educated women were destined to play a pivotal role in converting the world to Protestant Christianity and in building the Kingdom of God on earth.

EARLY YEARS AND EDUCATION

As a farm girl in Massachusetts, Mary Lyon spent a lot of time thinking about God and death and sometimes preached to other children. Indeed, she experienced a difficult childhood. Her father, Aaron Lyon, died when she was five and the family had to work hard to make ends meet. While her brothers worked outside, Mary Lyon, her mother (Jemima Shephard Lyon), and her sisters spent long hours churning butter, baking bread, spinning yarn, making clothes and candles, and doing wash. When Mary Lyon was thirteen, her mother remarried and moved away, while her older brother inherited the farm. Mary Lyon stayed on to do the domestic work until her brother married two years later and started a family of his own.

As factory goods began to replace many things women used to make at home, Mary

An 1845 daguerreotype of Mary Lyon. The Mount Holyoke College Archives and Special Collections.

Lyon, as did many other young, single women in early nineteenth-century New England, faced the prospect of being an economic and emotional burden to her family. Fortunately, new teaching opportunities for women were also becoming available as laws mandating public support for children's education came into effect and district schools began to open their doors to girls. Lyon saw these new teaching opportunities as evidence of God's hand in history. "Without this wide and increasing field of usefulness," she later wrote, "that would be a dark providence, which, by manufacturing establishments, has taken from families so much domestic labor, which had its influence in forming the character of our maternal ancestors. But 'providence meets providence,'" she added confidently (Porterfield 1997, 31). Could we not see, she asked, "the hand of One, wiser than Solomon, in all the labor-saving machinery of the present day?" (Porterfield 1997, 31).

Lyon loved learning, especially geology and chemistry, and did everything she could to become educated. As a teenager, she taught younger girls part time and eventually saved enough money from her teaching and spinning to attend the Ladies Seminary run by Joseph Emerson, a well-known religious teacher and advocate of women's education. While other private female academies taught drawing, dance, French, and other skills that contributed to women's decorative role in polite society, Emerson wanted to give young women a more substantive education, much like what young men at the best American schools received. He wanted his students to be good teachers of other young women but also wanted them to be agents of social and religious reform.

As a religious teacher, Joseph Emerson inspired in his students the idea that women had an important role to play in God's plan for the world. He instilled in Lyon a confidence in divine providence that rescued her from episodes of personal despair and prepared her to act on behalf of other young women in her society. Many aspects of Lyon's conception of Mount Holyoke evolved out of her exposure to these ideas. Like Emerson, Lyon established a boarding school that offered women new opportunities for employment. And like Emerson, she was committed to carrying forward the religious values associated with New England Puritanism. Still, Lyon also went further than Emerson in joining religious conversion with academic excellence and in joining enthusiasm for missionary work with advances in female education.

CAREER HIGHLIGHTS

Lyon's greatest achievement was the establishment of Mount Holyoke Female Seminary in South Hadley, Massachusetts in 1837. Traveling through the towns and villages in New England seeking small contributions from hundreds of people, she worked tirelessly to achieve her goal of founding an institution of higher learning for young women of modest means. Many of her donors were women who denied themselves a new carpet or bonnet to help give the next generation of women an opportunity for advanced education that they themselves had never had. Lyon asked for this kind of benevolent self-sacrifice and led the way in enthusiasm for the cause of assisting young women. As she wrote in 1834, "My heart has so yearned over the adult female youth in the common walks of life, that it has sometimes seemed as if there was a fire, shut up in my bones" (Porterfield 1997, 30).

Lyon worked to instill the principle of self-sacrificial benevolence in her students and teachers. She wanted her students to feel grateful to donors who had made personal sacrifices for them and to feel responsible for carrying this spirit of benevolence out into the world. To encourage this in her students, and to make tuition as low as possible, she assigned all of her students to domestic tasks in the kitchen and laundry. Furthermore, she sought out teachers whose own commitments to benevolent self-sacrifice made them glad to accept only a modest salary.

After the building, curriculum, and daily routine of the seminary were established, Lyon focused her attention on increasing her students' dedication to Christ and their interest in missionary work. When Fidelia Fiske, a teacher at Mount Holyoke and former student of Lyon's, accepted the call to become a missionary and opened a girls' school in Persia, many others were inspired to follow in her path. Soon after Fiske's departure in 1843, Lyon called all of her students to profess their dedication to Christ and commit their lives to His service. The revival of religious feeling that followed this call produced more commitments to missionary work among students. Before long, enthusiasm for missionary work became a way of life at Mount Holyoke and, by the time of Lyon's death in 1849, Mount Holyoke was famous for producing missionaries. Many nineteenth-century American women missionaries in Africa, Asia, the Middle East, and the American West had ties to Mount Holyoke.

MAJOR PHILANTHROPIC CONTRIBUTIONS

Through her establishment of Mount Holyoke, Lyon made major contributions to American higher education, to the American Protestant missionary movement, and to the advancement of female education worldwide. She did more than anyone to persuade the American public that teaching and missionary service were respectable fields of employment for women. Her strategy was to define teaching as a form of benevolence and to explain that God's plan for the redemption of human society required the agency of female teachers.

Lyon's success in gaining acceptance for women's education was also a result of her pragmatic instinct toward the political process. Unlike more radical reformers, she never criticized orthodox religion or challenged the conventional belief that women did not belong in public life. In defining new roles for American women as educators and missionaries, she never directly challenged male authority and never wavered in her belief that her women should obey their husbands, fathers, and ministers. Yet, if her teachers had lower status and less public authority than ministers, she believed their work was even more fundamental. "Fill the country with ministers," Lyon wrote in 1836, "and they could no more conquer the whole land and *secure* their victories, without the aid of many times their number of self-denying female teachers, than the latter could complete the work without the former" (Porterfield 1997, 47).

Carrying forward the combined commitments to benevolence, learning, religious enthusiasm, and female self-sacrifice taught at Mount Holyoke, early alumnae created sister institutions of Mount Holyoke in Ohio, Oklahoma, Persia, India, Africa, and elsewhere across the continent and around the world. Nineteenth-century alumnae of Mount Holyoke were among the vanguard in introducing or furthering women's education around the world, and in exporting

American culture abroad. In spreading ideas about historical progress as an essential part of God's plan, alumnae of Mount Holyoke also helped to shape the transition to modern industrial society in many parts of the world.

CONCLUSION

Mary Lyon is most admired today for her pioneering role in establishing women's higher education, for her particular commitment to the education of young women of modest means, and for her love of learning, especially her love of science. Her fervent belief in the complete triumph of Protestant Christianity is somewhat less compatible with American values today, as is her insistence on thoroughgoing self-sacrifice as an essential component of benevolence. Nonetheless, Lyon's intense religious zeal motivated her work as an educator and contributed to widespread acceptance of her belief in the importance of women's education.

Amanda Porterfield

FURTHER READING

Conforti, Joseph A. "Mary Lyon, the Founding of Mount Holyoke College, and the Cultural Revival of Jonathan Edwards." *Religion and American Culture: A Journal of Interpretation* 3, no.1, Winter 1993, 69–89.

Green, Elizabeth Alden. *Mary Lyon and Mount Holyoke: Opening the Gates.* Hanover, NH: University Press of New England, 1979 [reprint 1983].

Hitchcock, Edward, ed. *The Power of Christian Benevolence Illustrated in the Life and Labors of Mary Lyon.* Northampton, MA: Hopkins, Bridgman, 1852.

Porterfield, Amanda. *Mary Lyon and the Mount Holyoke Missionaries.* New York: Oxford University Press, 1997.

Sklar, Kathryn Kish. "The Founding of Mount Holyoke College." In *Women of America: A History,* ed. Carol Ruth Berkin and Mary Beth Norton. Boston: Houghton Mifflin, 1979, 177–201.

PAPERS

Mary Lyon's papers are located in the Archives of the Mount Holyoke College Library in South Hadley, Massachusetts.

M

COTTON MATHER
(1663–1728)

Clergyman, Theologian, and Author of Bonifacius: An Essay upon the Good

INTRODUCTION

"There needs abundance to be done, that the great GOD and His CHRIST may be more known and served in the world; and that the *errors* which are *impediments* to the *acknowledgments* wherewith men ought to glorify their Creator and Redeemer, may be rectified" (Mather 1966, 17). With these words, Cotton Mather summarized his understanding of public service. First and foremost, "doing good" was an expression of religious faith and an aspect of every reborn Christian's fundamental obligation to honor God.

EARLY YEARS AND EDUCATION

Cotton Mather was born into Puritan New England's most prominent clerical family in Boston on February 12, 1663, the son of Increase and Maria (Cotton) Mather. Increase Mather, the teacher of Boston's Second Church, one of its two ordained ministers, was widely known for his scholarship, piety, and ecclesiastical sway. Cotton Mather's grandfathers, Richard Mather and John Cotton, had also exercised rare influence as two of the leading clergymen of New England's first generation of settlers.

From the first, it seemed clear that Increase Mather expected his son to follow his illustrious father and grandfathers into the ministry. Cotton Mather was precocious both in his piety and in his intellect. He was already praying seriously by the age of three and was reading by the time he started school. The boy was adept in both Greek and Latin when he entered Harvard College in 1674, half a year before his twelfth birthday and, to that point, the youngest student to be admitted to the school. As accomplished as he was for someone of his age, he was apparently already struggling with parental pressure to succeed in the ministry. Before the age of ten, he began to stutter badly, an affliction that plagued him intermittently throughout

Engraver Peter Pelham created this portrait of Cotton Mather in Boston in 1727. Mezzotint, 1727, MHS image #2454. Courtesy of the Massachusetts Historical Society.

his life, although he worked hard, and with some success, to overcome it.

Mather graduated from Harvard College in 1678, and in keeping with both his family's expectations and his own wishes, he began to groom himself for the ministry through independent reading. In 1681, Harvard granted him the master of arts degree in recognition of this preparation. Four years later in 1685, at age twenty-two, the Second Church in Boston called him to be its pastor. For the next thirty-eight years, Cotton Mather and his father, as pastor and teacher, respectively, served the Second Church together as colleagues.

Mather married Abigail Phillips, the daughter of one of the leading citizens of nearby Charlestown, in 1686. She was the first of his three wives. After her death in 1702, he married Elizabeth Hubbard, the widow of a mariner. Following Elizabeth's death in 1713, he married Lydia George, the

widow of a Boston merchant. Cotton and Lydia Mather were estranged at his death in Boston of a pulmonary disorder on February 13, 1728, the day after his sixty-fifth birthday. By his first two wives, Cotton had fifteen children, of whom thirteen died before he did.

CAREER HIGHLIGHTS

In the late seventeenth century, Boston's Second Church numbered about 1,500 congregants, of whom nearly one-third had been admitted to communion. It was a large and visible religious society, and its importance across New England ensured the prominence of its ministers. From the day he ascended the church's influential pulpit, Mather was a man of consequence. By 1689, at age twenty-six, Mather was one of a small circle of Massachusetts dissidents who worked to remove their governor, Edmund Andros, an appointee of King James II. Mather and others welcomed England's Glorious Revolution, which deposed King James and resulted in both a new charter and a new governor for the Massachusetts Bay Colony. The residents of Massachusetts also turned to Mather for advice in 1692 and 1693 when charges of witchcraft in Salem Village resulted in the execution of twenty women and men judged in court to have been possessed by the devil. Mather believed in the possibility of diabolical possession, but he questioned the quality of the proof on which the court based its verdicts. Spectral evidence—testimony by accusers of incriminating visions—persuaded the court's judges but not Mather, who attempted to study witchcraft scientifically through observation and published reports. Never a strong supporter of the Salem witchcraft prosecutions, Mather nevertheless failed to express his reservations about the court's course.

Mather's scientific inquiry into witchcraft was typical of his approach to most topics. Interested in a broad variety of concerns, he researched and wrote widely. Whatever the subject, he believed that his writings expressed his Christian obligation to glorify

God, who manifested Himself in every aspect of the universe. Mather's most important publication, *Magnalia Christi Americana*, has been a significant source of information on the religious history of seventeenth-century New England since it appeared in 1702. His other publications include books and pamphlets on theology, education, public affairs, and natural science. A series of letters containing scientific observations, many of them published or abstracted in London's *Transactions of the Royal Society*, resulted in his election to membership in this eminent organization in 1713. *The Christian Philosopher*, published in 1721, offered a means of reconciling reformed theology with the latest in scientific research, including the discoveries of Sir Isaac Newton. Mather's list of publications numbers more than 400 titles, but two of his most important studies remained unpublished at the time of his death. *The Angel of Bethesda*, which did not appear in print until the twentieth century, ambitiously offered medical instruction. Written in the aftermath of a smallpox epidemic, during which he was an influential advocate of inoculation, a controversial practice in the early 1720s, the manuscript reveals Mather's wide reading in his day's medical literature. *Biblia Americana*, a vast scriptural commentary in six manuscript volumes, remains unpublished to this day although Mather considered it his most important project.

Mather's contemporaries recognized his wide knowledge and, on two occasions, when the presidency of Harvard College was vacant, he was a candidate to fill the opening. Throughout his career, however, he had made many political and ecclesiastical enemies, and the college's corporation, which selected the president, passed him over each time as too controversial.

MAJOR PHILANTHROPIC CONTRIBUTIONS

The piety that Cotton Mather believed to be central to every reborn Christian's relationship with God permeated his understanding of philanthropy. To produce "GOOD WORKS," Mather instructed, "the ONE thing, that is *needful*, is a glorious work of GRACE on the soul, renewing and quickening of it, and *purifying* of the sinner, and rendering him *zealous of good works*" (Mather 1966, 27). In other words, Mather believed that only reborn Christians were truly capable of good works. Like all Puritans, Mather worried whether he was predestined to be saved. He was certain, though, that every reborn Christian expressed his faith through his good deeds to others.

Mather's contributions to his community's philanthropic life included practical initiatives, but his pen provided the most important of them. An active transatlantic correspondent, Mather was aware, very early, of the development of reform societies in England, after the Glorious Revolution of 1688; some reform societies strove to relieve societal problems and others to promote the moral health of their own members. In the 1690s and early 1700s, Mather took the lead in introducing such organizations to New England. From time to time, he also wrote sermons and pamphlets about the importance of "doing good," that is to say, of promoting the spiritual, moral, and physical well-being of family members, friends, neighbors, and others. When Elihu Yale made the first major contribution to the American college that eventually bore his name, Cotton played a significant role in persuading the Connecticut-born London merchant that his support was an appropriate expression of philanthropy.

Bonafacius: An Essay upon the Good was Cotton's most important treatise on public service. Published in 1710, the book of about 200 pages was a practical instruction manual outlining every reborn Christian's obligations toward others. Relationships are at the heart of Mather's analysis of public service. By virtue of their stations in life, he taught, relatives, neighbors, masters and their apprentices, ministers and their parishioners, instructors and their pupils, public officials and citizens, physicians and their patients, the rich and the poor, and the saved and the unconverted all had special mutual responsibilities. For example, every husband had a particular duty to promote his wife's spiritual, moral, and physical welfare at the same time that she had a reciprocal obligation toward him. *Bonafacius* also included useful suggestions to aspiring philanthropists. A minister who made pastoral visits to the homes of poor families in his congregation at dinnertime, for example, might be able to tell whether or not they had enough to eat.

CONCLUSION

Although Mather believed that "a glorious work of GRACE on the soul" was necessary for "good works" (Mather 1966, 27), and he addressed *Bonafacius* explicitly to reborn Christians, a much wider audience eventually read and benefited from the book's practical advice. During Boston's smallpox epidemic in the early 1720s, for example, **Benjamin Franklin**, still a sixteen-year-old apprentice working for his brother James, mocked Mather in a series of satirical essays on Mrs. Silence Dogood, a fictional busybody. Yet Franklin, who never experienced religious conversion, had taken at least a portion of Mather's message to heart. As Franklin later acknowledged in his autobiography, Mather's lessons on doing good had been a formative influence during his youth. For generations of readers, Mather's injunctions to "do good" to one another encouraged beneficence whether or not they believed their souls to be saved.

Conrad Edick Wright

FURTHER READING

Foster, Stephen. *Their Solitary Way: The Puritan Social Ethic in the First Century of Settlement in New England.* New Haven, CT: Yale University Press, 1971.

Levin, David. *Cotton Mather: The Young Life of the Lord's Remembrancer, 1663–1703.* Cambridge, MA: Harvard University Press, 1978.

Levy, Babette M. *Cotton Mather.* Boston: Twayne Publishers, 1979.

Mather, Cotton. *Bonifacius: An Essay upon the Good*, ed. David Levin. Cambridge, MA: Harvard University Press, 1966.

Middlekauff, Robert. "Cotton Mather." In *American National Biography*, vol. 14, ed. John A. Garraty and Mark C. Carnes. New York: Oxford University Press, 1999, 682–684.

———. *The Mathers: Three Generations of Puritan Intellectuals.* New York: Oxford University Press, 1971.

Miller, Perry. *The New England Mind: From Colony to Province.* Cambridge, MA: Harvard University Press, 1953.

Silverman, Kenneth. *The Life and Times of Cotton Mather.* New York: Harper & Row, 1984.

Wright, Conrad Edick. *The Transformation of Charity in Postrevolutionary New England.* Boston: Northeastern University Press, 1992.

PAPERS

The American Antiquarian Society (Worcester, MA) holds the majority of Cotton Mather's surviving papers. A smaller but important collection, including the manuscript of Mather's *Biblia Americana*, is at the Massachusetts Historical Society (Boston, MA).

OSEOLA MCCARTY
(1908–1999)

Laundress, Higher Education Supporter, and Traditional African-American Giver

INTRODUCTION

"When I leave this world, I can't carry . . . nothing away from here. Whatever I have, it's going to be left right here for somebody.

Some child can get their education . . . because you can't do nothing now unless you get your education. . . . The only thing I regret is that I didn't have that much more to

Oseola McCarty carries the Olympic torch through Columbia, Mississippi, in May 1996. AP Photo/Steve Coleman.

give" (University of Southern Mississippi, 1999, n.p.). Words like these demonstrate Oseola McCarty's incentive for giving $150,000 to the University of Southern Mississippi in 1995. People in her hometown of Hattiesburg, Mississippi were surprised to learn that McCarty, an African-American woman in her late eighties, made what was later cited as the largest philanthropic gift from an African American in the University of Southern Mississippi's history. Certainly, no one expected the retired laundress to have accumulated such great wealth in her lifetime. A caring, concerned woman, McCarty follows in the long, rarely noted, tradition of African-American giving in the United States.

EARLY YEARS AND EDUCATION

McCarty was born in Wayne County, Mississippi on March 7, 1908. She was heavily influenced by her mother, who worked hard to support her family. As a child, McCarty attended Eureka Elementary School and held a job, ironing for people in the neighborhood. With the money earned from this job, she began a lifelong habit: saving money. According to McCarty, "I would go to school and come home and iron. I'd put money away and save it. When I got enough, I went to First Mississippi National Bank and put it in. I just kept on saving" (University of Southern Mississippi, 1999, n.p.). McCarty also enjoyed learning and had dreams of working in the health profession: "I loved school . . . I wished I had gone on and gotten my education. . . . I wanted to be a nurse . . . wearing those big ol' white caps and a stiff white apron" (University of Southern Mississippi 1999, 1). Her dreams were deferred, however, when her childless aunt became ill and was hospitalized. McCarty needed to care for her aunt, who was no longer able to walk on her own, and she never returned to school.

CAREER HIGHLIGHTS AND MAJOR PHILANTHROPIC CONTRIBUTIONS

Throughout her life, McCarty lived simply and frugally. She never owned a car or learned to drive. In fact, she only added an air-conditioner to her small, wood-frame house during the last years of her life. Never earning more than $9,000 a year as a laundress, she understood what it was like to live in poverty and how difficult it is for the less fortunate to acquire an education. In 1995, McCarty chose the University of Southern Mississippi as the recipient of her donation. Although that institution had not admitted African Americans for most of its history, the University of Southern Mississippi was the only one she knew and she wanted to help young people who lived near her. In making the contribution, McCarty asked that it be used to help those students in need, giving priority to African Americans. Her gift created much excitement across the country and inspired many others to give over $380,000 to that same institution. These additional donations allowed the university to offer scholarships from the Oseola McCarty Endowed Scholarship Fund prior to McCarty's death in 1999; nine students received McCarty scholarships between the announcement of the gift in 1995 and her passing. A deeply religious person, McCarty also gave 10 percent of her assets to her church. Clearly, a belief in the importance of education and religion was the focal point of her life.

In 1996, with the assistance of an Atlanta-based publisher, McCarty expressed her thoughts in a book entitled *Simple Wisdom for Rich Living*. This work was the first time that many people became acquainted with McCarty's ideas. Although a shy public speaker, in writing she was very pointed about the principles essential to success. McCarty spent most of her ninety-one years saving. She believed in taking responsibility for herself and encouraged others to save to prepare for the emergencies in life. Still, McCarty created a legacy of saving for more than just a rainy day. Her life was an example of how to share one's time, wealth, and wisdom. McCarty summed up her motivations and philosophy best in saying "It seems pretty basic to me. If you want to feel proud of yourself, you've got to do things you can be proud of" (University of Southern Mississippi 1999, 1).

Although she received an enormous amount of attention as a result of her contribution (including a Presidential Citizen's Medal from Bill Clinton and honorary degrees from the University of Southern Mississippi and Harvard University), McCarty's gift was not an aberration for African Americans. She followed in a long tradition of African-American philanthropic giving that began over 200 years ago. Emmett D. Carson has noted that black philanthropy has received scant coverage by researchers for two main reasons: the smaller sums involved and the fact that the majority of early charitable activities related to blacks were channeled secretly through churches during slavery. Carson also argued that African-American giving has taken place through four specific venues: the black church,

mutual-aid organizations set up by ministers, sociopolitical organizations like the National Urban League, and community organizations such as civic and social clubs. Black churches, in particular, acted as collection points for money, services, and goods that were pooled and redistributed. Black philanthropy has been instrumental in underwriting important black social movements throughout history. For example, African Americans, through the Afro-American League, raised funds to test the legality of Jim Crow laws in the South.

CONCLUSION

Following in the African-American philanthropic tradition, McCarty gave both to her church and to education. Meanwhile, organizations such as the African American Legacy Program in Michigan, the Black Family Reunion Institute at Temple University (studying the use of the family reunion as an occasion to bolster philanthropy), and the Black United Fund have been encouraging and highlighting African-American giving for many years. The miraculous nature of McCarty's contribution helps draw attention to previously ignored philanthropic efforts by African Americans.

Marybeth Gasman

FURTHER READING ON OSELOA MCCARTY

McCarty, Oseola. *Simple Wisdom for Rich Living*. Atlanta: Longstreet Press, 1996.

Mercer, Joye. "Retired Laundress Gives U. of Southern Mississippi $150,000." *The Chronicle of Higher Education*, August 11, 1995, A31.

University of Southern Mississippi. *Press Kit*, 1999. Contact: Public Relations, Box 5016, Hattiesburg, MS 39406–5016.

FURTHER READING ON AFRICAN-AMERICAN GIVING

Carson, Emmett D. *A Hand Up: Black Philanthropy and Self-Help in America*. Washington, DC: Joint Center for Political and Economic Studies Press, 1993.

———. "The Evolution of Black Philanthropy: Patterns of Giving and Voluntarism." In *Philanthropic Giving: Studies in Varieties and Goals*, ed. Richard Magat. New York: Oxford University Press, 1989, 92–102.

———. "Patterns of Giving in Black Churches." In *Faith and Philanthropy in America: Exploring the Role of Religion in America's Voluntary Sector*, ed. Robert Wuthnow and Virginia A.

Hodgkinson. San Francisco: Jossey-Bass, 1990, 232–252.

Smith, Bradford, Sylvia Shue, Jennifer L. Vest, and Joseph Villarreal. *Philanthropy in Communities of Color*. Bloomington: Indiana University Press, 1999.

NETTIE FOWLER MCCORMICK
(1835–1923)

Businesswoman and Religious and Educational Benefactor

INTRODUCTION

In her teens, Nettie Fowler McCormick wrote, "I want to be somebody. . . . During the past year, I have read many biographies of eminent individuals—and while reading I have burned to be great and good. I will be" (Burgess 1962, 10). This strong drive to succeed led McCormick to become not only one of the earliest American businesswomen, but also one of the leading philanthropists of her time. She had a major role in the development of a great American invention, the mechanical reaper, as her husband's partner. After her husband's death, she used the profits to give away more than $8 million to institutions and individuals in America.

EARLY YEARS AND EDUCATION

"Nettie" McCormick was born Nancy Maria Fowler in a northwest frontier town of New York State in 1835. She was the youngest of three children and the only daughter. Her parents, Melzar and Clarissa Fowler, were dry-goods merchants. When she was only seven months old, a horse killed her father. Subsequently, her mother ran the business and cared for the children until her own death six years later.

At age seven and an orphan, she and her brother, Eldridge Merick Fowler, went to live with the family of their uncle and their maternal grandmother in Clayton, New York. Their uncle, Eldridge Merick, was a prominent shipbuilder and a temperance ac-

Nettie Fowler McCormick. State Historical Society of Wisconsin, (X3)37518.

tivist, and both guardians were recognized in their community as philanthropists. Indeed, Nettie Fowler entered a family who strongly supported the local Methodist Church and assumed an active role in both the Methodist Sunday school and church.

Nettie Fowler attended the local yellow schoolhouse until she was fifteen. From 1850 to 1855, she attended three different schools:

Falley Seminary (Fulton, NY); Emma Willard's Troy Female Seminary (Troy, NY); and Genesee Wesleyan Seminary (Lima, NY). She also began her first venture in philanthropy when she was at Genesee Wesleyan Seminary, prominently serving in the missionary society. In fact, she must have been one of the most promising mission students, as she was one of three to whom the school appropriated money to make them life members of the parent mission society.

She also seemed to have a special inclination toward education and children. For instance, she spent one year, when not away at school, as the teacher at the same yellow schoolhouse where she had been a student. She wrote on her first day: "This morning, I commenced my school. Teaching, is something I have, from childhood, loved to think of. I always loved children and to preside over a body of children and 'to go to Italy' was once the ambition of my life" (Roderick 1956, 30).

CAREER HIGHLIGHTS

While on an extended visit to Chicago, she met the inventor of the mechanical reaper, Cyrus Hall McCormick. He was a strong Presbyterian and more than twice her age. Within six months, she had begun attending the Presbyterian Church. Six months later, on January 26, 1858, the couple was married. Although she wanted to be a good housekeeper and a good wife, the majority of her journal documents the trials of her marriage. Both Cyrus and Nettie McCormick were considered to be strong-willed individuals by those who knew them.

Despite any marital discord, the two had a highly productive business relationship. She quickly became her husband's silent, but closest, business associate. At night, the two of them would stay up for hours to formulate and write business correspondence. By 1860, Nettie McCormick was an active participant in her husband's many activities. Besides the growing reaper business, his interests included a theological seminary, publishing activities, and the Presbyterian Church. These interests now became Nettie McCormick's as well.

Following the Chicago fire of 1871, Nettie McCormick, at age thirty-six, began to take a more visible role. When the McCormick Harvesting Machine plant was destroyed, Cyrus McCormick intended to retire. Consequently, Nettie McCormick oversaw the construction of the new plant, guided her husband's investments, and began to plan future ventures. Ultimately, she consolidated the farm machinery industry under the International Harvester Company. After a neck operation in 1878, Cyrus McCormick never returned to work; Nettie McCormick served as untitled director and president of the International Harvester Company until his death in 1884. Then her son, Cyrus McCormick, Jr., took the helm, and she continued as an active business advisor. Interestingly, Nettie McCormick abruptly ended her journal the same year as her husband's operation. Possibly, she no longer needed the emotional crutch upon which she had leaned for twenty years while cut off from a life of action.

During this time, she not only concentrated on business interests, but also became more involved in charitable work. After the fire, she organized aid for the destitute, listened to requests for clothing and bedding, and cooperated in distribution of supplies. In the late 1870s, she helped found the Women's Presbyterian Board of Missions of the Northwest. She subsequently served as treasurer, vice-president, and honorary vice-president of the organization. She also persuaded her husband to provide the mission group with free office space in one of his publishing houses for more than ten years.

MAJOR PHILANTHROPIC CONTRIBUTIONS

McCormick was motivated to a life of philanthropy for numerous reasons, including her commitment to religion and education. She also felt that she had a debt to repay to society because her uncle and grandmother had taken her in as an orphan. Probably encouraged by her grandmother and uncle,

McCormick developed her love for education early in life. Her family's strong religious belief was another reason for her commitment to education. Both Methodists and Presbyterians believed that knowledge was essential to a full Christian life.

After she became wealthy, her desire to do charitable works only increased. She felt that profit was acceptable, if she did "a great deal of good to the poor, the homeless and the orphan" (Burgess 1962, 33). She viewed her money as a sacred trust for which she would one day have to give an accounting to God.

Following her husband's death in 1884, his will stated that his wife and their son were to keep the estate intact for five years and "to make such reasonable donations therefrom to charitable or benevolent purposes as in their judgment I would have made as living" (Roderick 1956, 157) Her husband had given away $550,000 in his lifetime in well-defined areas: the Presbyterian Church, McCormick Theological Seminary, and church colleges. McCormick honored her husband's wishes, focusing on these causes and giving away a total of $475,000. In 1890, however, she was freed from the philanthropic confines in his will and could become a philanthropist in her own right. Now she gave, regardless of religion or sectarian association, to any entity dedicated to spiritual and educational progress. She gave to orphanages, schools, colleges, hospitals, relief agencies, and individuals of a wide range of affiliation.

McCormick's charitable giving was marked by both a painstaking attention to detail and a giving of self. She was known for her strong involvement in the planning and construction of projects. Although she felt it was her duty to give, she clearly cherished the act of giving her time, money, thoughts, and prayers. At the same time, her gifts were highly selective and restrictive. She felt that worthy individuals and institutions deserved support, but not necessarily all the many thousands in need. And who did she consider worthy? She had several criteria: (1) Was there a moral purpose behind the request? (2) Would the person or institution benefit spiritually or educationally? (3) Would the gift help the person or institution achieve his or her own success?

McCormick also viewed philanthropy as an intensely personal matter. She was reluctant to discuss her many gifts and often genuinely preferred anonymity, never inviting or receiving publicity. This giving behavior was most evident in her *Chicago Daily Tribune* obituary, which identified her as a woman who had supported more than six schools in the country. In reality, she was a philanthropist who supported more than forty institutions. Indeed, she focused her giving on education because she viewed such gifts as the best way to improve the world. In only eight of her thirty-four years of giving did education fail to receive greater financial support than any other interest. Generally, these gifts went to denominational institutions—typically Presbyterian ones—and to rural areas. She was particularly concerned with the inadequate educational facilities in the rural Midwest, in the frontier regions of the West, and the highlands and other backward areas of the South. For instance, she took on the development of a group of schools in the mountains of Tennessee and North Carolina, giving money to establish—what she felt were sorely needed—domestic science departments. Throughout her entire life, and despite some of her untraditional activities, McCormick felt that housekeeping was to be a woman's crowning achievement. Yet, as a woman who was always hard on herself, she believed she lacked domestic skills. Perhaps, she hoped her efforts could ensure that other young women would not feel inadequate.

CONCLUSION

Unlike such contemporary female philanthropists as **Margaret Olivia Sage**, McCormick neither promoted the cause of social welfare nor created a foundation. Yet, she was a dynamic factor in American philanthropy at the turn of the century, giving away more than $8 million. The history of education in certain fields would have been different without her. She donated nearly $4 million to forty-six private schools and institutions in America. Certain international religious efforts, particularly the missions work of both the Presbyterian and Methodist churches, deeply felt her influence as a giver of money, ideas, counsel, and spiritual guardianship. Many of her contributions also went to foreign mission educational endeavors and scholarships for students to attend seminary. She offered sustained support to McCormick Theological Seminary and came to be known as the principal donor of the Presbyterian Church.

Throughout her life, she had an incredible drive to touch the lives of others. As a young woman, McCormick wrote in her journal, "Usefulness is the great thing in life. . . . To do something for others leaves a sweeter odor than a life of pleasure" (Burgess 1962,

14). As an older woman, she put this belief into practice.

Lynn O'Connell

FURTHER READING

Albertine, Susan A. "Nettie Fowler McCormick." In *American National Biography*, Vol. 11, ed. John A. Garraty and Mark C. Carnes. New York: Oxford University Press, 1999, 920–921.

Burgess, Charles O. *Nettie Fowler McCormick: Profile of an American Philanthropist*. Madison: State Historical Society of Wisconsin, 1962.

Roderick, Stella Virginia. *Nettie Fowler McCormick*. Rindge, NH: Richard R. Smith Publisher, 1956.

PAPERS

Nettie McCormick's papers are in the McCormick manuscript collection as part of the State Historical Society of Wisconsin (Madison, WI).

MELLON FAMILY

Andrew W. Mellon (1855–1937)

Banker, Secretary of the Treasury, Art Collector, and Founder of the A.W. Mellon Charitable and Educational Trust, Mellon Institute for Industrial Research, and the National Gallery of Art

Ailsa Mellon Bruce (1901–1969)

Art Collector and Founder of the Avalon Foundation

Paul Mellon (1907–1999)

Art Collector, Founder of the Old Dominion Foundation and the Bollingen Foundation, and Chairman of the A.W. Mellon Charitable and Educational Trust and the National Gallery of Art

INTRODUCTION

In 1967, Paul Mellon gave a lengthy interview to *Fortune*'s Charles J.V. Murphy as part of a series about the Mellon family. "If I ever had to write an essay on the ingredients of my personal philosophy," Mellon said, "the honest statement would be that I am more interested in the foundations than I am in business, and I am more interested

in general in the arts and humanities than I am in science" (Murphy 1967, 134). That comment expressed, with Paul Mellon's traditional understatement, his philosophy of giving. Indeed, Paul Mellon was continuing in large measure his father Andrew Mellon's philanthropy. Given the lengthy lives of both Andrew Mellon, his son Paul Mellon, and his daughter Ailsa Mellon Bruce, the Mellon family made substantial philanthropic contributions in every decade of the twentieth century. Prominently, they established and developed one of the world's greatest collections of art, the National Gallery of Art.

ANDREW W. MELLON

The Mellon fortune began with Thomas Mellon. Born in Ireland, Thomas Mellon emigrated to America at age five and settled with his parents on a farm twenty-one miles east of Pittsburgh. He started several short-lived businesses and was elected (as a Republican) to the first of several terms as a judge in the Pittsburgh Court of Common Pleas in 1859. Thomas Mellon quit the judiciary in 1870 and founded T. Mellon's Sons, a private bank that was later to evolve into the Mellon National Bank. This bank ensured that Mellon would be able to pass on about $2.5 million to his children.

The sixth child (of eight) produced by Thomas and Sarah Jane Mellon, Andrew W. Mellon was born in Pittsburgh on March 24, 1855. He attended the Western University of Pennsylvania (now the University of Pittsburgh), but left the university without graduating to work with his father at the family bank. He would remain involved with the bank until his death.

Andrew Mellon was one of the greatest entrepreneurs of the late nineteenth and early twentieth centuries. Most great philanthropists created one giant business enterprise. Mellon either created or maintained five important businesses: the Mellon National Bank; Gulf Oil (now part of Chevron); the Aluminum Company of America (now Alcoa); Koppers, a leading mining company; and Carborundum, an industrial manufacturer. Mellon was, in effect, the first venture capitalist. Business journalist John K. Barnes, in a 1924 article, described the business practices forged by Mellon. "Find a man who can run a business and needs capital either to start or expand. Furnish the capital and take shares in the business, leaving the other man to run it except when it is in trouble. . . . The Mellon fortune has grown into a kind of re-

Andrew W. Mellon (left), then secretary of the Treasury, photographed in December 1930 with his daughter Ailsa Mellon Bruce and his son Paul Mellon. © Underwood & Underwood/CORBIS.

volving fund for the promotion of enterprises and the employment of workers" (Denton 1948, 15).

Mellon's first great triumph was investing in Charles Hall, who perfected techniques that allowed aluminum to be refined cheaply in 1889. Hall's company, now Alcoa, was a cornerstone of the Mellon fortune. Another major triumph was investing in the wildcatters who discovered the Spindletop oil strike in 1901, creating Gulf Oil. In fact, the **Pews** of Philadelphia became millionaires shipping and refining the oil discovered with Mellon money. Since the Mellons were minority shareholders in scores of enterprises, few at the time realized how wealthy they really were. In addition, Andrew Mellon was a private man who preferred to stay out of the limelight.

In 1920, after the Mellon National Bank contributed $1.5 million to the Republican National Committee, President Warren G. Harding rewarded Mellon by naming him Secretary of the Treasury. Most reporters had never heard of Mellon; few even knew whether his middle initial was "J," "G," or "W." Still, Mellon, once he had stepped down from the boards of fifty-one corporations, turned out to be a brilliant Secretary of the Treasury. When Mellon arrived in Washington, he found the federal government saddled with World War I debts and taxpayers burdened with some of the highest tax rates in U.S. history. "High taxation means a high price level and high cost of living," Mellon wrote in his only book, *Taxation: The People's Business* (Mellon 1924, 76). "A reduction in taxes, therefore, results not only in an immediate saving to the individual or property directly affected, but an ultimate saving to all people in the country" (Mellon 1924, 76). Under Mellon's leadership, tax rates were slashed and the national debt fell from $6.5 billion to $3.5 billion. By 1928, Mellon proudly announced that a childless single man with a $4,000 income saw his tax bill fall from $120 in 1920 to $5.63 in 1928. Had Mellon stepped down in 1929, he would have possessed a spotless reputation. However, he made the mistake of staying on with President **Herbert Hoover**. At the time, he was blamed for instigating the Great Depression.

Major Philanthropic Contributions

For most of Mellon's life, he appears to have been personally very generous. Longtime family friend Lucius Beebe told Stewart Holbrook that most of these small acts of charity—paying hospital bills and college educations, buying pianos for college students—were not publicized because of Mellon's "patrician hatred for anything savoring of personal popularity or seeming to cater to good will" (Holbrook 1953, 229). Among Mellon's acts of kindness, according to Beebe, was burning the invoices of small creditors every Christmas. According to Mellon biographer Philip H. Love, part of the reason for Mellon's reticence was the fear of being hounded by people wanting handouts. He quoted long-time Mellon personal assistant David Finley, who said in 1928 that Mellon

received thousands of letters each week asking for aid. "Naturally, he cannot grant all of the requests made in these letters," Finley said, "and not being able to grant all of them, the only fair thing to do is to grant none of them" (Love 1929, 130).

Mellon, in collaboration with his brother Richard Mellon, performed his first major act of charity in 1909 when he created the Mellon Institute for Industrial Research. That year, Mellon received a letter written in French (a language he could barely read) that promised new discoveries. He sent the letter to a Gulf chemist, who said that there was nothing useful in the letter and reinforced his point by enclosing a copy of *The Chemistry of Commerce* by University of Kansas chemistry professor Robert Kennedy Duncan. In the book, Duncan proposed that businesses could advance science by funding research. Fascinated by Duncan's ideas, Mellon invited him to Pittsburgh. He then agreed to fund an industrial research institute lead by Duncan. In 1911, the institute opened in a ramshackle building at the University of Pittsburgh. After Mellon saw a scientist being hoisted into an attic with a block and tackle, he agreed to fund a new building, which opened in 1913. With that building's opening, the Mellon Institute became an independent educational institution.

From the start, the Mellon Institute's method of funding, in which corporations paid the institute and in return received proprietary business information, was highly controversial. Harvey O'Connor, author of a critical biography of the Mellons, charged that the institute "solved admirably the research problems of the Mellon corporations" (O'Connor 1933, 247). Others ridiculed some of the institute's findings, such as the study that reduced the amount of yeast needed in commercial breadmaking by half and the perfection of cellulose-based hot dog casings. Since much of the research was shared by the corporations that funded it, the Mellon Institute did a great deal to advance basic science. Research on petrochemicals was commissioned—and rejected—by Gulf, and then picked up by and perfected for rival

Union Carbide. In addition, the institute funded a great deal of nonproprietary research: on artificial rubber, pollution-reducing devices, and sleep research.

Like most wealthy men of his generation, Andrew Mellon collected great art. When he was treasury secretary, however, Mellon began to accumulate the collection that was to become the core of the National Gallery of Art. Those close to Mellon are divided about when he decided to donate his paintings to the United States. David Finley, who later became director of the National Gallery of Art, traced the decision to 1927. Baron Duveen, the British art dealer who sold Mellon many of his paintings, said in a court case that Mellon made the decision in 1929. John Walker, Finley's successor as director of the National Gallery of Art and a man who knew Andrew Mellon well, provides the most definitive evidence. Walker believed that Mellon decided late in 1927. He provides two pieces of evidence: a letter of Mellon's to the Duchess of Rutland in 1926 in which he states that he is not collecting "for public purposes," and an entry from Mellon's diary in early 1928 in which he writes that his daughter Ailsa calls and "asks if I have given art gallery to the Government" (Walker 1974, 108).

The National Gallery of Art marked the culmination of a lifetime of collecting by Mellon. Walker observes that Mellon's taste evolved over time. Up until 1916, according to Walker, Mellon bought "overvalued Barbizon painters and their entourage" (Walker 1974, 105). However, in 1916, Mellon moved to a mansion in Pittsburgh's East End that somewhat resembled an English country house. He then began to buy great art such as paintings by Gainsborough and Sir Joshua Reynolds. Mellon, Walker writes, "seems to have wanted paintings which would offer him an escape into an ideal world filled with civilized human beings, often portrayed in the midst of beautiful scenery. Passing much of his life in Washington among uninspired bureaucrats and in Pittsburgh where day after day he faced the smoke and dirty fog which produced his wealth, he wished to dream of a pleasanter environment" (Walker 1974, 106).

From the late 1920s onward, Mellon began buying art in earnest but he kept his philanthropic goal a secret for nearly five years. There is no reference to Mellon's art collecting in Harvey O'Connor's muckraking *Mellon's Millions* (1933). Philip Love, in his 1929 biography of Mellon, states that art was Mellon's "expensive hobby" and that "only his most intimate friends are privileged to view" his paintings and "only on the condition they tell no one about them" (Love 1929, 130).

In 1930, Mellon made two dramatic steps toward the creation of a National Gallery of Art in the United States. He created the A.W. Mellon Educational and Charitable Trust and he purchased seventeen great paintings from the Soviet Union's Hermitage Museum, including three Rembrandts, two Raphaels, and three Van Dycks. In 1932, Mellon left the Treasury Department to serve as U.S. Ambassador to Great Britain. He spent a great deal of time in Britain's National Gallery, and also built a relationship with British art dealer Baron Duveen.

Mellon returned to Washington in 1933. A year later, he was indicted for allegedly understating his 1931 income taxes by $3 million. During the trial, it was revealed that Mellon had contributed $3 million in paintings to his foundation, but had not taken any deductions during 1931. When government lawyers tried to prove that Mellon had acquired these paintings purely for his own pleasure, Mellon was forced to reveal that he was planning a national gallery in Washington. He publicly offered to donate his paintings as well as a $10 million endowment to the United States if a suitable spot on the National Mall would be available. President Franklin Roosevelt accepted Mellon's offer in December 1936, and the National Gallery of Art was formally created in March 1937. With his plans revealed, Mellon and Duveen began a business relationship that was so close that Duveen rented an apartment one floor below Mellon's at 1785 Massachusetts Avenue and began to display paintings that

Mellon could inspect at his leisure. Mellon also began buying from other dealers as well. By the fall of 1936, he had 369 paintings in his collection.

Mellon not only secured the site for the National Gallery; he hired the architect, John Russell Pope, and selected the Tennessee limestone to be used in the building. He also insisted that the building not bear the Mellon name, according to historian David Doheny, "since he felt that it might prevent it from receiving major collections then at the hands of other American collectors" (Doheny 1999, 17). Ultimately, the National Gallery of Art would not open until 1941, four years after Mellon's death in Washington, DC, on August 26, 1937. David Doheny estimates that Mellon spent $21 million on paintings for the National Gallery of Art, $10 million on the endowment, and $15 million on the building. As for the tax trial, it ended four months after Mellon's death; he was acquitted of all charges, although the estate paid $560,000 as part of the settlement.

AILSA MELLON BRUCE

In 1901, Andrew Mellon's oldest child, Ailsa Mellon, was born in Pittsburgh, Pennsylvania. In the early 1920s, she married David Bruce, the son of a U.S. senator, who became a prominent diplomat during the Kennedy administration. They divorced in the mid-1940s.

When Andrew Mellon died, both Ailsa Mellon Bruce and her brother Paul Mellon set up foundations. While Paul Mellon started the Old Dominion Foundation, Ailsa Mellon Bruce established the Avalon Foundation but she was a much less systematic philanthropist than her brother, in part because—particularly in her last decade—she suffered from severe pain from arthritis. Still, she was a patron of the arts. She purchased scores of paintings for the National Gallery of Art, most notably Leonardo da Vinci's *Ginevra de Benci*, and also donated generously to the gallery's endowment. She was also a major patron of the Carnegie Institute of Pittsburgh, who acquired most of her personal collection upon her death. A conservationist, she and her brother also purchased a substantial amount of land in North Carolina and donated it to the nation for the Cape Hatteras National Seashore.

When Bruce died in 1969, the Avalon Foundation absorbed the Old Dominion Foundation and the A.W. Mellon Educational and Charitable Trust to form the Andrew W. Mellon Foundation. Following Bruce's example, her children and grandchildren were also philanthropists. Her only child, Audrey Bruce Currier, created the Taconic Foundation, which the *New York Times* described as funding "programs to further equal opportunity with emphasis on housing and jobs for young people" (Pace 1998, C23). A grandson, Michael Currier, also practiced philanthropy, setting up a fund that loaned money to Tibetan exiles in the United States who wanted to start small businesses.

PAUL MELLON

The only son of Andrew Mellon was born on June 11, 1907, in Pittsburgh, Pennsylvania. His mother, Nora McMullen Mellon, was the daughter of a prominent British brewer. In 1912, the Mellons divorced, and one condition of the divorce settlement was that Ailsa and Paul Mellon spend eight months in America with Andrew Mellon and four months in Britain with Nora Mellon. This experience ensured that Paul Mellon would possess a love of England, British painters, and the English countryside throughout his life.

After studying at the Choate School, Paul Mellon went to Yale University, graduating in 1929. After receiving a second bachelor's degree at Clare College, Cambridge University in 1931, Paul Mellon briefly went to work for some of the companies created by his father. After a brief—and disastrous—attempt to create a chain of cheap restaurants offering five-cent hamburgers in 1932, he abandoned the business world. He then went back to Cambridge University, where he received a master's degree in 1938. Prior to achieving that graduate degree, Mellon married Mary Catherine Brown (1935). They had two children, Catherine and Timothy. After Mary Mellon's death in 1946, Mellon married Rachel Lambert "Bunny" Lloyd, who survived him. Aside from serving in World War II (he joined the Office of Strategic Services, rising to the rank of major), Mellon spent most of his career as a full-time philanthropist.

Mellon's principal philanthropy was the National Gallery of Art. In 1938, he became the gallery's first president, resigning in 1939 to join the military. He then rejoined the gallery's board of directors in 1945 and became vice-president in 1961. Two years later, he accepted the position of president for a second time, serving in this capacity from 1963 to 1979. He became the gallery's chairman in 1979 and finally retired from the board in 1985. While spending two days a week as the museum president, Mellon was also the gallery's most generous donor. Both personally and as chairman of the A.W. Mellon Educational and Charitable Trust and the Old Dominion Foundation, Mellon kept giving gifts to the gallery: 113 paintings in 1947 and 351 oil sketches by George Catlin in 1959 as well as Cezannes, van Goghs, and Degases. In addition, the A.W. Mellon Educational and Charitable Trust and its successors contributed $84 million to the National Gallery of Art between 1930 and 1980—much donated under Paul Mellon's supervision.

The National Gallery of Art housed only part of Paul Mellon's collection. He was a major collector of British art; at one point in the 1960s, as many as 300 British paintings from the eighteenth and nineteenth centuries went across the Atlantic to Mellon's American homes. He richly endowed the Yale Center for British Art in the United States and the Paul Mellon Centre for Studies in British Art in Great Britain to house his paintings and to fund art historians conducting substantial research. Mellon was also interested in ancient art. In 1961, he created and endowed Harvard's Center for Hellenic Studies to aid scholars studying ancient Greek coins, art, and history. Returning to one of his father's philanthropic creations, Mellon was forced to close the Mellon Institute, which was ailing as corporate research and development funding increased in the 1950s and 1960s. In 1966, the Mellon Institute merged with Carnegie Tech to form Carnegie-Mellon University.

Perhaps Mellon's most controversial philanthropic institution was the Bollingen Foundation. Begun in 1945, the foundation was named for the village in which Carl Jung spent his summers. In 1939, Paul and Mary Mellon spent their summer in Switzerland, taking courses from Carl Jung. They vowed to promote and translate Jung's works in America. Between 1945 and 1969, the Bollingen Foundation published scores of important works (including literature authored by Jung). Many of these books were arcane, which led U.S. Representative Wright Patman to denounce the foundation as "spending thousands of dollars abroad for the translation of trivia into nonsense" (Hersh 1978, 512). The Bollingen Foundation also published one bestseller, *The I Ching* (1950). In 1946, the foundation also established a major poetry prize, which received some criticism when the first recipient was Ezra Pound, interned at the time in St. Elizabeth's Hospital as a fascist sympathizer.

Paul Mellon died in Upperville, Virginia on February 11, 1999. He left $280 million in his will to charity. He left $75 million and 113 artworks (including two van Goghs and three Seurats) to the National Gallery of Art, and an additional $75 million and 155 paintings to the Yale Center for British Art. Other major beneficiaries include Carnegie-Mellon University ($20 million), Choate Rosemary Hall School ($20 million), and Cambridge University's Fitzwilliam Museum ($8 million).

CONCLUSION

"I have been an amateur in every phase of my life," Paul Mellon wrote in his 1992 memoir, *Reflections in a Silver Spoon*, "an amateur poet, an amateur scholar, an amateur horseman, an amateur farmer, and amateur soldier, an amateur connoisseur of art, an amateur publisher, and an amateur museum executive. The root of the word 'amateur' is the Latin word for love, and I can honestly say that I've thoroughly enjoyed all the roles I've played" (Mellon 1992, 366). When Paul Mellon wrote these words, he used traditional Mellon understatement. Paul Mellon was not a true amateur and neither were his father and sister. The Mellon family did not approach philanthropy blindly. They were systematic, dedicated, and intelligent givers. As a result, the Mellons made substantial and lasting contributions to art, science, and scholarship.

Martin Morse Wooster

FURTHER READING

Denton, Frank R. *The Mellons of Pittsburgh*. New York: Newcomen Society of England, American Branch, 1948.

Doheny, David A. *David E. Finley: Statesman of the Arts*. Washington, DC: National Trust for Historic Preservation, 1999.

Hanchette, D. Quinn. "Philanthropist Paul Mellon's Many Bequests to Charities Include Artworks, $280 Million." *Chronicle of Philanthropy*, February 15, 1999, 24–25.

Hersh, Burton. *The Mellon Family: A Fortune in History*. New York: William Morrow, 1978.

Holbrook, Stewart. *The Age of the Moguls*. Garden City, NY: Doubleday, 1953.

Love, Philip H. *Andrew W. Mellon: The Man and His Work*. Baltimore: F. Heath Coggins, 1929.

Mellon, Andrew W. *Taxation: The People's Business*. New York: Macmillan, 1924.

Mellon, Paul, with John Baskett. *Reflections in a Silver Spoon*. New York: Morrow, 1992.

Mellon Institute: Dedication of the New Building for Science and Humanity. Pittsburgh: Mellon Institute, 1937.

Murphy, Charles J.V. "The Mellons of Pittsburgh: Part III, Paul Mellon." *Fortune*, December 1967, 132–134, 170–184.

O'Connor, Harvey. *Mellon's Millions: The Biography of a Fortune*. New York: John Day, 1933.

Pace, Eric. "Michael Currier, 37, Philanthropic Rancher who Helped Tibetans." *New York Times*, September 22, 1998, C23.

Walker, John. *Self-Portrait with Donors: Confessions of an Art Collector*. Boston: Atlantic Monthly/Little, Brown, 1974.

PAPERS

Correspondence of Andrew W. Mellon can be found in the National Archives (Washington, DC), the Warren G. Harding Papers at the Library of Congress (Washington, DC), and the Carter Glass Papers at the University of Virginia (Charlottesville, VA). As of the present, the papers of Alisa Mellon Bruce and Paul Mellon have not been deposited in an archive.

JESSE E. MOORLAND
(1863–1940)

African-American Clergyman, Bibliophile, Pioneer Secretary of the Colored Department of the Young Men's Christian Association, and Founder of the First African-American Research Library

INTRODUCTION

In a speech entitled "Giving," Reverend Jesse E. Moorland stated, "Men must make giving just as much a fundamental principle of Christianity as prayer and faith. When that day comes, and it is rapidly breaking, genius will not be hampered: every child will have a fair chance to begin the race of life whether he can keep up or not. Men will see that they can ill afford not to give liberally to character-making enterprises. In this great awakening, may all of God's stewards be faithful to do his will" (Jesse E. Moorland Papers, Folder 398, Moorland-Spingarn Research Center). For over twenty-five years, Moorland was a faithful steward to the thousands of African-American men and boys whose lives he enriched through his Young Men's Christian Association (YMCA)

Jesse E. Moorland in his study in Washington, DC, c. 1910. Moorland-Spingarn Research Center, Howard University.

work. Indeed, Moorland's greatest legacies were the establishment of modern YMCA buildings for African Americans in most of the large cities across the United States (as a result of his fifteen-year fund-raising campaign) and the donation of his private library to Howard University, which became the "first research library in an American university devoted exclusively to materials on the Negro" (Winston 1982, 451).

EARLY YEARS AND EDUCATION

Moorland was born on September 10, 1863, in Coldwater, Ohio. He was the only child of Nancy Jane Moore and William Edward Moorland and part of a family of successful farmers who were prominent in local community affairs. His grandparents on both sides were born near New Bern, North Carolina. In 1807, the Moores left North Carolina and settled in Stewart County, Tennessee, where they became landowners and exercised the right to vote. In 1858, his maternal grandfather moved to Ohio because new restrictions were being imposed on free Negroes in Tennessee. While Jesse Moorland

was an infant, his mother died. Soon after, his father left the farm in Coldwater and his maternal grandparents raised Moorland there. Later in life, he recalled that his grandfather played an important role in his education. Grandfather Moores's daily routine included reading aloud to Moorland from The Bible and from such books as Frederick Douglass' autobiography, *My Bondage and My Freedom*. As a result, he read widely in literature, politics, history and geography for the rest of his life.

Moorland's early education took place in a small county school near the farm in Coldwater, Ohio. Later, Moorland attended Northwestern Normal School in Ada, Ohio, where he met his future wife, Lucy Corbin Woodson. The Moorlands were married in 1886. They both taught for a brief period in the public schools of Urbana, Ohio, before moving to Washington, DC to attend Howard University. Jesse Moorland enrolled in the Department of Theology and his wife enrolled in the Normal (teaching) Department; he graduated as salutatorian of his class in 1891 and she graduated in 1893. After his graduation, Jesse Moorland was ordained a

Congregational minister, organizing a church in South Boston, Virginia. The same year, he was appointed secretary of the colored branch of the Young Men's Christian Association in Washington, D.C., where, he wrote later, his "reward was found in the lives of the young men he helped" (JEM Papers, Folder 124). He stayed in this position for two years, resigning to become pastor of Howard Chapel in Nashville, Tennessee, a Congregational church supported by the American Missionary Association in New York. In 1896, he was chosen pastor of the Mount Zion Congregational Church in Cleveland, Ohio. He stayed with this congregation until 1898, when William Alphaeus Hunton, secretary of the recently created Colored Men's Department of the YMCA, offered Moorland a position as administrator and fund-raiser for colored "Y's" in the major cities.

A widely read man, Moorland was "in the vanguard of progressive American Protestant clergymen of the 1890s who wanted to adapt Christian theology to the practical needs of their congregations" (Winston 1982, 448). He believed that the church should not only be responsive to the changing social conditions, but should be a catalyst for change. Such progressive ideas made Moorland eminently suited to "Y" work. Under Moorland's direction, the YMCA became a refuge for African-American men and boys who had migrated from the rural areas of the South to the larger towns and to the crowded cities of the North in their search for an alternative to sharecropping, disenfranchisement, and racial discrimination and injustice. Most of those who migrated to urban areas were poor and uneducated. To these men and youth, the "Y" served as an interpreter of their new urban environment by promoting a program of civic, economic, educational, health, and religious development. In most cases, the YMCA was also the sole recreational facility in the racially segregated cities of the North and South.

CAREER HIGHLIGHTS AND MAJOR PHILANTHROPIC CONTRIBUTIONS

At the time Moorland began his career in the YMCA, most of the Negro associations did not own the often-rundown buildings in which they met. About these early years Moorland wrote, "The work was small then; only one residence was owned by the Association for Black men in the entire country. . . . Often it was hard to get an Association secretary or president [who were white] to give you ten minutes' time to talk about establishing a colored YMCA. The days were dark, and it seemed there was little hope for equipment or supplies; secretaries came and went" (JEM Papers, Folder 124). Moorland resolved to emphasize the construction of buildings designed specifically for YMCA purposes. His first major success was in Washington, DC, where the oldest colored YMCA had been established in 1853. In 1909, he embarked on a fund-raising campaign in which he first garnered the support of the black leadership, presenting the drive as a challenge to their race pride, after which he solicited funds from white philanthropists looking for opportunities to fund Negro self-help programs. In the "Monster Men's Meetings," which he convened, Moorland exhorted to his audiences: "Save your young men and you save your race. Save your young men and you save your country. Save your young men and you save the world" (JEM Papers, Folder 1091). This formula proved to be a success. For the new Washington, DC Twelfth Street YMCA, which was ready for occupancy in 1912, Moorland raised $26,000 from the community, $25,000 from **John D. Rockefeller, Sr.**, $25,000 from **Julius Rosenwald**, and $25,000 from the National Council of the YMCA.

In 1910, Moorland was called to Chicago to head a fund-raising drive for the construction of a building there. While there, he met with Julius Rosenwald to discuss his fund-raising efforts, convincing Rosenwald that the Chicago and Washington campaigns could be models for the nation. As a result, Rosenwald agreed to donate $25,000 to any city that could raise $75,000 for the construction of a YMCA building. This offer was to be valid for five years. Over the next few years, Moorland, an efficient administrator and popular leader, was able to rally the people of America, black and white, to donate more than $2 million to finance the building program of the YMCA in fourteen cities across the country.

The foundation of Moorland's fundraising was his "Watch the Clock—$50,000 in Ten Days" campaign in which he announced, via fliers, letters, and local newspapers, the goal of the building fund. He used the newspapers to keep the communities apprised of the campaign's progress. Headlines such as "Negroes' Fund Now $30,960" in the *St. Louis Argus* on December 16, 1915 and "Negroes Have Raised $41,448" two days later challenged the readership to give until the goal was reached (JEM Papers, Folder 1141). In many cities, the goal was even surpassed.

In one of his early fund-raising brochures titled "Meeting the Challenge," Moorland described the campaign as a "comprehensive challenge . . . that the Colored people have never had . . . to meet before. It has called forth latent energy that has been waiting for a task that would call out true heroism. It has called out earnest workers for an unselfish cause and has brought to light a number of people who have been frugal and yet are not stingy, but liberal of heart" (JEM Papers, Folder 1141). He cites as evidence of genuine interest, for example, a donor from Washington, DC, "born a slave, now a laborer in Government service, who was the first Colored man to give $500," and an employee of the Chicago Telephone Company, who was the first colored man to give $1,000, representing "nearly thirty years of saving" (JEM Papers, Folder 1141). Moorland not only organized the effort to match the grants, he also personally supervised the construction of fourteen YMCA buildings.

Upon the death of his friend and associate William A. Hunton in 1916, Moorland became the senior secretary of the Colored Men's Department. By that time, Moorland

had helped to build the department into a significant national institution. In 1919, it included 29 buildings, 107 college student chapters, 39 city associations, 14 industrial associations, and 2 railroad associations. In 1923, Moorland retired from the YMCA at the mandatory retirement age of sixty. He had moved from Washington to New York City four years earlier to work at the national headquarters. Upon his retirement, Moorland devoted himself to the work of such organizations as the National Health Circle for Colored People, the Association for the Study of Negro Life and History, and Howard University (on whose Board of Trustees he had served since 1907). In the 1930s, he held the chairmanship of the Executive Committee of Howard University's Board of Trustees.

In 1914, Moorland donated his private library and personal papers, at that time considered to be one of the most significant collections of black-related materials in existence, to Howard University. One of several black bibliophiles and collectors in the country, Moorland had amassed a collection of 6,000 books, pamphlets, manuscripts, sheet music, photographs, and artifacts documenting blacks in Africa and the United States. His donation reflected the efforts of African Americans to take a leadership role in the documentation, preservation, and study of their own history and culture. In fact, it was hoped that his generous gift would support research and instruction in black studies. Indeed, Moorland's collection on the "Negro and Slavery" provided the catalyst for the centralization of the university library's other black-related materials, which became known collectively as the Moorland Foundation. In a letter to the president of the university, Moorland stated that his collection "has been regarded by many experts as probably the largest and most complete yet gathered by a single individual. I have spent many years and considerable means in getting this collection together. . . . I am giving this collection to the University because . . . it is the place where our young people . . . should have the privilege of a complete Reference Library on the subject" (JEM Papers, Folder 124).

In 1946, Howard University acquired the large personal library of Arthur B. Spingarn, an attorney, social activist, and prominent collector of books and other materials produced by black people. The Moorland-Spingarn Research Center is named for those two benefactors whose collections provided the foundation upon which later development could be built. Today, the Moorland-Spingarn Research Center is widely known as one of the world's largest and most comprehensive repositories for the documentation of the history and culture of people of African descent in Africa, the Americas, and other parts of the world.

CONCLUSION

Following a heart attack two weeks earlier, Moorland died on April 30, 1940, in New York City. In life, he devoted himself to the expansion of YMCA work among African-American men and boys. Although he was opposed to the racial segregation within the organization, Moorland recognized the positive aspects of having the facilities to train young black men for leadership roles through volunteer and paid positions at the "Y." During his tenure, the growing number of all-black branches became a force for education and enlightenment in the black communities. They provided residence halls, recreational activities, adult education, job training, Bible study, and summer camps to a population that had been denied the benefits and advantages that white Americans took for granted. Clearly, Moorland saw his "Y" work as an opportunity to serve his community but he also served that community by sharing his private library of African-American heritage.

Joellen El Bashir

FURTHER READING

Moorland, Jesse E. "The Young Men's Christian Association among Negroes." *Journal of Negro History*, April 1924, 127–138.

Moorland obituary notice. *Journal of Negro History*, July 1940, 401–403.

"A Tribute to the Memory of Jesse E. Moorland." *Howard University Bulletin*, July 1940, 12.

Winston, Michael R. "Jesse Edward Moorland." In *Dictionary of American Negro Biography*, ed. Rayford W. Logan and Michael R. Winston. New York: W.W. Norton, 1982, 448–452.

PAPERS

Jesse E. Moorland's papers are located in the Manuscript Division of the Moorland-Spingarn Research Center, Howard University (Washington, DC).

JOHN MUIR
(1838–1914)

Naturalist, Preservationist, and Founder of the Sierra Club

INTRODUCTION

"The world we are told was made for man—a presumption that is totally unsupported by facts. . . . Nature's object in making animals and plants might possibly be first of all the happiness of each one of them, not the creation of all for the happiness of one. Why ought man to value himself as more than an infinitely small composing unit of one great unit of creation? And what creature of all that the Lord has taken the pains to make is not essential to the completeness of that unit?" (Teale 1976, 316–317) This passage from John Muir's memoir of his trek from Indiana to Florida in 1867 serves as an eloquent expression of the philosophy that guided his entire adult life. Muir's tireless defense of America's disappearing wilderness as sanctuaries for the "thousands of tired, nerve-shaken, over-civilized people" in urban

America continues to echo today through the efforts of the Sierra Club, the organization he founded in 1892 (Muir 1901, 15).

EARLY YEARS AND EDUCATION

Born in Dunbar, Scotland, on April 21, 1838, John Muir grew up in a household governed by his severe and pious father, Daniel Muir. The first son in a family of eight children, Muir's early childhood passed amid the wild nature of the Scottish coast. Indeed, Muir later attributed this early exposure as a catalyst for much of his spiritual connection to the natural world. Muir's tumultuous passage through the violent grammar school system of mid-nineteenth-century Scotland also played a role in the development of his reverence for all life. When ten-year-old John Muir embarked with his father and two older siblings for North America in 1849, he viewed the change as an escape, a chance to learn not from books but from the natural world he had seen in the sketches of John James Audubon. Daniel Muir saw the move as an opportunity to recreate the primitive conditions of early Christianity and thereby induce greater piety in himself and his family.

Settling in Marquette County, Wisconsin, the Muirs engaged in the environmentally destructive agricultural practices of frontier America, more than once wearing out a piece of land through overfarming. This insensitivity to the limits of nature grated on John Muir. His formal education had ended when the family immigrated but, in his limited spare time, he rambled through the countryside observing the flora and fauna. He also developed a keen interest in mechanics and invention. Both hobbies became a source of tension between John Muir and his increasingly fanatical father. The pressure of unfulfilled promise and stifled ambition built during John Muir's teenage years. At last, in 1860, John Muir (at the age of twenty-two) left the family farm to exhibit some of his inventions at the state fair in Madison, Wisconsin.

The trip to the fair opened many doors for Muir. He received a job as a mechanic in a

John Muir, c. 1900. © CORBIS.

boat workshop and then began studying at the newly chartered University of Wisconsin. There, he studied botany, chemistry, geology, and biology; the latter two were just then being transformed by Charles Darwin. His hunger for learning was insatiable (by his own account he slept only four or five hours a night); he struggled to reconcile the observation and experimentation of science with his religious convictions. This struggle resulted in the peculiar fusion of pantheist/ Christian ideas that infused his later writing and underwrote his advocacy for wilderness preservation. Punctuated by a stint as a teacher in a rural school and summertime botanizing expeditions, Muir's career at the University of Wisconsin was distinguished. In the summer of 1863, he decided to pursue a medical degree at the University of Michigan. However, the threat of being drafted into the Union Army was growing with each passing month. Not yet even an American citizen (he did not become one until circumstance compelled him to at the age of sixty-five, when he embarked on a world tour), he felt no allegiance to the Union or its Civil War efforts. In early 1864, after learning of a new draft order, Muir left Wisconsin for Canada. Although he did not know it at the time, his formal education had ended.

CAREER HIGHLIGHTS

Muir spent the rest of the Civil War in the future Canadian province of Ontario, first as something of a fugitive and then as a machinist in a woodworking factory. His skills in woodworking and mechanical engineering eventually took him to Indianapolis, Indiana, where he became supervisor of a wagon factory by the end of 1866. Despite his passion for botany and the outdoors, Muir's work ethic and fascination with all things mechanical were leading him toward a career in industry. A late-night accident in March 1867, which temporarily blinded Muir, led to weeks of soul-searching. In the end, Muir decided to give up his promising career in the factory and travel to South America to botanize along the Amazon. In no hurry, he decided to walk to the Gulf of Mexico to catch a steamer abroad. His 1,000-mile trek convinced him that his future lay in such rambles and in studying the natural world he encountered along the way.

Muir never did make it to South America. After reaching the Gulf and falling desperately ill of a fever (perhaps malaria), he eventually wound up on a steamer to California. Still beckoned by the tropics, Muir planned to stay only a few months. The mountains of the Sierra Nevada proved a stronger draw and he made California his home. Initially, Muir supported himself with odd jobs that kept him close to the mountains, primarily as a sawyer (sawing wood) and shepherd. He used the freedom such work allowed to explore the mountains of northern California, especially the Yosemite Valley. Never had Muir felt such a sense of belonging to a place. Willfully isolated from other people, he developed an acute sense of the grandeur and sacredness of every species he encountered. He began to believe that the nonhuman na-

ture he interacted with each day had enormous therapeutic value for human beings, most of whom were cut off from wildness. Thus, he began a career of public nature advocacy that would continue the rest of Muir's life.

MAJOR PHILANTHROPIC CONTRIBUTIONS

Through newspaper and magazine articles, Muir began to disseminate his gospel of nature to millions of readers around the country. Beginning in the late 1880s, the powerful Robert Underwood Johnson, editor of *Century* magazine, helped Muir agitate for wilderness preservation throughout the West. Indeed, Muir was instrumental in the foundation of Yosemite National Park in 1890, the United States' second national park (after Yellowstone). His advocacy for national parks and preserves set the tone for wilderness preservation throughout the twentieth century. Alternatively, adherents to the philosophy of natural resource conservation believed that forests, mountains, and rangeland were valuable economic commodities that needed managing but should still be exploited for their riches. Gifford Pinchot, the first Chief Forester of the United States and Muir's great adversary in the debate over conservation versus preservation during the late 1890s and early 1900s, saw Muir's beloved forests and rivers in these economic terms. However, Muir believed much more was at stake than the appropriate management of the nation's natural patrimony. For Muir, the very soul of America would be lost if the wilderness was tamed, or, worse, destroyed altogether. In this sense, he proved a direct philosophical descendant of the Transcendentalist Henry David Thoreau, who had voiced the same concerns fifty years earlier.

To enlist others in his cause and to provide an organization for fellow nature enthusiasts, Muir helped found the Sierra Club in May 1892, remaining president until his death twenty-four years later. The charter of the organization made explicit these goals: "To explore, enjoy, and render accessible the mountain regions of the Pacific Coast; to publish authentic information concerning them; and to enlist the support and cooperation of the people and government in preserving the forests and other natural features of the Sierra Nevada" (Cohen 1988, 10). The foundation of this organization remains Muir's greatest contribution to what would later become known as the environmental movement. The Sierra Club has grown steadily in membership and influence during its more than 100 years of existence. Today, the Sierra Club tops the list of dozens of environmental organizations that help shape public policy in ways Muir would have found unimaginable. In fact, the environment consistently rates among the top concerns of American citizens, a legacy of the efforts initiated by Muir a century ago.

CONCLUSION

John Muir helped to define a new dimension of civil society: the value of a healthy natural environment for the physical and psychological well-being necessary for a thriving democracy. As an explorer, naturalist, writer, and activist, Muir also contributed to a vision of philanthropic action that focuses on the natural world rather than the people who inhabit it.

Michael B. Smith

FURTHER READING

Cohen, Michael P. *The History of the Sierra Club: 1892–1970.* San Francisco: Sierra Club Books, 1988.

Fox, Stephen. *The American Conservation Movement: John Muir and His Legacy.* Madison: University of Wisconsin Press, 1981.

Muir, John. *Our National Parks.* Boston: Houghton Mifflin, 1901.

Teale, Edward Way. *The Wilderness World of John Muir.* Boston: Houghton Mifflin, 1976.

Wilkins, Thurman. *John Muir, Apostle of Nature.* Norman: University of Oklahoma Press, 1995.

Wolfe, Linnie Marsh, ed. *John of the Mountains: The Unpublished Journals of John Muir.* Boston: Houghton Mifflin, 1938.

PAPERS

John Muir's papers are located at the Holt-Atherton Department of Special Collections, University of the Pacific Libraries (Stockton, CA).

O

JOHN M. OLIN
(1892–1982)

Industrialist, Advocate of Free Enterprise, and Founder of the John M. Olin Foundation

INTRODUCTION

"My greatest ambition now," John M. Olin told a *New York Times* reporter in 1977, "is to see free enterprise re-established in this country" (Mullaney 1977, 3). When the Midwestern industrialist passed away five years later, the United States had elected a president more committed to that goal than any American leader since the pre–New Deal era. Through a grantmaking strategy focused on supporting intellectuals and political activists, the foundation he created not only had a lot to do with that transformation, but also helped produce a lasting change in the nation's public philosophy.

EARLY YEARS AND EDUCATION

Nothing about John M. Olin's early life, or even most of his career, suggested he would play such a historically significant role. Born November 10, 1892, in Alton, Illinois, he was the second son of a successful am-munition manufacturer, Franklin W. Olin. After a boarding school education, he enrolled at Cornell University, earning a B.S. degree in chemistry in 1913. Olin subsequently joined his father's Western Cartridge Company as a chemical engineer. In 1917, he married Adele Louise Levis; their marriage lasted until 1935 and produced three daughters, one of whom died in childhood. In 1940, he married Evelyn Niedringhaus, who had a daughter from a previous marriage. The couple remained married until his death.

CAREER HIGHLIGHTS

At the Western Cartridge Company, John M. Olin applied his scientific training to developing improved ammunition, including the "Super-X" shotgun shell, which became a favorite of wildfowl hunters. Altogether, he was credited with two dozen patents. In 1944, Olin succeeded his father as president of what had become Olin Industries, which included the Winchester Repeating Arms

John M. Olin. Courtesy of Olin School of Business, Washington University in St. Louis.

Company, manufacturer of "the gun that won the West," as well as the M1, the principal rifle used by American soldiers during World War II. Under his leadership, the company rapidly increased its sales and diversified, moving into making aluminum, paper for cigarettes, roller skates, and flashlights, among other products. Following a 1954 merger, Olin became chairman of the Olin Mathieson Chemical Corporation, then the fifth largest chemical company in the United States, which was headquartered in New York City and, later, in Stamford, Connecticut. He became honorary chairman in 1963, but remained active in what eventually became the Olin Corporation until his death on September 8, 1982.

From his youth, Olin was an avid hunter and outdoorsman. In 1958, John and Evelyn Olin were featured in a *Sports Illustrated* magazine cover story. Concerned about the increased popularity of hunting following World War II, Olin developed Nilo Kennels and Farms outside Alton to show how train-

ing dogs to recover lost and crippled game, coupled with the restocking and management of preserves, could prevent the depletion of wildlife. This "vast national experiment in conservation," as *Sports Illustrated* called it, proved successful, inspiring rapid growth in shooting preserves and instructional programs modeled after Nilo Farms (Kraft 1958, 34). In addition, one of the dogs Olin trained, a Labrador retriever named King Buck, won a record eighty of eighty-two field trials in which it participated and was immortalized on a U.S. postage stamp.

Olin also led a campaign to preserve the Atlantic salmon and raised thoroughbred racehorses, including one, Cannonade, which won the one hundredth running of the Kentucky Derby in 1974. He belonged to numerous civic clubs, sat on the boards of several charities, and otherwise undertook the kinds of activities expected of a person of his wealth and standing in the business world of the 1950s. During the turmoil of the 1960s, however, Olin's philanthropic interests became very different from those of most of his contemporaries.

MAJOR PHILANTHROPIC CONTRIBUTIONS

In 1953, Olin established a general-purpose foundation. For its first twenty years, the John M. Olin Foundation served principally as a vehicle for his gifts to organizations with which he was personally involved. Among the beneficiaries were such well-established institutions as the American Museum of Natural History, Johns Hopkins and Cornell Universities, various hospitals and medical programs, and the Episcopal Church.

Starting in the mid-1970s, however, the foundation's priorities changed. It began providing funding for a variety of projects focused on public policy issues. Among the major initiatives were: a series of law-school programs aimed at bringing legal theory and practice into closer alignment with economic reasoning; studies, conferences, and professional development efforts dealing with American defense strategy; and faculty chairs, graduate fellowships, and publications addressing religious, cultural, and philosophical questions. The nation's most prestigious universities and colleges received support, as well as an increasingly influential network of Washington think tanks, such as the American Enterprise Institute, the Heritage Foundation, and the Center for Strategic and International Studies. Those involved in foundation programs included the famous—such as Nobel Prize–winning economists Milton Friedman, George Stigler, and Ronald Coase; best-selling philosopher Allan Bloom; editors William F. Buckley, Jr., and Irving Kristol; and former government officials William J. Bennett and Robert H. Bork—and the unknown, particularly numerous young scholars, such as Francis Fukuyama, John D'Iulio, and Dinesh D'Souza, whose work on Olin-funded projects frequently brought them to public attention.

These grantees shared two characteristics. In the first place, their views were generally in tune with those held by Olin and his foundation staff, which favored more freedom for business, a smaller role for government in social and economic matters, a stronger American effort against communism, and traditional cultural values such as the importance of individual responsibility, the family, and religion. On the last issue, the world's problems "would easily be solved," Olin said, "if all mankind adopted belief in a Supreme Power" (Mullaney 1977, 3). This did not mean that all of his recipients were of one mind; to the contrary, differences among Olin grantees could be substantial and long lasting. Or that the foundation simply gave money to anyone who happened to agree with it; more than a few who thought they shared Olin's outlook found their applications turned down because they were lacking in quality. Still, those who did get awards formed a group that held strong views on American life and public policy.

At the same time, most grantees were also genuine intellectuals. To be sure, the foundation supported a number of public-interest lawyers, political activists, and polemical journalists as well. However, the bulk of its grants went to scholars and writers at universities or other kinds of research institutions and high-quality magazines. Because of their views, many recipients were looked on unfavorably by their colleagues, but they could not easily be dismissed as inferior academics or propagandists, let alone thinkers for hire. Indeed, they included scholars who were widely acknowledged to be among the top minds in their fields and whose work, however unpopular, was their own and had to be taken seriously.

Why a Midwestern industrialist, best known for his interest in hunting and horse breeding, decided to devote his funds to underwriting such people remains obscure. With the controversy over the Vietnam War, Watergate, and economic stagnation, the late 1960s and early 1970s were a tumultuous period in American life, causing large portions of the public to worry about the nation's future. As a strong supporter of Richard M. Nixon and trustee of one of the universities (Cornell) caught up in student protests, Olin may have been more deeply affected than most people. The idea of using philanthropy to help restore confidence in the United States was also being discussed at the time; in well-publicized comments, both **David Packard** and Henry Ford II called on their fellow businessmen to do so (though neither of them proved as resolute as Olin). A scientist by training, Olin seems to have valued research and analysis, and throughout his life paid attention to political and economic writings, particularly on the effects of socialism and government regulation.

He also was adept at picking his associates. The first executive director of the foundation was Frank O'Connell, a long-time employee of the Olin Corporation, who prepared a lengthy memorandum, based partly on consultations with executives and trustees at **Pierre Goodrich**'s Liberty Fund and other organizations that emphasized the importance of supporting scholarly work. A young educator, Michael Joyce, succeeded him in

1978 and worked closely with Olin to develop the foundation's program and build a network of advisors and consultants throughout the intellectual world. In 1985, a former college professor, James Piereson, replaced Joyce as executive director.

However, Olin made his most critical appointment in 1977, when he persuaded outgoing U.S. Treasury Secretary William E. Simon to become president of the foundation. A Wall Street financier before entering government, Simon had earned a reputation in Washington as a critic of government spending and regulation. In his best-selling book, *A Time for Truth*, published shortly after he joined the board, Simon wrote that he shared the foundation's objectives: "to contribute to the battle of ideas—to the ongoing war between the free society and those who would make it less free or destroy it altogether—by seeking and supporting scholars and programs which would competently and persuasively expound those ideas" (Simon 1978, 244). Although he was also involved in extensive business activities throughout his tenure, Simon provided direction, energy, and leadership for the foundation's program until he passed away in the spring of 2000.

Although Olin just knew him casually before recruiting him, Simon's "fundamental thinking and philosophy" were "almost identical" to his own (Mullaney 1977, 3). Yet, Olin's views ultimately shaped the foundation. As board chairman, he continued to be active until his death, meeting regularly with the staff and having the dominant voice among the trustees. Although his son-in-law, Eugene F. Williams, Jr., a prominent St. Louis banker who had married his stepdaughter, served on the board and was elected chairman in 2000, Olin's wife and other members of his family had virtually no role in the foundation. Without making a formal commitment, Olin also indicated that the foundation's lifetime should be limited so that it would not drift from his intentions after he had passed away.

The close tie between Olin's views and the foundation's activities led to criticism that its grants were really designed to advance its donor's business affairs, rather than sound public policy. "Given the source of the foundation's money and the interlocking boards," one writer charged, "it takes quite a willing suspension of disbelief to overlook the intimate links between the financial and legal problems of the corporation [with government regulation] and the recipients of the foundation's largesse" (Stone 1979, 19). Others accused the foundation of interfering with academic freedom by limiting its support to scholars who shared its ideological beliefs.

From the right side of the political spectrum, however, came the complaint that the Olin Foundation and others allied with it were not ideological enough. "For years, conservatives had wandered in the wilderness," wrote two such critics, "but now, just as they were about to reap the reward for their suffering, a set of 'Johnny-comelatelies' were taking the lion's share" (Gottfried and Fleming 1988, 73). Instead of being a reliable source of support for rightthinking scholars and organizations, Olin had opened its doors to "neoconservatives" and others who may have been talented academics, but whose sympathies were not always with free enterprise and conservatism, as they had traditionally been defined.

CONCLUSION

Olin did not live to hear most of these criticisms, though those who knew him say he was prepared for controversy. During his lifetime, in fact, the Olin Foundation was relatively small, never exceeding $3 million in grants annually. After his death and a sizable increase in its assets (to be followed after his widow's passing by another large infusion of funds), the foundation's spending rose rapidly, topping $14 million by the mid-1980s (and eventually $20 million in the 1990s). With this growth came greater visibility. Yet, while the number of grantees expanded, the pattern of support for scholars, think tanks, and high-quality magazines remained much as Olin himself had set it in the late 1970s.

What did change was American society. The ideas about American foreign, economic, and social policy underwritten by the Olin Foundation were increasingly influential in public policy discussions and on government actions. Many of its grantees had become prominent figures in public life, as well as in the academy. "Conservative policy ideas and political rhetoric continue to dominate the nation's political conversation," observed Sally Covington, of the left-of-center National Committee on Responsive Philanthropy (Covington 1997, 3). If the powers of government had not returned to their pre–New Deal (or even pre-Great Society) state, the spirit of enterprise had acquired new and extensive appeal, even within the philanthropic world.

How much of this change would have occurred without the work of the John M. Olin Foundation and its allies is impossible to know. Still, veteran foundation watcher Waldemar Nielsen has written, "Though many may disagree with his social and political outlook, Olin was until his death in 1982 one of the most effective and influential philanthropists in recent times" (Nielsen 1996, 207). And he did it largely the old-fashioned way, using a philanthropic strategy that goes back to the earliest foundations: supporting research, writing, and publicity about the ideas and conditions he believed were most harmful in American life.

Leslie Lenkowsky

FURTHER READING

Covington, Sally. *Moving a Public Policy Agenda: The Strategic Philanthropy of Conservative Foundations.* Washington, DC: National Committee for Responsive Philanthropy, 1997.

Gottfried, Paul, and Thomas Fleming. *The Conservative Movement.* Boston: Twayne, 1988.

Kraft, Virginia. "A Man, a Dog, and a Crusade." *Sports Illustrated*, November 17, 1958, 32–40.

Mullaney, Thomas E. "Olin: Staunch Fighter for Free Enterprise." *New York Times*, April 29, 1977, section 4, page 3.

Nielsen, Waldemar A. *Inside American Philanthropy: The Dilemmas of Donorship.* Norman, OK, and London: University of Oklahoma Press, 1996.

Simon, William E. *A Time for Truth.* New York and Chicago: Reader's Digest Press and McGraw-Hill, 1978.

Stone, Peter H. "The Counter-Intelligentsia: The 'Free Enterprise' Think Tanks and the Holy War on Government.'" *Village Voice*, October 22, 1979, 14–19.

PAPERS

The John M. Olin Foundation's papers have not been deposited in an archive, nor have John M. Olin's papers. William E. Simon's papers, including many related to his work at the foundation, are at Lafayette College (Easton, PA).

OWEN FAMILY

Robert Owen (1771–1858)

Industrialist and Utopian Socialist

Robert Dale Owen (1801–1877)

Politician and Social Reformer

INTRODUCTION

For British manufacturers, the Industrial Revolution meant increased wealth and prosperity. For both adult and child laborers, however, it meant unemployment, misfortune, and poverty. As a manufacturer, Robert Owen emerged as an advocate for the working class. He believed that those with wealth must "either give the poor a rational and useful training or mock not their ignorance, their poverty and their misery, by merely instructing them to become conscious of the extent of the degradation under which they exist" (Owen 1927, 75). This conviction led attempts to develop legislative reforms, establish means for industrial philanthropists to assist the poor, and formulate plans to change the structure of modern society.

Owen's son, Robert Dale Owen, entrenched himself in the confines of established power to achieve reform. Though their ideologies diverged, for a short time they worked together to establish one of the most important social experiments of the nineteenth century in New Harmony, Indiana, which firmly planted the utopian impulse on American soil.

ROBERT OWEN

Early Years and Education

Robert Owen was born on May 14, 1771, in Newton, Wales. He was the sixth child of Anne Williams and Robert Owen, a saddler and ironmonger. Attending day school from an early age, he excelled in his studies. Like most poor children living at the start of the Industrial Revolution, Owen had but two options after leaving school: he could become either a factory laborer or an apprentice. Consequently, after he left school at age ten, he spent a year as an apprentice at a haberdashery selling men's clothing. He then relocated to the town of Stamford to assist a producer of women's clothing. At Stamford, he spent much time reading in his employer's extensive library and he subsequently began to doubt the validity of the Christian faith and to form secular ideas about morality and ethics. At the conclusion of this apprenticeship, Owen relocated to Manchester.

Career Highlights

At the age of nineteen, while working in Manchester, Robert Owen became the su-

Robert Owen. Indiana Historical Society.

perintendent of a large mill and soon after entered into a partnership with the owners of the Chorlton Twist Company. During this time, Owen, while visiting Glasgow, encountered David Dale, the owner of large cotton mills in New Lanark, Scotland and his daughter, Ann Caroline Dale, whom Owen later married (1799). In 1799, he and several partners purchased Dale's New Lanark mills.

Owen's ideas about the condition of the working class, children, and society at large developed while he was at New Lanark and during the height of the Industrial Revolution (1760–1830), which marked the shift in labor from human to mechanical. Both in Manchester and in Glasgow, Owen participated in literary societies where he interacted with social theorists including James Mill, Jeremy Bentham, and William Goodwin. Although there were material benefits resulting from the Industrial Revolution, many of these thinkers, including Owen, believed it also contributed to moral debasement. They considered this new manufacturing system a destabilizing force in society. Indeed, Owen saw, in the behavior of the New Lanark employees, the social ills that industrialization had created. Still, he continued to believe that the process could be beneficial if only the factory owners themselves would promote some form of social control.

Major Philanthropic Contributions

When Owen purchased the cotton mill at New Lanark, it employed between 1,500 and 2,000 people, including 500 children. Mill owners were responsible for the welfare of children in their service, but regularly neglected their duties. Accidents, exceedingly long hours, and poor working conditions were common. As a result, the children they employed were sickly, small, and usually illiterate. Owen shortened the working day at his mill, initiated a minimum age requirement for child workers, built new houses for his employees, and improved sanitary conditions in New Lanark village. He also imposed a paternalistic system of moral standards intent on reducing drunkenness and monitoring work performance. Many employees resisted the more imposing of Owen's policies, such as random body searches and house inspections.

Owen understood that these reforms might temporarily improve social conditions but they would not have much effect until the character of the poor and laboring classes was transformed: dramatic change could be accomplished only through a national system of education focused on the role of environment on the mind and growth of the individual. Although Owen always maintained that his ideas about the affect of industrialization on living conditions and human character were wholly unique, his approach to solving social problems seems to have its roots in Enlightenment thinkers such as Rousseau and Locke, who believed that if all contaminating influences were removed from a child's life, the child would develop into a moral, reasoning adult.

Based on this theory, Owen founded the Institution of the Formation of Character at New Lanark in 1816, which pioneered new methods of teaching, focusing on children's experience. Through an education based on positive experiences, children could be "ultimately molded into the very image of rational wishes and desires" (Owen 1927, 22). Many of Owen's views influenced not only the foundation of schools in Owenite communities but also the whole infant school movement, bringing to popular education a degree of humanity and establishing the right of the poor to be educated.

Parallel to his child welfare reforms, Owen developed remedies for unemployment and poverty, which he publicized in the *Report to the Committee of the Association for the Relief of the Manufacturing and Labouring Poor* (1817). Given to a group charged with reforming the British Poor Laws, he proposed founding communal settlements of 1,200 paupers in the countryside with rectangular groupings of buildings and agricultural land. Through work and collective living, these villages would transform the character of the destitute by reviving the agrarian way of life. These ideal communities would practice sexual equality in education, rights, privileges, and personal liberty. Owen viewed contemporary society, especially organized religion, as consisting of irrational concepts and institutions that contrasted with his hope for a society based on scientific reasoning and logical thought. Therefore, he called for the liberation from what he called the " 'trinity' of evils; private or individual property—absurd and irrational systems of religion—and marriage" (Pitzer 1997, 89). Fearing the sort of brutality that occurred during the French Revolution, Owen hoped for a peaceful and gradual transition to his new moral world through the influence of small successful experiments, phasing out current systems while introducing new ones. These communities, where everyone's well-being depends on that of the other community members, where competition is replaced by cooperation, where the traditional family is restructured, and where a rational system of education is available to all from infancy, would pave the way to utopia.

After 1813, Owen became frustrated with legislative apathy and the New Lanark partners' unwillingness to experiment further with social change. Deciding to distance himself from his managerial role at the mills and focus on achieving reforms national and international in scope, he expanded his movement in 1817 from communities for the poor and unemployed to the overall reconstruction of society. Owen approached numerous groups in Britain with his proposal, but none would fund his plan. Dissatisfied with the response at home, Owen turned to America to test his theories. Concurrently, a time of prosperity and progressive thinking in America lent itself to an abundance of philanthropic activity, social innovation, and participation in voluntary associations. Across the Atlantic, several religious communities that practiced common labor, including the Shakers and Moravians, were already prospering when Owen first envisioned his ideal community. One of these groups, the Rappites, a German religious sect from Württemburg who settled Harmonie, Indiana on the east bank of the Wabash River, practiced celibacy, common ownership of property, and cooperative manufacturing. After ten years in Indiana, their leader, Father George Rapp, decided to relocate the community to Pennsylvania in 1824.

In January 1825, Owen purchased Harmonie, Indiana for $125,000, the bulk of his fortune. The purchase comprised 20,000 acres, a complete village including houses, churches, dormitories, four mills, a textile factory, distilleries and a brewery, mechanics shops, vineyards, and orchards. The utopian experiment at New Harmony began officially on April 27, 1825. By June, more than 800 people of all social and economic backgrounds had flocked to join the community.

The New Harmony experiment was the earliest of at least nineteen American villages as well as nine British communities based on Owen's ideas. Indeed, New Harmony was the earliest and most ambitious of the American communal secular experiments. During the early months of the community's existence, Owen did not spend much time on the premises and left his second son, William Owen, in control. Virtually from the beginning, the group was an economic disaster. A lack of efficient laborers and the absence of capable administrators brought work in the once-profitable Rappite industries to a standstill. A shortage of food in September 1825 made it necessary to purchase goods from outside sources and the community fell into debt. Meanwhile, members awaited Owen's return and hoped he would be the solution to all of their difficulties.

When Owen did return in January 1826, William Maclure, a wealthy industrialist turned geologist, accompanied him. After some coaxing by Owen, Maclure had decided to invest in New Harmony and hoped to start the first manual labor school. They led a "Boatload of Knowledge," a keelboat commissioned *The Philanthropist* that transported educational reformers, scientists, musicians, and artists from Pittsburgh to New Harmony. This migration of intellectuals, moving further west than any American college, made New Harmony an educational and scientific center for years to come. Nonetheless, the mixture of intellectuals, wealthy aristocrats, and Western farmers, laborers, and artisans did not create the harmonious community Owen had envisioned. By March 1826, factions began to spring up in New Harmony. Maclure, who disagreed with Owen on many issues, proposed forming separate communities based on occupation. After an unsuccessful effort to reorganize the community in 1827, Owen departed, selling much of the land and disconnecting himself from the venture. The utopian phase of the community came to an end in June 1827.

As the first socialistic community in America, both the successes and the shortcomings of the New Harmony experiment influenced all nonsectarian communal settlements that followed. Although some of the equality and freedom promised to members was not granted, the most significant problems came from Owen's failure to unite members with a common ideological and economic purpose or to provide a solid form of governance. Clearly, his absence for all but seven months of New Harmony's communal existence was not conducive to stable conditions. Owen was also indifferent to the types of people admitted to the community: there was a shortage of skilled labor and a lack of diversity in the residents' talents. Both insiders and outsiders' hostility toward Owen's unconventional ideas about marriage and religion may have also contributed to the demise of the community. Although these weaknesses were considerable, New Harmony's success in establishing educational reform, providing sexual equality, and restructuring economic policies, as well as its rejection of traditional social organizations, motivated many other groups to undertake their own experiments.

After the New Harmony experiment, Owen's activities shifted from the realm of utopian communalism to the trade union movement. During the 1830s, Owen's theory that labor was the source of all wealth, and consequently that the wage system should be abolished with the end product of labor belonging to the workers, permeated the working-class movement in Britain. A return to his communal aspirations, however, was to follow. In the 1850s, Owen was again writing about the improvement of society based on cooperative living. In addition, many contemporary reformers adapted and reinterpreted his ideas, publishing works based on his communal and industrial theories. Though the communal stage of New Harmony did not survive much longer than two years, Owenism as a reform movement was not dead. Indeed, some Owenite communities survived after New Harmony, but few beyond the late 1830s. Many American Owenites, such as Owen's son, Robert Dale Owen, realized that it was necessary to find new methods beyond communitarian living to enact change.

ROBERT DALE OWEN

The eldest son of Robert Owen and Ann Caroline Dale's seven children, Robert Dale Owen was born in Glasgow, Scotland in 1801. His formative years were greatly influenced by his father's philosophical idealism and his renunciation of Christianity. Dale Owen acquired a progressive education at a college in Switzerland known for its broad

Robert Dale Owen. Indiana Historical Society.

and revisionist curriculum, which embraced traditional subjects as well as exhorting the principles of tolerance and democracy. Upon his return from college, Dale became his father's second in command, both in the field of business and in humanitarianism. At this time, much of his father's time was occupied with reform activities, so Dale took over managing the New Lanark mills and school.

Dale Owen worked closely with his father on the formation of the community at New Harmony. When New Harmony residents began to split off into factions and the community's future began to look bleak, Dale took over full-time publication of the *New Harmony Gazette*, the newspaper he had founded in October 1825, which was focused on social problems rather than current events. Dale thought it was his duty to expose every popular prejudice that created misery in the world, or which slowed down society's progress. In his writings, he openly questioned Christianity and strict divorce laws, called for reform of female dress by advocating the ankle-length pantaloons later termed "bloomers," and criticized Indiana politicians for not supporting the funding of public schools.

Dale Owen began his life imitating the work of his father, but over time their ideas diverged and Dale developed his own brand of social reform. After 1827, Dale could no longer be called a socialist. He did not participate in the communistic utopian resurgence that took hold in the 1840s because he no longer accepted communalism as the cure for all social problems. In fact, his work after New Harmony adjusted Owenite social radicalism into a process of gradual reform.

Dale's relationship with the reformer Frances Wright, whom he met in New Harmony, directly correlates with his shift from a socialist into a freethinker. In 1825, she founded a community devoted to the emancipation of slaves in Nashoba, Tennessee, and after New Harmony dissolved, Dale accompanied her there. He worked with her among the "Free Enquirers," a group opposed to evangelical religion and advocating wider access to education and the even distribution of wealth. Then, he moved to New York and changed the name of the *New Harmony Gazette* to the *Free Enquirer*. Soon after, he joined his father in England and they jointly edited a prolabor periodical called *The Crisis*.

Returning to New Harmony in 1833, Dale began a career in politics, serving three terms in the Indiana legislature (1836–1838), where he secured significant funding for the state's public schools. He was elected to the U.S. Congress in 1842 as a Democrat and served two terms before being defeated for a third. As a U.S. representative, he introduced the bill founding the Smithsonian Institution. This organization, intended for the popular dissemination of scientific information, illustrates the survival of Owenite influence in Dale Owen's later work. He also advocated property rights for married women and emancipation. Later in life, he served as a trustee of Indiana University and ambassador to Naples. Dale Owen married twice, in 1832 to Mary Jane Robinson, and after her death to Lottie Walton Kellogg in 1876.

He fathered seven children, two of whom died at a young age.

CONCLUSION

Although Owenite communities never flourished, the ideals embodied by Owenism significantly affected the collective American conscience. Religious groups such as John Humphrey Noyes' Oneida perfectionists and secular communalists such as the Icarians at Nauvoo and Fourierists at Brook Farm contributed to the resurgence of communitarianism in the 1840s. These groups embraced the communal impulse envisioned by Owen in attempting to pave their own path to a perfect society.

Owenites functioned both within and beyond their communities to effect social reform in the United States. They advocated women's rights, birth control, the abolition of slavery, and the formation of public libraries and museums. The influence of Robert Owen and Robert Dale Owen's ideas for social reform spread beyond the confines of experimental communities and into the mainstream of society. It was Robert Owen's utopian vision, not his precise plan for the perfect community, which substantially affected future philanthropic activities and voluntary actions in America.

Alexis Manheim

FURTHER READING

Bestor, Arthur E. *Backwoods Utopias: The Sectarian Origins and the Owenite Phase of Communitarian Socialism in America, 1663–1829.* Philadelphia: University of Pennsylvania Press, 1950.

Harrison, John F. *Quest for the New Moral World: Robert Owen and the Owenites in Britain and America.* New York: Scribner, 1969.

Leopold, William R. *Robert Dale Owen: A Biography.* New York: Octagon Books, 1940.

Owen, Robert. *A New View of Society and Other Writings.* Introduction by G.D.H. Cole. London: J.M. Dent & Sons, 1927.

Pitzer, Donald E. *America's Communal Utopias.* Chapel Hill: University of North Carolina Press, 1997.

OWEN FAMILY

PAPERS

Manuscripts relating to Robert Owen and New Harmony are located in the New Harmony Collection of the Indiana Historical Society Library (Indianapolis, IN) and the New Harmony Workingmen's Institute Library (New Harmony, IN). Robert Dale Owen's papers are located in the Manuscript Division of the Indiana State Library (Indianapolis, IN).

P

DAVID PACKARD (1912–1996)
and LUCILE PACKARD (1914–1987)

Technology Entrepreneurs and Founders of the David and Lucile Packard Foundation

INTRODUCTION

"I think you get the most satisfaction in trying to do something useful. After you've done that, you ought to forget about it and go on to something else. You shouldn't gloat about anything you've done, you ought to keep going and try to find something better to do" (Fisher 1996, 20). Those self-effacing and practical words by David Packard influenced his work as the founder of Hewlett-Packard and creator of one of the world's largest private foundations. Integrity, respect for all people, a belief in individual leadership, an enduring commitment to effectiveness, and the capacity to think big are the values that David and Lucile Packard embodied during their lives. Those same values were reflected in the formation and growth of Hewlett-Packard—one of the most influential companies in the history of American business—and the establishment of the David and Lucile Packard Foundation.

EARLY YEARS AND EDUCATION

David Packard was born in Pueblo, Colorado, on September 7, 1912, the son of a lawyer and a high-school teacher. His mother always had a large garden and he spent a great deal of time outside as a boy. He had fond childhood memories of roaming the desert and discovering horned toads, cactus, and rattlesnakes. Packard often credited the early Pueblo years with developing his lifelong interest in nature, farming, and ranching. Years later, he could be found operating a bulldozer on his ranches in Idaho and California. From an early age, Packard was also intensely interested in science, mathematics, and inventions. While quite young, he began his first experiments with explosives and electrical devices. Radio was another early fascination. Packard was an accomplished ham radio operator and attended the state convention by the time he was in high school.

A summer trip to California in 1929

proved to be pivotal in the young life of David Packard. He visited Stanford University between his junior and senior years of high school with a family friend and was intrigued to find that they had an excellent electrical engineering program. Subsequently, he was accepted into Stanford at the then-steep tuition of $114 per quarter. A natural athlete, Packard lettered in a number of varsity sports at Stanford, including football, basketball, and track. To earn money, he also worked as a "hasher," serving meals at the Delta Gamma sorority house. At Delta Gamma, he met Lucile Salter, his future wife.

Lucile Salter was born in San Francisco on July 30, 1914. At the height of the Great Depression, she attended Stanford University and graduated in 1935 with a degree in English. As a sophomore, she met David Packard, and their courtship flourished even as Packard graduated in 1934, took a job with General Electric, and moved to Schenectady, New York. Lu, as family and friends called her, went to business school after graduation and began to work for Stanford University. By the spring of 1938, David Packard and Lucile Salter decided to get married. Thus, she journeyed to Schenectady.

CAREER HIGHLIGHTS

While at Stanford University in the fall of 1930, David Packard met a fellow student named William Hewlett. Together, they shared a love of science and mathematics and began what was to be a lifelong friendship and business association. After graduation, Packard secured his first job at General Electric (GE) while Hewlett did graduate work at the Massachusetts Institute of Technology (MIT). After Packard married Lucile Salter in 1938, Professor Fred Terman, an early mentor of Packard, arranged for him to return to Stanford for a fellowship. More important, it reunited him with Hewlett. They began their partnership in a one-car garage in Palo Alto, which has since been designated as a California historical landmark and the "birthplace of Silicon Valley." In their early days, as they decided what to develop and manufacture,

they worked on audio oscillators, signaling devices, and other electronic products. They also discovered that their skills were complementary: Hewlett's strengths were in circuitry design and Packard was better trained and experienced in manufacturing processes. When the time came, they flipped a coin to determine how the company should be named—thus, the Hewlett-Packard Company was born in 1939.

Lucile Packard was an integral part of the fledgling company. She left her job at Stanford University and was a combination secretary, accountant, and personnel manager for the young company. She even baked metal panels for the company in her kitchen oven. Since much of the equipment that Hewlett-Packard manufactured was purchased by the military, such as audio-signal generators, the company grew rapidly during World War II and well into the 1950s (due to the Korean War). They also continued working on new product development, as well as manufacturing. HP, as the company came to be known, did early work with microwave technology, which eventually enabled the company to be in the forefront of the microwave instrument business. Innovative technological advances came to be the hallmark of Packard and Hewlett's young company. As they moved into laser technology, calculators, computers, and printers, HP dramatically expanded into global operations and eventually employed over 100,000 people worldwide.

As the company was growing, so too was the Packard family. Lucile and David Packard had a son and three daughters: David Woodley (1940), Nancy (1943), Susan (1946), and Julie (1953). Lucile Packard volunteered tirelessly in the community as she raised her young family. A special passion for children's health care was born when she became affiliated with the Stanford Home for Convalescent Children, which treated children with tuberculosis. Lucile Packard also continued her active involvement at HP, creating a family atmosphere in the company, where she organized annual picnics and remembered employees' birthdays. A compassionate and caring woman, she reflected those qualities in her work at Hewlett-Packard as well as in her volunteer activities. As a young girl, Julie Packard thought her mother worked full time. Later, she realized that her mother was a full-time volunteer.

David Packard felt strongly that a good measure of a life was to do something useful and make a contribution. In 1968, Melvin Laird, then secretary of defense, called and asked Packard to serve his country as deputy secretary of defense. Feeling he could make a contribution to the country and to the war effort, he agreed to serve and did so until 1971, when he returned to California and resumed his position as chairman of the board at Hewlett-Packard. However, he remained a prominent advisor to the White House on defense procurement and management and was a member of the Trilateral Commission from 1973 to 1981.

Hewlett-Packard was widely known and respected not only for its technical prowess and commercial success, but also for a management style that came to be known as the "HP Way." Dave Packard and Bill Hewlett believed in the ability of employees to excel if they were given the right tools and allowed to express their creativity. They pioneered a close relationship between management and employees. Indeed, Packard became famous for not spending much time in his own office because he was out walking around on the production floor, talking to employees. Shunning pomposity, when the senior HP managers traveled to New York to celebrate the listing of the company stock on the New York Stock Exchange in 1961, Packard insisted that they all take the subway to Wall Street. In his 1995 book *The HP Way*, Packard wrote that one of the objectives of the company was "to maintain an organizational environment that fosters individual motivation, initiative and creativity, and a wide latitude of freedom in working toward established objectives and goals" (Packard 1995, 81). Hewlett-Packard was one of the earliest companies to embrace responsiveness to workers' needs, profit-sharing programs, flexible scheduling, and an open-door policy

with senior executives. Now one of the largest computer companies in the world, Hewlett-Packard remains a model company widely studied in business schools throughout the United States.

MAJOR PHILANTHROPIC CONTRIBUTIONS

As young adults, David and Lucile Packard lived through the Great Depression and felt a commitment to giving something back and making a useful contribution. Consequently, they formed the David and Lucile Packard Foundation in 1964. The foundation grew slowly over the next several years, enabling the Packard children to gradually learn about foundations and charitable giving. The children were invited to serve on the foundation board when they were twenty-one and Susan Packard Orr fondly refers to family board service as "a life sentence" (*Lucile Packard: A Woman of Grace*, 1997).

Lucile Packard was the operational head of the foundation, reviewing proposals, writing letters, and making site visits to each applicant organization. Indeed, she knew many of the grant recipients personally. Meanwhile, David Packard was quite busy building and running HP, but he always handled the foundation finances and was involved in decision making. Cole Wilbur, the foundation's first employee, was hired as executive director in 1976 and worked closely with both Lucile and David Packard in shaping the grant making and subsequent growth of the foundation over the next twenty years. Wilbur observed that they had a deep commitment to involving the family early on, giving them responsibility, and allowing them to grow into the work of the foundation.

As she continued raising her own family and working in the foundation, Lucile Packard remained an active volunteer with the Blood Bank, Junior Red Cross, Children's Health Council, San Francisco Symphony, and Wolf Trap National Park for the Performing Arts. Still, she is prominently remembered for her work with the Children's Hospital at Stanford University, where she served on the board from 1964 to 1987. Lucile Packard was integrally involved in the planning, design, and decision making for a new facility in Palo Alto. Indeed, she insisted that all rooms have extra-large windows so that children could see flowers, trees, and people while they were recuperating. Unfortunately, she never lived to see the new hospital built.

In 1986, Lucile Packard was stricken with cancer. She died in May 1987 and her eulogies noted her deep devotion to her family and her tireless work for children. In 1996, the Lucile Salter Packard Foundation for Children's Health was created through a gift of the Lucile Salter Packard Children's Hospital to Stanford Health Services and is the San Francisco Bay area's only foundation dedicated exclusively to the health of children. When Stanford University Children's Hospital and University of California–San Francisco Hospital merged in 1997, it was agreed that patient care for children at both campuses would be named Lucile Salter Packard Children's Health Services.

With two of the Packard daughters trained as marine biologists, undersea exploration was another natural focus for the Packards. David and Lucile Packard provided $55 million to design and build the Monterey Bay Aquarium and also founded the Monterey Bay Aquarium Research Institute in 1987. Believing that the earth and its inhabitants formed a fragile ecosystem, the Packards recognized the problems of the planet's growing population had a profound effect on families, the environment, and the stability of developing nations. Improved access to family planning and reproductive choice, at home and abroad, is a funding focus of the Packard Foundation to this day.

After his wife's death, David Packard decided to donate all of his Hewlett-Packard stock to the Packard Foundation. He formulated new ideas and strategies for the foundation but felt strongly that he should not overly direct foundation funding. He felt that the world continually changes and to try to determine now what his successors should do in twenty or thirty years was foolish. Above all, he enjoyed learning and remained, in a very real sense, a student throughout his long life. "Don't be afraid to make mistakes; if you don't make mistakes, you're not reaching far enough" was a common refrain that Packard voiced to colleagues (personal conversation with Cole Wilbur, first Executive Director of the David and Lucile Packard Foundation, August 21, 2000).

CONCLUSION

Upon Packard's death in 1996, the Packard Foundation received over $6 billion in assets. He had also appointed his daughter, Susan Packard Orr, to be the next chairman. The Packard Foundation, now one of the largest foundations in the world, serves as a lasting legacy to David and Lucile Packard. The grants made by the foundation continue to support such issues as conservation, population growth, science, and children. Clearly, the ideals and values that David and Lucile Packard demonstrated during their lifetimes continue to guide the goals and aspirations of the Packard Foundation.

Kathleen Odne

FURTHER READING

Fisher, Lawrence M. "David Packard, 83, Pioneer of Silicon Valley, Is Dead." *New York Times*, March 27, 1996, Section D, 20.
Packard, David. *The HP Way: How Bill Hewlett and I Built Our Company.* New York: HarperCollins, 1995.

PAPERS

David and Lucile Packard's papers are located at Hewlett-Packard (Palo Alto, CA).

FREDERICK DOUGLASS PATTERSON
(1901–1988)

College President and Founder of the United Negro College Fund

INTRODUCTION

"Could black colleges, perhaps through a united effort, make a case for the needs of black youth now being severely restricted and handicapped by lack of resources?" (Patterson 1991, 65) In 1943, in his column for the *Pittsburgh Courier* entitled "The Southern Viewpoint," Frederick Douglass Patterson wrote about an idea that had been brewing in his mind for some time. He asked presidents of black colleges to "pool their small monies and make a united appeal to the national conscience" (Patterson 1943, n.p.). This simple, but overlooked, idea would be the start of the United Negro College Fund.

EARLY YEARS AND EDUCATION

In 1901, Frederick Douglass Patterson was born in Washington, DC, to William Ross Patterson and Mamie Brooks Patterson. His father named him after the well-known African-American journalist and abolitionist Frederick Douglass. Both of his parents were educated at Prairie View State Normal and Industrial Institute in Texas. His father also graduated from law school at Howard University but did not live long enough to practice law. In fact, Frederick Douglass Patterson's parents died of tuberculosis shortly after his birth. Despite losing them at an early age, young Patterson was influenced by his parents' interest in education. With the help of his sister, Bessie Patterson, a music teacher, he moved to Texas and attended Prairie View High School. Meanwhile, Bessie Patterson secured a teaching position in the music department of Prairie View High School. While living on campus with his sister, Frederick Douglass Patterson met Dr. Edward Evans, a veterinarian. His skill and

Frederick Douglass Patterson in a 1962 publicity photo for the Children's Aid Society. Library of Congress; LC-USZ62-114998.

knowledge impressed Patterson and, as a result, he developed an interest in veterinary medicine. When he enrolled at Iowa State College, he was the only African-American student in the veterinary science program. Graduating in 1923, Patterson secured his first job as a teacher at Virginia State College in Petersburg, Virginia. In 1926, he received a fellowship from the **John D. Rockefeller, Sr.**–sponsored General Education Board, enabling him to complete a master's degree at Iowa State College.

After five years of service at Virginia State

College, he was offered a veterinary science position at Tuskegee Industrial and Normal Institute (Tuskegee Institute) in Alabama. In 1931, he received a second fellowship from the General Education Board to study bacteriology at Cornell University. Upon receiving a Ph.D., he returned to the Tuskegee Institute in 1935 to be director of the Department of Agriculture. Coincidentally, Dr. Robert Moton, president of Tuskegee Institute, decided to retire that year. Although he did not know that he was being considered for the position of president and did not even consider himself prepared, Patterson was chosen to replace Moton in October 1935.

Shortly after becoming president, Patterson married Catherine Moton, the daughter of Robert Moton, and they would subsequently raise one son (Frederick Douglass Patterson, Jr.). During the couple's honeymoon, Patterson received a telegram from the chairman of the board of trustees that read, "Come at once to New York to discuss the problems of the budget" (Patterson 1991, 42). This interrupted vacation would mark the beginning of Paterson's struggle to solve the financial problems of black colleges.

CAREER HIGHLIGHTS AND MAJOR PHILANTHROPIC CONTRIBUTIONS

Patterson was only thirty-four years old when he became president of Tuskegee Institute. He lacked the fund-raising skills and personal ties of past Tuskegee presidents **Booker T. Washington** and Robert Moton. Typically, a new president would look to the trustees of an institution for assistance with fund-raising, but Tuskegee Institute's trustees had become accustomed to a more passive role owing to the strong abilities of both Washington and Moton. Patterson found it difficult to run Tuskegee Institute in an efficient manner while meeting the needs of poor black college students—many of whom lacked the means to afford tuition. After much frustration, Patterson began to correspond with a cadre of black college presidents about the challenges of fund-raising and possible solutions to these prob-

lems. The majority of college presidents wrote back to him detailing their dire financial situations. From his correspondence, Patterson realized that black college presidents were competing for the same small pool of funds; everyone was soliciting the same organizations and the same donors.

Meanwhile, two of the largest supporters of black higher education—the General Education Board and the **Julius Rosenwald** Fund—were turning their attention to other funding priorities. Without the support of these two philanthropic organizations, black colleges would have to broaden their search for funds. Therefore, the task of fund-raising could not be left to the president alone. After a failed funding request to the state of Alabama, Patterson proposed a united appeal for private black colleges carried out by an organization specifically created for fund-raising. The National Foundation for Infantile Paralysis' March of Dimes Campaign, which pushed giving in a new direction by reaching out to the small donor rather than focusing exclusively on the small number of wealthy Americans, inspired this plan. Patterson stated, "The idea occurred [to me] that this was the direction of national philanthropy, with the masses brought together to contribute. Only by going beyond any immediate constituency such as alumni and trustees could a campaign have a national appeal" (Patterson 1991, 65).

In 1943, Patterson called an exploratory meeting to measure the feasibility of a combined appeal for black colleges. His comments in the *Pittsburgh Courier* were the guiding words for the establishment of the United Negro College Fund (UNCF), which was incorporated on April 25, 1944, with twenty-seven member colleges and a combined enrollment of 14,000 students. According to Patterson, "The coming together of the private black colleges out of concern for our needs; the fact that we were not going to get the amount of money we had been receiving from our former sources; and the innovative fund-raising practices of other organizations—all of these factors contributed to the formation of the UNCF"

(Patterson 1991, 135). He also thought it was important to reach those who were interested in educating black youth but did not know about black colleges. Working together, the college presidents had many more connections and a greater influence.

As a result of his previous interactions with the General Education Board, Patterson was able to get **John D. Rockefeller, Jr**. to publicly endorse the United Negro College Fund. This action, according to Patterson, was key to the UNCF's fund-raising success. "Leadership is the key to any campaign. If the top one or two or three people in the community identify themselves with it, their endorsement will make an important difference in its success" (Patterson 1991, 131). Although the UNCF's efforts proved successful, it has not been without criticism. During the early years of the UNCF, for example, several college presidents told him that his idea would not work. Perhaps the most intense criticism stemmed from limitations on independent fund-raising by member institutions. The fund's policy restricted individual solicitations by college presidents during its annual campaign period, which made it very difficult for black college presidents to meet endowment challenges set forth by their own funders: there simply was not enough time left in a year after the UNCF's annual campaign. In spite of these drawbacks, the UNCF continues to successfully raise funds. Today, the UNCF is the largest and most well-known African-American higher education assistance organization, consisting of thirty-nine private, accredited four-year black colleges, and continues its commitment to the principles set forth by Patterson.

In addition to his accomplishments as president of Tuskegee Institute (1935–1952) and the United Negro College Fund (1964–1966), Patterson made other important contributions to the field of education. During his tenure at the Tuskegee Institute, he introduced military aviation to the curriculum. After promoting black participation in established Air Corps training programs and seeing no results, Patterson worked to create a new program at Tuskegee. This program gave blacks access to the field of aviation and ultimately supported the famed Tuskegee Airmen: a group of over 900 black military aviators who were an important part of American air power during World War II. Due to the rigid patterns of segregation during the war, the Tuskegee airmen were not trained within the white military ranks. Instead, they were schooled at an isolated airfield near Tuskegee Institute. Patterson also established the School of Veterinary Medicine at Tuskegee Institute, which now graduates more black veterinarians than all of the other eighteen American veterinary schools combined.

Patterson also served as director (1953–1958) and president (1958–1969) of the Phelps Stokes Fund. In this position, he worked to improve the status of blacks throughout the world by providing scholarship and fellowship opportunities as well as training and professional development programs.

In the 1970s, Patterson became concerned with the plight of small independent colleges. These institutions, which included both historically black and predominantly white colleges, were becoming more and more reliant upon the government for assistance. As a potential remedy, he developed the College Endowment Funding Plan. This plan was based on the concept of combining grant income with long-term loans to create more endowment monies and immediate capital. Patterson's idea was well received and President Ronald Reagan honored him for his work in 1987. Furthermore, Patterson became an instrumental force in the creation of the Robert R. Moton Institute, an organization that helped colleges to recruit and retain students as well as manage institutional finances.

CONCLUSION

In 1987, Patterson received the Presidential Medal of Freedom in recognition for his lifelong efforts in the field of education. Clearly, Patterson made major contributions to the future of black colleges and the strategies for funding them. He was concerned not only with the individual advancement of African Americans through education but with the overall leadership of his race.

Marybeth Gasman

FURTHER READING

Enck, Henry S. "Tuskegee Institute and Northern White Philanthropy: A Case Study in Fund Raising, 1900–1915." *Journal of Negro History*, 65 (4), Autumn 1980, 336–348.

Goodson, Martia G., ed. *Chronicles of Faith: The Autobiography of Frederick D. Patterson.* Tuscaloosa: University of Alabama Press, 1991.

McQuiston, John T. "Frederick D. Patterson, Founder of Negro College Fund, Dies at 86." *New York Times*, April 27, 1988, 8.

Patterson, Frederick D. *Chronicles of Faith: The Autobiography of Frederick D. Patterson.* ed. Martin G. Goodson. Tuscaloosa: University of Alabama Press, 1996.

———. *The College Endowment Funding Plan.* Washington, DC: American Council on Education, 1976.

———. "Southern Viewpoint: Would It Not Be Wise for Some Negro Schools to Make Joint Appeal to Public for Funds?" *Pittsburgh Courier*, January 30, 1943, n.p.

Williams, Lea E. "The United Negro College Fund in Retrospect—A Search for Its True Meaning." *Journal of Negro Education*, 49, Autumn 1980, 363–372.

PAPERS

Frederick Douglass Patterson's papers are available at the Library of Congress (Washington, DC), Tuskegee University Special Collections, Tuskegee University (Tuskegee, AL), the Oral History Collection, Oral History Research Office, Columbia University (New York City), and the Frederick D. Patterson Research Institute (Fairfax, VA).

GEORGE PEABODY
(1795–1869)

Merchant, Banker, Creator of the Peabody Education Fund, and a Founder of Modern Philanthropy

INTRODUCTION

On March 12, 1862, George Peabody, in a letter founding the $2.5 million Peabody homes for London's working poor, wrote, "I [early] resolved that if my labors were blessed with success I would devote a portion of my property to promote the intellectual, moral, and physical welfare of my fellowmen wherever their need was greatest" (*Peabody Donation* 1862, 5). Peabody, a bachelor, earned $20 million and gave half of his wealth to philanthropy and half to relatives. While such generosity is laudable, Peabody also gained acclaim as a founder of modern philanthropy. In fact, historians cite the principles of his $2 million Peabody Education Fund (1867) for public education in the former Confederate states as significantly influencing later U.S. funds and foundations.

EARLY YEARS AND EDUCATION

Peabody was the third of eight children born to a poor family in Danvers, Massachusetts (renamed Peabody in 1868). He attended school for four years (1803–1807) and was apprenticed for four years in a general store (1807–1810). In 1811, his father died in debt and the loss of the family home forced his mother and siblings to live with relatives. Eleven days later, a town fire ended his job in a dry-goods store in Newburyport, Massachusetts. At age seventeen Peabody migrated to what is now the Georgetown neighborhood of Washington, DC, where he opened a dry-goods store and was also a peddler.

CAREER HIGHLIGHTS

A brief service in the War of 1812 led a fellow soldier, an older merchant named Eli-

George Peabody. Photograph courtesy Peabody Essex Museum.

sha Riggs, Sr., to make Peabody (at age nineteen) a partner in the Riggs, Peabody & Co. located in Georgetown. The firm imported merchandise for sale to U.S. wholesalers, moved to Baltimore in 1815, and by 1822 had Philadelphia and New York City warehouses. When Elisha Riggs, Sr. left the firm to become a banker (1828), his nephew Samuel Riggs replaced him.

Through this business venture, Peabody paid his father's debts and restored his mother and family to their home in 1816. He also paid for the education of younger relatives. For instance, he enabled nephew Othniel Charles Marsh to become the first U.S. paleontologist at Yale University as well as another nephew to become a Harvard-trained lawyer. Responding to one relative's request for help in attending Yale University, Peabody reflected, "Deprived, as I was, of the opportunity of obtaining anything more than the most common education, . . . willingly would I now give twenty times the expense attending a good education could I now possess it. . . . I can only do to those who come under my care, as I could have

wished circumstances had permitted others to have done by me" (May 18, 1831, letter, Peabody Papers, Peabody Essex Museum, Salem, Massachusetts).

During the last of his five buying trips to Europe (1827–1837), Peabody was also Maryland's agent to sell its $8 million bond issue to finance the Chesapeake and Ohio Canal and the Baltimore and Ohio Railroad. The Panic of 1837, however, caused Maryland and eight other states to stop interest payments on their bonds sold abroad. Peabody urged defaulting states to resume interest payments retroactively while reassuring foreign investors. After interest payments were resumed, Marylanders learned that, not wanting to burden their state treasury, Peabody had declined his $60,000 commission. In 1847, the Maryland legislature voted him unanimous thanks.

After February 1837, Peabody remained in London the rest of his life, except for three American visits. He founded George Peabody & Co., London, a banking firm, which sold state and other bonds to finance U.S. roads, canals, and railroads from 1838 to 1864. He also helped sell Mexican war bonds; bought, sold, and shipped European iron and later steel rails for U.S. railroads; and helped finance the Atlantic Cable Co. In October 1854, he took Boston merchant Junius Spencer Morgan as a partner. Morgan's nineteen-year-old son, John Pierpont Morgan, began his banking career as a New York City agent for George Peabody & Co. On retirement, October 1, 1864, Peabody withdrew his name from the firm. Later, J.P. Morgan headed J.S. Morgan & Co. Consequently, George Peabody & Co. was the foundation of the J.P. Morgan international banking firm.

MAJOR PHILANTHROPIC CONTRIBUTIONS

Given his attachment to England and the United States, Peabody became an important benefactor in both countries. When the London press ridiculed U.S. exhibitors at the Great Exhibition of 1851 (London) for their large unadorned exhibit area, Peabody's timely $15,000 loan enabled American art and industry to be displayed to a world audience. In addition, his lavish American-British friendship dinners in connection with the Great Exhibition, repeated in later years, brought together distinguished Englishmen and visiting Americans and won him friends and informants.

In 1862, Peabody amazed Britons by establishing a $2.5 million Peabody Trust to build model apartments for London's working poor (where 34,500 low-income Londoners still lived in 2001). In announcing Peabody's "unusual act of beneficence," London's leading newspaper stated, "Such an act is rare in the annals of benevolence" (*London Times*, March 26, 1862, p. 9, c. 6). Among the awards subsequently recognizing his philanthropy, Peabody became the first American to receive the Freedom of the City of London and be honored with a statue in London (at the Royal Exchange).

While impressing his English neighbors with his charitable endeavors, Peabody did not neglect his fellow American citizens. For the 1852 centennial celebration of the separation of his hometown, Danvers, from Salem, Massachusetts, he sent, from London, a check to found the first Peabody Institute Library in his hometown (now Peabody, Massachusetts). Along with the check, Peabody enclosed a motto that explained his valuation of libraries and other education institutions: "Education: a debt due from present to future generations" (Parker 1995, 59). Peabody also created public libraries that remain today in Danvers, Newburyport, and Georgetown (all in Massachusetts); in Thetford, Vermont; Washington, DC; and Baltimore, Maryland.

Besides the aforementioned libraries, Peabody devoted $1.4 million to create the Peabody Institute of Baltimore (founded 1857 and opened 1866), which contained a superior reference library, lecture hall and fund, art gallery, and conservatory of music. After it opened during Peabody's 1866–1867 American visit, Baltimorean Johns Hopkins asked for Peabody's philanthropic advice.

Soon after, Hopkins founded Johns Hopkins University. In 1982, Baltimore's Peabody Library and Conservatory of Music merged with Johns Hopkins University.

Continuing to demonstrate his strong support of education, Peabody also founded museums at Harvard (anthropology) and at Yale (natural science) in 1866. In 1867, he created the Peabody Essex Museum—with maritime history and Essex County documents—in Salem, Massachusetts. Peabody further endowed professorships at Kenyon College, Ohio (1866), and at what is now Washington and Lee University, Virginia (1869).

Americans visiting England brought Peabody news of the approaching Civil War. This news caused Peabody to delay his 1859 idea of a large fund for public schools for New York City's poorest children. Early in his 1866–1867 American visit, Peabody, witnessing Civil War devastation in the South, determined instead to found his most influential American gift, the $2 million Peabody Education Fund (1867–1914), to promote public elementary and secondary schools and teacher education in the eleven former Confederate states plus West Virginia.

Former South Carolina Governor William Aiken, one of three southerners of the sixteen original trustees, wrote to Peabody via a friend: "The South is ruined . . . its destruction is certain" (Aiken to Peabody via W.W. Corcoran, January 5, 1867, Corcoran Papers, Library of Congress). Besides a ruined economy, the private academies on which the South had relied had closed. Unlike northern public schools flourishing since the 1840s, the South had few schools for whites or blacks to help revive the region. Peabody Education Fund trustee President Robert Charles Winthrop's herculean task was to use the fund's relatively small income to help revive the South through tax-supported public schools. Winthrop, a respected former speaker of the Massachusetts House of Representatives and of the U.S. House of Representatives, needed a policy strategy and an administrator. In 1867, he found both in a chance meeting in Boston with Brown University President Barnas Sears. Asked for advice, Sears presented a plan that immediately impressed Winthrop, who convinced Sears to become the Peabody Education Fund's first administrator.

Sears, who had succeeded Horace Mann as Massachusetts' education secretary, moved to Virginia and toured the South. He offered officials of larger towns a rising scale of grants, based on enrollments, to initiate public schools, required town and state leaders to provide matching funds, and required that such schools be sustained through legislation as state public schools. He also formed a network of agents among dedicated school officials to act on behalf of the fund. Through them, Peabody Education Fund grants were extended to outlying unschooled or little schooled areas, thus perpetuating the fund's work through its forty-seven years of existence.

Thus, the Peabody Education Fund used relatively small grants as levers to initiate, stimulate, sustain, and perpetuate tax-supported elementary and later secondary, public schools; one-week and two-week teacher-training institutes; and ongoing teacher-training normal schools for white and black children. Peabody's expressed wish to prohibit religious requirements became a standard for future large funds. Winthrop carefully orchestrated favorable publicity to awaken and sustain public awareness of the fund's challenges and accomplishments. By granting 3,645 Peabody scholarships for teacher training at Peabody Normal College during 1877–1904, the fund set a precedent in selecting, supporting, and channeling able, ambitious, dedicated students—regardless of income or status—into higher education. These Peabody scholars formed a small but important core of southern education leaders. When the Peabody Education Fund ended in 1914, its principal enriched education departments in southern state universities. The fund earlier created the Peabody Normal College, Nashville, Tennessee (1875–1909), and also endowed its successor, George Peabody College for Teachers (1914–1979), adjoining Vanderbilt University in Nashville. Since 1979, Peabody College has flourished as part of Vanderbilt University.

President Andrew Johnson thanked Peabody for the Peabody Education Fund, regarding it as a national gift. The U.S. Congress also voted him a unanimous resolution of thanks and a gold medal. Yet his philanthropy to the former Confederacy also drew disapproval from those bent on punishing the South. In particular, abolitionist William Lloyd Garrison criticized his gift to Baltimore as "made to a Maryland institution, at a time when that state was rotten with treason." (New York City *Independent*, November 11, 1869, p. 4, c. 1). Later, Garrison even characterized Peabody as a pro-slavery sympathizer. Earlier Peabody replied to such charges by stating, "I . . . publicly . . . avow that during the war my sympathies were with the Union—that my uniform course tended to assist but never to injure the credit of the Union. At the close of the war three-fourths of my property was invested in United States Government and State securities, and remain so at this time" (*New York Times*, October 27, 1866, p. 5, c. 1–2).

CONCLUSION

Gravely ill and much honored on his last American visit (summer 1869), Peabody died in London on November 4, 1869. His death evoked public clamor for funeral honors despite bitter American-British tensions over the *Alabama* claims. The United States demanded compensation (and in 1871–1872 received $15.5 million) for British-built Confederate raiders, such as the CSS *Alabama*, which caused vast losses of Union lives, ships, and treasure. Meanwhile, Peabody's will required burial in Massachusetts. British and American officials vied to outdo each other in an unprecedented ninety-six-day transatlantic funeral, partly to honor his philanthropies, his $10,000 gift for a U.S. expedition to search for lost British Arctic explorer Sir John Franklin (1852–1853), and his United States-England friendship efforts, but also to soften *Alabama* claims tensions.

Today, the Peabody Education Fund is often recognized as the first major multimillion-dollar foundation in the United States. In its forty-seven years of existence, many of the fifty-plus Peabody Education Fund trustees were also influential trustees of later and larger funds and foundations as well as initiators of other charitable institutions. Trustees Anthony Joseph Drexel and Paul Tulane acknowledged that their Peabody Education Fund experience influenced their founding of Drexel University, Philadelphia, and Tulane University, New Orleans. Enoch Pratt, a Peabody Institute of Baltimore trustee, was influenced to found Baltimore's Enoch Pratt Free Library. Meanwhile, Johns Hopkins University's first president, Daniel Coit Gilman, cited Peabody's example as influencing the founding of the John F. Slater Fund, **John D. Rockefeller, Sr.**'s General Education Board, **Andrew Carnegie** foundations, and the Russell **Sage** Foundation. "Almost . . . all of these foundations," Gilman wrote, "have been based on principles that were designated by Mr. Peabody" (Gilman 1907, 657).

Franklin Parker

FURTHER READING

Burk, Kathleen. *Morgan Grenfell 1838–1988: The Biography of a Merchant Bank.* Oxford: Oxford University Press, 1989.

Flexner, Abraham. *Funds and Foundations: Their Policies Past and Present.* New York: Harper & Brothers, 1952.

Garrett, John Work. *Address Delivered on the 30th of January, 1888, before the Young Men's Christian Association of Baltimore on the Occasion of Their Thirtieth Anniversary.* Baltimore: News Steam Printing Office, 1883.

Gilman, Daniel Coit. "Five Great Gifts." *The Outlook* 86, no. 13, July 27, 1907, 648–652, 657.

Hidy, Muriel Emmie. *George Peabody, Merchant and Financier, 1829–1854.* New York: Arno Press, 1978.

Mortuary Honors to the Late George Peabody in Portland, Maine. Portland, ME: Loring, Short & Harmon, 1870.

Parker, Franklin. *George Peabody: A Biography.* Nashville, TN: Vanderbilt University Press, 1995.

Parker, Franklin, and Betty J. Parker. "*George Peabody A–Z*" (CORE) Collected Original Resources in Education. Microfiche journal, Carfax Publishing, Abingdon, Oxfordshire, U.K., vol. 23, no. 3, October 1999, Fiche 11 C10.

Peabody Donation. London: E. Couchman & Co., 1862.

Peabody Education Fund. *Proceedings of the Trustees of the Peabody Education Fund from Their Original Organization on the 8th of February 1867.* 6 vol. Boston: John Wilson & Sons, 1875–1916.

Winthrop, Robert Charles. *Eulogy, Pronounced at the Funeral of George Peabody, at Peabody, Massachusetts, February 8, 1870.* Boston: John Wilson & Son, 1870.

PAPERS

George Peabody's papers are in the Peabody Essex Museum (Salem, MA), the George Peabody Library, the Johns Hopkins University (Baltimore, MD), the Peabody Museum Archives at Harvard University (Cambridge, MA), and the Peabody Museum Archives at Yale University (New Haven, CT).

PEW FAMILY

J. Howard Pew (1882–1971)

President of Sun Oil Company, Founder of the Pew Charitable Trusts, and Anonymous Donor

Mary Ethel Pew (1884–1979)

Founder of the Pew Charitable Trusts and Anonymous Donor

Joseph N. Pew, Jr. (1886–1963)

Vice President of Sun Oil Company, Founder of the Pew Charitable Trusts, and Anonymous Donor

Mabel Pew Myrin (1889–1972)

Founder of the Pew Charitable Trusts and Anonymous Donor

INTRODUCTION

In 1958, Robert Hayes of the Grace Hartley Memorial Hospital in Banner Elk, North Carolina wrote J. Howard Pew to thank the Pew Memorial Trust for its "generous gift to our new hospital project" and inform him that the hospital wished "to announce contributions that have been received and from whom" (December 28, 1957, letter from Robert G. Hayes to J. Howard Pew, Pew Papers, Hagley Museum and Library). Five days later, J. Howard Pew wrote a letter to Hayes in which he stated that "the Board of the Pew Memorial Trust do not like any publicity given to contributions which they make. Therefore I must ask that you do not mention our name in connection with the contribution to the Grace Hartley Memorial Hospital" (January 3, 1958, letter from J. Howard Pew to Robert G. Hayes). Since Americans customarily observe public recognition of and honors for philanthropists' gifts, Pew's response may be a bit surprising. However, J. Howard Pew and three of his siblings, unlike industrial giants **Andrew Carnegie** and **John D. Rockefeller, Sr.**, gave away their tremendous business profits while subscribing to one of the oldest philanthropic traditions, anonymous giving.

EARLY YEARS AND EDUCATION

The four individuals who created what is presently known as the Pew Charitable Trusts were the children of Joseph Newton (J.N.) Pew and Mary Catherine Anderson. During the 1870s, J.N. Pew, a former schoolteacher, traveled to the site of the first oil gusher—Titusville, Pennsylvania. In 1881, J.N. Pew created the Keystone Gas Company and sold natural gas, an oil by-product, to oil fields and the town of Bradford, Pennsylvania. Soon, Pew sold natural gas to other towns and cities, particularly Pittsburgh. Thereafter, his Sun Oil Line Company and Diamond Oil Company provided oil products throughout the Midwest. After the discovery of the tremendous Spindletop gusher in Texas, J.N. Pew also sent a nephew to investigate the situation and then partnered with the United Gas Improvement Company of Philadelphia to build the Marcus Hook Refinery, located along the Delaware River, and ship the oil to the refinery by tanker.

As J.N. Pew's business progressed, his growing family moved from Bradford, to Pittsburgh, and then finally settled in Philadelphia in 1904. J.N. and Mary Catherine Pew raised five children (Arthur, J. Howard, Mary Ethel, J.N., Jr., and Mabel) in a close-knit and highly religious environment. Members of the Presbyterian denomination, the family was known to conduct daily worship in the home and J. Howard remembered that his "father saw to it that I never missed attending Sunday School and church" (Sennholz 1975, 15). The Pew parents also strongly valued education. All five children attended private schools and four also earned college degrees: Arthur (Princeton University, 1896), J. Howard (Grove City College, 1900), J.N. Jr. (Cornell University, 1908), and Mary Ethel (Bryn Mawr College, 1906).

CAREER HIGHLIGHTS

After graduating from Grove City College in 1900, eighteen-year-old J. Howard Pew

J. Howard Pew in 1970. AP Photo/files.

attended the Massachusetts Institute of Technology for a year and then joined the family business. As a young engineer, J. Howard Pew developed a successful lubricating oil known as Sun Red Stock as well as a process that produced the first commercially successful petroleum asphalt (known as Hydrolene). In 1912, J.N. Pew died of a heart attack. With elder brother Arthur Pew, who died four years later, ill, the Pew family made J. Howard Pew the new company president. Educated as an engineer and only four years out of college, younger brother J.N. Pew, Jr. became vice president of the company.

Over the next three decades, the two brothers would work together to expand Sun Oil. In 1916, they wanted to ensure the global distribution of their product and created a shipyard that ultimately became the largest producer of oil tankers in the United States. In 1942, for instance, they built two-thirds of all oil tankers created that year. As the number of automobiles grew and the corresponding need for gasoline rose in the

1920s, the company renamed itself the Sun Oil Company (1922), began to own hundreds of filling stations, and promoted Blue Sunoco (a single-grade gasoline that competed with the multiple grades of other brands). With $50 million in assets, Sun Oil Company issued common stock on the New York Stock Exchange in 1925. The next year, the Pews offered a stock-sharing plan for employees, believing ownership would produce better workers. During the 1930s, J.N. Pew, Jr. built a pipeline to Pittsburgh, Cleveland, and Syracuse to move their refined products to markets. Continually investing in their company, the brothers followed the business philosophy known as vertical integration, controlling numerous steps in the production and distribution of their products, by owning oil wells, tankers, refineries, pipelines, and gas stations. In 1947, J. Howard Pew retired from the presidency of the hugely successful company.

While the Sun Oil Company expanded, the Pew family grew as well. J. Howard Pew married Helen Jennings Thompson in 1907. Subsequently, the couple adopted three children: George T., Roberta, and Frances. In 1916, J.N. Pew, Jr. married Alberta Caven Hensel and they raised Mary Caven, Eleanor Glenn, Joseph Newton (J.N.) III, J. Howard, and Alberta Hensel. The Pew sisters, however, never had any children of their own. Mary Ethel Pew never married and Mabel Pew married H. Alarik Myrin, who did have two children from a previous marriage, in 1919.

A staunch Republican family, the Pews ventured into politics and supported conservative candidates who promoted the free-enterprise system and fought government involvement in the activities of businesses and individuals but also derided monopolies and approved government intervention in such instances. Although J. N. Pew, Jr. initially agreed to work with President Franklin Roosevelt on petroleum industry guidelines for the National Recovery Act, he broke with Roosevelt over his desire for price controls. J.N. Pew, Jr. even became the Republican political boss of Pennsylvania and graced the cover of the May 6, 1940 issue of *Time* magazine as a leading critic of Roosevelt's New Deal. The cover story author wrote that Pew believes the New Deal will "raze U.S. businesses to a dead level and debase the citizenry into a mass of ballot-casting serfs . . . robbing U.S. voters of their precious heritage of independence" (*Time* May 6, 1940, 17). J.N. Pew, Jr. is even quoted as saying, "The Republican Party stands today where the Continental Army stood at Valley Forge" (*Time* May 6, 1940, 17). Although J.N. Pew, Jr. made substantial financial contributions to the Republican Party, his political leadership proved largely inept. Still, his family would always remain steadfast in their conservative outlook. During the New Deal and after, J. Howard Pew, for instance, would give speeches on the values of free-enterprise and individualism as well as the dangers of a welfare state.

MAJOR PHILANTHROPIC CONTRIBUTIONS

In 1948, the four remaining children of J.N. Pew created the Pew Memorial Foundation in memory of their parents and with 880,000 shares of Sun Oil stock. While the four Pews clearly had charitable goals in mind, they also wished to use the foundation as a way to shield themselves from inheritance tax and ensure that their company would remain firmly in family hands. Over time, their charitable vehicle became managed by the Glenmede Trust Company (1956)—to provide more coordination as well as ensure the privacy of their giving— and developed into multiple trusts: the Pew Memorial Trust, the Mary Anderson Trust, the J. Howard Pew Freedom Trust, the J.N. Pew, Jr. Charitable Trust, the Knollbrook Trust, the Mable Pew Myrin Trust, and the Medical Trust. Finally, the investment and grantmaking operations of the trusts became separate divisions of Glenmede Trust Company in 1987, with the grantmaking division known as the Pew Charitable Trusts.

Although the four Pew siblings gave personal money away before and after forming the Pew Memorial Foundation, they also ran the foundation as a close-knit and personal venture. With a foundation mission broadly defined as benefiting charitable endeavors, a review of their grants shows that they often gave to local charities and causes that at least one Pew knew well. The foundation, for instance, made substantial donations for cancer research and care because their mother died of cancer in 1935 and Mary Ethel Pew's giving focused on that area. Since their father substantially donated to and served as chairman of the trustees of Grove City College (in addition to J. Howard Pew being an alumnus), the Pews made some of their largest gifts to this private religious college.

During the three decades that the four Pews ran their foundation, J. Howard Pew not only served as the president of the trustees but was the undisputed leader of their family philanthropy until his death in 1971. Although the Pews were giving away considerable amounts and numerous grants, they still reviewed and approved every grant at quarterly board meetings. In fact, they resisted but eventually hired some professional staff to aid them in their philanthropy. The foundation primarily gave yearly grants and even supported charities' construction projects but would not donate to an endowment. J. Howard Pew firmly detested endowments because he believed they eventually allowed institutions to undertake projects that donors to those endowments would never have funded. Thus, he preferred charitable institutions with small or no endowment and even promoted a free-market system for nonprofits. "My experience is that an institution which is really serving the public well will obtain the funds necessary for its budget every year; and if they don't serve the public well then they should not exist" (March 15, 1948, letter from J. Howard Pew to Wm. D. Anderson, Pew Papers).

Predictably, the Pew family foundation favored small religious colleges, particularly those with substantial Bible instruction and daily chapel. J. Howard Pew believed "that freedom can succeed only in a community where people generally accept the attributes of Christianity as a rule of their conduct" (J. Howard Pew, Pew Memorial Foundation document entitled "Social Sciences," May 6, 1955, Pew Papers). Besides support for health care, black colleges, the Boy Scouts, and numerous other major charities, they also substantially aided evangelistic Christian training and outreach through such organizations as the Moody Bible Institute, the Gordon-Conwell-Theological Seminary (J. Howard Pew even purchased land for their new campus in South Hamilton, Massachusetts), and the Billy Graham Evangelistic Association. In the latter case, the Pews were friends with Billy Graham as well as early and longtime donors to his ministry.

With such a fervent Christian outlook, it may not be surprising the Pews choose to follow the teachings of the Bible and conduct their charitable giving anonymously. According to Mary Sennholz, the Pews tailored their philanthropy according to verses one through three of the sixth chapter of the Gospel of Matthew:

> Take heed that you do not your alms before men, to be seen of them: Otherwise, ye have no reward of your Father which is in Heaven. Therefore, when thou doest thine alms, do not sound a trumpet before thee, as the hypocrites do in the synagogues and in the streets, that they may have the glory of men. Verily, I say unto you, they have their reward. But when thou doest alms, let not the left hand know what thy right hand doeth. (Sennholz 1975, 34)

Indeed, J. Howard Pew's foundation correspondence includes a number of instances where grant recipients or potential grant recipients expressed their desire to publicize a grant or name something after the Pew family or foundation. In almost every case, J. Howard Pew responded similarly, "At the outset, let me say that nothing would distress us more than to have you use the name 'Pew' in connection with any of your buildings" (Letter from J. Howard Pew to H.W. Prentis, Jr., October 14, 1957, Pew Papers).

The practice of anonymous giving actually stems from numerous religious traditions, which promote the virtue of such an act because the recipient's dignity is protected—he or she is not beholden to anyone—when the donor is not recognized and does not know the recipient(s). For instance, the medieval Jewish scholar Moses Maimonides, who compiled the farming law code, according to the Talmud and Jewish legal literature, in *The Book of Agriculture*, included a section on the Eight Stages of Tsedakah (righteousness and charity). In that section, anonymous giving is placed as one of the highest forms of giving.

Besides religious reasons, donors certainly give anonymously for other reasons. Some may giving anonymously to reduce the number of appeals they receive, to ensure their safety if their donations are radical or even life-threatening (such as the case of **Booker T. Washington**), or to hide a particular agenda that they do not want to make public. Perhaps due to the latter motive, the public is occasionally suspicious of anonymous giving and the Pews were not exempt from such concerns. In *The Golden Donors*, Waldemar Nielsen wrote that some supposed "the real purpose" of the Pews's anonymous giving "was to hide the use of philanthropic funds for ideological and political purposes" (Nielsen 1985, 174). The author of an article on the Pew Charitable Trusts in *Foundation News* even described the foundation as operating under an "odd policy of secrecy" (Williams 1991, 20).

Nonetheless, the policy was not odd but quite traditional. Moreover, the Pews' foundation primarily funded groups that were not broadly defined as political. In fact, the foundation actually resisted funding social sciences research for numerous years after its creation because they saw such grants as political. Still, J. Howard Pew's conservatism and concern about communism could be characterized as extreme at times, but the Cold War, and the communist hysteria that began in the 1940s, helped shape such a mindset in numerous people. In 1957, he did create the J. Howard Pew Freedom Trust to counter what he saw as liberal grant making by foundations started by **Carnegie**, the

Ford family, and the **Rockefeller** family. Expectedly, this new trust promoted values such as limited government, free markets, and its founder's belief that freedom and Christianity were ex- plicitly linked and funded conservative groups such as the Hoover Institution.

CONCLUSION

Today, the Pew Charitable Trusts are not only one of the larger foundations in the United States but also one of the most well known. During the 1960s and 1970s, the Pew foundation slowly changed its anonymous giving policy. After J.N. Pew, Jr. died in 1963, the three remaining founders and other members of the Glenmede Committee on Grants honored him at their June 19, 1967 meeting. On that day, they approved the J.N. Pew, Jr. Trust's name on a bronze plaque that recognized it as one of the donors of Lou Henry Hoover Building at Stanford University. In late 1971 and early 1972, J. Howard Pew and Mable Pew Myrin passed away. With three of the four founders deceased, the December 18, 1972, Committee on Grants meeting approved a Pew Memorial Trust plaque for a gift to St. Luke's and Children's Medical Center (Philadelphia) and soon allowed such publicity for other grants. After Mary Ethel Pew died in 1979, the foundation issued their first annual report in 1980. Nonetheless, the four Pew siblings are noteworthy for their decades of adherence to an old charitable tradition.

Robert T. Grimm, Jr.

FURTHER READING

Fleeson, Lucinda. "How a Foundation Reinvented Itself." *Philadelphia Inquirer*, April 27, 1992, A1.

———. "Trusts' New Direction Leaves Region Behind." *Philadelphia Inquirer*, April 26, 1992, A1.

Gardner, Joel. *A History of the Pew Charitable Trusts.* Philadelphia: Pew Charitable Trusts, 1995.

Nielsen, Waldemar A. *The Golden Donors: A New Anatomy of the Great Foundations.* New York: Truman Talley Books, E.P. Dutton, 1985.

"Pennsylvania: Mr. Pew at Valley Forge." *Time*, May 6, 1940, 15–18.

Pew, J. Howard. "Preserving the Free Enterprise System." *Vital Speeches*, New York: City News Publishing Company, February 1, 1941, 244–247.

Rottenberg, Dan. "The Sun Gods." *Philadelphia Magazine*, October 1975, 111–120, 182–196.

Sennholz, Mary. *Faith and Freedom: The Journal of a Great American J. Howard Pew.* Grove City, PA: Grove City College, 1975.

"Sun Oil." *Fortune*, February 1941, 50.

Williams, Roger M. "From Inside Right to Outside Front." *Foundation News*, May–June 1991, 20–25.

PAPERS

The papers of the Pew family and of the Pew Charitable Trusts (and earlier forms of the Pew family foundation) are located at the Hagley Museum and Library (Wilmington, DE).

R

JAMES HERMAN ROBINSON
(1907–1972)

Minister and Founder of Operation Crossroads Africa

INTRODUCTION

"It is not merely a question of the practical moves needed to win Africa or to hold back the nefarious hosts that seek to seduce Africa, it is a question of morality, of human decency, of Christian love, and the matching of our protestations with our deeds" (Robinson 1962, 79). More than any other ideological motivation, this quote explained James Robinson's missionary-style work in Africa and his efforts toward social reform in the United States.

During the early 1960s, at the height of the Cold War, American policymakers viewed Africa as a strategic player on the global chessboard between capitalism and communism. As a result, the U.S. State Department and a number of other governmental and nonprofit organizations dramatically increased aid to the continent as scores of African colonies rapidly achieved independence. Robinson responded to the urgency of these times by establishing Operation Crossroads

Africa (OCA). Begun in 1958, OCA brought college students to Africa each summer to work on housing, health care, agriculture, and education projects. Inspired by OCA, the Kennedy administration created the Peace Corps in 1961, thereby ensuring Robinson's mark upon the history of public service and philanthropy.

EARLY YEARS AND EDUCATION

Born in Knoxville, Tennessee, in 1907, James Herman Robinson grew up in the segregated American South. He was introduced to Christianity through his parents, who were members of a sanctified church. By World War I, his family had moved to Cleveland, Ohio, where Robinson attended school with the children of working-class poor immigrants. Despite his intelligence, he frequently missed school, working to support his family, and became active in a street gang. In 1929, he finally graduated from high school at the age of twenty-two.

James Herman Robinson. The Amistad Research Center at Tulane University, New Orleans, Louisiana.

During that year, Robinson met a black Methodist minister named Russell Brown. Inspired by Brown's self-help message and desperate to leave street life, Robinson joined his church. He preferred Brown's style of Christianity to that of his parents because of its social emphasis. Mindful of his own experiences, Robinson started an after-school club for troubled boys. Within a few months, he began seven more clubs at other Cleveland churches. Hearing about his work, a highly impressed Presbyterian minister talked to Robinson about joining the ministry and offered to pay for his education. Robinson jumped at the chance and enrolled at Lincoln University, a historically black Presbyterian college in Pennsylvania, in 1931.

At Lincoln, Robinson was noted for his diligence in the classroom and became a student leader on campus. He even led an unsuccessful effort to introduce a "Negro History" course. In the summer of 1933, Robinson returned to Tennessee and re-ceived permission to pastor at a small church in Beardon, a town south of Knoxville. In addition to his preaching, Robinson taught English and mathematics to the area's African-American residents, informed church members about civil rights groups such as the NAACP, and tried to start a credit union. Hearing about his efforts, local whites grew resentful, threatened his life, and finally drove him out of town. He returned to Lincoln and graduated from there in 1935.

Deciding to attend graduate school in New York City, Robinson was accepted to Union Theological Seminary. A training ground for many liberal ministers, Union was the base of leftist minister and professor Harry Ward, who later became Robinson's mentor. Ward believed in Social Christianity, which argued that the key to personal salvation lay in pursuing an agenda of social reform that championed rights of the poor and the oppressed. Situated next to Harlem during the Great Depression, Robinson and Ward found numerous opportunities to promote their agenda among African Americans and unemployed workers. Robinson had also begun to believe that being a Christian minister meant working for racial desegregation.

CAREER HIGHLIGHTS AND MAJOR PHILANTHROPIC CONTRIBUTIONS

After graduating from Union in 1938, Robinson accepted an offer to pastor the Morningside Presbyterian Church in Manhattan. Soon after, he decided to change the church's name to the Church of the Master. The new name represented his belief that the word "Master" represented God, which meant that all human beings were God's children and were welcomed in his church, regardless of race or class. The formerly all-white neighborhood around the church had become majority black by the late 1930s, and Robinson decided to retain as many white members as possible while attracting new black members. Within months, he had enlarged its membership from twenty to over 200, and brought in white students from

Union, Columbia University, and Barnard College to volunteer at the church.

Adopting as his personal motto "personal salvation is impossible without social salvation" (Robinson 1950, 211), Robinson began a number of community service programs. He started a social services department that provided housing and employment information, guidance counseling for juveniles, a credit union, a cooperative store, and after-school programs. Hearing about Robinson's work, an elderly white couple donated 470 acres of New Hampshire land to his church, which led to the establishment of the Morningside Summer Camp for children in 1942. It opened as an interracial camp, and Robinson recruited black and white volunteers from New England colleges to operate it. Like the future Operation Crossroads Africa, the volunteers paid their expenses, raised funds for the camp, constructed camp buildings, and worked as counselors.

Robinson also helped found the African Academy of Arts and Research in 1943. Like many African Americans, he had an interest in Africa, due to his skin color and heritage, which blossomed more fully during his years at Lincoln University and as a Union graduate student near Harlem. The academy held parties, lectures, and informal gatherings for African students, intellectuals, and other New Yorkers who had an interest in Africa. When Robinson developed OCA, the academy provided crucial contacts. Indeed, the academy's governing board included First Lady Eleanor Roosevelt; Bethune-Cookman College President **Mary McLeod Bethune**; American Civil Liberties Union President **Roger Baldwin**; and Nnamdi Azikiwe, a Nigerian intellectual who would later become the first president of an independent Nigeria in 1960, with Robinson serving as chairman of the board.

Robinson's community work, his interest in African affairs, and his attempts to develop integrated institutions attracted many admirers. In 1951, the Presbyterian Board of Foreign Missions chose Robinson to go on a fact-finding eight-month tour through Asia. Robinson was to assess the church's role in countries that were becoming independent following World War II. After his return in 1952, he began speaking and publishing his ideas on African and Asian nationalism. Contrary to Cold War hawks that viewed the world in stark terms between capitalists and communists, Robinson argued that nationalism had to be taken seriously. He predicted that Africa and Asia would become independent regardless of communist help. In his mind, the key issue was whether Americans had enough faith in themselves and in God to help Africans and Asians gain independence. He argued that assistance to the Third World should be seen as an act of Christian love, not as a defense against communism. Robinson also linked racism in the United States with European colonialism. Like many African Americans, he argued that African and Asian oppression was the same as racial oppression in the United States, and he warned that American racism and support for European interests in Africa and Asia enhanced the appeal of communism to non-whites. To remedy this problem, he called for black employment in diplomatic, missionary, and business operations in Africa and Asia.

In 1954, Robinson traveled to Africa for the Presbyterian Church. Following his return, he argued for the creation of a voluntary grassroots service program that would send committed individuals to Africa. The new program would be open to all regardless if they were religious or not. In his mind, these new secular missionaries should not force American or religious ideals upon Africans, but that they should help achieve a more democratic world. Although Robinson was a minister, he reminded his audiences that what Africa needed most were doctors, nurses, engineers, accountants—in short, skilled workers and professionals who could help run a government, not establish a new church. By 1957, he actively worked around the country to establish his program. In his writings and speeches, Robinson particularly noted that industrialization had created a whole range of urban problems that Africans were ill prepared to deal with.

Nevertheless, Robinson found it difficult

to sell his idea. Most Americans were only vaguely interested in Africa; for many, their only images were from Tarzan movies and the panicked reports about the Mau Mau rebellion in Kenya. However, Robinson had intrigued several prominent Americans, such as U.S. Supreme Court Justice William Douglas, with his idea. In addition, a number of events had transpired by 1957 to make Africa a foreign-policy priority, such as Egypt's threatened takeover of the Suez Canal and the independence of Ghana.

As a result, Robinson's idea for a service program in Africa had gained considerable support by the end of 1957. He recruited several influential Americans, such as Justice Douglas, former U.S. Ambassador to India Chester Bowles, Atlanta University President Rufus Clement, and University of Notre Dame President Theodore Hesburgh, to serve as honorary national co-chairs. Robinson served as director and Israel Moshowitz, a rabbi from the Hillcrest Jewish Center in Jamaica, New York, served as associate director. Robinson also recruited several African government officials in support of his plan, many of whom had participated in the African Academy's gatherings a decade earlier, such as Nnamdi Azikiwe, Kingsley Mbadiwe, and Akiki Nyabongo. The U.S. State Department endorsed the plan and British and French officials assured him of their cooperation. In the summer of 1958, the first group of sixty students arrived in Cameroon, Ghana, Liberia, Nigeria, and Sierra Leone. Within a year, the project's name officially became Operation Crossroads Africa.

By 1960, news magazines such as *Time* and *The Economist* had begun reporting on OCA. They described how more than 100 interracial students paid their own expenses to work for ten weeks in Africa digging ditches, building schools, and developing friendships with Africans. In their editorials, the magazines praised Crossroaders for helping to dispel the notion of the United States as a completely racist country following conflicts over racial desegregation in the American South.

Although its programs were entirely dependent on volunteers and charitable contributions, OCA continued to gain in size and notoriety throughout the 1960s. By the early 1970s, more than 4,000 students and volunteers had participated in the program. Crossroaders not only comprised college and graduate students, but increasingly included professionals, such as doctors and nurses who volunteered for OCA's health clinics in Sierra Leone, business education teachers who worked at a school in Liberia, and social workers who staffed a welfare office in Nigeria. Furthermore, agricultural and public works specialists were sent to Kenya and folklorists were sent to Uganda. Indeed, OCA found itself unable to fill all of the African nations' requests for its services.

In addition to its work in Africa, OCA ambitiously created two new programs and influenced the operation of another. In 1964, Robinson and OCA (with the help of the U.S. State Department) brought a group of African youth leaders to the United States for an eight-week study tour. The program became permanent the following year, and by the early 1970s, it had brought more than 400 African students to the United States from thirty-seven countries. Aware that many Caribbean and Latin American nations contained millions of African descendants, OCA created a diaspora component in 1969. The program conducted similar work camp projects like its African twin, with operations primarily in Brazil, Haiti, and Jamaica. Meanwhile, the Kennedy and Johnson administrations utilized Robinson as a consultant in the creation of the Peace Corps. As the government agency grew in size, it drew more frequently on Robinson's developing expertise in African affairs, and recruited OCA veterans as Peace Corps volunteers.

CONCLUSION

James Robinson died on November 6, 1972. Although he derived great satisfaction from his life's work, he was perhaps all too aware of its limits. "The projects which we shall undertake—to work with our hands, and build as a continuing monument to our faith in Africa—will not be very pretentious, but the impact of their influence will be far beyond any measure of their size, because they will be a reminder in the years to come of our willingness to serve and learn from Africa" (Brown 1973, 160). OCA continued to operate following Robinson's death, and it remains committed to its original mission decades later. Although OCA was officially created in the 1950s, its concepts were forged during years of state-enforced racial segregation and Depression-era unemployment. Robinson's experiences and faith in Christian service motivated him to persevere in the hope of one day establishing **Martin Luther King's, Jr.**'s idea of the "beloved community."

Damon W. Freeman

FURTHER READING

Brown, Laverne. "James H. Robinson's Unfinished Task." *The Crisis* 80, May 1973, 159–161.

Isaacs, Harold. *Emergent Americans: A Report on "Crossroads Africa."* New York: John Day, 1961.

Lee, Amy. *Throbbing Drums: The Story of James H. Robinson.* New York: Friendship Press, 1968.

Plimpton, Ruth. *Operation Crossroads Africa.* New York: Viking Press, 1962.

Robinson, James Herman. *Adventurous Preaching.* Great Neck, NY: Channel Press, 1956.

———. *Africa at the Crossroads.* Philadelphia: Westminster Press, 1962.

———. *Love of This Land: Progress of the Negro in the United States.* Philadelphia: Christian Education Press, 1956.

———. *Road without Turning: The Story of Reverend James H. Robinson.* New York: Farrar, Straus, 1950.

———. *Tomorrow Is Today.* Philadelphia: Christian Education Press, 1954.

PAPERS

The James Herman Robinson papers and the Operation Crossroads Africa archives are located in the Amistad Research Center at Tulane University (New Orleans, LA).

JOHN D. ROCKEFELLER, SR.
(1839–1937)

Standard Oil Mogul, Founder of the Rockefeller Foundation, and the Architect of "Scientific Giving"

INTRODUCTION

Wallace Buttrick, the genial Baptist minister who was one of John D. Rockefeller, Sr.'s chief advisers, loved to repeat a favorite story, which began with someone asking a friend, "What would you do if you had a million dollars?" "Do?" the other replied, "I wouldn't do a thing!" (Records of the Rockefeller Foundation, Series 900, The Rockefeller Archive Center) While his audience chuckled, Buttrick drove home his point: often, those with great fortunes did not use them well. John Davidson Rockefeller, however, lured Buttrick from his pulpit by preaching about the social responsibility of wealth, which Rockefeller practiced during a long life that spanned a momentous period in American history. Indeed, Rockefeller greatly shaped the United States of his time, first as one of the founders of Standard Oil and then, as the world's richest man, the architect of "scientific giving": the idea that business principles, not individual whim, should organize charity. One of the early twentieth century's most famous, and most reviled, men, Rockefeller was also the era's most generous philanthropist.

EARLY YEARS AND EDUCATION

In his old age, John D. Rockefeller, Sr. grew thinner, and his face took on the appearance of an ancient bird. He seemed to

John D. Rockefeller, Sr., in September 1911. Courtesy of the Rockefeller Archive Center.

epitomize the Baptist maxims of frugality, temperance, and respectability by which he lived. Who could have imagined that Rockefeller was in fact the son of an earthy, fiddle-playing, itinerant patent medicine salesman who abandoned his first wife and children to marry bigamously under the assumed name "Dr. Levingston"?

The signs that William Rockefeller would not be a faithful husband to Eliza Rockefeller were abundantly apparent. In 1839, John D. Rockefeller was born in the small upstate village of Richford, New York, which was also the year that William Rockefeller's mistress gave birth to the first of John Rockefeller's illegitimate stepsisters. If the boy was not blessed with family stability, he grew up in an era rich in opportunity for those able to see it. By 1855, the habitually absent "Doc" Rockefeller had departed for good, leaving the care of Eliza Rockefeller, as well as four younger brothers and sisters, to his exceptionally serious, sixteen-year-old eldest son. By then, the family had relocated to Cleve-

land, Ohio, and John Rockefeller, a tall, bony boy, set out to make his fortune.

He had no personal connections in Ohio, no money, and only the training in penmanship, double-entry bookkeeping, and commercial law that a three-month course at a proprietary business "college" had provided. Still, Rockefeller made up in ambition what he lacked in tangible assets. He was a striving young man in the right place at the right time and soon found employment as a clerk. In the late 1850s, Cleveland was a bustling town about to boom. Immigrants from the Eastern seaboard and abroad poured into what soon became a Midwestern transportation hub—with connections to Lake Erie and the Ohio Canal.

By the outbreak of the Civil War, Rockefeller was no longer a clerk. He was already a partner in a Cleveland wholesale produce company, and, like many other prominent nineteenth-century Americans, had hired a substitute for $300 and did not serve in the Union Army. Rather, staying in Cleveland, he grew rich as a military supplier. In 1864, he married Laura Spelman, a fellow Baptist from a reform-minded abolitionist family. "Cettie" Rockefeller would remain his beloved wife for the next fifty-one years, bearing him one son and four daughters. By 1865, he had expanded his investments to include oil. At war's end, he was well positioned to invest even more money into oil refining.

CAREER HIGHLIGHTS

Throughout his life, Rockefeller was a man blessed with good timing. He invested in the wholesale food business on the eve of a war that would cause the value of his inventory to soar. In like fashion, he saw opportunities, also boosted by the Civil War, in a new fuel for interior lighting. The sectional conflict had disrupted the whaling industry, doubling prices and curtailing the North's ready access to southern turpentine. Kerosene, a derivate of petroleum, filled the gap. It was a northern product, abundant in Pennsylvania.

John D. Rockefeller convinced his brother William Rockefeller and fellow Clevelanders

Henry Flagler and Stephen Harkness that the oil business had a bright future. Indeed, it did. By the turn of the new century, John D. Rockefeller and his associates were among America's richest men. As the head of Standard Oil, Rockefeller helped forge one of the world's first great multinational corporations, emphasizing that the key to success was control of all phases of production, from the refinery to the retailer. In 1910, when the U.S. Supreme Court determined that the Standard Oil empire acted illegally to restrain trade, the company was one of country's biggest and most powerful. The corporation was worth at least $660 million, able to produce 40,000 barrels of refined oil per day, and in possession of hundreds of thousands of miles of company-owned pipelines as well as a fleet of 100 tankers that supplied a huge world market. Ironically, Standard Oil's dissolution, which split the trust into thirty newly created, independent companies, made its founder the world's wealthiest man, as the formerly closed corporation's heirs began trading stock on Wall Street.

MAJOR PHILANTHROPIC CONTRIBUTIONS

Rockefeller had always taken religious admonishments to charity seriously. Even as a young man, he gave generously, especially to Baptist missions and to efforts to improve economic and educational opportunities for freed slaves in the defeated South. However, in midcareer, and at midlife, he decided to impose the broad vision and organizational structure that had made Standard Oil an industrial colossus on his benevolence as well.

Once again, timing was crucial. By the time he retired from business, Rockefeller was almost sixty years old but also a seasoned corporate in-fighter, ruthlessly successful, and eerily calm in the face of crisis. He brought all the skills acquired as the founder of a corporate empire to the creation of an equally influential group of incorporated philanthropies. Like many other Big Business philanthropists, he too had felt hounded by pleas for help, but unlike most others, he had

another motivation for placing his capital in charitable foundations. They gave him a crucial arm's-length distance at a time when he was one of America's most notorious capitalist tycoons.

In the early twentieth century, the philanthropic foundation was still a novel device, structured on a business model, with a board of trustees, a managerial staff, and a government-issued charter. Until the 1880s, states remained leery of the new economic institution, demanding that any corporate charter state the nature of the business enterprise in detail. The idea that a charter could be granted to a corporation that did not seek to make a profit only gained legislative acceptance after 1900. Rockefeller was among the first to make large-scale use of the incorporated foundation and declare that his purpose was to solve national and world problems (scientific giving), not ameliorate individual suffering.

Until a major reorganization in 1928–1929, which merged many of the Rockefeller philanthropies under the umbrella of the Rockefeller Foundation, the six most important Rockefeller foundations operated independently. The Rockefeller Institute for Medical Research, the General Education Board, the Laura Spelman Rockefeller Memorial, the International Health Board (successor to the Rockefeller Sanitary Commission), the International Education Board, and the Rockefeller Foundation itself helped set the agendas and policies of educational and medical institutions for much of the twentieth century. Unlike his presumed rival, **Andrew Carnegie**, Rockefeller never sat as a managing member of any board he created. In fact, he made a point of never attending meetings of any of his foundations. This action did not signal disinterest, but rather a conviction that a philanthropist should launch programs with the hope of their eventual complete independence, a task Rockefeller felt could best be accomplished through trusted surrogates and experts, such as chief aides Frederick T. Gates and Abraham Flexner.

The Rockefeller philanthropies promoted the selective improvement of a restricted number of good schools, seeking to make them models for future private and public institutions. The idea worked best at the college level, where scientific giving helped shatter the reputation of American universities as inferior to those in Europe. The University of Chicago, which Rockefeller co-founded with a gift of $600,000, was just the best known of several universities around the country that quickly reached world-class status with the help of Rockefeller's deep pockets. This funding also came with demands. By the 1930s, higher and professional education had been transformed. Schools, which had emphasized Greek and Latin in 1900, now offered the elective system pioneered at Rockefeller-supported universities like Chicago and Yale. Students took a wide range of required courses, and then declared a "major"—often in a new discipline, like sociology or psychology, promoted by the Laura Spelman Memorial and other Rockefeller foundations. In league with the Carnegie Corporation and Carnegie Foundation for the Advancement of Teaching, Rockefeller philanthropy endorsed more rigorous and standardized training for the professions.

This was especially true in medicine, the second focus for Rockefeller's benefactions. Rockefeller philanthropy's partnership with medicine was its most important achievement. The Rockefeller Institute for Medical Research, founded in 1901, was the first American institution devoted to pure research in biological sciences. It quickly became one of the world's premier facilities. After 1965, the Rockefeller Institute became Rockefeller University, but remained a magnet for some of the best scientists in the world.

Under Rockefeller sponsorship, hundreds of medical discoveries, from vaccines to prevent yellow fever to maps of the nervous system, enhanced a growing American reputation for research leadership in biomedical sciences. Moreover, from the American South to China, Rockefeller philanthropies encouraged the translation of medical innovation into public health practice. The

Rockefeller Sanitary Commission and the International Health Board led campaigns that defeated several water- and fecal-borne parasitic diseases. It was a fittingly ironic achievement for the man whose feckless father had traveled the backroads of New York state and Ohio in the nineteenth century selling useless "cures" for many of the same ailments.

CONCLUSION

By his death in 1937, John D. Rockefeller, Sr. split his enormous fortune roughly in half—giving $540 million to charity and $500 million to his family, principally his only son, **John D. Rockefeller, Jr.** Each of these sums was equivalent to at least $5 billion in late-twentieth-century calculations. As a businessman, Rockefeller concentrated his energies on the oil business, revolutionizing the structures of world commerce. As a philanthropist, he focused on American education and medicine, greatly altering both.

Judith Sealander

FURTHER READING

Berliner, Howard. *A System of Scientific Medicine: Philanthropic Foundations in the Flexner Era.* New York: Tavistock, 1985.

Chernow, Ron. *Titan: The Life of John D. Rockefeller, Sr.* New York: Random House, 1998.

Collier, Peter, and David Horowitz. *The Rockefellers: An American Dynasty.* New York: Scribner, 1976.

Corner, George. *A History of the Rockefeller Institute, 1901–1953.* New York: Rockefeller Institute Press, 1964.

Ettling, John. *The Germ of Laziness: Rockefeller Philanthropy and Public Health in the New South.* Cambridge, MA: Harvard University Press, 1988.

Fosdick, Raymond. *The Story of the Rockefeller Foundation.* New Brunswick, NJ: Transaction Publishers, 1989.

Harr, John Ensor, and Peter Johnson. *The Rockefeller Century: Three Generations of America's Greatest Family.* New York: Scribner, 1988.

Sealander, Judith. *Private Wealth and Public Life: Foundation Philanthropy and the Reshaping of American Social Policy from the Progressive Era through the New Deal.* Baltimore: Johns Hopkins University Press, 1997.

PAPERS

The Rockefeller Archive Center (Sleepy Hollow, NY) houses a number of personal papers and organizational archives useful to gain insights into the life of John D. Rockefeller, Sr. Among the most important: General Files: Offices of the Messrs. Rockefeller, Papers of John D. Rockefeller, Sr., Papers of William Rockefeller, Records of the General Education Board, Records of the Laura Spelman Rockefeller Memorial, Records of the Rockefeller Foundation, and Records of the Rockefeller Sanitary Commission for the Eradication of Hookworm Disease.

ROCKEFELLER FAMILY

John D. Rockefeller, Jr. (1874–1960)

Founder of the Bureau of Social Hygiene, International Education Board, and Several Other Philanthropic Institutions

Abby Aldrich Rockefeller (1874–1948)

Art Collector and Patron and Cofounder of Museum of Modern Art

John D. Rockefeller 3rd (1906–1978)

Founder of JDR 3rd Fund, Population Council, and Several Other Philanthropies

ALSO MENTIONED:

Abby "Babs" Rockefeller Mauzé (1903–1976)

Founder of the Greenacre Foundation

Nelson A. Rockefeller (1908–1979)

Governor of the State of New York, Art Collector and Patron, Founder of the Museum of Primitive Art, and Several Other Philanthropies

Laurance S. Rockefeller
(1910–   )

Venture Capitalist and Environmentalist

Winthrop Rockefeller (1912–1973)

Rancher and Governor of Arkansas

David Rockefeller (1915–   )

Bank Executive, International Businessman, and Civic Leader

Peggy Dulany (1947–)

Founder of Synergos Institute

INTRODUCTION

"Giving," John D. Rockefeller, Jr. wrote to his biographer, "is the secret of a healthy life—not necessarily money, but whatever a man has of encouragement and sympathy and understanding" (Fosdick 1956, 414). His sometimes-wayward son, Winthrop Rockefeller, would write to his own son in a similar vein: "I have enjoyed the personal use of money. But I have gotten the greatest satisfaction from using it to advance my beliefs in human relations—human values. . . . The biggest returns from the investment of money come in what we can call philanthropic achievements, in the encouragement of people who make our business grow, making jobs and security for others, and in the development of men, their happiness, their usefulness and their freedom" (Winthrop Rockefeller, "A Letter to My Son," n.d., unpublished manuscript, 5–6).

For members of the Rockefeller family, charity and philanthropic giving have been essential duties, part of a set of basic human values transmitted from generation to generation. **John D. Rockefeller, Sr**. imparted a philanthropic legacy to his only son, John D. Rockefeller, Jr.; he and his wife, Abby Aldrich Rockefeller, deepened the tradition as they passed it to their six children. By the year 2000, a fifth generation of Rockefellers had become active philanthropists. Accepting an award on behalf of the five Rockefeller brothers in 1967, John D. Rockefeller 3rd, the eldest brother, described this process of transmission. He noted that his grandfather and father "bequeathed to us not only our name and material resources, but also certain basic values":

> Several of these values have given shape and meaning to philanthropy to me. One of them is a sense of responsibility, of considering the resources passed on to us as a trust. Our task was to grow into this responsibility, to develop the ability to manage this trust in active efforts to promote human welfare.
>
> Another value is the importance of being relevant to the problem and needs of one's time. One could be very busy as a philanthropist, and yet be relatively ineffectual. Thus, fifty years ago, the dominant concerns of philanthropy were health and welfare. Today, they are in such areas as overpopulation, urban decay, civil rights, conservation, the arts.
>
> A third value is to give of one's self. We were taught that it is not enough to give only of one's name or material resources. One must also become involved personally, to contribute one's time and thought and energy. To me, this is the spirit of giving. And I know of no other way to stay relevant and be effective (Harr and Johnson 1988, 6–7)

Perhaps no other American family has sustained such an active tradition of philanthropy over so many generations. The Rockefellers have done so in part by creating institutions to help the members of each successive generation grow into the role of an active philanthropist and to foster the values of responsibility, relevance, and personal involvement.

JOHN D. ROCKEFELLER, JR.

John D. Rockefeller, Jr. (JDR, Jr.) was born in Cleveland, Ohio, on January 29, 1874, the fourth child and only son born to Laura Spelman Rockefeller and John D. Rockefeller, Sr., the founder of the Standard Oil Company. In 1874, the elder Rockefeller was in the process of consolidating the oil industry in America and building one of the nation's largest fortunes. In 1884, the family moved to New York City, where JDR, Jr. attended several schools, the most important of

John D. Rockefeller, Sr., and his grandchildren, c. 1916. Standing in the back row from left are Abby; John D. Rockefeller, Jr.; and John D. Rockefeller 3rd. Seated from left are Laurance; John D. Rockefeller, Sr., holding David, Winthrop; Abby Aldrich Rockefeller (John D., Jr.'s wife); and Nelson. Courtesy of the Rockefeller Archive Center.

which was the Browning School (1889–1893). His devout Baptist parents instilled in him "values of thrift, sobriety, aloofness from worldly temptations, and individual responsibility for salvation" (Harr and Johnson, 1988, 39). Laura Rockefeller took charge of her son's character development, instructing him in his religious duties and moral obligations, and protecting him as much as possible from temptations toward sin and sloth. His father introduced his son to the world in ways that reinforced religious and moral teachings. At an early age, he involved his son and daughters in charitable giving by reading to them the letters of appeal that he received, and he encouraged them to make charitable donations to needy causes from their allowances.

When he entered Brown University in 1893, JDR, Jr. possessed a contemplative religious temperament and self-discipline, but he was shy and ill at ease socially. By the time he graduated in 1897, his perspective on the world and his place in it had been enlarged.

JDR, Jr. worked to improve his social skills; met and courted his future wife; and came under the influence of the school's president, E. Benjamin Andrews, a progressive social reformer who challenged the limited world view of the young Rockefeller and encouraged him to become involved in the social issues of his day. Following his graduation in 1897, JDR, Jr. joined his father's office. Although he was given no clear role or specific duties, he was expected to learn how to handle business and philanthropic matters for his father. He soon found that he had little stomach for the business side of his father's interests and, following a nervous collapse in 1904, decided to devote his efforts to philanthropy.

JDR, Jr.'s education in philanthropy continued under the tutelage of the second progressive thinker to influence his life, the Rev. Frederick T. Gates, who had become his father's chief advisor in philanthropy and some business matters. A minister who had been a successful fundraiser for Baptist causes, Gates brought a scientific point of view to social problems, to religion, and to philanthropy. He sought to manage Rockefeller's giving according to the guidelines the elder Rockefeller had elaborated but also to administer it scientifically to make it more effective. Gates wanted philanthropy to do more than relieve misery and distress temporarily: scientifically applied, philanthropy should seek to cure problems at their root cause. He urged the elder Rockefeller to practice "wholesale," not "retail," philanthropy: to establish philanthropic institutions staffed by experts that would attack problems intelligently and systematically, rather than giving to a number of institutions that would only treat the symptoms that a problem caused. Convinced of the value of Gates's approach to philanthropy, JDR, Jr. worked with Gates to persuade the elder Rockefeller to create several major institutions with his increasing personal wealth: the Rockefeller Institute for Medical Research in 1901, the General Education Board in 1903, the Rockefeller Sanitary Commission for the Eradication of Hookworm Disease in 1909, and the Rockefeller Foundation in 1913. JDR, Jr. served as a trustee of each of these organizations and shaped each to a greater or lesser degree over the next several decades. Meanwhile, the philanthropic office that Gates created for the elder Rockefeller in the Standard Oil building in Manhattan (and later housed at Rockefeller Center) was the beginning of a family institution that would provide an expert staff for JDR, Jr., and subsequent generations, to draw upon for advice and counsel. As JDR, Jr.'s sons began their careers, this office also served as training ground in philanthropy.

The transfer of wealth from John D. Rockefeller, Sr. to his son was a gradual process that took place largely between 1916, when the cautious elder Rockefeller was seventy-seven and his son forty-two, and 1921. By 1922, when the transfer was completed, JDR, Jr.'s net worth was about $500 million. JDR, Jr.'s first foray into philanthropy on his own came as a result of his

service as foreman of a grand jury investigating organized prostitution in New York City in 1910. When JDR, Jr. realized that the grand jury's hard work and investigations would produce little change from politicians or the police, he took the initiative to raise funds to support further research, as well as rehabilitation work among the victims of the "white slave trade."

In 1913, he established the Bureau of Social Hygiene for "the study, amelioration and prevention of those social conditions, crimes, and diseases which adversely affect the well-being of society, with special reference to prostitution and the evils associated therewith" (Bureau of Social Hygiene Articles of Incorporation, The Rockefeller Archive Center). Before it closed in 1940, the bureau studied and made policy recommendations about narcotics, police corruption, criminology, crime reporting, penology, juvenile delinquency, and other aspects of social hygiene. The bureau was a pioneer among the new organizations that brought the spirit of progressive, scientific research into new areas of social reform. It enhanced understanding and treatment of behaviors considered outside the social norm or detrimental to public health. Rockefeller money and the bureau supported the research of prison reformer Katharine Bement Davis at the Laboratory of Social Hygiene, New York State Reformatory for Women at Bedford Hills, and it advocated for publicly supported sex education as a public health measure, publishing and distributing such informational booklets as *Social Hygiene vs. the Social Plagues*. It also supported basic research into human sexuality, funding the Committee for Research in Problems of Sex through 1933 and funding the research that resulted in Davis's highly influential book, *Factors in the Sex Life of Twenty-two Hundred Women* (1929). The Bureau also quietly provided support for **Margaret Sanger**'s work on birth control.

JDR, Jr.'s increasing interest in social welfare stemmed in part from a tragedy in Colorado, where miners from thirty companies went on strike in 1913. The Rockefellers held a controlling interest in the largest company involved, the Colorado Fuel and Iron Company, and JDR, Jr. was a member of the board of directors. On April 20, 1914, two weeks after he had strongly supported management's view of the strike in testimony before a congressional subcommittee, a furious battle between strikers and the National Guard resulted in the deaths of two women and eleven children at a miners' camp in Ludlow. Not only did JDR, Jr. become the focus of criticism and the recipient of death threats as a result of the "Ludlow massacre," but he began to take more clear-cut and independent action on his own to ensure that he received adequate information about business and social affairs, and to take more of an active role as a civic leader on social issues. He hired a public relations man, Ivy Lee, to both provide him with information and help him respond to the public. He also brought in an expert on labor-management relations, W.L. MacKenzie King, to help him respond to the strike at Colorado Fuel and Iron. In September and October 1915, the three men traveled to Colorado to meet with the miners and to unveil their forward-looking "industrial representation plan" for the company, which the employees approved overwhelmingly. Since the plan had been developed under the auspices of the Rockefeller Foundation, it appeared to the public as though "the Rockefellers were using monies placed in a trust to bail themselves out of a personal problem" (Harr and Johnson 1988, 144). As a result of this controversy, the Rockefeller Foundation was reorganized to operate independently from the family, although JDR, Jr. and family advisors continued as trustees.

JDR, Jr. created several other philanthropic organizations on his own: the International Education Board (1923), the Davison Fund (1934), and the Sealantic Fund (1938), and he helped his sons by endowing their foundation, the Rockefeller Brothers Fund in 1952. Rockefeller's biographers estimate that JDR, Jr.'s total giving amounted to $537 million, of which $192.2 million went to the aforementioned foundations. The International Education Board may represent the most significant foundation he created. Between 1923 and 1928, the International Education Board promoted the development of science and agriculture in thirty-nine countries and allowed more than 600 promising scholars and scientists to pursue additional studies with leaders in their fields.

Rockefeller did not channel all of his philanthropic giving through foundations, however, and his personal philanthropy ranged across the country and around the world. His causes varied widely, from gifts to colleges and universities ($58.4 million in America, $13.2 million abroad) to support for churches and religious organizations ($71.7 million), especially the promotion of liberal religious thought and ecumenism (unity and cooperation among religious groups), such as the founding of Riverside Church in New York City. His support for conservation and the development of national parks ($44.4 million), such as Acadia in Maine and the Grand Teton National Park, led analyst Stephen Fox to call him "the most generous philanthropist in the history of conservation" (Winks 1997, 75). He also funded the restoration of three French landmarks damaged or neglected during World War I, Rheims Cathedral and the buildings and gardens at Versailles and Fontainbleau ($2.5 million), and the restoration and preservation of historic sites in the United States ($63.3 million) through such organizations as Colonial Williamsburg, Inc., in Virginia and Sleepy Hollow Restorations (now Historic Hudson Valley—three of whose four historic properties are in Westchester County, New York). Libraries and museums ($35.1 million), cultural organizations ($12.1 million), hospitals ($11.8 million), and relief agencies ($9.5 million) also received Rockefeller's financial assistance. Another $22.8 million went to a variety of "miscellaneous" causes, such as housing developments for working-class people, the temperance movement (until

Prohibition proved to be a failure), Alcoholics Anonymous, and the National Urban League.

JDR, Jr. did not simply offer money in support of causes that he valued; he often offered his time and energy in fund-raising campaigns for such organizations as the United War Work Campaign during World War I and the United Negro College Fund created by **Frederick Douglass Patterson**. On July 8, 1941, in a radio broadcast appeal on behalf of the United Service Organizations and the National War Fund, he offered a concise statement of his philosophy that was widely reprinted under the title "I Believe":

I believe in the supreme worth of the individual and in his right to life, liberty, and the pursuit of happiness.

I believe that every right implies a responsibility; every opportunity, an obligation; every possession, a duty.

I believe that the law was made for man and not man for the law; that government is the servant of the people and not their master.

I believe in the dignity of labor, whether with head or hand; that the world owes no man a living but that it owes every man an opportunity to make a living.

I believe that thrift is essential to well ordered living and that economy is a prime requisite of a sound financial structure, whether in government, business or personal affairs.

I believe that truth and justice are fundamental to an enduring social order.

I believe in the sacredness of a promise, that a man's word should be as good as his bond; that character—not wealth or power or position—is of supreme worth.

I believe that the rendering of useful service is the common duty of mankind and that only in the purifying fire of sacrifice is the dross of selfishness consumed and the greatness of the human soul set free.

I believe in an all-wise and all-loving God, named by whatever name, and that the individual's highest fulfillment, greatest happiness, and widest usefulness are to be found in living in harmony with His will.

I believe that love is the greatest thing in the world; that it alone can overcome hate; that right can and will triumph over might. (*The Story of Rockefeller Center* 1987, 37)

Rockefeller died in Tucson, Arizona, on May 11, 1960. In 1962, his creed was inscribed on a commemorative plaque at Rockefeller Center, where the words continue to inspire visitors from around the world.

ABBY ALDRICH ROCKEFELLER

On October 9, 1901, after a lengthy courtship, John D. Rockefeller, Jr. and Abby Greene Aldrich were married in Warwick, Rhode Island. Born on October 26, 1874, to Abby Pearce Chapman and Nelson W. Aldrich, she had been educated at home by a Quaker governess until 1891, when she entered Miss Abbott's School for Young Ladies. She pursued its rigorous academic courses until 1893, when she made her debut and continued her education at the lyceum (an educational institution that provided lectures, discussions, and concerts), in her father's library, and at Europe's museums and historic sites. She also worked on behalf of several social welfare institutions in Providence and, as her mother retired from public life, assumed the role of hostess for her father, a powerful U.S. senator from Rhode Island.

The self-confident, outgoing bride complemented and relaxed her retiring, earnest husband. She was not awed by the Rockefeller wealth or put off by the Baptist rectitude; she took both in stride and seemed to humanize both. The couple had six children, for whom she supplied the affection and joy while JDR, Jr. was the loving but stern disciplinarian, teaching thrift and attention to detail by auditing the children's account books to make sure each had reconciled allowance income and earnings with expenditures. Abby Rockefeller laughed off his suggestion that she keep an account book as well.

During World War I, Abby Rockefeller renewed her interests in social welfare, working with the Red Cross to provide bandages and clothing for soldiers at the front and working on housing for women war workers through the YWCA. As the chairperson of the housing committee of the YWCA's War Work Council, she led efforts to build demonstration housing for women workers, opening the first in Charleston, South Carolina. After the war, affordable housing for women became one of her personal philanthropic concerns. As chairperson of the YWCA's Emergency Housing Committee, she worked to develop "a very much enlarged and perfected rooms registry, more and better boarding homes for young girls in shops and industry, hotels for business women and players houses for the girls of the stage" (Kert 1993, 179). She also chaired the YWCA's committee that built the Grace Dodge Hotel for business and professional women in Washington, DC, in 1921–1922. In 1919–1920, she used some of her own funds as well as a contribution from JDR, Jr. to build Bayway Cottage, a model home for a working family in Elizabeth, New Jersey, near a Standard Oil plant. Beginning in 1928, the cottage was expanded into a community center with meeting rooms, clinics, a nursery school, and recreational facilities. Abby Rockefeller's total contribution to the project was estimated at $200,000 over twenty years. Like her husband, she gave not only her money, but her time, energy, and leadership to projects that interested her.

Abby Rockefeller shared her father's passionate interest in art, and she became JDR, Jr.'s unofficial aesthetic consultant on a variety of projects, including his construction of a home for his father near Tarrytown, New York, which became known as Kykuit; the restoration of Colonial Williamsburg; and the construction of Rockefeller Center. Nonetheless, her husband did not share her passion for modern art, which she began to collect in 1924, or her devotion to the Museum of Modern Art, which she helped to organize in 1929 with Lillie Bliss and Mary Sullivan. As treasurer, she raised funds for the new museum. As an active art collector, she acquired drawings, watercolors and prints that she donated to its collections. Her commitment to the museum earned her husband's respect and support for the institution at crucial points in its development, including the donation of family land for expansion, but his hostility to modern art itself never waned. In addition to modern art, Abby also collected folk art and gave her extensive collection to Colonial Williamsburg in 1939.

THE BROTHERS' GENERATION

In 1934, imminent changes in the tax law regarding gift and estate taxes prompted JDR, Jr. to begin the transfer of wealth to his children earlier than he had planned. He established seven trusts, one each for his wife and six children, which provided them with an income during their lifetime, enabled his sons—after the age of thirty—to draw from the trusts' capital with the approval of the appointed trustees, and provided a tax-free inheritance for his grandchildren. As Rockefeller family historians John Ensor Harr and Peter J. Johnson note, the creation of these trusts resolved a dilemma JDR, Jr. faced by "taking advantage of the tax incentive and hedging against possible future tax increases by transferring assets out of his hands, yet guarding against his deep fear of irresponsible spending by his heirs in the restrictions that could be placed in the deeds of trust" (Harr and Johnson 1988, 358).

With varying degrees of intensity, the daughter and five sons of JDR, Jr. and Abby Aldrich Rockefeller used their wealth to pursue their own philanthropic interests. Abby "Babs" Rockefeller Mauzé disappointed her father by not showing sustained interest in philanthropy, but she joined her brothers in the work of the Rockefeller Brothers Fund in 1955 and contributed to established Rockefeller concerns, including planned parenthood programs, the Rockefeller University, and Memorial Sloan-Kettering Cancer Center, giving the latter an estimated $8.8 million over twenty years. She also was an officer and financial supporter of the Rehearsal Club, a New York City institution that provided housing for young women pursuing careers in the performing arts. Her most distinctive philanthropic endeavor was the creation of the Greenacre Foundation (1968), which developed Greenacre Park on East 51st Street in Manhattan in 1971.

Nelson A. Rockefeller had several careers, including expanding the family's tradition of public service into politics as governor of New York (1959–1973) and vice president of the United States (1974–1977). As a philanthropist, art and Latin America were his specialties. In 1932, he joined his mother as one of the leaders of the Museum of Modern Art; besides being a lifelong trustee (1932–1979), he also served as treasurer (1935–1939), and as president twice (1939–1941, 1946–1953). Nelson Rockefeller also established his own art collection. In 1954, he founded the Museum of Primitive Art in New York City. At the end of 1974, he closed the museum and transferred the 3,300 pieces of art, the library, and photographic archives to the Metropolitan Museum of Art for its Michael C. Rockefeller Wing, named for his son who disappeared in New Guinea while collecting indigenous art.

Nelson Rockefeller began a lifelong interest in the social and economic welfare of Latin America in 1937, when, as a director of Creole Petroleum, the Venezuelan subsidiary of Standard Oil, he visited several countries in South America. He fell in love with the peoples, their cultures, and the land, but he was dismayed by the way in which U.S. businessmen distanced themselves from the local population. He returned to New York and lectured Standard Oil executives on the social responsibilities of business: "The only justification for ownership is that it serves the broad interests of the people. We must recognize the social responsibilities of corporations and the corporation must use its ownership of assets to reflect the best interests of the people. If we don't they will take away our ownership" (Reich 1996, 169).

During the 1940s, he turned to government, philanthropy, and business organizations in an attempt to improve relations between the United States and Latin American nations and the social and economic welfare of Latin Americans, but also to counter Naziism and Soviet communism's impact on the region. President Franklin D. Roosevelt appointed Nelson Rockefeller to be the Coordinator of Inter-American Affairs in 1940 and he became Assistant Secretary of State for American Republic Affairs in 1944. In 1946, Nelson Rockefeller established the American International Association for Economic and Social Development (AIA) as a philanthropy to promote "self-development and better standards of living together with understanding and cooperation" in Latin America (Dalrymple 1968, 10). The following year, he created a for-profit corporation, the International Basic Economy Corporation (IBEC). The articles of incorporation included a preamble that made its mission— "promote the economic development of various parts of the world . . . increase the production and availability of goods, things and services useful to the lives or livelihood of people," and "better the standards of living" (Reich 1996, 408)—seem more like that of a philanthropy than a business to some people. Both organizations worked most intensively in Venezuela and Brazil. Rockefeller served as president of the AIA and IBEC until 1953, when he accepted an appointment from President Dwight D. Eisenhower as Undersecretary of the Department of Health, Education, and Welfare. IBEC developed businesses in a variety of industries, including agricultural services, housing, manufacturing, wholesale and retail food distribution, and investment banking, while AIA worked on rural economic development and education, forming partnerships with more than 230 organizations and government departments in thirty countries and enrolling more than 160,000 members in rural youth clubs. When it ceased operations in 1968, AIA left behind self-sufficient vocational education programs in Venezuela and Chile and agricultural development programs in Venezuela and Brazil.

Laurance S. Rockefeller, a venture capitalist, made his philanthropic mark in cancer research and as a conservationist, both fields in which his father had been involved. In 1947, Laurance Rockefeller joined the board of the Memorial Hospital for Cancer and Allied Diseases and, in 1949, was elected to the board of the Sloan-Kettering Institute for Cancer Research. A proponent of the consolidation of cancer research, cancer treatment, and cancer education, he became chairman of the reorganized Memorial Sloan-Kettering Cancer Center (MSKCC) in 1960 and embarked upon a campaign for the integration and expansion of its services and facilities. By 1973, a successful fund-raising campaign transformed MSKCC into "the largest privately operated non-profit institution in the country dedicated to the conquest of cancer," with a 565-bed hospital and a staff that included 200 scientists and 300 physicians (Moscow 1977, 317). In addition to increasing resources and support for MSKCC, Laurance Rockefeller also joined forces with Mary Lasker, Elmer H. Bobst, and Benno C. Schmidt to make a cure for cancer a national public policy priority. The four successfully lobbied both President Richard Nixon and the U.S. Congress to increase annual federal funding for cancer research.

Assuming his father's role in conservation and national park development, Laurance Rockefeller was affiliated with more than fifty organizations devoted to conservation, the earliest being the New York Zoological Society (trustee 1935–1986), the Palisades Interstate Park Commission (1939–1979), and Jackson Hole Preserve, Inc. (beginning as president in 1940). He also founded the American Conservation Association, Inc. (1958), the Grand Teton Lodge Company (1956), the Woodstock Foundation (1968), and was cofounder of the Conservation Foundation (1948), which eventually merged with the World Wildlife Fund. He played major roles in the development or growth of the National Park Trust Fund (later the National Park Foundation), Resources for the Future, Inc., and the American Committee for International Wildlife

Protection. He also purchased the land that became the core of the Virgin Islands National Park and helped to expand Haleakala National Park on the Hawaiian Island of Maui. While "the physical impact of his work has been enormous," historian Robin Winks has argued that Laurance Rockefeller's "most lasting influence . . . on America's landscape" may be in raising its status as a public policy issue, for "his persistence in espousing reasonable change within the system helped move concern for nature from obscurity to a full place on the cabinet table, the congressional caucuses, and the corporate board rooms without the rancor of revolution" (Winks 1997, 204).

Winthrop Rockefeller, viewed by some as the "black sheep" of his generation, contributed money and time to a number of philanthropic projects that the family favored, but by 1953 he needed a change of scenery and settled permanently in Arkansas. He bought land on the Petit Jean Mountain and established Winrock Farms; he also undertook several philanthropic projects to promote the development of education and public health in Arkansas, creating the Rockwin Fund in 1956 (renamed the Winthrop Rockefeller Foundation in 1974) to fund such projects. By 1966, his charitable donations in Arkansas totaled more than $8 million. In 1955, Governor Orval Faubus appointed him to lead the new Arkansas Industrial Development Commission; during his tenure (1955–1964), the state enjoyed a period of industrial growth, with the construction of 600 new industrial plants and the creation of more than 90,000 jobs. Service on this commission led him to run for governor, and in 1966 he won election as the first Republican governor of Arkansas since the Reconstruction era; he won reelection in 1968 but lost a bid for a third term in 1970. As governor, Winthrop Rockefeller had some legislative victories that modernized state government and raised taxes modestly, and he increased the presence of African Americans in politics and state government. He had, however, less success with prison reform and other efforts to fight corruption in government. He died from cancer in 1973, and in his will he challenged the trustees of his estate to be "venturesome and innovative" in using his bequest to develop institutions to help people help themselves (*Winrock International Annual Report* 1988, 48, The Rockefeller Archive Center). The trustees responded in 1975 by creating the Winrock International Livestock Research and Training Center, focusing on research and training in farming. In 1985, it merged with two other Rockefeller-related agricultural programs—John D. Rockefeller 3rd's Agricultural Development Council and the Rockefeller Foundation's International Agricultural Development Service—to create the Winrock International Institute for Agricultural Development. Winrock International now describes its goal as "to increase economic opportunity, sustain natural resources, and protect the environment" (*Winrock International Annual Report* 1999, Inside Front Cover, The Rockefeller Archive Center).

David Rockefeller made his career in banking and economics, becoming president of the Chase Manhattan Bank, but he had varied interests in philanthropy. He joined the board of trustees of the Rockefeller Institute for Medical Research in 1940 and, as chairman, oversaw its transformation into Rockefeller University. He took a special interest in foreign affairs, joining the Council on Foreign Relations in 1941, participating in the annual Bilderberg meeting of international leaders, and forming the Trilateral Commission in 1973, which brings together leaders from North America, Europe, and Japan to recommend policies that would promote economic and political cooperation between these regions. He made New York City a special focus of his philanthropic leadership. He spurred efforts to revitalize both Lower Manhattan's financial district and the Morningside Heights neighborhood. Following the urban unrest of the mid-1960s, David Rockefeller was among the civic leaders in New York City who founded the Urban Coalition to deal with problems of social inequality, due to racial discrimination in employment and housing, that the riots made

apparent. He further undertook efforts to promote various kinds of philanthropic work among his colleagues in business, including the Business Committee for the Arts in 1966—to foster more corporate patronage of the arts—and the International Executive Service Corps in 1964. The latter, sponsored by 126 corporations and nicknamed "the paunch corps," in contrast to the youthful Peace Corps, encouraged business executives, especially those in retirement, to volunteer their services and become unpaid advisors for businesses in the developing world that needed managerial and entrepreneurial expertise. Its mission was in keeping with David Rockefeller's favorite theme: "the social responsibility of the capitalistic system" (Moscow 1977, 239).

JOHN D. ROCKEFELLER 3RD

John D. Rockefeller 3rd (JDR 3rd) was more closely associated with philanthropy than his siblings. As the first-born male heir of JDR, Jr., JDR 3rd was expected to join his father in the family office and to take on many of his projects. He actively pursued philanthropy as a career: partly as a family obligation but also because he understood philanthropy as an effective means of meeting social needs and fostering understanding among the people of the world.

John D. Rockefeller 3rd was born in New York City. JDR, Jr. was a stern, formal, and moralizing father, and his oldest son reflected more of his father's influence than that of his mother. As a youngster, in the words of his biographers, he was "frail, excessively serious, . . . shy and self-conscious, overburdened with a sense of responsibility, and, above all, driven to please his father" (Harr and Johnson 1991, 10). He began his education at age six at the Roger Ascham School; after three years there, he moved to the exclusive but progressive Browning School for the next four years, then left New York City for a year at the Harvey School in Hawthorne, New York, and the next year at the Pine Lodge School in Lakewood, New Jersey. As his prep school, JDR 3rd attended the

Loomis Institute in Windsor, Connecticut, graduating in 1925. At Princeton University (1925–1929), he focused on economics courses dealing with government, international affairs, and labor; his senior thesis was "Industrial Relations Plans: A Study." He also took numerous classes in art, which he had considered as a major.

Following graduation in 1929, JDR 3rd spent several months traveling around the world. On December 2, 1929, the day after his return to New York, JDR 3rd began work at the family office, starting his apprenticeship to his father. In 1928, even before his graduation from Princeton University, his father put him on the boards of the Bureau of Social Hygiene and the Dunbar National Bank; in 1929, he took a seat on the boards of the New York International House and Industrial Relations Counselors and was named secretary of both the China Medical Board and Riverside Church. He subsequently became a trustee of the Rockefeller Foundation and the General Education Board in 1931 and the Rockefeller Institute for Medical Research and the Community Service Society in 1932. Against his father's advice, he accepted an invitation to join his first board outside of the Rockefeller orbit, that of the American Museum of Natural History (1933). By 1940, he was serving on more than twenty boards.

On November 11, 1932, JDR 3rd married Blanchette Ferry Hooker. The couple had four children: Sandra (1935), John (1937), Hope (1938), and Alida (1949). Having experienced the burden of expectations associated with carrying the famous name of his grandfather and father, JDR 3rd purposely did not give his son the middle name of Davison or the numerical designation that would be next in line. He would allow the son, who was known as Jay, to make that decision for himself when he came of age, and Jay Rockefeller decided to take the name John Davison Rockefeller IV.

Military service during World War II hastened the end of JDR 3rd's prolonged apprenticeship to his father. Following Pearl Harbor, JDR 3rd took a management position with the Red Cross in Washington, DC, but he soon joined the Navy, where, after a year in personnel, he secured positions dealing with what he described as "political-military affairs" related to policies on military occupation of enemy land, relief and rehabilitation, and the return to civil authority and peace (Harr and Johnson 1991, 418). This experience in planning for the postwar era led him to think seriously about his own role; he ultimately resolved to devote his efforts to four goals: strengthening democracy in the United States; changing the direction of the Rockefeller Foundation toward helping poorer nations; improving government administration and personnel; and attacking the problem of overpopulation. After several years of frustration working on these goals, events in 1951–1952 held out the promise of success. His election as chairman of the board of trustees of the Rockefeller Foundation in 1952, for example, enabled him to promote his ideas there more forcefully.

In 1951, JDR 3rd was invited to travel to Japan as a member of the American mission— led by John Foster Dulles—to conclude a peace treaty with Japan. Rockefeller was invited to work on the cultural, educational, and informational aspects of future relations between the United States and Japan. His report from that trip included recommendations for both government action and private-sector initiatives, including cultural centers in each nation, at least one International House in Japan, an exchange program for intellectuals, and English-language instruction in Japan.

The mission trip seemed to give JDR 3rd greater confidence and spurred his philanthropy in new and independent directions as he set about creating programs to improve relations between Americans and the Japanese. He revived the waning Japan Society in 1952, and he and Blanchette Rockefeller initiated discussions with both the Metropolitan Museum of Art and the Museum of Modern Art about exhibitions of Japanese art. His successes in this area led him to expand his efforts to improve understanding between Americans and the peoples of other Asian countries. Thus, he established the Asia Society in 1956 and the Asian Cultural Program of the JDR 3rd Fund (1963–1979), which was continued as the Asian Cultural Council following the Fund's dissolution. To help improve living conditions within Asia, he founded the Council on Economic and Cultural Affairs (1953), which became the Agricultural Development Council in 1963; it sought to strengthen professional capacity within Asia to deal with problems of agriculture and rural development. In both the arts and agriculture, projects sponsored by JDR 3rd's philanthropy developed the talents and skills of Asians through training programs and travel opportunities, fostered the development of Asian organizations, sponsored American professionals' travel to Asia to teach and study, and contributed to cross-cultural awareness and appreciation by supporting the traveling performances and exhibitions of the Asian arts in the United States and the American arts in Asia. Between September 1963 and August 1975, for example, the Asian Cultural Program of the JDR 3rd Fund spent nearly $5.5 million on project, fellowship, research, and travel grants that involved 636 Asians and 217 Americans. "Can there ever be effective interdependence without the tolerance, the respect, and the admiration that comes from a sensitive understanding and appreciation of other cultures?" JDR 3rd asked in a review of his work in Asia. "The fostering of cultural relations can be a form of insurance for the future of this dangerous but exciting world" (*The JDR 3rd Fund and Asia, 1963–1975*, The Rockefeller Archive Center, 1977, 8–9).

As early as 1934, JDR 3rd had set his sights on birth control and population issues as one focus of his philanthropic energies. In 1952, he established the Population Council to conduct research in human fertility and reproductive science; to develop more effective, easy-to-use, and inexpensive contraceptive devices and procedures; and to provide technical assistance to underdeveloped countries in creating and implementing family planning programs. During the 1960s, JDR 3rd actively promoted family planning to leaders in the underdeveloped world and became a widely known public advocate for population control, raising awareness of the issue in the United States and around the world. Historian Donald Critchlow argues that JDR 3rd was "pivotal in bringing [the family planning] movement together and orchestrating the campaign to change federal policy" so that it gave greater priority to family planning in the 1960s and 1970s (Critchlow 1999, 4).

Concurrently, JDR 3rd's military service made him question the quality of government personnel. "It seems imperative that every effort [should] be made to encourage competent civilians to enter Federal service as a career and to stimulate the sustained interest, growth, and development of those already in service," he wrote in 1951 (Harr and Johnson 1991, 50–51). Toward this end, JDR 3rd established the Rockefeller Public Service Award in 1952. Administered by Princeton's Woodrow Wilson School of Public and International Affairs, this award provided support for government employees to take a sabbatical and pursue additional training. The successful program and JDR 3rd's lobbying helped build support for the Government Employees Training Act, which passed through Congress and was signed into law in 1958. The law enabled federal employees to obtain government funding for further job-related training. The Rockefeller Public Service Award program continued, in different forms, until its funding expired a few years after JDR 3rd's death.

One of JDR 3rd's most public roles as a philanthropist, beginning in 1955, was his leadership in the development of Lincoln Center for the Performing Arts in New York City. He served as president of the project, was a trustee from 1955 to 1969, contributed his own funds to the project, and is credited with raising more than half of the $184.5 million in private funds needed to build the complex.

Since the 1950s, JDR 3rd had been concerned about the future of philanthropy as a vital pillar of American society. During the 1960s and 1970s, he became, in the words of his biographers, a "self-appointed . . . caretaker of philanthropy . . . exert[ing] leadership to protect, reform, and enhance philanthropy generally in the United States" in the face of increasing political attacks against foundations and the tax abuses of the wealthy (Harr and Johnson 1991, 289). In 1969, as Congress debated tax reform proposals that some feared would bring an end to charitable giving, JDR 3rd took the lead in creating the Commission on Foundations and Private Philanthropy, led by business executive Peter G. Peterson (the Peterson Commission), and lobbied against proposals for increased restrictions on foundations while acknowledging the need to correct abuses and misconduct. He saw these political attacks as symptoms of a mistrust of philanthropy and a lack of understanding about its role. To change these attitudes, JDR 3rd sought ways to educate the public and politicians. As a result, he founded the Commission on Private Philanthropy and Public Needs (1974), led by Aetna chairman John H. Filer (the Filer Commission), which issued its findings and recommendations in late 1975 as *Giving in America: Toward a Stronger Voluntary Sector.*

These discussions about "philanthropy" crystallized JDR 3rd's dislike for the term, and he began to talk of foundations and voluntary associations as comprising a "third sector" of American society, distinct from the private sector of profit-supported business and the public sector of tax-supported government. Focusing on philanthropy had been a mistake, he suggested, for it was but a means to an end, "the support mechanism which makes possible the third sector as we know it today" (Harr and Johnson 1991, 384). Thus, he argued, attention should be given to the third sector and understanding its role in American life. As a step in this direction, JDR 3rd funded a feasibility study (1975) at Yale University that led to the creation of Yale's Program on Non-Profit Or-

ganizations, to which he also contributed significant sums. This program was the first of what soon became a growing number of academic centers dedicated to the study of philanthropy and the "third sector." Unfortunately, JDR 3rd did not witness the growth of these educational programs; he was killed in an automobile accident near his home in Westchester County, New York, on July 10, 1978.

GENERATIONAL COOPERATIVE FUNDS

Rockefeller Brothers Fund

In 1940, taking their cue from JDR, Jr.'s Davison Fund, his five sons joined forces to establish the Rockefeller Brothers Fund to coordinate their philanthropy and enhance the effectiveness of their giving. Each brother made annual contributions to the fund for a "recurring citizenship program" of grants to such civic groups as the Boy Scouts, the Girl Scouts, the United Hospital Fund, and the Community Service Society. Their sister joined the organization as a trustee in 1955, and their father provided an endowment for the fund in 1952. From the beginning, the fund had a strong focus on New York City, which has persisted, but early on its founders began to fund international organizations as well. The program changed over time, adding new features in response to perceived changes in needs and opportunities, such as a West Africa Program (1957–1962) to foster economic development in the region, and Nelson Rockefeller's Special Studies Project (1956–1961), directed by Henry A. Kissinger, which brought together leading academics and public policy analysts to define the major problems and opportunities facing the United States and to clarify the nation's purposes and objectives in the midst of the Cold War. The reports prepared by the project's various panels were published as *Prospects for America: The Rockefeller Panel Reports* (1961). By the time the Rockefeller Brothers Fund marked its fiftieth anniversary in 1990, it had made grants totaling nearly $384 million to 1,342 institutions in 37 countries, and leadership of the Fund was passing to the Cousins' generation (*Rockefeller Brothers Fund Annual Report*, 1990, 8, The Rockefeller Archive Center).

Rockefeller Family Fund

Just as John D. Rockefeller, Sr. and John D. Rockefeller, Jr. collaborated to create the Rockefeller Foundation and John D. Rockefeller, Jr. helped his children create an endowment for the Rockefeller Brothers Fund, his children in turn helped their sons and daughters establish a new institution to address the concerns of their generation. The Rockefeller Family Fund was established in 1967 "to span," according to its first annual report, "the philanthropic interests of the third and fourth generations of the John D. Rockefeller family"—generally referred to as the Brothers and the Cousins generations (*Rockefeller Family Fund Annual Report for 1968 and 1969*, 4, The Rockefeller Archive Center).

During its early years, the Rockefeller Family Fund's grants during its early years "concentrated on projects attempting to come to grips with the problems of poverty, housing and education in the New York and Boston metropolitan areas," where many of the trustees lived (*Rockefeller Family Fund Annual Report for 1968 and 1969*, 4, The Rockefeller Archive Center). In June 1971, the trustees established five programs in which the fund would make grants for much of the next decade. Two of the programs—the Arts-Public Aesthetics Program and the Education Program—were short-lived. Three other programs continued into the next century, with some revisions to meet new needs. The Equal Opportunity—Women program was revamped in 1985 and renamed the Economic Justice for Women program. The Conservation Program was renamed the Environment Program in 1986 and given a new emphasis: how the environment affected health. The Institutional Responsiveness Program, a broad effort that

aimed to "build more responsive relationships between individuals and institutions," remained unchanged (*Rockefeller Family Fund Annual Report 1970–71*, 7, The Rockefeller Archive Center). The latter program supported efforts to hold corporations and government agencies accountable for their actions and be more responsive to the public interest. The Council on Economic Priorities was an early recipient of support under this program for its work monitoring the social responsibility of businesses in such areas as the environment and minority employment, and it has continued to receive frequent grants. By 1985, the program had supported "a program to make tobacco companies accountable for the health effects of smoking; a project to insure that individuals and organizations with diverse points of view gain access to over-the-air-broadcasting time . . . and efforts to increase the range of organizations receiving employee contributions from workplace solicitations" (*Rockefeller Family Fund Annual Report 1985*, 10, The Rockefeller Archive Center). From 1985 to 1998, Donald K. Ross, a lawyer and founder of the New York Public Interest Research Group, served as director of the Rockefeller Family Fund. Under Ross's leadership, the foundation developed new programs in Arms Control (1983–1989); Citizen Education and Participation, established in 1986; and, in 1993, Self-Sufficiency, which funded efforts by nonprofit groups to increase and diversify their financial support.

Generational transition has been one of the themes of the Rockefeller Family Fund's history. Dana Creel, a Rockefeller philanthropic advisor since 1940 and president of the Rockefeller Brothers Fund, served as the Rockefeller Family Fund's first director. Meanwhile, two members of the brothers' generation served as president of the Rockefeller Family Fund as mechanisms were developed to bring more members of the cousins' generation into leadership positions. In February 1971, David Rockefeller, Jr. became the first member of the cousins' generation to serve as president. In 1978, Gail O'Neill joined the board of trustees, the first member of the fifth generation to do so. By March 1999, when the Family Fund commemorated more than thirty years of grant-making, fifty-three members of three generations of the Rockefeller family had served on the board. Cousins continued to fill the presidency, as Anne R. Roberts (1974–1980), Richard Chasin (1980–1992), Richard G. Rockefeller (1992–1998), and Anne Bartley (1998–   ) subsequently succeeded David Rockefeller, Jr., and more members of the fifth generation became trustees.

In addition to the collective family philanthropy, certain members of the cousins generation also created their own philanthropic organizations—just as their parents had—to respond to their specific concerns. The best known of these organizations is the Synergos Institute, founded in 1987 by Peggy Dulany, daughter of David Rockefeller. Some members of the cousins' generation, who came of age during the politically and socially turbulent 1960s, found it difficult to feel at ease with the wealth, status, and power of their family amid contemporary critiques of American society: particularly the war on poverty, racial inequality and the civil rights movement, and the seemingly imperialistic war in Vietnam. Active in radical politics as a college student in the Boston area, Peggy Dulany decided to drop the last name of "Rockefeller" and sought to make her way on her own, without the automatic opportunities that the name itself might make available. Nonetheless, she found ways to use the wealth, status, and contacts of her family name in support of causes that mattered to her. Thus, the Synergos Institute was born in 1987. This organization describes itself as "an independent, nonprofit institute dedicated to developing effective sustainable solutions to global poverty," and is most active in Africa, Asia, and Latin America (*Synergos: A Decade of Accomplishment* 1998, inside front cover, The Rockefeller Archive Center). Creating partnerships and building bridges are the watchwords for Synergos. It seeks to connect those with needs to those with resources and expertise in a manner that is both culturally sensitive and cognizant of the local context of problems, casting off the assumption that experts from the developed world have ready-made answers for those in poorer nations.

Two members of the cousins generation—John D. Rockefeller IV (known as Jay), a Democrat, and Winthrop P. Rockefeller, Jr. (known as Win), a Republican—illustrate both the political diversity of their generation of Rockefellers and a certain family continuity as they follow Nelson and Winthrop Rockefeller's pursuit of politics as their chosen method of public service. Jay Rockefeller went to West Virginia in 1964 as a VISTA volunteer, working on community development projects in Emmons. He remained in the state and entered politics, winning election to the state House of Delegates in 1966 and to the statewide position of secretary of state in 1968. After a short period as president of West Virginia Wesleyan College (1973–1976), he successfully ran for the governorship in 1976 and won reelection in 1980. In 1984, he was elected to the U.S. Senate and won reelection in 1990 and 1996. Win Rockefeller (born in 1948) was elected the lieutenant governor of Arkansas in 1996 through a special election and was reelected to a full four-year term in 1998. In a fitting tribute to the continuity of values among the generations of Rockefellers, Win Rockefeller included his grandfather John D. Rockefeller, Jr.'s 1941 "I Believe" credo in his official lieutenant governor publicity material.

CONCLUSION

Concentrations of wealth and power traditionally make some Americans uneasy and suspicious of the goals and motives of its possessors. The Rockefellers have not been uncontested in either the development of or the uses to which they put their wealth and philanthropy. Rockefeller wealth, economic power, and philanthropy have aroused concern ever since John D. Rockefeller, Sr.'s business practices angered oil producers and competitive refiners in the 1870s and 1880s, leading to state and federal investigations, new regulations on business practices, and the antitrust law suit that ultimately dissolved the Standard Oil Trust in 1911. Muckraking journalism, particularly Ida Tarbell's series of articles in 1902–1903 on Standard Oil's business practices, increased antagonism toward Rockefeller, so that even his charity came under attack. In 1905, the Rev. Washington Gladden led a protest drive that urged the Congregational Board of Foreign Missions to return a $100,000 gift from Rockefeller, calling it "tainted money" because of the sinful greediness with which the Rockefeller fortune had been accumulated—"the most relentless rapacity known to modern commercial history," he claimed (Chernow 1998, 499). Meanwhile, Congress refused to grant the Rockefeller Foundation a federal charter (1910–1913), prompting it to turn to the state of New York for a charter in 1913.

By the 1960s, the brothers' wealth and their wide-ranging involvement in philanthropy, politics, banking, business investments, and international affairs led many critics on the left to associate the name Rockefeller with the democratically unresponsive "Establishment," while critics on the extreme political right worried that the Rockefellers were dangerous internationalists more concerned with profits and power than about United States' economic well-being and national sovereignty. Critics saw the family's philanthropy as essential to the power and influence certain family members enjoyed. "Philanthropy is the essential element in the making of Rockefeller power," Myer Kutz argued in *Rockefeller Power: America's Chosen Family* (Kutz 1974, 249). "It gives the Rockefellers a priceless reputation as public benefactors which the public values so highly that power over public affairs is placed in the Rockefeller's hands. Philanthropy generates more power than wealth alone can provide" (Kutz 1974, 249).

Over the generations, the number of heirs to the Rockefeller fortune has increased, thus diluting the concentration of wealth for any particular family member, and the Rockefeller fortune has been eclipsed by the development of other family fortunes (spurred by the growth of new industries). Yet, while members of the younger generations of Rockefellers may have both diminished financial resources when compared with their parents and a different sensibility toward wealth and power than did the brothers generation, they have displayed an abiding interest in philanthropy and public service and may well leave their own mark on the world through their philanthropy. Any such mark is likely to be fainter than those left by JDR, Jr. and the brothers' generation, for each of these men had sufficient resources to focus the attention of opinion and policymakers on particular issues, or to prompt them to rethink their attitudes toward the peoples and cultures of other countries, or to create organizations that could provide additional training for hundreds of professionals in diverse fields at home or abroad, as did the IEB, AIA, JDR 3rd Fund, and others. Nonetheless, perhaps the most significant accomplishment of Rockefeller philanthropy has been the ability to sustain itself over time and continue to foster the values of social responsibility, relevance, and personal involvement among successive generations in increasingly secular and self-indulgent times.

Kenneth W. Rose

FURTHER READING

Broehl, Wayne G., Jr. *The International Basic Economy Corporation*. Washington, DC: International Planning Association, 1968.

Chase, Mary Ellen. *Abby Aldrich Rockefeller*. New York: Macmillan Company, 1950.

Chernow, Ron. *Titan: The Life of John D. Rockefeller, Sr.* New York: Random House, 1998.

Collier, Peter, and David Horowitz. *The Rockefellers: An American Dynasty*. New York: Holt, Rinehart & Winston, 1976.

Commission on Private Philanthropy and Public Needs. *Giving in America: Toward a Stronger Voluntary Sector*. Washington, DC: The Commission.

Critchlow, Donald T. *Intended Consequences: Birth Control, Abortion and the Federal Government in Modern America*. New York: Oxford University Press, 1999.

Dalrymple, Martha. *The AIA Story: Two Decades of International Cooperation*. New York: American International Association for Economic and Social Development, 1968.

Davis, Katherine Bement. *Factors in the Sex Life of Twenty-Two Hundred Women*. New York: Harper & Brothers, 1929.

Dillard, Tom W. "Winthrop Rockefeller." In *The Governors of Arkansas: Essays in Political Biography*, ed. Timothy P. Donovan and William B. Gatewood. Fayetteville: University of Arkansas Press, 1981, pp. 226–234.

Ernst, Joseph W., ed. *Worthwhile Places: Correspondence of John D. Rockefeller, Jr. and Horace M. Albright*. New York: Fordham University Press for the Rockefeller Archive Center, 1991.

Fitch, Robert. *The Assassination of New York*. London and New York: Verso, 1993.

Fosdick, Raymond B. *John D. Rockefeller, Jr.: A Portrait*. New York: Harper & Brothers, 1956.

Harr, John Ensor, and Peter J. Johnson. *The Rockefeller Century: Three Generations of America's Greatest Family*. New York: Charles Scribner's Sons, 1988.

———. *The Rockefeller Conscience: An American Family in Public and in Private*. New York: Charles Scribner's Sons, 1991.

Humelsine, Carlisle H. *Recollections of John D. Rockefeller, Jr. in Williamsburg, 1926–1960*. Williamsburg, VA: Colonial Williamsburg Foundation, 1985.

The JDR 3rd Fund and Asia, 1963–1975. New York: JDR 3rd Fund, 1977.

Kert, Bernice. *Abby Aldrich Rockefeller: The Woman in the Family*. New York: Random House, 1993.

Kutz, Myer. *Rockefeller Power: America's Chosen Family*. New York: Simon & Schuster, 1974.

Longsworth, Amy P. "Rockefeller Brothers Fund." In *Foundations*, ed. Harold M. Keele and Joseph C. Kiger. Westport, CT: Greenwood Press, 1984, 361–364.

Moscow, Alvin. *The Rockefeller Inheritance*. Garden City, NY: Doubleday & Company, 1977.

Newhall, Nancy Wynne. *Contribution to the Heritage of Every American: The Conservation Activities of John D. Rockefeller, Jr.* New York: Alfred A. Knopf, 1957.

Reich, Cary. *The Life of Nelson A. Rockefeller: Worlds to Conquer, 1908–1958*. New York: Doubleday, 1996.

Roberts, Ann Rockefeller. *Mr. Rockefeller's Roads: The Untold Story of Acadia's Carriage Roads and Their Creator*. Camden, ME: Down East Books, 1990.

Rockefeller Brothers Fund. *Prospects for America: The Rockefeller Panel Reports*. Garden City, NY: Doubleday, 1961.

Schenkel, Albert F. *The Rich Man and the Kingdom: John D. Rockefeller, Jr., and the Protestant Establishment*. Harvard Theological Studies no. 39. Minneapolis, MN: Fortress Press, 1995.

The Story of Rockefeller Center: From Facts to Fine Arts. New York: The Rockefeller Group, 1987.

Synergos: A Decade of Accomplishment [1987–1997]. New York: Synergos Institute, [ca. 1998].

Winks, Robin W. *Laurance S. Rockefeller: Catalyst for Conservation*. Washington, DC: Island Press, 1997.

PAPERS

The Rockefeller Archive Center (Sleepy Hollow, NY) holds the papers of members of the Rockefeller family, including those of John D. Rockefeller, Jr., Abby Aldrich Rockefeller, John D. Rockefeller 3rd, and Nelson A. Rockefeller, as well as the records of many of their philanthropic organizations, most notably the Rockefeller Foundation, the Rockefeller Brothers Fund, and the Rockefeller Family Fund.

JULIUS ROSENWALD
(1862–1932)

President of Sears, Roebuck and Company and Founder of the Rosenwald Fund

INTRODUCTION

Julius Rosenwald loved to tell about the man who won a million dollars on number 14. Why that particular number? Well, Rosenwald continued, imitating the new millionaire, "I saw a great big 9 and a large 6 in my dreams and figured that 9 and 6 is 14" (Werner 1939, 357). The story illustrated Rosenwald's lesson: it did not take brains to be rich. The man who became one of the early twentieth century's wealthiest retail merchants was too modest, but he sincerely believed his fortune to be a gift, one that he should share with those most lacking opportunity. Thus, the Rosenwald Fund championed racial equality at a time when America remained firmly segregated.

EARLY YEARS AND EDUCATION

On the same Springfield, Illinois, street where one of his idols, Abraham Lincoln, had practiced law, Julius Rosenwald was born to Samuel and Augusta Rosenwald in 1862. The son of German Jewish immigrants, his father, Samuel Rosenwald, sold men's suits and woolen cloth with his brothers-in-law. The enterprise prospered, especially after large uniform orders from the Union Army allowed the new firm to move to much bigger quarters. Julius Rosenwald grew up working in his father's store, then, following family wishes, apprenticed with an uncle who sold seersucker and cotton cloth wholesale in New York City.

Intent on setting up his own business, Rosenwald returned to Illinois in 1885 and, with his father's help, opened a factory in Chicago that specialized in the manufacture

Julius Rosenwald photographed outside the White House in November 1929. Library of Congress; LC-USZ62-111719.

of men's summer clothing. For ten years, Rosenwald practiced the family trade, selling paper collars, linen shirts, and cotton suits. In 1869, he married Augusta Nusbaum (the daughter of another Chicago clothier). She would remain his wife until her death in 1929. The couple raised five children: Lessing Julius, Adele, Edith, Marion, and William. Julius Rosenwald remarried in 1930 to Adelaide Goodkind, his eldest son Lessing's widowed mother-in-law, but the marriage was brief, cut short by his own death in 1932.

CAREER HIGHLIGHTS

Rosenwald's life might have followed the typical path of a prosperous middle-class merchant had he not decided to enter into a partnership with Richard Sears in 1895 and undertake a new venture, the mail-order catalog business. Sears, a former watch salesman who had elevated an employee named Roebuck into the fictive role of an associate to make his letterhead look more impressive, convinced Rosenwald that a potential mass market existed for retail goods sold through the mail. As Sears envisioned, such a commercial endeavor reaped substantial profits. In the aftermath of Union victory in the Civil War, the nation's banking, currency, and railroad systems nationalized. As huge new department stores opened to the residents of the country's cities, the mail-order catalog became the equivalent for the majority of Americans who still lived in small towns, villages, and on farms.

Richard Sears was not an astute money manager, and several of his previous enterprises had failed. Indeed, he possessed more than a trace of the snake-oil salesman, and the first Sears, Roebuck catalog contained electric belts guaranteed to cure asthma and rheumatism, "gold" watches that were not, as well as elixirs for stammering and occasional deafness. Still, Sears possessed an advertising genius. He was the first to put the captivating phrase, "SEND NO MONEY," in large type at the top of copy, to offer prizes for orders, and to promise a year's supply of free thread with the purchase of a sewing machine.

When Rosenwald and his brother-in-law, Aaron Nusbaum, became Sears's partners, they did not change the company's name, but they did transform its practices, in the process making Sears, Roebuck and Company the nation's biggest mail-order retailer. Within ten years, the Sears, Roebuck catalog became the hefty book familiar to generations of rural Americans. In its hundreds of pages, customers could find almost any item they could imagine—from chocolate bars, cream separators, and ready-made clothing, to kits for constructing a single-family home, and, for a time, an inexpensive automobile named the "Sears Buggy." Rosenwald and Nusbaum also banished questionable products, imposed a money-back guarantee, and established the first quality control laboratory for merchandise in the country. As the business flourished, economies of scale allowed Sears, Roebuck to lower the prices of many goods: the same Sears sewing machine cost $17.55 in 1897 but only $10.50 in 1910. If rural Americans possessed two books, likely they were the Sears catalog and the Bible. Rosenwald subsequently became a millionaire many times over.

MAJOR PHILANTHROPIC CONTRIBUTIONS

Rosenwald contributed to Jewish charities throughout his life. As he became a well-known Chicago business leader, he took on civic good works as well, raising funds for education of orphans in the city and supporting **Jane Addams'** Hull-House settlement. However, a 1911 meeting with **Booker T. Washington** focused his philanthropy. Rosenwald had read the black educator's autobiography, *Up from Slavery.* When Washington came to Chicago to raise funds for his Tuskegee Institute, Rosenwald gave a luncheon for him, forcing Chicago's Blackstone Hotel to break its color barrier (at least for the guest of honor). Becoming an avid supporter of Tuskegee, Rosenwald traveled frequently to Alabama, sometimes chartering a private railway car to bring potential donors for a personal tour of the Tuskegee Institute campus.

In 1917, Rosenwald endowed the Rosenwald Fund, stipulating that the new foundation spend all its principal and interest within a generation after his death. Rosenwald adamantly opposed perpetual endowments. He even wrote frequently about their potential dangers, including a widely noted *Atlantic Monthly* piece entitled "Principles of Public Giving" (1929), but relatively few fellow philanthropists ever followed his advice. Nonetheless, Rosenwald thought it was possible to assess current needs, even to guess what a society's most pressing problems might be for a decade or two into the future, but additional foresight was not possible. Furthermore, he worried that philanthropic institutions without an ending date would become more concerned with their own self-perpetuation instead of achieving their mission. Rosenwald stated that a person's charity should be like "manna of the Bible, which melted at the close of each day" (Julius Rosenwald Papers, University of Chicago). At the close of a philanthropist's life, his beneficent enterprises should also begin to come to an end, though their missions, if worthy, should continue but be assumed by others. Thus, Rosenwald demanded that the Rosenwald Fund benefit his contemporaries and their children—no more.

From its creation until its dissolution in 1948, the Rosenwald Fund sought to improve the lives of black Americans. Rosenwald also continued his personal contributions to Tuskegee and other black schools and colleges but the Rosenwald Fund had a much more ambitious agenda: to convince state governments in the South to provide comparable schooling for black and white children. Between 1917 and 1939, the Rosenwald Fund contributed over $28 million for the construction of what became universally known as "Rosenwald Schools." By the end of the 1930s, in 5,300 schools scattered throughout fourteen southern states, almost three quarters of a million black children studied in clean, brightly lit, solidly built schoolhouses. To qualify for a "Rosenwald" building, a county or local public school district had to provide at least half the money needed for construction and guarantee future maintenance costs. The county or district also had to follow the architectural plans sent from the Rosenwald Fund's Chicago offices and hire teachers for a minimum five-month term annually. In addition to creating this network of model schools, the Rosenwald Fund sought to spur the training of black teachers by helping to develop four university centers strategically placed throughout the South: Howard University in Washington, DC, a federation of seven black colleges in Atlanta, Fisk University in Nashville, and Dillard University in New Orleans.

Finally, the Rosenwald Fund sponsored three health centers, again meant to act as regional demonstrations, to provide blacks with better health care. As late as 1930, most general hospitals, North and South, refused to admit African Americans. As for the tiny number of hospitals that admitted blacks, they isolated minority patients, even those able to pay, in overcrowded, shamefully underequipped, charity wards. With the Rosenwald Fund's backing, the Provident Hospital in Chicago, allied with the University of Chicago, became the nation's leading institution for the training of black physicians and nurses. At Flint-Goodridge Hospital in New Orleans and at the John Andrew Hospital in central Alabama, the Rosenwald Fund sought to encourage experimental public health practices that bettered health care for impoverished urban and rural black families. Among the innovations was a penny-a-day hospital insurance plan.

Black Americans enthusiastically greeted the efforts of the Rosenwald Fund. Throughout the South, churches kept "Rosenwald School" boxes in their vestries, to which people added their pennies and nickels every Sunday. In thousands of communities, black men gave in kind, donating their skills as carpenters, painters, and masons, and black women organized "Rosenwald" fish fries. During the New Deal, pictures of Franklin Roosevelt and Julius Rosenwald hung in a place of honor side by side in many black homes.

CONCLUSION

The Rosenwald Fund had meant its efforts to improve education and health care for blacks as object lessons for white officials. It always argued that real opportunity could be realized only when segregation ended. That certainly did not happen in Julius Rosenwald's lifetime or during the existence of the Rosenwald Fund. No southern state came even close to providing equal, even if separate, access for blacks to either state-sponsored medical care or education. In 1936, Edwin Embree, president of the Rosenwald Fund, estimated that the average southern school district spent $157 per white pupil, $37 per black pupil. Moreover, the low-cost insurance plans the Rosenwald Fund advocated to help the poor and people of moderate means pay hospital bills helped generate interest in the nonprofit Blue Cross system, which by 1948 had 27 million members, most of them white.

Angry critics, especially in the South, argued that Rosenwald should put his own house in order before inspecting theirs. Rather than spend his fortune on Rosenwald Schools, they argued that he should pay his own workers higher wages. Indeed, Rosenwald always refused to give his employees anything higher than the going rate: a near-poverty living for just-hired female clerks and warehouse workers. Under Rosenwald's leadership, however, Sears, Roebuck and Company had one of the country's most generous profit-sharing plans, and, unlike most early twentieth-century companies, shared the cost of health insurance with its workers and provided paid vacations.

Rosenwald's legacy, however, was not as an ideal employer. Instead, ahead of his time, this small man, famous for kind gestures but also well known "to be exhilarated when he had a good fight on his hands," fought against segregation and bigotry (Werner 1939, 359).

Judith Sealander

FURTHER READING

Belles, A. Gilbert. "The College Faculty, the Negro Scholar, and the Julius Rosenwald Fund." *Journal of Negro History* 54, 1969, 383–392.

Embree, Edwin, and Julia Waxman. *Investment in People: The Story of the Julius Rosenwald Fund*. New York: Harper, 1949.

Goggin, Jacqueline Anne. *Carter G. Woodson: A Life in Black History*. Baton Rouge: Louisiana State University Press, 1993.

Jarrette, Alfred. *Julius Rosenwald, Son of a Jewish Immigrant, a Builder of Sears, Roebuck and Company, Benefactor of Mankind: A Biography Documented*. Greenville, SC: Southeastern University Press, 1975.

Johnson, Charles. *Shadow of the Plantation*. Chicago: University of Chicago Press, 1934.

Rosenwald, Julius. "Principles of Public Giving." *Atlantic Monthly* 143, May 1929, 599–606.

Sealander, Judith. *Private Wealth and Public Life: Foundation Philanthropy and the Reshaping of American Social Policy from the Progressive Era to the New Deal*. Baltimore: Johns Hopkins University Press, 1997.

Werner, M.R. *Julius Rosenwald: The Life of a Practical Humanitarian*. New York: Harper & Brothers, 1939.

PAPERS

Both the personal papers of Julius Rosenwald and the organizational archives of the Rosenwald Fund are at the Archives of the University of Chicago.

BENJAMIN RUSH
(1746–1813)

Physician, Patriot, Abolitionist, and a Founder of the American Temperance Movement and One of the First Free Medical Clinics in North America

INTRODUCTION

In a letter to Jeremy Belknap on June 21, 1792, Benjamin Rush wrote: "I anticipate with a joy which I cannot describe the speedy end of the misery of the Africans, of the tyranny of kings, of the pride of ecclesiastical institutions. . . . Connected with the same events, I anticipate the end of war and such a superlative tenderness for human life as will exterminate capital punishments from all our systems of legislation. In the meanwhile let us not be idle with such prospects before our eyes. . . . the more active we are in bringing it about, the more fitted we shall be for that world where justice and benevolence eternally prevail" (Butterfield 1951, 1:620). Rush, Revolutionary era physician, patriot, and humanitarian, translated his Great Awakening upbringing into a "public spirit" and numerous republican commitments, including extensive participation in voluntary societies. In Revolutionary America, Rush advocated social reforms on behalf of African slaves and the poor (among others) and these actions were matched only by his vigorous promotion of education in the new nation.

EARLY YEARS AND EDUCATION

Of Quaker descent, Benjamin Rush was born on the farm of his father, John Rush, in Byberry, Pennsylvania—about fourteen miles northwest of Philadelphia—and baptized in the Church of England. After his father's death (when Benjamin Rush was six), his mother, Susanna Rush, joined the Reverend Gilbert Tennent's Second Presbyterian Church. At eight, Benjamin Rush attended Nottingham Academy, a boarding school run by his maternal uncle Samuel Finley, a middle-colony religious revival leader. When Rush was thirteen, he entered the College of New Jersey at Princeton and was much impressed by its president, the Reverend Samuel Davies, who urged graduates to commit to activities marked by a "public spirit" (Davies 1761, 4–5).

After consulting with Davies and Finley, Rush decided to pursue a career in medicine. From 1761 to 1766, he was apprenticed to Dr. John Redman of Philadelphia. Preparation for this vocation sent young Rush to that center of medicine in the Western world, Edinburgh, Scotland, where he earned the M.D. degree under renowned chemist Dr. William Cullen. Abroad, Rush was exposed

This portrait of Benjamin Rush was painted in 1783 by Charles Wilson Peale. Courtesy, Winterthur Museum, gift of Mrs. Julia B. Henry.

to the Scottish Enlightenment and to the Whig ideas of republicanism. On return to America in 1769, Rush was appointed professor of chemistry at the College of Philadelphia.

Through it all, Rush assumed that both medicine and republican social philosophy were natural outgrowths of his religious commitments, which had been formed early in life by revivals following the Great Awakening of the 1740s. By healing the sick, by promoting greater social freedom and equality, Dr. Rush believed that he was carrying out the divine will in his profession and in his philanthropic activities.

CAREER HIGHLIGHTS

In January 1776, Rush married Julia Stockton of Princeton, New Jersey; they subsequently produced thirteen children of whom nine, six sons and three daughters, lived to adulthood. In the summer of 1776, Rush signed the Declaration of Independence and was elected to the Continental

Congress. In 1777, he was appointed Surgeon General, then Physician General, of the Middle Department of the army. Ten years later, he was part of the Pennsylvania delegation to the Constitutional Convention. A charter member of **Benjamin Franklin**'s American Philosophical Society, Rush was the first American to hold an academic chair in chemistry as well as the first to publish on that subject. Rush also wrote the early textbook on psychology for which he has been dubbed the Father of American Psychiatry. Controversial therapy—bloodletting—during the Philadelphia yellow fever epidemic in 1793 led to accusations of malpractice; finally, Rush was exonerated through a lawsuit against British tabloid journalist William Cobbett. Although there were flaws in Rush's medical system, many acknowledged that Rush was one of the few doctors to remain in Philadelphia during the epidemic and that he was assisted courageously by African Americans loyal to him.

Toward the end of Rush's career, President John Adams appointed him head of the United States Mint (1797–1813). Indeed, lifelong friendships with Adams and Thomas Jefferson led to this opportunity. In the election campaigns of 1796 and 1800, when they ran against each other for the presidency, these two great founding fathers became bitter rivals. It was Benjamin Rush who, through a methodical series of letters to both men, coaxed them to renew their friendship. For fifteen years, until their deaths on July 4, 1826, Adams and Jefferson remembered the events of the revolution and the creation of the American republic through lengthy correspondence. Subsequently, these letters became classic documents of American history.

MAJOR PHILANTHROPIC CONTRIBUTIONS

Temperance, women's education, humane treatment of the poor, prison reform (abolishing capital and public punishments), founding of schools—these causes all stirred Rush. In 1772, he published *Sermons to Gentlemen upon Temperance and Exercise*. At this time, he donated his services to an almshouse. This commitment grew naturally out of his vocation and shaped a lifetime of charitable giving.

Early on, Rush also became involved in abolition. In 1773, he supported a bill at the Philadelphia Assembly to double the tax on importing slaves. In this way, he sought to make the practice of slavery uneconomical. Moreover, his pamphlet, *An Address to the Inhabitants of the British Settlements in America, upon Slave-Keeping* (1773), equated slavery with the British Parliament's abuse of American laborers. Clearly, Rush was deeply disturbed by the institution of slavery. Alongside his friend **Anthony Benezet**, the Quaker Abolitionist, and with help from Rev. Granville Sharp, the Anglican leader of the antislavery cause in England, Rush worked to persuade fellow Americans of the wrongs of slavery. He helped form the Pennsylvania Society for Promoting the Abolition of Slavery and the Relief of Free Negroes Unlawfully Held in Bondage (1774). In 1784, this society was reorganized; Rush rejoined it and served as secretary (1787–1803) and then as president from 1803 until his death in 1813.

Although Rush had an African-American house servant, it is also true that, owing to the man's age, Rush would not turn him out. Furthermore, Rush played a key role in the emergence of the African Methodist Episcopal Church. Blacks and whites at St. George's Methodist Church had fallen out over who would use the silver chalice given to the congregation by John Wesley (founder of Methodism). When African-American Methodists came calling, Rush not only became a chief subscriber to their fund-raising campaign but also helped secure land in South Philadelphia for the new building.

His 1784 essay *Inquiry into the Effects of Spirituous Liquors upon the Human Body, and Their Influence upon the Happiness of Society*, a milestone in an age of heavy drinking, became a much-used pamphlet during the temperance crusades of the nineteenth century. Rush cautioned about using liquor in his medical lectures and the College of Physicians, knowing his position, supported a

Temperance memorial (petition) to the state legislature. Rush was appointed chair of a committee to prepare the memorial, and the college adopted it in 1787. Others soon took up the cause. Quakers and Methodists limited the distribution of spirits in shops and at the harvest. In 1885, over 300 members of the Women's Christian Temperance Union met at Rush's grave to plant an oak tree and to remember the great founder of temperance reform. Though it was not taken up as a crusade, Rush, who had been surgeon general, also warned about the health hazards of tobacco.

Early in his career, Rush not only served an almshouse to bring medical care to the poor but participated in the Society for Inoculating the Poor. In 1786, Rush accepted a highly prestigious position at the Pennsylvania Hospital. The same year, he helped establish a free health care clinic for the poor. The Philadelphia Dispensary derived from the model of Rush's friend Dr. John Coakley Lettsom who, fifteen years before, had set up a free medical dispensary for the poor in London. The Philadelphia Dispensary was one of the first free medical clinics in North America and the first after the formation of the United States. The organization of six attending and four consulting physicians and surgeons, a treasurer, and an apothecary (pharmacist) allowed for patients to be seen in their own homes in an efficient and economical way. Affording the poor privacy was an important feature; many people went without medical care because they were unwilling to accept charity in public. Thus, the dispensary allowed those people living in "virtuous poverty" to be attended with dignity (Hawke 1971, 321).

Commitment to the principles of liberty and equality pervaded Rush's charity. As he organized associations, he wrote essays and letters on human treatment for the disenfranchised. In 1787, *An Enquiry into the Effects of Public Punishments upon Criminals, and upon Society* was read in Benjamin Franklin's living room to the founding members of the Society for Promoting Political Inquiries, largely concerned with prison reform. The

doctor's work led, in the same year, to the creation of the Philadelphia Society for Alleviating the Miseries of Public Prisons.

It should be noted that many voluntary associations in a city such as Philadelphia provided citizens with regular experiences in self-government. Members of these societies drafted constitutions and ratified the rules of their organizations. No matter the object of the association, this activity amounted to significant nation-building work, for it supplied the common citizen with an opportunity to participate in public life. Patriotism was as much a part of this work as was caring for the poor, relieving burdens of the insane or freeing the African. Rules of order in these societies often included guidelines for behavior. For example, a member was allowed to speak only twice on a subject, unless called upon to clarify or expand a comment. Thus, the public purpose of educating the citizenry for self-government was part of most, if not all, voluntary societies.

These activities, based on a new way of thinking about society, were nothing less than the application of republican social philosophy. With no hereditary king or nobility, republican society required self-government of its members. The object was res publica, the public good, and the virtue to choose that object over self-interest was needed of every citizen. Rush put the matter this way: "Every man in a republic is public property. His time and talents—his youth—his manhood—his old age—nay more, life, all belong to his country" (Runes 1947, 31).

In Philadelphia, no one was more active in the society movement than "public-spirited" Benjamin Rush. Indeed, these associations had permeable borders. A member of one would know another's work in several other contexts, so the lines of influence multiplied. Societies merged, reforming their roles, their laws, and their names. One interested in the new Enlightenment science might join the Society for Recovering Persons from Suspended Animation, a group that got merchants along the riverside to keep rescue equipment (grappling hooks, blankets) in their shops in case of emergency. Meanwhile, ice-skaters on the Delaware were trained to revive drowning victims. The society later merged with the city's skating club. Nearness to the riverbank was only part of the rationale for the merger—it was also part of the ongoing, fluid reforming and expanding of associations among citizens experimenting with democratic order. As such, these societies gave opportunities for Americans to try on a new kind of government. In 1783, this new group became the Humane Society of Philadelphia: Rush, a founder, contributed to its great reputation for a preventive approach to medicine.

Belief in education made Rush a promoter of schools in the new nation. The principal founder of Dickinson College in 1783, he also played a key role in the founding of Franklin College (later Franklin and Marshall). Rush's ideas on education can be found in "Of the Mode of Education Proper in a Republic" (1784), "A Plan for the Establishment of Public Schools" (1786), and "Thoughts upon Female Education" (1787). In these and other essays, Rush argued for free schools, available to every child, and the importance of women's education in a republic.

CONCLUSION

An avid participant of numerous charitable orders, moral societies, and voluntary associations, Rush was eulogized by his friend John Adams who knew "of no Character living or dead, who has done more real good in America" (D'Elia 1974, 6). Human rights and American freedoms were central to Rush's work in various aid organizations and moral associations in the new American republic. Committed to the claim that all were created equal, he sought more humane living conditions for those on the margins of society.

John M. Kloos

FURTHER READING

Abzug, Robert H. *Cosmos Crumbling: American Reform and the Religious Imagination.* New York: Oxford University Press, 1994.

Butterfield, Lyman H. "The Dream of Benjamin Rush: The Reconciliation of John Adams and Thomas Jefferson." *Yale Review* 40, 1950, 297–319.

———, ed. *Letters of Benjamin Rush.* 2 vols. Princeton, NJ: Princeton University Press, 1951.

Corner, George W., ed. *The Autobiography of Benjamin Rush: His Travels through Life Together with His Commonplace Book for 1789–1813.* Princeton, NJ: Princeton University Press, 1948.

Davies, Samuel. *Religion and Public Spirit: A Valedictory Address, September 21, 1760.* New York: J. Parker, 1761.

D'Elia, Donald J. *Benjamin Rush, Philosopher of the American Revolution.* Philadelphia: American Philosophical Society, 1974.

Goodman, Nathan G. *Benjamin Rush: Physician and Citizen, 1746–1813.* Philadelphia: University of Pennsylvania Press, 1934.

Hawke, David Freeman. *Benjamin Rush, Revolutionary Gadfly.* Indianapolis and New York: Bobbs-Merrill, 1971.

Kloos, John M. *A Sense of Deity: The Republican Spirituality of Dr. Benjamin Rush.* Brooklyn, NY: Carlson Publishing, 1991.

Runes, Dagobert D., ed. *The Selected Writings of Benjamin Rush.* New York: Philosophical Library, 1947.

PAPERS

The Library Company of Philadelphia has the largest collection of Benjamin Rush's unpublished papers; they are on deposit next door at the Historical Society of Pennsylvania.

S

MARGARET OLIVIA SLOCUM (MRS. RUSSELL) SAGE
(1828–1918)

Founder of the Russell Sage Foundation

INTRODUCTION

When eighty-nine-year-old multimillion-aire financier Russell Sage died in 1906, his physician commented, "In leaving his fortune to Mrs. Sage, Mr. Sage has left it to charity" (*Troy Record* July 28, 1906, 5). Sure enough, over the next eleven years, his widow, Margaret Olivia Sage, spent over $45 million in charitable donations, establishing herself as the greatest female philanthropist of her time.

EARLY YEARS AND EDUCATION

Although in her old age Sage was America's wealthiest woman, her early life had been haunted by her family's financial problems and by the struggle to support herself. Her Quaker father, Joseph Slocum, prospered in the boom times of canal building in upstate New York, but when the panic of 1837 struck the region, his stores, warehouses, and other businesses began to fail. In

1841, when his daughter Olivia (her preferred name) Slocum was thirteen, he sold 500 acres of land to pay his debts. For the next twenty-five years, Joseph Slocum traveled continuously, seeking sponsors for his improved agricultural machinery and other inventions as far as Russia, but his projects generally failed and he was never able to provide his family with adequate support, let alone financial security.

Despite these problems, and encouraged by her ambitious and protective mother (Margaret Pierson Slocum), Olivia Slocum managed to obtain an education as good as then available for girls. After attending private schools in Syracuse, she enrolled at Troy Female Seminary, borrowing the tuition money from a wealthy uncle. At the seminary, she studied an impressive range of subjects and came under the influence of the charismatic educator Emma Willard, who would remain her lifelong model and mentor.

Willard's Troy Female Seminary produced

Portrait of Margaret (Mrs. Russell) Sage. Courtesy of the Rockefeller Archive Center.

a generation of young women who thought of themselves as cultural and moral leaders. Many women went on to found their own schools on Troy Female Seminary principles, forming an "ever-widening circle" of feminist evangelical reformers whose impact on antebellum culture and society has yet to be fully appreciated (Crocker 1996, 254). This self-aggrandizing mission appealed to Olivia Slocum, who drew comfort from the thought that, despite present money problems, her family had a distinguished New England past, and perhaps some special destiny for the future. As early as 1847, she anticipated her role as a philanthropist when she praised "our distinguished inhabitants who spend their wealth in deeds of charity" in her graduation speech (Patton 1941, 12).

CAREER HIGHLIGHTS

For the next twenty years, Olivia Slocum supported herself as a teacher in Syracuse and Philadelphia while her father's financial situation went from bad to worse. Joseph Slocum's business ventures involved him in deals with some men smarter or less scrupulous than himself, including her future husband, Russell Sage. Financially ruined and gravely ill with tuberculosis, Joseph Slocum put the family home up for sale in 1857, forcing Olivia and her mother to move in with relatives.

During the Civil War, Olivia Slocum worked as a governess in Philadelphia, also volunteering her services in a hospital for the wounded. Her unremitting struggle to survive on a teacher's salary made her ready to accept a proposal of marriage from Russell Sage, an ex-congressman and multimillionaire twelve years her senior, who had recently lost his first wife to cancer. They married in 1869, when she was forty-one years old. Marriage transformed her fortunes and gave her the status of a wealthy New York matron, but it also connected her to a tireless workaholic whose frugal and eccentric lifestyle and uncanny skills on Wall Street as the business partner of hated railroad mogul Jay Gould, attracted both the ridicule and awe of the public.

Now Mrs. Russell Sage, she forged a public persona as a philanthropist that rivaled her husband's public persona as financier and miser. She took up public work, becoming what one journalist called one of that "New York type of well-to-do committee-working church women" (Gleason 1906, 8184). Olivia Sage donated hours of work to voluntary organizations such as the New-York Woman's Hospital, the first hospital specializing in the diseases of women, where she served in many capacities, including treasurer and board member. In 1891, she was among the founders of the Emma Willard Association, an alumnae organization for Troy Female Seminary, and she supervised the collection of biographical data for *Emma Willard and Her Pupils*, which contains information on the lives of 3,500 of the more than 12,000 women who attended Troy from 1822 to 1872. She also paid for its publication and distribution.

Voluntary activity by women, many historians believe, helped to propel the suffrage and feminist campaigns, for it involved fund-raising, studying public issues, holding meetings, and planning the "investment" of benevolent resources (money and time). Moreover, these voluntary associations provided middle- and upper-class women with opportunities to work and possess a public voice at a time when such activities, outside of benevolent work, were viewed as unladylike. Since she had recently experienced poverty and struggle, Sage used her public voice to call for women's economic emancipation and for female suffrage. She rejected the identity of the "lady of leisure," and embraced the idea of work and moral earnestness. Indeed, she found a voice as an advocate for moral reform and advancement for women, causes she considered identical. Her first full-scale interview with a reporter, published as "The Opportunities and Responsibilities of Leisured Women," provides a summary of her views about how women's influence would reform society and clean up politics. "Now the woman of to-day has demonstrated the quality of her talent, courage, and endurance," she said in 1905, "there is no excuse for her not working" (Sage 1905, 714).

MAJOR PHILANTHROPIC CONTRIBUTIONS

In 1906, Olivia Sage inherited virtually all her husband's fortune of $75 million, and her experience as a fund-raiser and treasurer in voluntary associations during her thirty-seven-year marriage gave her confidence in handling money. Now, she launched into an astonishing array of philanthropy, spending about $35 million in her eighties, about $1.5 billion in today's money.

Her first major donation came only six weeks after Russell Sage's death, when she gave New York University about $294,000 for women's education. Unfortunately, the gift deed was drafted poorly, and the university never applied the money as she specified. Often, as in this case, her philanthropy was diverted from the uses she intended. In some cases, the elderly widow was outmaneuvered

and outwitted by fund-raisers, so that she spent millions of dollars on *their* favorite schemes, leaving her own plans unfulfilled. She supported women's mission auxiliary associations, but gave far more to the male-dominated American Bible Society than to its female auxiliary. Additionally, she gave over $1 million to the Charity Organization Society (COS), presided over by her own lawyer, Robert W. de Forest. Isolated by deafness and suffering the physical limitations of old age, she was easily hoodwinked. In the end, her influence was even less than it might have been because she also generously funded thousands of worthy institutions and causes with modest amounts of money, rather than making one or two really major contributions.

Her great gifts often had multiple meanings. When she purchased Constitution Island off West Point and gave it to the nation in 1908, her action had, for example, at least four motives. First, it was an act of patriotism commemorating a Revolutionary War campaign; second, it saved the island home of Susan and Anna Warner, best-selling domestic novelists whose *The Wide, Wide World* (1850) was among her favorites; third, it thwarted plans of commercial development for the site, a prospect she deplored. Finally, the area's natural beauty had sentimental ties with her younger days. No single explanation would have sufficed for this gift.

Little of Sage's money went directly to poor people. Her donation of $10,000 a year for this purpose was administered through the New York Charity Organization Society. Her largest and most significant donation was a gift of $10 million to set up a Russell Sage Foundation for Social Betterment in April 1907. The Sage Foundation was to maintain a fund and apply the income to "the improvement of the social and living conditions in the United States of America . . . to use any means for that end which from time to time shall seem expedient . . . including research, publication, education, the establishment and maintenance of charitable or benevolent activities, agencies and institutions" (Hammack 1994, 3). For reasons that are still unclear, she insisted that the foundation should bear only her husband's name, altering early planning documents by scratching out "Margaret Olivia" and inserting "Russell." If she hid behind her husband's name, Sage nevertheless tried to harness her husband's money to her own purposes. At the first meeting of the board of trustees, she was overheard to declare, "I am nearly eighty years old and I feel as though I have just begun to live!" (de Forest 1918, 151). Thus, the elderly widow expressed her delight in being able to put her money to work for the public good.

Although it is impossible to say how much credit for the foundation should be given to Sage and how much to her advisor Robert W. de Forest, the Russell Sage Foundation clearly made a significant contribution to the development of the social sciences in America. In recruiting trustees and experts, the foundation gathered up the most important strands of postbellum reform from the overlapping charitable, academic, and evangelical elites. Russell Sage Foundation grants supported research and generated public policy in urban planning, public health, social work and social provision, and consumer economics. The most remarkable demonstration of this uniting of social science and reform was the foundation-funded Pittsburgh Survey, which employed dozens of social scientists to study an entire industrial region and improve the lives of its inhabitants. The result was the first empirically based study of urban problems, which drew attention to the need for more schools, better housing, and safer, healthier neighborhoods. The Russell Sage Foundation also played a crucial role in helping establish social work as a profession. It supported the publication of professional social-work journals, especially *Charities and the Commons* (renamed *The Survey* in 1909), and established training programs for "social workers" (then a new term), with Schools of Philanthropy (Social Work) in Boston, St. Louis, New York, and Chicago.

In addition to the foundation, Olivia Sage gave millions of dollars to educational institutions, including universities, colleges, and schools. She sometimes specified that her giving should be directed to help women, and donated dormitories and scholarships for women. She gave generously to women's colleges including Wellesley, Vassar, and Bryn Mawr, but she donated far more over her lifetime to Harvard, Yale, and Princeton, universities that would continue to exclude women well into the twentieth century. Her most characteristic donation came in 1916, when she gave $1 million to endow a new women's college in Troy, New York, the Russell Sage College of Practical Arts, with the goal of producing a generation of women that would enter the professions and business and achieve the economic and political participation that had always eluded its founder.

The terms of her will were extraordinarily generous. The legacy was divided into fifty-two equal parts. Of educational institutions named in the will, nineteen received one part, or about $800,000 each. Favorite institutions received huge legacies: the Emma Willard School, the Woman's Hospital, the Children's Aid Society, the Charity Organization Society, the Metropolitan Museum of Art, the American Museum of Natural History, and Syracuse University received $1.6 million each. The will also provided large donations to churches, missions, and other religious causes. Some of these gifts reaffirmed sentimental and intellectual ties to the "woman's domain" of religious auxiliary societies. The Woman's Board of Foreign Missions of the Presbyterian Church and New York City Mission and Tract Society (Woman's Board), for example, each got a whopping $1.6 million.

CONCLUSION

Olivia Sage practiced philanthropy in many ways. As a volunteer, a reformer, an investor, a patron, and a visionary, she was able to have a major impact on American society in the twentieth century. Using her husband's name, "Mrs. Russell Sage," while giving to many women's organizations, she presents a fascinating puzzle to historians for the way she went about the work of giving away the fortune her husband had spent his whole life to amass.

Ruth Crocker

FURTHER READING

Crocker, Ruth. "From Widow's Mite to Widow's Might: The Philanthropy of Margaret Olivia Sage." *Journal of Presbyterian History (American Presbyterians)* 74, no. 4, Winter 1996, 253–264.

———. "The History of Philanthropy as Life-History: A Biographer's View of Mrs. Russell Sage." In *Philanthropic Foundations: New Scholarship, New Possibilities*, ed. Ellen Lagemann. Bloomington: Indiana University Press, 1999, 318–328.

———. " 'I Only Ask You Kindly to Divide Some of Your Fortune with Me': Begging Letters and the Transformation of Charity in Late 19th Century America." *Social Politics* 6, Summer 1999, 131–160.

———. "Mrs. Russell Sage: 'Private Griefs and Public Duties.' " In *Ordinary Women, Extraordinary Lives: Women in American History*, ed. Kriste Lindenmeyer. Wilmington, DE: Scholarly Resources, 2000, 147–159.

———. *Splendid Donation: A Life of Philanthropist Mrs. Russell Sage*. Bloomington: Indiana University Press, 2003.

de Forest, Robert W. "Margaret Olivia Sage, Philanthropist." *The Survey* 41, 1918, 151.

Gleason, Arthur Huntington. "Mrs. Russell Sage and Her Interests." *The World's Work* 13, November 1906, 8182–8186.

Hammack, David C. "The Russell Sage Foundation, 1907–1947: An Historical Introduction." In *The Russell Sage Foundation: Social Research and Social Action in America, 1907–1947.* Frederick, MD: UPA Academic Editions, 1988, 1–14.

Hammack, David C., and Stanton Wheeler. *Social Science in the Making: Essays on the Russell Sage Foundation, 1907–1972.* New York: Russell Sage Foundation, 1994.

Patton, Julia. *Russell Sage College: The First Twenty-Five Years, 1916–1941.* Troy, NY: Press of Walter Snyder, 1941.

Sage, Margaret Olivia. "Opportunities and Responsibilities of Leisured Women." *North American Review*, 181, November 1905, 712–721.

———. "Mrs. Russell Sage's Plea." *New York Daily Tribune*, August 8, 1898, Section II, 7.

"Sage Will a Surprise." *Troy Record.* July 28, 1906, 5.

Sarnoff, Paul. *Russell Sage, the Money King.* New York: Ivan Obolensky, 1965.

Scott, Anne Firor. " 'The Ever-Widening Circle': The Diffusion of Feminist Values from the Troy Female Seminary, 1822–1872." *History of Education Quarterly* 19, Spring 1979, 3–25.

PAPERS

The main collections of Olivia Sage's papers are at the Rockefeller Archive Center (Sleepy Hollow, NY) and at the Emma Willard School (Troy, NY). Other scattered papers can be found at the Butler Library, Columbia University (New York City); the New York State Library (Albany, NY); New York University Archives (New York City); the New York Public Library (New York City); Rutgers University Archives (New Brunswick, NJ); U.S. Military Academy Archives (West Point, NY), and elsewhere.

MARGARET SANGER
(1879–1966)

Leader of the Birth Control Movement

INTRODUCTION

"To preach a negative and colorless ideal of chastity to young men and women is to neglect the primary duty of awakening their intelligence, their responsibility, their self-reliance and independence. Once this is established, the matter of chastity will take care of itself" (Sanger 1922, 249). With this challenging statement, Margaret Sanger declared her faith in the right and responsibility of individuals to manage their sexuality, in their self-interest, but always informed by social responsibility. Born into a society where the conduct of women was closely scrutinized and opportunities for personal expression and social achievement were restricted, Sanger helped to engineer a social revolution that gave women the right to leave the private sphere of the home for work and play with men in public.

To make this transition, she believed, women had to control their own bodies. Sanger dedicated herself to the deceptively simple proposition that access to safe and reliable means of preventing pregnancy was a necessary condition of women's liberation, and in turn, of human progress. She led a successful campaign to remove the stigma of obscenity from contraception and to establish a nationwide system of clinics where women could obtain reliable birth control services. She organized research to improve methods, won court battles that changed obscenity laws, laid the groundwork for acceptance of birth control by organized medicine, and finally, in the year before her death, witnessed the U.S. Supreme Court affirm her belief that there was a fundamental right to practice birth control (*Griswold v. Connecticut* 1965).

EARLY YEARS AND EDUCATION

Margaret Sanger was drawn to social reform through a series of vivid personal experiences that began in childhood. Born Margaret Louise Higgins in Corning, New York, on September 14, 1879, she was the sixth of eleven children and third of four daughters. Her father (Michael Hennessy Higgins), a freethinking political radical, earned a poor living as a stonemason, while her mother (Anne Higgins) struggled to make ends meet and maintained the Roman Catholic faith of her Irish ancestors. Margaret Higgins admired her father's rebelliousness, but she was also haunted by her mother's premature death from tuberculosis at the age of fifty, a result, in Margaret's view, of excessive childbearing. With the help of two older sisters, Margaret Higgins fled home after her mother's death, attended private schools, and was working her way

Margaret Sanger in 1961. Library of Congress; LC-USZ62-118519.

through nursing school in 1902, when marriage to architect William Sanger ended her formal education. Sanger survived a difficult first pregnancy complicated by tuberculosis. By 1911, she had three children and a suburban home in Westchester County, New York, but found life as a housewife stifling. In an effort to save their troubled marriage, the Sangers moved to New York City to participate in the radical activism and bohemian culture that they both found attractive. Margaret Sanger worked as a home nurse on the Lower East Side, and, as an activist in the Women's Committee of the New York Socialist Party, she participated in major labor struggles such as the 1912 strike of textile workers at Lawrence, Massachusetts.

Radical leaders such as William "Big Bill" Haywood of the International Workers of the World found Sanger especially effective because she did not fit the popular stereotype of the leftist agitator. She was a petite mother of three, native born, and a trained nurse. Sanger gradually lost the reticence expected of a lady as she linked issues of social justice with her developing enthusiasm for sexual liberation. Alienated both from her husband and from male comrades whose attitudes toward women seemed little different from those of other men, Sanger became convinced that women needed a distinctive voice representing them as an interest group and argued that control of their bodies was the paramount issue for women. Her emerging feminist consciousness was provoked when an article on syphilis and female hygiene for *The Call*, part of her series on "What Every Girl Should Know," was declared obscene by the U.S. Post Office under the Comstock Act of 1873, whose sweeping provisions banned information on contraception and abortion. Venereal disease exacted a terrible toll from women denied knowledge of their bodies, but the numerous abortion-related deaths among Sanger's slum-dwelling patients provided an even more horrifying symbol of female degradation. Sanger claimed that the death of one of her clients led her to focus all her energy on the single cause of reproductive autonomy for women. In the story of Sadie Sachs, a truck driver's wife who was scornfully refused contraceptive advice by a doctor and instructed instead to have her husband sleep on the roof, Sanger found a compelling myth that conveyed her outrage at the suppression of knowledge that women needed, whether their primary concern was the economic survival of their families or the desire for greater personal freedom.

CAREER HIGHLIGHTS AND MAJOR PHILANTHROPIC CONTRIBUTIONS

Although many nineteenth-century marriage manuals described contraceptive methods, most medical men and other social leaders were troubled by declining birthrates among native-born Protestant women and agreed that the public interest was best served by suppressing information on fertility control. Sanger's first task in the fight to win reproductive autonomy for her sex was to identify a safe, effective, female-controlled contraceptive. She hoped to mobilize a mass demand for legalized birth control through the publication—beginning in March 1914—of her militantly feminist journal, *The Woman Rebel* (where the term "birth control" was coined in the June 1914 issue). The post office declared the journal obscene even though it gave no specific contraceptive advice. After being indicted for violation of the postal code, Sanger departed for Europe in October 1914. Left behind were her instructions for mass distribution of her how-to-do-it pamphlet *Family Limitation*, which provided the most detailed and informed discussion of contraceptive techniques available in English.

During exile in Europe, Sanger became an intimate friend of Havelock Ellis, author of *Studies in the Psychology of Sex* (1897–1910). Influenced by Ellis and other British intellectuals, she began to develop a more cautious propaganda that exploited the rhetoric of social science and sought to win social elites to the cause of sexual liberation. In the Netherlands, Sanger found contraceptive advice centers staffed by midwives and attended classes in the fitting of the spring-loaded vaginal diaphragm, which became the primary method she recommended. Sanger returned to the United States and, in October 1916, opened a women's clinic in the Brownsville section of Brooklyn, where 464 mothers got contraceptive advice during the ten days before a police raid closed the center. Her trial and brief imprisonment made Sanger a national figure, and, in appealing her case, she won a clarification of the New York law that forbade distribution of birth control information. Judge Frederick Crane ruled that the 1873 statute under which Sanger had been arrested was reasonable because it allowed doctors to prescribe condoms for venereal disease. In rejecting Sanger's claim that the law was unconstitutional because it forced women to risk death in pregnancy against their will, Crane established the right of doctors to provide women with contraceptive advice for "the cure and prevention of disease," thus widening the venereal disease clause to include women.

Sanger interpreted the Crane decision as a

mandate for doctor-staffed birth control clinics. Although she continued to send revised editions of *Family Limitation* to those who asked for it, she adopted the strategy of lobbying for "doctors only" bills that removed legal prohibitions on medical advice. This pragmatic concession was bitterly opposed by Mary Ware Dennett, Sanger's chief rival for leadership of the birth control movement in the 1920s, but Sanger's willingness to cultivate support among doctors was part of her shift in strategy. Gradually, she broke her ties with old comrades, played down her radical past, stressed eugenic arguments for birth control that were in vogue among academics, and found financial angels among socialites and philanthropists. Such support allowed her to organize the American Birth Control League in 1921. Having divorced William Sanger in 1920, she completed her social transition in 1922 by marrying James Noah H. Slee, the manufacturer of Three-in-One Oil, who demonstrated his ardor for birth control by smuggling contraceptive devices into the United States from Europe and by making large donations to the cause.

By 1923, Sanger had developed the network of support that allowed her to open the Birth Control Clinical Research Bureau in New York City, and to keep it open despite a 1929 police raid. The first doctor-staffed birth control clinic in the United States, the clinic provided case histories that demonstrated the safety and effectiveness of contraceptive practice. Social conservatives' irresponsible claims that diaphragms caused cancer and madness, and did not work anyway, were refuted. The clinic also served as a teaching facility where hundreds of physicians received instruction in contraceptive techniques at a time when it was not a part of the medical school curriculum. Finally, the clinic was a model for the nationwide network of over 300 birth control clinics established by Sanger and her supporters by 1938. Staffed mainly by women doctors and supported by women volunteers, these clinics provided access to reliable contraceptive advice and were responsible for important improvements in the effectiveness of contraception.

During the 1930s, Sanger organized a major lobbying campaign to remove contraception from the federal Comstock Act. The effort failed because the ideal of reproductive autonomy for women was literally a joke among male legislators at a time when the birthrate had fallen below the level needed to maintain the existing population. Additionally, President Franklin Roosevelt's New Deal political coalition depended heavily on the votes of urban ethnics, who were often Roman Catholics and believed that efforts to separate sex from procreation violated natural law. Sanger was able to win a major revision in federal law, however, by opportunistic use of the courts, a public forum where the political power of Roman Catholics was minimized and success depended on finding a judge who recognized that the social mores of Americans had fundamentally changed since the late nineteenth century. In the early 1930s, Sanger's National Committee on Federal Legislation for Birth Control was participating in multiple court actions challenging bans on contraceptives. When a shipment of Japanese pessaries (diaphragms) intended for Dr. Hannah Stone, the medical director of the Birth Control Clinical Research Bureau, was confiscated, federal judge August Hand ruled in *United States v One Package* (1936) that the clinical data on the effectiveness of contraceptive practice made available since the passage of the Comstock Act mandated recognition of the right of physicians to receive contraceptive materials. This legal victory set the stage for a 1937 resolution by the American Medical Association that recognized contraception as an ethical medical service.

After the *One Package* case, Sanger played a less important role in the American birth control movement and retired to Tucson, Arizona. Her occasional calls for "birth strikes" until women got justice seemed out of step during a period of economic stagnation, which economists associated with the low birthrates of the Great Depression decade. Much to Sanger's chagrin, new leaders replaced "birth control" with "family planning" in the title of the national organization in an effort to broaden the appeal of the movement. Rapid world population growth after World War II brought new respect for Sanger's ideas and she was a founder and first president of the International Planned Parenthood Federation in 1952. Sanger raised subsidies for research in reproductive biology throughout her career. Vindication for her persistence came in the 1950s, when she brought the work of the biologist Gregory Pincus to the attention of her long-time ally and financial benefactor Katharine Dexter McCormick, who subsidized the development of the birth control pill first marketed in 1960.

CONCLUSION

Sanger was the voice linking feminism with sexual liberation in the early twentieth century. She left humble origins and radical associates behind as pursuit of her cause required that she accept and cultivate support from the society women and wealthy philanthropists whose funds made it possible to open clinics, win court cases, and conduct lobbying campaigns. Religious leaders and historians have criticized her move into the political mainstream as well as her association with academic eugenicists and racists who wanted to sterilize the mentally incompetent and to limit the numbers of the poor. While she did not advocate efforts to limit population growth solely on the basis of class, ethnicity, or race, and refused to encourage higher birthrates for the middle and upper classes, Sanger's reputation was tainted by her relationship with eugenicists, who, ironically, enjoyed the academic respectability and social standing that Sanger lacked.

Sanger was ahead of her time, however, in recognizing that the personal and the political cannot be separated. She did more than any other person to liberate women from sexual oppression and to provide them with the self-knowledge that they needed to compete with men in the modern world. The strongest argument used by antifeminists has been that biological necessity dictates that women bear children, with the implication that this reality must involve limitations on careers and activities outside of the home. Sanger believed that women could combine motherhood with social equality and led the way in her private life and public career.

James W. Reed

FURTHER READING

Chesler, Ellen. *Woman of Valor: Margaret Sanger and the Birth Control Movement in the United States.* New York: Simon & Schuster, 1992.

Forster, Margaret. *Significant Sisters: The Grassroots of Active Feminism, 1839–1939.* New York: Alfred A. Knopf, 1985.

Garrow, David J. *Liberty and Sexuality: The Right to Privacy and the Making of Roe v. Wade.* New York: Macmillan, 1994.

Gordon, Linda. *Woman's Body, Woman's Right: A Social History of Birth Control in America.* New York: Penguin Books, 1990 [1976].

McCann, Carole R. *Birth Control Politics in the United States, 1916–1945.* Ithaca, NY: Cornell University Press, 1994.

Reed, James W. *The Birth Control Movement and American Society: From Private Vice to Public Virtue.* Princeton, NJ: Princeton University Press, 1983 [1978].

Sanger, Margaret. *Margaret Sanger: An Autobiography.* Elmsford, NY: Maxwell Reprint Co., 1970 [1938].

———. *My Fight for Birth Control.* New York: Maxwell Reprint Co., 1969 [1931].

———. *The Pivot of Civilization.* New York: Brentano's, 1922.

PAPERS

The two largest collections of Margaret Sanger's papers are in the Library of Congress (Washington, DC) and the Sophia Smith Collection of Smith College (Northhampton, MA).

ELIZABETH ANN BAYLEY SETON
(1774–1821)

Founder of the Sisters of Charity and the American Parochial School System and Roman Catholic Saint

INTRODUCTION

"The promising and amiable perspectives of establishing a house of plain and useful education, retired from the extravagance of the world . . . an abode of innocence and refuge of affliction" (Dirvin 1990, 131). Part of a letter written in 1812, this statement by Elizabeth Ann Bayley Seton expresses what she envisioned as her life's work. Following God's will, Seton wished to educate and nurture the minds and souls of children. Since schools, then as now, create the basis for economic advancement and a better life; she founded the Sisters of Charity with the mission of improving people's lives through education and service to others. Thereafter, Seton and her fellow Sisters of Charity significantly shaped Catholic education in the United States.

EARLY YEARS AND EDUCATION

Born on August 28, 1774, in New York City, Elizabeth Bayley was the second of three children born to Dr. Richard Bayley and Catherine Charlton Bayley. Elizabeth Bayley would become, both by birth and by marriage, part of New York society's wealthy and influential families. Her father was an eminent and respected surgeon, and was the first professor of anatomy at Columbia University (then King's College). Due to his work, he was often away from home for long periods of time.

During her lifetime, death was a frequent companion. Consequently, she thought about God and eternity from an early age. By the time she was four years old, she had already lost her mother and her younger sister (Catherine Bayley). Her father soon remar-

Mother Elizabeth Seton. The University of Notre Dame Archives.

ried but she and her older sister (Mary Bayley) were sent to their uncle for long periods of her childhood. As a very busy physician who spent his life serving and caring for others (especially the poor), her father's example and influence had a direct impact on her life. Indeed, he possessed an extensive library for his time and directed her learning. Owing to her desire to please her father, she was a well-educated young woman for her time. Her father's influence and example as well as her education helped to shape a future life of service.

In 1794, she married William Magee Seton, the son of William Seton and Rebecca Carson Seton. The Setons were one of the wealthiest and most prominent families in

New York society. William Seton worked in the family import business, the shipping firm of Seton, Maitland, and Company. Within a few years, the young couple had five children: Anna Maria, William, Richard, Catherine, and Rebecca. Elizabeth Seton enjoyed this period of her life; she felt complete and blessed with her husband and children.

While a mother and wife, Seton was also active in her parish. As a parishioner of Trinity Episcopal Church, she sought ways to help those in need. In 1797, the Society for the Relief of Poor Destitute Widows with Young Children was established. Founded by Elizabeth Seton, her sister-in-law (Rebecca Seton), and several other parishioners, this group was so active in helping the poor that its members were sometimes called the Protestant Sisters of Charity. Betty McNeil stated: "This group became the first charitable organization managed by women in the United States. This association not only raised funds to benefit needy families but also spearheaded education for the children, employment for their mothers, and low-income shelter for needy families" (McNeil 1999, 26). As the organization's treasurer, Elizabeth Seton demonstrated the management skills that would serve her well in the future.

This charitable effort illustrated how Seton always sought to accept the will of God in her life, and to help those less fortunate than herself. She believed that one should serve the poor and those in need because such acts were serving Christ. She always, whether as an Episcopalian or later as a Catholic, strove to serve God and to do His divine will and work.

Within a short span of time, Seton's life changed dramatically. In 1798, her father-in-law died. Three years later, her father passed away. Furthermore, the Napoleonic Wars led to a decline in the fortunes of the firm of Seton, Maitland and Company. Bankrupt, and with her husband suffering from tuberculosis, Elizabeth Seton, her husband, and their oldest daughter (Anna) went to visit Antonio and Filippo Filicchi in Italy in 1803. The Filicchis were business associates and close friends of her husband, and she hoped

the climate in Italy would improve her husband's health. Unfortunately, they were placed in a quarantine prison in Leghorn, Italy as soon as they arrived because officials feared that William Seton was suffering from yellow fever. When he was released thirty days later, William Seton's health had so declined due to the Lazaretto confinement that he died a few days later on December 27, 1803.

The Filicchi brothers and their wives took in the young widow and her daughter. For the rest of her life, the Filicchis would continue to help Elizabeth Seton with their friendship, connections, and money. During her stay with the Filicchis, Seton observed the peace and joy that they found in their Catholic religion. She had always sought a closer spiritual relationship with Christ, and finally found it in the Eucharist of the Catholic Church. Seton returned to New York City in 1804, and began the journey that would change her life. Her conversion to Catholicism would bring her immense spiritual fulfillment, but it would also cost Seton her status in society and the life that she knew.

In 1805, Seton became a Roman Catholic and, as a result, was ostracized by most of her family and friends. Seton also began teaching her own children, afraid that their spiritual needs, as well as their education, would not be properly fulfilled if left to her wealthy Episcopalian relatives and friends. Indeed, she believed that all children needed a Christian education. Needing to support her children, she tried to teach at a few schools in New York City, but the anti-Catholic feeling of the time prevented her from keeping a position. In fact, Seton would have to move to Maryland to begin her life's work for God.

CAREER HIGHLIGHTS AND MAJOR PHILANTHROPIC CONTRIBUTIONS

Father Du Bourg of St. Mary's Seminary invited Seton to Baltimore, Maryland to start a school. In 1808, a Catholic school for girls was opened on Paca Street. Baltimore was America's leading Catholic city at that time, and Seton soon had plenty of pupils, as well as her own children, to teach. Soon, other women joined her, and they founded a religious community, the Sisters of St. Joseph. Seton took her vows in March 1809, and received the title of Mother. Meanwhile, Samuel Cooper, a Catholic convert, donated land—in Emmitsburg, Maryland—and money for the support and growth of Mother Seton's religious community as well as a school for poor children.

The educational opportunities of Seton's time were very different from today. Wealthy individuals were the only ones who could afford to educate their children. Furthermore, boys were expected to be well educated, preparing them for leadership roles in society and government. However, girls did not need an extensive education because their role in life was to be a good wife and mother. As well as reading, writing, and arithmetic, a girl's education probably consisted of learning to play the piano, speak English and French, create intricate and regular needlework, and run an efficient household for her future husband. In the male-centered world of the nineteenth century, women were dependent upon their fathers, husbands, or other male relatives to provide for them.

In June 1809, the sisters arrived in Emmitsburg, Maryland. On February 22, 1810, the first free Catholic school in the United States opened. While this educational institution was not the first Catholic elementary school, it would become the model and foundation for the Catholic parochial school system in the United States. Indeed, this school would become well known for providing its pupils (girls and boys) with an excellent education, academic and religious. Deeply involved in the education of her students, Seton taught, trained the sisters as teachers, wrote the textbooks, and translated books for lessons from French to English. Wishing to nurture both the minds and spirits of her students, Seton, and the sisters she trained as teachers, not only taught all of the academic subjects to the students, but also gave them a firm foundation in religion, including chapel time each day. To educate poor children and to help bear the expenses

of the community, Seton and her fellow Sisters of St. Joseph soon accepted those students whose parents could pay for their tuition. This policy enabled them to educate the poor or nonpaying children while also maintaining financial stability.

On July 19, 1813, the Sisters of Charity, the first American religious order, was officially established and made education its main mission. The order's constitution and rules, with modifications, were based on the rules of the Daughters of Charity founded by Vincent de Paul and Louise de Marillac in the seventeenth century. One of the modifications allowed Seton, who became the first mother superior, to remain the legal guardian of her children. Seton had devoted her life to serving Christ because she viewed Christ as the source and model of all charity, serving the poor, the sick, and children. Thus, her religious vows would include poverty, chastity, and obedience, but also the vow of service to the poor.

The first mission of the Sisters of Charity soon followed. Seton sent a few Sisters of Charity, under Sister Rose White, to Philadelphia in 1814 to assume the charge of Saint Joseph's Asylum, the first Catholic orphanage in the United States. She later sent Sisters to start Saint Patrick's Orphan Asylum in New York in 1817. Day schools soon followed. In 1818, the Sisters opened a free school for German Catholics in Philadelphia. This institution represented the first free parochial school taught by nuns in America, and was the forerunner of parish schools associated with Catholic churches.

CONCLUSION

Elizabeth Ann Bayley Seton died on January 4, 1821. In life, Seton championed the belief that education was important to all—not just those who could afford it—and religious education would be the foundation for a better life, preparing her students to be the leaders of tomorrow. Although she did not start the first Catholic school, she is regarded as the founder of the parochial school system in the United States. She and her Sisters of Charity became responsible for laying the foundation of Catholic education in almost every one of the early American dioceses as well as starting the parochial school system in the United States.

The Sisters of Charity were foremost teachers but they continually demonstrated a love for the poor and afflicted as well. Consequently, the Sisters of Charity also founded hospitals (including America's first Catholic hospital), sanitariums, orphanages, settlement houses, child-care centers, working girls' homes, training schools for nurses, deaf-mute institutes, homes for the aged, foreign missions, insane asylums, and a leprosarium. Clearly, Seton's influence lives on through the Sisters of Charity and the charitable works they perform. In recognition of Seton's works and legacy, Pope Paul VI canonized her as a saint on September 14, 1975.

Patricia E. McWilliams

FURTHER READING

Celeste, Marie, S.C. *The Intimate Friendships of Elizabeth Ann Bayley Seton: First Native-born American Saint (1774–1821)*. New York: Alba House, 1989.

Code, Joseph B. *Mother Elizabeth Seton*. New York: Paulist Press, 1950.

Dirvin, Joseph I. *Mrs. Seton: Foundress of the American Sisters of Charity*. New York: Farrar, Straus & Giroux, 1975.

———. *The Soul of Elizabeth Seton*. San Francisco: Ignatius Press, 1990.

Feeney, Leonard. *Mother Seton: Saint Elizabeth of New York (1774–1821)*. Cambridge, MA: Ravengate Press, 1975.

Fugazy, Irene M., S.C. *Elizabeth Ann Seton Saint*. Rome, Italy: Albagraf, 1997.

Kelly, Ellin, and Annabelle Melville, eds. *Elizabeth Seton: Selected Writings*. New York: Paulist Press, 1987.

McNeil, Betty Ann, D.C. *The Mountain and Valley of Saint Elizabeth Ann Seton*. Emmitsburg, MD: Daughters of Charity, 1999.

Reville, John C. *Mother Seton*. New York: America Press, 1921.

Sadlier, Agnes. *Elizabeth Seton, Foundress of the American Sisters of Charity: Her Life and Work*. Philadelphia: H.L. Kilner & Co., 1905.

White, Charles I. *Mother Seton: Mother of Many Daughters*. Garden City, NY: Doubleday & Company, 1949.

Wilson, Paul E. *Conscience of America: Saint Elizabeth Seton, American*. (New York): American Broadcasting Companies, 1975.

PAPERS

The largest collection of Elizabeth Ann Bayley Seton's papers is located at the Archives of the Daughters of Saint Vincent de Paul, Saint Joseph's Provincial House (Emmitsburg, MD). One can also find Seton papers at the St. Elizabeth Ann Seton Collection, 1798–1982, Northeast Province Archives, the Daughters of Charity of St. Vincent de Paul (Albany, NY) as well as the Robert Seton Collection, which includes Seton family papers from 1782 to 1908 and is located at the Notre Dame Archives, University of Notre Dame (South Bend, IN).

JAMES SMITHSON
(1765–1829)

British Chemist and Mineralogist and Founder of the Smithsonian Institution

INTRODUCTION

For decades after ratification of the Constitution, the scope and powers of the federal government remained a subject of intense debate, including disputes over the role of the federal government in matters involving education, health care, and scientific research. In 1835, a generous bequest to the federal government by British nobleman James Smithson and "for the establishment of an institution for the increase and diffusion of knowledge" intensified this debate (Rhees 1879, 2). Arriving at a time when Americans were sharply divided between the Jacksonian Democrats, who favored reducing the size of government, and the Whigs, who believed that government should play an active role in promoting "internal improvements," the controversy over the Smithson bequest helped to clarify ideas about the role of government and the nature of philanthropy. As finally established by Congress in 1846, the Smithsonian Institution—a private endowment controlled by public officials acting ex officio as trustees—represented a model of public philanthropy that would be widely emulated throughout the United States.

EARLY YEARS AND EDUCATION

Born in France in 1765, James Smithson was the natural son of Hugh Smithson, the first duke of Northumberland, and Mrs. Elizabeth Keate Macie, a granddaughter of Sir George Hungerford of Studley. Among the British aristocracy of the eighteenth century, an illegitimate birth was no obstacle to social and professional success. Graduating from the University of Oxford in 1786, he pursued a career as a gentleman scientist, devoting his life to travel and to research in chemistry and mineralogy, and never married. He was elected a fellow of the Royal Society, an acknowledgment of his contributions to the leading scientific journals, *Annals of Philosophy* and *Philosophic Transactions.*

CAREER HIGHLIGHTS

In the last decades of the eighteenth century—the high tide of the Age of Reason—the possibilities of science riveted the attention of ambitious men on both sides of the Atlantic. **Benjamin Franklin**, in combining careers as a scientist, entrepreneur, and statesman, had set a pattern that others strove to emulate. His younger countryman, **Benjamin Thompson** (better known as Count Rumford), after fleeing America with

James Smithson was an English mineralogist and founder of the Smithsonian Institution in Washington, DC. © Bettmann/CORBIS.

other Loyalists following the American Revolution, emerged as a major figure in physics, social reform, and diplomacy. Thompson was the chief promoter of a new kind of scientific organization, the Royal Institution—which described itself as "a Public Institution for diffusing the Knowledge and facilitating the general Introduction of useful Mechanical Inventions and Improvements, and for teaching by courses of Philosophical Lectures and Experiments, the Application of Science to the Common Purposes of Life" (Thompson 1970, V; 439). Established in 1799, the Royal Institution undoubtedly served as inspiration for the bequest that Smithson would make to the U.S. government thirty years later.

Smithson died in Genoa, Italy, in 1829. His estate, which exceeded $100,000, was bequeathed to a nephew with the stipulation that, should the nephew die childless, it should go "to the United States of America to found at Washington, under the name of the Smithsonian Institution, the establishment of an institution for the increase and diffusion of knowledge among men" (Rhees 1879, 2). When the nephew died in 1835, the American ambassador in London was notified of the bequest.

Little is known about Smithson's reasons for making this bequest. Inquiries made by Richard Rush, the American envoy placed in charge of representing the nation's interests as the estate made its way through the Court of Chancery, were unrevealing. "I have enquired if his political opinions or bias were supposed to be of a nature that led him to select the United States as the great trustee of his enlarged and philanthropic views" (Rhees 1879, 61). Writing the Secretary of State, Rush continued:

> The reply has been that his opinions, as far as known or inferred, were thought to favor monarchical rather than popular institutions; but that he interested himself little in questions of government, being devoted to science, and chiefly chemistry, that this had introduced him to the society of Cavendish, Wollaston, and others advantageously known to the Royal Society in London, of which body he was a member, and to the archives of which he made contributions. (Rhees 1879, 61)

As a scientist, Smithson is little more than a footnote in the annals of the physical sciences. During his lifetime, his philanthropy was negligible. Indeed, he only became a significant figure after his death, as Americans struggled over the best use of his legacy.

MAJOR PHILANTHROPIC CONTRIBUTIONS

Setting aside the unquestionable importance of the Smithsonian as a philanthropic and scientific institution, its greatest significance is as a catalyst in debates over the role of government and the nature of philanthropy. Although a handful of states had well-developed philanthropic traditions by the beginning of the nineteenth century, many Americans—especially adherents of the egalitarian doctrines of Jefferson and Jackson—worried that big government and private institutions supported by the wealthy were a threat to democracy. Furthermore, the federal courts had issued contradictory rulings on the status of philanthropy. Although the Supreme Court had upheld the trustees of Dartmouth College in their efforts to resist a takeover by the state of New Hampshire (*Dartmouth College v. Woodward*) in 1819, in the same term, in *Philadelphia Baptist Association v. Hart's Executors*, the court had upheld the Commonwealth of Virginia's limitations on philanthropic bequests. Although the court would ultimately affirm the idea of private philanthropy in 1844 by upholding the charitable bequest of **Stephen Girard** to the City of Philadelphia (*Vidal, Girard, et al. v. Philadelphia*), between 1838, when the Smithson bequest was received, and 1846, when Congress finally acted to establish the Smithsonian, both the legal and the institutional outcomes remained very much in doubt.

President Jackson notified Congress of the Smithson bequest on December 17, 1835. In a brief message, he noted, "The Executive having no authority to take any steps for accepting the trust, and obtaining the funds, the papers are communicated with a view to such measures as Congress may deem necessary" (Rhees 1879, 135). Thus, the bequest was referred to the Senate Judiciary Committee.

When the Senate moved to approve the Judiciary Committee's report, a bitter debate broke out, with Southern senators arguing that Congress lacked the power to accept the bequest and declaring that it should be beneath the dignity of the United States to receive gifts from foreigners. The bill authorizing the President to take steps to secure the Smithson bequest was passed by a large majority against the determined opposition of southern senators led by John Calhoun. In the meantime, the House of Representatives had taken up the matter, entrusting it to a select committee chaired by John Quincy Adams. The committee's report, authored by Adams, was an extraordinary meditation on the larger meaning and possibilities of the bequest, as well as on the implications of trusteeship—a concept foreign to most of Adams's colleagues. The concept of trusteeship Adams set forth was, despite the public nature of the body to which the trust was committed, a distinctly Bostonian version, which emphasized not only faithfulness to the intentions of the testator, but the sense of a more profound accountability to a higher power—the public good.

The debate over the propriety of accepting the fund was only the prelude to a protracted wrangling in which congressmen and civilians alike (including Adams himself) came forward with their favorite schemes. The most interesting aspect of this debate was the extent to which it entailed a broad-ranging appraisal of the nature and needs of American public culture, an assessment of the role of government in cultural and educational affairs, and an exploration of the available instrumentalities of cultural action. The opposite poles of the debate involved popular models, which would devote the funds to developing and disseminating *applied* knowledge—in the form of agricultural and mechanical arts—and elite models, which would emphasize scientific research carried out by trained specialists and the accumulation of collections of books and artifacts. Numerous institutional possibilities were offered, including a university and a public lecture series, as well as experimental farms and factories. As it became clear that Congress itself could never settle the question, the argument shifted from substantive to contextual grounds—from how the money should be spent to the question of who could most reliably and prudently make such a decision.

Early in 1839, the Senate resolved to incorporate a board of ex officio trustees consisting of the vice-president, the chief justice, the secretaries of state and treasury, the attorney general, the mayor of Washington, three members of the Senate, four from the House, and two "citizens of the United States." The matter was not settled so quickly or easily in the House, where both congressmen and their constituents continued to offer suggestions about the activities that the Smithsonian Institution should pursue.

CONCLUSION

In the course of the debate, the Smithson bequest fell prey to politics. "The apparent total indifference of Mr. [President] Van Buren to the disposal of the money" (Rhees 1879, 774), Adams wrote in his diary, is "so utterly discouraging that I despair of effecting anything for the honor of the country," and fear the bequest will be wasted (Rhees 1879, 775). In fact, the legacy was invested in Arkansas and Michigan state securities and lost when the states defaulted on their debts; Congress only reluctantly refunded the money after Adams and others shamed their colleagues into restoring it. This act did not mark an end to congressional debate over the Smithsonian. Every year, questions came up about the terms of appointment to its staff and governing board; controversy and scandal surrounded its acquisition of real estate and its letting of contracts for buildings. In an intensely political age, when virtually everything was seen as fair game for spoilsmen, it was only natural that the Smithsonian should have been subject to constant efforts—which continue to this day—to divert its resources to private purposes and undermine its autonomy.

Peter Dobkin Hall

FURTHER READING

Goode, George Brown, ed. *The Smithsonian Institution: The History of Its First Half Century.* Washington, DC; 1897.

Hafertape, Kenneth. *America's Castle: The Evolution of the Smithsonian Building and Its Institution, 1840–1878.* Washington, DC: Smithsonian Institution Press, 1984.

Rhees, William J. *An Account of the Smithsonian Institution, Its Founder, Building, Operations, Etc., Prepared from the Reports of Prof. Henry to the Regents, and Other Authentic Sources.* Washington, DC: Thomas McGill, Printer, 1859.

———, ed. *The Smithsonian Institution: Docu-*

ments *Relative to Its Origin and History.* Smithsonian Miscellaneous Collections XVII, Publ. No. 328. Washington, DC: Smithsonian Institution, 1879. [Republished in 1901 with more documents and two volumes.]

Thompson, Benjamin. "Proposals for Forming by Subscription in the Metropolis of the British Empire a Public Institution for Diffusing the Knowledge and Facilitating the General Introduction of Useful Mechanical Inventions and Improvements, and for Teaching, by Courses of Philosophical Lectures and Experiments, the

Application of Science to the Common Purposes of Life." in *Collected Works of Count Rumford,* vol. 5, ed. C. Brown Sanborn. Cambridge, MA: Harvard University Press, 1970, 439–470.

PAPERS

Although James Smithson's papers were not deposited in an archive, a small collection of letters, related to Smithson's bequest, is housed at the American Philosophical Society (Philadelphia, PA).

GEORGE SOROS
(1930–   )

Financier, President of Soros Fund Management, Promoter and Benefactor of "Open Societies," and Founder of Numerous Foundations and Other Charitable Organizations Collectively Known as the Soros Foundations Network

INTRODUCTION

Describing the evolution of his giving philosophy, George Soros stated, "I've always had this idea of an open society, which is based on the recognition that our understanding is imperfect and therefore we need democracy, we need a market economy, we need rule of law . . . when I made enough money for my personal needs, I set up a foundation to foster an open society, help open up closed societies and help correct the deficiencies of open societies" (*Nightline* 1997). Like many important philanthropists in the past, Soros garners considerable amounts of praise and criticism for his global philanthropy. One of the wealthiest men of his time, billionaire Soros achieved great wealth through high-risk investment and then marshaled huge portions of his wealth toward an equally high-risk philanthropic agenda. Although assessing the significance of a living philanthropist is fraught with dangers, Soros already deserves credit for using his resources to undermine certain totalitarian and communist regimes. Longtime Foundation critic Waldemar Nielsen even characterizes Soros as "the boldest and most

visionary major donor in the world at the present time" (Nielsen 1996, 77).

EARLY YEARS AND EDUCATION

In 1930, George Soros was born in Budapest, Hungary to Tivadar Soros and Elizabeth Szucs. During World War I, Tivadar Soros had been a prisoner in Russia but managed to escape and then survive during the Russian Revolution. George Soros later observed that such an experience helped his father save his family during World War II: "When the Germans came in, he was mentally better prepared than most others for the turmoil" (Weiss 1993, 50). In 1944, Tivadar Soros, a lawyer and fairly wealthy man, forged official papers and paid government officials money to conceal his family's Jewish heritage from German and Hungarian fascists, who killed hundreds of thousands of Jews. George Soros even posed as the Christian godson of an official in the Hungarian Agriculture Ministry and found himself traveling with the official as he confiscated Jewish property and sent Jews on to the extermination camp in Auschwitz. In 1947, George Soros left Hungary, wishing to avoid life un-

George Soros speaking during a press conference at the World Economic Forum annual meeting in Davos, Switzerland, February 1997. AP Photo/ Patrick Aviolat.

der a communist government, and traveled to London. Extremely poor, Soros graduated from the London School of Economics in 1952. After selling handbags and jewelry, Soros eventually gained a trainee position with the British investment bank of Singer and Friedlander.

CAREER HIGHLIGHTS

In 1956, Soros became an arbitrage trader at F.M. Mayer in New York City. Five years later, he became an American citizen. In 1961, Soros married Annaliese Witschak. Although the couple would eventually divorce, they produced three children: Robert, Andrea, and Jonathan. While working for various other firms, Soros became quite successful as a money manager. Consequently, he formed the Quantum Fund with James Rog-

ers. As an offshore hedge fund, which makes it exempt from U.S. regulation but off-limits to American investors, Soros could guide the Quantum Fund to high risk but also high returns on investment. Soros's skill at money management, particularly the area of currency speculation, fashioned a fund that produced outstanding rates of return. In 1973, Soros became president of Soros Fund Management, which included the Quantum Fund and other investment vehicles. Owing to his extensive philanthropic activity, Soros no longer engages in the day-to-day management of his investment funds but still remains a principal force in the firm.

MAJOR PHILANTHROPIC CONTRIBUTIONS

In the late 1970s and early 1980s, Soros encountered a low point in his life. Divorcing his wife (1981), breaking with his original partner, experiencing strained relationships with his children, and even losing money one year, he lived a rather isolated existence in his Manhattan apartment. Reflecting on that period in a *Time* magazine article, Soros said, "I underwent a serious change in my personality during that period. There was a large element of guilt and shame in my emotional makeup" (Shawcross 1997, 48). Although Soros had engaged in philanthropy previously, even started giving anonymously, the growth of his charitable giving seemed to correspond with a renewed enthusiasm. In fact, William Shawcross wrote that "philanthropy was the cure" for Soros's malaise (Shawcross 1997, 48). Meanwhile, Soros married Susan Weber in 1983 and they had two children, Alexander and Gregory.

In developing the parameters of his giving philosophy, he combined personal encounters with totalitarian and communist governments with the powerful inspiration and ideas of philosopher Karl Popper, a former professor, who published *Open Society and Its Enemies* (1945). Through these two major influences, Soros subsequently became a full-time philanthropist who travels around the world and makes substantial donations to foster open societies: marked by vigorous debates, respect for minorities, democratic governments, and vitality. Like his former teacher, Soros fears closed societies—totalitarian or communist—in which the state uses its power to stifle or end debates by foisting one viewpoint upon its people, ensuring a lethargic society. Nonetheless, he also believes that closed societies are inherently unstable and even limited but strategic actions can significantly open those societies.

Soros's early grants illustrate his productive and creative use of philanthropy to nudge so-called closed societies toward open societies. In 1979, he started anonymously giving scholarships to black students in the rigidly segregated South Africa. During the 1980s, however, some of his most exceptional grants were given in Hungary. Although already supporting dissidents in Central and Eastern Europe, Soros managed to develop a relationship with the communist government in Hungary that allowed him to establish the Soros Foundation–Hungary, the first private independent foundation within a communist country, in 1984. Over the next five years, Soros used the foundation to undermine the communists. The communist government hoped to use Soros's largesse, which offered study abroad scholarships, to elevate their scientific research but instead found individual grant recipients returning to Hungary with positive attitudes toward Western ideals such as democracy and a market economy. In 1985, Soros damaged the communists' control of information by offering to donate copy machines to Hungarian libraries on the condition that secret-service agents—as opposed to the past—did not monitor them. Strapped financially, the Hungarian government agreed to Soros's stipulation. As a result, the underground press could more easily get their message out.

With the end of the Cold War and the fall of communism from 1989 to 1991, Soros moved quickly to foster the development of open societies among the old and new nations contained within Central and Eastern Europe as well as the former Soviet Union. Soros observed, "Communism has tried to form a universal closed society. Now . . . it was possible to create a universal open society. The first few moments of creation are always the most important: that is when the pattern is set. . . . Not only did I recognize the significance of the moment, I also had the resources to make an impact" (Quigley 1997, 88–89). Thus, Soros formed a myriad of "national foundations" in formerly communist countries. Believing in the need for broad and local civic engagement to foster open societies, Soros, unlike many other foundations working in the area, structured these foundations so that local citizens mange them and serve as the board of trustees. Still, Soros primarily funds these foundations and is actively engaged in their operations, which varies but includes support for democracy building, human rights, educational initiatives, and nongovernmental organizations.

Soros and his foundations also work on a number of regional projects. In 1990, he created a regional university, the Central European University. This university offers full scholarships for graduate education aimed at developing the region's future leaders as well as research pertinent to the development of emerging democracies. Acknowledged as a highly risky venture, the university has also been recognized as one of the most valuable philanthropic projects in the region.

Perhaps more than domestic philanthropy, international philanthropy necessitates the careful balancing of complex diplomatic relationships because foreign governments, corporations, nongovernmental organizations, and citizens can easily ensure the failure of a philanthropic endeavor. Moreover, Soros is not your average international philanthropist. Since he has billions of dollars in assets, gives hundreds of millions dollars to his philanthropies annually, and would like to give all of his money before he dies, Soros is a financial force on par with past philanthropic giants such as **Andrew Carnegie** and **John D. Rockefeller, Sr**. In fact, the amount he donates to a country even makes him more important than some foreign nations and viewed by others as a serious threat. In 1997, for instance, Soros closed the Belarus Soros foundation after the Belarus government—quite unfavorable to open society ideals—undertook criminal investigations against foundation personnel and charged the foundation $3 million for tax fraud.

During the later part of the 1990s, Soros began to turn more attention and resources to the United States. Observing that even long-standing open societies require continual development and are endangered by excessive capitalism and individualism, Soros asserted, "The core of an open society is under attack in our laissez-faire society" (Miller 1996, A1). Intending to stimulate "rational debate" within the United States, Soros concentrated on immigrant rights, dying and death, the drug war, education, and the criminal justice system (Miller 1996, A1). In 1996, for instance, he largely funded successful ballot initiatives in California and Arizona, which approved marijuana use for medical purposes. Furthermore, Soros believes the American "war on drugs" is ludicrous—although he does not promote the legalization of drugs—because it overly criminalizes drug users, and he hopes his money will facilitate debate on the country's drug policy. Expectedly, initiatives, such as challenging the American drug war and excessive capitalism around the world, spur criticism from some quarters. Sighting liberal bias, conservatives, such as Forbes magazine, regard some of his giving as possessing "a rather nutty political side" (Morais 1997, 82). Still, Soros appears to enjoy serving as a lightning rod for criticism if it elevates the level of debate on his chosen domestic or foreign issue.

CONCLUSION

In reviewing Soros's giving, Kevin Quigley rightly observed that Soros epitomizes "an intensely personal, high-profile philanthropy" (Quigley 1997, 90). Though Soros's personal connections to the development of emerging democracies is obvious, even such domestic programs as reconfiguring Americans' understanding and treatment of death stem from his personal experiences with his parents' deaths. Although an overall evaluation of the success or failure of Soros's philanthropy would be premature, opening closed societies and building emerging democracies and civil societies is extremely difficult and slow work. Perhaps expectedly, the local members of some Soros foundations have been cited as quite inefficient. Nonetheless, some of Soros's high-risk giving in Central and Eastern Europe has already made him an important philanthropist.

Robert T. Grimm, Jr.

FURTHER READING

Baker, Russ. "George Soros's Long Strange Trip: A Philanthropist Defies Drug War Orthodoxy." *The Nation*, September 20, 1999, 32.

Greene, Stephen G. "Eastern Europe's Ambivalent Benefactor." *Chronicle of Philanthropy*, December 3, 1991, 6.

———. "The Frustrations of a Modern Carnegie." *Chronicle of Philanthropy*, May 3, 1994, 1.

Kaufman, Michael T. *Soros: The Life and Times of a Messianic Billionaire*. New York: Knopf, 2002.

Marshall, Toni. "Enigmatic Billionaire Donor Soros Makes Waves with a Broad Activist Agenda." *Washington Times*, November 9, 1997, A1.

Miller, Judith. "A Giver's Agenda: With Big Money and Brash Ideas, a Billionaire Redefines Charity." *New York Times*, December 17, 1996, A1.

Morais, Richard. "Beware of Billionaires Bearing Gifts." *Forbes*, April 7, 1997, 82.

Nielsen, Waldemar A. *Inside American Philanthropy: The Dramas of Donorship*. Norman: Oklahoma University Press, 1996.

Nightline. "The World According to George Soros—Billionaire, Speculator, Crusader." November 5, 1997. Transcript.

Quigley, Kevin F.F. *For Democracy's Sake: Foundations and Democracy Assistance in Central Europe*. Baltimore: Johns Hopkins University Press, 1997.

Shawcross, William. "Turning Dollars into Change Savvy Financier George Soros Gave Away $1 Billion in Europe. Now He's Turned

Homeward with Some Unusual Ideas and Deep Pockets." *Time.* September 1, 1997, 48.

Soros, George. *Open Society: Reforming Global Capitalism.* New York: Public Affairs, 2000.

———. *Soros on Soros: Staying Ahead of the Curve.* New York: Wiley, 1995.

———. *Underwriting Democracy.* New York: Free Press, 1991.

Weiss, Gary, et al. "The Man Who Moves Markets—Super-Investor and Benefactor George Soros Is the Scourge of Europe's Central Banks." *Business Week*, August 23, 1993, 50.

PAPERS

George Soros's papers have not been deposited in an archive.

LELAND STANFORD
(1824–1893)
and JANE LATHROP STANFORD
(1828–1905)

Founders of the Leland Stanford Junior University

INTRODUCTION

"The intelligent development of the human faculties is necessary to man's happiness, and if this be true, each individual should, if possible, have such a liberal education as to enable him to understand, appreciate, and enjoy the knowledge of others. We trust that the education in this institution will be of such a liberal and broad character" (Stanford University 1891, 10). Speaking on opening day of the Leland Stanford Junior University, October 1, 1891, Leland Stanford sought to convey his deep commitment to the institution he and his wife, Jane Stanford, had established and endowed in 1885 for the purpose of educating the children of California.

EARLY YEARS AND EDUCATION

Amasa Leland Stanford was born March 9, 1824, to Josiah and Elizabeth Phillips Stanford in the Watervliet township of New York's Mohawk Valley. Leland Stanford's grandfather, Lyman Stanford, left Massachusetts and settled in the Albany region in 1799. He kept a tavern on the Albany-Schenectady turnpike and was appointed justice of the peace in 1811. Josiah Stanford continued in his father's footsteps and made his living as a farmer and an innkeeper. Although, as a young man, Leland Stanford signed letters A.L. Stanford, he did not use the name Amasa and was known as Leland Stanford throughout his life. The fourth son of eight children, Leland Stanford would make his mark in the world through business, politics, and philanthropy.

Of the six sons who would survive into adulthood, Leland and brother Thomas Welton Stanford were chosen to pursue professional careers. Leland Stanford attended public schools until the age of twelve and received three years of further education from teachers who came to his home. At seventeen, he began studies at Clinton and Cazenovia preparatory academies in upstate New York. It was at Cazenovia Seminary, a Methodist academy near Syracuse, that Stanford would develop interests in philosophy and debate. Perhaps more important for future developments in his life, Stanford observed the benefits of the coeducational experience offered at Cazenovia.

In 1845, Stanford moved to Albany to study law at the office of Wheaton, Doolittle, and Hadley. Three years later, he passed the New York bar. Declining a position at the law firm in Albany, he determined to move West and establish his own law office in Port Washington, which was in the new state of

Jane and Leland Stanford at the laying of the cornerstone for Stanford University. Courtesy Stanford University Archives.

Wisconsin. On the shore of Lake Michigan, Port Washington was a rapidly growing community in a largely Democratic county. As a confirmed Whig, Stanford was largely unsuccessful in his bids for elected office, but did serve as a village trustee and as president pro tempore of the town council for nine months. After two years of successful practice, Stanford returned to Albany to marry Jane Lathrop.

Jane Elizabeth Lathrop was born August 25, 1828, in Albany, New York to Dyer and Jane Ann Shields Lathrop. She was the third child and eldest daughter in a family of seven children born to the prominent Albany merchant and his wife. Like most young women of her generation, "Jennie" (as her husband would call her) was raised and educated at home. However, she briefly attended the Albany Female Academy. Jane Lathrop also accompanied her father on visits to the Albany Orphans Asylum, which he founded. Following their marriage on September 30, 1850, Jane and Leland Stanford made their first home together in Port Washington.

The faltering fortunes of Port Washington, coupled with a devastating fire that destroyed Leland Stanford's law office and extensive library, turned the eyes of the young and ambitious Leland Stanford westward once again. In June 1852, Leland Stanford departed for California to join his five brothers, Josiah, DeWitt, Charles, Phillip, and Thomas Welton Stanford, in Sacramento, California. Over the next three years, he established a career in business, selling supplies to the miners in the gold fields of California, while his wife resided in the safety of her parents' home in Albany, New York.

CAREER HIGHLIGHTS

In June 1855, after learning of his father-in-law's death, Stanford returned to Albany to be reunited with his wife. The young couple decided to make Sacramento their home, exchanging one state capitol for another, and traveled to California in late 1855. In the fall of 1856, Leland Stanford bought the Stanford Brothers firm in Sacramento from his brothers Phillip and Josiah Stanford and built a substantial new fireproof building. In addition to his business, Leland Stanford re-entered the political scene and was among the founders of the state's new Republican Party (launched at a convention held in Sacramento in April 1856). For the remaining years of his life, he would juggle the demands of business and politics. In late June 1861, the Central Pacific Railroad was chartered in Sacramento by a group of businessmen, including Stanford. Just over two months later, on September 4, 1861, the thirty-seven-year-old New York transplant, who had stumped the state for Abraham Lincoln, was elected governor of California.

Stanford began his term as California's eighth governor in January 1862. During his two years in office (the term was changed to four years in 1863), he battled the state's financial difficulties with a narrowly divided legislature. A small Republican majority enabled significant reforms in the state's civil rights codes, but opposition to granting equal rights to blacks or noncitizens was strong. Stanford is also credited with keeping California in the Union during the Civil War, although the secessionist movement supporters were perhaps far better at voicing their ideas than acting upon them. During Stanford's second year in office, the Central Pacific Railroad began laying track eastward from Sacramento to the Sierra Nevada. Since construction across the mountain range was slow and dangerous, crews did not reach the California-Nevada border until 1868. Stanford, President of the Central Pacific Railroad, drove the ceremonial last spike (made of solid gold) at Promontory Summit, Utah on May 10, 1869, to connect the Central Pacific and Union Pacific railroads.

Jane and Leland Stanford both came from large, close-knit families but starting their own family proved difficult. On May 14, 1868, at age thirty-nine, Jane Stanford gave birth to a healthy son at their Sacramento home. Leland DeWitt Stanford, who later chose to be called Leland Stanford, Jr., proved to be the couple's only child and became a prominent focus of their lives. By the time of Leland Stanford, Jr.'s birth, Leland Stanford, Sr. was a well-established businessman, but over the next ten years he would purchase significant acreages in northern Cal-

ifornia and become involved in growing grapes and breeding horses. The Stanfords would also build a mansion on Nob Hill in San Francisco following the move of the Central Pacific Railroad offices from Sacramento to San Francisco in 1873.

The Palo Alto Stock Farm, as the San Francisco peninsula property acquired piecemeal by Leland Stanford would be named, was a place where Leland Stanford could offer his son the country life that had been part of his own childhood. The stock farm was a working ranch, which boarded as many as 600 horses at one point and produced trotting horses that set nineteen world records between 1880 and 1895. Stanford tested his theories about breeding and training at the farm and developed what became known as the "Palo Alto system" of training by driving horses at full speed for short distances rather than the standard practice of driving them longer distances at a slower pace.

During the 1880s, the Stanford family undertook two tours of Europe. Leland Stanford, Jr., though only in his early teens, used the trips to gather historical objects for the museum he hoped to someday establish in San Francisco. He met with museum curators, visited archaeological sites, and furthered his studies in French and German. During their second trip, which began in May 1883, Leland Stanford, Jr. received education in the rudiments of hieroglyphics by the Louvre's Egyptologist, Georges Daressy, and was introduced to Heinrich Schliemann, the Homeric scholar and excavator of Troy. Following their visit to Troy, the Stanfords traveled to Naples and then on to Florence in an attempt to find a better climate in which Leland Stanford, Jr. could recuperate from what doctors diagnosed as a mild fever. Three weeks after arriving in Florence, Leland Stanford, Jr.'s health declined rapidly and he died of typhoid fever on March 13, 1884.

Leland and Jane Stanford were devastated by the loss of their only child, but at the same time were inspired, by his intelligence and interests, to begin planning several projects in his memory. After their return from Europe, the Stanfords consulted with educators at major universities on the east coast regarding their desire to create an educational institution in California in memory of their son. Although they were impressed by the education offered at Cornell University and Massachusetts Institute of Technology as well as the curriculum reforms underway at places like Harvard University, the Stanfords intended, from the beginning, to found an institution of their own—on the Palo Alto Farm—that would serve the needs of the children of California.

MAJOR PHILANTHROPIC CONTRIBUTIONS

On November 11, 1885, Jane and Leland Stanford signed the *Grant Founding and Endowing the Leland Stanford Junior University* in their San Francisco home. The document states the university's object and purposes clearly: "to qualify its students for personal success, and direct usefulness in life; [and] to promote the public welfare by exercising an influence in behalf of humanity and civilization" (Stanford University 1987, 4). In the grant, Jane and Leland Stanford provided for the university's initial endowment, defined the scope, responsibilities, and organization of the institution, and named the first board of trustees. In contrast to the major eastern universities, they outlined an institution that was coeducational, nonsectarian, tuition-free (the university instituted tuition in 1920), and open to all students regardless of social position or economic status. The Stanfords intended to create an institution that was responsive to the changing needs of the American society and that would train young men and women for useful, practical careers. They were also strong proponents of the value of education and the contributions that educated people can make to society. "We believe that a wise system of education will develop a future civilization as much in advance of that of the present as ours is in advance of the condition of the savage" (Stanford University 1891, 8).

Jane and Leland Stanford's support of ed-

ucational efforts took forms other than their own university. In January 1885, Leland Stanford was elected to the U.S. Senate by the California state legislature and in 1891, the year the university opened, he was elected to a second term that would be cut short by his death. In 1890, he spoke in favor of a bill to extend federal aid to an effort to overcome illiteracy. "In my opinion our Government can have no higher object than to secure to the people a high degree of intelligence, thereby assisting them to the attainment of the possibilities of humanity" (Clark 1931, 457). Meanwhile, Jane Stanford was active in supporting educational institutions in the San Francisco area. She donated funds to the Golden Gate Kindergarten Association and inspired other society women to support charities for child care and education. She also promoted a school on the Palo Alto Farm and a night school for employees of the stock farm. In Albany, New York, Jane Stanford turned her parents' home into a shelter for working women and their children.

It was the Leland Stanford Junior University, however, which would benefit most greatly from the Stanfords' largesse. Despite his senatorial duties, Leland Stanford took an active role in the planning and construction of the university. He chose a site in the flatlands of the stock farm rather than the foothills, which landscape architect Frederick Law Olmsted had recommended. Stanford also selected the quadrangle plan for the university, with a building design and construction materials that reflected the California landscape. Jane Stanford focused her energy on the plans for a memorial museum on the campus, housing Leland Stanford Jr.'s collection of antiquities and ethnological artifacts and the Stanfords' own collection of European art and Western American landscapes.

Leland Stanford's educational philosophy came largely from his own life experience and fused an intellectual and spiritual education with practical training. He believed in the teaching of moral, religious (though not sectarian), and civilizing ideals together with the tools that would provide students the means to make a living. These ideals played an important role in the selection of the first president of the university and set the tone for the institution's early years. David Starr Jordan, the forty-year-old Cornell University-educated president of Indiana University, was recommended to Stanford by the president of Cornell University, Andrew Dickson White. The Stanfords and Jordan shared a commitment to career-oriented education and to the creation of an institution that would foster invention and research.

The Leland Stanford Junior University opened on October 1, 1891, with fifteen faculty and more than 400 students. On June 21, 1893, shortly after the celebration of the university's second commencement, Leland Stanford died at his Palo Alto home at the age of sixty-nine. Stanford's death created an unforeseen and significant financial crisis for the university because Stanford managed the university as if it were part of his estate. With his death, Leland Stanford's assets were frozen and all income to the university was halted. Jane Stanford refused to allow the university to close and used her own income, as executor of the estate, to support the university through six difficult years in which the federal government sought early payment on the long-term loans made in the 1860s for building the Central Pacific Railroad.

CONCLUSION

In March 1896, the U.S. Supreme Court rejected the government's claims against the estate of Leland Stanford and its assets were released from probate in December 1898. As surviving founder of the university, Jane Stanford granted control of the university's endowment and management to the board of trustees on June 1, 1902. She died less than

three years later, on February 28, 1905, in Honolulu.

Out of the monumental sorrow brought about by their only child's untimely death, Jane and Leland Stanford turned to philanthropy and created a major educational institution. Their decision to contrast Stanford University from many other educational institutions helped to reshape the field of higher education. Clearly, the Stanfords' legacy has benefited not only the children of California but also the children of the world.

Margaret J. Kimball

FURTHER READING

Bartholomew, Karen, Claude Brineger, and Roxanne Nilan. *A Chronology of Stanford University and Its Founders, 1824–2000*. Stanford, CA: Stanford Historical Society, 2001.

Clark, George T. *Leland Stanford: War Governor of California, Railroad Builder, and Founder of Stanford University*. Stanford, CA: Stanford University Press, 1931.

Davis, Margo, and Roxanne Nilan. *The Stanford Album*. Stanford, CA: Stanford University Press, 1989.

Elliott, Orrin Leslie. *Stanford University: The First Twenty-Five Years*. Stanford, CA: Stanford University Press, 1937.

Nagel, Gunther. *Iron Will: The Life and Letters of Jane Lathrop Stanford*. Stanford, CA: Stanford Alumni Association, 1985.

Stanford University. *Exercises of the Opening Day of the Leland Stanford Junior University*. Palo Alto, CA: Stanford University, 1891.

Stanford University. *The Founding Grant with Amendments, Legislation, and Court Decrees*. Stanford, CA: Stanford University, 1987.

Tutorow, Norman. *Leland Stanford—Man of Many Careers*. Menlo Park, CA: Pacific Coast Publishers, 1971.

PAPERS

Leland and Jane Stanford's papers are located in the Stanford University Archives (Stanford, CA).

HENRIETTA SZOLD
(1860–1945)

Zionist Leader, Founder of Hadassah, and Mother of the Youth Aliyah

INTRODUCTION

In 1910, Henrietta Szold stated that "colonization in the twentieth century must be a philanthropy—a philanthropist, a leader of his people, will lay out a big plan, in which the architect will not blunder, in which the engineer will engage his best talents, in which men of science must have a share" (Fineman 1961, 250). Szold devoted her life to such a "big plan" and became instrumental in assisting the settlers of prestate Israel, in an area known at the time as Palestine, to set up social structures by organizing philanthropic efforts within the American Jewish community. She facilitated major donations by wealthy Americans, but is largely remembered for the manner in which she organized Jewish women in the United States. Szold began Hadassah, the preeminent women's Zionist organization, which established hospitals and schools in Palestine. She is equally remembered for her direction of the Youth Aliyah, which brought thousands of children to Israel before and after the Holocaust. Though she had no children, many of the Youth Aliyah participants considered Szold their mother.

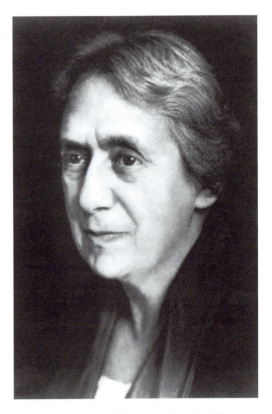

A 1944 portrait of Hadassah founder Henrietta Szold. Library of Congress; LC-USZ62-I20225.

EARLY YEARS AND EDUCATION

Szold was born on December 21, 1860, in Baltimore, Maryland, to Benjamin and Sophie Szold. Her parents emigrated from German-speaking Austria-Hungary so her father could become the Rabbi at Ohev Shalom Synagogue. The Szolds were part of an intellectual and social circle of progressive German Jews: dedicated to living both modern and intellectual lives as well as being observant Jews. Her father became a community leader in Baltimore, known as an abolitionist and participant in interfaith dialogues. His greatest influence, however, was on his daughter's life. He had six daughters and no sons, but Henrietta Szold became the son the Rabbi never had. He taught his oldest daughter German, Jewish history, and literature. Eventually, she helped him write his sermons, teach, and translate his work. Most important, Benjamin Szold taught her that she had an obligation to help her fellow-Jews to better themselves, their community, and society. Szold took these values as her own, never married, and dedicated her life to helping others.

Szold's early career can be characterized by her desire to help others gain the skills they would need to achieve well-rounded lives as American Jews. When Szold graduated from high school in 1878, she took a job teaching at Miss Adams' English and French School for Girls but also taught at her father's synagogue. At the same time, she began writing news, features, and editorials—under a pseudonym—for the *Jewish Messenger*, a weekly New York City publication. Soon, Russian Jews, who were not acculturated like their German peers, began immigrating to the United States. German Jews were more acculturated than Russian Jews because they immigrated earlier in the nineteenth century and came from western European cities. Most Russians came from rural areas and had not previously lived in an urban setting. Many Russian immigrants settled in Baltimore, where Szold established a night school in 1889 to teach English and American mores. Indeed, German-American Jews commonly helped newly arrived Eastern European Jews acclimate to American life.

In 1888, Szold was one of the founders of the Jewish Publication Society (JPS). This society published scholarly Jewish works in English to enable American Jews to pursue Jewish scholarship. Szold first served on the board of trustees, but became secretary for the JPS a year later, editing and translating works. In 1901, her father died. The next year, Szold, her mother, and her youngest sister moved to New York City so Szold could attend the Jewish Theological Seminary as a nonmatriculated student. Opened in 1901, this seminary wished to train rabbis to be—similar to Benjamin Szold—modern yet dedicated to tradition. Later, this branch of Judaism would be known as the Conservative movement. Szold continued to work for the JPS and began her interest in Zionism, which contended that the Jewish people should have a national homeland in Palestine, by joining a Harlem group in 1907 called Daughters of Zion. This study group discussed the work of the man credited with founding modern Zionism, Theodor Herzl.

CAREER HIGHLIGHTS AND MAJOR PHILANTHROPIC CONTRIBUTIONS

Fatigued by her work for the JPS and life at the Jewish Theological Seminary, Szold set out with her mother for a trip to Europe and Palestine in 1909. Szold's first trip to Palestine shaped the second half of her life. While abroad, she became convinced that Zionism represented the future of Judaism. She also realized that to help Zionism succeed, it was imperative that Jews around the world support the Jews living in Palestine. Thus far, the contributions to Palestine were given in a haphazard manner. As a result, the settlement of Palestine was uneven and the society's potential was not being realized. Jewish settlements, for example, founded and funded by European Jews were creating strong agricultural colonies. At the same time, poor sanitation, especially in Jerusalem, had caused diseases such as trachoma to become commonplace. However, such diseases could be alleviated with the building of hospitals and schools. Unfortunately, significant contributions to the Zionist cause had not envisioned such infrastructures. Szold realized the importance of laying the groundwork to improve the social and physical condition of the people.

Szold also encountered non-European Jews, known as Sephardim, during her first trip to Palestine. It was these Jews, more than the European Jews, who concerned her because they were typically poor and uneducated in European ways. Szold viewed Sephardic Jews as comparable to the Russian immigrants in the 1880s. She admired their piousness but believed they would need to be educated in modern Western European and American ways to flourish. Furthermore, she thought a weak infrastructure would make it difficult for diverse groups of Jews to successfully build a unified society and provide a refuge for Jews suffering abroad.

After Szold returned to the United States, she began delivering speeches to influential Jewish groups—mainly women's associations—about the importance of supporting Palestine financially. In her opinion, Jewish women in Palestine had a hard existence because male philanthropists were ignoring their needs. For example, farmers had the finest equipment available, but women were not given the tools to create modern and sanitary homes and schools for their children. After she began giving these popular speeches, she was asked to serve as secretary of the Federation of American Zionists. In that capacity, she began formally raising money for Zionist causes. At the same time, numerous study circles were created in American Jewish communities. Szold continued to organize more of these groups with the support of the Federation of American Zionists. These groups began calling themselves Hadassah, which is Hebrew for Esther, a Jewish heroine who is credited with saving the Jewish people of Persia from destruction. On February 24, 1912, Hadassah formally established itself as the national Zionist organization for women with Henrietta Szold as its chairperson.

In her capacity as founder and chairperson, Szold committed Hadassah to promoting public health in Israel: their first initiative sent two nurses to Israel to set up a clinic for women in Jerusalem. In 1916, the American Zionist Medical Union asked Hadassah to set up a staffed medical facility in Israel. Hadassah accepted the request and raised $500,000—over two years—to cover the project. To successfully achieve this goal, Szold secured funding from such well-known Jewish philanthropists as Baron DeRothchild, Louis Brandeis, Nathan Strauss, and the **Guggenheim** family. In addition, she raised 400 tons of donated goods through speaking and continuing to organize new Hadassah chapters.

At the same time, she accepted a position as secretary of Education of the Zionist Organization of America, which placed her in charge of Zionist education in America. With the funds raised and logistics arranged for the medical mission, Szold and a staff set up the Palestine medical facility in 1918. She also directed the further development of the infrastructure, opening several clinics and hospitals as well as the Nurses' Training School. This school, the first Hebrew-speaking establishment of its kind, opened in 1919. Later, Szold established the first Hebrew-speaking social-work school in Palestine. She fervently believed that education was the key to a society that could become the national home for all Jews.

Szold briefly returned to the United States to continue fund-raising and developing Hadassah as well as spend time with her family. In 1927, she returned to Palestine as an executive of the World Zionist Organization. Szold then concentrated her efforts on building programs that gave relief to struggling families, developing agencies to work with troubled youth, and continuing to work on issues of public health. She also worked to create environments that would foster healthier families, such as youth programs for children and Hebrew class for immigrants. Szold also encouraged American philanthropists to help finance her initiatives. Many Americans gave, even if they were not active Zionists, because they trusted the judgment and reputation of Szold.

In 1932, Szold's reputation as a Zionist, community builder, and social advocate inspired Recha Freir, a German woman, to contact her about creating the "Youth Aliyah." Germany had just enacted the Nuremberg Laws, which were legal restrictions on the activities of Jews, and many German Jews became nervous about their future in Germany and, led by Freir, began sending their children to Palestine before a mechanism could be set up to process the children. Szold became involved with Youth Aliyah because she believed it was important that these European teens be prepared for the difficult lives they would face in Palestine. At age seventy-three, Szold worked with the German community to develop a socially responsible way of resettling and educating the teens. Szold's efforts became more critical as Jews' situation in Europe worsened. Teens, and later younger children, immigrated to Israel and became placed in Youth Villages and Kibbutzim (Collectives). The Youth Aliyah also expanded to include all European Jewish children who were in danger and continued this policy well past World War II.

Ultimately, the Youth Aliyah was responsible for the immigration of over 155,000 children to Israel and Szold took personal responsibility for the safety and education of the children. In fact, the Youth Aliyah embodied Szold's most cherished values: service to her people, the social welfare of children, and strengthening the Jewish community.

CONCLUSION

Although she died in 1945, Hadassah and many of the other agencies Szold created still exist in the nation of Israel. Today, Hadassah continues to help improve the condition of women, children, and Israel as well as support the Hadassah Hospital, the premier institution in the Middle East. Clearly, Szold not only established important philanthropic institutions but also inspired others to give their time and money generously.

Robin Goldstein

FURTHER READING

Dash, Joan. *Summoned to Jerusalem: The Life of Henrietta Szold.* London: Harper & Row, 1979.

Fineman, Irving. *The Life of Henrietta Szold 1860–1945: Woman of Valor.* New York: Simon & Schuster, 1961.

PAPERS

Henrietta Szold's papers are located in the Hadassah Archives (New York City).

T

ARTHUR TAPPAN
(1786–1865)
and LEWIS TAPPAN
(1788–1873)

Evangelical Leaders, Abolitionists, and Business Innovators

INTRODUCTION

When Lewis Tappan founded the first national credit-rating agency in 1841, he meticulously recorded his reactions as he trudged through lower Manhattan to enlist store-keeping subscribers. At first, disappointment in winning new clients shook his faith in a benevolent God. Then, as the sun was setting, his fortunes miraculously improved. "I was surprised at my former unbelief & at the present revulsion in my feelings. I almost felt guilty. I applied to another customer, and he, after some persuasion, subscribed. My gratitude was now raised high, & I expressed it in ejaculatory prayer. The Lord, this day, has been better to me than my fears. Blessed be His holy name" (Wyatt-Brown 1997, 231). Tappan's unremitting determination to achieve both financial success and spiritual grace marked his life in business and religious work and contributed enormously to Northern evangelical reform. His brother Arthur Tappan shared these very same convictions. Yet, later in life, he was unable to generate the wealth he had formerly and lavishly expended on religious and educational causes.

EARLY YEARS AND EDUCATION

As the last two of eleven children, Arthur and Lewis Tappan, both born in Northampton, Massachusetts, were sons of former Bostonians: the merchant Benjamin Tappan, Sr., and Sarah Homes. Devout and strong-willed, Sarah Tappan had long worshiped at the town's First Church, where Jonathan Edwards had once famously presided. With unceasing zeal, Sarah Tappan prodded all her children to enroll as ardent and faithful advocates of Calvinist orthodoxy. The Tappan brothers attended the local schools before becoming apprentices to Boston merchants, who introduced them to commercial transactions and the intricacies of Italian double-entry bookkeeping. Afterward, shrewd maneuvers in shipping goods from Canada, at the start of the War of 1812, netted Lewis Tappan the capital to buy a hardware store in Boston. He married the well-born Susan Aspinwall (1813) and joined the Unitarian church, a decision that horrified his mother but doubtlessly assisted his social standing. Lewis and Sarah Tappan ultimately had six children, two sons and four daughters. In the meantime, Arthur Tappan, who never strayed from his mother's faith, married Francis Antill in 1810 (producing six daughters and two sons) and later migrated to New York City. There, after the War of 1812, he established a revolutionary style of merchandising. Arthur Tappan sold his goods to country merchants wholesale, offering competitively low prices. He could afford to do so because he traded in large volume while demanding cash only or extremely short-term notes. Soon, he was grossing $1 million a year and drawing handsome profits.

CAREER HIGHLIGHTS AND PHILANTHROPIC CONTRIBUTIONS

Events in the late 1820s brought the brothers into memorable collaboration. Sarah Tappan's death in 1826 and a collapse of risky business ventures led Lewis Tappan to reconsider both his religious faith and commercial interests. Sensing his change of heart, elder brother Arthur Tappan urged him to join his firm. He stipulated, however, that in exchange for assuming all of Lewis Tappan's debts, some $80,000, the younger brother would have to relinquish his Unitarianism. Convinced, as always, that God ruled both his fortunes and his heart, Lewis Tappan efficiently consented. When finances permitted, he moved his family from Boston to New York City. He began his career in helping his brother spend the New York City store's ample gains on philanthropic ventures while supervising the company's squad of underwear and straw-hat salesmen.

Not only did Lewis Tappan assist brother Arthur Tappan in the management of various evangelical societies, which distributed Bibles, tracts, and Sunday-school materials, but also accompanied and perhaps led his less outgoing, reticent older brother into new, radical directions. Their Magdalen Society sought to uplift the fallen women of the city. The mission, however, affronted the city's old land-holding elite: proprietors of the brothels and theaters where prostitutes met their clients. Likewise, local newsmen accused the Tappans of slandering New York City's good name. By organizing a campaign against delivery of U.S. mail on Sundays, the brothers courted further unpopularity. They objected to a policy that deprived postal workers the privilege of Sabbath worship and afforded the populace a tempting Sunday distraction. The howls of the impious against the Sabbatarian campaign, Lewis Tappan declared, gave sure "evidence of the righteousness of the cause" (Wyatt-Brown 1997, 70).

According to Lewis Tappan, these causes, along with temperance reform and stout defense of the Christian Cherokees against federal removal, would arrest the spread of a moral cancer in American politics. Still, the brothers concluded that the expansion of a slave economy and culture in the South represented the gravest problem. Aroused to action by young William Lloyd Garrison, whom Arthur Tappan had rescued from a Baltimore jail in 1830, the Tappan brothers were the earliest philanthropists to support the fiery editor's *Boston Liberator*. In 1833, the Tappans and Garrison helped to launch the American Anti-Slavery Society at a meeting in Philadelphia with Quakers and local African-American opponents of slavery. At its New York City headquarters, Lewis Tappan spearheaded drives for funds and took a major role in the management of the *Emancipator*, the society's chief organ. Arthur Tappan assumed the presidency of the new organization but he probably spent more time at the store, creating the means to finance this new and controversial enterprise against slavery. The antislavery leaders sought the elimination of the institution without compensation to owners, without an intermediary apprenticeship requirement, and, above all, without removal of freed slaves to Africa. The latter policy, to which the American Colonization Society was pledged, had once inspired the Tappans. In the late 1820s, however, they had become disillusioned with the expensive, piecemeal effort.

To reach members of the principal Protestant denominations, the pair enlisted the energies of a remarkable group of young evangelists. They included Elizur Wright, a later contributor to life-insurance reforms; the charismatic revivalist Theodore D. Weld, who was to marry the famous abolitionist and feminist leader, Angelina Grimké; the Rev. Joshua Leavitt, a gifted editor; and others. Recognizing the growing importance of the West, Arthur Tappan established, with a generous donation, an antislavery college in Ohio, Oberlin College, and induced the most prominent revivalist of the day, Charles Grandison Finney, to assume the chair of theology. At Oberlin College, Tappan Square, in the center of the campus, honors its patron.

Ignoring the perils of unpopularity, Lewis and Arthur Tappan also organized an evening service at the Chatham Street Chapel in early October 1833. Joined in prayer, whites and blacks defied the segregationist customs of the day. A riot ensued and mobsters chased the scattering worshipers around the church. Escaping through a back door, the brothers barely eluded a drunk armed with a dagger. The following year a much more widespread antiabolitionist riot erupted. In July 1834, mobs again took to the streets. They burned Lewis Tappan's household furnishings in the street, vandalized black churches, businesses, and homes, and assaulted Arthur Tappan's iron-shuttered and well-defended store. Still, this riot helped to publicize antislavery principles.

Perceiving that national unpopularity was better than indifference and obliviousness, the Tappans seized the chance to generate more publicity. Lewis Tappan was instrumental in organizing a massive postal campaign the following year. Tracts and papers reached thousands of influential figures in the free and slave states in the summer of 1835. Outraged, Southern slaveholders emboldened crowds to burn Arthur Tappan and Garrison in effigy and destroy the offending materials. Throughout Northern cities, proslavery speakers drew large crowds and cursed a program that, they predicted, would sever the Union and initiate a bloody race war. The protestors demanded postal censorship and President Andrew Jackson's administration happily complied. Such violation of free expression, however, gradually won the Tappans' cause a degree of sympathy in sundry Yankee quarters. Then, a massive petition campaign to Congress swiftly enlisted numbers of Northerners to antislavery. Yet, the famous Gag Rules prevented the thousands of petitions from reaching the House floor.

Even as the American Anti-Slavery Society, under Arthur Tappan's presidency, grew in numbers in the mid-1830s, the brothers faced a deterioration of their finances. Although his charitable gifts, many of them anonymous, had approached $50,000, Arthur Tappan could no longer maintain such generosity. His firm required $100,000 above expenses just to stay afloat. By 1840, the Pearl Street store was on the brink of insolvency. Suffering from severe migraines, Arthur Tappan grew listless and left management in the hands of his energetic brother. In 1841, Lewis Tappan left his desk, and Arthur Tappan took on a nephew as partner. Lewis Tappan's credit-rating strategy, however, soon generated a substantial yearly profit and provided him with the means to sustain his philanthropic interests. Meanwhile, Arthur Tappan spent his days at his residence in New Haven, Connecticut. Ever less frequently, he took the commuting steamer to his small, plain Manhattan cubicle.

In the new credit-assessing business, Lewis Tappan sought to combine the twin goals of his life: a sufficiency of wealth and a dedication to Christian stewardship. Resident agents, usually attorneys, throughout the North would inform his office regarding the financial reliability and sobriety of small-town and village entrepreneurs. At the New York headquarters as well as the Boston, Philadelphia, and Baltimore branches, across high counters, clerks read out from huge ledgers the reports on specific clients to inquiring subscribers. The agency's lawyers (Abraham Lincoln among them) would sue defaulting country storekeepers on behalf of the urban subscribers (mostly in dry goods). Tappan was convinced that his ingenious program had a moral impact. "It checks knavery, and purifies the mercantile air," Tappan proclaimed in 1843 (Wyatt-Brown 1997, 232). However, complaints were many: the Mercantile Agency's owner was too radical; the lawyers were dilatory and overcompensated; the credit seekers were falsely slandered; the subscribers were given incomplete or inaccurate information; and Tappan's clerks, some said, were surly (perhaps because of their low wages). Nonetheless, he had enlisted over 700 correspondents and produced for himself an income of $15,000 a year by 1846.

Aware of their reversal of fortunes, Lewis Tappan brought Arthur Tappan into the firm to permit himself time for more ennobling duties. He was, however, doubtlessly aware that his older brother's mental and physical ill health would not suit the go-getting climate of the operation. Yet, loyally Lewis Tappan marveled at his brother's business integrity, "Think of a man owing upwards of a million dollars divided among a hundred creditors and paying off every cent" with interest (Wyatt-Brown 1997, 241). By 1848, Lewis Tappan could afford retirement from business and sold out. Eventually, in 1859, the firm became the R.G. Dun Company. In 1932, it merged with Bradstreet, a competitor located in Cleveland, Ohio. Although he had founded a major innovation in business finance, Lewis Tappan's primary concern, like that of his older brother, was always the betterment of mankind in the name of Christian service.

Two years before establishing his Mercantile Agency, Lewis Tappan had begun his unceasing labors on behalf of the *Amistad* prisoners at a time when Arthur Tappan was withdrawing into chronic dejection. Within a few years, the *Amistad* cause evolved into a high point of Lewis Tappan's philanthropic work. In 1839, a supercargo of Mendi Africans killed the crew and commandeered *L'Amistad*, a Cuban slave ship. For weeks, the ship floundered in the western Atlantic until a U.S. naval crew boarded it off the tip of Long Island. A protracted series of court hearings and judgments offered the abolitionists the chance to publicize their crusade, expose the illegal foreign slave trade, and make a freedom-loving hero of Cinqué (the handsome young leader of the shipboard uprising). Among his innumerable activities for the captives, Tappan produced scores of articles for the Northeastern city papers and enlisted former President John Quincy Adams to argue the case before the U.S. Supreme Court. (Stephen Spielberg's otherwise remarkable film *Amistad* [1998] greatly diminishes Tappan's indispensable role.) In 1841, Adams won the case. Yet he accurately gave the credit where it truly belonged. The former President wrote Tappan, "The Captives are free! But thanks, thanks in the name of humanity and justice to *you*" (Wyatt-Brown 1997, 212).

Lewis Tappan also arranged for the Mendi Africans to return to their homeland. He hoped they would serve as Christian apostles to their heathen brethren. His vision, however, went further: the founding of a missionary body, combining the *Amistad* Committee with other small organizations. The purpose of such a group was to spread the antislavery gospel to all corners of the world. Under Tappan's supervision, the ecumenical American Missionary Association, as the new agency was called, developed antebellum missions in West Africa, East Asia, Canada, the British West Indies, Kansas, Kentucky, and the Minnesota Indian territory. During and after the Civil War, Tappan's organization founded and operated colleges and schools for Southern freed people, young and old. Among the more advanced institutions were Berea College, Kentucky, Tougaloo College, Mississippi, Fisk University, Nashville, and Howard University, Washington. Although in semiretirement by 1865, the year in which the Civil War ended and Arthur Tappan died, Lewis Tappan continued his work with the American Missionary Society. He rejoiced in its vast expansion to provide education, medical help, and religious sustenance to the needy former slaves. This vital work crowned his lifetime of relentless and effectual service to the cause of human freedom, an undertaking in which Arthur Tappan had once been so instrumental as well.

CONCLUSION

The abolitionist faction, for which the Tappans had so long striven, was by far the largest in the pre–Civil War period. About 100,000 to 250,000 citizens, chiefly Protestant churchgoers, belonged to or collaborated with the religious wing of the movement for immediate emancipation. These evangelicals formed the moral backbone, as it were, of the Republican Party when it arose amid the political chaos of the 1850s and then led the country through the bloody trials that followed. The Tappans undertook programs largely unsung but essential to the success of the antislavery movement. Always the optimist, before he died in 1873, eighty-five-year-old Lewis Tappan predicted that God would eventually bring about "the supremacy of the colored race & the humiliation of the proud and domineering Anglo-Saxons" (Wyatt-Brown 1997, 341). He underestimated the durability of human prejudice. Yet, both he and brother Arthur contributed more to trim its merciless influence than their obscurity in the American popular mind might suggest.

Bertram Wyatt-Brown

FURTHER READING

Abzug, Robert H. *Cosmos Crumbling: American Reform and the Religious Imagination.* New York: Oxford University Press, 1994.

Barnes, Gilbert H. *The Anti-Slavery Impulse, 1830–1844.* New York: D. Appleton-Century, 1933.

Friedman, Lawrence J. *Gregarious Saints: Self and Community in American Abolitionism, 1830–1870.* New York: Cambridge University Press, 1982.

McKivigan, John R. *The War against Proslavery Religion: Abolitionism and the Northern Churches, 1830–1865.* Ithaca, NY: Cornell University Press, 1984.

Stewart, James B. *Holy Warriors: The Abolitionists and American Slavery.* New York: Hill & Wang, 1976.

Wyatt-Brown, Bertram. *Lewis Tappan and the Evangelical War against Slavery.* Baton Rouge: Louisiana State University Press, 1997 [reprint].

PAPERS

Arthur Tappan left no documents and Lewis Tappan, in his *The Life of Arthur Tappan* (New York: Hurd & Houghton, 1870), attributes to his brother much of his own activities. The chief source for the study of the Tappans is the Lewis Tappan Collection at the Library of Congress (Washington, DC), which is now on microfilm. Tappan materials are also found in the Benjamin Tappan Papers, Ohio Historical Society (Columbus, OH); Charles G. Finney Papers and the college records in the Oberlin College Archives (Oberlin, OH); the Amos Phelps and William Lloyd Garrison Collections, Boston Public Library; the Gerrit Smith Papers, Syracuse University (Syracuse, NY); and the Theodore Dwight Weld Papers, William L. Clements Library (Ann Arbor, MI).

BENJAMIN THOMPSON, COUNT RUMFORD
(1753–1814)

British-American Scientist, Public Servant, and a Founder of the Royal Institution and Scientific Philanthropy

INTRODUCTION

"From the experience I have had in providing for the wants of the poor, and reclaiming the indolent and vicious to habits of useful industry, I may venture to consider myself authorized to speak," proclaimed Benjamin Thompson, Count Rumford in his 1796 essay, "Of the Fundamental Principles on which General Establishments for the Relief of the Poor May Be Formed in All Countries" (Thompson 1970, V: 102). The fact that the essay was simultaneously published in Geneva, London, and Paris (in English and in French) is indicative of the author's extraordinary career—in which he established an international reputation as a physicist, diplomat, public administrator, and philanthropist.

EARLY YEARS AND EDUCATION

On March 26, 1753, Benjamin Thompson was born in Woburn, Massachusetts to Benjamin and Ruth (Simonds) Thompson, part of a well-to-do farming family that had emigrated to the American colonies in the 1640s. Despite scant educational opportunities, Thompson was an able student. At the age of fourteen, he was "sufficiently advanced in algebra, geometry, astronomy, and the higher mathematics to calculate a solar eclipse within four seconds of accuracy" (*Encyclopedia Britannica* 1911, 23: 849). Apprenticed to merchants in Salem and Boston, he filled his spare time with chemical and mechanical experiments and attending the lectures of Harvard professor John Winthrop, then America's preeminent scientist.

Finding the prospect of a mercantile career too restricted for his ambitions, Thompson

Benjamin Thompson, Count Rumford. Dartmouth College Library.

turned his attention to teaching, working as a tutor to the children of wealthy local families. In 1772, at the age of twenty, he was invited to take charge of a large school in Concord, New Hampshire. Within months, he married Sarah Pierce, who was reputed to be the richest widow in Concord. As he would later write, "I might have been poor and unhappy all my life, if a woman had not loved me, if she had not given me a subsistence, a home, and an independent fortune" (Brown 2001, 8). Despite their difference in age (Pierce was fourteen years older than her husband), the alliance proved fortunate for Thompson. Drawn into the social circle of New Hampshire's governor, he was appointed a major in the Second New Hampshire Regiment.

CAREER HIGHLIGHTS

As tensions intensified between New Englanders and the British Crown, Thompson found himself drawn into politics as a Loyalist sympathizer. Subjected to threats by patriots, who twice tried him on the charge of "being unfriendly to the cause of Liberty," Thompson left his wife and young daughter (Sarah) behind in Concord and headed for Boston, then occupied by British troops, to seek his fortune. Gathering military intelligence for the British command, Thompson had to leave the city in the spring of 1776, when the king's forces evacuated Boston.

Thompson arrived in London in April 1776, a city that had become a world capital of culture and a hotbed of political intrigue. He attached himself to Lord Germaine, King George III's secretary of state, who appointed him to a succession of increasingly lucrative posts. He also continued to develop his scientific interests. In recognition of his experiments with ballistics and firearms, he was elected a fellow of the prestigious Royal Society in 1779. Two years later, he left the civil service, having been advanced to the position of Under Secretary of State for the Colonies, and purchased a colonelcy in the King's American Dragoons, a military company made of up Loyalists. During the fall of 1781, Thompson saw action in the Battle of Long Island.

With the British surrender in 1783 and with his patron, Lord Germaine, politically disgraced, Thompson had to seek new venues for exercising his considerable talents. Hoping to join the Austrian Army, then battling the Turks, he headed for central Europe. At Strassburg, he was introduced to Prince Maximillian, the Elector of Bavaria, who invited him to enter his military and civil service. During his sojourn in Bavaria,

Thompson served as minister of war, minister of police, and chief advisor to the prince. In this capacity, he took on the task of dealing with the country's poor.

MAJOR PHILANTHROPIC CONTRIBUTIONS

On the basis of a remarkable series of papers he wrote on the subject and his concrete accomplishments as a policymaker and institutional administrator, Thompson—who was made a count of the Holy Roman Empire in 1791—may justly be called the father of scientific philanthropy. Anticipating the charity reformers of the late nineteenth century, Thompson divided the poor into two groups, the "poor and distressed persons who have just claims on public charity" (Thompson 1970, V: 337) and "healthy individuals" who "live in idleness, without any fixed abode, concluding every day with schemes for defrauding the public of their subsistence for the next" (Thompson 1970, V: 336). For the worthy poor, he created a new institution—an almshouse operated by the military—where "all who are able to work may find employment and wages, and will be clothed and fed" (Thompson, 1970 V: 339). Thompson's military workhouses were more than mere custodial institutions: they provided literacy, vocational, and moral education intended to make the idle industrious.

Thompson believed that the "injudicious dispensation of alms" was the "real and only" cause of beggary—and favored institutional interventions designed to eradicate poverty rather than almsgiving that merely relieved suffering. Thompson encouraged citizens to give voluntarily to a fund for the "relief and support of the industrious, sick, and helpless poor." Thompson did not confine his interests in these institutions to policy and administrative matters. Determined that they should be operated with the greatest possible economy, he conducted experiments that resulted in important innovations in cooking methods, heating, ventilation, and nutrition. As he was not shy about publishing information about his inventions, they were widely adopted by Americans and Europeans alike.

Thompson returned to England in 1795, where he devoted himself to studying the physics of heat and its application to domestic heating. His plans for the design of fireplaces and chimneys (the well-known Rumford fireplace) have never been surpassed in efficiency.

In 1799, Rumford and fellow-expatriate Thomas Bernard proposed the organization of "a Public Institution for Diffusing the Knowledge and Facilitating the Introduction of Useful Mechanical Inventions and Improvements, and for Teaching, by Courses of Philosophical Lectures and Experiments, the Application of Science to the Common Purposes of Life"—an enterprise that would come to be known as the Royal Institution (Thompson, 1970 V: 439). Thompson recognized that, despite the extraordinary acceleration of scientific discovery in the eighteenth century, artisans and businessmen had few opportunities to learn about them or their application to the "arts and manufactures." Thompson wrote in the institution's prospectus, "I am only desirous that *science* and *art* [by which he meant the practical application of science] should once be brought cordially to embrace each other, and to direct their united efforts to the improvement of agriculture, manufactures, and commerce, and to the increase of domestic comfort" (Thompson 1970, V: 445). He believed that such improvements would, in promoting greater efficiency, produce greater prosperity—not only for the privileged, but also for the poor.

The institution was to be governed by a board of managers elected from among the institution's "founders and proprietors." It was to be supported by voluntary contributions, by life and annual memberships, and "by the sums that shall be received at the door from strangers who shall visit the repository [library and collections] of the Institution, or who shall obtain leave to frequent the philosophical lectures" (Thompson 1970 V: 458). Using his extensive connections among the highest reaches of British society, Thompson was able to enroll an extraordinary group of wealthy and influential backers and talented scientific researchers and lecturers.

In 1804, Thompson moved to France, where he married Marie-Anne-Pierette Paulze, the wealthy widow of the celebrated chemist Antoine Lavoisier. It was a stormy and unhappy marriage. The couple separated in 1808, when Thompson moved into his last residence at Auteuil, near Paris, where he died in 1814, at the age of sixty-two.

Despite his extraordinarily cosmopolitan life, Thompson never forgot his American origins. The fact of his birth "a Woburn pres de Boston en Amerique" was proudly inscribed on his tombstone. He left all his books, plans, and designs relating to military affairs to the U.S. Government "for use in any military academy that might be opened" (Brown 2001, 157). Having generously provided for his daughter during her lifetime, he left the remainder of his estate to Harvard University and for the establishment of a professorship, in his name, that would "teach by regular courses of academical and public lectures, accompanied by property experiments, the utility of the physical and mathematic sciences for the improvement of the useful arts, and for the extension of industry, prosperity, happiness, and well-being of Society" (Brown 2001, 157–158).

Americans too often forget that they have, from earliest settlement, been part of an Atlantic culture. Even with the formidable geographic obstacles to travel and communication existing before the steamship, airplane, and international telegraph, telephone, and radio, Americans and Europeans exchanged ideas with surprising ease and built international reputations. **Cotton Mather** was a fellow of the Royal Society and drew from the pages of its transactions the first reports of smallpox inoculation, which he immediately tried on his neighbors. **Benjamin Franklin**, who spent nearly a third of his long life abroad, carried back to Philadelphia the knowledge of voluntary associations, which he shared with his fellow-Americans. Through the eighteenth century, a steady flow of donations by generous Europeans nourished schools and colleges in the American colonies. In the early nineteenth century, the first American efforts to deal institutionally with poverty would be informed by the activities and writings of reformers like Thomas Chalmers and Benjamin Thompson, while Americans seeking advanced training as scholars and professionals would attend British, Scots, French, and German universities.

CONCLUSION

The philanthropic and scientific contributions of Benjamin Thompson not only serve to remind one of the extent to which American culture was an integral part of a larger Atlantic culture, but also that American philanthropy—like **James Smithson**'s and **John Lowell, Jr.**'s—cannot be understood without reference to Atlantic culture. In terms of its influence on American science and technology education, the Royal Institution was probably the most influential enterprise of its time. Its considerable resources—and the reputation of men like Thompson—enabled it to attract leading scientists as lecturers and resident scholars. It was the model for Philadelphia's Franklin Institute (founded in 1824), Boston's Lowell Institute (founded in 1839), and America's greatest national research and teaching facility, the Smithsonian Institution (founded in 1840). Thompson's bequest for an endowed Harvard University chair in applied science unquestionably helped to legitimate the study of "natural philosophy" (as physical science was called) in American colleges, as well as give attention to the value of exploring its practical applications. The nonacademic aspects of the Royal Institution, particularly the popular lectures it offered, set the precedent for the lyceums—popular lecture series—that played a vital role in the development of American intellectual culture in the decades before the Civil War. It is no exaggeration to say that Thompson is the founder of modern technical education and applied industrial research, both academic and popular.

Peter Dobkin Hall

FURTHER READING

Brown, G.I. *Scientist, Soldier, Statesman, Spy. Count Rumford: The Extraordinary Life of a Scientific Genius.* Gloucestershire, UK: Sutton Publishing, 2001 [1999].

Brown, Sanborn C. *Benjamin Thompson, Count Rumford.* Cambridge, MA: MIT Press, 1980.

Encyclopedia Britannica. Vol. 23. New York: Encyclopedia Britannica Company, 1911, 849–850.

Thompson, Benjamin. In *Collected Works of Count Rumford,* ed. Sanborn C. Brown. 5 vols. Cambridge, MA: Harvard University Press, 1970 [1968]

———. "Of the Fundamental Principles on Which General Establishments for the Relief of the Poor May Be Formed in All Countries." in *Collected Works of Count Rumford,* vol. 5, ed. Sanborn C. Brown. Cambridge, MA: Harvard University Press, 1970, 101–165.

PAPERS

The major collection of Benjamin Thompson/Count Rumford manuscripts is in the special collections of the Dartmouth College Library (Hanover, NH).

JOSEPH TUCKERMAN
(1778–1840)

Minister to Boston's Poor and a Prophet of Organized Charity

INTRODUCTION

"An impulse may be given to the poor by which their best efforts for self-support will be secured" (Hale 1971, 59). Although ill health often hampered his efforts, the Reverend Joseph Tuckerman served as minister to the poor of Boston from 1826 until 1839, striving earnestly to promote the self-reliance of impoverished Bostonians. His influential efforts, which affected and anticipated anti-poverty efforts for the next century and beyond, have led him to be called "America's first notable social worker" (Hawes 1986, 722).

EARLY YEARS AND EDUCATION

Joseph Tuckerman's family came from a long line of wealthy Americans. Indeed, the Tuckermans had been prosperous New England businessmen since the seventeenth century. His father, Edward Tuckerman, was a successful Boston merchant and public servant, who fought the British under Washington's command in the Revolutionary War. Joseph Tuckerman was educated at Boston Latin School, Phillips Andover Academy, and Harvard University. At Harvard University, he befriended William Ellery Channing, who was to become the founder of American Unitarianism, and Joseph Story, who was to attain prominence as a Supreme Court justice and legal commentator.

Tuckerman left Harvard University with a master's degree in 1801 and became the pastor of a Congregationalist church in the Boston suburb of Chelsea. Like his friend Channing, Tuckerman became a Unitarian. Unitarians rejected the Calvinist view that some people were unalterably destined for damnation. In its stead, they proclaimed a belief in the freedom of the will and the potential perfectibility of all human beings. These theological beliefs were to underlie Tuckerman's social service to the poor in important ways.

CAREER HIGHLIGHTS AND MAJOR PHILANTHROPIC CONTRIBUTIONS

Tuckerman became an important philanthropic figure almost by accident. His health was always frail, and a throat ailment in 1826 made it impossible for Tuckerman to continue to fulfill his duty to preach often and extensively to his congregation. Thus, he gave up his Chelsea pulpit. At the request of his friend Channing, Tuckerman then became minister at large to the poor of Boston, under the auspices of the American Unitarian Association. As minister at large, Tuckerman worked with poor Protestant families that were unaffiliated with a church. By the end of 1827, he serviced 170 such families—at a time when there were about 65,000 inhabitants of Boston.

Tuckerman's work with the poor consisted chiefly of personal visits. During the visits, he strove to understand the problems facing poor families and to offer solutions to them. He offered a range of moral and practical advice. Tuckerman declared that the objects of the ministry at large should be "to teach and to encourage cleanliness, temperance, economy, forethought; to aid in providing employment for those, the young and adults, who cannot obtain it for themselves; . . . and to be . . . an adviser and friend in whom they could confide" (Tuckerman 1838, 80). Tuckerman offered moral counsel to all the poor, even the most self-destructive among them. He never despaired, instead holding out hope for everyone, because in principle

Tuckerman believed that all could be redeemed. "I do not indeed believe there ever was, or that there is the human being, in whom there was or is no element of goodness; no element of moral recoverableness; no unextinguished spark of moral sensibility, which, with God's blessing may not be blown into a flame. There is no one so corrupted that there are no moral remains in him" (Tuckerman 1838, 89).

Although Tuckerman offered moral advice, he did not believe that poverty invariably resulted from vice or that prosperity was always a sign of moral virtue. Instead, he realized that many among the poor "have been industrious, temperate, and upright, as well as frugal," but nevertheless suffered when they were "thrown out of employment" (Hale 1971, 71–72) during hard economic times. He recognized that unemployment and low wages were major causes of poverty. Thus, he declared that a minister at large should be someone "who will know how to avail himself of the facilities which men in business can give him of obtaining employment for the poor, of extricating them from temporary difficulties, and of bringing them into the way of self-support" (Hale 1971, 54). He also called on employers to raise their workers' wages, which he thought were often unfairly low.

Tuckerman also believed that poor people without significant disabilities should strive for self-reliance. Therefore, he opposed the granting of cash relief payments to the able-bodied poor; he thought that their self-reliance was sapped when they were offered and accepted such payments. He did, on the other hand, believe that material assistance was essential for poor people who were rendered dependent by age or illness. Tuckerman also took a great interest in the problems of poor children. As a result, he was an early advocate of the expansion of public education, which he hoped would improve the prospects for impoverished youths. He also played a key role in establishing a reform school and a vocational school in Boston.

The demands upon the ministry at large soon expanded beyond Tuckerman's capacity to meet them. To better meet the needs of the poor, Tuckerman enlisted the cooperation of ministers in other Protestant denominations (Congregationalists, Methodists, Baptists, Episcopalians), who supplemented the Unitarians' efforts. Since Protestant hostility toward Catholicism ran high in the early nineteenth century, it is particularly noteworthy (and praiseworthy) that Tuckerman also sought to cooperate with Catholic clergy in assisting Boston's Catholic poor. Tuckerman took an active role in organizing Boston's charitable efforts, to prevent duplication of efforts among some twenty-six different philanthropic organizations, and to ensure that their funds were expended more efficiently and economically. His efforts in this direction foreshadowed attempts at charity organization that were to become far more common in American cities two generations later.

Although Tuckerman's service to the poor for the most part took place in the private sphere, he also held government posts. In 1830, he was elected one of the overseers of the Boston poor. In that capacity, he distributed relief to the sick and destitute residents of his ward. In 1833, commissioned by the Massachusetts House of Representatives, he also wrote a report on the Massachusetts Pauper System. In the report, he opposed a state system of support for the poor, which he thought undermined their self-reliance; instead he advocated charitable relief for the poor that was undertaken and administered on the local level.

CONCLUSION

As one of the earlier figures in the American philanthropic tradition, Tuckerman is notable because his practice of philanthropy anticipated approaches that were to characterize the charity organization movement (spearheaded by **Josephine Shaw Lowell**) that flourished a half-century after his death. Long before the charity organization movement, Tuckerman coordinated charitable efforts (to ensure that different organizations' efforts did not overlap). He also fostered interdenominational cooperation among religious charities: not only among rival Protestant groups, but also (remarkably for an era in which Protestants were deeply suspicious of Catholicism) between Protestants and Catholics. Furthermore, Tuckerman strove to assist the poor through personal interactions with them. Thus, Tuckerman anticipated the charity organization movement's contention that aid should be extended to the poor in ways designed to promote, rather than to replace, their self-help.

Nonetheless, Tuckerman's legacy relates not only to philanthropy in the late nineteenth century, but to philanthropy in the early twenty-first century. Tuckerman's philanthropy embodied an attitude toward the poor—respect and even reverence for them, coupled with insistence that the poor help themselves, and assistance in helping them to help themselves—that should be emulated in all times.

Joel Schwartz

FURTHER READING

Channing, William Ellery. "A Discourse on the Life and Character of the Rev. Joseph Tuckerman, D.D." In *The Works of William E. Channing, D.D.* Boston: American Unitarian Association, 1903, 578–599.

Hale, Edward Everett, ed. *Joseph Tuckerman on the Elevation of the Poor: A Selection from His Reports as Minister at Large in Boston.* New York: Arno Press and *New York Times,* 1971 [1874].

Hawes, Joseph M. "Joseph Tuckerman." In *Biographical Dictionary of Social Welfare in America,* ed. Walter I. Trattner. Westport, CT: Greenwood Press, 1986, 721–722.

Howe, Daniel Walker. *The Unitarian Conscience: Harvard Moral Philosophy, 1805–1861.* Cambridge, MA: Harvard University Press, 1970.

McColgan, Daniel T. *Joseph Tuckerman: Pioneer in American Social Work.* Washington, DC: Catholic University of America Press, 1940.

Schwartz, Joel. *Fighting Poverty with Virtue: Moral Reform and America's Urban Poor, 1825–2000.* Indianapolis: Indiana University Press, 2000.

Tuckerman, Joseph. *The Principles and Results of the Ministry at Large in Boston.* Boston: James Munroe & Co., 1838.

PAPERS

The most important collection of the papers of Joseph Tuckerman can be found at the Massachusetts Historical Society (Boston, MA).

LILLIAN D. WALD
(1867–1940)

Public Health Nurse, Social Reformer, Founder of Henry Street Settlement and Visiting Nurse Service of New York

INTRODUCTION

"Say to yourself, 'If there is a wrong in our midst, what can I do?' " (Dufus 1938, 71). Following her intense description of the problems associated with tenement housing and factory working conditions, these words by Lillian Wald demonstrate the commitment to immediate personal action and social justice that characterized her entire adult life. With what friends described as a sunny and irresistible personality, Wald also inspired others to join in her efforts to improve the lot of the less fortunate.

EARLY YEARS AND EDUCATION

Born in Cincinnati, Ohio on March 10, 1867, Lillian D. Wald was one of four children—the second daughter and third child—in a closely-knit family. After moving from Cincinnati to Dayton, Ohio, the Wald family finally settled in Rochester, New York when she was eleven. Lillian's father, Max D. Wald, was a dealer in optical goods; he had emigrated from Germany following revolutions in his home country as well as other European countries in 1848. Her mother, Minnie Wald, was a generous, charitable woman who moved into the Henry Street Settlement in her later years. The Walds were Jewish, however Lillian has been described as ambivalent about her Jewish identity. During her school years, she was assimilated and secure as part of Rochester's social set.

As a child, Wald was indulged, but she was also bright and energetic. She entered Miss Cruttendon's English and French Boarding and Day School for Young Ladies and Little Girls when she was eight years old and received a good education. At sixteen, Wald applied to Vassar College and was rejected on the grounds that she was too young. Disturbed by this rejection, she never applied to college again. Uncertain in her goals, Wald remained at Miss Cruttendon's and traveled;

A 1937 portrait of Lillian D. Wald. Library of Congress; LC-G412-9448-006.

she was restless and bored in the social setting surrounding her. However, her sister's difficult pregnancy helped Wald to redirect her life: the nurse who came to help Julia (Wald) Barry inspired Lillian to begin a career in nursing, and she entered the New York Hospital School of Nursing in August 1889. She graduated a year and a half later and became a staff nurse at the New York Juvenile Asylum. Appalled by the miserable conditions experienced by children in the asylum, Wald soon quit her position, enrolling in the Women's Medical College in New York City.

While at the Women's Medical College, Wald volunteered to teach weekly home-nursing classes in the Lower East Side. After a little girl took the inexperienced Wald to her hemorrhaging mother in a nearby tenement, Wald decided to move to the East Side and care for families in an "organic" relationship with their neighborhood. In summer

1893, Lillian D. Wald and Mary M. Brewster, a nurse and fellow-student, lived temporarily at the College Settlement (Rivington Street) and then settled into rooms in a nearby fifth-floor walkup. They began providing nursing services for their neighbors, but—as word of their work became known—visitors came to their apartment to be sociable as well. In a time of depression, they subsequently dealt with a range of problems faced by poor immigrant families. These activities led to the founding of two institutions that exist to this day, the Visiting Nurse Service of New York and the Henry Street Settlement, organizations only formally separated in 1944.

CAREER HIGHLIGHTS AND MAJOR PHILANTHROPIC CONTRIBUTIONS

In 1895, Brewster and Wald moved into a house at 265 Henry Street, which still is the core of the Henry Street Settlement. At that time, the settlement was called the "Nurses Settlement," but some unfriendly voices taunted "Noices! Noices!" and for that and other reasons the name Henry Street Settlement was adopted. Before long, Brewster left because of poor health; under Wald's direction, the settlement continued to provide nursing care in people's homes, which included advice about disease prevention, sanitation, and education.

The initial purchase of the house on Henry Street and its refurbishing were paid for by the financier Jacob Schiff, who was to remain Lillian Wald's friend and mentor throughout her career. Indeed, Wald's work was possible because she was able to secure the support and counsel of wealthy Jewish leaders in New York, starting with Mrs. Solomon Loeb and Jacob Schiff; ultimately she received invaluable assistance from the Loebs, Schiffs, Warburgs, and Morgenthaus. At the start, she was required to account to Jacob Schiff regularly; within a few years, however, he grew to trust her and reports became less frequent and less detailed. In these years, Henry Street depended entirely on private contributions, and it was said to be expensive to sit next to Lillian Wald at dinner.

According to R.L. Dufus, the "family" of the settlement included nine nurses, only some of whom were paid, and others, "nonnurses," who were considered members of the "laity" by 1898. Among the most famous of lay residents was **Florence Kelley**, brilliant attorney and fiery activist, who moved from Chicago's Hull-House to Henry Street, bringing intellectual breadth and a social agenda with her. From the 1890s onward, Wald was surrounded by strong-minded women who were deeply attached to her, including Lavinia Dock. Wald worked with Dock and other suffragists to secure the vote for women, and she sought improvement of labor conditions for women. However, only in recent years has a serious effort been made to define Wald as a feminist.

In shaping the Henry Street Settlement, Wald has been described as moving "energetically from one activity to another" (Daniels, 1989, 46). As Head Worker (her preferred title), she was responsible for a proliferation of programs at Henry Street, including the first playground in the nation (1902), lectures, arts and crafts for children, and a theater-and-dance program begun by the Lewisohn Sisters, which developed into the famous Neighborhood Playhouse. Henry Street also served as a union meeting place. In fact, Wald helped to found the National Women's Trade Union League in 1903. She later joined the Executive Committee of the New York City League.

Although Henry Street, like other settlements, had a "Negro" branch, African Americans were welcome at Henry Street. In 1909, the settlement hosted a landmark event, the National Negro Conference, which led to the formation of the National Association for the Advancement of Colored People (NAACP). In the next few years, Wald worked with Florence Kelley and others to draw attention to the needs of children in the United States: her skills as a persuasive negotiator were considered critical in helping to establish the federal Children's Bureau in 1912.

In the field of health, Wald did more than organize a district nursing service associated with the Settlement. In 1900, she pressured the New York City Board of Education to have special education for disabled and handicapped children. She even persuaded the Department of Education to hire its first school nurse in 1902, resulting in what she called "the first municipalized nurses in the world," which later led to the formation of a Bureau of Child Hygiene and an expansion of nursing services by the New York City Department of Health (Wald 1915, 53). Wald also helped to inaugurate a public-health-nursing lecture series at Teacher's College, leading to the establishment of the Columbia University Department of Nursing and Health (1910). In 1912, she served as the first president of the National Organization for Public Health Nursing, of which she was one of the founders. In 1916, Wald worked with the Henry Street nurses to help mobilize an all-out effort against a polio epidemic.

By 1913, Henry Street Settlement, with an annual budget around $500,000, extended into seven buildings and had become a community of research-informed individuals working for social reforms. Wald was involved in reform activity in the community, the city, and the nation, and that year she was also given the medal of the National Institute of Social Sciences for "distinguished services rendered to humanity" (Dufus 1938, 135). By this time, Wald was in frequent contact with **Jane Addams** of Hull-House (Chicago) on issues of common concern, and activists like *Commons* editor Paul Kellogg and the minister John Haynes Holmes. Famous socialists, such as Sydney Webbs of England, were visitors to the house, as were many philanthropists, including the **Rockefellers**, Morgenthaus, and Belmonts, all of whom Wald helped educate about the urban poor.

Despite her generally good rapport with her supporters, and particularly with Jacob Schiff, there were times of tension. Early on, she found it difficult to persuade Schiff that collective action by labor was beneficial, but he eventually supported a worker's strike. In 1914, Schiff also seems to have lost his temper with Wald over Christmas-related events and decorations at the settlement; he reminded her that she was a Jewish woman but was mollified when he recognized her desire to serve Christian as well as Jewish children.

During the period before America entered World War I, Wald lost supporters because of her pacifist activity. In 1916, Wald joined Jane Addams and Ida Tarbell in support of Woodrow Wilson's presidential bid. After he was elected, she headed a delegation that delivered a congratulatory message from the American Union against Militarism. Wald persisted in efforts to prevent America's entry into the war and became disillusioned when President Wilson declared war on April 6, 1917. During the war, however, she chaired the Nurses Emergency Council and organized nursing groups for the war effort. After the war, Wald went to Europe and represented the Children's Bureau at a conference called by the Committee of Red Cross Societies to develop "an extended program of activities in the interest of humanity" around the world (Dufus 1938, 206). At this conference, Wald stressed the importance of public-health nurses in promoting programs for the protection of children.

Now an internationally known figure, Wald accepted an invitation to Russia in 1924. She came away deeply concerned about conditions in that country. The next year, Wald went to Mexico with Jane Addams and even met with its president. Owing to the grueling demands of the trip, she became ill before returning home. She subsequently endured deteriorating health and retired in 1933.

CONCLUSION

Wald died on September 1, 1940. Her *New York Times* obituary was titled "Lillian Wald Dies: Friend of the Poor." Although not considered introspective, Wald wrote two books about her experiences as a settlement house leader and reformer: *The House on Henry Street* (1915) and *Windows on Henry Street* (1934). Both works demonstrate how social work in a community can lead to action on larger social issues. In particular, *The House on Henry Street* remains an inspiration for those interested in Wald's story.

Meanwhile, Wald's heritage is actively present today. The Visiting Nurse Service of New York is flourishing. In fact, there are 13,000 visiting-nurse programs nationwide. Concurrently, Henry Street Settlement remains a model community organization. With both private contributions and government support, the settlement serves a diverse population, including Asian Americans, African Americans, Latinos, and immigrants from other countries, and continues its tradition of caring for the community.

Eleanor L. Brilliant

FURTHER READING

Coss, Clare, ed. *Lillian D. Wald: Progressive Activist.* New York: Feminist Press of the City University of New York, 1989.

Daniels, Doris Groshen. *Always a Sister: The Feminism of Lillian D. Wald.* New York: Feminist Press of the City University of New York, 1989.

Davis, Allen F. *Spearheads for Reform: The Settlements and the Progressive Movement, 1890–1914.* New York: Oxford University Press, 1967.

Dufus, R.L. *Lillian Wald: Neighbor and Crusader.* New York: Macmillan, 1938.

Epstein, Beryl Williams. *Lillian Wald: Angel of Henry Street.* New York: J. Messner, 1948.

Hall, Helen. *Unfinished Business in Neighborhood and Nation.* New York: Macmillan, 1971.

Siegel, Beatrice. *Lillian Wald of Henry Street.* New York and London: Macmillan and Collier Macmillan, 1983.

Wald, Lillian. *The House on Henry Street.* New York: Holt, Rinehart & Winston, 1915. [Reprint edition, with an Introduction by Eleanor Brilliant, New Brunswick, NJ: Transaction Press, 1991]

———. *Windows on Henry Street.* Boston: Little Brown & Co., 1934.

PAPERS

Lillian Wald's papers are located at the Lillian D. Wald Papers, Rare Book and Manuscript Library, Butler Library, Columbia University (New York City) and the Lillian Wald Papers, Manuscripts and Archives Division, New York Public Library (New York City).

MADAM C.J. WALKER
(1867–1919)

Entrepreneur, Women's Advocate, and Civil Rights Activist and Benefactor

INTRODUCTION

"My object in life is not simply to make money for myself or to spend it on myself in dressing or running around in an automobile, but I love to use a part of what I make in trying to help others" (Bundles 2001, 136). As a pioneer of the modern hair care industry and as one of the wealthiest African Americans and female entrepreneurs of her day, Madam C.J. Walker surely had the means to indulge herself with luxuries. However, the destitution of her early life had made her so sensitive to the profound needs of her community that she contributed generously to a wide range of social, educational, and political causes.

EARLY YEARS AND EDUCATION

On December 23, 1867, Walker was born Sarah Breedlove in Delta, Louisiana, on a Mississippi River cotton plantation that had been occupied by General Ulysses S. Grant during the 1862–1863 Siege of Vicksburg. The fifth of Owen and Minerva Anderson Breedlove's six children, she was the first freeborn member of her family. Since no public schools were funded for black children in Madison Parish, Louisiana during her early childhood, whatever formal education she received likely came from her family's church, which had been founded by Rev. Curtis Pollard, a black Reconstruction-era state senator. With both parents dead before her eighth birthday, Sarah Breedlove was left in the care of her twenty-one-year old sister, Louvenia Breedlove Powell.

At fourteen, she escaped what she called her "cruel" brother-in-law by marrying Moses McWilliams, with whom she had one child, Lelia (later known as A'Lelia Walker),

in 1885. By 1888, Sarah Breedlove McWilliams was a twenty-year old widow, and the details of her husband's death, like those of his life, are unknown. Soon after his death, she moved to St. Louis where her three older brothers already had established themselves as barbers. Like more than half of all employed black St. Louis women of the era, she found work as a washerwoman. Between 1894 and about 1903, she was married to John Davis, a laborer who was said to have physically abused her. Despite—or perhaps because of—his treatment of her, she became increasingly ambitious and sought the assistance of the middle-class black women of St. Paul AME Church. These women encouraged her efforts to educate her daughter and to improve her life.

During the final decade of the nineteenth century, she was also faced with a crisis that would transform her life. Suffering from untreated scalp disease, she became nearly bald and ashamed of her appearance. After praying to God to restore her hair, and after experimenting with several products that were already on the market, she claimed that a hair-growing-and-conditioning formula was revealed to her in a dream. Annie Pope-Turnbo Malone, another black woman whose hair care products she sold during this same period, would later claim that she had actually cured her ailment. (In truth, neither woman had originated the centuries-old petrolatum and sulfur remedy, but both would create successful businesses from its sale and distribution.) Long separated from Davis, Sarah Breedlove McWilliams Davis moved in July 1905 to Denver, where she joined her widowed sister-in-law and nieces and continued peddling Malone's products. In January 1906, she married Charles Joseph Walker, a newspaper sales agent whom she had met in

St. Louis. The same year, she established her own line of products and began calling herself "Madam" C.J. Walker, adopting a title that was commonly used by businesswomen—especially hairdressers—of the day.

CAREER HIGHLIGHTS

As president of the Madam C.J. Walker Manufacturing Company, Walker created marketing plans, training and franchising opportunities, and distribution strategies for her curative ointments and shampoo as innovative as those of any entrepreneur of her era. Acutely aware of the desires of an increasingly urbanized black populace—especially of those women eager to purchase the cosmetics and hair care aids that were being manufactured by an emerging American beauty products industry—she launched an extensive campaign throughout the South and Midwest between 1906 and 1908 to train commission agents and to develop her customer base. After settling briefly in Pittsburgh, where she founded Lelia College (the first of a chain of beauty schools for Walker hair culturists), Walker moved to Indianapolis in early 1910 and continued coast-to-coast sales trips. Three years later, she established an international market for her products when she traveled to Central America and the Caribbean. In 1913, in partnership with her daughter, she also opened an impressive beauty salon and office in Harlem.

As an early advocate of women's economic independence, she provided lucrative incomes for thousands of African-American women who otherwise would have been consigned to jobs as maids, laundresses, and sharecroppers. Frequently, she urged black women "to rise above the laundry and kitchen . . . and to aspire to a place in the world of commerce and trade" (Bundles 2001, 153). Indeed, she continually argued that "the girls and women of our race must not be afraid to . . . wring success out of a number of business opportunities that lie at their very doors" (Bundles 2001, 153). Eventually, Walker would claim 20,000 sales agents.

Often described by the press and others as the first self-made American woman millionaire, even though her estate was actually worth between $600,000 and $700,000, Walker certainly was aware of the powerful symbolism of her achievements. In her Indianapolis office and factory, she established progressive employment practices: instituting paid vacations and subsidizing medical care. After organizing her sales agents into local and state clubs, she convened a national assembly of the Walker Beauty Culturists Union in August 1917, both to enhance their professional skills and to encourage them to set aside part of their earnings for charity. Walker later remarked, "I have insisted on the benevolent side of this convention, because I want my agents to feel that their first duty is to humanity" (Bundles 2001, 231). Furthermore, she wanted to "let the world know that the Walker agents are responsive to every human appeal, always ready to do their bit to help and advance the best interests of the Race" (Bundles 2001, 231). In adopting such a stance, she envisioned what few had ever imagined: a large-scale enterprise controlled by black women and organized around the principles of corporate responsibility, social betterment, and racial justice. In the aftermath of the deadly July 1917 East St. Louis riots, the union—as one of its first official acts—sent a telegram to President Woodrow Wilson, urging him to support legislation to make lynching a federal crime. The following year, in response to the backlash against the large World War I–era influx of black southerners into northern cities, she told her agents: "It is my duty, your duty, to go out in the back alleys and side streets and bring them into your home . . . where they can feel the spirit and catch the inspiration of higher and better living" (Bundles 2001, 231).

MAJOR PHILANTHROPIC CONTRIBUTIONS

Walker's philanthropic motivations stemmed from deeply held Christian beliefs that were influenced significantly by her participation in St. Paul AME Church's Mite Missionary Society, an organization whose members had assisted her when she first arrived in St. Louis. "She takes great stock in the theory that the Lord loves a cheerful giver," a reporter once wrote ("The Life of Mme. C.J. Walker," in *The Freeman: A National Illustrated Colored Newspaper*, December 26, 1914, 1). Walker's charitable contributions were numerous, ranging from orphanages and retirement homes for former slaves to stipends and commissions for promising young artists and musicians. She was particularly interested in black educational institutions including **Mary McLeod Bethune**'s Daytona Normal and Industrial Training School for Girls, Charlotte Hawkins Brown's Palmer Memorial Institute, and **Booker T. Washington**'s Tuskegee Institute, where she supported six students.

When she appealed to several leading black organizations for an endorsement of her company during the summer of 1914, she said—in a pioneering corporate philanthropy fashion—"I simply want to ask a favor of you in order that I, in turn, may be able to do more favors for our race . . . [and because] it will help me to be of more practical service to the several worthy causes in which I am particularly interested" (Bundles 2001, 153). While many of her contributions were spontaneous and sentimental, some were carefully calculated to bring attention to certain issues. As part of the national campaign to build YMCAs in the black communities of major American cities, Walker astonished the citizens of Indianapolis in October 1911 when she personally pledged $1,000, an amount equivalent to nearly $20,000 today and the same size donation made by some of the city's much wealthier white citizens. Newspaper headlines, heralding her gift as the largest ever contributed to the YMCA by a black woman, catapulted her into national recognition and challenged others to match her generosity. A few years later, when her usually prompt annual gift to the YMCA's Colored Men's Department was delayed, Secretary **Jesse Moorland** wrote, "I hate to lose Mrs. Walker, not merely for the amount of the money but for the fine effect it has on our work in general among both white and colored. . . . I regard Madam Walker as one of our strongest friends and one who has had as much or more to do with building up this work as it is, than any other member of our race" (Moorland to F.B. Ransom, December 27, 1916, Indiana Historical Society).

In an early effort at historic preservation, her 1918 contribution to the National Association of Colored Women helped save the home of abolitionist Frederick Douglass. Today, the home, which is in the Anacostia section of Washington, D.C., stands as a National Historical Landmark. During World War I, she mobilized her network of customers and agents to purchase Liberty Bonds and Victory Bonds. Fully aware of the patriotic message such a gesture would convey to the White House and the War Department, she stated, "Let us in this last campaign subscribe so promptly and liberally when called upon by the campaign workers that there will be no uncertainty as to where the Negro stands in these, the closing days of this great crisis" (Bundles 2001, 270). In early May 1919, less than three weeks before she died, Walker made the most substantial donation of her life, a $5,000 pledge to the NAACP's antilynching fund, equivalent to $51,000 in today's dollars, and a tenth of the organization's annual budget. Clearly, these three gifts illustrate her use of philanthropy as a powerful symbol: encouraging the generosity of others and the advancement of her race.

Walker's will stipulated that two-thirds of her company's net profits be held in trust for charity and for the maintenance of Villa Lewaro (her Irvington-on-Hudson, New York estate). Although the trustees honored all of her bequests and continued to contribute to her favorite charities, an unexpectedly heavy postwar tax burden and lowered company revenues during the Great Depression of the 1930s prevented them from dispensing the large sums she had envisioned. The original Walker Company remained in business until

1986, when it distributed its remaining cash assets to several charitable organizations in Indianapolis. Today, Walker's legacy survives through two national historic landmarks: Villa Lewaro and the Madam Walker Theatre Center in Indianapolis, which was the headquarters of her manufacturing company until 1979 and then became a multipurpose cultural arts and business center.

CONCLUSION

By the time Walker died at Villa Lewaro in 1919, she had become one of America's wealthiest businesswomen and had established herself—along with Annie Pope-Turnbo Malone, Helena Rubinstein, and Elizabeth Arden—as a founder of today's multibillion-dollar cosmetics industry. Equally important, Walker's particular approach to philanthropy helped reconfigure the philosophy of giving among African Americans, who were more accustomed to contributing the bulk of their charitable dollars to religious and fraternal organizations rather than to secular institutions and polit-

ical causes. Her strategically targeted donations—and the publicity they generated—provided symbolic and psychological impact far beyond their monetary value because they signaled the potential for future giving within the African-American community.

A'Lelia Bundles

FURTHER READING

Bundles, A'Lelia. *On Her Own Ground: The Life and Times of Madam C.J. Walker.* New York: Scribner, 2001.

Giddings, Paula. *When and Where I Enter: The Impact of Black Women on Race and Sex in America.* New York: William Morrow, 1984.

Peiss, Kathy. *Hope in a Jar: The Making of America's Beauty Culture.* New York: Henry Holt, 1998

Rooks, Noliwe M. *Hair Raising: Beauty, Culture, and African American Women.* New Brunswick, NJ: Rutgers University Press, 1996.

PAPERS

Most of Madam C.J. Walker's papers are located at the Indiana Historical Society Library (Indianapolis, IN). Some papers and photographs are included in the author's Walker Family Collection.

BOOKER TALIAFERRO WASHINGTON
(1856–1915)

African-American Leader and Educator

INTRODUCTION

In his autobiography *Up from Slavery*, Booker T. Washington remarked on the unselfishness of his teachers at Hampton Institute, his alma mater: "It was hard for me to understand how any individuals could bring themselves to the point where they could be so happy in working for others. Before the end of the year, I think I began learning that those who are happiest are those who do the most for others. This lesson I have tried to carry me with ever since" (Washington 1996, 34). With this outlook, Washington built

Tuskegee Institute as the center of an educational and economic empire in the early twentieth century.

EARLY YEARS AND EDUCATION

Booker Taliaferro Washington was born on April 5, 1856, in Franklin County, Virginia. His father was an unknown white man; his mother, Jane, was the slave cook of James Burroughs, a small planter. Washington spent his first nine years as a slave on the Burroughs farm. Following the end of the Civil

Booker T. Washington, c. 1890s. Library of Congress; LC-USZ62-119897.

War, his mother took her family to Malden, West Virginia, to join her new husband, Washington Ferguson. At the age of nine, he began working in Malden's salt and coal mines. In 1871, he found work as a houseboy for the wife of Gen. Lewis Ruffner, owner of the mines. Mrs. Ruffner became an important influence on Washington's life, instilling in him Victorian ideals of cleanliness and orderliness.

In West Virginia, Washington acquired an education, partly through his own efforts and partly by attending school while continuing to work in the mines. In 1872, he entered the Hampton Normal and Agricultural Institute in Virginia. Founded by Gen. Samuel Armstrong as an industrial school for newly freed slaves, the school's philosophy called for a practical and utilitarian education for African Americans. At the same time, this education would teach its students the values of character, cleanliness, and morality. Wash-

ington traveled most of the distance from Malden to Hampton on foot and arrived penniless. He worked as a janitor on campus to pay for his room and board, and Armstrong arranged for a white benefactor to pay Washington's tuition. At Hampton, Washington learned academic subjects and agriculture, and began to develop the educational philosophy that later came to dominate his life. He graduated in 1875 and returned to Malden to teach.

CAREER HIGHLIGHTS AND MAJOR PHILANTHROPIC CONTRIBUTIONS

In 1881, the Alabama state legislature authorized the establishment of a school to train African-American teachers in a small town called Tuskegee. Located in the heart of the "Black Belt" (named at first for the color of the soil), the Tuskegee Institute would become one of the most significant educational institutions for African Americans. The legislature first approached General Armstrong about naming a white person to head the school, but Armstrong recommended Washington. Named the first principal of Tuskegee, Washington arrived to head a school that had no land or buildings. The state contribution of $2,000 was appropriated only for teacher salaries.

Undaunted by these adverse circumstances, Washington went to work selling the school to the area's residents. He attempted to recruit African Americans who believed in the concept of industrial education, and he sought financial support from whites who agreed with his idea. The school opened in a shanty that had been donated by a local church. Washington also convinced his former teacher at Hampton, General Armstrong, to make a loan for the purchase of an abandoned plantation on the outskirts of the town as a permanent site for Tuskegee.

Like Armstrong, Washington believed in teaching his students the values of self-help and self-reliance. He and his students built a kiln to make bricks, and within a few years, a classroom building, a dining hall, a girls' dormitory, and a chapel had been built entirely with student labor. Since the Tuskegee kiln was the only one of its kind in the area, the students were able to sell bricks to raise more funds. By 1888, the school owned 540 acres of land and enrolled 400 students. It offered training in skilled trades such as carpentry, cabinetmaking, printing, and shoemaking. The school also emphasized the teaching of agriculture for boys and cooking and sewing for girls.

Washington also believed that education should teach students the values of personal hygiene, manners, and character building. Students rose each morning at five o'clock and went to bed at nine-thirty in the evening. Although the school was nondenominational, Washington required all students to attend daily religious services. In many ways, Tuskegee replicated Hampton in its program and emphasis. However, unlike Hampton, the staff at Tuskegee was all black, and most of them were Hampton graduates. By the early 1900s, the school's name and influence had spread far beyond Alabama's borders. Beginning in 1892, annual Tuskegee Negro Conferences were held that drew thousands of rural African Americans to learn better farming methods. Later in the decade, the opening of a hospital and a nursing school brought further services to southern blacks. By 1915, Tuskegee had an endowment of $1,945,000, a student body of 2,000, and a staff of 200. Noting the success of Washington's efforts over a span of little more than three decades, other black schools—modeled after Tuskegee—were started across the South. Many of these institutions employed Tuskegee graduates, and a few students took their newly acquired skills to Africa and the Caribbean.

Much of Washington's time was spent in raising money for the school. Most, if not all, of Tuskegee's students were poor, rural African Americans who could not afford tuition, meals, housing, or sometimes even basic necessities such as clothing. As a result, unlike other colleges that relied on wealthy parents and alumni, the institution created a huge scholarship fund that could pay for students' education. Washington's success in publicizing Tuskegee and raising funds for the institution were remarkable. Through his efforts, he became acquainted with industrial and philanthropic giants such as clothing retailer John Wanamaker, businessman **Andrew Carnegie**, and mail-order retailer **Julius Rosenwald** as well as the **Peabody** Education Fund. Washington used his contacts to increase the school's endowment, and many of Tuskegee's buildings were named after white benefactors.

Washington's philosophy for obtaining money was very simple and direct. He would often personally approach wealthy residents in such municipalities as Boston, New York City, and Philadelphia and talk with them in the privacy of their homes. According to Washington, his activity did not constitute begging and should not be viewed as such. "My experience and observation have convinced me that persistent asking outright for money from the rich does not, as a rule, secure help. I have usually proceeded on the principle that persons who possess sense enough to earn money have sense enough to know how to give it away, and that the mere making known of the facts regarding Tuskegee, and especially the facts regarding the work of the graduates, has been more effective than outright begging" (Washington 1996, 84).

These ideas concerning philanthropic fund-raising, and his belief that many of the best people in society were almost always the wealthiest, were repeated again and again in Washington's speeches and writings. A prolific speech maker, Washington continuously focused on three demographic groups in his talks: southern whites, wealthy northern whites, and African Americans. He constantly praised what he called "the best class" of southern whites, and addressed them in conciliatory terms. To northern whites, Washington optimistically forecasted a rosy picture in American race relations and complimented industrial growth while criticizing union organizing. Nonetheless, he saved his harshest criticism for African Americans. They were responsible, in his opinion, for their own welfare, and he gave the impression that only blacks could improve race relations through ignoring injustices and disavowing attempts to secure political rights. Although much of what Washington said appeared to be simple and straightforward, a closer reading reveals his understanding of human psychology and the society in which he was forced to live. The views he expressed were essentially the views that many white Americans, sons and daughters of Civil War veterans, wanted to hear. Although many African Americans were furious at Washington's suggestions that they were responsible for much of the racial hatred directed at them at the beginning of the twentieth century, others were drawn to his message of self-help and independence. As a result, he was able to navigate successfully, if rather tenuously, between white and black constituencies who made widely divergent and difficult demands on him.

Washington's ultimate moment in popularity occurred in Atlanta in 1895 when he gave a fifteen-minute speech appearing to endorse racial segregation. The oration occurred at a crucial moment in American history. Many Americans, for instance, desired to put the divisions caused by the Civil War behind them. At the same time, the recognized leader in black America during the nineteenth century, Frederick Douglass, had just passed away. White newspaper writers and intellectuals, eager to highlight a new African-American leader for the industrial age, cited Washington as the exemplar. His emphasis on industrial education, his willingness to put aside the issues of racial equality raised by the Civil War (unlike Douglass) in favor of self-help, and his praise of wealthy industrialists was enthusiastically reported by the white press and propelled him to a position of national leadership.

After the Atlanta address, Washington was in such demand as a speaker that he spent a majority of his time either lecturing, raising funds, or both. He wrote an autobiography, *Up from Slavery*, that instantly became a bestseller and was translated into a dozen languages. He also became involved in politics and was an advisor to Presidents Theodore Roosevelt and William Taft. He founded the National Negro Business League in 1900 to encourage black entrepreneurship and secretly funded dozens of black newspapers in both the North and South.

Yet Washington's projects occurred at a time when many blacks could not vote, hold political office, open a business, or use public facilities such as a restaurant. In many areas, both northern and southern, law and custom segregated African Americans. A small group of black intellectuals, such as W.E.B. Du Bois, **Ida B. Wells-Barnett**, and William Monroe Trotter, argued that Washington's work and ideas were ultimately self-defeating. Even worse, some charged that he helped bring about an increased sense of inferiority among African Americans through his acquiescence to racial segregation. Black activists also argued that Washington's program of industrial education would actually sentence African Americans to a life of perpetual servitude: they would not develop the necessary skills to become a part of the managerial middle class that would be necessary to lead business enterprises. These intellectuals encouraged a more aggressive stance toward African-American civil and political rights, and excoriated Washington and his followers for suggesting otherwise.

In spite of the cautious stance he publicly maintained, behind the scenes Washington actively fought for efforts against disfranchisement and racial discrimination. Research done by several of his biographers since the 1970s has shown that he secretly financed discrimination lawsuits in several southern jurisdictions. He also paid for legal assistance in cases involving the exclusion of blacks from Alabama juries and supported efforts to secure greater rights for black landowners. However, he carefully concealed these activities from white contemporaries, and only a handful of African Americans knew of his work.

For instance, as black disfranchisement became the order of the day in southern states between 1890 and 1910, Washington secretly funded two Alabama test cases, *Giles v.*

Harris (1903) and *Giles v. Teasley* (1904). Brought by black plaintiffs, these two cases challenged the constitutionality of Alabama's disfranchisement law. Washington chose and paid the only lawyer involved and used one secretary for communicating with him. The lawyer, Wilford Smith, and Washington used code names in case their letters were intercepted. Although the *Giles* cases were unsuccessful, they are clear evidence of Washington's ability to hide his civil rights activism from friends and foes.

CONCLUSION

Booker T. Washington died of heart disease in Tuskegee on November 14, 1915. Although diagnosed years before, he suffered continuously from exhaustion and overwork. Washington attempted to build an institution at a time when most Americans frowned upon the thought of higher education for African Americans. Indeed, many blacks were lynched, their homes burned and destroyed, and their lives torn apart by whites for less important, or even trivial, issues. Washington knew that any wrong moves on his part in a nation hostile to black interests could result in the destruction of his beloved Tuskegee. In the end, perhaps this knowledge, and the tension that resulted in living with this burden, hastened the end of his life.

Damon W. Freeman

FURTHER READING

Andrews, William L., ed. *Up from Slavery: An Authoritative Text, Contexts, and Composition History*. New York: W.W. Norton, 1996.

Baker, Houston A., Jr. *Turning South Again: Rethinking Modernism/Re-reading Booker T.* Durham, NC: Duke University Press, 2001.

Bontemps, Arna Wendell. *Young Booker; Booker T. Washington's Early Days*. New York: Dodd, Mead, 1972.

Boone, Theodore S. *The Philosophy of Booker T. Washington*. Fort Worth, TX: Manney Printing Co., 1939.

DeLaney, William H. *Learn by Doing: A Projected Educational Philosophy in the Thought of Booker T. Washington*. New York: Vantage Press, 1974.

Denton, Virginia Lantz. *Booker T. Washington and the Adult Education Movement*. Gainesville: University of Florida Press, 1993.

Friedman, Lawrence J. "Life 'In the Lion's Mouth': Another Look at Booker T. Washington." *Journal of Negro History* 59, Fall 1974, 337–351.

Harlan, Louis R. *Booker T. Washington: The Making of a Black Leader, 1856–1901*. New York: Oxford University Press, 1972.

———. *Booker T. Washington: The Wizard of Tuskegee, 1901–1915*. New York: Oxford University Press, 1983.

Hawkins, Hugh. *Booker T. Washington and His Critics; The Problem of Negro Leadership*. Boston: Heath, 1962.

Mathews, Basil Joseph. *Booker T. Washington, Educator and Interracial Interpreter*. College Park, MD: McGrath, 1948.

Meier, August. *Negro Thought in America, 1880–1915: Racial Ideologies in the Age of Booker T. Washington*. Ann Arbor: University of Michigan Press, 1963.

Scott, Emmett J. *Booker T. Washington, Builder of a Civilization*. Garden City, NY: Doubleday, Page, 1916.

Smock, Raymond, ed. *Booker T. Washington in Perspective: Essays of Louis R. Harlan*. Jackson: University Press of Mississippi, 1988.

Spencer, Samuel R. *Booker T. Washington and the Negro's Place in American Life*. Boston: Little, Brown, 1955.

Thornburgh, Emma Lou. *Booker T. Washington*. Englewood Cliffs, NJ: Prentice-Hall, 1969.

Washington, Booker T. *My Larger Education, Being Chapters from My Experience*. Miami, FL: 1st Mnemosyne reprint, 1969.

———. *The Story of My Life and Work*. Naperville, IL: J.L. Nichols & Company, 1900.

———. *Up from Slavery*. New York: W.W. Norton, 1996.

———. *Working with the Hands*. New York: Arno Press, 1911, 1969.

Wintz, Cary D., ed. *African American Political Thought, 1890–1930: Washington, Du Bois, Garvey, and Randolph*. Armonk, NY: M.E. Sharpe, 1996.

PAPERS

See Louis R. Harlan, ed., *The Booker T. Washington Papers*, 14 vols. (Urbana: University of Illinois Press, 1972–1989). This edited collection contains Washington's autobiographical writings, speeches, correspondence, and writings concerning him from 1860 to his death in 1915. The original Booker T. Washington papers are located in the Manuscript Division of the Library of Congress (Washington, DC).

IDA B. WELLS-BARNETT
(1862–1931)

Journalist and Antilynching Activist

INTRODUCTION

Reflecting on her anti-lynching efforts, Ida B. Wells-Barnett wrote, "I felt that one had better die fighting against injustice than to die like a dog or rat in a trap. I had already determined to sell my life as dearly as possible if attacked. I felt if I could take one lyncher with me, this would even up the score a little bit" (Wells-Barnett 1970, 62). Wells-Barnett was arguably one of the most prolific and outspoken journalists, activists, and public speakers of her era. At times, her efforts to combat racial prejudice threatened her life and career but she continued to fight for civil rights.

EARLY YEARS AND EDUCATION

Born in Holly Springs, Mississippi, to parents who were slaves, Ida B. Wells was one year old at the time of the Emancipation Proclamation (1863), which gave freedom to slaves living in states that comprised the Confederacy. Throughout her childhood, Wells attended Shaw University (later renamed Rust College), one of the institutions run by white missionaries for the education of freed blacks of all ages during Reconstruction (roughly 1865–1877). After Wells's parents and one sibling died during a yellow fever outbreak, Wells—only in her mid-teens—insisted upon teaching school so that she could support her five younger siblings.

Two events appear to have influenced the direction of Wells's life. On the way to a teaching job, she was forced to leave her seat in the first-class train car because non-first-

Ida B. Wells-Barnett. © Bettmann/CORBIS.

class train cars, reserved for tobacco smoking, were supposed to be the seating area for blacks. Wells subsequently sued the C&O Railroad for such treatment. Although she won in the lower court, the Tennessee State Supreme Court eventually overturned that verdict. After Wells moved to Memphis, Tennessee, three of her friends, black male grocers in Memphis, were lynched after they provided competition to a nearby white grocer. The horrible nature of the murders appalled her and spurred her to become an outspoken critic of lynching. Moreover, the combination of these two experiences formed the groundwork for her future efforts against racism.

CAREER HIGHLIGHTS AND MAJOR PHILANTHROPIC CONTRIBUTIONS

Wells was part of an entire movement of black women journalists in the last half of the nineteenth century. Gloria Wades-Gayles observed that many of these women, like Wells, were not paid for much of their careers, and supported themselves by teaching or writing on a volunteer basis. Wells and her colleagues led the way for the next generation of black journalists. By the beginning of the twentieth century, over ninety African-American publishers printed newspapers, magazines, and periodicals.

Wells, however, stood out from the rest. In Wells's first paying work as a journalist for an American Baptist newspaper, her talents earned her praise as "The Princess of the Press." In fact, Wells became editor and co-owner of the militant *Free Speech and Headlight*, a Memphis weekly, when she was only twenty-one. However, her candid editorials soon subjected her to a strong racist backlash. By criticizing conditions in the segregated African-American schools, she lost her teaching job. In addition, her articles condemning lynching led to her newspaper office being burned and her subsequent exile from Tennessee. Told she would be lynched if she returned to the South, Wells worked to organize antilynching societies, lecturing throughout other parts of the United States. Wells also spoke throughout Britain and Scotland to raise awareness of lynching in the United States and to form antilynching societies in Europe. Throughout her exile, she continued to write for northern newspapers as southern newspapers published criticism of her work.

"Lynch law," or mob rule, was arguably the subject about which she was most outspoken. In 1892, Wells led the first antilynching campaign in the United States. She authored *Southern Horrors: Lynch Law in All Its Phases* (1892) and *A Red Record* (1895), both of which gave detailed accounts of southern lynching and its history. After the lynching of the Memphis grocers, she wrote articles telling black citizens of Memphis to leave and travel West—and hundreds did. As a result, white business leaders, facing the loss of much of their business from black patrons, met with Wells and asked her to encourage the blacks to return. Instead, she congratulated the community on a job well done. Wells argued tirelessly that lynching was allowed to occur without interference because northerners believed that poor and uneducated blacks were probably guilty of many crimes, especially the rape of white women. Wells pointed out that few of those lynched had even been accused of rape and that women and children were among the lynch victims. "Crimes against women is the excuse, not the cause," Wells argued (Thompson 1990, 261). She also asserted that the word "rape" was being used in some instances when white women sought out black men for relationships.

Along with her activism, Wells raised a family. In 1895, Wells married Ferdinand Lee Barnett, a lawyer and the founder and publisher of the *Chicago Conservator*. The *Conservator* was the first black newspaper in Chicago and she bought the paper from her husband after the marriage. While raising two children from Barnett's previous marriage, the couple had four children of their own. After she became a mother, she continued her work as an activist.

In addition to being a leader in the antilynching movement, Ida B. Wells-Barnett became an instrumental figure in the women's club and women's suffrage movements. Influenced by English women's civic groups, she participated in the black women's club movement, notably the Association of Colored Women's Clubs. In this movement, black women formed civic organizations to share community resources and promote civic purposes. Along with other peers, Wells-Barnett worked to organize the National Association of Colored Women in 1896. Wells-Barnett also helped found the Alpha

Suffrage Club, the first African-American women's suffrage organization, and the Ida B. Wells Club in Chicago, a civic community organization. Other clubs, named after her, sprung up across the country.

In addition to her active leadership in these women's organizations, Wells-Barnett mobilized people in the establishment of the National Association for the Advancement of Colored People (NAACP) in 1910. While promoting racial integration, she encouraged, as evidenced by the colored women's clubs, African Americans to use the resources of their community and supported the opening of the first African American kindergarten in Chicago. After discussions with an adult men's Sunday school class, Wells-Barnett started the Negro Fellowship League (1910) to provide a community gathering place for young African Americans at a time when settlement houses and YMCAs were closed to blacks. Despite Wells-Barnett's commitment, the Negro Fellowship League did not receive the support (either financial or otherwise) that Wells-Barnett wanted, especially from the middle- and upper-class black community.

In fact, Wells-Barnett's brand of activism sometimes found few proponents. Indeed, she often opposed one of the most well-known African Americans of her time, **Booker T. Washington**, and sided—at one time or another—with prominent African Americans of differing and radical ideologies, including W.E.B. Du Bois, Marcus Garvey, and T. Thomas Fortune. By working whole-heartedly for integration and against accommodation, she did not gain much support from white philanthropists, who often favored Washington's accommodationist philosophies. Wells-Barnett, however, was not concerned with currying the favor of white elites: she had conducted her U.S. speaking tour completely financed by African Americans. Nonetheless, Wells-Barnett's vigilance and unwillingness to compromise with others made her a formidable organizer, but an advocate who was often abandoned by the very organizations she mobilized.

CONCLUSION

Wells-Barnett worked throughout her life for civil rights. She investigated, wrote, and spoke about injustice to educate others and motivate them to take action. Through her uncompromising work as a journalist and speaker, she challenged some conservative philanthropic approaches to American racial issues. Despite the obstacles she faced, her activism profoundly influenced her own generation and has benefited succeeding generations.

Rebecca Roth

FURTHER READING

Carlson, Shirley J. "Black Ideals of Womanhood in the Late Victorian Era." *Journal of Negro History*, Spring 1992, 61–73.

Peebles-Wilkins, Wilma, and E. Aracelis Francis. "Two Outstanding Black Women in Social Welfare History: Mary Church Terrell and Ida B. Wells-Barnett." *Affilia: Journal of Women & Social Work*, Winter 1990, 87–101.

Schechter, Patricia A. *Ida B. Wells-Barnett and American Reform, 1880–1930*. Chapel Hill, NC: University of North Carolina Press, 2001.

Thompson, Mildred. *Ida B. Wells-Barnett: An Exploratory Study of an American Black Woman, 1893–1930*. Brooklyn, NY: Carlson Publishing, 1990.

Wade-Gayles, Gloria. "Black Women Journalists in the South, 1880–1905: An Approach to the Study of Black Women's History." *Callaloo*, February–October, 1981, 138–152.

Wells-Barnett, Ida B. *Crusade for Justice: The Autobiography of Ida B. Wells*. Alfreda M. Duster, ed. Chicago: University of Chicago Press, 1970.

PAPERS

Ida B. Wells-Barnett's papers are located at the Regenstein Library of the University of Chicago.

GERTRUDE VANDERBILT WHITNEY
(1875–1942)

Sculptor and Founder of the Whitney Museum of American Art

INTRODUCTION

At the founding of the Whitney Museum of American Art, Gertrude Vanderbilt Whitney stated, "In making this gift to you, the American public, my chief desire is that you should share with me the joy which I have received from these works of art" (Healy 1960, 104). An artist herself, Whitney was uniquely placed to urge Americans to recognize the creativity springing from its own soil. Certainly the status of American art would be very different without her determination and vision.

EARLY YEARS AND EDUCATION

That Gertrude Whitney, known as "the richest girl in the world," might become a philanthropist was not unexpected, but her choice of service was most unconventional. Born in 1875, Gertrude Vanderbilt was the fourth of seven children of Alice Gwynne and Cornelius Vanderbilt II. Her pious and charitable parents, committed to social propriety, eschewed creativity or risk. Indeed, their daughter's passionate and sensitive nature confused them. Raised in mansions in New York City and Newport, Rhode Island, she was closely chaperoned and prevented from expressing her natural exuberance.

Gertrude Vanderbilt's education, however, exposed her to an intriguing world beyond her parents' narrow bounds. Educated first by governesses, then at the prestigious Brearley School, she took her studies seriously, filling journals with exquisitely detailed accounts of her feelings and perceptions. During her visits to museums and historic sites in Europe, her artistic self-awakening gradually developed. On first viewing Michelangelo's sculptures, she marveled that "a

mere boy could put into his work something that generations would seek in vain. He could cover all provinces with deft fingers, fashion worlds past, present, and to come" (Stasz 1991, 102). Enthralled by the fine arts, she discovered she had both an aesthetic eye and an empathy with the creator. Yet, she continued to write about caged birds with clipped wings, a metaphor for her sense of powerlessness.

When she came of age, the pressure to marry was immense and complicated by her wealth. When, on August 25, 1896, she wed Harry Payne Whitney, the brilliant, athletic, and charming son of family friends, journalists praised her for breaking recent practice by choosing an American over a foreign titled husband. The couple would be married for thirty-four years and have three children: Cornelius Vanderbilt, Flora Payne, and Barbara. Despite delight in motherhood, Gertrude Whitney found the social obligations of her class dull and her marriage disappointing. While working with decorators on her house, she met local artists and turned to them for friendship. When sculptor Henrik Anderson took her to his studio, she felt admitted into a secret society and decided to take up the art. Despite her family's disapproval of her sculpting naked human figures, she defied them. In 1901, she began serious study by traveling for five months to Europe by herself. Though a devoted mother, she realized her sanity demanded she also nurture her muse.

CAREER HIGHLIGHTS

It was 1904 before Whitney committed to being an artist. "I cannot be the sort of person which my life demands me to be—so why not try and be my own self" (Stasz

1991, 187). This decision led to splitting her time between high society and bohemia (a group of artists and writers who defy conventional society). Now a close friend of such independent painters as Robert Henri and John Sloan, she created a pied-à-terre and sculpture studio on MacDougall Alley in Greenwich Village in 1907. Highly disciplined, she rapidly advanced her technique. That year, she won first prize in an architectural competition and garnered commissions for fountains and bas-reliefs.

Whitney established a second studio in Paris, whose avant-garde society further inspired her. Admiring her monastic commitment, August Rodin gave her study models. In 1911, her *Spanish Peasant* was accepted for the highly selective Paris Spring Salon. The current vogue in orientalism and modernism also began to influence her art, which became more stylized and abstract. These changes were evident in her first "one-man" show in New York City in 1916.

Whitney's career gained national notice with the 1912 award to sculpt the *Titanic Memorial*, which would be placed in Washington, D.C. In 1915, her *El Dorado Fountain*, in the center of the Panama-Pacific Exposition, was accompanied by a seventy-five-foot-long frieze depicting the myth of the search for gold. Other noted public works included an equestrian *Buffalo Bill* (also known as *The Scout*) for Cody, Wyoming in 1924, a memorial to the American Expeditionary forces above the harbor of Saint-Nazarre, France in 1926, and a massive *Columbus* in Huelva, Spain in 1929. She also created and exhibited many small works, among the most notable being a collection of soldiers from World War I.

By 1930, monumental and representational art were losing their appeal. Thus, Whitney seldom exhibited during the 1930s even though she continued to sculpt small works. Her final public art pieces were *Peter Stuyvesant* at Second Avenue and Sixteenth Street in New York City and *Spirit of Flight* for the New York World's Fair of 1939. Before her death from a cardiac infection on April 18, 1942, Whitney received honors from the National Academy of Design and the National Sculpture Society, along with four honorary doctorate degrees.

During her lifetime, critics seldom addressed Whitney's art objectively. She was attacked in sexist tone for making her pieces too masculine, too feminine, or for even sculpting at all. Others assumed a wealthy person's attempts could be no more than dabbling. The support of fellow-artists helped her continue despite unfair criticism. After her death, reevaluation has led critics to acknowledge the significance of her smaller studio works over her public monuments, and place her squarely among the better sculptors of her day in that regard.

MAJOR PHILANTHROPIC CONTRIBUTIONS

At the turn of the century, art collectors and museums in the United States still looked to Europe for artistic talent. They limited their approval of American art to the conservative academic style, which emphasized idealized portrayals of figures, events, and landscapes to proclaim America's glory. Whitney admired the daring of her artist friends, many of whom had studied abroad to absorb the latest innovations. She determined to break the wall of indifference toward American art. Of liberal bent, she supported both the social realists of the Ashcan School, which depicted gritty urban scenes, and abstract modernists, who used color and form rather than known objects as the focus of their art. Whitney was perceptive in recognizing that these artists needed opportunities to exhibit as much as financial support. Thus, her first major philanthropy began in 1907 with shows at her sculpture studio. Nonetheless, her patronage of artists always included a private element, such as paying off a home mortgage, equipping a studio, or covering hospital bills. More publicly, she helped sponsor the revolutionary Armory Show of 1913, created the Whitney Studio Gallery in 1914, and helped form the Friends of Young Artists to encourage others to become patrons. As sculptor Jo Davidson recalled, she "was extraordinary, how she gave one the feeling that what you did was the only thing that mattered" (Friedman, 1978, 326). This forward thinking also included support of modernist composers and musicians such as Edgar Varese.

Whitney's philanthropy was furthered by a complete involvement in her many projects as well as her able organizational skills. Because Whitney spent part of each year at her studio in Paris, she responded immediately to the needs of France in World War I. In 1914, she contributed a completely furnished and staffed field hospital at Juilly for the American Ambulance Service. She helped set up the hospital and corresponded with staff on every detail. Her creativity extended to producing unique artistic events to raise funds on behalf of war relief and the field hospital. Consequently, though an underwriter of the Society of Independent Artists, she was a member of its board of directors for fifteen years because of her fund-raising capabilities.

Whitney also underwrote *The Arts* in 1922 when it threatened to cease. This influential magazine was the dominant new voice against the academic art establishment. She served modern art in other ways as well. She led a campaign to force the U.S. Customs Bureau to label Brancusi's streamlined sculpture *Bird in Space* as art instead of a kitchen utensil. This action was a key bureaucratic change for the importation of nonrepresentational work.

Whitney's establishment of the Whitney Studio Club in 1918 provided a unique catalyst for American artists. Growing to 400 members, its services ensured a vigorous creative community during its twelve years of existence. Whitney's commitment to democracy meant the elimination of prizes so prevalent then. With her assistant Juliana Force, she also introduced unusual themes, such as the Indigenous Art Show, to stimulate cutting-edge work. Cognizant of the special difficulties women artists faced, she was careful to include them in her exhibits and support. Although Whitney's enthusiasm could lead her to confuse talent and fashion, critics soon came to acknowledge that the Whitney

Club shows were the best place in New York City to find excellent new artists.

The Whitney Studio Club was so successful in launching artists, that many found space to exhibit in uptown galleries by 1928. Consequently, Whitney decided to close the club and donate the 600 works of American art she had collected to the Metropolitan Museum of Art. The museum's director, Edward Robinson, rejected her offer in so insulting a manner that she decided to create her own museum. She explained it would have a mission to present working artists rather than wait until they had been "deadened by age" or been accepted by other museum's "sacred portals" (Stasz 1991, 288). The museum, which opened on November 16, 1921, was housed in a set of remodeled town houses on Eighth Street in Greenwich Village, its foyer decorated by a stylized American eagle to alert visitors to its focus.

Like Gertrude Whitney herself, and her very able colleague Juliana Force, the policies and practices of the museum were experimental and dynamic—remaining so long after her death. Rather than socialites or business people, she insisted that the museum's main advisers would be artists. She eliminated prizes, and encouraged both the rental and the purchase of exhibited works, a decision deemed by critics to be "of incalculable benefit in America where there are no dealers in American art" (Healy 1960, 215). She tried various innovations, such as having artists select the work to be shown at Biennials.

Furthermore, Whitney sponsored traveling exhibitions around the country. Despite the financial drain of her resources resulting from the onset of the Great Depression in 1929, she steadily expanded the facilities. After her death in 1943, the Whitney Museum board met with the Metropolitan Museum board and agreed to explore a merger. Artists and critics decried the potential loss of so unique an institution, and worked to keep it independent. In 1948, the Whitney trustees canceled the planned merger because there were grave doubts that its liberal tradition could continue under Metropolitan management.

Since then, the Whitney has continued on its original course, to further contemporary American art through exhibits and research.

CONCLUSION

Gertrude Whitney's struggle to break away from convention led to her identifying with American artists of widely differing inclinations. Her warmth, generosity, and sense of inventive organization established the careers of many American artists and created an institution that has furthered her vision. The Whitney Museum continues her commitment to living art, and its sometimes-controversial exhibitions would only delight her.

Clarice Stasz

FURTHER READING

Berman, Avis. *Rebels on Eighth Street: Juliana Force and the Whitney Museum of American Art.* New York: Macmillan, 1990.

Conner, Janis, and Joel Rosenkranz. *Rediscoveries in American Sculpture: Studio Works 1893–1939.* Austin: University of Texas Press, 1989.

Friedman, B.H., with the research collaboration of Flora Miller Irving. *Gertrude Vanderbilt Whitney: A Biography.* Garden City, NY: Doubleday, 1978.

Healy, Daty. "A History of the Whitney Museum of American Art, 1930–1945." Ph.D. diss., New York University, 1960.

McCarthy, Kathleen. *Women's Culture: American Philanthropy and Art, 1830–1930.* Chicago: University of Chicago, 1991.

Stasz, Clarice. *The Vanderbilt Women: Dynasty of Wealth, Glamour, and Tragedy.* New York: St. Martin's Press, 1991.

PAPERS

Gertrude Vanderbilt Whitney's papers are available and on microfilm from the Whitney Museum of American Art (New York City). A small collection, not yet microfilmed, is at the Archives of American Art (Washington, DC).

FRANCES ELIZABETH CAROLINE WILLARD
(1839–1898)

Reformer, Feminist, and President of the Woman's Christian Temperance Union

INTRODUCTION

"We are all of us raw material, carried on long voyages, landed at strange ports, rattled over noisy pavements, always on our way to be made more useful and of higher value" (Leeman 1992, 186). Despite the inclusive language, Frances Willard's call to service in her 1897 presidential address to the Woman's Christian Temperance Union sprang from her particular and literal experience. Rattling over thousands of miles of road and track, she emerged as America's preeminent reformer in the late nineteenth century.

EARLY YEARS AND EDUCATION

Born in upstate New York to Josiah Flint and Mary Thompson (Hill) Willard, Frances Willard moved to a Wisconsin farm with her family in 1846 and remained a loyal Midwesterner the rest of her life. Like many rural girls in the nineteenth century, she had little formal schooling, but received a good education from her mother. Young Frances Willard read deeply and aspired to a literary career. As a teenager, she saw her work published in local newspapers and farm journals. At age seventeen, she and her younger sister Mary Willard were enrolled briefly at the Milwaukee Normal Institute, and the following year entered North Western Female College at Evanston, Illinois. The entire Willard family soon moved to Evanston and Frances Willard was awarded a "laureate of science" after three terms. At North Western Female College, Willard was an exceptional student, but not a model one. She recalled that while her

Frances Willard, c.1890s. The Schlesinger Library, Radcliffe Institute, Harvard University.

sister was conspicuous by her obedient and lady-like behavior, she herself "was ranked with the 'Ne'e-do-weels,' that is, those who did not go to prayer-meeting on Sunday evening, when all the good students assembled in the library; and did not give devout attention to the seventy rules of the institution" (Willard 1889, 107).

Ambitious and intelligent, Willard nevertheless faced an uncertain future. She expressed a growing interest in social reform, and particularly in "the woman question," the nineteenth-century term for the nascent women's movement, but did not make a career of reform at the outset. Against her father's wishes, she began teaching, working brief stints at institutions in Illinois and New York. She was also engaged twice, the first time to Charles Fowler (at the time a promising young Methodist seminarian), but Willard broke off both engagements. In 1862, her sister Mary died, followed by her father Josiah Willard's death in 1868, both of consumption. Mary's death was particularly hard on Frances, but it inspired her to write her first book the following year, *Nineteen Beau-*

tiful Years, a sentimental tribute to her sister. Her father's death was also a terrible blow, but it, too, opened doors for his surviving daughter. In 1868, Willard left for Europe on a two-year tour with Kate Jackson, the first of the female companions who would provide both emotional and financial support to Willard throughout her career.

The tour was the capstone of Willard's education. The women studied languages, art, architecture, and history, and Willard wrote copiously about their travels for American newspapers. Her European tour also directly affected Willard in two key ways. It further focused her attention on the issue of women's role in society and qualified her for her first prominent position. She met and corresponded with prominent reformers, and her published reports from Europe made her familiar to a growing American audience. Soon after her return to Evanston, Willard was appointed president of her alma mater, now named the Evanston College for Ladies and newly affiliated with Northwestern University.

CAREER HIGHLIGHTS AND MAJOR PHILANTHROPIC CONTRIBUTIONS

The new college was to have a new campus, and President Willard set to work, developing her skills at organizing, development, and fund-raising. The Women's Educational Association was created to secure a site and raise funds. Willard and her colleagues approached the Evanston authorities, who donated a city park for the building site. They planned a fund-raiser for July 4, and sent out letters to prospective donors. In advance of her "Women's Fourth of July," Willard managed to get thousands of dollars worth of free advertising from the Chicago press to promote the event. The rest of that summer, Willard divided her time between seeking financial support for the new college, recruiting students, and planning the curriculum for the upcoming fall term.

Her position as a college president brought Willard into the national spotlight, and she subsequently began to cultivate relationships within the reform community that would serve her well throughout her career. However, she did not remain long at the Evanston College for Ladies. Conflicts surfaced with the trustees and the administration over the relationship of the women's college with Northwestern University. Personality clashes and real differences regarding the education of women led her to resign in the spring of 1874.

It was at this point that Willard made the choice that fixed her on the path of her life's work. She received an offer to become the principal of a girls' school in New York. Instead, she chose to begin working earnestly for temperance. Although she had taken a temperance pledge as a girl (and had insisted that her family do likewise), Willard had not remained a strict abstainer during her travels. She reported that her attendance at a temperance meeting after her return to the United States was a pivotal event in her decision to join the crusade, but her motives were likely more complex. Many Midwestern Protestant women had been brought to the reform by the spontaneous rebellion in 1873 of several Ohio women against the saloons. Temperance work could reasonably be seen as an extension of the nineteenth-century view of women as moral leaders in the home. Throughout her career, Willard embraced a number of reform measures, but the abolition of alcohol remained at the center of her vision of a better society. She was offered, and accepted, the presidency of the newly organized Chicago Woman's Christian Temperance Union (WCTU). Looking back on the decision, she wrote: "Instead of peace I was to participate in war; instead of the sweetness of home, never more dearly loved than I had loved it, I was to become a wanderer on the face of the earth; instead of libraries I was to frequent public halls and railway cars; instead of scholarly and cultured men I was to see the dregs of saloon and gambling house and haunt of shame" (Willard 1889, 342).

Willard's rise to prominence within the Woman's Christian Temperance Union was swift, but not without challenges. She re-

ceived very little direct compensation from the organization, and had to depend on money from speaking engagements to support herself and her mother. At the organization's first national meeting, she was selected as corresponding secretary, a position she held for three years. This position gave her nearly as much visibility as Annie Wittenmyer, the Union's first president. It also made her responsible for holding together the national organization and promoting the growth of local unions. At these efforts, she worked tirelessly, and membership increased dramatically. Despite the organization's growth and increasing national visibility, divisions in the leadership began to become apparent. Willard supported female suffrage, a reform that Wittenmyer opposed. In 1879, the conservative members were overwhelmed and Frances Willard was elected president of the WCTU.

Willard spent the next decade traveling, speaking, and organizing. On average, she delivered a speech a day. She made several tours through the southern states and the West, building her voluntary association into the largest women's organization in the nation. Her 1883–1884 tour, billed as the "Crusade Roundup," took her and her companion and secretary Anna Gordon to every state in the nation. Press coverage, even among papers not particularly sympathetic to her cause, was extensive and adulatory. By the end of the decade, she was the most famous woman in America.

Willard worked to expand the WCTU's scope well beyond the temperance crusade. She promoted a "Do Everything" policy, which over the course of the decade came to include female suffrage, dietary reform, school reform, labor organization, and public sanitation. She endorsed the Knights of Labor and was a prominent figure in the Prohibition Party. She struggled unsuccessfully for a fusion of reform parties in the early 1890s.

Willard remained president of the WCTU until her death in 1898, but in her last years she expanded her attentions well beyond the borders of the United States. In 1891, she convened the first World Woman's Christian Temperance Union conference in Boston. She worked closely with her friend and financial supporter Isabel Somerset to build the British Woman's Temperance Association, an organization that Somerset headed. Somerset led Willard into international philanthropic work; the two women aided Armenian refugees in 1895 and lobbied their respective governments for assistance. Willard's work in England kept her away from the United States much of the time during her final years, yet she still was able to retain her leadership of the American temperance movement.

CONCLUSION

When Willard died in 1898, the press coverage, the funereal spectacle, and the genuine public outpouring of grief were greater than that for any American since the assassination of Lincoln. Yet today, many people regard her as a minor and quaint figure in American history. The reasons for this decline in her reputation are readily discerned. Temperance advocates did not achieve political success until after they had abandoned Willard's broad and ambitious reform agenda and concentrated on a single political solution. After the failure of national prohibition, they, and Willard with them, were relegated to the role of historical failure. On the other hand, by the opening of the twentieth century, American feminists, even those who advocated temperance, saw Willard's chosen cause as a side issue, which might only detract from the more important issue of suffrage.

Temperance reform and legal prohibition of alcohol were the central features of Willard's reform agenda, but her career as a reformer ranged much more widely. In her autobiography, she offered the hope that "the blossoming of women into deeds of phi-lanthropy gives us a hint of the truer forms of society that are to come" (Willard 1889, 333). Under her leadership, the Woman's Christian Temperance Union grew into the largest women's voluntary association in the world, providing the training ground for a generation of female reformers who, like Willard, viewed temperance as but one of the many issues that merited their attention. Indeed, Frances Willard devoted her life to developing a society that would give women a voice in all facets of reform.

James D. Ivy

FURTHER READING

Bordin, Ruth. *Frances Willard: A Biography.* Chapel Hill: University of North Carolina Press, 1986.

———. *Woman and Temperance: The Quest for Power and Liberty, 1873–1900.* Philadelphia: Temple University Press, 1981.

Earhart, Mary. *Frances Willard: From Prayers to Politics.* Chicago: University of Chicago Press, 1944.

Gifford, Carolyn De Swarte. *Writing Out My Heart: Selections from the Journal of Frances E. Willard, 1855–96.* Urbana: University of Illinois Press, 1995.

Leeman, Richard W. *"Do Everything" Reform: The Oratory of Frances E. Willard.* Westport, CT: Greenwood Press, 1992.

Willard, Frances. *Glimpses of Fifty Years: The Autobiography of an American Woman.* Chicago: Woman's Temperance Publishing Association, 1889.

PAPERS

Frances Willard's diaries and the National WCTU Papers are collected at the Willard Memorial Library (Evanston, IL). A large collection of Willard's papers, correspondence, and other WCTU papers and publications are in the Woman's Christian Temperance Union National Headquarters Historical Files (joint Ohio Historical Society–Michigan Historical Collections). The collection has been microfilmed and is available for interlibrary loan.

JOHN WINTHROP
(1588–1649)

Colonizer, Governor, and Author of "A Model of Christian Charity"

INTRODUCTION

"Love is as absolutely necessary to the being of the body of Christ, as the *sinews* and other ligaments of a *natural* body are to the being of that body" (*Winthrop Papers* 1929, 2: 292). John Winthrop's invocation of love, expressed aboard the *Arbella*, the flagship of the fleet that brought a colony of settlers to the Massachusetts Bay in 1630, summarized his understanding of the social and spiritual foundations of a Christian community. Through his teachings about the nature of community, he made a significant contribution to Americans' understanding of philanthropy.

EARLY YEARS AND EDUCATION

John Winthrop was born on January 12, 1588, in Edwardstone, Suffolk, England, the son of Adam and Anne (Browne) Winthrop. The elder Winthrop was the lord of Groton Manor, an estate about sixty-five miles from London. Adam Winthrop, a man of local influence, was his son's role model, showing him by example both how to manage his property and how to serve the public interest. Trained as a lawyer, Adam Winthrop presided over manorial courts both on his own estate and for neighboring lords. He also handled the financial records of two of the colleges of the University of Cambridge, St. John's and Trinity.

Trinity College was John Winthrop's destination when he matriculated at Cambridge in 1603. He remained at Trinity for a year, then left without a degree. On April 16, 1605, he married at seventeen, taking Mary Forth as his bride. John and Mary Winthrop made their home at Groton Manor and in Great Stanbridge, Essex, where he managed

Charles Osgood's portrait of Governor John Winthrop. Oil on canvas, 1834, MHS image #53. Courtesy of the Massachusetts Historical Society.

family lands. In 1613, Winthrop resumed his education, entering Gray's Inn in London, where he read law. Mary Winthrop died in 1615, but the same year he married Thomasine Clopton, who died after childbirth in 1616. Winthrop's third marriage, to Margaret Tyndal in 1618, lasted until her death in 1647. For his fourth wife, he took Martha Coytmore; she survived Winthrop at his death in 1649. Winthrop's marriages produced sixteen children, only half of whom survived to maturity.

As a major landowner with a liberal education, Winthrop, even as a young man, was one of the leading figures in Suffolk County, northeast of London. In 1615, at twenty-seven, he became one of the county's justices of the peace. Men of Winthrop's high social station ordinarily took responsibility for the community's less fortunate members; Winthrop recognized this duty by donating land in 1618 for the construction of a poorhouse and by service, a few years later, on a committee of justices of the peace charged with reviewing the local administration of poor relief.

Until the late 1620s, Winthrop devoted most of his energy to managing his estate in Groton. In 1627, his appointment as an attorney at the royal Court of Wards and Liveries, which oversaw the estates of orphans, provided him with a source of handsome legal fees, earnings that helped him support a growing family.

Before his first marriage, Winthrop had committed himself to a set of religious doctrines that emphasized human depravity, divine omnipotence, and the necessity for salvation of a conversion experience or spiritual rebirth. At Trinity College, in Groton, and in London, he associated with Puritans, a movement of men and women intent on reforming the established Church of England. When a circle of Puritans obtained a royal charter in 1629 permitting the establishment of the Massachusetts Bay Company to colonize a swath of the North American continent, Winthrop was an early participant. The royal government assumed that the Company would be based in England, where under Crown supervision its officers would manage the activities of its American colony. Between March and October 1629, however, intending to evade this oversight, the Company's leaders audaciously planned to resettle it in the New World.

CAREER HIGHLIGHTS

On October 20, 1629, the shareholders of the Massachusetts Bay Company elected John Winthrop its governor, or chief executive officer, for the coming year. Winthrop hurriedly wrapped up his affairs in London and Groton and prepared to transplant himself and his family, along with a colony of settlers, to the New World. The party of about 1,000 men, women, and children required eleven ships. On March 22, 1630, Winthrop and two of his children set sail with the first four vessels, embarking on a voyage that took sixty-six days. His wife, who was pregnant, delayed her departure until the following year. The extensive journal that Winthrop began on board ship and continued through the rest of his life provides the most detailed source of information on the early years of the Massachusetts Bay colony.

After examining the Massachusetts coastline and visiting Salem, a small town established by an advance group of Puritans in 1628, Winthrop and other leaders determined to settle their party at the mouth of the Charles River. When Governor Winthrop chose to build his house on a peninsula of land jutting into the harbor and at the opening of the river, that community, Boston, became the colony's dominant settlement.

As the company's elected chief magistrate, Winthrop was the central figure in the establishment of the new colony. He took the lead in determining the location of towns, assuring food supplies, communicating with supporters at home in England, advising potential immigrants, and dealing with other American communities, both native and settler.

After deciding where to build the settlement, the next task was to determine how it would be governed. The Massachusetts Bay Company was a private enterprise, a joint-stock venture owned by its shareholders who selected its company officers at annual meetings of its General Court, which could also fix its laws. Settlers who were not also stockholders in the company did not possess a vote in the colony's affairs. In May 1631, and at Winthrop's urging, the General Court opened the franchise to all male church members, a measure that soon encompassed most of the colony's adult men.

Between 1631 and Winthrop's death in 1649, the voters of the colony elected him to eleven more annual terms as governor. The survival and stability of the small settlement were his primary concerns as chief magistrate. At several points, when he perceived threats to its security, he urged the banishment of dissidents. In 1637, on the most important of these occasions, he effectively exiled Anne Hutchinson and a circle of followers for views about salvation that he considered heretical.

MAJOR PHILANTHROPIC CONTRIBUTIONS

As a youth and young man in Groton, Winthrop had learned the obligation of a community leader to assist neighbors in need. In Massachusetts in the early 1630s, land for farming was widely available and the demand for labor outstripped its supply, meaning that unemployment was uncommon. Widows, orphans, and newly arrived settlers nevertheless required assistance, which Governor Winthrop often provided out of his own pocket. His most important philanthropic contribution, however, was not a practical act but a theoretical statement.

Aboard the *Arbella* in 1630, as the settlers pondered what was in store for them, Winthrop instructed them on their Christian obligations toward one another. Winthrop was never ordained a minister, but "A Model of Christian Charity," the sermon he preached as a layman, outlined every believer's role in the community they planned to establish.

"A Model of Christian Charity" is a blueprint for a society of believers. Winthrop instructed that love is the connecting tissue that holds every society together, but he added that those who had experienced God's saving grace feel a special love for one another, a sentiment infinitely more powerful and selfless than the emotion that links those whom the Lord has not spared. Winthrop's audience consisted largely of pious men and women who had reason to hope that they would join God in heaven, and he addressed his words directly to those of the "household of faith," or community of sincere believers (*Winthrop Papers* 1929, 2: 284). Within this community, men and women occupied many different stations and everyone had a specific role. Winthrop taught: "God *Almighty* in his most holy and wise providence hath so disposed of the Condition of *mankind*, as in all times some must be rich some *poor*, some *high* and eminent in power and *dignity*, others *mean* and in *subjection*" (*Winthrop Papers* 1929, 2: 282). No matter what their means, reborn Christians were obliged to do whatever they could to promote the best interests of other members of the community of the faithful.

As Winthrop used the word, "charity" was not synonymous with alms. By the term, he meant the emotional bond, or "ligament," that connected believers to one another. Charity understood as divine love could be expressed in many ways, including the compassionate efforts of the poor to help the wealthy in times of personal or family crisis.

CONCLUSION

Winthrop's model of Christian charity provided New Englanders with a useful way to envision charitable relationships as long as most men and women felt or anticipated feeling God's saving grace. By the middle of the seventeenth century, though, as the first generation of settlers passed away, their children came to dominate the region. Under the influence of their faith, the settlers had uprooted themselves and their families, intent upon the establishment of a Christian society. There was, however, no guarantee that their children would experience their faith with the same power. As the settlers' sons and daughters, in increasing numbers, failed to undergo a spiritual rebirth, Winthrop's specific plans for a charitable community of faithful Christians began to appear dated and increasingly irrelevant. Nevertheless, his broader injunction to draw on love as the principal bond of society has continued to inspire many men and women from his day to the present.

Conrad Edick Wright

FURTHER READING

Cohen, Charles L. "John Winthrop." In *American National Biography*, vol. 23, John A. Garraty and Mark C. Carnes, ed. New York: Oxford University Press, 1999, 660–665.

Dunn, Richard S. *Puritans and Yankees: The Winthrop Dynasty of New England, 1630–1717.* Princeton, NJ: Princeton University Press, 1962.

Dunn, Richard S., James Savage, and Laetitia Yeandle. *The Journal of John Winthrop, 1630–1649.* Cambridge, MA: Harvard University Press, 1996.

Foster, Stephen. *Their Solitary Way: The Puritan Social Ethic in the First Century of Settlement in New England.* New Haven, CT: Yale University Press, 1971.

Morgan, Edmund S. *The Puritan Dilemma: The Story of John Winthrop.* Boston and Toronto: Little, Brown & Company, 1958.

Winthrop Papers. Boston: Massachusetts Historical Society, 1929–. Six volumes to date.

PAPERS

The Massachusetts Historical Society (Boston, MA) holds most of the papers of the Winthrop family, but the earliest surviving draft of John Winthrop's "A Model of Christian Charity" (titled, in seventeenth-century English, "A Modell of Christian Charitie") belongs to the New York Historical Society (New York City).

Appendix 1: A Timeline of American Philanthropy

1600s
The indigenous Lakota encounter Europeans in western Wisconsin and Minnesota. Along with other American Indians, the Lakota practice one of the oldest giving traditions in North America.

1630
While sailing toward America, Puritan leader John Winthrop preaches his famous "A Model of Christian Charity." The sermon outlines their future society in America as well as his conception of charity.

1638
John Harvard's bequest provides half his estate and his library to a fledgling college in Cambridge, Massachusetts.

1656
Robert Keayne dies and makes one of the earliest charitable bequests in America, illustrating the Puritan ethic.

1690s
Influenced by reform societies that developed in England after the Glorious Revolution of 1688, Cotton Mather begins to promote similar voluntary associations (also known as Neighborhood Benefit Societies) in America.

1710
Minister Cotton Mather publishes his important and practical work on public service, *Bonafacius: An Essay upon the Good*.

1727
Influenced by works such as *An Essay on Several Projects* and *Bonafacius: An Essay upon the Good*, Benjamin Franklin founds the Junto Club in Phil-

adelphia. The club serves as a catalyst for numerous civic improvements.

1750
Anthony Benezet begins teaching free African Americans in his home and devotes over thirty years to such educational endeavors, including the founding of the African School.

1751
Pioneering the matching-grant concept, Benjamin Franklin persuades the Pennsylvania Assembly to offer matching funds if private contributions for a hospital reach a certain level. The Pennsylvania Hospital opens the following year.

1754
Anthony Benezet founds the first school in Pennsylvania history that offers more than an elementary-level education for girls.

1775
Anthony Benezet creates one of the earliest American antislavery societies, the Society for the Relief of Free Negroes Unlawfully Held in Bondage.

1784
Benjamin Rush publishes *Inquiry into the Effects of Spirituous Liquors upon the Human Body, and Their Influence upon the Happiness of Society*, a work that makes him known as the founder of American temperance efforts.

1786
Benjamin Rush helps found the Philadelphia Dispensary for the poor, which represents one of the first free medical clinics in North America.

1790
Benjamin Franklin's death sets in motion a fund

for apprentices in Philadelphia and Boston. During the next 200 years, these funds receive much praise and criticism.

1799

American expatriates Benjamin Thompson (Count Rumford) and Thomas Bernard propose the creation of what comes to be known as the Royal Institution. Through this important action as well as others, Thompson, who could also be called a father of scientific philanthropy, influences the course of American philanthropy and typifies the Atlantic culture's affect upon American philanthropy.

1810

Elizabeth Seton and the Sisters of St. Joseph create the first free Catholic school in the United States in Emmitsburg, Maryland. The school becomes the model for the Catholic parochial school system in the United States.

1812

Returning from a trip to Sierra Leone, African-American merchant Paul Cuffe lands in the United States, encourages American blacks to assist (collectively) blacks in Sierra Leone, and enlists the strong support of black shipbuilder James Forten. Within a number of American cities, Cuffe also spurs the creation of African Institutions, black associations that wish to develop transatlantic mutual-aid initiatives.

1813

Elizabeth Seton officially founds the Sisters of Charity, the first American religious order, and focuses its efforts on education.

1819

After the state of New Hampshire passed a bill that took over the assets of Dartmouth College and replaced members of the board of trustees, because the state wished to transform the small liberal arts college into a school that offered practical training in agriculture and engineering, the former Dartmouth College trustees appeal the case up to the U.S. Supreme Court. In *Trustees of Dartmouth College v Woodward*, the U.S. Supreme Court sided with the old trustees and established corporations (nonprofit or for-profit) as entities afforded considerable protection from government interference.

Rebecca Gratz organizes the Female Hebrew Benevolent Society, the first independent Jewish women's charitable association.

1825

Robert Owen establishes the secular communal experiment of New Harmony, Indiana.

1826

Joseph Tuckerman gives up his pulpit and become a minister to Boston's poor. Anticipating the organized charity movement, he subsequently enlists the collaboration of Protestant denominations and Catholics.

1827

Despite the efforts of Robert Owen and Robert Dale Owen, the utopian community of New Harmony fails but it inspires other communal settlements as well as social reforms within American society.

1831

Abolitionist William Lloyd Garrison begins to publish *The Liberator*, a paper significantly funded by black entrepreneur James Forten as well as white entrepreneurs Arthur and Lewis Tappan.

1833

Impressed by Samuel Gridley Howe's work with the blind, Thomas Perkins donates his mansion as well as $50,000 to aid Howe's efforts. Howe subsequently travels the country promoting the education of and schools for people with blindness.

Along with others, Arthur and Lewis Tappan establish the American Anti-Slavery Society. Arthur Tappan is named the first president of the association and Lewis Tappan provides significant direction for the society's main publication, the *Emancipator*.

1835

Evangelist Lyman Beecher delivers *A Plea for the West*, an important piece on religion's place in public life and the value of voluntary associations but also an example of the religious prejudice of the time. During antebellum America, Beecher probably did more than anyone else to promote the use of voluntary associations.

James Smithson's bequest to the United States stirs much controversy and debate about the role of government and philanthropy.

1837

Mary Lyon establishes Mount Holyoke Female Seminary (later named Mount Holyoke College), which pioneers higher education for women in the United States.

1838

Rebecca Gratz establishes the Hebrew Sunday School, the first Jewish Sunday school in the United States.

1839

Per John Lowell's bequest, the Lowell Institute provides its first public lecture. Thereafter, the

Lowell Institute becomes a major cultural force in nineteenth- and twentieth-century Boston as well as a model of elite cultural philanthropy.

1841

In a case that provides notoriety for the abolitionist movement, the U.S. Supreme Court's decision in the famous *Amistad* case allows the Mendi Africans to return to their homeland. Lewis Tappan not only persuades former President John Quincy Adams to plead the Mendis' case before the U.S. Supreme Court, but is a major benefactor of the *Amistad* cause.

1844

In the landmark *Vidal, Girard, et al. v. Philadelphia*, the U.S. Supreme Court sides with Stephen Girard's controversial will and ensures private individuals' right to have their donations acted upon per their intent.

The U.S. Congress creates the Smithsonian Institution—its first act in what would become a pattern of public philanthropy.

1847

Leonard Bacon authors what is possibly the first detailed treatment of charitable trusteeship.

1848

By this time, Dorothea Dix has traveled over 60,000 miles, in the United States and Canada, advocating hospitals for people with mental illnesses.

Stephan Girard's secular boarding school for children, Girard College, opens.

Samuel Gridley Howe and Walter E. Fernald found and head the first residential school for American children with mental retardation.

1853

Charles Loring Brace launches the Children's Aid Society in New York City. Later devising a controversial "placing-out" program, the society relocates tens of thousands of children to new homes (often in the American West).

1854

After Dorothea Dix successfully lobbies the U.S. Congress to pass a bill that would provide a total of ten million acres of public lands to "several states" for the support of mental hospitals, President Franklin Pierce vetoes the bill because he worries "that if Congress have the power to make provision for the indigent insane . . . it has the same power to provide for the indigent who are not insane, and thus to transfer to the federal government the charge of all the poor in all the States." Until the Great Depression, the state and local governments as well as private charities remained responsible for social welfare.

1859

Hoping to help the poor and working class advance themselves, Peter Cooper founds the Copper Union in New York City, which offers such services as free night classes, lectures, and concerts. Andrew Carnegie later praises Cooper's school as an example of the proper use of wealth and philanthropy.

1861–1865

During the Civil War, the Christian Commission and the United States Sanitary Commission worked to improve the lives of soldiers. Spurred by considerable giving and volunteering, the Christian Commission provided soldiers with spiritual guidance and material goods, while the Sanitary Commission—employing a scientific philanthropy approach—focused its efforts on eliminating environmental conditions that produced suffering, disease, and death in military camps and hospitals.

1867

Concerned about Southern education after the Civil War, George Peabody establishes the $2 million Peabody Education Fund. Often recognized as the first modern foundation, the Peabody Education Fund influences the founding and principles of subsequent foundations.

1879

Francis Willard is elected president of the Woman's Christian Temperance Union (WCTU). Over the next two decades, her "Do Everything" reform approach and tireless travel and speeches make the WCTU the largest women's voluntary association in the world.

1881

Clara Barton establishes the American Association of the Red Cross, which becomes the American Red Cross, and quickly undertakes numerous relief efforts for national disasters.

Andrew Carnegie establishes his first public library in Dunfermline, Scotland. Ultimately, Carnegie provides money for the creation of 1,681 public libraries in the United States as well as 828 public libraries in other English-speaking countries.

Henry Lee Higginson founds the Boston Symphony, the first permanent symphony in the United States.

Helen Hunt Jackson publishes *A Century of Dishonor*, a documentary on the abuses experienced by Native Americans. This work and others authored by Jackson inspire others to promote the rights of Native Americans.

1882

Josephine Shaw Lowell takes a leading role in creating the Charity Organization Society of New York, the "flagship" of the charity organization movement.

1883

Bernice Pauahi Paki Bishop writes a will that leaves the vast amount of her estate, including 9% of the land in Hawaii, to the creation of the Kamehameha Schools and for native Hawaiians.

1884

Arguing for organized charity, Josephine Shaw Lowell publishes *Public Relief and Private Charity*.

1885

Disturbed by the lack of educational opportunities available to Baltimore girls, Mary Elizabeth Garrett and four other female friends launched the Bryn Mawr School for Girls, which becomes an exemplary college preparatory institution for young women.

1887

Bernice Pauahi Paki Bishop's Kamehameha Schools is established and becomes the largest private prekindergarten through twelfth-grade school in the United States.

1889

Jane Addams and Ellen Gates Starr found the Hull-House settlement in Chicago, which becomes the model social settlement.

Andrew Carnegie's well-known work, "The Gospel of Wealth," is published in the *North American Review*.

1890

John D. Rockefeller, Sr. and the American Baptist Education Society create the University of Chicago. With years of Rockefeller support, the university becomes recognized as a premier educational institution.

1891

"Millionaire nun" Katharine Drexel founds the Sisters of the Blessed Sacrament For Indians and Colored People.

Wishing to create an educational institution that differs from major Eastern universities and to memorialize their son, Leland and Jane Stanford found the Leland Stanford Junior University.

1892

To preserve America's wilderness, John Muir founds the Sierra Club.

Ida B. Wells-Barnett orchestrates the first anti-lynching campaign in the United States.

1893

Pioneers of public-health nursing, Lillian Wald and Mary Brewster, move into rooms in a fifth-floor walkup located on New York City's East Side and start providing nursing services for their neighbors, which leads to the creation of the Visiting Nurse Service of New York and the Henry Street Settlement.

Mary Garrett's philanthropy opens the Johns Hopkins University Medical School. By attaching specific conditions to her donation, she transforms medical education while ensuring that men and women are admitted and educated equally.

1895

Jane Addams, Florence Kelley, and other Hull-House colleagues publish *Hull-House Maps and Papers*, an important and early effort to connect reform to social science research. Efforts, such as this publication, lead to schools of social work and the social-worker profession.

1896

Ballington and Maud Booth break away from William Booth's Salvation Army and form the Volunteers of America. Thereafter, Maud Booth performs valuable prison reform work.

1901

Wishing to engage in "wholesale philanthropy" (solving societal problems at their source) instead of "retail philanthropy" (alleviating individual suffering temporarily), a philosophy promoted by his philanthropic advisor Frederick T. Gates, John D. Rockefeller, Sr. founds the Rockefeller Institute for Medical Research. This organization and subsequent Rockefeller philanthropies, such as the General Education Board, significantly shape American medicine and education.

1903

Booker T. Washington secretly finances *Giles v. Harris* and then funds *Giles v. Teasely* the following year; both cases challenge black disenfranchisement. Throughout his life, Washington secretly funds numerous black newspapers and racial discrimination cases within a highly racist society.

1904

Wishing to elevate the education of black females, Mary McLeod Bethune starts and heads the Daytona Literary and Industrial School for Training Negro Girls.

Evangeline Booth becomes the head of the American Salvation Army. Building on the work of Ballington and Maud Booth as well as Emma and Frederick Booth-Tucker. Evangeline Booth spends the next thirty years transforming the Salvation Army into one of America's most popular religious charities.

1907

Using $10 million, Margaret Olivia Sage founds the Russell Sage Foundation, which becomes a pivotal institution in the development of the social sciences and social work.

1910

Jane Addams publishes her highly acclaimed autobiography, *Twenty Years at Hull-House.*

1911

During a fund-raising campaign for a Colored YMCA in Indianapolis, Madam C.J. Walker amazes the city by pledging a gift ($1,000) equal to the amount pledged by wealthy white citizens.

Concerned that he would die rich and disgraced, Andrew Carnegie creates the Carnegie Corporation of New York, giving it most of his remaining assets ($125 million).

1912

As the anonymous "Mr. Smith," George Eastman provides a new campus for the Massachusetts Institute of Technology. Preferring to give with little or any attribution, Eastman spends much of his life donating around $125 million to his hometown of Rochester, New York as well as to many other localities related to his Eastman Kodak Company's work.

At her Savannah mansion, Juliette Gordon Low founds the Girl Scouts of America with eighteen girls.

Henrietta Szold formally establishes Hadassah, a national Zionist organization for women.

1914

Concerned about "dead hand" philanthropy, Frederick Goff founds the Cleveland Foundation, which becomes the first community foundation.

Herbert Hoover establishes and leads the Commission for Relief in Belgium (CRB), which distributes food to more than nine million Belgian and French civilians during World War I.

Creating the first African-American research library, Jesse Moorland donates his substantial collection of books, artifacts, and numerous other black-related materials to Howard University.

1917

Roger Baldwin establishes the Civil Liberties Bureau, which eventually becomes the American Civil Liberties Union (ACLU).

Julius Rosenwald creates the Rosenwald Fund to promote racial equality.

1918

Tithing advocate George Draper Dayton creates the Dayton Foundation.

1919

After the success of victory chest drives during World War I, a dramatic growth of community chests occurs across the United States in the 1920s. Ultimately, these united fund-raising vehicles become known as United Ways.

1920

Herbert Hoover's American Relief Administration European Children's Fund initiates a fund appeal, which raises close to $30 million in the United States. In the early 1920s, this private agency provides food for up to 3 million children on a daily basis.

1921

Herbert Hoover's American Relief Administration offers relief to famine victims in Soviet Russia. At its peak, during its activities from 1921 to 1923, the American Relief Administration feeds over 10 million people a day.

Troubled by the prejudice against contemporary American art, Gertrude Vanderbilt Whitney founds the Whitney Museum of American Art.

1923

Mary McLeod Bethune's Daytona Beach school merges with the Cookman Institute, forming the Bethune-Cookman College; Bethune becomes the president of this college for black women.

In New York City, Margaret Sanger opens the Birth Control Clinical Research Bureau, which represents the first doctor-staffed birth control clinic and the model for hundreds of future birth control clinics.

1924

After studying existing foundations, Sebastian S. Kresge establishes the Kresge Foundation, which diverges from the activities of many foundations that preceded it.

1925

Roger Baldwin's ACLU orchestrates the famous Scopes Monkey Trial.

Katharine Drexel and her Sisters of the Blessed

Sacrament start Xavier University of Louisiana, which remains the only historically black Catholic university.

Advised by three former Rhodes scholars, Simon Guggenheim creates the John Simon Guggenheim Memorial Foundation, which offers competitive one-year fellowships to scholars aged 25–35. From 1925 to 1945, the foundation's inventive decision to offer grants to individuals successfully supports notable novelists, painters, composers, and scientists.

1926

Influenced by his aviator son Harry Guggenheim, Daniel Guggenheim establishes the Guggenheim Fund for the Promotion of Aeronautics. Within a few years, the foundation's work develops the first successful commercial air passenger service.

1927

Robert Brookings creates the Brookings Institution by merging the Institute for Government Research and the Institute of Economics.

1928–1929

Many Rockefeller philanthropies merge into the Rockefeller Foundation.

1929

Advised by Charles Lindbergh and largely directed by Harry Guggenheim, the Daniel and Florence Guggenheim Foundation provides grants to support Robert Goddard, a rocket scientist who pioneers American space travel.

Henry Ford dedicates what will become the Henry Ford Museum and Greenfield Village at Dearborn, Michigan.

Abby Aldrich Rockefeller co-founds the Museum of Modern Art.

1930

W.K. Kellogg founds the W.K. Kellogg Foundation with the goal of improving the lives of young people.

1933

Dorothy Day and Peter Maurin start publishing *The Catholic Worker*, which leads to the Catholic Worker Movement.

At the age of seventy-three, Henrietta Szold begins efforts to help European Jewish children emigrate to Palestine. During World War II, her rescue efforts save thousands of Jewish children's lives.

1936

Edsel and Henry Ford establish the Ford Foundation. Although the founders had focused on Michigan philanthropy, their sizable gifts to the foundation—upon their deaths in the 1940s—ultimately make it an international organization and one of the most influential twentieth-century foundations.

President Franklin Roosevelt accepts Andrew Mellon's offer to establish a National Gallery of the Art on the National Mall in Washington, D.C. For many years, Mellon had collected art with the goal of creating such an institution.

1937

Along with brother J.K. Lilly, Jr. and father J.K. Lilly, Sr., Eli Lilly establishes the Lilly Endowment, a foundation that reflects Eli Lilly's tendency for personal philanthropy by favoring grants to his hometown, Indianapolis, and home state, Indiana.

1938

Paul Mellon becomes the first President of the National Gallery of Art. Developing his father's vision, he donates a considerable amount of artwork, time, and money during the next sixty-one years.

1939

Ima Hogg founds the Hogg Foundation for Mental Hygiene, which offers mental heath services and education throughout Texas.

1944

After observing common fund-raising problems among black colleges and suggesting a united appeal for black colleges, Frederick Douglas Patterson serves as the guiding force in the creation of the United Negro College Fund.

1946

Five Dayton brothers institute an annual policy of giving 5 percent of Dayton's pretax profits to charity. Their company subsequently becomes a model of corporate philanthropy.

1947

New York University alumni donate various businesses to their alma mater, including the C.F. Mueller Company, a gift that makes New York University the largest manufacturer of macaroni in the world and the recipient of harsh criticism from the U.S. Congress.

1948

Hector P. Garcia founds the American G.I. Forum, which becomes an organization that fights for the civil rights of all Latinos.

J. Howard Pew, J.N. Pew, Jr., Mary Ethel Pew, and Mabel Pew Myrin form the Pew Memorial Foundation, which eventually becomes known as the Pew Charitable Trusts. During their lifetime, the four Pew siblings largely ensure that their foundation grants are given anonymously.

An opponent of perpetual endowments, Julius Rosenwald's Rosenwald Fund follows its founder's instructions and sunsets, having used all of its principal and interest.

1952

Advancing the Rockefeller family's philanthropic tradition, John D. Rockefeller, Jr. assists his five sons in endowing the Rockefeller Brothers Fund. Subsequent Rockefeller generations continue to form foundations to foster their brand of philanthropy.

John D. Rockefeller 3rd becomes chairman of the Rockefeller Foundation and re-directs its goals to strengthening democracy, assisting underdeveloped countries, promoting government efficiency, and addressing overpopulation.

Longtime leader of the birth control movement, Margaret Sanger serves as a founder as well as the first president of the International Planned Parenthood Federation.

1953

In *Barlow et al. v. A.P. Smith Manufacturing*, the New Jersey Supreme Court upholds for-profit corporations' right to make charitable contributions even if the gifts do not offer a "direct benefit" to the corporation.

1954

John M. Olin founds the John M. Olin Foundation, which eventually becomes highly effective at shaping public policy.

1955

Martin Luther King, Jr. becomes the head of the newly formed Montgomery Improvement Association and leads a sustained bus boycott in Montgomery, Alabama, by promoting nonviolent voluntary action. An acknowledged leader of the civil rights movement, King spends the remainder of his life promoting civil rights and social justice through nonviolent voluntary action.

1957

After years of efforts, Hector P. Garcia is able to end the Texas public schools' segregation of Mexican Americans by combining the efforts of the American G.I. Forum and the League of United Latin American Citizens behind *Hernandez v. Consolidated ISD*.

1958

James Herman Robinson forms Operation Cross-roads Africa, which inspires the Kennedy Administration to establish the Peace Corps.

1959

After twenty years of effort by Solomon Guggenheim and his nephew Harry Guggenheim, the Solomon R. Guggenheim Museum opens in New York City and within its Frank Lloyd Wright designed structure.

1960

Believing in "the power of ideas," Pierre Frist Goodrich founds the Liberty Fund.

1962

Cesar Chavez founds the National Farm Workers Association, which becomes the United Farm Workers.

1964

David and Lucile Packard create their family foundation, the David and Lucile Packard Foundation.

1965

Fighting for wage increases and improved working conditions, Cesar Chavez and the National Farm Workers Association start a strike against grape growers in California. Ultimately, these efforts spur a nationwide boycott of grapes and concessions by grape growers.

1974

Sensing that the public and government lack an understanding of philanthropy, John D. Rockefeller 3rd creates the Commission on Private Philanthropy and Public Needs (the Filer Commission). At the end of the following year, the commission reports their findings in the important work *Giving in America: Toward a Stronger Voluntary Sector*.

1975

At Yale University, John D. Rockefeller funds a feasibility study that leads to the Program on Non-Profit Organizations (PONPO), the first of many university-based academic centers that currently study issues pertaining to philanthropy and the nonprofit sector.

1977

Although pleased with many Ford Foundation accomplishments, Henry Ford II resigns from the board of trustees because he is troubled by the foundation's focus on what he perceives as liberal causes.

1984

George Soros negotiates the creation of Soros Foundation–Hungary, the first private independent foundation within a communist country.

Over the next five years, Soros provides grants to purchase materials, such as copy machines, that undermines the communist government.

1987

Due in part to its strong tradition of corporate philanthropy, the Dayton-Hudson Corporation is able to fend off a hostile takeover.

1988

To highlight the dangers of pesticides, Cesar Chavez fasts on water for thirty-six days.

1995

Mississippi laundress Oseola McCarty becomes a national figure by making a surprising gift of $150,000 to the University of Southern Mississippi. McCarty's action highlights the philanthropic capacity of "average" citizens as well as the African American giving tradition.

1997

Kenneth Dayton and Joe Selvaggio found the One Percent Club. The following year, Kenneth Dayton caps his wealth and details *The Stages of Giving*.

1999

Deciding to combine the William H. Gates Foundation and the Gates Learning Foundation, Bill and Melinda Gates form the Bill and Melinda Gates Foundation, quickly becoming the largest charitable organization in the world and possessing great philanthropic potential.

Appendix 2: Videos

JANE ADDAMS

The House that Jane Built. Chicago: WTTW, and New York: The Corporation for Public Broadcasting, dist. by Cinema Guild, 1990.

Jane Addams. Bala Cynwyd, PA: Schlessinger Video Productions, 1995.

Women of Hull-House. Chicago: Jane Addams' Hull-House Museum, University of Illinois at Chicago, 1992.

ROGER BALDWIN

The A.C.L.U.—A History. Princeton, NJ: Films for the Humanities and Sciences, 1998.

Traveling Hopefully. Wilmette, IL: Films Incorporated, 1981.

CLARA BARTON

Clara Barton. Bala Cynwyd, PA: Schlessinger Video Productions, 1995.

MARY McLEOD BETHUNE

Mary McLeod Bethune, Educator. Bala Cynwyd, PA: Schlessinger Video Productions, 1994.

BERNICE BISHOP

The Will of a Princess: Preserving the Legacy of ke ali'I Bernice Pauahi Bishop. Honolulu, HI: Kamehameha Schools/Bernice Pauahi Bishop Estate, 1995.

CHARLES LORING BRACE

The Orphan Trains. New York: Edward Gray Films, and Boston: WGBH Educational Foundation, 1995.

ANDREW CARNEGIE

Andrew Carnegie and the Age of Steel. New York: A&E Home Video, 1997.

The Richest Man in the World. Alexandria, VA: PBS Video, 1997.

CESAR CHAVEZ

Cesar Chavez. Bala Cynwyd, PA: Schlessinger Video Productions, 1995.

The Fight in the Fields: Cesar Chavez and the Farmworkers' Struggle. San Francisco: Paradigm Productions, 1997.

DOROTHY DAY

Dorothy Day: Blessed Are the Poor. Sparkill, NY: Hallel Communications, 1992.

Entertaining Angels: The Dorothy Day Story. Mahwah, NJ: Distributed by Paulist Press, 1997.

KATHARINE DREXEL

Blessed Mother Katharine Drexel. Philadelphia: WHYY Wilmington/Philadelphia, 1990.

GEORGE EASTMAN

George Eastman: An American Snapshot. New York: Lou Reda Productions for A&E Home Video, 2001.

HENRY FORD

Henry Ford. New York: A&E Home Video, 1999.
A Job at Ford's. Alexandria, VA: Distributed by PBS Home Video, 1993.
Model "T". New York: A&E Home Video, 1996.

BENJAMIN FRANKLIN

Ben and Me. Burbank, CA: Walt Disney Home Video, 1989
Benjamin Franklin, Citizen of the World. New York: A&E Home Video, 1999.
Benjamin Franklin, Scientist and Inventor. Irving, TX: Nest Entertainment, 1993.

W.K. KELLOGG

The Cornflake Story. San Diego, CA: The Media Guild, 1988.

MARTIN LUTHER KING, JR.

Martin Luther King, Jr.: The Man and the Dream. New York: New Video Group: A&E Home Video, 1997.
Memphis Dreams: Searching for the Promised Land. Stamford, CT: ABC Video, 1999.
Kearns, Kell. *In Remembrance of Martin*. Alexandria, VA: PBS Home Video, 1999.
The Speeches of Martin Luther King. [S.l.]: MPI Home Video, 1990.

MARY LYON

Harris, Julie. *Mary Lyon, Precious Time*. Chicago: International Film Bureau, 1987.

ANDREW MELLON

Sage, DeWitt. *The Quiet Collector, Andrew W. Mellon Remembered*. Washington, DC: A Francis Thompson Production for the National Gallery of Art, 1984.

JOHN MUIR

John Muir: The Man, the Poet, the Legacy. Beverly Hills, CA: Chronicle Broadcasting Co., 1981.

DAVID AND LUCILE PACKARD

Lucile Packard: A Woman of Grace. Los Altos, CA: The David and Lucile Packard Foundation, 1997.
A Tribute to David Packard. Los Altos: CA: The David and Lucile Packard Foundation, 1996.

ROCKEFELLER FAMILY

The Rockefellers. New York: A&E Home Video, 1994.
The Rockefellers. Arlington, VA: PBS Home Video, 2000.

MARGARET SANGER

Margaret Sanger. Princeton, NJ: Films for the Humanities & Sciences, 1998.
Margaret Sanger, a Public Nuisance. New York: Women Make Movies, 1992.

ELIZABETH SETON

A Time for Miracles. Los Angeles: American Broadcasting Company/Charter Entertainment, 1986.

LILLIAN WALD

Lillian Wald: At Home on Henry Street. Tacoma, WA: Pacific Lutheran University Television, 1996.

MADAM C.J. WALKER

Madame C.J. Walker. Highstown, NJ: American School Publishers, 1990.
Madam C.J. Walker, Entrepreneur. Bala Cynwyd, PA: Schlessinger Video Productions, 1992.

Two Dollars and a Dream. New York: Filmakers Library, 1987.

BOOKER T. WASHINGTON

Booker. Northbrook, IL: Disney Educational Productions, Distributed by Coronet MTI Film & Video, 1990.

Booker. Salt Lake City, UT: BWE Video, 1996.
Booker T. Washington, the Life and the Legacy. New York: Your World Video, 1986.

IDA B. WELLS-BARNETT

Ida B. Wells: A Passion for Justice. Alexandria, VA: PBS Video, 1990.

Appendix 3: Children's Books

JANE ADDAMS

Gleiter, Jan. *Jane Addams*. Milwaukee: Raintree Children's Books, 1988.

Kittridge, Mary. *Jane Addams*. New York: Chelsea House, 1988.

McPherson, Stephanie Sammartino. *Peace and Bread: The Story of Jane Addams*. Minneapolis: Carolrhoda Books, 1993.

Peterson, Helen Stone. *Jane Addams, Pioneer of Hull House*. Champaign, IL: Garrard, 1965.

Wheeler, Leslie. *Jane Addams*. Englewood Cliffs, NJ: Silver Burdett Press, 1990.

CLARA BARTON

Kent, Zachary. *The Story of Clara Barton*. Chicago: Children's Press, 1987.

Quackenbush, Robert M. *Clara Barton and Her Victory over Fear*. New York: Simon & Schuster Books for Young Readers, 1995.

Rose, Mary Catherine, and E. Harper Johnson. *Clara Barton: Soldier of Mercy*. New York: Chelsea Juniors, 1991.

Tilton, Rafael. *Clara Barton*. San Diego, CA: Lucent Books, 1995.

Whitelaw, Nancy. *Clara Barton: Civil War Nurse*. Springfield, NJ: Enslow Publishers, 1997.

MARY McLEOD BETHUNE

Greene, Carol. *Mary McLeod Bethune: Champion for Education*. Chicago: Children's Press, 1993.

Greenfield, Eloise, and Jerry Pinkney. *Mary McLeod Bethune*. New York: Crowell, 1977.

Kelso, Richard, and Debbie Heller. *Building a Dream: Mary Bethune's School*. Austin, TX: Raintree Steck-Vaughn, 1993.

McLoone, Margo. *Mary McLeod Bethune: A Photo-Illustrated Biography*. Mankato, MN: Bridgestone Books, 1997.

Meltzer, Milton. *Mary McLeod Bethune: Voice of Black Hope*. New York: Viking Kestrel, 1987.

BERNICE BISHOP

Williams, Julie Stewart, and Robin Yoko Burningham. *Princess Bernice Pauahi Bishop*. Honolulu, HI: Kamehameha Schools/Bernice Pauahi Bishop Estate, Intermediate Reading Program, Community Education Division, 1992.

BOOTH FAMILY

Fellows, Lawrence, and Janet Beller. *A Gentle War: The Story of the Salvation Army*. New York: Macmillan, 1979.

Lavine, Sigmund A. *Evangeline Booth: Daughter of Salvation*. New York: Dodd, Mead, 1970.

Ludwig, Charles. *General without a Gun: The Life of William Booth, Founder of the Salvation Army, for Teens*. Grand Rapids, MI: Zondervan, 1961.

CHARLES LORING BRACE

Orphan Trains: Traveling West to a New Life. Peterborough, NH: Cobblestone, 1998.

ANDREW CARNEGIE

Kent, Zachary. *Andrew Carnegie: Steel King and Friend to Libraries.* Springfield, NJ: Enslow Publishers, 1999.

CESAR CHAVEZ

Collins, David R. *Farmworker's Friend: The Story of Cesar Chavez.* Minneapolis, MN: Carolrhoda Books, 1996.

Davis, Lucille. *Cesar Chavez: A Photo-Illustrated Biography.* Mankato, MN: Bridgestone Books, 1998. (Also available in Spanish.)

Gonzales, Doreen. *Cesar Chavez: Leader for Migrant Farm Workers.* Springfield, NJ: Enslow Publishers, 1996.

Strazzabosco, Jeanne. *Learning about Justice from the Life of Cesar Chavez.* New York: PowerKids Press, 1996.

PETER COOPER

Gurko, Miriam. *The Lives and Times of Peter Cooper.* New York: Crowell, 1959.

PAUL CUFFE AND JAMES FORTEN

Diamond, Arthur. *Paul Cuffe.* New York: Chelsea House, 1989.

Douty, Esther Morris. *Forten, the Sailmaker: Pioneer Champion of Negro Rights.* Chicago: Rand McNally, 1968.

Johnston, Brenda A., and Don Miller. *Between the Devil and the Sea: The Life of James Forten.* New York: Harcourt Brace Jovanovich, 1974.

Johnston, Johanna, and Elton C. Fax. *Paul Cuffee: America's First Black Captain.* New York: Dodd, Mead, 1970.

DOROTHY DAY

Collins, David R. *Dorothy Day, Catholic Worker.* Cincinnati, OH: St. Anthony Press, 1981.

KATHARINE DREXEL

Muller, Gerald F. *More Than Money Can Buy: A Story of Mother Katharine Drexel.* Notre Dame, IN: Dujarie Press, 1959.

GEORGE EASTMAN

Joseph, Paul. *George Eastman.* Minneapolis, MN: Abdo & Daughters, 1997.

Mitchell, Barbara, and Jan Hosking Smith. *CLICK!: A Story about George Eastman.* Minneapolis, MN: Carolrhoda Books, 1986.

HENRY FORD

Aird, Hazel B., Catherine Ruddiman, and Wallace Wood. *Henry Ford, Young Man with Ideas.* New York: Aladdin Books; London: Collier Macmillan, 1986, 1960.

Gourley, Catherine. *Wheels of Time A Biography of Henry Ford.* Brookfield, CT: Millbrook Press, 1997.

Harris, Jacqueline L. *Henry Ford.* New York: F. Watts, 1984.

Quackenbush, Robert M. *Along Came the Model T!: How Henry Ford Put the World on Wheels.* New York: Parents' Magazine Press, 1978.

BENJAMIN FRANKLIN

Adler, David A., and Lyle Miller. *Benjamin Franklin—Printer, Inventor, Statesman.* New York: Holiday House, 1992.

Foster, Lelia Merrell. *Benjamin Franklin, Founding Father and Inventor.* Springfield, NJ: Enslow Publishers, 1997.

Giblin, James and Michael Dooling. *The Amazing Life of Benjamin Franklin.* New York: Scholastic Press, 2000.

Osborne, Mary Pope. *The Many Lives of Benjamin Franklin.* New York: Dial Books for Young Readers, 1990.

Quackenbush, Robert M. *Benjamin Franklin and His Friends.* New York: Pippin Press, 1991.

IMA HOGG

Gurasich, Marj. *Did You Ever—Meet a Texas Hero?* Vol. 2. Austin, TX: Eakin Press, 1996.

HERBERT HOOVER

Emery, Anne. *American Friend; Herbert Hoover.* New York: Rand McNally, 1967

HELEN HUNT JACKSON

Jackson, Helen Hunt. *Bits of Colorado: Helen Hunt Jackson's Writings for Young Readers.* Palmer Lake, CO: Filter Press, 2000.

FLORENCE KELLEY

Saller, Carol. *Florence Kelley.* Minneapolis, MN: Carolrhoda Books, 1997.

W.K. KELLOGG

Epstein, Rachel. *W.K. Kellogg: Generous Genius.* New York: Children's Press, 2000.

MARTIN LUTHER KING, JR.

Boone-Jones, Margaret, and Roszel Scott. *Martin Luther King, Jr.: A Picture Story.* Chicago: Children's Press, 1968.

Haskins, James. *The Day Martin Luther King, Jr., Was Shot: A Photo History of the Civil Rights Movement.* New York: Scholastic, 1992.

———. *I Have a Dream: The Life and Words of Martin Luther King, Jr.* Brookfield, CT: Millbrook Press, 1992.

McNatt, Rosemary Bray, and Malcah Zeldis. *Martin Luther King.* New York: Greenwillow Books, 1995.

Rowland, Della. *Martin Luther King, Jr.: The Dream of Peaceful Revolution.* Englewood Cliffs, NJ: Silver Burdett Press, 1990.

JULIETTE GORDON LOW

Behrens, June. *Juliette Low: Founder of the Girl Scouts of America.* Chicago: Childrens Press, 1988.

Brown, Fern G., and Marie De John. *Daisy and the Girl Scouts: The Story of Juliette Gordon Low.* Morton Grove, IL: A. Whitman, 1996.

Kudlinski, Kathleen V., and Sheila Hamanaka. *Juliette Gordon Low: America's First Girl Scout.* New York: Viking Kestrel, 1988.

Shultz, Gladys Denny, and Daisy Gordon Lawrence. *Lady from Savannah: The Life of Juliette Gordon Low.* Philadelphia: Lippincott, 1958.

MARY LYON

Rosen, Dorothy. *A Fire in Her Bones: The Story of Mary Lyon.* Minneapolis, MN: Carolrhoda Books, 1995.

COTTON MATHER

Lutz, Norma Jean. *Cotton Mather.* Philadelphia: Chelsea House, 2000.

Wood, James Playsted. *The Admirable Cotton Mather.* New York: Seabury Press, 1971.

JOHN MUIR

Force, Eden. *John Muir.* Englewood Cliffs, NJ: Silver Burdett Press, 1990.

Graves, Charles Palin and Robert Levering. *John Muir.* New York: Crowell, 1973.

Stewart, John. *Wind in the Woods: The Story of John Muir.* Philadelphia: Westminster Press, 1975.

Tolan, Sally. *John Muir: Naturalist, Writer, and Guardian of the North American Wilderness.* Milwaukee, WI: G. Stevens Books, 1990.

Wadsworth, Ginger. *John Muir, Wilderness Protector.* Minneapolis, MN: Lerner Publications, 1992.

ROCKEFELLER FAMILY

Laughlin, Rosemary. *John D. Rockefeller: Oil Baron and Philanthropist.* Greensboro, NC: Morgan Reynolds, 2001.

Myers, Elisabeth P., and Al Fiorentino. *John D. Rockefeller, Boy Financier.* Indianapolis, IN: Bobbs-Merrill, 1973.

Segall, Grant. *John D. Rockefeller: Anointed with Oil.* New York: Oxford University Press, 2001.

MARGARET SANGER

Lader, Lawrence, and Milton Meltzer. *Margaret Sanger: Pioneer of Birth Control.* New York: Crowell, 1969.

Topalian, Elyse. *Margaret Sanger.* New York: F. Watts, 1984.

Whitelaw, Nancy. *Margaret Sanger: "Every Child a Wanted Child."* New York: Dillon Press, 1994.

ELIZABETH SETON

Grunwell, Jeanne Marie, and Mari Goering. *Saint Elizabeth Ann Seton: Daughter of America*. Boston: Pauline Books and Media, 1999.

Power-Walters, Alma. *Mother Seton and the Sisters of Charity*. New York: Guild Press, 1963.

Stone, Elaine Murray. *Elizabeth Bayley Seton: An American Saint*. New York: Paulist Press, 1993.

LELAND STANFORD

Hoyt, Edwin Palmer. *Leland Stanford*. New York: Abelard-Schuman, 1967.

HENRIETTA SZOLD

Krantz, Hazel. *Daughter of My People: Henrietta Szold and Hadassah*. New York: Dutton, 1987.

Kustanowitz, Shulamit E., and Robert Masheris. *Henrietta Szold: Israel's Helping Hand*. New York: Viking, 1990.

LILLIAN WALD

Block, Irvin. *Neighbor to the World: The Story of Lillian Wald*. New York: Corwell, 1969.

Siegel, Beatrice. *Lillian Wald of Henry Street*. New York: Macmillan, 1983.

MADAM C.J. WALKER

Bundles, A'Lelia. *Madam C.J. Walker: Entrepreneur*. Philadelphia: Chelsea House, 1991.

Colman, Penny. *Madam C.J. Walker, Building a Business Empire*. Brookfield, CT: Millbrook Press, 1994.

McKissack, Pat, Frederick McKissack, and Michael Bryant. *Madam C.J. Walker: Self-Made Millionaire*. Hillside, NJ: Enslow Publishers, 1992.

Taylor, Marian. *Madam C.J. Walker*. New York: Chelsea Juniors, 1994.

BOOKER T. WASHINGTON

Amper, Thomas, and Jenni Reeves. *Booker T. Washington*. Minneapolis, MN: Carolrhoda Books, 1998.

McKissack, Pat, and Frederick McKissack. *The Story of Booker T. Washington*. Chicago: Children's Press, 1991.

Schroeder, Alan. *Booker T. Washington*. New York: Chelsea House, 1992.

IDA B. WELLS-BARNETT

Fradin, Dennis B., and Judith Bloom Fradin. *Ida B. Wells: Mother of the Civil Rights Movement*. New York: Clarion Books, 2000.

Lisandrelli, Elaine Slivinski. *Ida B. Wells-Barnett: Crusader against Lynching*. Springfield, NJ: Enslow Publishers, 1998.

Medearis, Angela Shelf. *Princess of the Press: The Story of Ida B. Wells-Barnett*. New York: Lodestar Books, 1997.

Welch, Catherine A. *Ida B. Wells-Barnett: Powerhouse with a Pen*. Minneapolis, MN: Carolrhoda Books, 2000.

FRANCIS WILLARD

Mason, Miriam Evangeline. *Frances Willard, Girl Crusader*. Indianapolis: Bobbs-Merrill, 1961.

JOHN WINTHROP

Connelly, Elizabeth Russell. *John Winthrop: Politician and Statesman*. Philadelphia: Chelsea House, 2001.

Index

Note: Page references to main entries are in **boldfaced** type.